Lollards and Reformers

LOLLARDS AND REFORMERS

Images and Literacy in
Late Medieval Religion

MARGARET ASTON

THE HAMBLEDON
PRESS

Published by The Hambledon Press
35 Gloucester Avenue, London NW1 7AX
1984

ISBN 0 907628 03 6 (Cased)
       0 907628 18 4 (Paper)

History Series 22

British Library Cataloguing in Publication Data

Aston, Margaret
    Lollards and reformers: images and literacy in
    late medieval religion. – (History series; 22)
    1. Lollards – History   2. England – Church
    history – 14th century   3. England – Church
    history – 15th century   4. England – Church
    history – 16th century
    I. Title   II. Series
    280'. 4'0942   BX4900

Printed and bound in Great Britain by
Robert Hartnoll Ltd., Bodmin, Cornwall

CONTENTS

ACKNOWLEDGEMENTS

All but two of the chapters in this book were originally published elsewhere and are reprinted by the kind permission of the original publishers.

1   *Past and Present*, 17 (1960), 1-44; subsequently reprinted in *Peasants, Knights and Heretics: Studies in Medieval English Social History*, ed. R.H. Hilton (Past and Present Publications, Cambridge, 1976), 273-318. World Copyright: The Past and Present Society, Corpus Christi College, Oxford, England.

2   *Journal of Ecclesiastical History*, 31 (1980), 441-61.

3   *Catholic Historical Review*, lxviii (1982), 469-97.

6   *History*, 62 (1977), 347-71.

7   *History*, 49 (1964), 149-70.

8   *Past and Present*, 30 (1965), 23-51. World Copyright: The Past and Present Society, Corpus Christi College, Oxford, England.

9   *The Reign of Richard II: Essays in Honour of May McKisack*, ed. F.R.H. Du Boulay and Caroline M. Barron (Athlone Press, London, 1971), 280-317.

10   *Journal of the Warburg and Courtauld Institutes*, xxxvi (1973), 231-55.

PERMISSIONS

Acknowledgement is due to the following institutions, by whose permission the illustrations are reproduced: the British Library (1a, 1b, 6, 9, 10, 11, 15a, 15b, 16, 20a, 20b, 26); the Trustees of the British Museum (3b, 17a, 17b, 17c, 17d, 23); the Trustees of the Ashmolean Museum, Oxford (3a, 4a, 4b, 5); the Syndics of the Cambridge University Library (18, 19); the Victoria and Albert Museum (14); the Committe for Aerial Photography of Cambridge (27a, 27b); Oxford Historical Society (32a).

LIST OF ILLUSTRATIONS

FOREWORD

The ten chapters of this book have been assembled as forming a reasonably united whole. Eight are previously published articles; the two which form the core of the book (Chapters 4 and 5) are new. The main theme is Lollardy, from its beginnings up to the Reformation period. The last two chapters, of a historiographical nature, veer away from this topic, though not at a complete tangent, in view of the fact that my interest throughout is to some degree historiographical (being as much concerned with the way events were viewed, as with events themselves), and bearing in mind the permanent imprint which the Reformation has left on our conception of the medieval church, and heresy in particular.

Without major revision it would not have been possible to bring all these chapters up to date. Chapter I was revised in 1976. For the rest I have tried to make the most needed corrections and additions by supplementary notes appended to the relevant chapters. These emendations make no claim to being exhaustive but will I hope alert readers to the more obvious shortcomings.

The notes reveal my many debts. I am grateful to the authors of several unpublished theses. James Crompton, to our loss, died without publishing his work on 'Lollard Doctrine, with special reference to the controversy over Image-Worship and Pilgrimages' (B. Litt. Thesis, Oxford, 1950), but this can now be read in typescript. Others, happily, I can thank in person: Dr. Jeremy Catto for information about William Woodford, as well as for kindly allowing me to quote from 'William Woodford, O.F.M. (c. 1330 - c.1397)' (D. Phil. Thesis, Oxford, 1969); Dr. Charles Kightly, for the valuable points and insights I have derived from his work 'The Early Lollards. A Survey of Popular Lollard Activity in England, 1382-1428' (D. Phil. Thesis, York, 1975); Rachel Pyper for most helpfully sending me texts and findings from her thesis in progress on 'Middle English Prose Commentaries on the Ten Commandments'. My biggest debt is to Dr. Anne Hudson for her constant readiness to answer questions, read and appraise, and for generously communicating unpublished material. Finally I want to take this opportunity to thank the friends who have helped and stimulated over the years: Professor John Bossy, Professor Elizabeth Eisenstein,

Barbara Everett, and Dr. Colin Richmond.

All history is hindsight and phrases like 'Lollardy and the Reformation', 'Wycliffe and the Reformation', carry dangerous overtones. Faced with the problem of derivations and connexions one need not hesitate to state at the outset that Lollardy had some influence on the course of reform in sixteenth-century England, or that Wycliffe's personality and writings were the starting-point of the late fourteenth-century heretical movement. What is in question, and has proved so difficult to establish, is the precise nature of the links between academic and popular theology from about the 1380s, between achieved reforms of the sixteenth century and would-be reformers of the fifteenth. Further work may elucidate these questions. For instance we still have no exact idea of the extent to which Wycliffe's Latin works were cited and used in the fifteenth century. Though we have learnt more about the use of repertories, detective work on the literary sources may yet tell us more about the transmission of Wycliffite writing from Latin into the vernacular.

Naturally the new heresy of the sixteenth century was judged in terms of the old. Much 'new learning' resembled, if it did not build on the old, and established terminology died hard. Parts of the ancient Lollard programme seemed to be taken up and pushed ahead with unheard of initiative in the later 1520s and 1530s. There was a merging of currents, or at least of the perceptible flow. What happened to the Lollards? If there were some who saw the advantage of linking old texts and ideas with new readers and promoters, that does not necessarily mean they subscribed to Protestant beliefs. Does the continuity of dissent in certain areas and communities suggest an ingrained tradition that carried on through the changes of the Reformation period? Was a puritanical separatist attitude the true heritage of the Lollards? Certainly it is a mistake to think of some Reformation finishing-post as terminating the Lollard course, though it needs to be remembered that scriptural roots have tended to give a family likeness to dissenters of different periods.

As knowledge of Lollardy and its sources has increased, we have learnt to see more clearly the dangers of our categories, to become more aware of the hazards of definition. The fourteenth century combined wide-ranging speculative criticism with lack of clarity about where orthodoxy ended and heresy began; the doubtful shared doubts with the devout. The force of events moulded contemporary views and steadily redefined the limits of the permissible. It was not the work of a day. And just as those called Lollards differed among themselves, so those who were troubled by their existence found themselves on a moving frontier as they struggled to establish the boundary line between the heretics and the orthodox.

The heretics as such may have been few, a tiny proportion of the population at large, but we cannot estimate the significance of Lollardy in terms of numbers — though if we were to try we should start with a count of texts. Ideas cannot be measured numerically. Orthodoxy has always been formed by its rubs with the heterodox, and fifteenth-century England was no exception. Lollardy was part of the climate, impinging on the faith of all believers, affecting society as a whole.

ABBREVIATIONS

BIHR	*Bulletin of the Institute of Historical Research*
BJRL	*Bulletin of the John Rylands Library*
BL	British Library
BLR	*Bodleian Library Record*
CUL	Cambridge University Library
DNB	*Dictionary of National Biography*
EETS	Early English Text Society
EHR	*English Historical Review*
Engl. Wycl. Writings	*Selections from English Wycliffite Writings,* ed. Anne Hudson (Cambridge, 1978)
Foxe, *AM*	John Foxe, *Acts and Monuments,* ed. J. Pratt (London, 1853-68)
JEH	*Journal of Ecclesiastical History*
JHI	*Journal of the History of Ideas*
JTS	*Journal of Theological Studies*
JWCI	*Journal of the Warburg and Courtauld Institutes*
Norwich Heresy Trials	*Heresy Trials in the Diocese of Norwich, 1428-31,* ed. Norman P. Tanner (Camden Society, Fourth Series, 20, 1977)
PBA	*Proceedings of the British Academy*
PL	*Patrologia Latina*, ed. J. P. Migne
PMLA	*Publications of the Modern Language Association of America*
PRO	Public Record Office
RP	*Rotuli Parliamentorum*
RS	Rolls Series
SCH	*Studies in Church History*
STC	*Short-Title Catalogue of Books printed in England....1475-1640,* compiled A. W. Pollard and G. R. Redgrave (London, 1926)
STC2	*Short-Title Catalogue,* 2nd edn., revised by W. A. Jackson, F. S. Ferguson, Katharine Pantzer (London 1976)
TRHS	*Transactions of the Royal Historical Society*
VCH	*Victoria County History*
Wilkins, *Concilia*	David Wilkins, *Concilia Magnae Britanniae et Hiberniae* (London, 1737)

LOLLARDY AND SEDITION, 1381-1431

BEFORE 1381, THOUGH THE ENGLISH GOVERNING CLASSES HAD encountered heretics as well as rebels against society, they had never had to deal with either on a large or concerted scale. By the end of May 1382 both had been on their hands, and heresy (in the event) had come to stay. Wycliffe, who before he moved on to full consideration of the Eucharist had found employment and patronage in the highest political quarters, had already passed the watershed of his career by the time of the outbreak of the Peasants' Revolt. But nothing is heard of those adherents of his views who, though hardly perhaps his true successors, form the mainstay of the Lollard movement, until the country had been shaken by the achievements of the lower classes in the summer of 1381. Then, when Archbishop Courtenay had taken the place of the murdered Sudbury, proceedings were begun which revealed the establishment of Wycliffe's followers elsewhere than in the university, and then, too, Wycliffites appear for the first time being publicly abused as "Lollards".[1] A heretical movement and a major upheaval among the lower orders of society had arrived, in point of time, together.

Did this coincidence of timing at all affect the attitude of the government, secular and ecclesiastical, towards the double challenge? Was the reception of the heresies of Wycliffe and his followers conditioned by the shock of the unprecedented happenings of 1381, by the fears engendered in that resounding year, as well as by their inherent political implications? Was Lollardy itself in any sense a doctrine of social revolt, involved in and responsible for rebellion and sedition? And was the course of the Lollard movement influenced by the political crises and disturbances of the later

---

* I am grateful to Mr. K. B. McFarlane for his criticism and advice.

[1] *Fasciculi Zizaniorum*, ed. W. W. Shirley (Rolls Series, 1858), p. 312. On 15 June 1382 the chancellor of Oxford suspended the Cistercian, Henry Crump, and "accused him of a disturbance of the peace, because he called the heretics Lollards". The earliest official use of the word appears to be in a letter of Bishop Wakefield of Worcester of 10 August 1387; D. Wilkins, *Concilia Magnae Britanniae et Hiberniae*, (London, 1737), iii, pp. 202-3. For the meaning and derivation of the name see H. B. Workman, *John Wyclif*, (Oxford, 1926), i, p. 327, and M. Deanesly, *The Lollard Bible*, (Cambridge, 1920), pp. 70 note i, 273-4. Bishop Buckingham began proceedings against the heretics at Leicester in the early months of 1382, before the meeting of the Blackfriars Council; K. B. McFarlane, *John Wycliffe and the Beginnings of English Nonconformity*, (London, 1952), p. 121.

fourteenth and early fifteenth centuries, as well as by its "own" rebellion of 1414, and another, less recognised, attempted rising which followed? These are indeed controversial questions; it would be a rash historian who claimed to have answered any of them. But unanswerable questions are not always the least deserving of attention, particularly if they were raised by contemporaries. Lollardy was, of course, in origin and remained throughout primarily and essentially a theological movement, to which its own considerable literature and the records of ecclesiastical proceedings bear abundant witness. But the structure of medieval politics and political theory were such that extreme and penetrating statements on the nature of the church and the priesthood could hardly fail to have some bearing upon society and upon the state. And this did not pass unnoticed at the time.

*   *   *

There can be no doubt, from the views expressed on both sides of the matter, as to whether contemporaries were aware of the social and political implications of Wycliffe's teaching. From the first admonitory papal missive there appeared in official documents a number of solemn warnings that it was the whole of society, and not the church alone, whose position was at stake. Such sentiments were echoed, amplified and broadcast in the works of pamphleteers and versifiers who reflected the orthodox point of view, while on the other side, Lollard tractarians found a constant cause of complaint in the slanderous accusations to which they were being subjected. As Daw Topias put it, when defending his fellow friars against the Lollard polemic of Jack Upland:

> "But sith that wickide worme,
> Wiclyf be his name,
> began to sowe the seed
> of cisme in the erthe,
> sorowe and shendship
> hath awaked wyde,
> in lordship and prelacie
> hath growe the lasse grace".[2]

Among the papal letters condemning Wycliffe's teaching which were sent from Rome in the spring of 1377, was one addressed to the archbishop of Canterbury and the bishop of London, enjoining them, among other things, to take steps to indicate to the English

---

[2] *Political Poems and Songs*, ed. T. Wright (R. S., 1859-61), ii, p. 45. These exchanges have been dated to 1401-2. ("Shendship" means disgrace or ruin).

government the danger of the views being developed in its midst. The king, his sons, the princess of Wales and other magnates and royal counsellors, were to be fully informed and shown that the condemned conclusions were not only theologically erroneous but, if properly understood, threatened to destroy the whole state.[3] It may have been no accident that the eighteen propositions chosen from Wycliffe's writings for special reprobation emphasised the subversive nature of his ideas on the question of temporal, as well as ecclesiastical, lordship: "God cannot give civil dominion to man for himself, and his heirs, in perpetuity" . . . "Charters of human invention concerning perpetual civil inheritance are impossible".[4] It is not difficult to see the radical implications of these statements, and, as the papal letter indicates, it was nothing if not easy to read into Wycliffe's philosophy ideas for a programme of devastating revolution. His theories upon dominion, on the grace of the righteous as the basis of authority, the exaltation of the power of the state over the church, and the right of temporal rulers to correct ecclesiastics, were, as the church was not slow to realise, far-reaching. And their implications, as subsequent writers and events were to demonstrate, were not confined to the church and its members. If property could be removed from a delinquent church in time of necessity, might not the same argument equally well be applied to secular owners? If tithes could be withheld from a sinful priest, could not rents and services be withheld from a tyrannical and unjust overlord? And if lay lords could and should correct churchmen, might not others in turn claim the power to correct them? Such later interpretations could be — and were — denied, but more than one prophet has made his reputation on what he did not say. We can hardly blame contemporaries for doing Wycliffe an injustice: if they were prejudiced they were also, in the main, less subtle than the great schoolman. And after the insurrection of 1381 had happened — and Pope Gregory, had he still been alive, might have pointed a certain moral — they do not seem to have been over-scrupulous in attributing the blame.

Yet, whatever the obscurities and controversies which surround his reputation and writings, Wycliffe himself was most emphatically not the advocate of revolution on the lines of 1381. After the revolt, for all his vituperance, (and he did not hesitate to draw his own deductions),[5] he showed himself as an undoubted member of

---

[3] *Chronicon Angliae*, ed. E. M. Thompson (R. S., 1874), p. 176.
[4] *Ibid.*, pp. 181-2.
[5] In *De Blasphemia*, written soon after the revolt, Wycliffe was saying, in effect, that if more attention had been paid to him none of this need ever have

the establishment which had suffered. The clergy were certainly
to blame, indeed they deserved worse . — but the people were
unjustified in proceeding to murder; temporal lords had offended in
the impositions they had imposed — but such things as had been
done should never be attempted against them; it was treachery to
God and the church for an archbishop to be chancellor — but that
did not excuse the manner of his death.⁶ The "reformer" himself,
however abusive in language and revolutionary in theory, clearly did
not envisage taking the enemies' house by such a storm, or overthrowing "Caim's Castles"⁷ in one great insurrectionary outburst.
Had he done so his career — and that of the early Lollard movement
— might have been very different.

The St. Albans chronicler was, like Wycliffe, anxious to derive
the lesson from 1381 — though in his case it was tinged with personal
animosity directed towards the memory of one for whom he cherished
scant respect. For the first cause of the rising to which Walsingham
drew attention was the failure of the late Archbishop Sudbury to
suppress the heresy of Wycliffe and his followers, who had "spread
their preaching and defiled the people far and wide through the
country" with their erroneous views on the Eucharist.⁸ Later he
tells us that John Ball, who had been preaching for over twenty years
and pleasing the people by his abuse of both ecclesiastical and secular
lords, himself "taught the perverse doctrines of the perfidious John
Wycliffe"; and that his end was delayed by Bishop Courtenay

happened. If the temporal lords had (carefully) removed temporalities from
the offending church, the people would not then have had to be taxed beyond
their capacity. "Nec dubium quin moderate et prudenter predonans temporalia
posset totum hoc malum faciliter extinxisse". And it was not too late.
Indeed, it seemed probable that God had ordained the whole disturbance so
that the kingdom might be regenerated in such a way. In the transfer of
property which Wycliffe was advocating as a "theoretical remedy", the temporal
lords were to have been compensated for their losses (caused by clerical
usurpation), but a sufficiency was to be allowed to the clergy. "O quam gloriosa
foret hec comutacio bonorum comunium, qua, reservato clero usque
sufficienciam ad alimentum et tegumentum, satisfieret wulgo per bonum cleri
residuum!": *Johannis Wyclif Tractatus de Blasphemia*, ed. M. H. Dziewicki
(Wyclif Society, 1893), pp. 190-1, 199, 267-9. It is interesting to compare
these suggestions, (and Wycliffe's intentions are, as usual, highly debatable),
with those of John Ball and the rebels of 1381, who were also intending to leave
churchmen "lour sustenance esement", but in their case the spoils were,
apparently, to be divided among parishioners — a significant difference of
emphasis: *The Anonimalle Chronicle*, ed. V. H. Galbraith (Manchester, 1927),
p. 147, cf. pp. 137-8.
    ⁶ *De Blasphemia*, pp. 189-99, 267-9.
    ⁷ The four orders of Carmelites, Augustinians, Jacobites, (the Preachers,
called after their Paris convent of St. James), and Minorites, as disparagingly
referred to by Wycliffe and Lollard writers.
    ⁸ *Chronicon Angliae*, pp. 310-11, cf. p. 117.

out of anxiety for the state of his soul.[9]   By the end of the century
the story had gained in standing.   Though less venomous and
extreme, Henry Knighton saw Ball as Wycliffe's John the Baptist, ⸙
preparing the ways for the master, "and he also, it is said, disturbed
many by his doctrine".[10]   From another source comes the (unverified)
story of how the hero of Blackheath, Wycliffe's "beloved follower",
when he was condemned publicly confessed that "he had been a
disciple of Wycliffe for two years, and had learnt from him the
heresies which he taught", and that "there was a certain company of
Wycliffe's sect and doctrine who had arranged a sort of confederacy,
and had organised themselves to go round the whole of England
preaching the matters which Wycliffe had taught, so that the whole
country should together agree to their perverse doctrine".[11]   The
chorus is so remarkably united that it may seem rather like a refrain
— but even untrue refrains may be remembered and repeated with
effect.

The chroniclers, who could afford the luxury of a certain
irresponsibility, and were habitually discriminating with their
solicitude for reputations, were prepared to be specific.   Parliament,
it seems, was not.   If, as some thought, the parliament of November
1381 expressed views about the ways in which church matters might
have affected the revolt, these were not officially recorded, but by
the following spring, with the immediate problems solved and time
to reflect, a new parliament was able to return to the question of how ⸙
to prevent the recurrence of such a catastrophe.

> "For fawte of lawe yif comouns rise,
> Than is a kyngdom most in drede".[12]

No such reminders can have been necessary.   And one of the
important outcomes of this parliament was the legislation which
gave statutory authority for the issue of commissions to sheriffs and
other local officials, upon certification of a bishop in chancery, to
⸙ arrest and imprison troublesome preachers.   No names were given,
but the terms of the statute surely leave little doubt what sort of
people its framers had in mind.   It has been found, it states,
(referring to the Blackfriars Council, where twenty-four of Wycliffe's
conclusions had just been condemned), that various ill-disposed
persons "in certain habits under the guise of great holiness" have
been going from county to county and from town to town without

---

[9] *Ibid.*, pp. 320-1.
[10] *Chronicon Henrici Knighton*, ed. J. R. Lumby (R.S., 1889-95), ii, p. 151.
[11] *Fasciculi Zizaniorum*, pp. 273-4.
[12] *Twenty-Six Political and other Poems*, ed. J. Kail (Early English Text
Society, Original Series, No. 124, 1904), p. 10.

any proper ecclesiastical licence, and preaching not only in churches and cemeteries, but also in fairs, markets, and other public places, endangering souls, the faith, the church and the whole realm. "Which persons", it continues, "preach also diverse matters of slander to make discord and dissension between the various estates of the realm, both temporal and spiritual, to the commotion of the people and the great peril of the whole realm".[13] The borrowed phraseology —taken from letters of Archbishop Courtenay[14]—makes it certain that it was intended to include among these anonymous and peripatetic speakers, Lollard preachers, whose beguiling appearance was habitually described in official pronouncements of the succeeding generation in these, or similar, words: "*sub magnae sanctitatis velamine*" became the regular advertisement to warn the unwary away from these most seductive of whited sepulchres.[15]

The charge is there — with plenty of plaintiffs. But there are no defendants. For there are no grounds to believe in John Ball's alleged association with Wycliffe, and considerable research has yielded no evidence to support the view that Wycliffe's teaching or

---

[13] *Rotuli Parliamentorum*, ed. J. Strachey (London, 1767-77), iii, pp. 124-5.

[14] The commissions issued after this parliament refer to the archbishop's petition pointing out the dangers of these preachers, and asking for the assistance of the lay arm. This petition has not survived, but the passage in the parliament rolls may be compared with the letter sent by the archbishop to the bishop of London on 30 May, 1382, in Wilkins, *Concilia*, iii, pp. 158-9. There is a further similarity of phraseology in a letter sent by Bishop Arundel of Ely to his official on 20 May, about the activities of false preachers, who were said to have been holding forth in churches, chapels, oratories, cemeteries, towns, villages and open spaces; Bishop Arundel's Register (Ely), ff. 41 v.-42 r. Arundel was not in London at this time, and this letter therefore suggests that the clerical plea had already taken shape at the Blackfriars meeting by about 18 May — on which day Bishop Brinton of Rochester, preaching most probably to this very council, delivered a sermon on the text "*Vigilate*", in which he warned his clerical audience to beware of the false prophets who touched on "*subtiles materias*" in preaching to the laity, and, if necessary, to invoke the secular arm to keep such wolves out of the fold. *The Sermons of Thomas Brinton*, ed. M. A. Devlin (Camden Third Series, lxxxv-vi, 1954), ii, pp. 458-62; read 1382 for 1381, p. 458.

[15] See for example, Wilkins, *Concilia*, iii, p. 158 (the archbishop's letter of 1382); *ibid.*, p. 202 (Bishop Wakefield's letter of 1387); *ibid.*, p. 252 ("sub simulate sanctitatis colore", in the clerical petition which preceded *De Heretico Comburendo*). Oldcastle was described in these terms, (*Henrici Quinti Angliae Regis Gesta*, ed. B. Williams (English Historical Society, 1850), p. 6, and so were the followers of Perkins in 1431 (p. 34 below). Cf. also *Pol. Poems and Songs*, i, p. 232, ("Sub sanctitatis specie Virus vomunt malitiae"), and descriptions such as those by Knighton (*Chronicon Henrici Knighton*, ii, pp. 184-5), and Gower (*Pol. Poems and Songs*, i, p. 347), which — often quoting the famous passage in Matthew vii, "beware of false prophets . . ." — stress the deceptiveness of the Lollards' outward simplicity. The fact that so many contemporaries went out of their way to make this point suggests that there were many Lollards who maintained puritanical standards.

Lollard preaching were either significant instruments, or in any way connected with the 1381 revolt.[16] Even so, it is possible to be impressed by the charge alone, for it represents a considerable and undeniable body of contemporary opinion which apparently believed, and acted on the belief, that there was such a connection. "It is noteworthy", added one writer as an afterthought, looking back on the events of 1381-2, "that so much division and dissension was created everywhere in England by John Wycliffe and his associates, that catholics were afraid that their preaching would lead to a new rising against the lords and the church".[17] Such fears were not easily dispelled. Those who had "leide heore jolité in presse"[18] when the commons began to rise could never shake it out again with quite the same abandon, and heretics were gravely compromised by the folds. Somehow, through deliberate falsification, fixed prejudice, or plausible hypothesis, the conviction seems to have become established that Lollardy was associated with revolt. And opinions once lodged are themselves historical facts: and, as such, may influence events.

If it was possible, not long after the happenings of 1381, to regard Wycliffe's followers as potential rebels and instigators of sedition, later events seemed to add substance to the interpretation. Adam Usk's memory was not very clear when, after a lapse of some thirty-five years, he came to chronicle the history of Richard II's minority, which he had seen himself as a young man, near the beginning of his career. But, having recently experienced a genuine Lollard rebellion, he entertained few doubts that Wycliffe's disciples "by preaching things pleasing to the powerful and rich, namely the withholding of tithes and offerings, and the removal of temporalities from the clergy", had sown the seed of "many disasters, plots, disputes, strife and sedition, which last until this day, and which I fear will last even to the undoing of the kingdom . . . The people of England, wrangling among themselves about the old faith and the new, are every day as it were, on the very point of bringing down upon their own heads ruin and rebellion".[19]

[16] In particular A. Réville, *Le Soulèvement des Travailleurs d'Angleterre en 1381*, (Paris, 1898); cf. C. Petit-Dutaillis, "Les Prédications Populaires, les Lollards et le Soulèvement des Travailleurs Anglais en 1381", in *Etudes d'Histoire du Moyen Age dédiées à Gabriel Monod*, ed. E. Lavisse (Paris, 1896), pp. 373-88. For another allegation of the connection see *Pol. Poems and Songs*, i, p. 235.
[17] *Fasciculi Zizaniorum*, p. 273.
[18] *Pol. Poems and Songs*, i, p. 250.
[19] *Chronicon Adae de Usk*, ed. E. M. Thompson (London, 1904), pp. 3-4.

After the first quarter of the fifteenth century the common repute of a Lollard was even less enviable than it had been a generation earlier. When Chaucer was writing the Canterbury Tales it was still a light — almost friendly — jesting matter for the host to "smelle a loller in the wind".[20] But in the summer of 1413 Margery Kempe's enemies were able to taunt her with threats of the fire, and when she was accused of Lollardy four years later (probably when Oldcastle, no longer officially Lord Cobham, was still at large), she was arrested by two yeomen of the duke of Bedford, who alleged that "she was Cobham's daughter and was sent to bear letters about the country".[21] By then the Lollards had produced open rebels and traitors, and as secular proceedings became more common, so false accusations and summary treatment of innocent persons became more easy. And, as the Lollard programme itself developed, the burden of disrepute carried in the name was cumulative. While in 1411 Lollards and heretics are mentioned alongside homicides and other malefactors,[22] in 1417 the commons, complaining of disturbances to the peace caused by violent breaking of forests, chases and parks, remarked that the offenders were "probably of the opinion of Lollards, traitors and rebels".[23] By 1425 there was no doubt that Lollardy was on a par with treason, felony, "or any such other high poynt",[24] and six years later Lollards were described as "traitors and enemies of the king".[25] To be called a Lollard — as to be called a Quaker or a Ranter — was to be abused at the outset in the very derivation of the name, but the name had grown in content. Opinion and legislation must here have reacted upon each other, and those who were deemed sufficiently dangerous to be punished as rebels and traitors naturally tended to become equated with such.

It was undoubtedly true that a Lollard might endanger a good deal more than his own and his neighbour's soul. But it is also undeniable that if current opinion represents a deformity of this truth, it was a deformity which those in authority had every reason to cultivate, and which the nature of our sources may tend to exaggerate. The

---

[20] *The Complete Works of Geoffrey Chaucer*, ed. W. W. Skeat (Oxford, 1894-7), iv, p. 165, the Shipman's Prologue. Significantly, the host's remark was provoked by the parson's objection to an oath, and accompanied by fears of a sermon. See below p. 16 and note 61.

[21] *The Book of Margery Kempe*, ed. S. B. Meech and H. E. Allen (E.E.T.S., Original Series, No. 212, 1940), pp. 33, 36, 132, 316.

[22] *Rotuli Parliamentorum*, iii, p. 651.

[23] *Rotuli Parliamentorum*, iv, pp. 113-4.

[24] *Ibid.*, p. 292.

[25] P.R.O. E.403/700, m. 11.

stress which churchmen and statesmen laid upon the seditious and treasonable aspects of certain Lollard aspirations is likely to reflect their concern to warn those in responsible positions away from dalliance with the sect. The movement certainly found adherents and patrons in high places, and long before Sir John Oldcastle is known to have given it his allegiance, two independent sources provide between them the names of ten reputed Lollard knights, (including a group attached to the royal household), some at least of whose guilt seems established.[26] Material is not lacking to show how the Lollard case was being presented to attract the support of just such persons. But, when argument was translated into action and issued in rebellion, the evidence for Lollard deeds and intentions comes almost completely from the other, and hostile, side.[27] The story can hardly be a whole one when we have to watch it at moments of crisis from an entirely adverse viewpoint. And throughout it is necessary, of course, to make a particular discount for the racy exaggerations with which — in terminology of impending disaster — men of affairs and preachers alike, were then accustomed to spice their arguments.

* * *

What were the aspects of the Lollard movement which fostered or facilitated the growth of such fears ? Lollardy was a variable creed — if indeed its heterogeneous and ill-assorted conclusions can be dignified by such a name — and seems at some points certainly to refute this contemporary interpretation. For example there is the pacifism which formed one of the twelve articles of the 1395 manifesto: objections to Christian fighting Christian, and to

[26] For the names of the suspects, and an examination of the case against them see W. T. Waugh, "The Lollard Knights", *Scottish Historical Review*, xi (1914), pp. 55-92. Cf. K. B. McFarlane, *op. cit.*, pp. 145-7. In a series of lectures delivered after the publication of his book, Mr. McFarlane reviewed both Waugh's and other evidence, and found further reasons to give weight to the chroniclers' accusations.

[27] The *Coram Rege* Rolls and the Ancient Indictments are the main sources for 1414 and 1431, and it has been shown from such evidence relating to London after the Peasants' Revolt, that these indictments might falsify the facts to make a particular case. When it comes to determining the aims and intentions of the Lollard rebels one is usually not in a position to verify the facts. If the accusations sometimes seem improbable it should be remembered that they also included much circumstantial detail, and when (as in the proceedings against those who had been in contact with Oldcastle in 1417), the jurors were themselves sympathetic, the case is not likely to have been grossly overstated. In general the presentments had at least to be credible enough to make conviction possible, and some of the more sweeping statements of the Lollards' intentions may have been derived from their own claims; see below, p. 36 and note 132.

"homicide through war or alleged law of justice in a temporal cause, without spiritual revelation",[28] could, logically, have been associated with passive resistance in domestic issues.   There were, too, Lollard teachers who (like Wycliffe himself) stressed the duty of obedience owed by the oppressed servant to the tyrannical master: "if thou be a laborer, lyve in mekenesse, and trewly and wylfully do thi labour".[29] Hard in any circumstances to construe into a doctrine of revolt.   But evangelical fervour does not tend towards systematic thinking, and if some Lollards posed so defiantly as defenders of the peace it was, in part anyway, because the dangers in the other direction were obvious.

First there is the question of temporalities, which, under John Ball's direction had assumed an ugly shape, and a prominent place in the rebels' demands, in 1381.   As a primary feature of the Lollard programme the repercussions of disendowment proposals were naturally discussed and emphasised by both supporters and opponents. Wycliffe, who like many great men, was never afraid to repeat himself, returned to the matter with relentless and exhausting insistence, and Lollards likewise (in this at least true to the spirit of the master) never tired of inveighing against the temporal endowments of the church, and of stressing the duties of lords and knights to bear up holy church "rigt as the see bereth up schippes",[30] the meaning of which they did not hesitate to elucidate — including the possible storms.   Many works made no doubt that among the first of the laity's obligations to the church was that of restoring its spiritual inheritance by relieving it of its undue load of temporal acquisitions, the which were as antipathetic as fire and water, and "rigt as water holdyng hymsilf hool in receyvyng of fier quenchith it, so seculer power igove to the clergie . . . distruyith seculer lordis, & most gendrith dyvycioun in the puple & stirith the puple to arise agen' her lordis . . ."[31]   For this same reason others after Wycliffe echoed him in thinking it therefore, "No wondur thanne thof ther ben grete discencouns in tyme of suche pristis bishopis as risyngis of the puple & comunes agen hem, & the lordis, as doolfully we sawen late".[32] The Lollard theorists had their own answers ready for the "blabering"

---

[28] *Fasciculi Zizaniorum*, p. 366.

[29] *Select English Works of John Wyclif*, ed. T. Arnold (Oxford, 1869-71), iii, p. 207. This quotation comes from one of the large number of English Lollard writings which, without adequate foundation, have been fathered on Wycliffe.

[30] Brit. Mus. Add. M.S. 41321, f. 19 v.

[31] Brit. Mus. Add. M.S. 24202, f. 5 v. (The tract in which this passage occurs was probably written before 1389).

[32] *Ibid.*, f. 41 r.

clergy who denied the legality of the action they were advocating. Among the favourites was a *reductio ad absurdum* derived from the king's power to amerce delinquent clerks. For, it was incautiously argued, if the king were unable to fine clerks by as much as a penny or farthing, they would be free to commit what sin or treachery they pleased, "and thus no worldly lord may lette hem to conquer alle the worldly lordschipe in this londe, and forto slee alle lordis and lauedyes . . . blode".[33] Few perhaps would have been seriously frightened by the notion that "worldly clerks" were out to amortise the whole land. But it is not so hard to envisage the attraction of schemes designed to restore property to the heirs of defrauded almsgivers, and to relieve oppressed commoners of taxation. Nor was this aspect of the poor preachers' insight into their more worldly-minded lay audience lost upon contemporaries.

Arguments such as these had, in fact, an unfortunate tendency to turn into two-edged swords. While the Lollards were busy with allegations that the suppression of their virtuous proposals was a source of discord, and endangering all the lordships in the realm, those whom they chose to describe as "Antecrist and his meynee"[34] saw precisely the same points in reverse. "Thei seyen", it was bitterly complained, "that seculer lordshipis asken degrees; for yif alle weren oon, ther weren noon ordre, but ilche man mygte ylyche comaunde to other, and so seculer lordship wer fully destryed".[35] As William Wodeford wrote in the riposte commissioned by Archbishop Arundel, it followed from Wycliffe's arguments that "the people could lawfully remove the possessions of kings, dukes, and their lay superiors, whenever they habitually offended".[36] And when, soon after their appearance, the Dominican Roger Dymoke embarked on his lengthy rejoinder to the conclusions of 1395, he dwelt tellingly upon the revolutionary and destructive aspects of disendowment, depicting the promoters of the plan as setting temporal lords at loggerheads with ecclesiastical, and inciting the whole people to rise against both as misappropriators of property.[37] Removal of ecclesiastical possessions, if not carried out by legal means, which,

[33] *Ibid.*, f. 35 v. Cf. *Select English Works*, iii, pp. 313-4, 515-6, where the same argument appears.
[34] The title of a tract printed in *Three Treatises by John Wycklyffe*, ed. J. H. Todd (Dublin, 1851). As in most cases the insults were mutual, and the Lollards were themselves called the followers of Antichrist by their opponents.
[35] *Select English Works*, iii, p. 434.
[36] *Fasciculus Rerum Expetendarum & Fugiendarum*, ed. O. Gratius, revised E. Brown (London, 1690), i, p. 231.
[37] *Rogeri Dymmok Liber Contra XII Errores et Hereses Lollardorum*, ed. H. S. Cronin (Wyclif Society, 1922), pp. 13, 27-8.

he said, was impossible, could only damage the whole land by ending in insurrection or tyranny. For if the commons took action "it is probable that they would also usurp for themselves the lordships of others, and thus civil war would arise"; and if the lords did so "no one thenceforward in this kingdom would possess his lordships in safety, since anybody would be able to rise against another when he wished . . ."[38] Whatever the means, it seems, there could only be dire results.

Closely connected with temporalities, and also, as Adam Usk suggested, with perturbing implications, is the matter of tithes. The history of tithe disputes and the troubles attendant on them was already a long one before the Lollards made their contribution, and there were many others, apart from heretics, who held strong views on the question — capable of turning, in a later age, into an "issue of blood".[39] We do not know that any of the blood which John Ball helped to spill was lost on this account, though he, it seems, had drawn attention to the question of tithes, by directing that parishioners should withhold payment if their rector or vicar were richer, or of less virtuous life, than themselves.[40] The similarity with Wycliffe's statement that "tithes are pure alms, and parishioners may withhold them on account of the sins of their curates, and freely bestow them on others",[41] needs no elaboration. As an uncomplicated and obviously attractive proposition it was repeated, with fewer variants than many of Wycliffe's ideas, by disciples like William Swinderby, Walter Brute, William White and others, sometimes with the master's proviso that the withholding should be done with prudence.[42] But that other, and more insidious deductions could be read into it, appears from the following complaint in the Lollard tract *"Of servants and lords"*.

"But yit summe men that ben out of charite sclaundren pore prestis with this errour, that servauntis or tenauntis may lawefully withholde rentis & servyce fro here lordis whanne lordis ben opynly wickid in here lyvynge. & thei maken this false lesyngis upon pore prestis to make lordis to hate hem . . . & this is a feyned word of anticristis clerkis that, yif sugetis may leffully

[38] *Ibid.*, p. 177. Another possibility which Dymoke considers is that the king should carry out such a spoliation of the church without process of law, which would have the evil result that he would "degenerate into a tyrant".

[39] As stated by General Monk; cf. M. James, "The Political Impoitance of the Tithes Controversy in the English Revolution, 1640-60", *History*, New Series, xxvi (1941-2), pp. 1-18.

[40] *Chronicon Angliae*, pp. 320-1.

[41] One of the twenty-four conclusions condemned in 1382. *Fasciculi Zizaniorum*, pp. 280-1.

[42] *Johannis de Wiclif Tractatus de Officio Pastorali*, ed. G. V. Lechler (Leipzig, 1863), p. 16, where Wycliffe makes this proviso; cf. *Fasciculi Zizaniorum*, p. 428, for William White's repetition of it.

withdrawe tithes & offryngis fro curatis that openly lyven in lecherie or grete othere synnes & don not here office, than servauntis & tenauntis may withdrawe here servyce & rentis fro here lordis that lyven opynly a cursed lif".[43]

One is reminded of the fears of those who, looking back from the seventeenth century to the German precedent of a peasants' rebellion, remarked in no small anxiety that "Land-lords' rent, and Tythe-rent (like Hypocrates' twins) will stand or fall both together".[44]   And though in post-Reformation times these controversies were embittered by the worries of lay impropriators, the problems were essentially similar: tithes and other forms of property were at all times too closely connected for the one not to reflect upon the other.   Indeed Bishop Peacock, in his defence of ecclesiastical endowments against the arguments of the Lollards, likened tithes to "a free rente of money".[45]   Even at this period, moreover, there were circumstances in which a layman might himself be receiving tithes.[46]   "Antichrist" once again appears to have hastened to point the moral.

But the winds of alarm were stirring on account of the manner as well as the matter of Lollardy.   Wycliffe, for all his defects as a reformer, had done some radical rethinking and introduced a fundamental challenge: the deposition of the sacraments and the hierarchy for the elevation of scripture and preaching of the word. Individual interpretation was put before priestly adminstration, and every layman became the advocate of Christ: the change was a change of method as much as a change of doctrine.   But questioning based on the Bible did not begin or end with the peccability of the pope and the fallibility of the fathers, nor did it need renaissance learning and reformation experience to see that "divers naughtie and erronyous opynions"[47] secular as well as ecclesiastical, might arise

[43] *The English Works of Wyclif Hitherto Unprinted*, ed. F. D. Matthew (E.E.T.S., Original Series, No. 74, 1880), p. 229.
[44] R. Culmer, *Lawles Tythe-Robbers Discovered*, (London, 1655), p. 13.
[45] *The Repressor of Over Much Blaming of the Clergy*, ed. C. Babington (R.S., 1860), ii, p. 391.
[46] For example through tenure of the lands of alien priories, among the holders of which appears Sir John Cheyne, the suspect Lollard knight, (*Cal. Pat. Rolls*, 1399-1401, p. 111), whose anti-clericalism was feared by Archbishop Arundel in 1399; see *Annales Ricardi Secundi et Henrici Quarti*, ed. H. T. Riley (R.S., 1866), p. 290, and p. 393 for Arundel's rebuke on the subject of the alien priorities mentioned below, p. 24. Laymen might also be in receipt of tithes in lieu of a pension payable by a religious house; *The Wiltshire, Devonshire and Dorsetshire Portion of the Lewes Chartulary*, ed. W. Budgen and L. F. Salzman (Sussex Record Society, 1943), pp. 46-7. And there were less reputable circumstances in which it could happen; Wilkins, *Concilia*, iii, p. 274, for a case of a layman illegally holding a church at farm.
[47] *Statutes of the Realm*, iii, p. 896.: 34 and 35 *Henry VIII*, c.1.

once the new approaches to belief were popularised. Those whose learning dethroned the pope might one day try to dethrone the king. Roger Dymoke, presaging such dangers in the Lollard statement that the miracle of the sacrament induced idolatry, remarked that disrespect for the efficacy of the Eucharist tended to destroy respect for all law and authority, and thereby to undermine the unity of the state.[48] The view that sin invalidates the sacrament, and the right — or duty — of the parishioner to judge whether the life and morals of his curate accorded with scriptural precept, ultimately indeed not only destroyed the faith, but "put all in doubt".[49] As Archbishop Arundel, with his ripe experience of Lollard methods, asked William Thorpe in 1407, (according to the latter's account); "Why losell! Wilt not thou and other that are confedered with thee, seeke out of holie Scripture and of the sence of doctours, all sharpe authorities against lords, knights, and squiers, and against other secular men, as thou doest against priests ?"[50] Those who were actively advocating the maxims that "hooly scripture conteyneth al prophitable treuthe", and that "it is leful and nedful to the pepel for to knowe Goddis lawe and the feith of holy chirche in here langage", were well aware of what their opponents were saying, and sometimes tried to forestall criticism by refutation of the arguments "that lewed men mowe soon erre", and "that holy writ in Englische wole make cristen men at debate, and sugettis to rebelle ageyns her sovereyns".[51]

There is no doubt that the Lollards were avid in their reading, and they derived plenty of errors from the Bible. John Purvey, Wycliffe's secretary, who may have been involved in the translation of the Bible, certainly found there the origin of his idea that "it belongs to the king to ordain bishops and priests"; he had also somehow decided that "if our kingdom elects a bastard to be king, providing he fulfills the office well, God will make him king".[52] By 1443 Lollards in the diocese of Salisbury — whose scriptural interests were revealed by more than one bishop — had received the opportunity of familiarising themselves with the fundamental concept that "holichirche catholike is congregacioun of trewe men wiche only shulbe saved".[53] And only a few years earlier William Wakeham

[48] *Rogeri Dymmok Liber*, pp. 89-92; Dymoke's answer to the fourth conclusion.
[49] *Pol. Poems and Songs*, i, p. 238.
[50] *The Acts and Monuments of John Foxe*, 4th edn., revised J. Pratt (London, 1877), iii, p. 272; cf. pp. 261-2.
[51] *The Holy Bible*, ed. J. Forshall and F. Madden (Oxford, 1850), i, pp. 49, xiv-xv, note k.
[52] *Fasciculi Zizaniorum*, pp. 396, 391. The second of these views was derived from his theories on the sacrament of marriage.
[53] Bishop Ayscough's Register (Salisbury), f. 53 v. (The renunciation of a heretic who was born in Bristol, had recently been living in Oxford, and had been teaching in various places, especially Windsor and Wallingford).

of Devizes, who admitted to having "gaffe entendaunce by many yerys" to English Bible readings in secret places, had been arguing with weavers in a house at Marlborough about his unusual conclusions that "*terra est supra celum*"; "the soul of man is the church of God"; and that "it is no better for laymen to say the *pater noster* in Latin than to say 'bibull babull'."[54] Such erratic thinking could develop along many channels. The Bible, as Henry VIII discovered, was too large and sage a book to leave the safely conservative hands of clerks and aristocrats. Even if the Lollards did not go to it in search of political systems there was no knowing what they might not stumble upon through intensive study in their schools and conventicles, and the archbishop who, in 1409, put controls on the translation and study of scriptural texts, was performing a service which did not benefit the church alone.

While Bible study and personal devotion were to bring men and women more closely into the fold of the church, the primary duty of their keepers was no longer to be prayer, or administration of the sacraments, but preaching. "Evangelization", Wycliffe had said, "exceeds prayer and administration of the sacraments to an infinite degree"; and it was not only "the special work of the curate"; it was also "the work of laymen".[55] Whatever else the Lollards failed in they cannot be accused of forgetting this. Though some thought that the priests of their reformed church would, like those in More's Utopia, be "of exceding holines and therefore very few",[56] they were undoubtedly to form a "godly preaching ministry", and, as far as it existed, theirs was the missionary church *par excellence.* Even if the inauguration of a priesthood of "poor preachers" — and it seems unlikely that there ever was such a conscious ceremony — was no more Wycliffe's own work than the translation of the Bible, the indirect responsibility for these devotional travellers is, equally decidedly, his.

Lay preaching had already achieved popularity during Wycliffe's lifetime: it had taken a firm hold by the time of Archbishop Courtenay's visitation of Leicester in 1389, where he found Lollards maintaining that "any layman can preach and teach the gospel anywhere".[57] The heretics' literature is full of near-theological

[54] Bishop Neville's Register (Salisbury), ff. 52 r. - v., 57 v. ("Bibull babull", idle or empty talk, prating; *Ox. Eng. Dict.*, *sub voce* Bibble-babble, gives 1532 as first reference for the expression, common in the sixteenth century).

[55] *De Officio Pastorali*, p. 33.

[56] For example, John Bath, accused of heresy in 1418, had a book which stated that "A resonable nombre taught in godd' lawe is sufficiant to do the sacrament and preche only goddis lawe in word and dede were y nowe too the churche . . ." Bishop Chandler's Register (Salisbury), f. 18 r.

[57] Wilkins, *Concilia*, iii, p. 208.

arguments justifying their frequent evasion of the law on this matter. Lay participation in the Lollard church included more, however, than preaching. Those laymen who had been educated to think that they could dispute on what seemed (to them) to be a level of equality with bishops and clerks,[58] were challenging the clergy in ways more serious. John Purvey, for instance, had taught before 1401 that "every man holy and predestined to eternal life, even if he is a layman, is a true minister and priest ordained by God to administer all the sacraments necessary for the salvation of man, although no bishop shall ever lay hands upon him".[59]

But was this ever more than a remote ideal? Had the Lollards tried to organise themselves to meet all the spiritual needs of a separate society of believers? Rare moments of vision into the Lollard underground certainly reveal direction of their preaching missions, and of the methods by which their literature was produced, circulated and advertised. The continuity of their programme, as well as the dissemination of their ideas make "some rudimentary form of organisation at least probable".[60] Contemporary authorities, at all events, were in agreement, not only as to the pastoral style affected by the Lollard missionaries, but that they were affiliated into a "sect". Numerous (and not only hostile) descriptions — among which it seems wholly probable that Chaucer's poor parson should be placed[61] — tell how the Lollards went on foot about their work, poorly clad, unshod, staff in hand. What is harder to establish is whether the chroniclers were justified, who concluded further that those who clothed themselves outwardly in gowns of poor russet cloth, as a symbol of their inward scriptural riches, did so by virtue of some sort of centralization.[62]

---

[58] Swinderby's dealings with Bishop Trefnant, (McFarlane, *John Wycliffe*, pp. 131-2), and Thorpe's with Archbishop Arundel, (Foxe, *loc. cit.*), are paralleled in the case of laymen. William Wakeham for instance, boasted to his fellow weavers that "he was before venerable men of the church, and disputed with them, and proved before them that the earth is above the sky". (Neville's Register, f. 52 v.).

[59] *Fasciculi Zizaniorum*, p. 402, cf. pp. 387-9. Purvey also renounced in 1401 the opinion that "every holy priest of God is truly a bishop, prelate, and curate of the faithful": (*ibid.*, p. 403).

[60] McFarlane, *op. cit.*, p. 179.

[61] The Lollard inclinations of the parson must strike anyone with an acquaintance of Lollard literature, as they struck the host himself, (see p. 8 and note 20 above). For an argument of the case (combined, however, with the unconvincing suggestion that the portrait is of Wycliffe) see D. V. Ives, "A Man of Religion", *Modern Language Review*, xxvii (1932), pp. 144-8.

[62] See above p. 5; also *Thomae Walsingham Historia Anglicana*, ed. H. T. Riley (R.S., 1863-4), i, p. 324, and for a more cautious version *Chronicon Henrici Knighton*, ii, p. 184.

Though it would be rash to presume upon a few examples, on occasion the Lollards did undoubtedly resort to ordination. Walsingham, who tells the story of how John Claydon had made his son (or daughter) a priest to celebrate mass in his own house for his wife, rising from childbirth,[63] was certainly not inventing — though he may unwarrantably have generalised from his news — when he recorded under the year 1389 that the Lollards had been making their own priests, *more pontificum*, in the diocese of Salisbury.[64] In July this year there appeared before Bishop Waltham in his manor house at Sonning (Berks.), a heretic by the name of William Ramsbury, who renounced a large number of errors which, he said, he had learnt from a certain Thomas Fishburn, who had tonsured him "with priestly tonsure, and invested him with a certain habit, namely a tunic of russet with a mantle of the same cloth, giving him power both to preach and to celebrate masses". There is no doubt that William Ramsbury had taken his office and its duties seriously. He had not merely practised as well as preached "that it is of greater merit for priests to go through the countryside with a Bible under their arm, preaching to the people, than to say matins, or celebrate masses, or perform other divine offices". For, during the four years before his ministry was discovered he had covered a considerable part of Wiltshire and Dorset, visiting over twenty towns and villages, where he not only expounded Lollard doctrines in churches, cemeteries, and private "confabulations" and drinking parties in taverns, but also celebrated masses according to a special unauthorised Lollard version, full of significant gaps and silences.[65]

Those with similar aspirations and temperaments, if they are not the best of friends, always make the worst of rivals. Perhaps there was too much in common between the Lollards and the mendicants, who embittered the souls of Wycliffe's successors as sorely as they had embittered the soul of Wycliffe himself. The example of William Ramsbury shows that Lollardy could seem to some suspiciously like an attempt to found a new order, and the feelings of the Franciscans cannot have been improved by the deviations of some of their own members in the same direction. The result was

---

[63] *Historia Anglicana*, ii, p. 307, and *The St. Albans Chronicle*, ed. V. H. Galbraith (Oxford, 1937), p. 89. Walsingham wrongly calls him William.
[64] *Historia Anglicana*, ii, p. 188. John Badby had to answer in 1410 for having held that John Rakier of Bristol had as much power to make Christ's body as any priest; Wilkins, *Concilia*, iii, pp. 326-7.
[65] Bishop Waltham's Register (Salisbury), ff. 31 r. - 32 v.

a long battle of mutual recriminations, in which the Lollards never tired of extolling and exhorting their own humble advocates of God's law, or of pouring scorn and hatred on those allies of Antichrist, the friars, who stuffed and sweetened the anecdotal substance of their sermons with "japes, lesynges and fablis" — deceits fit for no man's ear, and damaging to all. For, apart from mendicancy, preaching was the most obvious field for rivalry,[66] and here the Lollards felt that the law was a double perversion of justice: the righteous were excluded so that the evil-doers should inherit the kingdom. And (as they saw it) those hypocritical leaders of the church who feared the revelation of their own shortcomings were busy making the laws under their very eyes.

There were good reasons for this enmity. Against Lollards, as against Wycliffe, the friars were one of the church's chief bulwarks of defence. The very year after the passing of the Oxford constitutions, which tightened up the restrictions on the licensing of preachers, the four orders of the friars were given complete freedom, notwithstanding any legislation to the contrary, to preach throughout the realm.[67] Doubtless there were also personal hostilities, and one may suppose that the friars, like others since, were irritated by a certain arrogance which, to outsiders, must always seem to be inherent in the doctrine of predestination.[68] Probably then, it was for a complexity of causes that annoyance was sometimes fanned into open disturbance. The Lollardy of Peter or William Pattishall, the Austin friar whose detractions of his order caused a riot in London in 1387, and his own summons before the council, rests only on the assertion of a Benedictine chronicler, with an evident relish for the tale.[69] But Lollards were certainly involved in a similar stir, long after, in Coventry.

In November 1424 a preaching tour was given in the midlands

[66] Knighton drew attention to these rivalries, *op. cit.*, p. 188; cf. *Eulogium Historiarum*, ed. F. S. Haydon (R. S., 1858-63), iii, p. 355. Losses of alms due to hostile preaching led to proclamations in favour of the friars in September and October 1399; T. Rymer, *Foedera*, (London, 1704-35), viii, p. 87; *Cal. Cl. Rolls*, 1396-9, pp. 523-4; *Cal. Cl. Rolls*, 1399-1402, p. 1.

[67] Wilkins, *Concilia*, iii, p. 324, from which it appears that the regulations of 1409 were never intended to apply to the friars; cf. *Eulogium Historiarum*, iii, p. 417.

[68] Cf. Arundel's alleged remark to William Thorpe; "For you presume that the Lord hath chosen you only for to preach, as faithfull disciples and speciall followers of Christ"; (Foxe, *Acts and Monuments*, iii, p. 260): or William Ramsbury's statement that he "and his followers were and are in the true faith, and no others"; (Waltham's Register, *loc. cit.*). See also the remarks in Thomas Netter's *Doctrinale*, ed. F. B. Blanciotti (Venice, 1757-9), i, pp. 16-17.

[69] *Historia Anglicana*, ii, pp. 157-9; *Cal. Pat. Rolls*, 1385-9, p. 386, which shows that Pattishall had apostasised. Cf. McFarlane, *op. cit.*, pp. 138-9.

by a "brother" with heretical inclinations called John Grace,
(reputed by certain of his hearers as sometime monk and friar),
which created such disturbances that the Franciscans who opposed
him went in fear of their lives, and here too the council intervened,
with expressions of surprise that no action had been taken by
the authorities in Coventry, where the matter had come to a head.[70]
The mayor, for his part, was disposed to make light of the affair,
as having been grossly exaggerated, but in London it was viewed
differently. John Grace was arrested and imprisoned in the Tower,
and the following May and June securities were taken from about
fifty artisans of Coventry that they would be obedient to the
mayor and bailiffs of the town, that they would not favour or sustain
Lollardy or any heretical opinions, and would not make riotous
congregations or illicit conventicles there, to the disturbance of the
peace. More than half of these persons were also being called upon
to answer for contempt of the peace by having participated in unlawful
assemblies.[71]

Such happenings provide some justification for the Carmelite
collector of Lollard tares, who wrote (retrospectively) of Wycliffe's
early followers; "they were always spreading dissension and inciting
the people to insurrection, so that it was hardly possible for any one
of them to preach without their hearers being provoked to
blows, and discord would arise in towns".[72] Lollards, like
Cathars and earlier continental heretics, and like the friars themselves,
flourished along the main roads, and found supporters among the
trades-people of large towns. The midland boroughs of Coventry and
Northampton (both of them being involved in 1431) can be numbered
with Leicester, among the strongholds of the sect. Bristol, prominent
in 1414, was another such centre. And as the movement became
increasingly artisan, so it gained a footing in both rural and urban
districts in the various branches of the woollen industry, where the
heretics' strength probably reflects the predominance of that trade,
rather than any special activity or predilection on their part. Weavers
in England were never in danger of becoming synonymous for heretics
as they were abroad, and Lollards were to be found in many other
trades, as is witnessed by the suspect girdle-makers, shoemakers,

[70] *The Coventry Leet Book*, ed. M. D. Harris (E.E.T.S., Original Series,
Nos. 134, 135, 138, 146, 1907-13), i, pp. 96-7; *Cal. Pat. Rolls*, 1422-9, pp. 275-6;
F. Devon, *Issues of the Exchequer*, (London, 1837), p. 390; *Vict. County Hist.
Warwicks*, ii, pp. 20-1. John Grace was called a "false prophet" but not a
Lollard.
[71] P.R.O. K.B.27/655, *Rex* m. 6 v.; K.B.27/656, *Rex* mm. 6 r. - 8 v., 16 r.;
K.B.27/657, *Rex* mm. 4 r., 6 v., 10 r. - v.
[72] *Fasciculi Zizaniorum*, p. 272.

whittawers and wire-drawers in Coventry in 1425, who easily out-numbered the weavers, dyers and woolmen.[73]   Among such persons and in such places there were plenty of debatable matters which Lollard views and disciples might inflame.   For as long as people were "governed by pulpits more than the sword in times of peace"[74] the openings for trouble were manifold, and when the pulpit was occupied by Lollard preachers it sometimes threatened to transform times of peace into something very different.

*   *   *

The idea of disendowment as practicable politics was by no means purely, or originally, Lollard.   Proposed by hothead anti-clericals as well as by visionaries, it was aired in the political scene at least twice in the later fourteenth century, at times when the clergy were resisting attempts to subject them to conditions in taxation.   But in the hands of the Lollards disendowment was advanced, elaborated, discredited and, for long, defeated, and if the actual proposals seem to anticipate "in the strangest manner"[75] the achievements of the reformation which in a later day succeeded, the circumstances of their advancement and reception may do much to explain that earlier reformation which failed.   Though it is usually difficult to discover how far such programmes were taken, there is no doubt that they were designed to appeal to a lay audience and — for many years — intended for parliamentary hearing.   To be chary of allowing the possibility of parliament entertaining or even inspiring these schemes is to discount both the precedent of 1371[76] (when the parliament rolls are silent), and the continuance of anti-clericalism in high places.   For, as was demonstrated by the examples of John of Gaunt, or the two friars who addressed an anti-clerical parliament about the laity's right to deprive the church in times of need, those who never wavered in matters of doctrine might for a number of reasons turn extremist when they contemplated great ecclesiastical possessions.   The optimistic knights who in 1385 were urging the king to deprive the recalcitrant clergy even got as far as wrangling about the distribution of the spoils, according to the angry chronicler who heard one of them swearing

---

[73] Whittawers, or white-tawyers. Tawing — treating skins with alum — was an important stage in the processing of leather.

[74] As stated by Charles I. S. R. Gardiner, *History of the Great Civil War*, (London, 1901) iii, p. 135.

[75] M. D. Knowles, *The Religious Orders in England*, (Cambridge, 1948-59), ii, p. 107.

[76] V. H. Galbraith, "Articles laid before the Parliament of 1371", *Eng. Hist. Rev.*, xxxiv (1919), pp. 579-82.

that he would have an annuity of a thousand marks from the temporalities of St. Albans.[77] Here surely, lay the richest bait to hook or hold a Lollard knight, and if churchmen were afraid perhaps they were aware of their weakness.

It is not possible to be sure of the exact moment when the Lollards drew up their detailed suggestions for the redistribution of the church's possessions, or of the occasion when these were first published for a wider audience. The text explaining how clerical temporalities could be used to find 15 earls, 1,500 knights, 6,200 esquires and 100 almshouses, as well as maintenance for 15 universities and 15,000 priests, and additional revenues for the king, is placed by several annalists under the year 1410, but the plan had almost certainly been in existence some years before then, and there is reason to suppose that its appearance or that of something very similar, in 1395, was responsible for some of the reactions of that year. For it would be wrong indeed to judge the potential alarm of Richard II's government at this moment only from the terms of the twelve conclusions which were posted up when parliament was in session, on the doors of Westminster Hall and St. Paul's. Rightly they have been dubbed a manifesto, since they were, avowedly, not a complete programme, and while the tenets listed were expanded — and presumably circulated as far as possible — in a longer book, the proposals about temporalities (which formed the subject of the first article) were alleged to be already in the king's hands.[78]

We have been warned into scepticism of the story that Richard II returned from Ireland to meet the Lollard menace.[79] The clergy, certainly, were jolted into new and uncomfortable awareness of the unsatisfactory nature of their position, and when Boniface IX received a copy of the conclusions he wrote to the king, pointing out (and this was the passage which Walsingham thought worthy of notice), that those pseudo-Christians who were grieving the pope's heart were not only deceiving the souls of the faithful, but also leading their bodies to destruction, and preparing ruin for temporal lords as well. "*Age igitur . . .*" he concluded, having wrapped up his spur to action in the politely involved verbosity of the Roman curia.[80] Action, however, had been taken. For already, before the arrival of these letters, a number of Lollard sympathisers had found themselves the object of most unwanted governmental concern.

[77] *Historia Anglicana*, ii, p. 140.   [78] *Fasciculi Zizaniorum*, pp. 364, 368-9.
[79] See the examination of these events by Cronin in *Rogeri Dymmok Liber*, pp. xxvi-xlii, and cf. McFarlane, *John Wycliffe*, pp. 147, 149-50.
[80] *Cal. Papal Letters*, 1362-1404, pp. 515-6; *Registrum Johannis Trefnant*, ed. W. W. Capes (Canterbury and York Society, xx, 1916), pp. 406-7.

After Richard was back steps were taken to put the royal house in order, when a renunciation of Lollardy was received from John Croft, one of his esquires, and, if Walsingham is to be believed, the "certain matters" objected to the chamber knight, Sir Richard Sturry, by the king at Eltham on 15 August, were no other than countenance of Lollardy.[81]   Before this, and among the first business to be transacted after the king's return to England in May, there had taken place the arrest and examination by the council of John Claydon, later described, not long before he was burnt in 1415, as a Lollard leader.[82] He seems to have been kept in custody in London until early in July, when he was sent, with strict orders that no one should have communication with him, to the safely remote prison of Conway Castle, whence he was transferred, after two years, to be reincarcerated in the Fleet until 1399.[83]   Likewise escorted to confinement in another Welsh castle this summer, were "certain persons called Lollards", who included a group of fellows of Merton College,[84] at least one of whom was subsequently deprived of his fellowship.[85] Orders were given on 26 May for the arrest, and on the following day for the imprisonment at Beaumaris, of Richard Whelpington, Thomas Lucas and John Gamlingay. Thomas Lucas, as will be seen, reappears in suspicious circumstances twenty years later. John Gamlingay's arrest had already been ordered the previous December, together with that of William James, another fellow of Merton

[81] P.R.O. E.403/551, m. 16.

[82] *Cal. Pat. Rolls*, 1391-6, p. 591. H. T. Riley, *Memorials of London*, (London, 1868), pp. 617-8; *Cal. of Letter-Books of the City of London*, ed. R. R. Sharpe (London, 1899-1912), I, pp. 140-1.

[83] *Cal. Cl. Rolls*, 1392-6, p. 430.   Claydon is not here referred to as a Lollard or heretic, but the account given at his trial before Archbishop Chicheley in 1415 shows that he was sent to Conway at this time.   *The Register of Henry Chichele*, ed. E. F. Jacob (Cant. and York Soc., xlii, xlv-vii, 1937-47), iv, p. 132.   In view of their connection with these events it may be noted that both Claydon and Thomas Lucas were later accused of holding erroneous views about clerical possessions.

[84] P.R.O. E.403/551, m. 13. Payment on 2 July to John Ellingham, serjeant-at-arms, escorting certain Lollards to Beaumaris: no names were recorded, but on 27 May orders were given for Ellingham to conduct to this castle a group of persons, including those here referred to, and no one else appears to have been imprisoned at Beaumaris this summer. *Cal. Pat. Rolls*, 1391-6, p. 591; *Cal. Cl. Rolls*, 1392-6, p. 344.

[85] Gamlingay was at some date expelled from Merton, and there seems to be no evidence that he returned after this spell in prison. According to A. B. Emden, *A Biographical Register of the University of Oxford to 1500*, (Oxford, 1957-9), ii, p. 1170, there is no evidence for the expulsion of Lucas after 1408, (as stated by G. C. Brodrick in *Memorials of Merton College*, Oxf. Hist. Soc., iv, 1885, p. 223), but the indictment brought against him in 1417 might have provided grounds for ejection, if he had not already ceased to be a fellow of the college.   This seems possible, since he was then described as Thomas Lucas, M.A. of Andover, Hants.   See below p. 27.

College, whose long profession of Lollardy interrupted his residence on more than one occasion. James was apparently (and it may be thought suggestively) in Bristol when he was arrested on 16 July, two days before the king wrote to the chancellor of Oxford ordering the expulsion of all Lollards in the university, and in particular that of Robert Lechlade. Both James and Lechlade were banished from Oxford until Henry IV's accession brought them (like John Claydon) a change of fortune, and restoration to their fellowships.[86] There remains at least a gist of truth from the chronicler's story: somehow, whatever the reasons, the government had decided that there were certain Lollards with whom it was wiser to take no chances. And Courtenay's purge of the university in 1382, and his visitation of Merton College in 1389, appear to have left a nest of suspects who were still thought to have hopes of finding a more than academic audience.

Although it may have been 1410 before the Lollards returned to a prominent parliamentary manoeuvre, signs are not wanting that threats of clerical deprivation were made publicly on earlier occasions. There is, perhaps, a suspicious similarity in the stories of how, at Worcester in 1402 and 1405 — both times of royal need and clerical reluctance to pay — various knights proposed sending home all the bishops who were present, penniless and horseless.[87] The suggestion certainly had an authentic Lollard ring about it: it might well have issued from those who believed that, "hit is noght lefall bishopes or other men of the chirche to have possessionis, ne to have hors and ride, but thei shulde goe oon fete as criste and his apostilis dede".[88] Again, though the proof is lacking, it is not out of the question that the knights in the Coventry Parliament of 1404, which was considering a resumption of another kind,[89] entertained the idea of a year's resumption of the temporalities of the church. If so, they were speedily informed that excommunication would be their first reward, and the rebuke put by Walsingham into the mouth of Archbishop

[86] *Cal. Pat. Rolls*, 1391-6, pp. 586, 651; *Cal. Cl. Rolls*, 1392-6, p. 434. *Cal. Pat. Rolls*, 1399-1401, pp. 75, 84. William James' Wycliffite views were displayed in 1382, when he is described as being chancellor Rigg's *familiarissimus*. *Fasc. Ziz.*, p. 307. He was welcomed back to Merton in 1399, but his continuing Lollardy is witnessed by his submission to Chicheley in 1420, after which he was confined to the archbishop's manor of Maidstone; *Chichele's Register*, iv, pp. 203-4: Emden, *op. cit.*, ii, pp. 741, 1012-3, 1184.

[87] *Annales Henrici Quarti*, pp. 373, 414.

[88] Bishop Ayscough's Register (Salisbury), f. 53 v.

[89] It was in this parliament that a group of "parliamentary knights" proposed resuming into the king's hands all the landed resources held in absolute possession by the crown since 1366. B. P. Wolffe, "Acts of Resumption in the Lancastrian Parliaments 1399-1456", *Eng. Hist. Rev.*, lxxiii (1958), pp. 586-90.

Arundel, uses the example of the alien priories to suggest that the
common good was not likely to be the first interest to be served by
such proposals.   But this did not deter Mr. William Taylor, Principal
of St. Edmund Hall, Oxford, from preaching publicly at St. Paul's
Cross when parliament was in session in 1406, that religious should
not have temporal possessions, and that there were cases when
temporal lords could lawfully deprive them.   And, it was later said,
by his "dissembling words and metaphors" he advocated the seizure
of clerical property "by the violent rebellion of the people".[90]   These
propositions received public refutation, not only in another sermon
given the following day in the same place,[91] but also in parliament,
where the speaker set forth a petition of the prince of Wales and
the lords, complaining that the Lollards, "both in public sermons and
also in conventicles and secret places called schools, have wrongly and
evilly excited and publicly provoked the people of your realm to
remove and take away their temporal possessions from the prelates
and ministers of holy church"; and, if they were not speedily deflected
from this purpose, it was probable that they would go on similarly to
incite the people "to remove and take away from the temporal lords
their possessions and inheritance, and so to make them common, to
the open commotion of your people, and the final destruction and
subversion of your kingdom for all time".[92]   If similar arguments
were used to defeat the scheme of 1410 they escaped record: the
reply, it seems, was a definitive "*le roi s'avisera*".[93]

Not many years later the ominous prognostications of 1406 must
have seemed to be amply justified.   Though Oldcastle's rebellion
was a movement with which not all Lollards could have fully
sympathised, there may have been many, heretics and otherwise, to
whom it appeared the expected outcome of Lollard pretensions, the
open declaration of the "bateil of god", which meant the "violent
withholding & takyng awey of ther temporel goodis bothe meblis
& unmeblis, the whiche is cause of thor bateil",[94] from all who
hindered the fight.   The long advocated programme for spoliation

---

[90] Archbishop Arundel's Register (Lambeth), ii, f. 118 v.   Cf. A. B. Emden,
An Oxford Hall in Medieval Times, (Oxford, 1927), pp. 125-33 for Taylor's
career and his citation by Arundel.
[91] *The St. Albans Chronicle*, pp. 1-2.   William Thorpe was apparently
present at Thomas Alkerton's sermon, and did some heckling.   It seems also
that Taylor's sermon was widely circulated.   Foxe, *Acts and Monuments*, iii,
p. 278   [92] *Rot. Parl.*, iii, p. 583.
[93] *The Great Chronicle of London*, ed. A. H. Thomas and I. D. Thornley
(London, 1938), p. 90; *The New Chronicles of England and France by Robert
Fabyan*, ed. H. Ellis (London, 1811), pp. 575-6.
[94] Brit. Mus. Add. M.S. 24202, f. 38 v.

of the church now moved on to a different level: direct and forceful action superseded peaceful parliamentary persuasion. And ecclesiastical temporalities were not the sole objective.

None of the bills written "in his favour" which were advertised and circulated by Sir John Oldcastle and his accomplices seems to have survived, but the judicial proceedings taken after the revolt provide the names of persons who wrote and distributed them, (such as Thomas Ile of Braybrooke), as well as indications of the aims of the rebels, which, presumably, they contained. The objectives there described were "wholly to annul the royal estate as well as the estate and office of prelates and religious orders in England, and to kill the king, his brothers, (Thomas, duke of Clarence, and John and Humphrey of Lancaster), the prelates and other magnates of the kingdom, and to turn men of religion, after they had abandoned divine worship and religious observances, to secular occupations: totally to despoil cathedrals and other churches and religious houses of their relics and other ecclesiastical goods, and to level them completely to the ground".[95] Oldcastle himself — the royal family destroyed and disinherited — was to be appointed regent, and various other unspecified rulers (whom the accusers may have suspected of including Sir Roger Acton, Sir Thomas Talbot, and the more elevated supporters of the rebellion), were to be appointed at the will of the rebels, "as a people without a head". And, as is well known, the adherents to these plans proposed to meet together, from various parts of England, "to the number of 20 thousand men", at St. Giles' Fields, on 10 January 1414.

Walsingham, situated once again in uncomfortable proximity to stirring events, heard that his life as well as his livelihood were in danger. Westminster, St. Paul's, and all the London friaries were said to have been proscribed, together with St. Albans, from which house one of its neighbours had actually managed to obtain a roll belonging to the precentor, to help identify the monks he was out to exterminate. He did not expect this work to go unrewarded; his gilded spurs were prepared in readiness for his knighthood.[96] Another Lollard, Thomas Noveray of Illston on the Hill (Leics.), evidently like this brewer of Dunstable, thought to have a good return for investment in the rising; he was reputed to have sold his goods before taking up arms.[97] Examples like these did not

---

[95] P.R.O. K.B.27/613, *Rex* m. 25 r., *Rot. Parl.*, iv, pp. 107-110. My treatment of Oldcastle's rebellion is summary since it has been described elsewhere. In particular see McFarlane, *John Wycliffe*, and W. T. Waugh, "Sir John Oldcastle", *Eng. Hist. Rev.*, xx (1905), pp. 434-56, 637-58.
[96] *The St. Albans Chronicle*, p. 79.   [97] P.R.O. K.B.27/613, *Rex* m. 6 v.

escape adverse notice; they helped to make the cause resemble a treasonable scramble for property and preferment. And though there were Lollards who did not participate in these activities, the movement emerged into the open, as its opponents had long been predicting, as the rebellious enemies of the king and lay lords, not only of clerical possessioners. Nor, despite the aspirations of some of his assistants, did Oldcastle's pretensions help to refute the idea that community of property was the logical outcome of disendowment: as Hoccleve told him in 1415, after the Lollards' chief *campiductor* had gone to earth:—

> "Presumpcion of wit, and ydilnesse,
> And covetyse of good, tho vices three
> Been cause of al your ydil bysynesse.
> Yee seyn eeke: 'goodes commune oghten be'."[98]

It was possible at the time to think that Oldcastle's unknightly and "unkyndly" actions had turned the "sory sekte of lollardie" to confusion.[99] But this was not obvious, particularly to those in positions of authority, for many years to come. The aftermath of the 1414 rebellion, especially while Oldcastle was still in hiding, gave rise to a number of ill-authenticated reports. In July 1415 Lollard collaboration was supposed to have been promised in the Southampton plot. Two years later, when Lollard activity subjected several towns to house-to-house propaganda, it was stated that Henry Greyndor, described as Oldcastle's messenger, had presented the king with a bill requesting the resumption of ecclesiastical temporalities, and that the Scottish attacks on Berwick and Roxburgh were due to Lollard arrangements which included plans for the appearance of the northern version of Richard II. It may also have been hostile intent which led to the further allegation that Oldcastle himself, at the end, maintained that his liege lord Richard II was still alive in Scotland. But while his own actions, during his last days of freedom, had included a visit to north Wales to discuss matters "contrary to his allegiance" with the son of Owen Glendower,[100] more than one of his supposed adherents was accused of treacherous dealings with Scotland.

The petition of a loyal subject of Henry V advanced many years later to the council of his son, described how he had contrived the capture of Oldcastle's clerk and "chief counsellor", Thomas Payne of

---

[98] *Hoccleve's Works*, ed. F. J. Furnivall (E.E.T.S., Extra Series, Nos. 61, 72-3, 1892-7), i, p. 22.
[99] *Pol. Poems and Songs*, ii, pp. 244, 247.
[100] H. G. Richardson, "John Oldcastle in Hiding, August-October 1417", *Eng. Hist. Rev.*, lv (1940), p. 437.

Glamorgan, who having escaped unscathed in 1414, was (four or five years after) in the act of arranging to release the Scottish king from his confinement at Windsor, and escort him back to Scotland.[101] Thomas Payne spent a number of years in prison for this exploit, and — after escape and recapture — was still awaiting trial in 1422.[102] Mr. Thomas Lucas, despite his own previous spell of imprisonment, was more fortunate. Though he had certainly returned to Oxford since 1395, he may no longer have been a fellow of Merton College when he came up for trial before the King's Bench at Easter 1417, on several serious charges. It was presented that on 14 August 1416, at Westminster, he was conspiring the king's deposition and death, both by sending a letter to the Emperor Sigismund (who was then in England negotiating the Treaty of Canterbury),[103] containing among other things that religious should not have or enjoy temporal possessions, and that Richard II was alive in Edinburgh, and also by scattering bills with these suggestions in the streets of London, Canterbury and elsewhere. He was further said to have induced Richard Benet, "Wolman", John Whitlock, with other unknown persons, to destroy Henry V. And in addition, "the said Thomas was and is in agreement with, acting with, counselling and abetting, all the works of John Oldcastle, both in opinions of Lollardy and in all his other evil deeds, treacherously purposed and imagined by the said John Oldcastle towards the king".[104] Thomas Lucas put himself on the country and was acquitted. But both his alleged agents had already been brought to justice.

Benedict Wolman of London, ostler and late under-marshal of the king's marshalsea, described as a Lollard in one source, was drawn through the city and hanged at Tyburn on 29 September 1416.[105] Together with Thomas Beckering of Beckering (Lincs.), "gentleman", (who died in Newgate prison awaiting judgement), he had pleaded not guilty to a charge of conspiring in London since 18 April 1416, on

[101] James I of Scotland was a captive in English hands 1406-1424.

[102] *Proceedings and Ordinances of the Privy Council*, ed. N. H. Nicolas (Rec. Com., 1834-7), v, pp. 104-6; Devon, *Issues*, pp. 373, 375; *Cal. Pat. Rolls*, 1422-9, p. 186; *Rot. Parl.*, iv, p. 196; J. H. Wylie and W. T. Waugh, *The Reign of Henry the Fifth*, (Cambridge, 1914-29), iii, p. 395.

[103] Sigismund arrived at Dover on 1 May 1416; on 26 June Henry V left for Southampton and the emperor went to stay at Leeds Castle in Kent. The treaty was signed at Canterbury on 15 August 1416. E. F. Jacob, *Henry V and the Invasion of France*, (London, 1947), pp. 109-24; *Henrici Quinti Gesta*, pp. 82, 89, 93.

[104] P.R.O. K.B.27/624, *Rex* m. 9 r.

[105] *The St. Albans Chronicle*, p. 102, repeated by Capgrave, *The Chronicle of England*, ed. F. C. Hingeston (R. S., 1858), p. 316.

behalf of Thomas Ward of Trumpington, alleging him to be
Richard II and in the custody of the duke of Albany in Scotland,
and of having sent a petition (which Sigismund had delivered to
Henry V) asking the emperor's assistance in deposing the king.[106]
The third party named in Lucas' indictment had been imprisoned
three months after Henry V's accession, and was brought for trial
soon afterwards, in the summer of 1413.   John Whitlock, groom and
yeoman of Richard II, was accused of conspiring with others against
Henry IV and Henry V continuously since 1406, of adhering to the
king of Scotland, the duke of Albany, and Thomas Ward of
Trumpington, and escorting to Westminster Scottish envoys and with
them spreading the news across England and Wales that Richard was
alive, and about to return to England.   Further, Whitlock was said in
the reigns of both kings to have been posting bills at Westminster and
elsewhere in London, at times of parliament, in one of which produced
at his trial, he declared his readiness, after long service with Richard
and residence in Scotland, to prove to members that the late king was
still alive.[107]

Neither Wolman nor Whitlock is known to have been officially
accused of Lollardy, and Lollards were certainly neither first, nor
foremost, in advocating the case of the Scottish pretender Thomas
Ward, whose usefulness as a figurehead seems to have outlasted his
own existence.[108]   It is possible, however, that John Whitlock's
endeavours at parliamentary lobbying which were later, at least,
attributed to a Lollard connection, throw some light on the anxiety
of the parliament of 1406, which associated Lollards with the
purveyors of lies who were accused of publishing falsely that
Richard II was still alive, and of spreading false prophecies to the great
commotion of the king's subjects, including that "celuy fool q'est
en Escoce" was Richard himself.[109]   The Lancastrian accession,

---

[106] Riley, *Memorials,* pp. 638-41, *Cal. Letter-Books,* I, pp. 165-6.   A Benedict
Wilman, possibly the same, was accused with others in 1410, of plotting the
death of Prince Henry and his brothers, and of sending agents and letters on
behalf of Richard II (allegedly in Scotland), to Scotland, France, Wales and
Flanders, and to various parts of England.   P.R.O. K.B.27/595, *Rex* m. 3v.;
cf. mm. 1 v. 8 r. 11 v. for similar accusations.

[107] *The Fifty-Third Annual Report of the Deputy Keeper of the Public Records,*
(London, 1892), pp. 28-30; *Cal. Cl. Rolls,* 1413-19, p. 31.   Whitlock was
imprisoned together with Thomas Clerk, possibly the Thomas Payne *alias*
Clerk mentioned above.

[108] A reputed Lollard was associated with a plot on Ward's behalf in 1420.
One of the two plotters was taken, and when questioned about the identity of
Thomas Ward maintained that the matter was immaterial, since he had been
dead some time.   R. R. Sharpe, *London and the Kingdom,* (London, 1894-5),
i, p. 248.

[109] *Rot. Parl.,* iii, pp. 583-4, and below p. 314.

though it brought respite to several Lollards, hardly benefited the fortunes of the sect as a whole. It seemed to leave some of its members, together with other would-be legitimist plotters, on the wrong side of dynastic disputes. And no doubt Oldcastle's doings seemed to strengthen the grounds for connecting Lollardy with positive treason.

After 1417 the authorities remained watchful, and their continued vigilance was not misplaced. Oldcastle's plans died neither with his rebellion, nor with him when he went to the stake three years after. Kent, the seat of his Cobham estates, long continued to produce heretics, and some of his adherents who had escaped notice, or been pardoned in 1414, intermittently attracted attention. In 1421, when Oldcastle had been dead four years, securities not to maintain heresy were taken from John Prest who, as vicar of Chesterton (Warwicks.), had sheltered the leader of the sect two years before his capture, and also from one John Reynald, a taylor (probably of London) who undertook not to be of the assent or "covin" of the late Sir John, and not to hold or preach his opinions.[110] A decade after this, legal proceedings were still in progress against Thomas Tiperton of Cheshire, "gentleman", a member of Oldcastle's entourage, who had been appealed with others of various treasons by an approver of the previous reign.[111]

Richard Wyche, the Lollard martyr of 1440 and another of Oldcastle's probable accomplices (but not implicated in his rising), may have helped to keep the word alive in Kent, where he held livings in the 1420's and 1430's. In 1428 the archbishop of Canterbury made a determined effort to track down a large number of Kentish suspects, many of whom seem to have managed to evade him.[112] But among the heretics who were brought up in convocation that year was Ralph Mungyn, said to have been defamed of heresy for about twenty years, and to have had Lollard connections in Oxford and London (where he had been suspended from a cure of souls), as well as in Kent. Those with whom he was accused of having illicit communication included Bartholomew Cornmonger, who had already been cited by the archbishop that summer, and Nicholas Hoper, sometime servant of Sir John Oldcastle, and one of

---

[110] *Cal. Pat. Rolls*, 1416-22, p. 372; *Cal. Cl. Rolls*, 1419-22, pp. 206, 215.
[111] P.R.O. K.B.27/655, *Rex* m. 5 r.; K.B.27/680, *Rex* m. 10 v.; K.B.27/683, *Rex* m. 10 v.
[112] *Chichele's Register*, iv, pp. 297-301; but it is possible that those here referred to were caught, for a contemporary tells of a great anti-Lollard movement in the diocese of Canterbury in 1428, when the archbishop "riding several days and nights" caught and imprisoned at least thirty; *ibid.*, i, p. cxxxvii.

the twelve persons excepted from the general indemnity of March 1414.

Evidence was given at Mungyn's trial that he had made statements in the house of a citizen (late alderman) of London, to the effect that "all goods should be held in common, and no one ought to be allowed to have property".[113]   He was not the only Lollard nurturing ideas which had received special publicity in 1414.   The same convocation in which he was tried heard Robert, rector of Hedgerley (Bucks.), confessor to the "notorious" thief and robber of churches, William Wawe, return a "doubtful" reply to the question of whether it was lawful for spiritual men to have temporal possessions.[114] Robert Hook, rector of Braybrooke (Northants.), whose living had been a centre of Lollard propaganda efforts in Oldcastle's rebellion, was answering for his Lollard opinions for the third time when he appeared before the convocation of 1425.   Among the errors which he agreed to abjure publicly in London and Northampton was that "lordes temporell' been holden by the lawe of god to have all' thinges in commun".[115]   Likewise renouncing his Lollardy in this assembly was Thomas Drayton, rector of Snave (Kent), who as rector of Drayton Beauchamp was another of those who failed to receive pardon in 1414, though he had submitted to a commissary of the bishop of Lincoln the following year.   One of the ways in which he had gone back on this was by associating, as he admitted, with Mr. William Taylor, who had been twice cited by Archbishop Arundel as the result of his sermon of 1406, and released on bail in 1421 after appearing before Archbishop Chicheley.   Taylor was finally condemned in 1423, in the presence of the duke of Gloucester and the earls of Warwick and Vendôme, and one of the articles for which he went to the fire sounds remarkably consistent with the views imputed to him seventeen years earlier: "civil dominion, or secular, which according to me is the same as civil, is so imperfect that in no way can it rightfully accord with priestly perfection, and in no way does Christ wish priests of the church so to rule".[116] The bishop of Lincoln testified to having heard him state also that the civil dominion of kings and temporal lords enjoyed only God's

[113] *Ibid.*, iii, pp. 197, 200, 202-4.

[114] *Ibid.*, iii, p. 188.   Orders for the arrest of William Wawe, who was himself suspected of heresy, as well as of consorting with heretics, were sent out in 1427; Devon, *Issues*, pp. 398-9; *Cal. Pat. Rolls, 1422-29*, p. 422.

[115] *Chichele's Register*, iii, p. 111.

[116] *Ibid.*, iii, p. 169, and above p. 24, note 90. Taylor was burnt on 2 March 1423. His long unorthodoxy on the question of temporalities, and his citation in March 1410 invite speculation on his possible connection with the 1410 proposals. But no mention of them was recorded at his trial.

permissive, but not his benevolent, approval. Lollard ideas — whose academic origin was still, though more tenuously, in evidence — could demonstrate, like Lollard preachers, disquieting obstinacy. Such continuity of personnel and opinions helps to explain the maintenance and revival of schemes for another full scale, if less distinguished, Lollard rebellion. This, discovered and repressed just as it was on the point of maturing in the spring of 1431, brought to light the foiled plans of 1414 persisting in a debased and still more subversive shape.

William Perkins' projected rising produced fewer martyrs than that of Sir John Oldcastle, but this was not because it was less ambitious, and may not have been because the cause was less popular. It lacked conspicuously, it is true, leaders of social distinction, and we only know the names of a few who died. But the subsequent indictments list, besides active participants, more than a score of others who would have benefited from the plot, and if the government of Henry VI's minority saw fit to execute only a handful or so of ringleaders, there is evidence that it felt considerable alarm — alarm which, skilfully exploited by the duke of Gloucester, provided strong grounds for a handsome annuity, not to mention other rewards.[117]

All too little, unfortunately, can be discovered of the Salisbury heretic, John Keterige, "notoriously suspect" and afterwards convicted of heresy and error, whose capture by the late mayor of that town revealed the treason and promoted the capture of John Long and William Perkins *alias* Mandeville, both of Abingdon.[118] John Long had evidently been helping to distribute the seditious Lollard leaflets by which the insurgents had been propagating their plans in London, Oxford, Coventry, Northampton and Frome, as well as Salisbury, where one of the recipients turned informer. The fuller of Abingdon and two men from Westbury who were among those accused of plotting at Salisbury, may have been similarly engaged. One of the latter, Thomas Puttok, clerk, caught in Staffordshire in July, was condemned (like a Wiltshire weaver a

---

[117] The duke and duchess of Gloucester received various presents on 20 May 1431, from the city of Coventry, including a silver and gilt cup, and four pipes of wine. *The Coventry Leet Book*, i, pp. 137-8.

[118] *Proceedings and Ordinances of the Privy Council*, iv, pp. 99-100. Richard Gatour, late mayor of Salisbury, duly received the £20 awarded to him for his action; (P.R.O. E.404/48/125 and E.403/700 m. 13). Orders for the proclamation promising this reward (together with half the goods of anyone convicted), for those producing the writers of seditious bills, had gone out on 13 May (*Cal. Cl. Rolls*, 1429-35, p. 123), and met with a quicker response than similar measures to secure the arrest of Oldcastle. Cf. William Warbleton's assistance in arresting Perkins, for which he too was granted £20. *Proceedings and Ordinances*, iv, pp. 107-8; Brit. Mus. Cott. Ch. iv, 24.

month before), to be hanged, burnt and quartered at Salisbury.[119]
A mercer called John Orpud, reputed to have long held heretical
opinions, but acquitted on the charge of conspiracy, came from the
village of Steventon in Berkshire, which only three years earlier
had produced a heretic defamed of spreading erroneous literature.[120]
Other suspects, likewise acquitted, included a dyer of Frome and
a labourer of Thatcham in the Kennet valley.[121]   William Perkins,
the foremost leader of these and other men, who chose as his popular
pseudonym the title of "Jack Sharpe of Wigmoreland",[122] was a
weaver, and may have derived his particular hostilities towards the
abbot and monks of Abingdon from a professional connection with
the monastery.[123]

Another leader, who was executed at Tyburn nearly two months
after the deaths of Long and Perkins, is a somewhat less obscure
figure whose chequered career takes us back to the after-events of
Oldcastle's rebellion, and shows something of the workings of that
disreputable underworld of intrigue, crime, and high treason plotted
in lowly places, in which some Lollardy was sustained.   John
Russell — described variously as woolman, woolmonger and
woolpacker — had been involved with the law for over fifteen years
before he finally went to his death in July 1431, and there is reason
to credit as substantially true the accusations of the jury which then
presented him as having for long held heretical opinions, and been
plotting the destruction of the king and his laws.   Russell's association
with the heretical baker, Richard Gurmyn, is clearly indicated in the
action which he and two other Londoners brought at Easter 1416
against the king's escheator, for wrongful seizure of various goods
(including a box of deeds and charters), after this heretic had been
burnt on 9 September 1415.   It was alleged by Russell and his

---

[119] P.R.O. K B.9/227/Pt. ii, 1-3; Devon, *Issues*, p. 413.   The other rebel
condemned to be drawn, hanged, and thereafter beheaded, quartered and to
have his entrails burnt, was John Kymrygge, a weaver of Salisbury.

[120] P.R.O. K.B.27/682, *Rex* m. 18 r .   Bishop Neville of Salisbury on 15 June
1428 ordered proceedings to be taken against William Fuller of Steventon,
defamed of Lollardy, of possessing heretical literature, and of publicly teaching
and preaching heretical opinions.   Bishop Neville's Register (Salisbury), f. 77 v.

[121] P.R.O. K.B.9/227/154; K.B.27/686, *Rex* m. 1 v.

[122] The title — which in fact, if not by intention, commemorates a long-lasting
Lollard association with the marches of Wales, and Oldcastle's native country
— may possibly be evidence of a wish to be identified with the duke of York and
the Mortimer claim to the throne; cf. Jack Cade *alias* Mortimer in 1450. (I owe
this suggestion to Mr. McFarlane.)

[123] He is reported to have been bailiff of Abingdon; *A Chronicle of London*,
ed. E. Tyrrell and N. H. Nicolas (London, 1827), p. 119; *Fabyan*, p. 602;
cf. A. E. Preston, *The Church and Parish of St. Nicholas, Abingdon*, (Oxf.
Hist. Soc. xcix, 1935), p. 63.

fellow pleaders that Gurmyn had made over to them, before his conviction, all his movable and immovable possessions, which included properties in Lichfield, Shrewsbury and Shropshire, the deeds to which had been seized.[124] This connection provides an interesting link in the Lollard movement, which leads back at least to 1395, for Gurmyn's friendship and alliance with John Claydon, who went to the stake the day after him, was recorded at the latter's trial. The escheator who was attempting to enforce the crown's rights in taking possession of the goods was Thomas Fauconer who, as mayor of London, had been instrumental in the proceedings brought against Gurmyn and Claydon in the summer of 1415. In July 1416 (by which time Russell and the others had probably lost hope of winning their case), Fauconer found himself committed to the Tower and put to a fine of £1,000, on the basis of a rumoured charge that he had caused Richard Gurmyn to be burnt together with a royal pardon. Russell was running a risky course: for spreading this report he was condemned to the pillory, and then retired to sanctuary at Westminster until he confessed and submitted the following April.[125] But a year later he was back in sanctuary, and there took to false moneying, a pursuit in which he was still engaged at the time of the preparations of March 1431.

The objectives of these insurgent Lollards included, as earlier, religious disendowment. In one source there is preserved the "most evil supplication presented by John Sharpe to Humphrey duke of Gloucester, protector of the realm, to the subversion of the church".[126] The document which follows is none other than the scheme of 1410. This is the more interesting in view of the similarity between the plans of William Perkins and those of Sir John Oldcastle, as revealed in the indictments presented after the revolt had been quelled, and, though there are no doubt grounds why such present-ments should not always be taken at their face value, there is every reason for historians to consider the charges as seriously as did

---

[124] P.R.O. K.B.27/620, m. 7 r-v. Fauconer's case was that in 1407-8, when Gurmyn had been accused of heresy and was a debtor to the king and others, he was indicted for felony, and had entered into a collusive action to make over to Russell and the other two all his goods and chattels. But, it was alleged, he had never given them livery either of the goods, or of the deed of conveyance. Already before this action, in January 1416, Gurmyn's goods had been granted to a yeoman of the king's chamber; *Cal. Pat. Rolls*, 1413-16, p. 388.

[125] Riley, *Memorials*, pp. 630–4; *Cal. Letter-Books*, I, p. 180; see above, p. 22 and notes 82, 83.

[126] Brit. Mus. M.S. Harl.3775, ff. 120 r. - 121 v. Printed in *Annales Monasterii S. Albani a Johanne Amundesham*, ed. H. T. Riley (R.S., 1870-1), i, pp. 435-6. This text, like Fabian's version of the 1410 proposals, omits the suggestion for founding fifteen universities.

Henry's lieutenant, particularly in view of the known antecedents of one of the leaders. If the 1410 petition was indeed among the bills circulated by Perkins to gather his supporters he must have been ostensibly and with one hand campaigning for parliamentary disendowment, while privily and with the other, he was plotting the destruction of the very persons who would have had to carry it out. The rebels' true aims, were they in fact those described so circumstantially by the indictments, could never have had much hope of a sympathetic parliamentary hearing. But, radical as they were, one can hardly suppose that even the most foolhardy of leaders would have canvassed too openly for their realisation: "totally to destroy the estate and person of the king, as well as the estate and office of prelates and religious orders in the kingdom of England", and "to despoil both churches and religious houses of relics and other goods and chattels found in them, and to fill the said churches with secular persons of their own circle (*covina*) and opinion; and to move and make insurrection in the said kingdom, and such commotion of people between the king and his subjects against their due allegiance, that these traitors could at their own lust and will rule and kill the king, his lords, temporal and spiritual, and the religious orders".[127]

This is more than an echo of 1414. Jack Sharpe and his "meyne of rysers" were alleged to have found that the proposals for the complete destruction of religious persons and houses which they had produced, "under colour of sanctity", could not be put into effect "as long as the royal power and regal state of the king, and the state and office of prelatical dignity continued in prosperity in the kingdom".[128] Oldcastle's treason had been explained likewise. But William Perkins and his accomplices had gone a significant step beyond the known aims of 1414. They were going to be sure that there was a vested interest in their reformation, and it might have been more difficult to suppose in 1431, as Hoccleve had in 1415, that community of property was the Lollards' slogan. For though there is evidence to suggest that this conception was being advocated in London and Northampton not long before, the disciples of Robert Hook and Ralph Mungyn might have hesitated to join in the train of William Perkins and John Russell, who had not only drawn up a long list of proscribed secular and ecclesiastical lords, but had also worked out in detail the manner in which they were "themselves to take possession of the property of others of the king's faithful lieges".[129] Secular

---

[127] P.R.O. K.B.9/225/2; K.B.27/681, *Rex* m. 8 r.
[128] P.R.O. K.B.27/681, *Rex* m. 8 r.
[129] *Ibid.*

disestablishment; the disendowment of lay lords together with ecclesiastical; the accession of Lollard nominees to property as well as to government: such, apparently, was the plan.

The royal uncles were the first to be done away with, as they were to have been (in a different capacity) in 1414, and on other occasions. Now, likewise honoured by inclusion in the list, were nine abbots, three priors, the dukes of Norfolk and York, and the earl of Huntingdon. Though it is clear from all accounts that Perkins was to "take upon himself as a prince"[130] the division of the spoils, we are not told what positions the leaders themselves had intended to take, and the details of the scheme, which survive in the accusations against John Russell, may have been modified by him after his fellow plotters (Perkins and Long) had gone to their deaths. At all events, the twenty or so "certain poor people" named as successors elect of those condemned were almost all Londoners — against whom no subsequent proceedings appear to have been taken, on the grounds that they were "totally ignorant" of the rôles assigned to them. Those appointed to succeed the dukes of Bedford, Gloucester and Norfolk, (holding in addition respectively, Glastonbury, Westminster, and Bury St. Edmunds), were John Byle of Chipping Norton, John Cook, a London weaver, and Richard Stowe of London. Lordships and offices were allocated in the same way to the rest of the obscure individuals predestined for sudden preferment in this territorial lottery, some of them being selected for the mysterious posts of *regis controrotulator*, *embasiator*, *custos London'*, and *capitalis hered'*, as well as two to be masters of the Lollard chancery, and one to be secretary. As in 1410 the requisitioned properties did not touch certain ecclesiastical possessioners, such as cathedral chapters, colleges, chantries, and the charterhouses, but some additions had been made, notably of London friaries, including (significantly, since it was expressly excluded in Jack Sharpe's supposed bill) that of the Crutched Friars.[131]

Careful thought seems also to have gone into the means of achieving this astonishing programme. Here, Perkins may have taken into account the experience of 1414. For, though London and Londoners featured to a large extent in the rebels' plans — meetings having been held not only at Abingdon but also continuously in March and April at Finsbury and "other hidden and suspect places" in Middlesex, where indeed the plotting probably began — the place of assembly appointed for 22 May was far distant from the capital. The

[130] P.R.O. K.B.27/686, *Rex* m. 1 v; K.B.9/227/154 and pt. ii/1.
[131] P.R.O. K.B.27/681, *Rex* m. 8 r.; K.B.9/225/2.

"diverse unknown rebels to the number of 20 thousand men"[132] were to assemble in warlike array in a field called "Gyldynmylle" in the village of East Hendred in Berkshire. From there the first objective (before the various "armies" of rebels continued their course of destruction through the realm), was the abbot, monks and buildings of the abbey of Abingdon.[133] The irony was certainly intentional which ordained that William Perkins, after his arrest at Oxford, should be sent to be executed, with others, at Abingdon, on the very day when they were to have risen. Meanwhile in the capital (which had earned the gory spectacle of Perkins' head), hopes — or suspicions — died hard, to judge by the charge brought that autumn against Richard Leyk, holy water clerk, of Westminster, an associate of the late John Russell, of having on 26 July dispersed subversive literature, and nominated and created certain persons in the parish of St. Clement Danes to be bishops, dukes, earls and barons, including one to be treasurer of England.[134] It makes a pathetic postscript to a not very glorious affair.

The ramifications of this abortive plot were widespread, and though some of its intentions now appear wild in the extreme, the previous history both of the Lollards and of the arguments used by their opponents, help us to understand, as we cannot doubt, the anxious reactions of the government. The duke of Gloucester sent a special commissioner to deal with the heretics in Coventry, where more of them were executed, and himself returned to the midlands in the summer to make enquiry into Lollard activities, visiting both Leicester, and Coventry (where he had been in May). Meanwhile proceedings were started in Wiltshire and Somerset, and the abbot and bishop of Ely met with others in special session at Hertford[135] on the same day that John Orpud was indicted, and William Perkins executed, at Abingdon, under the direction of the king's lieutenant. It appears both from Gloucester's movements, and from the indictments, that Abingdon, Salisbury, London, and the midlands were the chief centres of the rebellion. But the royal letters sent in

---

[132] Cf. above, p. 25 for the same unrealistic figure which likewise appears in the indictments after Oldcastle's rebellion. It is possible that the number was derived from the Lollards' own claims; Walsingham says their bills in 1413 included statements that they had a hundred thousand supporters, (*St. Albans Chronicle*, p. 70), and cf. the remarks in a Lollard letter in *Snappe's Formulary*, ed. H. E. Salter (*Oxf. Hist. Soc.*, lxxx, 1924), p. 132.

[133] When Archbishop Chicheley visited the abbey of Abingdon in 1423 he found much in need of correction, and Ralph Ham, the abbot of 1431, was removed from all the offices he then held. *Chichele's Register*, iii, p. 512; A. E. Preston, *op. cit.*, pp. 60, 62.

[134] P.R.O. K.B.27/682, *Rex* m. 15 v.

[135] *Chronicon Rerum Gestarum*, in *Annales . . . Amundesham*, p. 64.

July to the alderman and bailiffs of Bury St. Edmunds, show that alarms and suspicions which were circulating that summer about "the malicious entent and purpos of goddis treitours and oures" extended further afield.[136]

Unlike 1414, no members of the landed gentry are known to have lost their lives in the venture of 1431. This does not mean to say, however, that none was thought to be implicated. There are indeed signs that one knightly family, whose name had previously been mentioned in connection with the heresy of the Lollards, was placed under particular surveillance at this time. On 19 June commissioners were sent to Buckinghamshire to arrest and bring Sir John Cheyne before the council, to seize his manors of Grove and Drayton Beauchamp, together with all his books and suspicious memoranda, and to investigate the nature of his armoury. Both Sir John and his brother Thomas Cheyne were committed to the Tower until 4 August.[137] They belonged to a family which had long been under suspicion of heresy, and which had patronised the Thomas Drayton who abjured in 1415 and 1425. And they had both been implicated in 1414, when John had gone to the Tower with their father Sir Roger Cheyne, and Thomas was excepted from the king's pardon. The treatment they now received emphasises the fact that the government looked upon these rebels as Oldcastle's successors, fearing, as the king expressed it to the townsmen of Bury, their intent to "distroie alle men of estate, thrift, and worship, as thei purposed to have do in oure fadres daies, and of ladds and lurdains wolde make lordes . . ."[138] But by the autumn, when some of them were acquitted, the "ladds and lurdains" had been put in their proper places, and the crisis was over.

No doubt as they lost influence the Lollards also lost moderation. If they lacked strong knightly support they could hardly look so hopefully to parliament, and the levels of society from which they were recruiting were perhaps less likely to do so. The more artisan the movement became, the more easily its radical elements could predominate. Those who died as rebels and traitors in these ambitious exploits may have been only a small minority of extremists, who were not at the heart of the continuing doctrinal movement. Some, strictly speaking, may not have been heretics at all. But, to those who had long been saying, or hearing, that revolution and radicalism were the likely outcome of the heretics' beliefs, the

[136] *Archaeologia*, xxiii (1831), pp. 341-3; (from a register of Bury St. Edmunds, now Brit. Mus. Add. M.S. 14848).
[137] *Cal. Pat. Rolls*, 1429-36, p. 153; *Cal. Cl. Rolls*, 1429-35, p. 89.
[138] *Archaeologia*, xxiii (1831), p. 342.

development and debasement of their programme and distinctions within the sect, must have mattered less than the fulfilment of unpleasantly prophetic utterances; 1431 must have seemed very much like 1381, as well as 1414, starting all over again. If the Lollards had advocated reform, they had tried — and tried more than once — something which was more like revolution: if they had denied the authority of the pope they had also attacked the king: from making their own priests they had turned to the creation of dukes and earls. Perhaps the story does not even end with Jack Sharpe's sorry fiasco. If the Lollards avoided involvement in the rising of 1450 this does not prove that they had given up all hope of another rebellion of their own. Indeed, as William and Richard Sparke admitted to Bishop Chedworth, Lollards in the diocese of Lincoln were still in 1457 confederating together and gathering sworn followers into a secret society, in the hope of overthrowing Antichrist.[139] Left wing Lollards who helped to give the movement such prominence and discredit may have persisted as long as the heresy itself.

*   *   *

Lollardy did not bring England the Inquisition. But, not surprisingly, the methods of repression were similar; an increase of episcopal powers, the assistance of the friars, and the support of the lay arm. The rôle of the state, though the early stages of its participation have been described, remains nevertheless somewhat enigmatic. Why, when the church seems to have made the way open, was it so long before England acquired the power which existed elsewhere to burn heretics? And if "it is unlikely that fresh measures would be taken against heretics except upon a petition from the clergy",[140] why did three independent chroniclers on three different occasions attribute the initiative in the new proceedings to the commons?[141] Chroniclers, unfortunately, may often seem to be getting away with an untruth or half-truth for the lack of means to prove them wrong. Such evidence as there is, however, certainly suggests that both in 1382 and 1401 the first moves were made by ecclesiastics, and that the chronicles, if taken at their face value, are

[139] *Lincoln Diocese Documents*, ed. A. Clark (E.E.T.S., Original Series, No. 149, 1914), p. 92.
[140] H. G. Richardson, "Heresy and the Lay Power under Richard II", *Eng. Hist. Rev.*, li, (1936), p. 10.
[141] *Fasciculi Zizaniorum*, p. 272, (reference to a petition which, allegedly, spurred Courtenay to call the Blackfriars meeting): *Chronicon Henrici Knighton*, ii, p. 263, (a request of lords and commons in 1388): *Annales Henrici Quarti*, p. 335, (a petition of the commons in 1401).

either mistaken or misleading. But either way their words are interesting, for at the very least they provide reason to suppose that there were moments when the commons acted as the willing co-operators of the clergy. In 1401 at any rate, to judge by their petition to this parliament, the commons were anxious that an example should be made of any man or woman arrested for Lollardy, "pur legerement cesser lour malveis predications".[142] If, on the other hand, there were members of the commons who were actively hostile to the clergy, who would resent putting more power into their hands, and might even contemplate taking some away, then the passage of anti-Lollard legislation would not always have been plain sailing. Signs that some, anyway, of the commons had qualms about what was happening seem evident in a petition to the October parliament of 1382, in which they asked for repeal of the statute passed the previous May on the grounds not only that they had not agreed to it, but also because it was not their intention "to bind themselves or their successors to the prelates more than their ancestors in the past".[143] Or again, there is the request of 1410, when the commons asked to have returned a petition "touchant l'estatut nadgairs fait des Lollardes".[144] This may have been the petition which, Walsingham reports, was produced after the failure of a demand for convicted clergy to be put in royal and lordly, not episcopal prisons, and asked for modification of the procedure for heretical preachers provided in 1401. If so, it was withdrawn under a threat that if it was pressed the penalties provided would be aggravated rather than reduced. Such afterthoughts, whatever their origins, were displeasing to ecclesiastical chroniclers, who were anxious for commoners, as well as lords, to be the sound and undivided friends to a church in need. The truth was perhaps that the laymen were not considering the church's needs alone, nor attributing powers to it alone. If their views were seldom united, and varied with the times, they were most likely to approach unity when the dangers seemed most common. And if the clergy indicated the general form the legislation should take, they waited on the pleasure of statesmen to decide upon its precise terms, as well as the moment when it should be passed.

[142] *Rot. Parl.*, iii, pp. 473-4.
[143] *ibid.*, p. 141.
[144] *ibid.*, p. 623. Cf. *The St. Albans Chronicle*, p. 56. (Kingsford thought that the petition which was withdrawn was the 1410 disendowment scheme, and that this explains the latter's absence from the rolls of parliament. It seems probable, however, that there were other reasons why such radical proposals would not have been likely to find their way to formal enrolment. Cf. *Chronicles of London*, ed. C. L. Kingsford (Oxford, 1905), p. 295).

Historians have long since noticed that Archbishop Courtenay pressed home the first successful campaign against Lollardy in the reaction following the revolt of 1381, and it can hardly have been only the advent of a new archbishop which brought the movement so prominently into view for the first time in the spring of 1382. The fact that "subverters of all kinds became suspect at a time of general subversion",[145] affected not only Wycliffe but a number of others, who found their hitherto obscure careers given a sudden and glaring publicity. When the publicity was next renewed it was by an administration which was concerned to meet the endemic fears of revolt by constructive improvements in the labour laws. The comprehensive legislation of the Cambridge Parliament of 1388 shows that the lords appellant — who had themselves come to power on a dangerous wave of rebellion, and had been told in the Merciless Parliament that there would soon be a new rising unless remedy was given for the recent "leve et rumour" of the "petitez gentz" of the realm[146] — intended to provide fully for the general maintenance of law and order. The new commissions, of laymen as well as ecclesiastics, appointed to deal with Lollardy, (several of them sent out while the Merciless Parliament was in session), would have accorded well with this interest, as well as with that of the two archbishops, one of them also chancellor and brother of one of the older appellants. Itinerant preachers, who in 1382 had been made liable to immediate arrest and imprisonment in secular prisons, now came under further lay supervision: the commissions were given the task of hunting out not only Wycliffite works, but also those teaching or studying them; at the same time local officials (sheriffs, mayors, bailiffs, etc.) were made generally responsible for assisting such enquiries. And offenders were subject to forfeiture as well as imprisonment.

If there was a background of social and political unrest to this earliest legislation against heresy, the precedents of 1382 and 1388 were fully followed on subsequent occasions. Moves in the direction of more extreme measures started in 1395, when the clergy of the southern province petitioned the two archbishops to approach the king, so that he might bring the assistance of the lay arm to deal with the Lollard sect. But though, as has been seen, Richard did not disregard Lollard activities, he took no steps to meet this plea, or another clerical request two years later, when the king and lords of parliament were asked for legislation to introduce the death penalty

[145] M. McKisack, *The Fourteenth Century*, (Oxford, 1959), p. 514.
[146] *Chronicon Henrici Knighton*, ii, pp. 266-7.

for heretics. When *De Heretico Comburendo* finally went through not only had the archbishop returned to stronger standing with a different king: the new king had also had a significant taste of political instability and disturbance.

The act which in 1401 gave England the death penalty for relapsed and impenitent heretics was also designed to meet the "damages, dangers and scandals" threatening the kingdom from the activities of the new sect, which, as the clergy pointed out to parliament, "basely instructs and informs the people, and incites them to sedition and insurrection as far as they are able, and makes great dissensions and divisions in the people . . ."[147] But Henry IV did not need instruction about the hazards of the pulpit. Already, in May 1400, writs had been sent to the sheriffs throughout England ordering proclamation to be made that no chaplains, apart from parochial chaplains in their own churches, were (under pain of imprisonment and forfeiture) to presume to preach without due licence from their diocesan, as some, it was learnt had been doing, spreading heretical views to the disturbance of the people and injury of the faith.[148] There was cause for alarm. But there long had been, and was it perhaps something more than the souls of his subjects which was causing the king this anxiety, and leading him to anticipate — if not precipitate — action in a sphere which more properly belonged to the church? 1400 was a year of widespread troubles, and Henry IV had already dealt with his first major rebellion. He may well have feared the influence of the pulpit on his own position.

To some contemporaries the restrictions imposed upon teachers of heresy in 1401, seemed quite as important as the introduction of burning which continental practice had already made familiar. The statute was framed to deal both with unauthorised preachers who escaped episcopal control by moving from diocese to diocese, and also with the holding of illicit "conventicles and confederations", meetings which had borne a sinister content at an earlier time of anxiety, twenty years back, and about which the king and some of the lords had lately expressed their concern to convocation.[149] Private Lollard study groups were certainly no new development at this time, and it is significant that they were given such prominent

[147] *Rot. Parl.*, iii, pp. 466-7.
[148] *Cal. Cl. Rolls*, 1399-1402, p. 185.
[149] Wilkins, *Concilia*, iii, p. 254. The word "conventicle" bore the opprobrious meaning of a private meeting for an unauthorised purpose, and was not only applied to heretical gatherings. (See Du Cange, *Glossarium*). 1381 shows its use in the sense of conspiratorial groups and assemblies. For examples see *The Peasants' Rising and the Lollards*, ed. E. Powell and G. M. Trevelyan (London, 1899).

attention at a moment when secret gatherings of any kind were liable
to be viewed with suspicion.   Revolution; sedition; suspicion; and
once again legislation was passed against the Lollards.   Once again,
too, there had been an exchange of powers.   Transgressors who
participated in the prohibited schools and conventicles of the heretics,
or who preached without episcopal licence were subjected to a
royal fine: but the right of immediate arrest and imprisonment of
suspects was now given to the bishops.[150]

It was not long before these provisions were also found to be
inadequate.   The ghost of Richard II which lingered so long, and
haunted the Lancastrians in such uncomfortably material forms was
already abroad in the spring of 1402.   Various mendicant preachers
went to their deaths that year, not for denying the faith but for
denying the rightful king, teaching that ghosts could walk, and,
given sufficient support, walk back to the throne.   And as we have
seen, suspicions of Lollard complicity in these matters did not take
long to settle.   The parliament of 1406, which found compelling
reasons for drawing attention to the danger of Lollard sermonising,
ordained as a temporary measure that anyone found preaching
or writing in favour either of disendowment, or of Richard II's
continued existence, should be arrested and imprisoned without bail,
taken before the chancellor, and brought to be judged by the king
and lords in the next parliament.   The statute also empowered the
lords spiritual and temporal, the justices and keepers of the peace,
and all local officials to make enquiries and arrest all such persons
without further commission.   When, the following year, Archbishop
Arundel drafted the improvements upon the clerical machinery for
licensing preachers which were published in 1409, though he brought
the legislative action of the church to bear on the problem in a way
which the Lollards found thoroughly objectionable, he can hardly be
said to have been demonstrating ecclesiastical initiative.

The propagators of heresy, for reasons more than one, increasingly
became one of the responsibilities of secular officials.   The final and
logical step was taken in 1414 when parliament met at one of the
centres of heresy, in a mood of little tolerance towards the heretics
from whose recent traitorous purpose not only the estates and
ministers of the church, but "all the temporal estates of the realm were
also on the point of being finally and completely destroyed, with all
manner of policy therein . . ."[151]   The outcome of these deliberations
was to make heresy hunting a normal duty of the chancellor,

---

[150] *Statutes of the Realm*, ii, pp. 125-8: 2 Henry IV, c. 15.
[151] *Rot. Parl.*, iv, p. 15.

treasurer, justices, and all local officials, who were to be sworn into this obligation when taking office. Secular courts were authorised to receive indictments for heresy, and the justices were henceforth to be commissioned with full powers of enquiry into the activities of all who in sermons, schools, conventicles, congregations and confederacies, as well as by writing, were maintaining heresy. Two years later Archbishop Chicheley followed suit, providing for clerical enquiries to be held twice a year in every rural deanery. The mesh of controls which persistent heretics had to evade was now closer, and also double. Laymen as well as churchmen were regularly involved in the surveillance of Lollards, with all their attendant aspirations. The legislation ends here, after the mêlée at St. Giles' Fields, not because heretics had ceased to be a danger, but because England had acquired a full complement of laws to deal with the offending sect — laws which Mary Tudor re-enacted for heretics of a different breed.

*   *   *

As it turned out the contemporary was right who wrote so confidently:—

> "And, pardé, lolle thei never so longe,
> Yut wol lawe make hem lowte;
> God wol not suffre hem be so stronge
> To bryng her purpos so abowte".[152]

Oldcastle's revolt proved, in the end, to have been the Lollards' day of judgement. They could nearly boast such another rebellion, but not such another leader. Among the reasons why they never lived to see God's doom enacted after their own desires must surely be set the lingering echoes of an old refrain. If Lollardy emerged full grown from the head of rebellion the church had thereby acquired most strong defensive armour. We shall never know how many recruits joined or left the Lollard movement not only for the stimulus of its devotional creed, but also because it provided the promise of rewarding but treasonable action in rebellious times. But extremism, as the Anabaptists later showed, might discredit, if not kill reform. "Pore phantasticals", complained Calvin, "have hyndered and disturbed us";[153] what was needed was strong moderate influence to win the day. Lollardy was persistent, but such hopes as it ever had of achievement always hung upon a single thread, for the heretics no more than their opponents needed telling that the lay lords were the keystone

[152] *Pol. Poems and Songs*, ii, p. 245.
[153] J. Calvin, *A short instruction for to arme all good Christian people agaynst the pestiferous errours of the common secte of Anabaptistes*, (London, 1549), from the Prologue.

to success; if they refused persuasion when living they were to do service by their deaths. The names of suspect Lollard knights are few, and there could certainly have been a number of reasons for this apart from the church's long schooling that a Lollard reformation would bring them losses and not gains. But the final outcome, as it stood, was shaped by more than hopes of the recompense or fears of the fires awaiting in a world to come.

This is not, at all, to deny that there was, throughout, a very genuine alarm for the salvation of souls, and concern for the maintenance of the orthodox faith; nor to say that this aspect of the Lollard movement was not, and is not, the first to be considered. But the nature of the heresy, of the society in which it spread, and of the government which had to deal with it, were such that its religious implications could not be considered alone. And other happenings of the period ensured that they were not. Sedition and dissent had come of age together.

NOTE, 1976

A full contemporary notice of Perkins' rising, which I only discovered after the publication of this article, is to be found in the volume of collected papers of Nicholas Bishop of Oxford (Cambridge University Library, Ms. Dd. 14. 2). Anthony Wood, who knew the collection through Brian Twyne's excerpts, described Nicholas Bishop as an author "not unworthy the taking notice of, and as yet unknown to the world".[1] Nicholas was the son and heir of Bartholomew and Isabella Bishop of Oxford, and his book was primarily a personal cartulary though it also incorporated matters of wider interest, including the brief chronicle of English kings from which the following extracts are taken.[2] The compilation can be dated from internal references to 1432. At Oxford Nicholas Bishop was situated not far from the centre of Perkins' activities, and though he remains singularly silent about occurrences in the city (including Perkins' capture), his account is valuable by reason of its proximity both in time and place to the events mentioned. The first paragraph on the rising appears to be derived from an official document but Bishop goes on to add some details not recorded else-

---

[1] *Anthony Wood's Survey of the Antiquities of Oxford*, ed. A. Clark, ii (Oxf. Hist. Soc., xvii, 1890), p. 291; cf. *Anthony Wood's Life and Times*, coll. A. Clark, iv (Oxf. Hist. Soc., xxx, 1895), p. 193.

[2] Bartholomew Bishop, whose will was dated 1395, seems to have died about 1396, and Nicholas to have been born some time after 1368. For their holdings in Oxford see H. E. Salter, *Survey of Oxford* (Oxf. Hist. Soc., N.S. xiv, xx, 1960, 1969), esp. i, pp. 22-6, 144-5.

where. From him we learn that the wife of a mayor was among those executed at Coventry,[3] while at Warwick a Chipping Norton minstrel, Hendy Clarener, lost his life having been found guilty of harbouring Lollard books and of disparaging the eucharist. Bishop also adds to the dimension of events in London, with his report of seventeen arrests including a rich man of Cheap, and the rescue of Perkins' head from London Bridge by two men who were caught in the act. He tells of a ceremonial book-burning later that same summer. And finally, this account lends weight to the view that it was suspicions of Lollard sympathies which placed members of the Cheyne family under arrest at this time.[4]

I am most grateful to Mrs. Dorothy Owen for kindly checking this transcript (in which I have extended obvious abbreviations), and thank the Librarian of the Cambridge University Library for permission to publish.

CAMBRIDGE UNIVERSITY LIBRARY MS. DD. 14. 2.

f. 286[r–v]

In the thursday next after the closyng of Easter, in the yer regnyng of our kyng Harry the sixte the ix yer[5] at Abyngdon in the counte of Berk' bethin the kynges yerd, John Perkyn alias Sharp de Wygmorelond, John Long Couper of Chepyng Norton, a webbe of Stevynton smytsmart, Goqwyt[6] wyth hur felshyp to them i socied the numbre of xx m[l] as Lollardes fals heretikes common traytoures rysarrs conspiratours ymagined and to geders confederid oon with many tho thenn i socied and felouns of hur covyn and hur false malis before thaught as common liggers in a wayte of high weyes and the feyth of holy church to destruye there falsliche traytourlich as common traytures and felouns of our kyng lete dude wryte divers fals bulles and fals scriptures and gilful and many contraris the doctrine of christyn feyth conteynyng, and thenn to the puple of our kyng to be publich and to be comuned follysch dampnablysch in divers places that is to [f. 286[v]] wytyng in citees of London of Salebur' and of townys Coventre Marleburgh wikkydliche have set styked cast to ground, and every day so to wryte

---

[3] Cf. the report in Gregory's Chronicle about some of Perkins' followers being hung, drawn and quartered in Coventry, "and a woman was be-heddyd at the galous". *Historical Collections of a London Citizen*, ed. J. Gairdner (Camden Soc., N.S. xvii, 1876), p. 172.

[4] Cf. J. A. F. Thomson, *The Later Lollards, 1414-1520* (Oxford, 1965), pp. 60-1, 147.

[5] Marginal note: "traytours".

[6] *Sic.* The sense requires "gathered".

procureth to styke to draw to ground cessit nat ne dredith in grete
offens the high maieste of god and of dignite of corowne regal and
derision of christian feith in disturbaunce of the kynges pese and wrong
and contempt of al chistian pepele, and thenn with hur fals imaginacouns
wikkedlich by hur fore thaughtes to the world and to the multitude
xx m^l and overe of pueple etc.

Where a pon this chevynteyns as now at instawns of Umfray Duk of
Glowcestre buth draw hanged hedyd quartered[7] and in divers countreys
hur quarteres i hanged up in tokyn here of this tresun thus for to be
eschwed fro this tyme forth.   Al so a minstrell of Chepyng Norton by
name Hendy Clarener at Warewyk for this cause i drawe hanged hedid
quartered and so i send ford, as is a bove told.   A womman a mayreswyf
of Coventre for this cause al so be hedyd.   Al so the lord Cheyne for
thes causes is a restud and lad to the Tower of London.

f. 288^r

Sir John Cheyne knyght Thomas his brother sqwyer[8] for this seyd
Lollardy buth a restud and lad to the tower of London at the
comaundement of [the] Duke of Glowcestre lew tenaunt of kyng Harry
the sixt and uncle to the kyng at his wyll in the moneth of June anno ix^o
this was dun.   Al so a worthi man and a riche of Chepe in London is
a restud for this lollardy and xvi men wyth hym a peched.   Al so this
seyd Perkyn his heed fro London brigge by twey wel faryng men was
take fro thennis and soon a pon that thees twey men wer take ther with
and a rested and buth at poynt to be hange draw and quartered ther
fore, and do with as is a for seyd.   Al so Hendy Clarenere a hanged
draw and quartered for be cause that he sad that godys body myght nat
be grounde in a mille and that he kept counseil in huydyng of Lollard
bokes.

f. 290^r

... at the same procession[9] lollardes bokes weren brend as many as
a man myght ber.

---

[7] Marginal note: "treson — traytours".
[8] Marginal note: "Henry the sixt".
[9] Seemingly that at St Paul's on 4 July 1431, referred to ff. 288^v, 289^v.

Additional Notes to Chapter 1

2   See now for this text and its date *Jack Upland, Friar Daw's Reply and Upland's Rejoinder*, ed. P.L. Heyworth (Oxford, 1968), quote at p. 75.

26   See K.B. McFarlane, *Lancastrian Kings and Lollard Knights* (Oxford, 1972), for the posthumous edition of these lectures, edited by J.R.L. Highfield.

65   Anne Hudson, in 'A Lollard Mass', *Journal of Theological Studies*, N. S. xxxiii (1972), pp. 407-419, has now published this text and elucidated the significance of Ramsbury's form of the mass.

126   Anne Hudson, in *Selections from English Wycliffite Writings* (Cambridge, 1978), pp. 203-4, thinks the Harley manuscript's association of the 1410 bill with 1431 should be rejected.

Postscript to Note, 1976

These extracts from Nicholas Bishop's manuscript were already in print (as I discovered later). S. B. Meech's article, 'Nicholas Bishop, an Exemplar of the Oxford Dialect of the Fifteenth Century', in *Publications of the Modern Language Association of America*, Vol. xlix (1934), pp. 443-59, printed Bishop's historical notes (ff. 286r – 290r of CUL Ms. Dd. 14.2) on pp. 457-9, preceded by two English passages concerning his quarrel with the abbot of Osney. However, since Meech's interest was linguistic, not historical (which may help to explain why historians failed to notice this piece) and since the extracts given above are particularly relevant to my argument, I have let them remain. Two additional points supplement my notes to Bishop's account:

4   The Buckinghamshire Cheynes were connected with the Cheynes of Gloucestershire, whose Lollardy (in particular the suspicions of Sir John Cheyne of Beckford and his son Edward) is considered by McFarlane, *Lancastrian Kings and Lollard Knights*, pp. 163, 191, 210-11, 214 (the index, p. 251, hopelessly confuses these families).

9   Sentence had also been solemnly fulminated against the Lollards by the archbishop of Canterbury and ten bishops in procession at Paul's Cross on Sunday 11 March this year, during the final days of parliament. *Annales....Amundesham*, ed. Riley (RS, 1870-71), i, p. 59; M. E. Cornford, *Paul's Cross: A History* (London, 1910), p. 25.

2

LOLLARD WOMEN PRIESTS?

The role of women in heresy has long been a matter for observation and comment. It must be attributed to historians' lack of interest, rather than lack of evidence, that the Lollards have until now escaped analysis on this front.[1] There are certainly grounds for supposing that they, like Cathars and Waldensians, derived a large measure of support from members of the female sex. In the fourteenth and fifteenth centuries, as earlier, unorthodoxy offered women outlets for religious activity that were not to be found in the established church.[2] But, while the sources can tell us a good deal about women participating in the Lollard movement as learners, readers and expounders of the gospel and other vernacular texts, the question of whether they ever advanced to the point of acting as priests is less easily answered. We know, indeed, very little about Lollard rites of any kind, and this makes it all the more worth while exploring fully what evidence we have. This little is enough to show that at one formative stage at least in Lollard development, claims were being advanced for women as capable of priesthood.

Contemporaries were in no doubt that lay women were actively caught up in Lollardy alongside lay men. Women became evangelists, expounding as well as studying the word of the anglicised gospel. Henry Knighton was one of the first to draw attention to this. 'Women who know how to read' were among those 'swine' whose trampling on the

---

[1] We now have Claire Cross. '"Great Reasoners in Scripture": the activities of women Lollards 1380–1530', In *Medieval Women*, ed. Derek Baker (*Studies in Church History* (hereafter cited as *S.C.H.*): Subsidia I), Oxford 1978, 359–80, which appeared after my article was written. I wish to thank Anne Hudson for drawing my attention to this paper and for her comments and suggestions.

[2] For comments on the role of women in earlier heretical movements see M. D. Lambert, *Medieval Heresy: Popular Movements from Bogomil to Hus*, London 1977, 76–7, 86, 90. 114–16, 158; Brenda Bolton, 'Mulieres Sanctae', *S.C.H.*, x (1973), 77–95, esp. 77, 80; G. Koch, *Frauenfrage und Ketzertum im Mittelalter: Die Frauenbewegung im Rahmen des Katharismus und des Waldensertums und ihre sozialen Wurzeln (12–14 Jahrhundert)*, Berlin 1962. For the role of women in seventeenth-century sects see Keith Thomas, 'Women and the Civil War Sects', *Past and Present*, xiii (1958), 42–62.

evangelical pearl he so deplored.[3] The Lollards, he insisted, seduced members of both sexes by their insidious teaching, and such was the method of their madness that 'both men and women were suddenly transformed into doctors of evangelical doctrine by means of the vernacular'.[4] The same point was made by a late fourteenth-century preacher who stated in one of his sermons that women as well as men were to be heard spreading the Word in his time.

> Behold now we see so great a dissemination of the Gospel, that simple men and women, and those accounted ignorant laymen in the reputation of men, write and learn the Gospel, and, as far as they can and know how, teach and scatter the word of God.[5]

Would God, he wondered rhetorically, appoint such persons as these to confound the pride of the worldly as a sign of the apocalyptic ending of the world?

Another such charge comes from Friar Daw's reply to Jack Upland. The heretics' frequently repeated censure of the friars as wife-stealers is here countered by the accusation that they were just as bad themselves.

[3] *Chronicon Henrici Knighton*, ed. J. R. Lumby, Rolls Series (hereafter cited as R.S.), London 1889–95, ii. 152; see my 'Lollardy and Literacy', *History*, lxii . Below, 206. In the heresy trials of Coventry and Lichfield in 1511–12, nearly one-third of the accused were women; John Fines, 'Heresy Trials in the Diocese of Coventry and Lichfield, 1511–12', *J. E. H.*, xiv (1963), 161. In the Norwich trials of 1428–31 the proportion was about half this; 9 out of 60 accused were women. A point to bear in mind when considering women heretics is the possibility that they received more lenient treatment before the law than men. This seems to be the case in the Norwich trials in respect not only of punishment, but also of procedure. Except in the case of Hawise Moon, who specifically requested an itemised point-by-point abjuration (which like that of her husband and other male heretics was recited by the accused or his spokesman), the female suspects were apparently expected to give only a general abjuration of the heresies imputed to them, after these had been read out by a court official. *Heresy Trials in the Diocese of Norwich, 1428–31*, ed. Norman Tanner (Camden Society, 4th Ser., xx, 1977) (cited hereafter as *Norwich Heresy Trials*), 24, 139, cf. 178–9. Cross, *art. cit.*, 379, suggests that the total of Lollard women sentenced to burning (perhaps less than twelve) was disproportionately small considering the number who appear to have relapsed. On the relatively greater immunity of women from the law in a later period see the remarks of Peter Clark, 'Popular Protest and Disturbance in Kent, 1558–1640', *Economic History Review*, 2nd Ser., xxix (1976), 376–7.

[4] *Knighton*, ed. Lumby, ii. 186; cf. 187 for the same emphasis on the Wycliffite address to 'both men and women'. There was of course a natural tendency to exaggerate in reporting such events; cf. the description of the heretics of Périgueux about 1160 that 'nobody is so stupid that if he joins them he will not become literate within eight days . . .': R. I. Moore, *The Birth of Popular Heresy*, London 1975, 80.

[5] 'Ecce iam videmus tantam disseminacionem evangelii quod simplices viri et mulieres et in reputacione hominum laici ydiote scribunt et discunt evangelium et quantum possunt et sciunt docent et seminant verbum dei.' Cambridge Univ. Lib., MS Ii. 3. 8 fo. 149r.; quoted by G. R. Owst, *Preaching in Medieval England*, Cambridge 1926, 5–6, 135.

Who marrith more matrimonie, ye or the freris?
With wrenches and wiles wynnen mennes wyves
And maken hem scolers of the newe scole,
And reden hem her forme in the lowe chaier;
To maken hem perfit thei rede your rounde rollis,
And call on men for ther lessouns with 'Sister, me nedith'.[6]

Likewise the poet Hoccleve, dressing down Sir John Oldcastle in 1415, blamed women for contributing to contemporary questioning of faith and scripture.

Some wommen eeke, thogh hir wit be thynne,
Wele argumentes make in holy writ!
Lewde calates! sittith down and spynne,
And kakele of sumwhat elles, for your wit
Is al to feeble to despute of it![7]

Lollard teaching certainly helped to produce some well-schooled women in the fifteenth century. They included the Norfolk housewives Margery Baxter and Hawise Moon, whom Margery praised as 'a very discreet and very wise woman' in her knowledge of the teaching of William White.[8] The arrogant self-confidence of female fundamentalists was noticed in passing by Reginald Pecock. Conceivably he had himself experienced the difficulties of discourse with

those women which make themselves so wise by the Bible, that they will allow no deed to be virtuous and to be done in man's virtuous conversation. save what they can find expressly in the Bible, and are most haughty of speech regarding clerks, and vaunt and advance themselves when they are in merriment and in their own houses to argue and dispute against clerks.[9]

Dogmatic assertiveness is perhaps not a surprising attitude among individuals whose textual skills brought them fame and leadership in

[6] *Jack Upland, Friar Daw's Reply and Upland's Rejoinder*, ed. P. L. Heyworth, Oxford 1968, 76. Cf. Pecock's remark about Lollard scripture-spouting 'upon their high benches sitting'; *The Repressor of Over Much Blaming of the Clergy*, ed. C. Babington, R. S., London 1860, i. 129. On Lollard 'rolls' (*schedulae*), the most ephemeral form of their literature which could, however, serve as compendia of doctrine see Anne Hudson, 'Some Aspects of Lollard Book Production', *S.C.H.*, ix (1972), 149–50. In his comment on this passage Heyworth (p. 141) notes the pedagogic metaphor but says that 'the references to a *lowe chair* and *rounde rollis* probably imply that the women's instruction was not religious but amorous'. Traducers of heretics rarely missed an opportunity to cast a slur of sexual misbehaviour, and that there are such insinuations in these lines seems obvious. This need not, however, exclude a genuine pedagogic setting, and the charge makes more sense if we accept the presence of women in Lollard schools.

[7] *Hoccleve's Works. The Minor Poems*, i. ed. F. J. Furnivall (E.E.T.S., Extra Series 61, 1892), 13.

[8] *Norwich Heresy Trials*, 41–51, at 47; J. A. F. Thomson, *The Later Lollards, 1414–1520*. Oxford 1965, 123ff. For these and other examples see Cross, 'Great Reasoners in Scripture'.

[9] Pecock, *Repressor*, i. 123; V. H. H. Green, *Bishop Reginald Pecock*, Cambridge 1945, 90.

their close-knit heretical communities—witness the sixteenth-century example of Alice Colyns described by Foxe.[10] But did women ever advance beyond reciting, reading and teaching to the exercise of priestly functions? Claims were certainly made on their behalf.

According to Walter Brut or Brit,[11] who was arrested in 1391 and submitted in early October 1393, 'women have power and authority to preach and make the body of Christ, and they have the power of the keys of the church, of binding and loosing'.[12] A major argument in defence of this thesis was the ability of women to give baptism, on the grounds that since this was the most necessary of all the sacraments, if they could administer 'this chief sacrament, I dare not say they cannot administer the other sacraments'—in the absence of a competent ecclesiastical person.[13] Moreover, whatever St Paul said about women not being allowed to teach, their ability to do so was another matter. For 'women, holy virgins, steadfastly (*constanter*) have preached the word of God and converted many to the faith, while priests hearing them dared not say a word.'[14] And since women who baptise absolve from sin, they must, having this power, have the power to bind and loose. Women were therefore not excluded from the Christian priesthood, though their power was restrained (*refrenetur*) in the presence of others ordained to these offices. Why should they not administer extreme unction, given their admitted right in baptism? So logically, concluded Brut, 'I dare not exclude them from the possibility of administering the body of Christ, though they ought not to proceed to do this while there are others constituted in the church for this purpose'.[15] In the face of these

[10] Claire Cross, *Church and People, 1450–1660*, Glasgow 1976, 34, 37; Aston, 'Lollardy and Literacy', 355. Below, 201.

[11] See below notes 18 and 19 for variants of his name. At his trial, where he is named Brut, the heretic made the most of his 'British' ancestry. *Registrum Johannis Trefnant Episcopi Herefordensis* (hereafter cited as *Reg. Trefnant*), ed. W. W. Capes (Cant. and York Soc., xx, 1916), 285, 293–5.

[12] Ibid., 364, no. 30; cf. 279 where the first of the points of which Brut was defamed was his assertion 'quod quilibet Christianus eciam mulier extra peccatum existens potest conficere corpus Christi ita bene sicut sacerdos'. On Brut's examination see K. B. McFarlane, *John Wycliffe and the Beginnings of English Nonconformity*, London 1952, 135–8.

[13] *Reg. Trefnant*, 345. On the ecclesiastical law providing that laymen, including women (in the absence of a man), could baptise in cases of necessity see W. Lyndwood, *Provinciale*, Oxford 1679, 241ff., Lib. III, tit. 24, esp. 241, n. b, *Propter necessitatem*, and 242, n. a, *Foemina*; also *Councils and Synods*, ed. F. M. Powicke and C. R. Cheney, Oxford 1964, 140, 896–7, cf. 182, 233, 368, 452, 634, 702–3. There were, of course, Lollards who objected to baptism as an unnecessary rite.

[14] *Reg. Trefnant*, 345. Variants of this passage appear in B.L. MS Harl. 31: fo. 201v 'mulieres ymmo et virgines constanter predicaverunt verbum dei et multos ad fidem converterunt sacerdotibus tunc non audentibus [audientibus, corrected] loqui verbum'; cf. fo. 219r 'multe mulieres constanter predicaverunt verbum quando sacerdotes et alii non audebant verbum loqui et patet de Magdalena et Martha . . .' Brut cites St Paul in 1 Tim. ii. 11–12 (cf. 1 Cor. xiv. 34–5) saying that 'docere mulieri *non permittit* neque dominari in virum'. But, comments Brut, Paul does not say 'quod tamen *non possunt* docere neque in virum dominari' (my italics).

[15] *Reg. Trefnant*, 345–7.

arguments there is no surprise in Brut's further conclusion that there was
no reason why women should not 'pray and bless equally with priests'.
Brut therefore rested this case for women's ability to administer the
sacraments on unorthodox, as well as orthodox practice. In addition to
the long-established right of mothers and midwives to baptise in cases of
necessity, he adverted to the successes of women preachers, hinting that
a preaching pastorate might open the door to a fuller ministry.

Brut's case attracted a lot of attention.[16] The bishop of Hereford, John
Trefnant, collected quite a galaxy of university men, including fifteen
doctors of theology, to refute the interminable outpourings of this ✱
educated layman, and the hearings were reported at unusual length in the
bishop's register.[17] The assertions about women here form one of the
thirty-seven points charged against Brut. The gravity of this error also left
its mark elsewhere. Walter Brut's dual conclusions that women had the
power and authority both to preach and to consecrate the body of Christ
were fully answered in two sets of *questiones* which survive in manuscript.
Both texts are anonymous and both pair the controversial issue of women
priests with the commoner Lollard claims about preaching. In one case
the discussion of 'whether women can, as true priests, make the
sacrament of the eucharist' followed arguments as to 'whether every just
layman is a priest of the new law'. In the other the question of 'whether
women are suitable ministers to make (*ad conficiendum*) the sacrament of
the eucharist', was linked to the issue of 'whether women are allowed to
teach a public gathering of men'.[18] Both these discussions (which alike

[16] In addition to the determinations considered below and William Woodford's reply to
Brut (below, n. 18), the 37 condemned conclusions of the heretic were registered at the
end of a late fourteenth-century repertory of canon law belonging to the abbey of
Reading. B.L. MS Royal 10 D X, fo. 312r–v

[17] Brut's case occupies pp. 278–394 in the published register (fos 106v–128r). Much of
the record consists of the defensive treatise Brut penned with his own hand after (he says)
'I was required to write a reply in latin to all these matters' (p. 285). Perhaps the
authorities did not realise what they were letting themselves in for!

[18] Both texts are in B.L. MS Harl. 31; fos 194v–196v 'Utrum liceat mulieribus docere
viros publice congregatos'; fos 196v–205r 'Utrum mulieribus sint ministri ydonei ad
conficiendum eukaristie sacramentum'; fos 216r–218r 'Utrum quilibet laicus iustus sit
sacerdos nove legis'; fos 218r–223r 'Utrum mulieres conficiunt vel conficere possunt ut
veri sacerdotes eukaristie sacramentum'. There is another copy of the latter pair of
determinations in B.L. MS Royal 7 B III, fos. 1r–4v (to which Anne Hudson kindly drew
my attention). Bale, followed by Tanner, suggested as the author of the former pair the
Carmelite Walter Hunt (d. 1478), who has to be dismissed on grounds of date. John Bale,
Scriptorum illustrium maioris Brytannie Catalogus, Basle 1557–9, i. 615–16; Thomas Tanner,
Bibliotheca Britannico-Hibernica, London 1748, 423. Another suggested candidate, William
Woodford (various of whose works are in MS Harl. 31), is rejected for stylistic reasons by
J. I. Catto, 'William Woodford, O.F.M. (*c.* 1330–*c.* 1397)', (unpublished Oxford D.Phil.
thesis 1969), 314. Woodford certainly participated in the refutation of Brut. He refers
himself to his discussion of tithes, offerings and clerical temporalities in the 'letter' or
'history' which he sent to the bishop of Hereford against the book of 'Walter Britte'. O.
Gratius, *Fasciculus Rerum Expetendarum & Fugiendarum*, ed. E. Brown, London 1609, 220,
222 (referring also to a 'certain determination'); A. G. Little, *The Grey Friars in Oxford*,
(Oxford Hist. Soc., xx, 1891), 248.

focused their main attention on the topic of women as priests) were undoubtedly framed as answers to Walter Brut. One text refers to 'Walter Bryth' by name, quotes and answers him in the second person, and while the other generalises this to 'the Lollards' it also deals unmistakably with Brut's conclusions, similarly quoting both phrases and arguments to be found in the recorded trial.[19] The overlapping between the two paired disputations is sufficiently close to suggest a common, or related authorship.

It seems likely on the face of it that the author, or authors, of these discussions were among the large body of academics (both regulars and seculars) present at Brut's trial.[20] Among these perhaps the most probable candidates are Masters John Necton and William Colville, respectively chancellor and ex-chancellor of Cambridge, to whom was committed the task of answering the heretic's diffuse speculations. The two masters seem to have divided their forces, since they produced two sets of replies to Brut's thirty-seven condemned conclusions which, while much more concise than the heretic's own writings, still took up a substantial part of the trial record.[21] Both replies to some extent regrouped the heresies listed by the bishop in his condemnation on 6 October 1393, and together they provided a comprehensive counter-argument. Only the second rebuttal, however, deals with the question of women priests, and it does so in a way which suggests that the complete presentation of the case extended beyond the limits of the registered version. Having indicated that Brut's assertions about women celebrants needed to be considered with his view of the sacrament and his denial that only priests could celebrate, the reply briefly stated the orthodox view of the eucharist, indicating that not only women but unordained men were excluded from celebrating this office. 'The doctors also establish', ended

[19] There are references to 'Walterus Bryth' in MS Harl. 31, fos. 201v, 202r, and twice on fo. 204v; cf. fos 219r, 222r–v for allusions to Lollards. For parallels with the record in the bishop's register cf. *Reg. Trefnant*, 345–7, and MS Harl. 31, fos 201v–202r, 220r–v. The links between the two manuscript disputes, not only in argument, but in some passages of close verbal similarity (see below notes 34, 36 and 39) are such that I think one must postulate, if not common authorship, shared debate.

[20] See *Reg. Trefnant*, 359–60 for the list of those present at the trial in October 1393, described by McFarlane, *John Wycliffe*, 137, as 'an absurdly large body of doctors'. Cf. ibid., 135 and idem, *Lancastrian Kings and Lollard Knights*, Oxford 1972, 170 for the suggestion (also made by Foxe) that Brut was a graduate of Oxford. Trefnant was a learned man himself; see A. B. Emden, *Biog. Reg. of the Univ. of Oxford*, Oxford 1957–9, iii. 1900–2. The large number of academics at the trial opens wide the possibilities of authorship, which include Nicholas Hereford, whose presence here may be presumed to have contributed to the attack on him as a turncoat (*Reg. Trefnant,* 394ff). This question must therefore remain open; what is more important is that we can pinpoint the context of the debate. Since it is impossible here to give more than a summary I have given more attention to the heretical arguments, as being the more novel.

[21] *Reg. Trefnant*, 368–76 and 376–94 (an editorial error makes this section, wrongly, a reply to Swinderby). On Colville and Necton see A. B. Emden, *Biog. Reg. of the Univ. of Cambridge*, Cambridge 1963, 151, 419.

this paragraph, 'that women do not have the power or authority to preach or make the body of Christ, and also that they do not have the power of the keys of the church, of binding and loosing, and the faithful ought to hold these conclusions and to shun the opposite as heresy.'[22] This sentence could be read almost as a summary of the two related manuscript disputations on this topic.

Whoever penned the *questiones*, the role of the Cambridge doctors at Brut's trial certainly increased the likelihood of his extravagances being ventilated and controverted in that university. Lollard debates were not alien to Cambridge in the 1390s, for it was in this decade that John Devereux (or Deverose) was putting together the case for images against Lollard iconomachs.[23] Perhaps it is also worth bearing in mind a negative point. The rebuttal of Brut's case for women teachers and women priests gives no hint of the actual existence of either; the whole debate was academic, confined to the realm of theory. Yet the theory itself is interesting, airing as it did so remarkably fully arguments for and against the spiritual equality of women.

You will not admit a point, objected Brut's opponents, unless it is founded in holy scripture or natural reason.[24] The case for and against women ministrants therefore traversed both these grounds and included a full statement (looking back to Aristotle's *Politics* among other sources) of the physical and mental inferiority which made women by nature unfit for priesthood.[25] The defence of women preachers naturally made the most of arguments from scripture, both in specific examples (in the Old Testament the prophesyings of Deborah and Huldah, wife of Shallum, or from the New Testament the cases of Mary Magdalen and the four daughters of Philip the evangelist, 'virgins, which did prophesy') and also in general injunctions, which meant that anyone in possession of wisdom and learning was duty bound to teach the ignorant, and that teaching,

---

[22] *Reg. Trefnant*, 382–3; also below p. 61.

[23] Emden, *Biog. Reg. Cambridge*, 186; James Crompton, 'Lollard doctrine with special reference to the controversy over image worship and pilgrimages', (unpublished Oxford B. Litt. thesis 1950), 167ff. Foxe suggests, needlessly, that Brut's articles were 'sent to the university of Cambridge to be confuted'; *Acts and Monuments*, ed. J. Pratt, London 1853–68, iii. 187.

[24] MS Harl. 31, fo. 204r, 'tu non vis admittere nisi scripturam sacram vel racionem naturalem . . .'; cf. fo. 219r, 'hac regula est lollardorum hoc non habetur ex sacra scriptura neque ex racione naturali ergo hoc non est ponendum'. Cf. Brut's protestations that he will freely submit to corrections 'ex auctoritate scripture sacre aut probabili racione in scriptura sacra fundata . . .' *Reg. Trefnant*, 285–6, 358.

[25] References to Aristotle's *Politics* in the context of women's deficiency of reason and unsuitability for the rule of bodies (and therefore, much more so, of souls) appear in MS Harl. 31, fos 200r, 218r. Cf. *The Politics of Aristotle*, trans. Ernest Barker, Oxford 1946, 35–6, 75–6; St Thomas Aquinas, *In Libros Politicorum Aristotelis Expositio*, ed. R. M. Spiazzi, Turin and Rome 1951, 49, para. 159, 72, para 218, 99–100, paras. 301, 303. For a summary of the biblical and other grounds for this traditional theory of female subjection see D. S. Bailey, *The Man–Woman Relation in Christian Thought*, London 1959, 15–16, 62–4, 157, 293–6.

being a work of mercy, was not forbidden to anyone.[26] To prophesy was
to preach and the women prophets of the Bible were therefore precedents
for women preachers.

The claim for women to be priests was partly an extrapolation from
this overriding obligation to preach. The heretics argued, according to
their opponents, that every priest can *ex officio* preach the gospel publicly;
women can also rightfully preach; therefore they are priests.[27] But there
was also another major line of approach—the Donatist one, which
impugned the ministry of evil priests and grounded office on merit.
'Every holy person is a priest' and 'every good elect woman is holy;
therefore every such one is a priest.' The argument from worth, *bonitas*,
operated both positively and negatively, both to choose and exclude. 'A
good layman and good woman is worthier than an evil priest, and
therefore more suited to the worthy work of consecrating, for making the
body of the lord is the worthiest work and therefore the good layman and
good woman is more suitable for it.'[28] Virtue singled out the righteous
and the operations of the evil were worthless. The sinful priest, on
account of his lack of goodness, *defectum bonitatis*, does not consecrate,
whereas the virtuous lay woman, effectively ordained by the sacramental
words ('Take, eat . . . this do in remembrance of me': 1 Cor. xi. 24) was a
proper ministrant. The holy spirit operates 'more through the good
layman and the holy woman than through the evil priest'. 'So if a woman
has goodness of life and is ordained, why can she not consecrate?'[29]

Brut's opponent devoted considerable attention to refuting this
heretical view of sacerdotal office, showing what complete confusion it
would lead to. And, though the administration of the eucharist was the

[26] MS Harl. 31, fos 194v–196r, citing Judges iv. 4ff; 2 Kings xxii. 14ff; Acts xxi. 8–9; 1
Cor. xi. 5 ('every woman that prayeth or prophesieth . . .'); 1 Cor. xiv. 5 ('I would that ye
all spake with tongues, but rather that ye prophesied . . .'), and 1 Peter iv. 10 ('minister the
same [gift] one to another . . .'). In reply to these claims it was stated that there were three
cases in which women could publicly teach (which explained these examples): i. by special
privilege, as in the example of Huldah; ii. to bring ignominy on effeminate men, as in the
example of Deborah; iii. when there was a shortage of preachers and teachers (as in the
New Testament examples). MS Harl. 31, fos 196r, 221r.

[27] Ibid., fo. 199r, where Brut's casuistry on 1 Tim. ii (see note 14 above) is dealt with. ('Et
nota quod non dicit statuo quasi ex suo statuto primitus emanasse sed dicit non permitto
simple sicut nec Christus hoc permisit . . .') The case against Brut cited this passage against
him, reversing the argument. If women were priests they would be allowed to preach,
which (as 1 Tim. ii showed) is heretical. Ibid., fo. 218r.

[28] Ibid., fo. 196v; 'omnis sanctus est sacerdos'; 'omnis mulier electa bona est sancta
ergo omnis talis est sacerdos'; 'magis dignus bonus laicus et mulier bona malo presbitero
ergo magis aptus ad opus dignum conficiendi. Conficere autem corpus dominicum est
opus dignissimum ergo ad illud est laicus bonus et mulier bona magis apta'. The Lollard
arguments on this point—against which a large part of the reply was addressed—are
summarised fos 196v–197r. For some of Brut's arguments against the ministry of evil
priests see *Reg. Trefnant*, 349.

[29] 'magis vult [spiritus sanctus] operari per bonum laicum et pro illo et per mulierem
sanctam quam per malum presbiterum'; 'si ergo mulier habeat bonitatem vite et ordinetur
cur non potest consecrare'. MS Harl. 31, fos 196v–197r.

principal priestly power, it was also necessary to answer the claim that women could administer other sacraments, especially confession and baptism. Brut, who like a good many other Lollards denied the necessity of oral confession to a priest and the utility of priestly absolution, conjoined these heresies with claims for a lay ministry. He found in Christ's words, 'Receive ye the Holy Ghost . . .' (John xx. 22–3) the right of baptised Christians to forgive sins, and among the powers he attributed to women was that of binding and loosing. Central to this argument were the assertions about baptism, since 'everyone who baptises has the keys of the kingdom of heaven, and the layman in baptism thus equals the priest'. Hence the claim that the right of women to perform this sacrament in times of need conferred on them competence to perform other sacraments, the eucharist included.[30] The main argument against this was the inherent difference between baptism and the eucharist: one being essential for salvation, the other not.[31] In any case, as Brut himself conceded (a point not missed by the other side),[32] the permission to lay persons was only granted in the absence of a competent cleric, and though God could indeed act through a woman pronouncing the baptismal words, she did not by that process herself confer grace. Women's role in baptism had no bearing whatsoever on the office of the eucharist.

The heretical case took the argument from history beyond the Bible. Besides claiming that *presbiterisse et sacerdotisse* had existed in the early Church,[33] Brut rashly advanced in support of women's ability to confer orders the example of the mythical Pope Joan. If, he maintained, the Church denied her ordinations, then subsequent priestly orders must be in doubt; contrariwise, to accept them was tantamount to accepting good women as priests. Brut's opponent, taking aim at this easy target, replied that the alleged two-year reign of the female pope, if it ever existed, argued exactly the opposite of what was claimed. For, as the rest of Joan's story showed, any acts she might appear to have performed with priestly powers were void and quashed by the Church, and if office were to be based on merit, the final scandal of this woman—reportedly chosen for her excellence of learning and character—pointed in the opposite

[30] *Reg. Trefnant*, 330; cf. Foxe, *Acts and Monts.*, iii. 168, 179. As reported in *Reg. Trefnant*, 345–6, Brut's claims for the female ministrant mentioned all the sacraments except confirmation. Cf. also 324–36 for his discussion of the related questions of the power to bind and loose, confession and baptism, and 362–3, nos. 9, 16 and 19 of the charges against him. The counter-arguments are to be found in MS Harl. 31, fos 201v ff., and 219r ff. and *Reg. Trefnant*, 370–1, 384–5.

[31] For Wycliffe's arguments on these lines see below p. 68.

[32] MS Harl. 31, fos 201v, 202r. Cf. *Reg. Trefnant*, 345–7, where this proviso is mentioned four times. One might reflect that it could make little difference to a heretical ministry which would *ipso facto* exclude those competent in the church.

[33] MS Harl. 31, fo. 197r. On the development of the female diaconate in the East during the patristic age see Bailey, *Man–Woman Relation*, 66–9.

direction. 'I am amazed', concluded the rejoinder, 'that he believes this deed strengthens his case, when it is annulled and reprobated by God and the whole church.'[34]

Walter Brut's eccentric learning led his defence of women into some remarkable quirks. On the example of the Virgin and women's capacity to generate and nourish the flesh he attempted to construct a defence of female powers to make the body and blood of Christ. Assertions about the irrelevance of sex to priestly office were linked with postulates on the possible transmigration of souls between the sexes and the feasibility of physical sexual change.[35] He was learnedly controverted at all points, not least on the grounds of logic. To claim that women could consecrate the eucharist was the equivalent, said the opposition, to saying that a woman can contract matrimony simultaneously and singly with her father and son; that a nun consecrated to God can marry a professed religious or even the supreme pontiff; that women can make the sun and moon and stars, raise up a great mountain and cast it into the sea; that any woman can conceive and bring forth God and redeem the world; make the blind to see, the deaf to hear, and the dumb to speak. The monstrosity of these propositions was such that anyone preaching them deserved to have his tongue cut out.[36] Women should not preach, and no ministry could belong to them. Such rights as they had to instruct were strictly limited to private occasions and the hearing of women and children. The teaching of *men* in *public* was utterly forbidden them.[37] Woman, imperfect in

[34] MS Harl. 31, fo. 204v 'miror ergo quod ipse credit pro se valere hoc factum quod a deo et tota ecclesia dei adnullatum est et reprobatum'; cf. fo. 222v and B.L. MS Royal 7 B III, fo. 4r for the similar conclusion in the other disputation; 'miror ergo quomodo lollardi hanc historiam pro se audent allegare per quam oppositum propositi illorum a deo et universali ecclesia declaratur'. Brut's case on this matter (*Reg. Trefnant*, 346) is summarised in MS Harl. 31, fos 202r, 220r, no. 12. Cf. below p. 68 for Wycliffe on Pope Joan, whose imaginary ninth-century reign was finally disposed of by J. J. I. von Döllinger, *Die Papst-Fabeln des Mittelalters*, Stuttgart 1890, 1–53. In the story the choice of a woman was explained by her great intellectual capacity, but after two years' reign she gave birth while processing to the Lateran.

[35] MS Harl. 31, fos 198r–v, 219v, 222v. This last point was supported by reference to Albert the Great's *De Animalibus*. Cf. *Albertus Magnus de animalibus libri xxvi*, ed. Hermann Stadler (Beiträge zur Geschichte der Philosophie des Mittelalters, vols. xv–xvi, Münster 1916–21), 1226, lib. xviii, tract. 2, cap. 3. The same work (cf. 573, lib. viii, tract. 1, cap. 1) was also cited by Brut's opponent (MS Harl. 31, fo. 219r) on woman's contentiousness and instability. For a view of woman's superiority as having conceived God, see Eileen Power, 'The Position of Women', in *The Legacy of the Middle Ages*, ed. C. G. Crump and E. F. Jacob, Oxford 1951, 402.

[36] I have here conflated the parallel passages in MS Harl. 31, fos 202r–v, and 220v, both of which, pursuing their case through distinctions of *posse* (*logicum, politicum, phisicum* and *iuridicum*), listed these extravagances to demonstrate the extremity of the heretical error, alike concluding that 'talis predicatoris lingua meretur amputari'.

[37] Ibid., fo. 196r, after elucidating the circumstances in which women were allowed to teach (e.g. abbesses those subject to them in the cloister, and housewives other women and children). The main biblical passages were 1 Cor. xiv. 34–5 and 1 Tim. ii. 11–12.

nature, physically impure,[38] formed for subjection and unfit for authority, was totally debarred from priestly orders. How was it possible that throughout the whole history of the Church up to the present, women had been excluded from the priesthood, unless this was according to divine precept?[39]

Thanks to Walter Brut's heady theologising and the seriousness with which it was viewed, we can learn a lot about his heretical defence of women. To that extent his case was exceptional. He was not alone, however, in making claims for women priests. One of the charges laid against William White in September 1428 was that he had taught 'that all pious and just livers, of either sex, have equal jurisdictional power to bind and loose here on earth; so that the power of binding and loosing granted to priests does not exceed the power of other perfect, men or women'. White confessed to this. He utterly denied, however, another more serious accusation that followed. According to this he had believed, affirmed and taught that 'every faithful person in Jesus Christ is a priest of the elect church of God' (*quod quilibet fidelis in Christo Jesu est sacerdos electae ecclesiae Dei*). Also, it was alleged (with circumstantial detail) he had practised what he preached to the point that on the previous Easter Sunday, in his room in the parish of 'Bergh', he had shown a lay disciple how to celebrate a domestic communion, breaking bread, giving thanks and distributing to those present with the words, 'take and eat in memory of Christ's passion'.[40]

White's denial notwithstanding, a number of his followers admitted, during the months of intensive investigation that followed his condemnation and death, to holding just such views of the priesthood. Margery Baxter, for instance, a close disciple of William White, had

---

[38] Woman's menstrual impurity disqualified her from a ministry which required physical purity under the new law as under the old (citing Leviticus xxi on the physical requirements for priests); on this taboo see Joan Morris, *Against Nature and God*, London 1973, 105–12. MS Harl. 31, fos 199v, 219r.

[39] Ibid., fos 199v–200r 'Non est verisimile quod ecclesia dei a Christo usque modo totum genus mulierum exclusissimum a sacerdocio et suscepcione ordinum et a tam nobili actu sine precepto Christi ergo cum per ecclesiam omnes mulieres ab huiusmodi excluduntur videtur quod hoc ecclesia faciat ex precepto divino'; cf. fo. 219r (= MS Royal 7 B III, fo. 2v) 'Non est verisimile quod a principio mundi tam in veteri lege quam nova totum genus mulierum fuisset exclusum a sacerdocio sine auctoritate dei vel racione naturali. Sed a principio mundi usque modo totum genus mulierum a sacerdocio fuerat exclusum ergo hoc factum est auctoritate dei vel auctoritate racionis naturalis et sive unum sive aliud detur hoc factum est auctoritate dei ergo auctoritate dei mulieres a sacerdocio sunt excluse'. (The transcriber seems to have omitted a word after 'huiusmodi' in the former passage).

[40] It is implied, therefore, that he omitted the words of institution, 'Hoc est enim corpus meum'. *Fasciculi Zizaniorum*, ed. W. W. Shirley, R.S., London 1858, 422–4; Tanner, *Norwich Heresy Trials*, 33, n. 14 identifies the place as probably Bergh Apton, Norfolk. The wording of Article xii, which White denied, is close to Wycliffe; see below, pp. 68–9.

evidently learnt from him her view that 'every man and woman who share
the opinions of the said Margery are good priests'. Sybil Godsell
likewise believed that 'every faithful man and every faithful woman is a
good priest and has as good power to make the body of Christ as any
ordained priest', and Hawise Moon (whose husband, like Sybil's, gave
accommodation to schools of heresy, which Hawise attended) also
endorsed this opinion. Nor was it only women who spoke of women's
capacities. Sybil's husband, John Godsell, a parchment-maker of
Ditchingham in Norfolk, held this view, as did John Skilly, miller of
Flixton, a few miles across the county boundary in Suffolk, who confessed
that 'I held and affirmed that every true man and woman being in charity
is a priest, and that no priest hath more power in ministering of the
sacraments than a lay man hath.' Both Skilly and Godsell had received
William White in their houses, and both were given the severe
punishment of seven years' imprisonment, suggesting serious
commitment to the sect. Another of White's lay disciples to confess and
abjure this error was John Skylan of 'Bergh'. He was a member of the
heretical school in the village where the illicit communion was said to
have been celebrated.[41]

Statements of this kind (which were still being uttered at the end of the
fifteenth century)[42] might be taken not so much as claims for a new
universal priesthood, as denials of the claims of the existing priesthood.
Anti-sacramentalism was common among the heretics,[43] and denials of
priestly powers were accompanied by attacks on the pope as Antichrist
and on the evil lives and vices of those 'called priests' who were 'no
priests'.[44] The idea of every true Christian man and woman as priest was
in a sense a negative as well as a positive proposition. Negatively it derived
from the heretics' rejection of the traditional ministry and sacraments (of
baptism, confirmation, marriage and penance) as obstructions between
the individual and God. Positively, and more important, the concept of
the lay elect as ordained of God was the direct result of regarding the
Church as the congregation of all true believers, Wycliffe's *universitas*

---

[41] *Norwich Heresy Trials*, 49 (cf. 42), 57 (cf. 52), 60–1, 67, 140, 142, 147.

[42] One example is the assertion abjured in 1499 by John Whitehorne, rector of Letcombe
Basset (Berks.), that Christ at his ascension 'left his power with his Apostles and from them
the same power remaineth with every good true Christian man and woman living
virtuously as the Apostles did, so that priests and bishops have no more authority than
another layman that followeth the teaching and good conversation of the Apostles'.
Claude Jenkins, 'Cardinal Morton's Register', in *Tudor Studies presented . . . to A. F. Pollard*,
ed. R. W. Seton-Watson, London 1924, 48; Thomson, *Later Lollards*, 80, 82, 85–6.

[43] Ibid., 244–5; Lambert, *Medieval Heresy*, 268–9. The Norwich heresy trials of 1428–31
illustrate the anti-sacramental aspect of Lollardy very clearly.

[44] *Norwich Heresy Trials*, 141, cf. 147.

fidelium predestinatorum.[45] It was to be defined spiritually, not structurally, individually rather than formally.

Lollard priests were therefore less than 'priestly'. For by their very definition, the sacerdotal role was greatly altered—diminished as well as impugned in orthodox eyes. 'No priest in earth has power to make the sacraments . . .'; 'No priest has power to make God's body in the sacrament of the altar, but God made all priests, and no priest has power to make God, for God was made long time ere the priests were made'.[46] The ministry that mattered above all was the ministry of the Word.

A preaching ministry—male or female—was very different from a celebrating ministry, and the administration of the sacrament of the altar was critical. As the doctors who replied to Brut's heresies and errors pointed out at his trial, his arguments about the priestly powers of women had to be considered together with his denial of the sacrificial nature of the mass.[47] There was an integral connection between the denial of transubstantiation and the claim for a female priesthood. If one denied, as Brut did, that the mass was other than commemorative,[48] the administration of the sacrament did not involve the miraculous change of elements. The priestly role was accordingly depreciated.

Looking at it slightly differently, one might say that the idea of a priesthood of all believers, in which men and women were equal participants, was a logical concomitant of denying transubstantiation. Taking the miracle out of the eucharist reduced this sacrament to the level of the others and opened it to the ministry of every Christian believer, regardless of sex. This idea was given particular publicity in the twelve conclusions of 1395. The fourth point of this manifesto attacked the idolatry of the 'fained miracle of the sacrament of bread', referring to Wycliffe's words in the *Trialogus*; 'quod panis materialis est habitudinaliter corpus Christi'. A further deduction followed. 'For we suppose that on

[45] *Johannis Wyclif Tractatus De Ecclesia*, ed. J. Loserth (Wyclif Soc., London, 1886), 37, cf. 2. Cf. the view of John Burell 'quod ecclesia catholica est anima cuiuslibet boni Christiani' (*Norwich Heresy Trials*, 77), or that of William Wakeham, in *Peasants, Knights and Heretics*, ed. R. H. Hilton, Cambridge 1976, 287. The genuine historical case behind this redefinition of the Church was doubtless less important for such Lollards than it was for Wycliffe. For a helpful discussion of the concept of priesthood in the early centuries of the Church (when laymen were seen as able to baptise and offer liturgical sacrifice in case of necessity), showing how the *character indelebilis* developed with sacramental doctrine, see Hans von Campenhausen, *Tradition and Life in the Church: Essays and Lectures in Church History*, trans. A. V. Littledale, London 1968, 217–30.

[46] *Norwich Heresy Trials*, 81, 115.

[47] *Reg. Trefnant*, 279, 284, 336–41, 364. While it is clear that Brut's view of the mass denied a change in the substance of the bread, the opponents of his thesis about women devoted a lot of attention to showing that women could not convert the bread and wine into the body and blood of Christ.

[48] For William White's denial of transubstantiation see *Fasc. Ziz.*, ed. Shirley, 418–19, 423. This was of course one of the common heresies of the Lollards.

this wise may every true man and woman in God's law make the sacrament of the bread without any such miracle.'[49]

Roger Dymoke took up this point in his answer to the manifesto. Were the heretics denying that the usual priesthood was descended from that instituted by Christ? If they were not, what justification could there be for altering the Church's traditional forms? If they were, such a change of essence amounted to destroying the evangelical law, failing to be Christian. This, by implication, was what the heretics were doing in asserting that every good Christian could make the body of Christ in the sacrament and in denying the established priesthood the power to bind and loose. Christ instituted no such priesthood among his apostles, nor did any such exist in Rome, like that of the heretics in their conventicles at Oxford and London, 'where *women* (whom they call virgins, but in fact their whores) have, I cannot say *celebrated, but rather profaned masses, of which they are publicly and manifestly convicted,* for "as with the people, so with the priests"' (cf. Isa., xxiv. 2).[50]

Was there anything more than rhetoric in this accusation? Were the heretics' vindications of women priests ever acted on, or did they remain confined to the sphere of theoretical discussion? There are a few pieces of evidence which may be brought to bear on Dymoke's statement and the possible existence of women celebrants.

First there is an extraordinary episode related by Henry Knighton under the year 1391—the year when Brut first appeared before the authorities in Hereford. 'In those days', wrote Knighton,

> there was a certain matron in the city of London who had an only daughter whom she instructed to celebrate mass, and she set up an altar with its furnishings in her secret chamber, and got her daughter for many days to dress as a priest and go to the altar and to celebrate mass after her manner; but when she reached the sacramental words she prostrated herself before

[49] *Rogeri Dymmok Liber*, ed. H. S. Cronin (Wyclif Soc., London, 1922), 89–90; for Wycliffe's view of the eucharist in his *Trialogus* see Gordon Leff, *Heresy in the Later Middle Ages*, Manchester 1967, ii. 555; *Selections from English Wycliffite Writings*, ed. Anne Hudson, Cambridge 1978 (cited hereafter as Hudson, *Selections*), 25 and notes p. 152; cf. 19, 22, 148 for the much more restrained view advanced on this point in another Lollard text (though one wonders whether this is to be taken at face value or whether it should be seen as a casuistical argument intended to help heretics under threat of examination). It is worth noting that in the third of the twelve conclusions (cf. also no. 11) priestly chastity was attacked on the grounds that the law of continence was invented 'in prejudice of women'. William White, who married after his abjuration in 1422, was one who acted on this belief. (*Fasc. Ziz.*, 420–1, 425–6). Another was William Ramsbury, on whom see below and Lambert, *Medieval Heresy*, 239.

[50] *Rogeri Dymmok Liber*, 63–4 (my italics), cf. 108–9. Dymoke alludes to conclusion 2 on existing orders and conclusion 9 on the power to bind and loose. In view of the reports of London events discussed below it is relevant to note that Dymoke, an Oxford doctor of theology, was by 1396 regent of the Dominican convent of Blackfriars in London. Emden, *Biog. Reg. Oxford*, i. 617.

the altar and did not consecrate the sacrament; but rising completed all the rest of the mass to the end with her mother assisting and attending her devotion.[51]

This went on for some time until the secret escaped through a woman neighbour who had attended the ceremony. Report came to the bishop of London (Robert Braybrooke). The priestess was discovered, her priestly tonsure[52] exposed to public view, and she herself was put to penance.

It is conspicuous, particularly in view of the extended treatment which he gives to the development of Wycliffite heresy, that Knighton recounts this story without a mention of Lollardy. He leaves the tale as it stands—an isolated event, from which the reader might draw his own conclusions. We might, however, set this incident (as Knighton almost certainly could not) beside the case of William Ramsbury, a layman who had been proceeded against for heresy by the bishop of Salisbury two years earlier. He too had received an illicit priestly tonsure; he too had been celebrating unorthodox masses in orthodox vestments; he likewise was not named a Lollard, though in Ramsbury's case there is sufficient additional material to make it clear that he must be accounted such. Also, which is worth particular notice, we know from details of the manner in which he celebrated mass that William Ramsbury did so without the words of institution.[53] This omission, to which Knighton drew attention in the celebration of the London woman was, as I have indicated, wholly consistent with the Lollards' denial of transubstantiation—a denial which Ramsbury had to abjure.

If the London incident could once (like Thomas Walsingham's reporting of the Salisbury case) have been verified in official records, that option no longer seems open to us. Word of such scandals certainly got round, however. Curiously similar to Knighton's tale is the curt notice given by Walsingham in his mention of the heretic John Claydon, a skinner of London who was burned in the city, after twenty years' heresy, in 1415. Claydon, Walsingham tells us (misnaming him William), had taken his heretical insanity to the extent of making his daughter a priest to celebrate mass in his own house, on the day that his wife, rising from childbirth, should have gone to be churched. The same story is repeated in the later abbreviated version of the chronicle, though in the printed version

[51] *Knighton*, ii. 316–17; for a comment on the incident see B. L. Manning, *The People's Faith in the Time of Wyclif*, Cambridge 1919, rep. 1975, 138. It seems from what Knighton says, that Braybrooke preached against these doings in St Paul's.

[52] It was argued against Brut (MS Harl. 31, fos 199r, 218r) that if a woman were to be priest she would be capable of the tonsure, which would be against 1 Cor. xi. 6 ('. . . shame for a woman to be shorn or shaven'). Brut himself, however, indicated rather that tonsure might be a 'sign of Antichrist', and contrary to the practice of the early Church. *Reg. Trefnant*, 341–4.

[53] For Ramsbury see Anne Hudson, 'A Lollard Mass', *J.T.S.* n.s. xxiii (1972), 407–19. Walsingham. *Historia Anglicana*, ed. H. T. Riley (R.S., London 1863–4), ii. 188, reports the incident—as Knighton does his—without names.

that we have (mistakenly taken from a poor recension) the unambiguous
filiam of the best manuscripts is changed to *filium*.[54] There is no mention of
any such offence in the full record that survives for Claydon's last trial in
1415. If, however, we allow for the possibility that the chronicler was
referring back to some earlier incident in Claydon's heretical career which
might have been dealt with in earlier proceedings, this lack would not be
inexplicable.[55] In any event these two independent stories from the
chroniclers of Leicester and St Albans deserve joint consideration. Is it
significant that in both cases it was reportedly the daughter who
celebrated? Whatever the Lollards said against vows of chastity, one
might perhaps link this with Dymoke's remark about virgins profaning
masses.

If the 1390s brought these goings-on into the limelight, their notoriety
was not forgotten thereafter. Three other contemporaries, two of whom
were writing in the 1420s, adverted to Lollard views on women priests.
One such charge (not precisely datable) comes from the pen of Friar Daw,
who accused the heretics—among their other sins—of upholding the
right of women to act as priests.

> And yet your sect susteynes wommen to seie massis,
> Shewyng to trete a sacrament as preestes that thei were,
> Reversynge holy doctours & decree of Holy Chirche.[56]

In reply Jack Upland rebutted this charge, accusing Daw of his habitual
wiles and of ignorance of those he despised. 'But as wele of her [their]
sacryng as wymmen syngynge messe/al wey thou usest the craft of thyn old
fader'; it was incumbent on Friar Daw to prove his charges.[57] Yet may
there not have been an element of evasion in the rejoinder? After all,

[54] *The St Albans Chronicle 1406–1420*, ed. V. H. Galbraith, Oxford 1937, 89; Walsingham,
Historia Anglicana, ii. 307. Riley, though well aware of its derivative nature chose
'inexplicably'—as Galbraith remarks—to base his text on Arundel MS vii in the College
of Arms (compiled c. 1422–30). Two earlier and better texts which both have a clear 'ut
eciam filiam propriam sacerdotem constitueret' where Riley prints 'filium proprium', are
Corpus Christi College MS 7, fo. 84r, and MS 195, fo. 447v. (See Galbraith's edition, pp.
x–xi, n 3, xxvi, lix, for these two manuscripts, the former of which contains probably the
earliest version of this section of the short chronicle, the latter being apparently copied
from it.)

[55] For the proceedings against Claydon see Thomson, *Later Lollards*, 140–2. Claydon
was imprisoned in Conway Castle in 1395, and the fact that his journey there was paid for
by Robert Braybrooke, bishop of London 1381–1404, suggests the possibility that action
was taken against him at this time by the latter. No record of this, nor of any other
heretical proceedings at this time, survives in Braybrooke's register, though we know from
other sources that he took action about now against William Thorpe; *John Lydford's Book*,
ed. Dorothy Owen, London 1974, 11, 108–12. If Braybrooke's proceedings of this kind
were recorded (as were, for instance, Bishop Alnwick's of 1428–31) in a separate register,
now lost, one can surmise that this might have covered the incident described by
Knighton.

[56] *Jack Upland*, 99; cf. notes on pp. 160–1. On the dating of this text cf. 9ff. esp. 17, and
cf. Hudson, *Selections*, 182.

[57] *Jack Upland*, 172.

singing masses was not at all the same as *saying* them, especially for Lollards who objected to mass and other offices being 'sung with high crying'.[58]
And it was the 'sacring', the consecration, which contained the critical words most likely of all to have been omitted in any heretical celebration.

The manifold ills which the preacher John Swetstock (if it was he) attributed to the Lollards in the reign of Henry v included their outrageous question: 'Why should not women be priested and enabled to celebrate and preach like men?' To this one reply was the stock answer that the Virgin, stainless as she had been, and sole repository of the faith as she was at the time of the crucifixion, had not been a priest. Women must not aspire to such heights. 'Take thee to thy distaff', advised the preacher, 'covet not to be a priest or preacher.'[59]

Lastly, there is the notice that was given to this matter by Thomas Netter in his *Doctrinale*. He alludes in a number of places to the Lollards' advancement of women, including statements by Wycliffe and the claims of John Purvey in a work called *De compendiis scripturarum*, that the office of preaching should extend to women as well as men.[60] Netter was in no doubt that Lollard women had responded to this call, not only through scriptural readings and preachings at heretical meetings, but also as women priests. The heresy gathered such strength that 'in the city of London the most foolish of women, set up on stools, publicly read and taught the scriptures in a congregation of men'.[61] In the populous capital there had also been young women celebrants.[62] Netter implies that these heretical priestesses existed in the plural, but his most specific references are singular. There was, he related, 'a certain girl, the daughter of a tanner in the city of London, who publicly celebrated masses in English

---

[58] For Lollard objections to church chanting and singing, including at the mass and other offices see *English Works of Wyclif*, ed. F. D. Matthew (E.E.T.S., 74, 1880), 169, 191–2 (quotation at 191); *Select English Works of John Wyclif*, ed. T. Arnold, Oxford 1869–71, iii. 203, 228, 479–82; Hudson, *Selections*, 23, 86, 149, 181–2; cf. also the arguments of William Thorpe in *Fifteenth Century Prose and Verse*, ed. A. W. Pollard, Westminster 1903, 140–2; Thomson, *Later Lollards*, 250.

[59] R. M. Haines, '"Wilde wittes and wilfulnes": John Swetstock's attack on those "poyswunmongeres", the Lollards', *S.C.H.*, viii (1972), 152; cf. Hudson, *Selections*, 125, 202. Cf. the case of John Yonge, a Bristol heretic who abjured in 1449, who claimed the right of free preaching except for women; Thomson, op. cit., 37. For other such remarks about keeping to the distaff see above p. 51(Hoccleve) and Thomas, 'Woman and . . . Sects', 60–1, n 70.

[60] Thomas Netter of Walden, *Doctrinale Antiquitatum Fidei Catholicae Ecclesiae*, Venice 1757–9, refers to this work of Purvey's, i, cols. 619, 637 (Bk. ii, caps. 70, 73), which he says included the claim that women could preach at will. This text (apparently now lost) is discussed by Anne Hudson in a forthcoming article on Purvey which I am grateful to her for showing me in typescript. See below pp. 67-8 , nn. 69, 71, for Netter on Wycliffe's defence of women.

[61] Netter, *Doctrinale*, i. col. 638 (Bk. ii, cap. 73). Once again (cf. above n 14 and p. 58) it was the teaching of *men* in *public* which was specially shocking, in view of the words of St Paul.

[62] Ibid., i. col. 296 (Bk. ii, cap. 12), iii. col. 199 (De sacramentalibus, cap. 28); cf. iii. col. 371 (De sacramentalibus, cap. 58).

before them'.[63] This incident had taken place long before, in the reign of Richard II, but report of it was still current. Whether or not, as seems very probable, Netter was thinking of the tale of John Claydon's daughter, it is worth noticing that he says the heretical masses were in English, and that London is the only location he gives for such priestesses.[64]

We are left, as so often, with more verbiage than substance. It seems most unlikely that there were ever many Lollards—either men or women—who resorted to administering the eucharist. We should certainly expect to learn more about it (in the way of formulated questions, if not answers) if they had, and the frequency with which they denied transubstantiation, coupled with their own belief in the sacramental value of the Word, makes it likely that such ceremony as they had centred upon preaching. 'For the Word is God and God is the Word', as John Whitehorne put it in 1499. 'And therefore whosoever receive devoutly God's Word he receiveth the very body of Christ.'[65] Silence in this matter is surely indicative. The fact that we hear so little, even polemically, suggests the extreme rarity of such proceedings as illicit ordinations or bowdlerised masses, conducted by male or female celebrants. Skilled the Lollards were in the arts of concealment, but the authorities would have been at their most vigilant to hunt out and suppress any operations so suggestive of a nascent counter-church.[66]

Yet the wisps of reporting that survive (repetitive though some of this may be) cannot be dismissed out of hand. At the very least they are indicative of a certain consistency of attitude among both the heretics and their opponents, and of the parallels between Lollards and earlier medieval heretics. Comparable developments had taken place among the Cathars and Waldensians. Cathar women were capable of receiving the *consolamentum* and of joining the ranks of the *perfecti*, a status which gave them precedence over other believers in the sect, even though they could not hold office in it. Women were also prominent in the Waldensian

[63] Ibid., ii. col. 71 (De sacramentis, cap. 7) 'ut tunc tempore regis Richardi II fama personuit, & usque nunc durat'; cf. col. 185 (cap. 28) '. . . sectatores ejus [Wycliffe], ut publica fama canit, in hac civitate Londoniarum olim instituerunt juvenculam quamdam pro festis diebus, & dominicis consecrare eis suam eucharistiam'.

[64] The period, location and trade (a tanner might well have been confused with a skinner) seem to point to Claydon, but Walsingham does not say the celebrations were in the vernacular.

[65] Jenkins, 'Cardinal Morton's Register', 48.

[66] On the little we hear of Lollard ritual see Lambert, *Medieval Heresy*, 270; Thomson, *Later Lollards*, 115, 161, 246–7. If the catch-phrase 'May we all drink of a cup' found among early sixteenth-century Coventry Lollards was a password one can point to the parallel with Cathars; Moore, *Birth of Popular Heresy*, 153. The questions about the eucharist framed *c.* 1428 for examining suspect Lollards, though pointing towards possible rejection of transubstantiation and orthodox consecration of the sacrament, did not envisage lay celebrants—which contrasts with the expectation of lay preaching and correction of clerical possessioners. Anne Hudson, 'The Examination of Lollards', *Bull. Inst. Hist. Research*, xlvi (1973), 153, 155 and comments 150–2.

movement, in which the ability to preach brought them equal leadership with men. The early fourteenth-century inquisitor Bernard Gui regarded Waldensian proclivities towards Donatism as responsible for heretical claims for women priests. 'They say', he wrote, 'that the consecration of the body and blood of Christ may be made by any just person, although he be a layman and not a priest ordained by a Catholic bishop, provided he is a member of their sect. They even believe the same thing concerning women, if they are of their sect, and so they say that every holy person is a priest.'[67]

Donatist (or near-Donatist) denials of the validity of the sacraments administered by unworthy priests led to claims for a lay ministry, and these in turn opened the way to further claims and counter-charges. There was a logic, if not a direct link, connecting the error of which Wycliffe was condemned in 1382, that a bishop or priest, if in mortal sin, does not ordain, consecrate or baptise,[68] and the supposition of the 1395 manifesto that every true man and woman in God's law could make the sacrament of the bread. Netter was surely right to look back to Wycliffe for the beginning of this story. His speculations—as usual hedged with provisos and in this case largely parenthetical—had set the ball rolling.

Wycliffe touched on the topic of lay celebrants, including women, in more than one work. It seems to me, objected the unfaithful and captious Pseustis in the *Trialogus*, that you deviate from the opinion of the Church and from scripture, in saying that a layman can consecrate (*conficere*) as a priest. To which the 'subtle and mature theologian', Phronesis, answers that it seems probable to many that a layman can consecrate. There was the example of St Cecilia who had turned her house into a church. More important, there was the evidence of scripture. I do not think you can show, wrote Wycliffe, that where we read of believers 'breaking bread from house to house' (Acts ii. 46), 'that those breads were not the body of Christ, or that only the apostles or priests (*presbyteri*) did this'. But, admitting this was uncertain, it was undoubted from 1 Corinthians (xi. 24ff.) that this office appertained to 'holy priests' (*sacerdotes sanctos*), on whom Christ had specially enjoined it.[69]

[67] *Religious Dissent in the Middle Ages*, ed. Jeffry Russell, New York 1971, 45, cf. 63; Lambert, 76–7 and, on the effects of Donatist leanings among the Waldensians, 79–80, 163.

[68] *Historia Anglicana*, ii. 58; H. B. Workman, *John Wyclif*, Oxford 1926, ii. 416. For an attempt to escape Donatist heresy while arguing that Christians should not receive the sacraments or attend divine services administered by open simonists, lechers, or other 'such vicious men' (putting the stress on the public nature of the sin), see *Remonstrance against Romish Corruptions in the Church*, ed. J. Forshall, London 1851, 120–34 (art. xxxv)—N.B. the mention of Donatists, 123.

[69] *Joannis Wiclif Trialogus*, ed. G. Lechler, Oxford 1869, 280–1; cf. 38 for the author's characterisation of the speakers in the text. For Netter's linking of this passage in the *Trialogus* with the 'profane priestess of the Lollard order' see *Doctrinale*, ii. col. 185 (De sacramento eucharistiae, cap. 28).

A few years before this Wycliffe had made some passing remarks about female ministrants in *De potestate pape*. These asides appeared as part of his argument that priestly orders were all of equal authority, so that a simple priest (*simplex sacerdos*) was on a par with bishop or pope in his ministry of the sacraments. The papal office resided in virtue, not rank, and anyone—in theory even a layman—could be pope. Christ had given the simple priest all necessary powers, and in case of need a layman was able to baptise.[70] It was in parenthesis, in considering and answering foreseeable objections to this thesis, that Wycliffe raised the topic of women priests. It is important to bear in mind the strictly academic nature of the context. Wycliffe was *not* discussing women priests as such; he was using this hypothetical contingency to counter possible objections to his view of the priesthood.

Firstly, he answered the argument that if a layman could baptise he was capable of administering the other sacraments, so that God could impart 'not only to a layman but to a woman or other irrational person the power of consecrating and administering any sacraments'.[71] Wycliffe denied this. His main reason was that later used against Brut. Baptism, because of its special scriptural authority and indispensability for salvation was unlike the other sacraments, so that arguments about lay ministrants deduced from lay baptism were of no validity. Could a woman be pope? What Wycliffe had to say about the story of Pope Joan in considering this question again seems closer to the view later expressed by Brut's opponent than to that heretic's own thinking. It could indeed be argued, said Wycliffe, that sin, not sex, was what chiefly disabled Joan, since monstrous sin in a ministrant or communicant was more serious an obstacle than physical deformity 'or the distinction of sex in a predestined woman of outstanding virtues'. But against this had to be set the fact that even the 'holy woman is not allowed, because of the weakness of her sex, to preach the gospel publicly in church', and that limitation excluded her, as much as any angel, from the headship of the Church.[72]

Wycliffe also dealt with the objection that his view of the priesthood was tantamount to abolishing priests and ordination. Not so, he maintained. If we look to Christ and the apostles, and to words of Augustine and Chrysostom, it is evident that all faithful Christians, the

[70] *Johannis Wyclif Tractatus de Potestate Pape*, ed. J. Loserth, London 1907, 307, 272. Leff, *Heresy in the Later Middle Ages*, ii. 531–3.

[71] *De Potestate Pape*, 308. Cf. Netter, *Doctrinale*, iii. col. 372 (De sacramentalibus, cap. 58) where Wycliffe's 'femine ac alii irracionali' has become 'femine sive bruto'. According to Netter (col. 371) 'ipse Wicleffus non erubuit libro suo *de Papa* pluries laborare pro femina, ut sit apta sacerdos ecclesie, episcopus, sive papa'. Cf. also cols. 376–7ff. Though Netter remarked on the ambiguity of Wycliffe's tortuous expressions, he does not seem to have made sufficient allowance for this in the deductions he drew from Chapter xi of *De Potestate Pape*.

[72] *De Potestate Pape*, 308, 271–2—referring to 1 Cor. xi. The example of angels was also used in the refutation of Brut's view of sacerdotal office (MS Harl. 31, fo. 216r–v).

holy people, were priests of God, and in that spiritual sense 'all holy men and women members of Christ are priests'; 'woman is priest'. The sacraments would not vanish if there were no pope; it is sin, not office, that differentiates between ministrants. 'Every Christian and specially a good priest is sacerdotal', but no one should presume to think himself directly ordained of God and the Church should rest content with the two orders of deacon and priest.[73]

Despite the tangential and perhaps confusing character of these remarks, they were set in a challenging context, and magisterial ambiguity was no bar to controversy. Where Wycliffe hinted others asserted and acted. His reformulation of the Church as the body of the elect brought him virtually to deny the existing order of priesthood and seemingly to elevate the virtuous layman over the constituted ministers of the Church. 'Every predestined layman is a priest.'[74] As was perceived at the time, the logical outcome of this view was a ministry of both the sexes. Some Lollards' fidelity to this most dangerous aspect of Wycliffe's thought carried them well beyond the heresiarch, yet still with a discernible continuity of intention. Those on the receiving end of heresy, whether or not they were sufficiently knowledgeable about continental heresies to anticipate such developments,[75] could scarcely have been taken by surprise.

Lollard women priests? The conclusion is indefinite. The Lollards, who produced some famous women preachers in their time and promoted the religious and educational equality of the sexes, had at least raised the theoretical possibility of having women priests. The theory was itself startling, shocking enough to prompt rumours as well as counter-arguments. Rumour there certainly was at that critical moment in the development of the sect in the 1390s, when academics and popular evangelisers were beginning to take diverging ways. If the exceptional extremist (or extreme feminist) did resort to surreptitious female rites, the most likely time was then, the most likely place London. Having not a single name to go on, we must leave the record as it stands—as plausible gossip. Yet the talk itself is remarkable enough, and gossip is also part of history.

---

[73] *De Potestate Pape*, 312–13, 315 ('Sicut enim omnis christianus et specialiter bonus presbiter est sacerdos . . .').

[74] From *De Eucharistia*, quoted Leff, *Heresy in the Later Middle Ages*, ii. 520, n 2; cf. 519–20, 525–6 for references to this and other such views described (p. 520, cf. p. 525) as 'the single most destructive and heretical feature of Wyclif's teaching'.

[75] For a suggestion of parallels between heresies of Waldensians and Lollards made by Thomas Palmer see *Reg. Trefnant*, 400.

Additional Notes to Chapter 2

2   See also R. Abels and E. Harrison, 'The Participation of Women in Languedocian Catharism', *Mediaeval Studies*, xli (1979), pp. 215-51.

11   For an account of Walter Brut's heretical career and doctrines see Glanmor Williams, *The Welsh Church from Conquest to Reformation* (Cardiff, 1976), pp. 158-9, 203, 205-9, 216, 235, 532-3.

16   I am indebted to Dr. Jeremy Catto for the information that a fragment of Woodford's reply to Brut – not on the topic of women priests – survives in Paris, Bib. Nat. Ms Lat. 3381. Cf. also (for publicity of another sort) the defence of Brut in *Pierce the Ploughmans Crede*, ed. W. W. Skeat (EETS, OS 30, 1867), p. 25.

55   Charles Kightly, 'The Early Lollards. A Survey of Popular Lollard Activity in England, 1382-1428' (D. Phil. Thesis, University of York, 1975) dates the entry relating to Thorpe in *John Lydford's Book* between 5 Jan. 1382 and 24 Jan. 1387, indicating that the action against him took place probably in 1386 (not *c*. 1395). I am grateful to the author for permission to quote this unpublished work, (cited at p. 438, n. 1).

60   See now Anne Hudson, 'John Purvey: A reconsideration of the evidence for his life and writings', *Viator*, 12 (1981), p. 364.

Postscript

In connection with Brut's teaching it may be worth considering some other charges brought against women in Wales and the marches about the turn of the fourteenth century. The offence of Agnes Hugy, excommunicated by the bishop of St. David's and said to be 'wickedly infecting the Lord's flock by her unlawful communications and persistently setting at naught the keys of holy mother church', remains obscure.[1] But Isabel Prustes, who in July 1397 renounced Lollardy before Bishop Trefnant, was said to have been a heretic and 'sedulous seducer' of the people and long excommnicate, 'wrongfully despising the keys of the church'.[2] Six years before this, in February 1391, two other women (Margaret Laybourn and Joan Smyth) were excommunicated for heresy by Trefnant – though their cases are not recorded in his register.[3] And the bishop's visitation of 1397 revealed an example of remarkable laxity on the Worcestershire-Herefordshire border. At Eardisley (midway between Almeley and – Whitney-on-Wye, both of which had – or were to have – Lollard patrons), one of the many charges against the vicar was the allegation that 'Agnes Knetchur and Isabel, servants of the said vicar, ring the bells and help the said vicar to celebrate, which is against the honour of the church'. (There were also suspicions about the vicar's sexual relations with these women).[4] Were conditions in these western regions perhaps peculiarly favourable to the reception of views such as Brut's?

1   *Episcopal Registers of the Diocese of St. David's*, ed. R. F. Isaacson (Cymmrodorion Record Series, No. 6, 1917-20), i, pp. 282-3; Williams, *The Welsh Church*, p. 210.

2   *Reg. Trefnant*, pp. 144-5; Kightly, 'Early Lollards', p. 179.

3   F. D. Logan, *Excommunication and the Secular Arm in Medieval England* (Toronto, 1968), p. 190; H. G. Richardson, 'Heresy and the Lay Power under Richard II, *EHR*, li (1936), p. 15. The signification of their excommunication was repeated in July 1392 and December 1393.

4   A. T. Bannister, 'Visitation Returns of the Diocese of Hereford in 1397. Pt. IV', *EHR*, xlv (1930), p. 447.

3

WILLIAM WHITE'S LOLLARD FOLLOWERS

Heresy Trials in the Diocese of Norwich, 1428–31. Edited from Westminster Diocesan Archives MS. B.2 by Norman P. Tanner. [Camden Fourth Series, Volume 20.] (London: Royal Historical Society. 1977. Distributed by Rowman and Littlefield, Totowa, New Jersey. 1980. Pp. vi, 233. $20.00.)

It is not often that we have the chance to investigate the followers of a heretical missionary. The volume of cases edited by Norman P. Tanner as *Heresy Trials in the Diocese of Norwich, 1428–31*,[1] provides such an opportunity, though it has not been presented as such. We can here gain some unusual insights into the diffusion and popularization of heretical opinion.

The prosecution of heretics undertaken by Bishop Alnwick of Norwich[2] between September, 1428, and March, 1431, is one of the exceptional records of a cumulative investigation to have survived from the Lollard movement.[3] The editor suggests, without exaggeration, that "it is perhaps the most important record of heresy trials in the British Isles before the Reformation."[4] While the enquiry itself has long been known from the account given of it by John Foxe, and recent historians have made good use of the manuscript (MS. B. 2 in Westminster Diocesan Archives), this is the first time the record has been edited in full. This careful and complete edition constitutes, therefore, a major source for the history of fifteenth-century Lollardy. It is accordingly important that we should be aware of its limitations as well as its undoubted value.

Norman Tanner has given us a meticulous and well-organized edition. He has rearranged the cases in chronological order, a decision which probably yields more advantages than otherwise, though it would have been helpful to have given the dates in modern form as headings in the body of the text, as well as in the list of

---

[1] Cited hereafter as *Trials*.

[2] William Alnwick was provided to the bishopric of Norwich on February 27, 1426, in succession to John Wakering (d. April 9, 1425), and held the see until September 19, 1436, when he was translated to Lincoln. For accounts of his career see *Dictionary of National Biography*, and A. B. Emden, *A Biographical Register of the University of Cambridge to 1500* (Cambridge, 1963), p. 11.

contents (pp. iv–v). The rearrangement of material also sometimes screens from view gaps in the manuscript that may well indicate missing portions of the proceedings.[5] I have noticed a few misprints that escaped the erratum slip (p. 74, 1. 6, *pisses* for *pisces*; p. 103, 1. 11, *ecclesiie* for *ecclesiis*; p. 183, n. 195, 29 Dec. for 29 Sept.; p. 196, 1. 15, *capenter* for *carpenter*). The editor has done an excellent job of identifying place-names throughout the text, though in the introduction it seems unnecessarily trying on the eye (or ear!) to keep calling the bishop's registrar John *Excestr*. There is a good index and a map that might have been improved (it lacks diocesan and county boundaries). Inevitably there is a good deal of repetition in the transcription of formalized documents, but it was certainly right to print the text in full, giving a firm basis for all future users of it.

It is misleading to refer to all these proceedings as 'trials.' The documentation relating to the fifty-one men and nine women suspects is of differing kinds and covers different stages of the investigative procedure. There are among the earlier cases some interrogations and examinations of suspects, two of which include the depositions of witnesses.[6] As the least formalized parts of the process these are the most interesting, but they are also the rarest. Much more common — indeed occupying almost the entire second half of the book — are the formal instruments of abjuration. In these cases the accused were being brought to court for judgment, to read or (more usually) listen to their listed errors being read out before the bishop, to give their solemn abjuration and be sentenced — usually to a public penance. We are presented therefore in some instances with suspects who appeared to be examined, possibly for the first time, and in others with those who had already been arrested and charged, and were reappearing (sometimes excommunicated) for sentencing.[7] This distinction between the different stages of procedure draws attention to another crucial point: the chronology of the antiheretical campaign.

From the beginning of March, 1430 (when the proceedings of the previous autumn were reopened),[8] nearly all those dealt with had either been held in deten-

---

[5]For example *Trials*, pp. 51, 64, 70, 72 (cf. Table 1, p. 3, for blank folios, or gaps in the folio numbers of the manuscript), where the cases of Margery Baxter (which goes only as far as the depositions of witnesses), John Godsell (whose English abjuration is lacking), John Cupper (case only started), and John Pyry (case halts at depositions) are all obviously incomplete.

[6]E.g., the cases of John Wardon, Margery Baxter, John Pyry, John Burell, William Colyn, and Robert Bert, *Trials*, pp. 32, 41, 71–72, 89, 98, of which the second and third include witnesses' depositions.

[7]A correct indication of this limitation to the contents of the manuscript was given by J. A. F. Thomson, *The Later Lollards, 1414–1520* (Oxford, 1965), pp. 120, n. 4, 223.

[8]In the preceding year also, proceedings were in the main broken off in the autumn to resume in the spring. Bishop Alnwick's attendance at convocation (where his presence is recorded in July and November–December, 1428, and October and December, 1429) had its effect on proceedings: William Colyn's hearing (*Trials*, p. 89) was started by John Exeter. *Register of Henry Chichele*, ed. E. F. Jacob (Canterbury and York Society, Vols. XLII, XLV– XLVII [London, 1938–1947]), III, 185, 189, 191, 196, 210, 212. Cf. John Foxe, *The*

tion or were very minor suspects whom the bishop did not bother with in person, but left to the discretion of his experienced vicar-general, William Bernham.[9] The record distinguishes throughout between the suspect who *"comparuit personaliter"* and those who were *"adductus,"* *"productus,"* or *"adductus in vinculis."* In the spring and summer of 1430 a large group of excommunicated individuals, some from the village of Loddon and a number of men from Beccles, appeared before the bishop to abjure, being brought in chains from prison, where they had been held for unspecified periods. (The only indication of time we are given is *diucius* or *aliquamdiu*, suggesting more than a matter of days, but we may assume the place was either Norwich Castle or the bishop's own prison in his palace at Norwich.)[10] While it is not possible to put an exact term on these detentions, it seems reasonable to connect them with a deposition of 1429 which survives only in Foxe (on whom more shortly), in which William Everden is reported to have made a Sunday trip, dressed in gentleman's attire, from Loddon to Norwich "to hearken how the bishop and his ministers used the poor Christians there in prison."[11] It is therefore misleading to think of the proceedings being spread out — unevenly and intermittently — over the two and a half years in question. The main impetus was concentrated in the months after September, 1428, to some point in 1429, during which period most of the suspects of significance had been rounded up and either brought to judgment or safely locked away. It was after they had had time to cool their heels and revise their opinions during a spell behind bars, that Bishop Alnwick devoted himself in the spring of 1430 to the tradespeople of Beccles, Loddon, and elsewhere, hearing their solemn abjurations and warning them of the danger of relapse. By the end of 1430 he felt sufficiently sure of his diocese to commit to his vicar-general a final mopping-up operation of the minnows, mostly

---

Acts and Monuments, ed. J. Pratt (London, 1853–1868) — cited hereafter as Foxe, *AM* — III, 599–600, where in the case of Nicholas Canon of Eye, heard by William Bernham at the end of November, 1430, penance was respited "until the coming of the bishop into his diocese."

[9]*Trials*, p. 9. William Bernham and John Exeter were both active in heretical proceedings during Wakering's episcopate, and both were present at the trial of William White (*infra*, pp. 85, 95). Exeter was an old hand with experience in the diocese reaching back to 1415, and Foxe, *AM*, III, 587, records his part in the arrest of six suspects in Bungay, Suffolk, who were imprisoned in Norwich Castle, apparently in 1428. For Bernham, who was Wakering's official in 1420 and vicar-general then and in 1424, see Emden, *op. cit.*, pp. 57–58; I. J. Churchill, *Canterbury Administration* (London, 1933), II, 253; *Reg. Chichele*, I, 321; Foxe, *AM*, III, 584, 586–587.

[10]*Trials*, pp. 105, 157; cf. pp. 200, 213, for references in later proceedings to individuals held in the prison of the episcopal palace in Norwich. For suspects held in Norwich Castle see *Trials*, pp. 52, 217; Foxe, *AM*, III, 587, cf. p. 596.

[11]Foxe, *AM*, III, 596; cf. p. 597 for the same deponent's report of William Everden's clothing and bedding being in the keeping of a man of Bergh Apton. On William Everden one of the leaders of the heretics, see below, pp. 81, 87, 95. This deposition by William Wright reports that William Taylor of Loddon, with whom Everden worked for a month tailoring, considered William Everden "the best doctor" after William White.

offenders or suspects in the village of Earsham, where there had been a Lollard school.[12]

The *Heresy Trials* printed here — as is evident from what I have said so far — form an incomplete record. Since this incompleteness has a critical bearing on the contents which has not been adequately spelt out by the editor, it seems worthwhile doing so here. We can demonstrate the lacks in two ways, the textual and the contextual — which do not necessarily point to the same totality.

First, the textual gaps. As the editor shows (p. 3) in his tabulation of the respective sequences of manuscript and printed text, the Westminster manuscript (which is a fifteenth-century transcript of original documents) has missing folios which appear to be irrevocably lost, and the contents of which are not known. All is not lost, however, since John Foxe, who used this record, not only abstracted the total number of cases (which he put at 120), but translated some of them at length.[13] Foxe's pages include material that is not present in the extant manuscript, but as the martyrologist reorganized his evidence more or less chronologically, like Dr. Tanner, it is not easy to try and work out how or where the *Acts and Monuments'* additions could have fitted into the Westminster manuscript. Our ability to assess Foxe's dependability is helped by his having transcribed some passages that we still have (e.g., notably, the case of Margery Baxter) as well as others that we do not. Foxe certainly edited his material, but comparison of his text with the Latin version leaves one with some respect for his over-all accuracy and detail, and surely encourages serious consideration of his additional matter.[14] We may well seek editorial guidance here, and it is a great pity that Dr. Tanner made no attempt (even in an appendix), to indicate where and how Foxe supplements his record. This omission is the more to be regretted in that (as I suggest below) Foxe includes valuable information that does not survive elsewhere.

Second, the contextual lacunae. One does not have to read far in the bishop of Norwich's proceedings to become aware that the enquiries recorded here form

---

[12]*Trials*, p. 8. Most of the minor suspects denied the charges and purged themselves.

[13]Foxe, *AM*, III, 587–600. In later editions Foxe translated documents (e.g., pp. 586–587, 592–593) that were left in Latin in 1563. Foxe's reference to "old monuments within the diocese of Norfolk and Suffolk" is not clear about their location, though Edwin Welch, "Some Suffolk Lollards," *Proceedings of the Suffolk Institute of Archaeology*, XXIX (1964), 156, took it to mean that the manuscript was in one of those countries. When Ussher transcribed part of the manuscript in the seventeenth century it was at Lambeth, where it may already have been when Foxe used it; J. A. F. Thomson, "John Foxe and Some Sources for Lollard History: Notes for a Critical Appraisal," *Studies in Church History*, ed. G. J. Cuming, II (London, 1965), 252–253. On the missing pages in the manuscript and Foxe's use of it see *Trials*, pp. 2, 5, n. 23, 8, 29, n. 252.

[14]This additional material is to be found in Foxe, *AM*, III, 592–593, 596–597, 599–600. Foxe's editing consisted (perhaps largely) in his omissions. Thomson, *art. cit.*, pp. 251–257, points out that it is unwise to reject the source-value of the *Acts and Monuments*, and credits Foxe with a reasonable degree of accuracy in his use of documentary sources. See also James Gairdner, *Lollardy and the Reformation in England* (London, 1908–1913), I, 158–159.

part of a larger whole. One after another the accused named their teachers and mentors—Willliam White, Hugh Pye, John Waddon, and others[15]—none of whom appears as defendant in these investigations. It is clear that we have to do here with suspects who were learners more than teachers, recipients, not makers, of heresy, the disciples of more important absentees. Those who were looked up to as leaders (or martyrs), who had given instruction and held Lollard schools in Norfolk and Suffolk must be sought elsewhere.

Why was it that Norwich, a diocese that—with the notable exception of William Sawtry—had hitherto been relatively untroubled by heresy (or antiheretical proceedings), became an area for such intensive investigation in the 1420's?[16] There is a considerable amount of external evidence alluded to, but not explored in the introduction to the *Trials*, which shows that the Norwich proceedings formed part of a wider campaign against the Lollards. The year 1428 saw action by the authorities in Kent, Essex, and Suffolk (where the bishop of Norwich initiated enquiries at Bury St. Edmunds, though this does not feature in the *Trials*).[17] It was also in the spring of this year that Bishop Fleming of Lincoln saw to the exhumation and burning of Wycliffe's bones.[18] All told, this seems, as Dr. Tanner points out (p. 7), to amount to "a concerted persecution of Lollardy all over the province of Canterbury." But what caused this remarkably co-ordinated initiative against the heresy, and why was convocation told in July, 1428, that it was growing unusually in strength?[19] The suggestion that this demonstration of orthodox vigor was put on for the sake of conciliar politics seems altogether unconvincing. "The persecution was no doubt stimulated by the English bishops' desire to show the forthcoming Council of Basle that they were tackling heresy."[20] Though this might have been a useful side effect, we can be sure that the primary motive was less disinterested and lay nearer home.

[15]Examples of the longest such lists of names appear in *Trials*, pp. 60, 66, 79, 85–86, 140, 146, 165, 176 (179). Cf. also the appended Table.

[16]On the absence of participants from this area in Oldcastle's rising see Thomson, *Later Lollards*, pp. 117–119; Charles Kightly, "The Early Lollards. A Survey of Popular Lollard Activity in England, 1382–1428" (D. Phil. Thesis, University of York, 1975), pp. 364–365, 380. I am extremely grateful to Dr. Kightly for permission to quote his unpublished work, which I have found most valuable. See Foxe, *AM*, III, 585, for Richard Belward's reported defense of Oldcastle as a true believer and falsely condemned.

[17]Thomson, *op. cit.*, pp. 120–121; see below, p. 95.

[18]H. B. Workman, *John Wyclif* (Oxford, 1926), I, xl, II, 319–320; "Gregory's Chronicle" in *Historical Collections of a Citizen of London*, ed. J. Gairdner (Camden Second Series, XVII [London, 1876]), p. 163. The date of this event is uncertain but W. Lyndwood, *Provinciale* (Oxford, 1679), p. 284, n. c (*Johannem Wickliff*), puts it in 1428, which would mean after March 25 that year. The event is referred to by Thomas Netter in his *Doctrinale Antiquitatum Fidei Catholicae Ecclesiae*, ed. B. Blanciotti (Venice, 1757–1759), III, col. 830, and cf. n. 57 below.

[19]*Reg. Chichele*, III, 185. Bishop Alnwick is among the bishops listed as present when this cause of convocation's meeting was declared on July 9.

[20]*Trials*, Introduction, pp. 7–8.

Undoubtedly, English and continental affairs were interwoven on these heretical questions. But it seems rather more likely that the currents of influence flowed in the reverse direction — fears of Bohemia's heresy enhancing fears of England's. It may well be that this was the case with the insistent letters sent by Martin V in December, 1427, to the bishop of Lincoln, the archbishop of Canterbury, and various secular authorities, ordering the publication of the sentence given against Wycliffe at the Council of Constance twelve years before. Martin, however, improved on the conciliar decree. He directed not only that Wycliffe's bones should be exhumed and cast far from ecclesiastical burial, but also (and this had not been commanded in 1415) that they should be publicly burned and the ashes so disposed of that no vestige or trace should remain.[21]

By the time he issued this order the pope was freshly informed of the importance of Wycliffe's heritage, thanks to the first two volumes of Thomas Netter's great work, both of which were dedicated and presented to him, and which he gratefully acknowledged.[22] The *Doctrinale antiquitatum ecclesie* (which was Netter's own title) was directed against continental as well as English followers of Wy-

[21]O. Raynaldus, *Annales Ecclesiastici* (Bar-le-Duc and Paris, 1864–1883), XXVIII, 55 (1427:14), cf. pp. 25–27 (1425:15–18); G. D. Mansi, *Sacrorum Conciliorum...Collectio* (Paris, 1901–1927), XXVII, cols. 635–636; *Calendar of...Papal Letters*, VII, AD 1417–1431, ed. J. A. Twemlow, p. 23. Martin issued these orders on December 9, 1427. (For his earlier actions against Wycliffe's works see *ibid.*, pp. 21–22.) Even now the English authorities seem to have taken their time to execute the papal order (see n. 18).

[22]The *DNB* life of Netter has been responsible for spreading error on the dating and presentation of his work. All three volumes were dedicated to Martin V, and the author's letters prefacing Vols. II and III gratefully acknowledge the pope's commendations of the first two volumes (comprising Books I–V of the work). Martin's letters acknowledging Vols. I and II are dated respectively April 1, 1426, and August 8, 1427, and they, as well as Netter's own references, show that both volumes were examined by "*solemnes viros.*" The pope wrote in both letters of Netter's work "against the Hussite heretics," and reported that he had given Vol. I to the legate responsible for combating heresy in Germany, for use in suitable cases. In the letter of August, 1427, Martin wrote that he looked forward to Vol. III, adding that "ut damnatas conclusiones Wicleffi securius valeas confutare, mittimus tibi bullam de damnatione librorum praedicti haeretici." (This was four months before the orders for exhuming Wycliffe and publishing his condemnation.) Netter's friend John Keninghale presented Vol. I and probably also Vol. II to the pope, and also one volume (? Vol. III, which was still being written in 1428, see below, n. 57) to Archbishop Chichele, who received it with much pleasure at a session of the king's council. (There is no reason why the Brother John, Carmelite, who presented the pope with Vol. II should be other than Keninghale, and the mistaken candidate, John 'Tacesphalus' or Titleshale, d. 1354, seems to have appeared thanks to a mistake of Trithemius.) Netter, *Doctrinale*, ed. Blanciotti, I, xviii–xix (cf. xvi–xvii), 1–4; II, 1–2; III, 1–2; *Monumenta Historica Carmelitana*, Fasc. 5, ed. B. Zimmerman (Lérins, 1907), pp. 444–445; A. B. Emden, *A Biographical Register of the University of Oxford to A.D. 1500* (Oxford, 1957–1959), II, 1035–1036, 1343–1344, III, 1880, s.n. Keninghale, Netter, Titleshale. See also the account of Netter and the *Doctrinale* in J. A. Robson, *Wyclif and the Oxford Schools* (Cambridge, 1961), pp. 223–224, 231 ff.

cliffe, Hussites as well as Lollards, illustrated from the author's direct experience of leading English heretics. And in the opening pages of Volume II (for which he was sent papal thanks and praise in August, 1427) Netter drew attention to the importance of the Constance decree as refutation of the Wycliffites' claim that their master had never been lawfully condemned.[23]

If Wycliffe was—provocatively to some—prominent in the news in the early months of 1428, so were the heretics of Bohemia. The convocation that met that summer simultaneously considered improvements to the procedures against Lollards and the grant of a subsidy for a crusade against the Hussites, being reminded of the need to strengthen the faith "and resist the malice of heretics, unusually spreading in various parts of the world."[24] It also heard the case of Ralph Mungyn, who had denied the lawfulness of fighting the Bohemian heretics.[25]

When the convocation of Canterbury met at St. Paul's in July, 1428, and reconvened the following November and December after the harvest recess, it studiously devoted itself (as is well known) to the deficiencies of the legal process for combating heresy.[26] This tightening of the mesh of provisions that had been de-

---

[23]Blanciotti dropped the reference to Wycliffites and Hussites that had been in the title of the 1532–1557 edition of the *Doctrinale*. For Netter's own title see *Doctrinale*, I, 2, and *Loci e libro Veritatum*, ed. J. E. T. Rogers (Oxford, 1881), p. 2. The continental prohibition of Wycliffe's writings was of course an ongoing cause, into which Netter injected his massive contribution. He certainly looked to Martin V for firm action ("Age jam, sancte pater: quod facturus es, fac citius," he concluded his prefatory letter to Vol. I; *Doctrinale*, I, 4; cf. col. 355). It seems possible that Netter's book, which was given careful consideration by the pope, had some direct bearing on the curial letters against Wycliffe, and it is therefore of some interest that Vol. II starts by listing twelve doctrines of the Wycliffites which include (3) their extolling of their master, (8) play on the fact that Wycliffe himself was not judicially condemned by the Church during his lifetime, (9) the claim that the proceedings against Wycliffe after his death were unjust—i.e., contesting the validity of the Constance decree, which Netter cited (*ibid.*, II, cols. 11–13, 22–27). The burning of Wycliffe's bones had been talked about before Constance. The fact that they had *not* been burned was part of the boast of the 1406 letter in Wycliffe's defense purporting to come from Oxford University, and in 1411 Archbishop Arundel asked the pope to order the exhumation of the heresiarch, and that his bones should be "cast on a midden or burned." David Wilkins, *Concilia Magnae Britanniae et Hiberniae* (London, 1737), III, 302; *Snappe's Formulary*, ed. H. E. Salter (Oxford Historical Society, LXXX [Oxford, 1924]), pp. 91, 133–135; J. H. Dahmus, *The Prosecution of John Wycliff* (New Haven, 1970), pp. 151–154.

[24]*Reg. Chichele*, III, 195–196; ". . . et ad resistenciam malicie hereticorum plus solito in diversis orbis partibus pullulancium;" cf. above, n. 19, for earlier harping on the unusual circumstances. For the outcome of the request for the Bohemian subsidy see *ibid.*, I, xlvii.

[25]*Ibid.*, III, 197, 200, 202–205. (Mungyn was condemned as an obstinate heretic to perpetual imprisonment.)

[26]On convocation's work on this matter see Thomson, *Later Lollards*, pp. 223–226; Anne Hudson, "The Examination of Lollards," *Bulletin of the Institute of Historical Research*, XLVI (November, 1973), 145–159. Convocation was considering both the form of procedure against heretics, and a specific form of abjuration (*Reg. Chichele*, III, 187, 191–192). The

veloped over the previous forty years was (as so often in the past) related to immediate circumstances. "Statutes and ordinances were issued in this convocation against the Lollards, who in many parts of England, as in Bohemia, were craftily scheming and working greatly to rage and rebel against the Christian faith," wrote the St. Albans chronicler.[27] We can do better than this vague assertion. A letter sent to William Swan, the English proctor at Rome, sandwiched a report of this convocation between matters of curial and personal business, and discloses interesting details of Lollard plotting.

> Convocation began in St. Paul's on 5th July last, in which my lord of Canterbury proceeded most determinedly against Lollards and heretics, among whom one Bartholomew Cornmonger, heresiarch, detected many Lollards in England, of whom some were taken and hanged as seditious, and others condemned to perpetual imprisonment. They confessed indeed that early on the feast of St. John the Baptist last [June 24] many thousands of heretics were to have gathered to the destruction of the English church but, God be praised, their proposal was wholly frustrated. For my lord of Canterbury, riding several days and nights, initially arrested these Lollards of whom he still holds in his prisons something like thirty, so that there is no doubt that shortly, by God's grace, he will exterminate all such heretics, and purge his province of evil men.[28]

What we know of the story begins early in May, 1428, with orders for the arrest of twenty-one named suspects from eight parishes centered on the Tenterden area of Kent, who were said to have held and taught heresy and error. Six, perhaps seven, of these were men later named as teachers in the bishop of Norwich's proceedings. One was Bartholomew Cornmonger, the reported informant. Two others may already have slipped away, since William White and John Fowlyn are referred to respectively as "late chaplain of Tenterden" and "late of Wittersham."

---

latter may have had some direct bearing on Alnwick's proceedings (*infra*, p. 97) though the specimen abjuration of Richard Monk (*ibid.*, III, 207–208) was not, like the Norwich ones, in the form of a chirograph.

[27]*Annales Monasterii S. Albani, a Johanne Amundesham, Monacho*, ed. H. T. Riley (Rolls Series [London, 1870–1871]), I, 32.

[28]"Quinto die Julii preterito incepit convocacio in ecclesia Pauli London' in qua dominus Cant' contra lollardos et hereticos valde realiter processit inter quos quidam dictus Bartholomeus Cornmonger heresiarcha plures in Anglia detexit lollardos, quorum quidam cogniti sunt et ut cediciosi suspensi, quidam vero perpetuis carceribus condempnati. Fatebantur vero quod in festo Johannis Baptiste ultimo preterito de mane in exterminium ecclesie Anglicane multa milia hereticorum fuissent congregata, sed deo laudes eorum propositum penitus dissipatum est, dominus vero Cant' ipsos lollardos equitando pluribus diebus et noctibus primo cepit, qui de eis adhuc habet in carceribus suis bene circa xxx lollardos, sic quod [non] dubium est quin in brevi cum dei gracia omnes huiusmodi hereticos exterminabit et provinciam suam malis hominibus purgabit. Iam nuper rex in persona propria cum multis proceribus suis et dominus Cant' cum pluribus confratribus suis cum cleri et populi innumerosa multitudine per civitatem London' solempnissimam et devotissimam fecerunt processionem." BL MS Cotton Cleop. C IV, fol. 198[r–v]. (I have supplied the word in square brackets.) For references to this letter see Jacob in *Reg. Chichele*, I, cxxxvii; Thomson, *op. cit.*, p. 175; Kightly, "Early Lollards," pp. 411–412. Dr. Kightly seems to be the

The archbishop's efforts to capture these suspects continued through the summer until finally, after convocation had adjourned for the recess, they were all, with the significant exception of Cornmonger, declared excommunicate on July 31.[29] However, ten days before this, the clergy had considered just before their departure the case of one escapee who failed to get away. William Harry of Tenterden, who was reported to have fled for fear of examination and to have been caught in London, was greatly suspect (especially for possessing English books). He confessed and abjured, but because he could not find sufficient surety for his good behavior he was imprisoned during pleasure.[30]

Bartholomew Cornmonger was captured between June 22 and July 31. His case is not recorded in the minutes of convocation, though his name came up in the trial of Ralph Mungyn, as one notoriously defamed.[31] Cornmonger's defection (whatever the hyperbole of the tale) was undoubtedly a break-through. His description of "heresiarch" receives some support from the Norwich *Trials*, in which six suspects named him as a Lollard teacher.[32] He was clearly a man who could give

only person to have drawn attention to the full significance of these events. The procession, said to have taken place "lately," is followed by an account of convocation being adjourned till Martinmas, in view of the impending harvest and the archbishop's great annoyance at the small remaining attendance of prelates and clergy. There is no report on the November session. It would seem likely that the letter was written during the recess. Was the reported procession, as Dr. Kightly suggests, in thanksgiving for the archbishop's success against the Lollards? If so, this is apparently its only record, since the only two processions chronicled during these months took place on June 2 and November 19, and were connected with other events. "Gregory's Chronicle" in Gairdner (ed.), *op cit.*, p. 162; *Reg. Chichele*, III, 193; Amundesham, *Annales*, I, 31. For William Swan and his letters see E. F. Jacob, *Essays in Later Medieval History* (Manchester, 1968), Chapter iii, pp. 58–78. For what may be another veiled reference to the rising by Netter see n. 57 below.

[29]*Reg. Chichele*, III, 297–301. Four men were arrested on May 23. They came from the parishes of Tenterden, High Halden, and Rolvenden, and two were not among the twenty-one named. The archbishop issued new orders for the arrest of the remaining nineteen suspects on May 25 and June 22, and, after they had again been fruitlessly cited, declared them contumacious and excommunicate on July 31 (when he was at Mayfield, Sussex). Cornmonger's name was now omitted from the list.

[30]*Ibid.*, III, 189–190 (on Wednesday, July 21, the last day before the adjournment). Harry's name was not in the list of May 4.

[31]*Ibid.*, III, 199. (Mungyn was said to have visited and communicated with Cornmonger, and claimed he had denounced him thrice to the bishop of London.) Kightly, *loc. cit.*, suggests that Cornmonger's capture was in the early summer, perhaps at the beginning of June. This, however, would make anomalous his inclusion in the archbishop's reissued citation of June 22. He may have been taken soon after that, though it does not seem necessary to suppose a date before the alleged rising. His fate is not known. Possibly his full confession helped him to escape serious punishment.

[32]*Trials*, pp. 60, 66, 79, 140, 146, 165. The homes of these defendants were in Bergh Apton, Loddon, and Ditchingham in Norfolk, and Nayland in Suffolk — which might have been a point of transit between Kent and Norfolk. William Harry was caught in London, and the capital was certainly a center for heretics from both sides of the Thames. (See *Trials*,

the authorities invaluable information, including on East Anglia where it must be assumed that his missionary activities (unlike those of other Kent Lollards) were now ended.

Archbishop Chichele's suspicions were aroused well before the reported midsummer rising was to have occurred. His prompt action apparently helped to foil Lollard plans, though he precipitated a heretical diaspora which convocation and other members of the hierarchy were left to cope with. The various Lollard prosecutions that followed must therefore be seen as the result of the reported new insurrection that had been successfully nipped in the bud. The circumstance, lost to sight thereafter (it is not mentioned in any of the surviving proceedings), deserves to be recalled since it accounts for the exceptional activity of the time.[33]

It is not clear at what moment the archbishop undertook his strenuous ride — apparently acting on the information obtained from Cornmonger. It could have been either in late June or the high summer, in August or even September, 1428, after convocation had adjourned and after the failure of his archdeacon's official to pick up the remaining fifteen men and three women who had been on the run since May.[34] Such a date would fit both the continued orders against the Tenterden suspects and also the fresh urgency attending the treatment of heresy after the summer recess. The new session started with a declaration to the assembled clergy of the need to provide adequate remedy against heretics, "whose malice increases from day to day in the province of Canterbury," and was likely to grow still further unless appropriate steps were taken.[35] The novel request was put forward shortly after this for the religious to provide additional prison accommodation for Lollard heretics — doubtless arising from the overcrowding of Chichele's own prisons.[36]

The Kent Lollards would seem to have had plenty of time in which to make good their escape. Some of them appear to have vanished for good. Of those who

---

p. 146, for a reference to Lollard schools in London, and Foxe, *AM*, III, 585, for a report of Richard Belward's books coming from London and of William Taylor of Loddon going to London with Hugh Pye.) But we should not leave out of account the possibility of sea-links between Kent and Norfolk (which could have taken in Colchester). There are some hints in the *Trials*: William White's books arrived via Yarmouth (p. 41 and below, p. 84) "sailing toward Yarmouth," a suspect broke his fast (p. 76 and below, p. 94); could the book that came "de partibus ultramarinis ad istas partes" (p. 75) have come from across the Thames estuary, rather than across the English Channel?

[33]Kightly, "Early Lollards," pp. 411, 418, points to Cornmonger's confession and the revelation of a new Lollard plot as having "triggered off prosecutions all over southern England." The charges against White and those in the *Trials* say nothing of the reported plot. But cf. Margery Baxter's reported expectation (*Trials*, p. 47), that White would preach at his execution "and make the people rise and kill all traitors" against him and his teaching.

[34]Chichele could scarcely have undertaken this mission while convocation was meeting, and it makes best sense to place it after Cornmonger's capture, in the summer recess.

[35]*Reg. Chichele*, III, 191.

[36]This request (on which the religious seem to have dragged their feet) was made on November 17 and again on November 23. *Ibid.*, III, 192, 195.

transferred to other missionary soil north of the Thames where they were already known, the most important, William White, is reasonably well recorded. He was already thought to be in East Anglia (or Essex) by July 6, 1428, to judge from the royal letters of that date quoted by Foxe, directing John Exeter and the keeper of Colchester Castle to arrest White and two other Lollard suspects.[37] The layman John Waddon (who left Kent with his wife Joan) was to die with White in Norwich in September the same year.[38] John Fowlyn taught six of Bishop Alnwick's suspects, but his fate is unknown, as is that of the two Everdens, Thomas and William, who likewise joined the heretical schools in Norfolk. John Abraham of Woodchurch in Kent (another on Chichele's list) may be the cordwainer of that name who held schools of heresy in Colchester and was executed there in 1428 or 1429.[39]

Bishop Alnwick was therefore taking up Archbishop Chichele's reins. His first concern must have been with the leaders and teachers of the heretics. We know just who these were from the names listed in a number of Dr. Tanner's *Trials*.[40] There were several men of importance besides the six already mentioned who came from Kent. Hugh Pye stands out above the others. Like White he was a priest, and when he was burned with him and Waddon, it was Pye whom the St. Albans chronicler thought the most important of the three.[41] Pye's trial is not extant, but we know something of his views from Foxe, who recorded his examination on July 5, 1424, when he was apparently chaplain at Loddon.[42] It seems a fair presumption that the heretics of Loddon, four of whom confessed their debt to Hugh Pye, owed at least as much to him as to White (with whom Pye's name was

---

[37]Foxe, *AM*, III, 586–587. The other two suspects were Thomas, late chaplain of Seething and William Northampton, priest. Conceivably the former is Thomas Pert, priest and chaplain, mentioned as teacher in the *Trials*; cf. Foxe, *AM*, III, 588.

[38]They were burned probably on September 13, 1428, at Bishop's Gate, Norwich, and John Exeter helped supply faggots for the occasion. *Records of the City of Norwich*, ed. W. Hudson and J. C. Tingey (Norwich, 1906–1910), II, 66; *Reg. Chichele*, I, cxxxvii, n. 4; Thomson, *op. cit.*, p. 122. According to a rather confused report in Foxe, *AM*, III, 587, Waddon was imprisoned at Framlingham Castle.

[39]See above, n. 11, and below, pp. **87, 95**, on Fowlyn and William Everden, and on Abraham, *Trials*, pp. 28, 45, n. 44, 152–153; Thomson, *op. cit.*, pp. 121–122. Another Kent heretic who went to the stake in Colchester in November, 1428, was William Chiveling. (He does not feature in the *Trials*.) *Red Paper Book of Colchester*, ed. W. G. Benham (Colchester, 1902), pp. 52–55; *Reg. Chichele*, I, cxxxvii, IV, 297–301; Thomson, *loc. cit.*

[40]See above, n. 15, and Table below.

[41]Amundesham, *Annales*, I, 29: "quorum principale nomen erat Hugo Pye." The suspects in the *Trials* bracket White and Pye together, suggesting their close association. Cf. Foxe, *AM*, III, 597, for a report that Pye bequeathed to Alice, servant of White, a New Testament that was in the keeping of a man of Colchester.

[42]Foxe, *AM*, III, 586 ("Ludney" is to be identified as Loddon). For one of the three points of which Pye was charged on this occasion see below, pp. **95-6**. The others were that people should not go on pilgrimage, nor give alms except to those who beg at their doors.

so often bracketed).[43] Another leader of importance (but even greater obscurity) who likewise was in orders was William Caleys: he was burned at Chelmsford in 1430.[44] A layman mentioned in the *Trials* as a teacher of heresy was Richard Belward, (whose family produced several suspects, including two Johns of Earsham who denied the charges against them in 1431). Here again Foxe extends the record, with an account of the articles brought against Richard Belward of Earsham in July, 1424, one of them (which he denied with the rest) being that of keeping a heretical school at Ditchingham, for which a parchment-maker brought books from London.[45] The man in question, John Godsell of Ditchingham, denied and purged himself of the same accusation at the same time. Foxe's report is substantiated by Tanner's evidence. The strong suspicion of heresy for which John Godsell had to answer in March, 1429, included the holding of Lollard schools and book-reading in his house at Ditchingham. And the independent record of a jail delivery a month before this reveals John Godsell and John Skylly of Flixton in Suffolk as having kept heretical schools at Earsham and elsewhere from 1424 to 1428. John Skylly and John Godsell were given the severest punishments of all Alnwick's sixty accused: seven-year prison sentences, surely linked with these facts.[46]

William Alnwick's investigations of 1428 and after were clearly, then, the continuation — if not the tail end — of earlier proceedings, conducted both inside his diocese by his predecessor, Bishop Wakering, and outside, in the diocese of Canterbury. Having traced the named leaders of the Lollard disciples collected in this round-up (leaders whom we can place in a tentative order of importance from their mentions in the *Trials*),[47] we may now go on to consider the heretical opinions imbibed in these teachers' schools.

[43]*Trials*, pp. 33, 140, 165, 176, for the cases of John Wardon, Edmund Archer, Hawise and Thomas Moon — who were all of Loddon and all named Pye as teacher, alongside White and others. In the case of John Pert of Loddon (on whom see below, pp. 95, 98), whose abjuration appears in the *Trials* (pp. 168–173), we learn from Foxe (*AM*, III, 597) that "he was the first that brought sir Hugh Pye into the company of the Lollards, who assembled oftentimes together at the house of the said Thomas Moon, and there conferred upon their doctrine."

[44]*Trials*, pp. 140, 146, 152, 165, 176, 179; Thomson, *op. cit.*, p. 122; Amundesham, *Annales*, I, 51; below, p. 87, for Caleys's link with White.

[45]Richard Belward seems to have been the most important Lollard of the family, though the two John Belwards, junior and senior, are the only ones to appear before the law in the *Trials* (pp. 47, 73–74, 86, 140, 146, 176, 179, 212–214). Richard appears to have been related (? as brother-in-law) to Hawise Moon. Nicholas Belward, named as a teacher by two suspects in the *Trials*, is reported by Foxe to have been the son of John, to have lived in the parish of South Elmham ("Southelem"), and to have had a New Testament which he bought in London for £2 16s 8d. Foxe, *AM*, III, 585–586, 597; *Selections from English Wycliffite Writings*, ed. Anne Hudson (Cambridge, 1978), p. 160; Thomson, *op. cit.*, p. 131.

[46]Foxe, *AM*, III, 586; *Trials*, pp. 51–64, and Appendix, pp. 217–219; cf. the editor's comment p. 24 on how Godsell and Skylly might "have considered their sentences unusually severe for their offences."

[47]See Table below.

TABLE OF HERETICS IN THE DIOCESE OF NORWICH c. 1428

Leading Teachers

(16) +WILLIAM WHITE K   (12) +HUGH PYE

Missionaries and Teachers in Lollard Schools

(8) +John Waddon K   (6) Bartholomew Cornmonger K   (6) John Fowlyn K   (5) +WILLIAM CALEYS   (5) THOMAS PERT   (5) Richard Belward   (5) William Everden K   (4) Thomas Everden K

Local Supporters and Hosts

(1) *John Godsell*   (4) *John Skylly*   *William & Margery Baxter*   (2) *Thomas & Hawise Moon*   (2) Thomas Burell   (5) *John Pert*   (3) *William Bate*   (3) *Edmund Archer*

Rank and File

KEY

CAPS.	in orders	
Ital.	a defendant in *Trials*	
( )	no. of cases in *Trials* that mention suspect	(excluding his own)
K	mentioned as being in Kent	
+	executed for heresy	

Dr. Tanner, who treats the tenets of the defendants at some length in his introduction (pp. 10–22), notes the "comparative uniformity" of their beliefs (p. 28), and the emphasis, unusual among the Lollards, of doubts about the sacraments. Foxe, who likewise observed the "agreement of doctrine to be found amongst them," decided it was unnecessary to detail many individual cases "because their articles and punishments were all one."[48] We cannot afford to leave it at that. If the heretics' "considerable measure of agreement on a number of topics, notably the sacraments"[49] is attributable, as Dr. Tanner supposes, to more than stereotyped questioning by the prosecutors, we are bound to consider the sources, knowing as we do that the sixty men and women had derived their views from their schooling. Though Wycliffe is doubtless properly to be seen as the *fons et origo* of Lollard opinions, it seems unreal to compare the defendants' alleged opinions with Wycliffe's Latin works when these, if known at all to the men and women of Loddon and Earsham and Ditchingham, were mediated to them through the teachings of others.[50] Tanner and Foxe both supply the essential clue, which neither follows up: the defendants' regard for William White.[51]

William White was a Lollard missionary of very considerable influence.[52] His claims are attested by both supporters and opponents. Margery Baxter, who knew him well (she had carried his books from Yarmouth to her village of Martham, and was present at his execution), called him a holy man, "a great saint in heaven, and a most holy doctor ordained and sent by God." Another suspect was charged with having received in his house the "condemned and notorious heretic," William White. White was named more often than any other leader by Alnwick's accused.[53] And Thomas Netter (who spoke from personal knowledge) called White

[48]*Trials*, pp. 10–22, 28; Foxe, *AM*, III, 589, 598; cf. p. 592.

[49]*Trials*, p. 20.

[50]*Ibid.*, pp. 11, 17, 21. While it is helpful to be directed to Wycliffe's views on the points in question, it is just as important to know how far the suspects' alleged statements diverged from him, e.g., on the eucharist, images and saints, and oaths, as compared with views of temporalities, tithes, the papacy, and excommunication. On this divergence of the heretics from Wycliffe see Welch, *art. cit.* (above, n. 13), pp. 164–165; *Selections*, ed. Hudson, p. 161.

[51]Cf. Dr. Tanner's remark (*Trials*, p. 21) quoted below, p. 88, and Foxe, *AM*, III, p. 590: "By which their consent and doctrine it appeareth, that they all received it of some one instructor, who was William White."

[52]Besides the account of White in Thomson, *Later Lollards*, see Gairdner, *Lollardy and the Reformation*, I, 157–158, neither of which seems to me to recognize his importance. Dr. Kightly, however, says of White that he "was to emerge as one of the more important national influences on post-Oldcastle Lollardy," and gives him his full due (*op. cit.*, pp. 406 ff.), pointing out his "immense influence" on Alnwick's suspects (p. 419).

[53]*Trials*, pp. 39, 41, 47, and see Table *above*. Cf. Foxe, *AM*, III, 596, for William Wright saying that "William White was a good and holy doctor." Margery Baxter was interrogated only three weeks after White's death. At the examination of John Wardon of Loddon (the earliest of Alnwick's *Trials*) William White and Hugh Pye are already, on September 2, 1428, referred to as "condemned heretics," though the surviving record dates White's condemnation September 13.

a "great satrap," "vassal," and "hanger-on" of Wycliffe, "a doctor" of the Lollards, and a "great satellite" of the Wycliffites.[54] It is fortunate (and probably not coincidental) that in the case of White alone among all these Norfolk leaders, evidence survives of his heretical teaching.

Our knowledge of White is limited, but enough to attest his standing. Apart from references in Chichele's register, which record his abjuration before convocation in 1422 (after he had been imprisoned by the archbishop as a Lollard suspect and excommunicated for his unlicensed preaching at Tenterden),[55] his last trial is known from two complementary and independent, though related, sources. There are various scattered references to White's errors in the third volume of Thomas Netter's *Doctrinale*. Netter was at White's condemnation on September 13, 1428—his presence itself being some indication of the significance of the accused—and he recorded the same year some of the views he had heard White voice in reply to the bishop of Norwich. The importance of this defendant was plain from the formidable team of experts assembled by Bishop Alnwick to hear his case, and it may be noted in passing that groups of these men reappeared for other cases in the following months (when likewise the number present on any single occasion is related to the character of the suspect).[56] Netter's remarks about White in his *Doctrinale* have the advantage of being written down soon afterwards, and at several points they complement the list of thirty points on which the heretic was condemned, to be found in the *Fasciculi Zizaniorum*. This record in a Carmelite book dating from about ten years after White's death probably owed something to the

[54]Netter, *Doctrinale*, ed. Blanciotti, III, cols. 412, 630, 795–796, 844: "Hoc anno tandem quidam magnus illorum [i.e., Wiclevistae] satelles *Willelmus* cognomento *Albus*, sacerdos..."; "sectatorum ejus doctor quidam et presbyter uxoratus"; "Wicleffus....et Guillelmus ejus satrapa magnus"; "Guillelmus vassallus ejus"; "Dixit ille clientulus Wicleffi Guillelmus Albus..." Cf. cols. 709–710, 789, for White's use of Wycliffe's *Trialogus* against praying to saints, and for his views on relics.

[55]*Reg. Chichele*, III, 85. White is here described as chaplain. (There is no record here of the points abjured, but three of them were referred to in 1428.)

[56]*Fasciculi Zizaniorum*, ed. W. W. Shirley (Rolls Series [London, 1858])—cited hereafter as *Fasciculi*—p. 417. On this "very strong court" to try White see Gairdner, *op. cit.*, I, 157. This impressive group of experts was mainly composed of university men, including nine or so doctors of theology, drawn about equally from both universities. Besides the bishop's registrar and vicar-general (see above, n. 9), regular attenders at Alnwick's later *Trials* who had also been at White's were William Worstede (prior of Norwich Cathedral Priory), Master John Thorp (Carmelite), John Elys (Franciscan), and Thomas Ryngstede (dean of St. Mary in the Fields, Norwich). In addition, some of White's examiners reappeared later for the trials of Margery Baxter (*Trials*, p. 41; Robert Colman, Franciscan, John Gaysle or Gasle, O.P., and James Walsingham) and John Skylly (*ibid.*, p. 51; Masters John Keninghale and Peter of S. Faith). Both these accused were heavily dependent on White; so was Robert Cavell (see below, p. 89), for whose hearing also it was thought desirable to assemble an impressive team. The cases of Matilda Fleccher, John Eldon, William Bate, Hawise and Thomas Moon (*ibid.*, pp. 131, 133, 139, 157, 175) were all thought to warrant a respectable judicial turnout. Cf. the editor's comments, p. 9. Netter had before this attended the trials of other important Lollards—Badby, Oldcastle, and William Taylor.

fact that four Carmelites (all with some Norwich connection) were present at the trial, one of them being Netter's close friend, John Keninghale.[57] The *Fasciculi* gives us the fullest account of White's views, though it is by no means a complete record, even of the final proceedings against him.[58] We learn from other sources of his burning.[59]

The judgment of 1428 and Netter's statements help to flesh out White's career in a few details. His earlier evangelizing in Gillingham and Tenterden in Kent had included eucharistic teaching and attacks on the mendicant orders and temporal possessions of the clergy, which all sound close to Wycliffe.[60] His association with the diocese of Norwich went back well before 1428. White took up residence in this area, abandoning his tonsure and clerical garb and living as if he were a married layman with his "wife" Joan, more than two years before September, 1428. And even before that he admitted to having been a visiting missionary, "ranging around and running about" to instruct people "in many parts" of the diocese of Norwich. This pushes back the known beginning of his heretical evan-

[57]References by Netter to "hoc anno," "vix. . .sex menses," and "infra annum" in his mentions of White's condemnation indicate the stages of his writing, not long after that event (*Doctrinale*, III, cols. 412, 630, 789, 844, and cf. col. 414 for White's *viva voce* reply). Netter cited verbatim four of the articles listed in the *Fasciculi*, naming White in three cases (*Fasciculi*, nos. 22, 25, and 26—Netter mixed up two of these numbers; *Doctrinale*, III, cols. 789, 844, 940, and below, nn. 76, 98; in the last instance Netter quotes White's conclusion "in libello suo"). The fourth passage (*Fasciculi*, no. 7 on the denial of church baptism and confirmation) is quoted by Netter (*Doctrinale*, III, col. 341) without White's name but with an interesting general reference to the proceedings against Lollards of Kent and Norwich diocese. He refers to Wycliffe as one head of the beast of the Apocalypse, "which when it was as it were killed, it brought itself back to life in death; and the blow of its death was cured by certain Lollards of woody Kent now recently taken under Henry archbishop of Canterbury, and again this year by others judged by holy prelates under William bishop of Norwich." The reference to the 1428 cure of Wycliffe's *plaga mortis* is suggestive of a link between the burning of his bones and the reported rising. This is the earliest of Netter's allusions to the Norwich heresies and conceivably he wrote his passage before attending White's trial, or before its conclusion (cf. col. 342: "Horum [i.e., Wiclevistae] tractatum nondum vidi"). On the dating of the *Fasciculi* and Netter's connection with this collection of documents see James Crompton, "*Fasciculi Zizaniorum* I and II," *Journal of Ecclesiastical History*, XII (April and October, 1961), 35–45, 155–166. For Keninghale see above, n. 22.

[58]*Fasciculi*, pp. 417–432, is clearly the formal instrument of White's condemnation, which one would expect to be completed by the declaration of his guilt and delation to the secular arm. It is possible that the interrogations which presumably preceded this final stage started over ten days earlier, and that by September 2 White was an excommunicated heretic, awaiting in prison the final sentence and degradation that took place on the day of execution. See above, n. 53, and below, p. 95, n. 103.

[59]See above, nn. 38, 41.

[60]*Fasciculi*, pp. 418–420. It is clear that these first three points were among those held and taught by White before his 1422 abjuration. Cf. the points listed in Foxe, *AM*, III, 591.

gelizing in Norfolk to about 1425.[61] It appears that Loddon became his chief base (a deposition in Foxe has him living with Thomas Moon), but he evidently also had a *pied à terre* in the neighboring village of Bergh Apton. The acknowledgments of his followers plot White's missionary path through the villages of Martham, Ditchingham, Earsham, Flixton, Beccles, and further south in Nayland (Suffolk), a few miles north of Colchester, and probably in Colchester itself.[62]

According to a story related by Netter (who brought it up as an example of the false pretension of Wycliffite evangelical poverty), White was found at his trial to have dissipated within a year the entire inheritance, worth about £40, of a young man he had won over.[63] The most intriguing of the charges recorded against him, one which White wholly denied, related to an incident that was alleged to have taken place in his room in the parish of Bergh Apton at Easter (April 4), 1428. It was stated that White had

> induced John Scutte, layman, your disciple, to perform the office of priest, and taught and made him break bread, and give thanks to God, and distribute this bread to you, your concubine, William Everden, John Fowlyn, and William Caleys priest, there present with you, offering it with these words: "Take and eat in memory of Christ's passion."[64]

Three of the participants in this alleged rite were sought for in Kent a month later, so the accusation, were it true, would argue for active correspondence between the two areas. White's "wife," Joan (stated by Foxe to have done her best to carry on her husband's teaching, and to have been harried by the bishop of Norwich as a result), is reported to have been escorted (perhaps after William's death) from Martham to a house in Seething by William Everden. Joan is mentioned by Netter in connection not only with White's rejection of priestly continence as an invention of Antichrist in the year 1000, but also with his confessed teaching on

[61]*Fasciculi*, pp. 420–421. It may be wondered whether the attention focused on the Tenterden area by the actions against Thomas Drayton, rector of Snave, in the summer of 1425, had any bearing on White's movements. *Reg. Chichele*, III, 107–109; Thomson, *op. cit.*, pp. 173–174.

[62]*Trials*, pp. 41, 52, 60, 66, 85–86, 79, 81, 146, 209; cf. 39, 73, 140, 165, 176, 179; Foxe, *AM*, III, 591; cf. p. 597 (referring to "the return of William White to Bergh"). The number of *Trial* references to White's school in Loddon lends support to Foxe's statement. Thomson, *Later Lollards*, pp. 125–126.

[63]Netter, *Doctrinale*, III, col. 630.

[64]*Fasciculi*, pp. 423–424; *Trials*, p. 33, n. 14, identifies the probable place. This is one of the extremely rare allusions to some sort of Lollard rite. See Anne Hudson, "A Lollard Mass," *Journal of Theological Studies*, N.S. XXIII (October, 1972), 407–419; cf. John Badby's remark that John Rakier of Bristol had as much power and authority to make Christ's body as any priest; K. B. McFarlane, *John Wycliffe and the Beginnings of English Nonconformity* (London, 1952), p. 154; Wilkins, *Concilia*, III, 326–327.

[65]Foxe, *AM*, III, 591, 597; Netter, *Doctrinale*, III, cols. 412, 420, cf. 414–417, 420–421, 850–851; *Fasciculi*, pp. 420–421, 425–426, nos. 5, 15–18.

the law of matrimony given by Christ to all three estates of clerks, knights, and laborers.[65]

The references to his tracts, booklets, and books[66] make it clear that White had been busy spreading heresy with his pen as well as by his voice. Besides his heresies on the sacraments of the eucharist and marriage, he was charged with false teaching on baptism and confirmation (which he denied), confession and penance, orders, and extreme unction. White was, in short, accused of error on all seven sacraments. In addition there were articles on the right of any faithful to preach and of temporal lords to remove church property; against fasting and Sunday observance, tithes, relics and images, and respect for St. Thomas of Canterbury; and on the unlawfulness of war and judicial execution. The debt to Wycliffe is clear in some of these points, and it was acknowledged (White admitted his description of "*beatus* Wycliffe"). In other articles, however, the views he had "held, affirmed, written, and taught" were individual to the point of idiosyncrasy. This personal note applies to his undermining of the sacraments, and to the expressions used on some other matters.[67]

William White was named as the heretics' instructor in sixteen out of Alnwick's sixty cases. This, however, is far from being the full extent of his traceable influence. The impact of his teaching is evident in the charges against thirty-four, possibly thirty-eight, of the forty-five suspects whose specific beliefs are stated. The editor indicated that "the defendants appear to have regarded William White, Hugh Pye, and a few others as their teachers."[68] It is possible to go further than this. We can show, both from the corpus of shared error and also from the verbal echoes, the heretics' common source. The peculiarities of this group of Lollards — their denials of the sacraments, and some of their more unusual opinions — have one identifiable source: William White.

It might be suggested that the explanation for the degree of verbal concordance is a common questionnaire that was administered to all the heretics from 1428 on, White included. Obviously there was such a list, or lists, of questions, but the evidence clearly points to White as the source. Firstly, one has to suppose some starting-point for a collection of tenets so peculiar and so unlike the other lists of

---

[66]*Fasciculi*, pp. 423, 432, refers to *tractatus et libelli* and *plures libros*, and cf. above, n. 57, and *Trials*, p. 39. (Lyndwood, *Provinciale*, p. 284, glosses *libellus* as "parvus liber vel codex"). Cf. Netter, *Doctrinale*, III, cols. 416, 940, 983.

[67]*Fasciculi*, pp. 417–432. (Baptism and confirmation are both dealt with in no. 7.) The reference to Wycliffe (my italics) appears in no. 24 (p. 429) on the right of every faithful (*quiscunque fidelis*) freely to preach the word of God.

[68]*Trials*, p. 21. My figures are reached by comparing the tenets charged against the defendants with those of White in the *Fasciculi*. The seven I have excluded from White's influence are William Colyn, Robert Bert, Thomas Ploman, John Fyllys, Thomas Love, Nicholas Drye, and John Goodwyn; the four doubtfuls are John Midelton, Richard Clerk, Thomas White, and Katherine Wright.

errors drawn up for interrogators at this time.[69] Secondly, the records make it plain that whereas White was being charged with teaching, preaching and writing his heresies and errors, the defendants in the *Trials* were all accused with having "learned, held, believed, and affirmed," "held and heard," "held, believed, and affirmed" their points of heresy.[70] On one side stands the man who taught; on the other the disciples who learned.[71] Thirdly, there is sufficient variety in the wording of the tenets charged against individual suspects for one to believe that they were specifically tailored to each of the accused. This testifies to the scrupulousness of the prosecutors,[72] and also enables us to see something of the beliefs of individual Lollards.

The case of Robert Cavell, chaplain, one of the most capable of the defendants (he was able to read out in court the Latin indenture of the articles he abjured), demonstrates this dependence with the utmost clarity. Of the eighteen points listed thirteen correspond closely to White's articles—and appear in the same order.[73] There can be no doubt whatever as to the source of Cavell's errors, and he admitted to having had frequent communication with White and Hugh Pye, and to having attended their heretical schools. This dependence may be demonstrated by juxtaposing three of the more out of the ordinary statements in this list with William White's.

> *Cavell*: Quod nulli licet pro iure suo hereditario vel pro patria pugnare nec placitare, quia sic facientes amittunt caritatem.
> *White*: ...quod nulli licet pro jure hereditario suo vel pro patria pugnare, dum talis cum pugnat caritatem perdit qua proximum diligeret, et sic in peccato mor-

[69]This problem of the questionnaire used by the examiners is considered by Dr. Tanner, *Trials*, pp. 19–20; cf. also Welch, *art. cit.* (above, n. 13), p. 162. It was under discussion at the time, being part of the improvements in procedure produced in 1428. The lists of questions prepared at this juncture (Hudson, "Examination of Lollards," no. 26 above) cover points salient in the *Trials*, including on some of the sacraments, fasting, and Sunday observance, but without any close verbal or general resemblance.

[70]There is a marked repetition in the phraseology of the *Trials*: "tenuit, credidit et affirmavit articulos" (p. 42); "manutenuisse et supportasse...didicisse, tenuisse et affirmasse articulos" (p. 52); "asseruit, tenuit et affirmavit" (p. 60); "tenuisse et audivisse ex informacione Willelmi White" (p. 71); "didicisse, tenuisse, credidisse et affirmasse errores et hereses" (p. 93). This contrasts with the accusations against White of having "held, affirmed, written, taught and preached" his errors and heresies; "scripsisti, tenuisti, dogmatizasti, et coram populo in publico predicasti...tenuisti, affirmasti, scripsisti et docuisti...tenuisse, affirmasse, scripsisse, docuisse et predicasse...fecisse et dictasse plures libros..."; *Fasciculi*, pp. 418, 423, 432.

[71]The word *discipulus* is used of John Scutte and John Godsell; *Fasciculi*, p. 423, *Trials*, p. 60.

[72]A point made by Richard G. Davies, *English Historical Review*, XCIV (July, 1979), 629.

[73]*Trials*, pp. 94–96; *Fasciculi*, pp. 421–423, 427–432, for White's articles nos. 7–9, 11, 20–23, 25–27, 29–30. In addition Cavell's article against clerical continence may reasonably be read as a summary of White's views.

tali existens totum dominium temporalis possessionis amittit, quia talis non est servus Dei sed peccati.

Cavell: quod reliquie sanctorum, scilicet carnes et ossa hominis mortui, nullo modo deberent a populo venerari, nec de monumento fetido extrahi, nec in capsa aurea vel argentea recludi, quia sic facientes committunt ydolatriam.

White: quod reliquie sanctorum, scilicet carnes et ossa hominis mortui, non debent a populo venerari, nec de monumento fetido extrahi, nec in capsa aurea vel argentea reponi; quia homines sic facientes non honorant Deum et sanctos ejus, sed committunt idolatriam.

Cavell: quod nullus honor est exhibendus ymaginibus crucifixi, Beate Marie nec alicuius sancti, eo quod arbores crescentes in silvis sunt maioris viriditatis et virtutis et eo cicius adorande quam lapis vel lignum mortuum sculptum ad similitudinem hominis.

White: quod non est honor aliquis exhibendus imaginibus crucifixi, Beate Marie Virginis, aut alicujus sancti. Nam arbores crescentes in silva sunt majoris virtutis et vigoris, et expressiorem gerunt similitudinem Dei et imaginem quam lapis vel lignum mortuum ad similitudinem hominis sculptum....[74]

The first of these points, "that it is not lawful to fight nor plead for heritage nor for a country" (as it was Englished in one case), was also abjured by three other defendants.[75] The wording of White's denials of relics ("bones of dead men, taken from the stinking tomb") and of images (contrasting the carving of dead wood with the strength of the growing tree) are altogether personal expressions. Both were singled out for quotation by Netter.[76] The denial of worshiping images was common to the heretics, but they seem in general more intent on refusing worship than on pointing to the godliness of sprouting trees. Two other disciples of White, John Skylly and Margery Baxter, echoed his phrases about "dead men's bones": "relics of saints," said Skylly, "that is to say flesh or bone of any dead man, should not be worshipped of the people nor shrined."[77]

There was a huge difference between the rank and file and the few most educated of Alnwick's suspects, such as Robert Cavell, or the chaplain of Bury St. Edmunds, Robert Bert, and John Midelton, vicar of Halvergate, both of whom

---

[74]*Trials, loc. cit.; Fasciculi*, pp. 431–432 (no. 30), 429 (no. 25), 429–430 (no. 26). (I have altered some of the punctuation of the *Fasciculi* passages.)

[75]*Trials*, pp. 53, 58, 61, 158, 160, for the views of John Skylly, John Godsell, and William Bate; cf. also p. 71 for John Pyry's view that it was not lawful to fight for any cause. One may wonder whether these views were in any way connected with Ralph Mungyn's denial of the lawfulness of raising arms and fighting against the heretics of Bohemia.

[76]Netter, *Doctrinale*, III, cols. 789 (confusing the numbers of arts. 25 and 22), 795–796, 940, 941, 983–985. Cf. Wyclif, *Sermones*, ed. J. Loserth (Wyclif Society [London, 1887–1890]), II, 165, for a remark on how the Church was seduced in the cult of "dead bodies and images."

[77]*Trials*, pp. 42, 58; cf. p. 53. Obviously one can find such phrases elsewhere (cf. John Mirk's recommending "dead men's bones oft to see"), but in the context it seems permissible to see the influence of White's emphasis. B. L. Manning, *The People's Faith in the Time of Wyclif* (1919, rep. Hassocks, 1975), p. 34.

denied the charges and purged themselves. Whatever else was taught by the masters of Lollard schools, they did not teach Latin. Vernacular theology had its hazards. Scholastic concepts inevitably shed some nuances as they reached a popular audience adventuring in English doctrine. The *Trials* present illuminating indications of the way in which carefully qualified phrases on that most difficult of all topics, the doctrine of transubstantiation, became lost or adulterated as they moved from academic utterance into an unschooled milieu.

The eleventh article against White (one of four relating to the eucharist, and one he confessed to) included the words:

> quod nullus sacerdos secundum ritum et consuetudinem ecclesie universalis ordinatus, . . . habet potestatem conficiendi corpus Christi; sed post verba sacramentalia a tali presbytero prolata, panis materialis remanet in altari.[78]

John Wardon of Loddon (charged in the month that White died) had apparently repeated this quite faithfully, apart from adding that the sacramental bread remained "panis *purus et* materialis."[79] But the accusation against Matilda Fleccher in April, 1430, shows the statement altered further:

> quod nullus presbiter habet potestatem conficiendi *verum* corpus Christi in sacramento altaris, sed quod post *omnia* verba sacramentalia, a *quocumque* presbitero *quantumcumque* rite prolata, remanet in altari *purus* panis materialis.[80]

Note the additional words which I have italicized (*all* the words. . .by *whatever* priest, *however* duly pronounced. . .). Another variant of White's statement was that attributed to John Reve, a glover of Beccles:

> quod nullus presbiter habet potestatem conficiendi corpus Christi in sacramento altaris ad missam, sed quod post verba sacramentalia, a presbitero in missa *quantumcumque* rite prolata, *nichil* remanet in altari *nisi tantum torta* panis materialis.[81]

In the vernacular version abjured by other offenders of Beccles in April this year (1430) this ran:

> that no priest hath power to make Christ's very body in the sacrament of the altar at mass, and that after the sacramental words said of any priest at mass, there remaineth nothing but only a cake of material bread.[82]

Such a view may, for all we know, have represented what White really thought

---

[78]*Fasciculi*, p. 423; cf. pp. 424, 418–419. White was here close to Wycliffe; cf. Gordon Leff, *Heresy in the Later Middle Ages* (Manchester and New York, 1967), II, 549–557, esp. p. 554; cf. also the first conclusion of which Wycliffe was condemned in 1382: "quod substantia panis materialis et vini maneat post consecrationem in sacramento altaris" (*Fasciculi*, p. 493).

[79]*Trials*, p. 33.

[80]*Ibid.*, p. 131; cf. pp. 196, 199, for the charges of 1431 against two defendants of Martham, both of which include the added "*quantumcumque*" and "*purus* panis."

[81]*Ibid.*, p. 107, cf. pp. 158 and 160.

[82]*Ibid.*, p. 115, cf. pp. 111, 121, 126, 134.

and taught. But it certainly debases and misconstrues the point as it was raised at his trial. He had there confessed to his denial of transubstantiation. The bread of the sacrament did not cease to be bread; it remained *"verus panis in natura."* As recorded, White never stated that the bread, though natural bread, was *only* or *merely* pure bread. He said it was *"corpus Christi in memoria,"* simultaneously the flesh of Christ and the substance of bread.[83] He seems to have remained substantially closer to Wycliffe than many of his followers.

Some of White's flock evidently had no time or taste for such refinements. To them the host was "only pure material bread," just "a cake of material bread"[84] — if not less or worse. The sacrament that priests call the true body of Christ has no eyes to see, ears to hear, tongue to speak, hands to touch, or feet to walk, but it is a cake made of wheat flour, said John Burell, servant of Thomas Moon.[85] Margery Baxter shows the process of debasement descending still lower. Priests were deceiving people with their elevation of the consecrated host and assertions that it was the true body of Christ, said Margery. If what they claimed were true there would be "infinite gods," a thousand priests would make a thousand gods, and afterwards all such gods, eaten and digested, were evacuated in base stinking privies.[86] One wonders whether the loss of the main teachers accentuated such theological crudities, and what other sources may have contributed to the formulation of these views.

The official record, formal and formalized though it is, did not put all the reported words into the mouths of the accused. It remains possible to trace something of the effect of vulgarization and the kind of transformation that took place as points of dogma inculcated in Lollard schools were mulled over in the chat of domestic hearth or tavern.[87] It was a process conducive to both simplification and

[83]*Fasciculi*, pp. 424, 418.

[84]*Trials*, pp. 147, 170.

[85]*Ibid.*, p. 73, cf. p. 77.

[86]*Ibid.*, pp. 44–45, 50–51. Yet even beneath these more extreme utterances there may be a learned substratum. Attacks on the multiplication of Christ's body in the sacrament were part of the case against transubstantiation from Wycliffe on, and Wycliffe himself was apparently responsible for scatological allusions in this context (reportedly calling an accident without a substance worse than rat excrement). *Fasciculi*, pp. 108–109, cf. 106; cf. *Joannis Wiclif Trialogus*, ed. G. Lechler (Oxford, 1869), p. 269. Margery's view might also be compared with that of John Badby, who said (1409) that if it were true that the consecrated host was Christ's body "then there are twenty thousand gods in England" (Wilkins, *Concilia*, III, 327). Cf. *Wycklyffes Wycket* (Oxford, 1828, rep. of 1546 edition) on how "the material bread hath an end . . . Christ said all things that a man eateth goeth down into the womb, and is sent down into the draught away, and it hath an end of rotting"; on the multiplication of Christ's manhood in the bread and wine meaning that "he should wax more in one day by cart loads than he did in 32 years when he was here in earth"; and also "if ye shall fetch your word at god, of god make god, there must needs be many gods": sigs. A 10^r, B 1^v, B 5^r–6^v.

[87]*Trials*, pp. 44, 90, refers to talk while Margery Baxter was "sitting and sewing in her chamber by the fireplace," and to William Colyn holding forth "publicly in the tavern."

also embroidery and eccentric variation. Being faithfully Lollard on one or two scores might combine (witness the skinner, William Colyn)[88] with wild theological assertions on matters quite unrelated to the main concerns of the sect.

Lollard schooling of humble lay people endangered theological priorities and whatever sense of purposeful direction may have existed in the heads of the heretics' leaders. An example that illustrates this fate of heresy on the ground, as it were, is the prominence that appears to have been given to the rejection of fasting. It is, of course, possible that this assumes unreal importance in the record since it was an easy way of identifying suspects.[89] But the impression remains that the heretics themselves set store by their defiance of this church rule — almost to the extent of turning their meat-eating at forbidden seasons into a kind of secret rite.

White had stated that none of the faithful (*nullus fidelis*) was obliged to fast in Lent, on Ember Days, the eves of saints, or in Advent, since Christ never did so and it was only after one thousand years that the popes had deceitfully introduced this observance. The faithful might therefore freely eat meat and other foods, even in the presence of the unfaithful, in order to convert them.[90]

White's followers took this teaching to heart and acted on it. They both rehearsed his words[91] and put them into their own down-to-earth vernacular. "Every Friday is a free day," they said, meaning free "to all manner meats, both flesh and fish indifferently," "as oft as lust and appetite cometh."[92] Margery Baxter, seeing it in housewifely terms, said it was better to eat Thursday's leftover meats on Friday than go to the market for fish.[93] The accused seem to have revelled in their fast-breaking. "In affirming of this opinion," confessed a man of Loddon, "I, Edmund Archer, with sir William White, sir William Caleys, sir Hugh Pye and with other heretics have eaten flesh and all manner of meats indifferently as oft as I had

---

[88]*Ibid.*, pp. 90–91; e.g., his assertion that the human race was more bound to the second person of the Trinity than to the Father, who created Adam, the cause of human damnation.

[89]Foxe, *AM*, III, 587, reports of the 120 who were examined that "some were only taken upon suspicion, for eating of meats prohibited upon vigil-days, who, upon their purgation made, escaped more easily away, and with less punishment." Cf. *Trials*, pp. 11, 15, and 103–105, for the cases of John Fyllys and Thomas Love, both suspect for meat-eating on the eve of St. Thomas.

[90]*Fasciculi*, pp. 427–248, nos. 20–21. (Friday is not included here, though the charge implies a general attack on fasting.) This is a point on which Wycliffe does not seem to have offered guidance. Was it peculiar to White's teaching? It would be interesting to know whether it had come to the fore earlier. According to Foxe, *AM*, III, 584, denial of fasting was one of the points charged against John Florence in 1424 (on whom see below, p. 95). In 1428 (probably) two questions about fasting featured in the Worcester list of articles for Lollard suspects. Hudson, "Examination of Lollards," p. 154.

[91]E.g., *Trials*, pp. 33, 52–53 (57), 61, 95 (all including Fridays in the listed fasting seasons).

[92]*Ibid.*, pp. 74, 78, 116, 121, 127, 142, 148, 154, 160.

[93]*Ibid.*, p. 46.

lust to eat, all such [forbidden] days and times."[94] We learn graphic details of their observance: Margery Baxter's Lenten bacon discovered simmering on the fire; Isabella Davy eating dove chicks, and others a barnacle goose from the marsh; some men partaking of their Saturday meat on a boat, sailing to Yarmouth.[95] We hear too of a secret repast that took place in Thomas Moon's cheesehouse chamber on Easter Eve, when the party consumed the best part of a quarter of pork. Present on this occasion was an unidentified man dressed in the coarse cloth known as russet that was regarded in some quarters as the uniform of the self-styled "poor preachers."[96]

The extent of the heretics' debts to William White having been ascertained, there remain a number of reiterated assertions for which no obvious source can be named. These include opinions on the sacrament of marriage, on excommunication, and on oaths.[97] A peculiar anomaly—which stands out all the more in such a remarkably homogeneous collection of tenets—is the divergence of view about Sunday.

White had taught that on Sundays and other feast days appointed by the Church it was lawful for the faithful to work, and do any bodily labor apart from servile works which would be sin and vice.[98] A number of heretics repeated this, some more parrot-wise than others.[99] Like other points, this error received its individual glosses. "No man is bound to hallow the Sundays nor none other festival days," asserted the tailor William Hardy, but all could lawfully work at such times since "priests ordained all holy days for covetousness to have offerings and tithes of the people."[100] John Pyry of Martham maintained that anyone busy or laboring on Sundays could perfectly well absent himself from church, "providing he thinks well about God, since it is other people's job to attend divine services on Sundays and feast days."[101] He was not the only Lollard whose Sunday observance entailed

---

[94]*Ibid.*, p. 165.

[95]*Ibid.*, pp. 50–51, 64, 72, 76.

[96]*Ibid.*, pp. 75–76, cf. 104–105, 108, for other examples of fast-breaking. The heretics' punishments were designed to correct this error, and a good many offenders were ordered to fast on bread and water on Fridays or other seasons for specified periods; e.g., pp. 119, 150, and see editorial comments, pp. 15, 23–24.

[97]Denials of excommunication clearly had a descent from Wycliffe: on oaths see below, n. 109. The charges relating to matrimony in the *Trials* go further than White's statements in the *Fasciculi* (i.e., in the assertion that assent between the parties sufficed, without need for solemnization in church), but it may be noted that White had apparently expressed views on secular marriage; Netter, *Doctrinale*, III, col. 412 (cf. col. 417). Views of marriage like those in the *Trials* were reported to have been voiced long before; see below, n. 117.

[98]*Fasciculi*, p. 428 (no. 22); Netter, *Doctrinale*, III, cols. 844–851 (this was the third of White's articles which Netter quoted verbatim (above, n. 57).

[99]*Trials*, pp. 33, 53, 61, 67, 108 (111), 135.

[100]*Ibid.*, p. 153.

[101]*Ibid.*, p. 71. Cf. Netter, *Doctrinale*, III, col. 847, on how "William [White] or some Wycliffite," demonstrated that the law concerning Sunday was made "only for clerks."

absence from church. According to William Wright's deposition (in Foxe), William Everden proved faithful to White's tenet during the month he spent tailoring at Loddon: "the first Sunday of the same month, the said William Everden did sit all day upon the table at work, saying . . . that he would not go to church to show himself a scribe or a pharisee."[102]

Sunday nonconformity, like fast-breaking, could betray adherence to the sect. Here as elsewhere we need to know more about the developing stages of Lollardy to be able to estimate William White's contribution. The antiheretical initiatives of 1428 certainly gave prominence to this point. Lollard suspects were to be asked what they thought about the need to observe Sundays and other feasts. And when Bishop Alnwick wrote to the abbot of Bury St. Edmunds on September 3, 1428, ordering enquiry into heresy in the town, he directed attention toward suspects holding private conventicles, making use of English texts, "or withdrawing themselves from church or social intercourse on feast days, or holding singular opinions about the faith or the sacraments."[103]

Alongside this train of thought existed another, less common and quite different. According to this school, represented by John Burell, Edmund Archer, John Pert, and John Wroxham, bodily works could lawfully be performed on all feasts ordained by the Church *with the exception of Sunday*.[104] All these defendants came from Loddon, where Hugh Pye was chaplain. Conceivably this variant opinion owed something to him. Another possible source is suggested by Foxe's record of one John Florence of Shelton, Norfolk, who in 1424 appeared before William Bernham (then vicar-general of Bishop Wakering) for views common to Alnwick's suspects, including "that there is no day to be kept holy, but only the Sunday, which God hath hallowed."[105]

One might also postulate that Hugh Pye had some influence on the iconomachy displayed by heretics at Loddon. A handful of these Norfolk Lollards had gone further than outspoken condemnation of images and pilgrimage and abuse of Thomas Becket. They were guilty of physical attacks on images, including burning a carving of St. Andrew, stolen from a church near Norwich and carried off to Bergh Apton. An old cross standing near the gate of Loddon Hall was bashed with

---

[102]Foxe, *AM*, III, 596 (on Everden see n. 11 above).

[103]Hudson, "Examination of Lollards," p. 154 (no. 38). BL Add. MS 14848. fol. 109[v]: "aut se diebus festivis ab ecclesiis vel a communi hominum conversacione subtrahentes seu opiniones singulares de fide aut sacramentis tenentes. . . ." It is tempting to link this order (which ran into trouble because of the abbey's claim to exempt jurisdiction) with the proceedings against White (see above, p. 81 and n. 58) and his associates. Cf. Netter, *Doctrinale*, III, col. 847, for the Wycliffites' contesting of the duty to attend church on Sundays.

[104]*Trials*, pp. 74, 77, 165, 170, 190; cf. p. 131 (Matilda Fleccher of Beccles). See introduction, p. 16.

[105]Foxe, *AM*, III, 584 (by a slip Foxe refers to William, instead of John [Wakering], bishop of Norwich). It is just possible that John Florence is the same as John Fowlyn (above, pp. 81, 87).

a faggot hook. And the clerk of Loddon was reported to have burnt images there. It is tempting to link these reports with the third error of which Hugh Pye had purged himself in 1424: "that the image of the cross and other images are not to be worshipped; and that the said Hugh had cast the cross of Bromehold into the fire to be burned, which he took from one John Welgate of Loddon."[106]

Finally, some general matters which hark back to our starting-point. The Norwich *Trials* cast interesting light on the bishop's misgivings about the efficacy of church procedures. Master Robert Bert, chaplain of Bury St. Edmunds, was cited on March 2, 1430, to reply concerning alleged errors and heresies in his copy of *Dives et Pauper*, and for associating with well-known heretics. Bert denied these charges (arguing for the good character of his text) and was given a day to purge himself, taking an oath that he would appear on the appointed date and being strictly admonished to hand over all his English books. On April 20 he duly appeared before Bishop Alnwick with his six compurgators (all rectors of Suffolk parishes) and after he had solemnly denied ever having held the heretical opinions attributed to him, the six clerics swore on the gospels that they believed the truth of his oath. That was not the end of the affair, however. After all this, "because the reverend father asserted that he held the said Robert strongly suspect of heresy, notwithstanding this purgation," on account of his possession of *Dives et Pauper*, which contained various errors imputed to Robert himself, still another oath was called for. Bert had to swear that he would never affirm heretical opinions or consort with heretics, and would make known to the bishop the names of any suspects he came across.[107]

Compurgation proved little and oaths were far from foolproof. Lollards held their own views on oath-taking, which perhaps helped them to equivocate their way through the courts. Certainly there were outstanding heretics who forswore themselves more than once.[108] One such perjured man appeared in the *Trials*. John Fynch of Colchester, who appeared before Alnwick in September, 1430, admitted that he had been before a commissary of the bishop of London in Col-

---

[106]*Ibid.*, III, 586; *Trials*, Appendix, p. 218; cf. pp. 76 and 46, n. 45.

[107]*Trials*, pp. 98–102; cf. Foxe, *AM*, III, 586, for the oath reported to have been taken from Richard Belward after his purgation in 1424. On the English work, *Dives et Pauper* (two volumes of P. H. Barnum's new edition have now appeared; Early English Text Society, Nos. 275, 280 [Oxford, 1976, 1980]) see my "Lollardy and Literacy," *History*, LXII **Below, 208, 211.**   The articles of which Bert was suspected (the suspicion being linked with the text) were: that tithes should not be paid to clerics in mortal sin; no honor was to be given to images of the crucifix, Virgin, or other saints; no pilgrimages should be made. It does seem possible that the discussion of image-worship in *Dives et Pauper* could have appeared dangerous to the authorities. For John Godsell, who apparently found compurgators in 1424 but continued his heresy, see above, **p. 82.**

[108]Thomas Drayton, Robert Hook, and William Taylor all abjured twice and reverted twice. *Reg. Chichele*, I, cxxxiv; Thomson, *Later Lollards*, pp. 24–25, 173–174, 235. On compurgation (and the rarity of its failure) see Peter Heath, *The English Parish Clergy on the Eve of the Reformation* (London, 1969), pp. 122–123, 126–133.

chester two years earlier and had sworn, albeit falsely, on a mass-book, that he never believed or affirmed the heresies and errors of which he was accused.[109]

We may see it as a reflection of these defects that eighteen of Alnwick's suspects who abjured were given indentured lists of their revoked errors, sealed with their own seals and that of the bishop. All but one of these were in English, and one (Hawise Moon) was the case of a woman. This method of documenting the process of abjuration was clearly intended to fortify the fears of recidivism: one-half of the document was to remain in the episcopal archive, the other to be kept by the accused to his or her life's end.[110] In theory at least, here was an infallible way of checking up on any of these eighteen who in future started to voice Lollard opinions.

One might also regard the use of these heretical chirographs as indirect acknowledgment by the authorities of the text-consciousness of the Lollards. There was, after all, more likelihood that such a potentially incriminating document would deter a person who could read, or had relatives and friends who could do so, than someone quite removed from comprehension of the written word. This makes it the more interesting that in all these cases except that of the clerk Robert Cavell, the defendant pleaded inability to read, so that a court official had to read through the document on his (or her) behalf. John Kynget of Nayland and Richard Fleccher of Beccles, who appeared within a week of each other in August, 1429, pleaded instead of the usual "being a layman and not knowing how to read," that they suffered from impaired vision.[111]

Without denying that eye diseases were doubtless common at the time, these pleas invite skepticism. Given that the possession and reading of English texts was a main grounds for suspicion of heresy, there was an obvious advantage in evading the avowal of literacy whenever possible. And it might well have seemed desirable to an individual defendant to "commit the power of abjuration" involved in a public recitation of itemized errors, allowing an episcopal official to "be the instrument of his voice."[112] Just as stumbling through the "neck-verse" could be the

---

[109]*Trials*, pp. 183–148, 185–186. Perhaps swearing on a mass-book was easier for a Lollard than taking an oath on the gospels. One of the points Fynch was accused of was the view "that it is not lawful a man to swear in any case." Cf. Henry G. Russell, "Lollard Opposition to Oaths by Creatures," *American Historical Review*, LI (July, 1946), 668–684.

[110]The indentures were also signed by the accused with a cross. This authentication had its own religious significance, which is brought home by the fact that Robert Cavell, who was fully literate, signed in this way, as well as the illiterate defendants. Cf. Charles Sisson, "Marks as Signatures," *The Library*, 4th Series, IX (1928–1929), 4–12. It was part of this process of abjuration for the signatory to be solemnly warned that the penalty for relapse would be relinquishment to the secular powers for burning.

[111]The usual phrases are "asseruit se fore laicum et nescire legere," or "asseruit se esse mere laicum et legere nescientem" (*Trials*, pp. 62, 114, 169). Kynget and Fleccher pleaded inability to read their abjurations because, respectively, "ipse tunc, ut asseruit, fuit oculorum visu debilitatus" and "asseruit se fore oculorum lumine aliqualiter caligatum" (*ibid.*, pp. 79, 85).

[112]*Ibid.*, pp. 109, 114, 128, 134, etc.

means of obtaining benefit of clergy,[113] so conversely perhaps there were circumstances in which it was wise to claim the benefit of mere laity — with its ostensible incompetence to read.

Foxe's additional evidence in the *Acts and Monuments* casts doubt on some of these disavowals of literacy. According to the deposition of William Wright (very likely the same as William Baxter, husband of Margery), Richard Fleccher was "a most perfect doctor in that sect, and can very well and perfectly expound the holy Scriptures, and hath a book of the new law in English, which was first sir Hugh Pye's."[114] It does not follow, of course, that he could read. The same deposition also stated of John Pert, who had likewise claimed that he was lay and a nonreader, that he "can read well, and did read in the presence of William White."[115] It is also worth noting that William Bate of Seething and Hawise Moon (both of whom had attended Lollard schools) were members of literate households, having respectively a son and a daughter whom William Wright reported to be vernacular readers.[116] One should not assume too much from that, but it does seem that we should be wary of taking at face value these heretical disclaimers of reading ability.

These Norwich *Heresy Trials* offer insights into the Lollard movement that are not easily found elsewhere. This source reveals a closely knit group of heretics whose views derived from a known circle of teachers, centered on William White. Thanks to a strenuous evangelizing mission that may have started in the early 1420's,[117] this seemingly exceptional leader implanted Lollard beliefs over a wide area of eastern England.

[113]Leona C. Gabel, *Benefit of Clergy in England in the Later Middle Ages* (Smith College Studies in History, XIV [Northampton, Massachusetts, 1929]), p. 72, n. 44 (the verse in question being the first of Psalm 51 — "Have mercy upon me O God...").

[114]Foxe, *AM*, III, 597. Cf. *Trials*, p. 29, for Dr. Tanner's suggestion that this deposition may indicate that the level of literacy among the defendants was higher than their claims of illiteracy seem to suggest. On the likely identification of William Baxter/Wright see *ibid.*, pp. 46, n. a, 72, 86, 140.

[115]Foxe, *AM*, III, 597, cf. p. 588 (on Hawise Moon and her daughter); *Trials*, p. 169.

[116]Foxe, *AM*, *loc. cit.*; *Trials*, pp. 140, 146, 176, 179.

[117]While the known evidence concerning White shows him at work in the Norwich diocese by c. 1425, Foxe's evidence cited above indicates that points similar to White's were already being voiced in the area by 1424. This does not invalidate the case I have made for White's influence on Alnwick's suspects. But it shows, as one must admit, that there is a lot we do not know. Apart from the exact date when White started evangelizing in East Anglia, there is a large question mark over his whole early life and education, and the derivation of his teaching. What was the exact nature of his debt to Wycliffe? Consider in the context of these unknowns the report, placed by Walsingham under the year 1402, of Lollard teaching about which Sir Lewis Clifford informed Archbishop Arundel. This included undermining the seven sacraments as "dead signs"; against the sacrament of the altar as "a morsel of dead bread," against church baptism and marriage (maintaining that assent between man and woman were sufficient); assertion of priests' duty to marry; and the rejection of purgatory and of hallowing Sunday or other holy days ("every day is equally free for working, eating and drinking"). This list constitutes a remarkable foreshadowing of the tenets of White and

Incomplete and formal though the Norwich record is, it takes us into the lower ranks of the heretics' cellular society, showing how humble followers of a regional missionary learnt and expressed their opinions. We can here inspect Lollardy at ground level—despite the fact that it is transmitted through official proscription and transcription. The documents in the *Trials* (supplemented by other sources) also make it possible to see something of the heretical hierarchy: or, if that is putting it too definitely, to arrange the suspects in tiers of importance. The penalties imposed on the accused complement the records of their repute, and sometimes court proceedings themselves highlight the capacities of individual Lollards. Greatest of all, though, is the interest of seeing how ideas filtered down through successive layers of the heretical following. We can observe heresy that was academic, more or less, in origin, passing through active proselytizing and Lollard schools into the sometimes limited intelligences of glovers and skinners, and into the domestic talk of enthusiastic women. As it did so, its content changed—and moved measurably further from Wycliffe. Dogma was weakened in the chain of repetition. Statements were simultaneously diminished and enlarged. They became simpler, less hedged with qualification, more thickened with verbiage, and more crudely anticlerical.

Popular theology cannot stand much refinement. The humbler followers of William White, however great their fidelity to this "holy doctor," could not help revealing the distance that divided them from him—alive or dead.

---

the defendants in the Norwich *Trials. Thomae Walsingham Historia Anglicana,* ed. H. T. Riley (Rolls Series [London, 1863–1864]), II, 252–253; cf. K. B. McFarlane, *Lancastrian Kings and Lollard Knights* (Oxford, 1972), p. 212.

Additional Notes to Chapter 3

32   Cf. allusions to the Firth of Forth as 'the Scottish sea'; *The Westminster Chronicle*, ed. L. C. Hector and B. F. Harvey (Oxford, 1982), pp. 66, 128.

113   For an instance in a secular court of the advantage of claiming illiteracy see the defendant's plea, in a case concerning obligations recorded in writing, that he was a layman 'with no knowledge of reading', in *Year Books of Henry VI.I Henry VI. AD 1422* ed. C. H. Williams (Selden Society, Vol. L, 1933), No. 7, pp. 23-24.

4

DEVOTIONAL LITERACY [1]

We have learnt a good deal recently about literacy as an agent of cultural and social change, and have begun to estimate the importance of its extension in medieval society. The increasing use and consciousness of letters in this period was a European phenomenon. In the fourteenth and fifteenth centuries more people, including those who had no intention of embarking on a religious or priestly career, were finding it desirable or necessary to learn to read or write (or ⁻ reckon) for business reasons, sometimes with motives that seem similar to those of today.

The extension of literacy in England, as abroad, owed much to the growth of government, towns and trade, and the practical secular needs of those involved in private and public affairs from the lowest officials and apprentices to the top levels of management.[2] When we look at municipal schools run by local townsmen, such as those at Hull, Ipswich and Bridgnorth, or the obligations on masters of guilds to have apprentices taught to read and write, we find ourselves in a setting that seems familiar.[3] We can see youths, and sometimes adults (like the thirty-year old wife of Francesco Datini, the merchant of Prato)[4] learning their letters to widen their interests and their prospects. Occasionally we have writing which seems to be the clumsy effort of a penman who had failed to master completely the difficult art of putting pen to paper (or parchment). Such are four letters from an apprentice called Goddard Oxbridge in the 1470s, poorly written and poorly spelt.[5] The survival of collections of fifteenth-century letters and

1 The orginal version of this paper was read at the University of Pennsylvania Lilly-Pennsylvania Program, 1980-81, Medieval Studies Colloquium on 'Literacy and Society in Medieval Europe'.

2 For a full exploration of the development of literary skills and concepts in the period up to the fourteenth century see M.T. Clanchy, *From Memory to Written Record: England 1066-1307* (London, 1979).

3 Joan Simon, *Education and Society in Tudor England* (Cambridge, 1966), pp. 21-22, 28, 32; Kenneth Charlton, *Education in Renaissance England* (London & Toronto, 1965), pp. 15, 254; Nicholas Orme, *English Schools in the Middle Ages* (London, 1973), pp. 204-5, 215.

4 Iris Origo, *The Merchant of Prato* (Harmondsworth, 1963), p. 213.

5 J.W. Adamson, 'Literacy in England in the Fifteenth and Sixteenth Centuries', in *'The Illiterate Anglo-Saxon' and Other Essays on Education, Medieval and Modern* (Cambridge, 1946), p. 39; *The Stonor Letters and Papers, 1290-1483*, ed. C.L. Kingsford (Camden Third Series, xxix-xxx, 1919), ii, pp. 4-6, 8-9, 49-50, nos. 164-5, 167, 213.

papers, like those of the Pastons, Stonors and Celys, concerned with the details of family affairs (the management of estates or the wool trade) seems to project us smoothly back into a world of lay readers and writers akin to our own.

> At great Calais on this side on the sea, the first of June, when every man was gone to his dinner, and the clock struck noon, and all our household cried after me and bade me come down: 'Come down to dinner at once!' And what answer I gave them ye know it of old.[6]

These concluding words of a letter from Thomas Betson (wool-trade partner of William Stonor), dashed off in the summer of 1476 to his future wife Katherine Ryche (then aged about twelve), bring him to us with an immediacy as vivid as any latter-day letter writer.

Such apparent familiarity is, however, dangerous. It makes it all too easy to assume that books and pages, pen and paper, were for these readers and writers much what they are to us. We all have a natural tendency to look for and find in the past, those kinds of behaviour and ways of thinking that have subsequently become habitual or important. If Goddard Oxbridge and Margherita Datini make us believe we are somewhere near the beginning of a race for the three Rs which has still not quite finished, we should stop and consider the rest of the picture. For one thing (as we have lately been reminded in an estimate of the still extensive illiteracy of the Tudor and Stuart age), the teaching of letters was a difficult art, even for a reader with a suitable text, and learning to read — let alone write — infinitely more demanding in the days of manuscript and fitful elementary education.[7] It should also be remembered that the vocational literacy of fourteenth-century lay learners was acquired in a society that had ancient and well-established assumptions about books and letters and learning. It was taken for granted that the child who conned his ABC was one 'willing to be a cleric'[8] — a budding churchman. The conventional view, which had so determining an influence on the course of literacy, is reflected in a letter of Archbishop Rotherham of York in 1483, when he founded a chantry college at his native town of Rotherham, providing for the

---

6   *Stonor Letters and Papers*, i, p. xviii, ii, p. 8.
7   David Cressy, *Literacy and the Social Order: Reading and Writing in Tudor and Stuart England* (Cambridge, 1980), pp. 19 ff., 40 ff., 52-3.
8   From *The Pore Caitif*: W.A. Pantin, *The English Church in the Fourteenth Century* (Cambridge, 1955), p. 249; M. T. Brady, '*The Pore Caitif*: An Introductory Study', *Traditio*, X (1954), p. 535.

teaching of writing and accounting as well as grammar. Because Yorkshire, wrote the archbishop, produces 'many youths endowed with the light of keen wit and not all of them wish to attain to the lofty dignity of the priesthood', they were to be trained for the mechanical arts and other worldly affairs.[9] Not all gifted adolescents wished to become clergy: the condition that the learning of the page was a clerical art was still bowed to, even in the escapement.

The acquaintance with letters that penetrated the whole of English society, markedly accelerating in the course of the thirteenth century, was not primarily the work of the church. Naturally clergy were at the forefront, and clearly ecclesiastical administration was developing its own processes of documenting and recording. But the single most important agency (as Dr. Clanchy has shown) in widening literate communication was the royal administration. The extension of literacy was preceded by growing awareness of the written word, and the precondition of that was the proliferation of documents.[10]

Thanks to the steady growth of royal requirement and the imitative methods of seigneurial estates — both secular and ecclesiastical — by 1300 written warrants and tally sticks were things that leading villagers could be expected to take in their stride.[11] Many individuals who did not regard it as their business to wield a pen, owned their own instrument of personal authentication — a signet. More and more people, peasants included, were coming into contact with documents and writings in the course of their daily lives, and some of such persons, in their capacity of manorial reeves or bailiffs, gained sufficient skill themselves to use or draw up administrative records. More of them, including the unfree, discovered the value of charters as a route to greater freedom. Even if the Bible had not yet come to represent for them some golden age of primeval equality ('when Adam delved and Eve span.....') there was another book of seemingly Biblical dimensions which began to loom large on the horizon of social justice — Domesday Book.[12]

It is a sign of this growing consciousness of letters as valuable

9   Adamson, *op cit.*, p. 48; Simon, *op cit.*, p. 50.

10   As in a later period (allowing for the very great difference of degree) people 'were increasingly touched ..... by the power of communication which only the written word makes possible'; T. Laqueur, 'The Cultural Origins of Popular Literacy in England 1500-1850', *Oxford Review of Education*, vol. 2 (1976), p. 255.

11   Clanchy, *op. cit.*, pp. 31-36, 187 ff., 197-8; N. Denholm-Young, *Seignorial Administration in England* (Oxford, 1937), pp. 32-40.

12   R. H. Hilton, *Bond Men Made Free* (London, 1973), p. 211; G. R. Owst, *Literature and Pulpit in Medieval England* (2nd edn. Oxford, 1961), p. 291.

tools, that the apparatus of literacy was itself turned into a religious metaphor. Things do not become metaphors until they have well and truly arrived. The way in which the instruments and forms of writing themselves appear in metaphorical dress in vernacular texts, shows how the extension of literary modes impinged on religious teaching. Christ's body, nailed on the tree of the rood, is compared to the child's horn-book, the ABC, nailed on its wooden panel. The body of the crucified Christ is seen as a lettered parchment. ('Come hither, Joseph, behold and look, / How many bloody letters ben written in this book'.) The saviour's wounds become the red letters limned on the vellum. ('How many letters thereon be / Read and thou may wite and see'.) In the early fourteenth century this literary device found its own idiom, in which the promise of salvation is presented as a charter, in some cases complete with an actual seal and modelled on the structural form of such a document.[13]

The legal deed of a medieval charter or land grant is transposed to the deed of Christ in the crucifixion. The whole elaborate parallel is pursued with loving detail; the transaction is inscribed on the parchment of Christ's body, with pens that are the scourges which pierced it; the letters are the wounds. And of course the seal, that instrument of personal identity which, we are told, was by 1300 possessed by 'all freemen and even some serfs',[14] was the saviour's blood. It was even possible to conceive of salvation in terms of a chirograph or indenture, divided between God and man. The latter's part of this (the copy of the original deed) consisted of the sacramental body of the Eucharist, while the other matching part (the original document) was the ascended body of the crucified Christ. Human holders of this holy indenture could 'come and claim when thou wilt /

---

13   M. C. Spalding, *The Middle English Charters of Christ* (Bryn Mawr Monographs, XV, 1914), pp. xlvii-xlviii, x, n. 10, 1, 60-61; J. E. Wells, *A Manual of the Writings in Middle English, 1050-1400* (New Haven, 1916), pp. 369-70, 821. On the literary commonplace in the thirteenth century of the comparison between Christ crucified and a manuscript see Beryl Smalley, *The Study of the Bible in the Middle Ages* (Oxford, 1952), p. 283, n. 3. For a late example which pursues in detail the analogy of crucifix and book see Fisher's sermon in *The English Works of John Fisher*, ed. J.E.B. Mayor (EETS, ES XXVII, 1876), pp. 388-428, esp. 393-6.

14   Clanchy, *op. cit.*, p. 184. For examples which show the frequent ownership of seals among fifteenth-century working people (who were ostensibly unable to read English) see *Heresy Trials in the Diocese of Norwich, 1428-31*, ed. N. P. Tanner (Camden Fourth Series, 20, 1977), pp. 59, 82, 88, 113, 117, 123, 128, 136, 143, 149, 155, 161, 171. These indentured abjurations of heresy were authenticated both by the seals of the accused and their signing with a cross. It is to be noted (see case of Robert Cavell, pp. 94, 97) that the latter is not of itself an indication of illiteracy. Cf. Charles Sisson, 'Marks as Signatures', *The Library*, 4th Series, IX (1928-29), pp. 4-12; Cressy, *op. cit.*, pp. 57-58.

the bliss that lost our former friend'.[15]

Such compositions — and the surviving manuscripts of these charters of Christ are fairly numerous — reflect the textual consciousness of the age. A literary conceit of this kind presupposes fluency with the form of a charter, the existence of a good many people who knew about and prized such writings. It is literary introversion of a sort that is very telling.

Christianity is a religion of the book and society was (at least in theory) Christian. From the church's point of view, however, there was no necessary connection between conversion and letters, between the Bible as the source of faith and the people's access to the faith. Nor, for that matter, was there any obvious connection between manorial administration and credal instruction. Ecclesiastical attitudes towards the role of books and the written word in the church's main task of making and teaching believers, had been fixed long before and were slow to change. They were geared to a world in which literacy was a preserve of the minority, and the minority were churchmen. The church had developed in a society whose culture was predominantly oral,[16] and in which it had to be assumed that the mass of believers were, and would remain, remote from the world of letters and learning.

The widespread dissemination of writings and the developing abilities of all sorts of people, peasants upward, to deal with them, may be regarded therefore in the light of a challenge to ecclesiastical tradition. It becomes necessary to ask how the church adapted itself to this changing society, how capable it was of moving with the times to meet the needs of believers who could learn in different ways. Did the growth of literacy prompt new forms of thought?[17] Did access to books, the knowledge or study of them, tend to distance people from traditional procedures or institutions? I pose these questions without hoping to do more than outline some approaches to answers.

To start with it is worth considering the circulation and availability of texts dealing with religious matters. We will return later to the topic of books, though it is important at the outset to remind

15   Spalding, *op. cit.*, pp. xv, xliii-xlv, lxxxv, 42-43. This work traces the spread of the analogy into the different forms of the 'charters of Christ', and argues that the archetype of the 'Long charter', of which the earliest extant manuscript is c. 1350, may be assigned to the early decades of the fourteenth century.

16   On early medieval oral biblical knowledge see Smalley, *op. cit.*, pp. xviii-xix; cf. also Ruth Crosby, 'Oral Delivery in the Middle Ages', *Speculum*, 11 (1936), pp. 88-110.

17   Cf. *Literacy in Traditional Societies*, ed. Jack Goody, (Cambridge, 1968), p. 44 ff. on the question of literacy among the Greeks and the appearance of a more critical attitude towards myths.

ourselves of the variety of reading-matter that existed, and the mistake
of thinking mainly or exclusively in terms of books. The book in the
shape of a volume, as opposed to smaller quires or single pages or rolls,
was precious, rare and expensive. This was true in general, of orthodox
and heterodox alike. It is as evident among the Cathars of the Pyrenees
in the early fourteenth century as among the Lollards in England in the
fifteenth. In the heretical society of Montaillou books were objects of
high regard, even veneration, in part because they were almost
inaccessible and only to be found in the hands of perfect or priest.[18]
Among the Lollards, though ownership of texts may have extended
among the rank and file, the probability is that many of the 'books' we
hear about were in the nature of tracts. Those who owned volumes, the
New Testament, or very occasionally the whole Bible, might be
assumed to be privileged members of the sect.[19] As in the early days of
printing, much reading matter was slight and perishable, valued as it was
by its possessor.[20] In fact, paradoxically, it may be that among
common readers (often those whose reading is attached to one or two
texts), it was the most used and cherished writings — those that gave
the most instruction or pleasure, or most helped the learning of letters
— which proved the most ephemeral. This aspect of literacy (though the
context is altogether changed) is to some extent still with us. The
investigator of popular literacy is therefore at a perennial disadvantage.

Among these lost ephemera were some of the documents posted in
public places. The idea that important matters should be seen as well as
heard, extended the practice of posting written copies of important

18   H. E. Bell, 'The Price of Books in Medieval England', *The Library*, 4th Series, XVII
(1936-37), pp. 312-332; E. Le Roy Ladurie, *Montaillou*, trans. B. Bray (London, 1978), p. 235.
The booklessness deduced from the evidence of wills by M. Deanesly, 'Vernacular Books in
England in the Fourteenth and Fifteenth Centuries', *Modern Language Review*, XV (1920) is
criticized by M. B. Parkes, 'The Literacy of the Laity', in *The Mediaeval World*, ed. D. Daiches
and A. Thorlby (London, 1973), p. 568. Also on the question of testaments as a guide to
book-owning see K. B. McFarlane, *The Nobility of Later Medieval England* (Oxford, 1973), pp.
235-8. J.T. Rosenthal, 'Aristocratic Cultural Patronage and Book Bequests, 1350-1500', *BJRL*,
64 (1981-2), pp. 522-48. On Lollard respect for books see below p. 110.

19   For the tracts, quires and rolls in use among the Lollards see Anne Hudson, 'Some
Aspects of Lollard Book Production', *Studies in Church History*, 9 (1972), pp. 147-57; *idem*,
'A Lollard Quaternion', *Rev. Eng. Studies*, NS XXII (1971), pp. 435-442. Cf. also my 'Lollardy
and Literacy', p. 200, and for a list of the 170 copies of the Lollard Bible known in 1850, see
The Holy Bible, ed. J. Forshall and F. Madden (Oxford, 1850), i, pp. xxxix-lxiv.

20   A 'book' may in fact not be a book at all. Cf. Eric A. Havelock, *Preface to Plato*
(Oxford, 1963), p. 55, n. 16 on references to books among the Greeks possibly indicating
something much smaller — single sheets, leaflets and manuals. And in the New Testament
writings *biblos* and its diminutive *biblion* refer both to books and documents; *Cambridge
History of the Bible*, Vol. i, ed. P. R. Ackroyd and C. F. Evans (Cambridge, 1970), p. 51. Even
today one finds people referring to throw-away magazines as 'books'.

1a   God in the book. Enemies of the law attack the lawbook, which corresponds with the word of God. As the author, squeezed between the pages, is kicked, God emerges from the volume. (pp. 112-13)

1b   Ceremony of swearing on relics (the presiding judge is seated on the right). Note the stylised gestures. (From the illustrated *Sachsenspiegel* of *c.* 1375. *Die Dresdener Bilderhandschrift des Sachsenspiegels*, ed. K. von Amira) (pp. 109-10)

2   St. Bernardino of Siena (d. 1464) proclaiming Christ. In his right hand he holds the emblem of the Holy Name. (French dotted print, 1454. Bibliothèque Nationale, Paris) (p. 113)

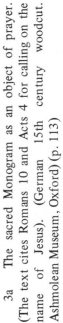

3a The sacred Monogram as an object of prayer. (The text cites Romans 10 and Acts 4 for calling on the name of Jesus). (German 15th century woodcut. Ashmolean Museum, Oxford) (p. 113)

3b The Visitation. (Devotional woodcut by Albrecht Altdorfer, c. 1515) (p. 119)

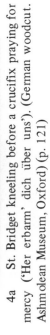

4b St. Bridget giving the rule to her order. (German 15th century woodcut. Ashmolean Museum, Oxford) (p. 132)

4a St. Bridget kneeling before a crucifix praying for mercy ('Her erbarm' dich über uns'). (German woodcut. Ashmolean Museum, Oxford) (p. 121)

5   Christ on the Cross with the Virgin and St. John. (German 15th century woodcut. Ashmolean Museum, Oxford) (p. 119ff.)

6   The crucifixion and its agony (Christ's body 'a dove-house of holes',
flowing with 'rivers of blood'). (The Holkham Bible Picture Book, early 14th
century. BL Add. MS 47682, f. 32ʳ) (p. 121)

7   The Prick of Conscience Window, *c.* 1410(?) showing the fifteen signs of the end of the world (from bottom left, the sea rising, to top right, the ultimate conflagration) according to the most popular Middle English poem. (All Saints, North Street, York) (pp. 121, 208)

8   Nicholas Blackburn and his wife Margaret. She holds a book with the words 'Domine labia mea aperies: et os meum annuntiabit laudem tuam' from Psalm 50 (now 51), part of the versicles and responses at the beginning of matins. (Early 15th century window in All Saints, North Street, York) (p. 123)

9   The alphabet in seven scripts, prefixing the paternoster, *ave*, creed and commandments, specially printed for the five-year old Prince Edward. (*Alphabetum Latino Anglicanum* [1543], title-page) (p. 125)

10   The owner of a Book of Hours as depicted in it, receiving the
sacrament. The altar with cross and painted retable, and the line of windows
above the decorated wall to the right, suggest a well-furnished private chapel.
(Book of Hours, *c*. 1435. BL Add MS 18192, f. 196^r) (pp. 123-4, 133)

texts in public. A process of publication that started with provisions of general concern (in 1279 copies of Magna Carta were ordered to be posted up in every cathedral and collegiate church),[21] was taken up and furthered by individual subjects. Clearly the development of this practice must be linked with the increasing numbers of individuals who could use and read documents. Nevertheless it would be mistaken to suppose that such advertising was premised on a rising percentage of literates, or to think in terms of yokels shouldering each other for views of texts.[22] It was a question rather of changing methods of publication and authentication. Legislation was published by being made visible to those to whom it applied, as well as by being heard by them: one witnessed by *seeing*, as well as by hearing an enactment. (The validation of corporate seeing, as opposed to paper documentation, is still with us in the marriage ceremony).

Individuals who wanted to advertise their views came to realize the value of such methods. Long before Luther, the practice of bill-posting on church doors (the most public and frequented door in every parish) had recommended itself to a variety of publicists and religious reformers — official and unofficial. Abroad there were distinguished reformers who had the idea of using pastoral placards for parochial evangelizing. John Gerson, for example, advocated posting up boards inscribed with essential religious doctrine in public places such as parish churches, schools and hospitals, and later in the fifteenth century Nicholas of Cusa hung in the church of St. Lambert at Hildesheim a large wooden panel on which was written the paternoster, creed and commandments.[23] In England such initiatives were often less official.

21   F.M. Powicke, *The Thirteenth Century* (Oxford, 1954), pp. 473-4, 476; Clanchy, *op. cit.*, pp. 171, 173, 213; cf. Pantin, *English Church*, p. 198 on how 'every parishioner was kept, or supposed to be kept, conscious of Magna Carta', and the excommunications involved in its transgression.

22   But perhaps one might visualize groups drawing together to listen to a competent individual reading out such a posted document. Professor John McKenna drew my attention to the passage in More's *History of Richard III*, which describes how the schoolmaster of St. Paul's cast doubts on the suspicious length and fair writing of the proclamation indicting Lord Hastings in 1483, as he stood with others to hear it read. *The Complete Works of St. Thomas More*, ed. R. S. Sylvester *et al.* Vol. 2 (New Haven & London, 1963), pp. 54, 228.

23   James L. Connolly, *John Gerson, reformer and mystic* (Louvain, 1928), p. 131, n. 2; E. Delaruelle *et al.*, *L'Eglise au temps du Grand Schisme et la Crise Conciliaire (1378-1449)*, (Paris, 1964), ii, p. 854, n. 25. Gerson's *Opus tripartitum de preceptis decalogi, de confessione et de arte moriendi*, concerning the essentials of religious instruction, was intended primarily for simple priests (*curatis minus instructi*) and also for the ignorant who had no adequate preaching. In the letter to the (unknown) bishop to whom he sent this work, Gerson suggested that it would be useful to have a summary of the law and the commandments painted on boards and set up in public places (parish churches, schools, hospitals and religious places), where the less competent clergy could use them to read and teach to their parishioners. Johannes Geffcken, *Der Bildercatechismus des fünfzehnten Jahrhunderts* (Leipzig, 1855), pt. i, p. 36, pt. ii, cols 30, 36. On commandment tables see below p. 112.

The Lollards pinned the text of their twelve conclusions in 1395 to the doors of Westminster Hall and St. Paul's, thereby intending to draw the attention of parliament to their wished-for reforms, and in 1417 they were reported to have delivered bills attacking the church to every large house and hospice in St. Albans, Northampton and Reading. Among the independent publicists who adopted such methods was the friar John Russell, who was convicted in 1424 of preaching error at Stamford, and of afterwards affixing a summary to the church door. (In this case the advertised conclusion was in Latin, though the sermon had been in English). Twenty years later another preacher, John Bredon, who had to disavow his offensive preaching in Coventry in 1445, confessed to bills he had made to be set on church doors in that city.[24] Long before the English world had become large enough, mobile enough, and literate enough to sprout signposts at country crossroads, the bill-board door had arrived.

For all the everydayness of some kinds of reading and writing and texts, there was still a sacred aspect to letters. This existed on many levels and included beliefs that were more magical than devout. We must not forget the ability of letters to be arcane: that is to conceal rather than reveal: to be symbols that enclosed a mystery rather than transmitting a message. This could be true of single letters, of letters grouped as monograms comparable to images, of texts, and of complete books. One can find examples of all these categories, which remind us that even for those who could construe a document or manage an account, there could still be an impenetrable aspect to letters. And in so far as this attitude was one of reverence, or at least respect for the remote, the contemporary church to some degree fostered it. One cannot assume that more letters necessarily imply more comprehension.

The Bible, the holy book containing the encyclopaedic word of God, was itself a sacred object. As a large and valuable volume it was also something that most people would not set eyes on. This was the epitome of writing that was holy, the central possession of the church, descended from prophets and evangelists inspired of God. *Sacra pagina,*

---

24   G. R. Owst, *Preaching in Medieval England* (Cambridge, 1926), p. 225, cf. pp. 77-79; D. Wilkins, *Concilia* (London, 1737), iii, pp. 428-31; *Thomae Walsingham Historia Anglicana,* ed. H. T. Riley (RS, London, 1863-64), ii, p. 317; Amundesham, *Annales,* ed. H. T. Riley (RS, London, 1870-71), i, p. 63. On Lollard bill-posting see my 'Lollardy and Literacy', p.196, n. 11, and for 'dynastic advertisement' by pictorial posters in French churches see J. W. McKenna, 'Henry VI of England and the Dual Monarchy: Aspects of Royal Political Propaganda, 1422-1432', *JWCI,* 28 (1965), pp. 145-62, esp. 151-2. For articles posted on church doors during the rebellion of 1405, which reportedly drew supporters to Archbishop Scrope 'when the people had read these articles', see *The Chronicle of England by John Capgrave,* ed. F.C. Hingeston (RS, London, 1858), p. 289.

sacra scriptura, the holy page, holy writ, was set apart as sacrosanct in the sense that it was only open to the understanding of those who were themselves dedicated and trained. Most lay people's knowledge of the Bible was what came to them from preachers, and they might often have been hard put to it to say which stories could or could not be found there. The nearest they got to the written text of scripture might have been a glimpse of the gospel book serving the altar of their parish church,[25] though after the thirteenth century this became less and less likely, given the inclusion of required liturgical readings of scripture in the various service-books. The evidence of 150 or so parish inventories in the diocese of Ely in the fourteenth century, which mention only two gospel books, suggests the rarity of such a possession.[26] The Gospel, receptacle of Christ's words, was the symbol of the Saviour; its entry at mass comparable to the entry of the Redeemer; and its placing on the altar (the most sacrosanct part of the consecrated building) mutually reinforced the divine presence in holy book and holy table.[27]

Laymen might also have encountered the New Testament through the ceremony of oath-taking. 'Lay thine hand on the book here before me and swear that thou shalt go out of my diocese as soon as thou may', Archbishop Bowet of York required of Margery Kempe.[28] This was to swear by the holiest of holies, the physical shrine of divine truths, an object far transcending a book of words. An alternative form of sanction for an oath — which draws attention to this aspect of the Bible as holy relic — was to swear on the relics or shrine of a saint (a practice we can see illustrated in a manuscript of the Sachsenspiegel,

---

25   *Cambridge History of the Bible*, Vol. 2, ed. G. W. H. Lampe (Cambridge, 1969), pp. 229-30; Smalley, *Study of the Bible*, pp. 26, 63, 294.

26   In the *Vetus Liber Archidiaconi Eliensis*, ed. C. L. Feltoe and E. H. Minns (Cambridge Antiquarian Society, XLVIII, 1917), the thirteenth-century inventories were kept up to date till about 1390. Only the churches of St. John's, Mill Street, Cambridge, and March, pp. 34, 146, list gospel-books, as opposed to missals, legends, antiphoners, graduals, psalters, manuals etc. These (not the gospels) were the books that parishes were expected to have; see W. Lyndwood, *Provinciale* (Oxford, 1679), pp. 251-2 for Winchelsey's constitution on this point (*Ut parochiani*). Lack of scripture texts in parishes was a Lollard complaint; see my 'Lollardy and Literacy', p. 201 and n. 34, p. 217.

27   'Codex etiam evangelicus super illud [i.e. altare] adaptatur, eo quod Evangelium ab ipso scilicet Christo sit editum, et ipse perhibeat testimonium'; W. Durandus, *Rationale Divinorum Officiorum* (Naples, 1859), Bk. I, cap. iii, sect. 33, p. 28; cf. p. 819 for Joannes Belethus, *Rationale Divinorum Officiorum*, cap. cxv; 'Altare quoque suis ornamentis decoratur, ut crucibus ordine collocatis, capsis, textibus evangelicis, philacteriis'.

28   *The Book of Margery Kempe*, ed. S. B. Meech and H. E. Allen (EETS, OS 212, 1940), p. 125; *The Book of Margery Kempe*, modern version ed. W. Butler-Bowden (London, 1954), p. 164.

dating from about 1375).[29] The Gospels were the most solemn sanction this world could give: *sic me deus adiuvet et haec sancta evangelia,* 'so help me God and these holy gospels':[30] words that bound the speaker to God's truth – and of course the practice of testifying on the holy book (Bible or Koran) still survives in English courts.

Book-conscious, Bible-enhancing Lollards were placed in a dilemma by this use of holy writ. The divine attributes of the Bible assumed heightened power in Wycliffe's thought,[31] and Wycliffites, who had so many reservations about worshipping the lifeless matter of dead images, seem to have been less than inhibited about revering the text of holy scripture. Kissing the holy book, as the priest kissed the gospel after reading it at mass, seemed to them a legitimate gesture of worship.[32] But, as was pointed out by their opponents, there was a certain inconsistency among the heretics for thus 'venerating, kissing and saluting the Gospel, revering the very manuscript', while simultaneously claiming that living trees were more worshipful than carved images. By the same token should not the care they bestowed on their texts, protecting them from dirty hands and drops of rain, more logically be bestowed on living creatures – sheep (rather than dead vellum), dogs, or flies?[33]

The text which for heretics was the highest sanction for testing holy church became, when they were themselves put to the test, the sanction of their own return to 'Antichrist'. A Lollard suspect who chose to abjure and be restored to the bosom of the church had to keep his or her right hand on the gospel book throughout the reading of the articles which were being revoked.[34] Many did so, but many also went back on this solemn commitment. Thomas Drayton, Robert Hook, and

---

29   M. Letts, 'The Sachsenspiegel and its Illustrators', *Law Quarterly Review*, XLIX (1933), pp. 555-574; for illustrations showing oaths sworn on relics see *Die Dresdener Bilderhandschrift des Sachsenspiegels*, ed. K. von Amira (Leipzig, 1902-26), Bd. I, pt.ii, Tafeln 140, 141, 181; J. C. Wall, *Shrines of British Saints* (London, 1905), p. 33. For the St. Asaph gospel-book being taken (as a relic) on fund-raising tours of the diocese see Glanmor Williams, *The Welsh Church from Conquest to Reformation* (Cardiff, 1976), p. 281.

30   I. J. Churchill, *Canterbury Administration* (London, 1933), I, pp. 183, 442.

31   William Farr, *John Wyclif as Legal Reformer* (Leiden, 1974), p. 20.

32   Prague Univ. MS X.E.9, f. 211[v] considers the parallel between kissing the gospel-book and the gestures of worship towards 'lay books' (images). I am indebted to Dr. Anne Hudson for a transcript of this manuscript.

33   Thomas Netter, *Doctrinale Antiquitatum Fidei Catholicae Ecclesiae*, ed. B. Blanciotti (Venice, 1757-59), iii, col. 942; cf. 'Lollards and Images', n. 63. Of course when it came to oaths Lollards were also inconsistent (it would seem), in regarding the gospel-book, like any other object, as a mere creature. (For charges about Lollards and flies see Amundesham, *Annales*, i, p. 230, ii, p. xxxviii, and *Memorials of Henry the Fifth*, ed. C.A. Cole (RS, London, 1858), pp. lvii, 159).

34   For examples of such solemn oaths see *Norwich Heresy Trials*, ed. Tanner, pp. 58-9, 97, 128, 209 etc.

William Taylor all managed to abjure and then renew their heresy twice over, and the fact that seemingly committed heretics were ready to take this course raises the question of whether members of the sect had devised some way of equivocating themselves out of this difficulty. 'Jurat, perjurat', versified Abbot Wheathampstead of St. Albans, 'secretum dummodo celat'.[35] Lollards certainly had their own philosophy about oaths, which helped them to disclaim the charge of perjury. They interpreted the second commandment in the light of Christ's injunction (Matthew 5; 37) to go no further than 'yea, yea, nay, nay'. And they saw the imposition of legal oaths as a contravention of the decalogue. 'The devil in his members constrains men to swear, and lay their hand on books', threatening them with burning if they should relapse: and so 'they that bring forth books on which men forswear themselves are guilty of this forswearing'.[36] It was a false clerical law that taught 'that a man to save his life, may forswear and lie'.[37] The burden of perjury rested with the judge, not the accused. Lollard suspects could salve their conscience about oaths imposed under duress. 'It is not lawful to swear in any case except where a man's life is in danger' said a suspect of 1429-30, while another at this time (Margery Baxter) maintained that oaths were ordained solely to save face before judges.[38]

As well as the holiness that attached to books on the altar, texts — biblical and otherwise — were sanctified by being inscribed on church

35   Amundesham, *Annales*, i, p. 230. On Drayton, Hook and Taylor see *Register of Henry Chichele*, ed. E. F. Jacob (Cant. & York, Soc., 1943-47), i, p. cxxxiv; J. A. F. Thomson, *The Later Lollards, 1414-1520* (Oxford, 1965), pp. 24-25, 173-4, 235; Charles Kightly, 'The Early Lollards. A Survey of Popular Lollard Activity in England, 1382-1428 (D. Phil. Thesis, York, 1975), p. 583. I am grateful to the author for permission to cite this unpublished work.

36   *The Lanterne of Light*, ed. L.M. Swinburn (EETS, OS 151, 1917), p. 88; cf. *The Lay Folks Catechism*, ed. T. F. Simmons and H. E. Nolleth (EETS, OS 118, 1901), p. 39, and H. G. Russell, 'Lollard Opposition to Oaths by Creatures', *American Hist. Rev.*, LI (1945-6), pp. 668-684 (including, pp. 673-4, on William Thorpe's arguments against swearing on the Gospel). For the Lollards' divergence from Wycliffe on this question see *ibid.*, p. 669 and E. Welch, 'Some Suffolk Lollards', *Proceedings of the Suffolk Institute of Archaeology*, XXIX (1964), p. 164; H. B. Workman, *John Wyclif* (Oxford, 1926), ii, p. 27.

37   Russell, *art. cit.*, p. 675; *The Praier and complaynte of the ploweman unto Christe* ([Antwerp], 1531 ?), sig. D 7ʳ.

38   *Norwich Heresy Trials*, ed. Tanner, pp. 42, 74, 78, 183-6. The duty of taking such oaths was reasserted by Archbishop Arundel in his Oxford Constitutions of 1408-9; 'iuramenta tactis sacrosanctis Dei evangeliis, et super ipsis in jure expressis, et in utroque foro usitatis, ab omnibus quorum interest legitime fore praestanda'. Lyndwood, *Provinciale*, iii, p. 67. On the questions framed for heretical suspects which included 'whether it was lawful to swear on a book?' and (in Martin V's bull of 1418) whether perjury committed to save ones own or someone else's life was a sin or not, see Anne Hudson, 'The Examination of Lollards', *BIHR*, XLVI (1973), p. 154; O. Raynaldus, *Annales Ecclesiastici* (1864-83), Vol. 27, p. 468 (1418, sect. 5); *Cal. Pap. Letters*, VII (1417-1431), p. 22; Foxe, *Acts and Mons.*, iii, p. 564.

walls or monuments. Though it was not until after the Reformation that the practice of ornamenting the altar wall with the text of the commandments became general, commandment tables were not unheard-of in the fifteenth century.[39] Biblical inscriptions were certainly to be found on church walls and tablets. The walls and roof of the chapel of Berkeley Castle were reported in the late fourteenth century to have been covered with the Apocalypse in both Latin and French, and the guild of the Blessed Virgin at Boston at the time of the Reformation owned seven tables with scriptures to hang on the altars.[40] In the thirteenth century sculptures of prophets and saints bore lettered scrolls as well as symbolic attributes to aid their identification. And of course there were the pious inscriptions of a more personal nature, placed by donors in the windows and on other monuments they gave to churches: inscriptions that were castigated by William Langland as blazons of worldly pride.[41] Parishioners were not without opportunities for alphabetic religious learning in church.

Letters were familiar, but they were also holy. The solemn awe attaching to holy writ and the reverence surrounding it spread into popular practices that we may regard as magical. The wearing of a text of scripture round the neck (for which in the sixteenth century the first chapter of St. John's gospel was a favoured extract), shows a veneration for the protective power of holy writ that had nothing whatever to do

---

39   J. C. Cox and A. Harvey, *English Church Furniture* (London, 1907), p. 356; H. M. Cautley, *Royal Arms and Commandments in Our Churches* (Ipswich, 1934), p. 109 ff.; J. T. Micklethwaite, *The Ornaments of the Rubric* (Alcuin Club Tracts, I, 1897), p. 45 (for an example of 1488). The altar, according to Belethus (above n. 27) was to be decorated with 'philacteriis', and a *philacterium* was a *chartula* on which the commandments were written. However, it appears from Durandus, *Rationale*, Bk. I, cap, iii, sect. 26, p. 27, that *philacteria* meaning a reliquary was what was in question in this passage. Such commandment tables may have been commoner abroad in the later fifteenth century than they were in England (where worries about vernacular scripture might have inhibited this development). For instance the *Manuale Curatorum* (1506) of Joannes Ulricus Surgant recommended that the parish priest should supplement his teaching of the vernacular Lord's Prayer, creed and commandments by writing the translated texts 'ad chartam vel ad kalendarium' and hanging them up on tables in the church where people could learn from them and copy them. Geffcken, *op. cit.*, pt. ii, col. 200, and cf. above n. 23. The commandments were also of course represented pictorially in churches.

40   The report of 1387 is by John Trevisa, chaplain to Thomas Lord Berkeley; *Trevisa's Dialogus*, ed. A. J. Perry (EETS, OS 167, 1925), pp. cxxiv-cxxvi; M. Deanesly, *The Lollard Bible* (Cambridge, 1920), p. 142; Workman, *John Wyclif*, i, p. 168. *English Church Furniture, Ornaments and Decorations, at the Period of the Reformation*, ed. E. Peacock (London, 1866), p. 206.

41   Emile Mâle, *The Gothic Image*, trans. D. Nussey (London, 1961), pp. 169, 285-6; E. H. Gombrich, *Aby Warburg: An Intellectual Biography* (London, 1970), p. 36; *The Vision of William concerning Piers the Plowman*, ed. W. W. Skeat (Oxford, 1886), I, pp. 66-69, 426.

with understanding.[42] Perhaps this helped to make it objectionable to those who were assured of scriptural priorities. At least one learned Wycliffite — a man who eventually died for his belief in the idolatry of contemporary religion — was said to have taught that 'whoever hangs any writing about his neck, thereby takes away the honour due only to God, and bestows it on the devil'.[43] It was a view that the authorities in 1421 condemned as savouring of heresy.

Books might be seen as giving priests inviolable defence against the devil. The mere presence of the Bible could be a protective power against the forces of evil.[44] Letters or texts could become talismans, relics, or images, and possibly this letter-magic reflects the regard for literacy extending down the social scale. Among the elevated, the Bible was a treasure comparable to a holy relic, something with a value that greatly surpassed its content as reading matter. The Gospel text was beautifully illuminated to praise God more than to please man. Charters likewise might be esteemed as holy objects, precious relics more than records, preserved in shrines, not filed away for reference.[45] The reverence that attached to letters as arcane or divine symbols continued alongside other more modern uses of the written word in a world that was simultaneously literate and illiterate. When in the second quarter of the fifteenth century St. Bernardino of Siena adopted as his emblem the monogram of the Holy Name (IHS inscribed in a sun), his preaching made it so popular on the piazzas of northern Italy that he was accused of sponsoring idolatry. Believers were thought to be worshipping the symbol.[46] Both the veneration and the fear are significant of contemporary attitudes to letters.

---

42   Alan Macfarlane, *Witchcraft in Tudor and Stuart England*, (New York, 1970), p. 103, quoting Scott's *Discoverie of Witchcraft* (1584). For an example of such a charm see Williams, *Welsh Church*, p. 335. Here again (see above p. 109) letters are being used as holy objects, quite unrelated to reading. Cf. *Literacy in Traditional Societies*, pp. 150, 193, 201-203, 227, 239 for examples of the magical use of characters, letters or portions of sacred texts in Kerala, the Western Sudan and Northern Ghana. It remains possible, of course, that such magical (or superstitious) uses of texts are related to the availability of writings in society, and the extent to which literacy is arrogated to a specialist or priestly caste.

43   *Reg. Chichele*, iii, pp. 67-68, 160; Thomson, *Later Lollards*, p. 26; Foxe, *AM*, iii, p. 582. Taylor was condemned in 1423. Cf. *An Apology for Lollard Doctrines*, ed. J. H. Todd (Camden Soc., xx, 1842), p. 92 ff.; *Lanterne of Light*, p. 132.

44   Delaruelle, *L'Eglise au temps du Grand Schisme*, ii, p. 872; Cressy, *Literacy and the Social Order*, p. 51.

45   Clanchy, *op. cit.*, pp. 114, 125-7, 226-7, 257, 263 on writings as works of art, and awe for liturgical books and script with sacred associations.

46   Iris Origo, *The World of San Bernardino* (New York, 1962), pp. 117-130; A. G. Ferrers Howell, *S. Bernardino of Siena* (London, 1913), pp. 157-164; John Moorman, *A History of the Franciscan Order* (Oxford, 1968), pp. 463-5.

Let us now go on to consider the church's view of lay people as readers, and to see how this related to practice. A useful entry into this question is provided by a sermon — attributed to St. Bernardino — that reflects the prevailing ideas of its time, in England as well as Italy and elsewhere in the west. 'There are four kinds of letters', said this preacher (very likely an Observant Franciscan), 'each better than the other', and he went on to explain.

> The first kind are gross letters for the rude people, such as pictures; the second, for men of the middle sort, are middle letters, and such are written letters; and these are better than the first. The third are vocal letters, found by those who desire actively to busy themselves for charity's sake, pleading and discoursing, in order that they may be learned and may teach others; and these are superior to the first two. Fourthly and lastly come the mental letters ordained by God for those who desire to persevere always in contemplation; and this sort is more perfect than the others and surpasses them all, since they were ordained for this end not the other way round.[47]

It was a popular expression of conventional theory — and valuable for that very reason. Addressing himself to the different forms of medieval communication and discourse, the preacher discerned simultaneously a parallel or equivalence, and a hierarchy, in his four modes. The symbolism of alphabetic letters was comparable on one side to representative symbols such as painting and to rhetorical persuasions (both of them part of the processes of learning and teaching), and on the other side to the mental images that communicated not with other people, but with God. At the same time the graphic arts, writing, speech, and mental imagery, were all part of the graded vocabulary of divine communing.

Investigating literacy inevitably at some stage lands one in treacherous questions of psychology and perception, and these were far

---

47   G. G. Coulton, *Art and the Reformation* (Cambridge, 1953), pp. 248-9; St. Bernardino of Siena, *Opera Omnia*, ed. J. de la Haye, 4 vols. (Venice, 1745), iii, p. 282. (I have altered Coulton's translation). Was this sermon (as Coulton assumed) really by St. Bernardino? I have not found it in *S. Bernardini Senensis.... Opera Omnia*, ed. P. Pacifici and M. Perantoni (Florence, 1950-65), but not having access to the first (Paris, 1635) edition of de la Haye, to which these editors address their detailed criticisms (I, pp. lvii-lxi, III, p. lvii, VI, pp. 59*-62*), I have not been able to pursue this problem. The topic *De Nomine Jesu* was appropriate to St. Bernardino's order, but its treatment decidedly popular. For imagery as laymen's 'writing gross and palpable' see 'Lollards and Images', n. 154.

from being alien to the middle ages. Our preacher was not the first to be guilty of muddling categories in this difficult terrain of words and letters.[48] His stratification of 'letters' seems to confuse ends and means, perceptual channels with intellectual and spiritual objectives. His hierarchy was a variant of the traditional mystical ladder of learning, at the bottom rungs of which the externals of the physical world assisted the contemplative on his way, while at the top clear spiritual vision enabled him to dispense with the support of even mental imagery.[49] Learning, teaching and contemplating were the steps of such an ascent. The techniques of the four sorts of 'letters', on the other hand, were simply the differing tools at the disposal of different sorts of learners.

This homiletic passage was in fact only elaborating on a very well-worn concept. For centuries the church had been expounding its view of the 'letters' of the 'rude people': the idea that the books of the laity were pictures. One can indeed trace back to antiquity this belief in the comparability of painting and speech, and though the context and content had changed enormously, some of the underlying assumptions of the tag *ut pictura poesis* were still present in the church's understanding of 'laymen's books'.

The most important ecclesiastical starting-point for this highly influential doctrine was a letter of Gregory the Great, written in the year 600 to Bishop Serenus of Marseilles, in which the pope justified the existence of imagery in churches.

> .... it is one thing to worship a picture, another to learn from the story depicted what should be worshipped. For what a book (*scriptura*) is to those who read, a picture (*pictura*) presents to the uneducated who observe, since in it the unlearned see what they ought to follow, and in it those who know no letters can read. Hence a picture serves as reading specially for the people.[50]

48   Cf. Eric A. Havelock, *Origins of Western Literacy* (Toronto, 1976), p. 10, on how the confusion between speech and visible symbols of speech is as old as Aristotle (who used the term *gramma*, letter, to mean a unit of sound).

49   Among the many works that deal with this mystical theory see Cuthbert Butler, *Western Mysticism* (lst pub. 1922, 3rd ed. London, 1967); H. O. Evennett, *The Spirit of the Counter-Reformation*, ed. John Bossy (Cambridge, 1968); L. L. Martz, *The Poetry of Meditation* (New Haven, 1954).

50   Gregory I, *Registrum Epistolarium*, ed. P. Ewald and L. M. Hartmann (Monumenta Germaniae Historica, 1891-99), II, p. 270. The last words of this passage – 'unde praecipue gentibus pro lectione pictura est' – are taken by J. W. Thompson, *The Literacy of the Laity in the Middle Ages* (Berkeley, 1939), p. 23, n. 86, to show that Gregory was thinking in terms of 'the lower classes and especially the foreign (i.e. the German) element in the population'. For the thesis that after the thirteenth century the growth of vernacular literacy and of a 'quasi-literate' public affected the relationship of written word and picture as outlined in Gregory's letter, and altered the function of narrative in pictorial art (as in literature) see F.H. Bäuml, 'Varieties and Consequences of Medieval Literacy and Illiteracy', *Speculum*, 55 (1980), pp. 237-65, esp. 259 ff.

Paintings were on a par with books in that they were picture-writing for the unlettered who could scan, construe, and gather information from them which the literate found in written texts. Pictorial symbols were for the ignorant what alphabetic symbols were for the learned: the means of instruction. From this critical and enormously influential text stemmed the church's long-continued justification of images as books of the laity. Its fully developed, more elaborate form, was expressed by Aquinas in the thirteenth century. The uses of imagery were now threefold: first for teaching – to instruct the simple who 'are taught by them as though by books'; secondly for remembering – to implant the mystery of the incarnation and the examples of saints more firmly in the memory by presenting them visually; and thirdly, for arousing feelings of devotion.[51]

A shift, however, took place as this theory was repeated and expounded over the centuries. The third part of the triad came to the fore. As devotional teachers these books of the people – the whole enormous multiplying range of ecclesiastical imagery – came to be regarded in some quarters as not merely the equals, but in some respects as *better* than lettered books. This is how it was put by Aquinas's contemporary, Bishop Durandus.

> It is seen that a painting moves the feelings more than what is written. In a painting some action is placed before the eyes; but in literature that action is recalled to the memory as it were by the hearing, which touches the feelings less. And so it is that in church we do not show as much reverence to books as we do to images and pictures.[52]

The visual image might be rated higher than the text.

Sight was the highest of the senses, seeing better than hearing. And, since reading was to be equated with hearing, learning through imagery could be more effective than learning through words. We find this point being made by Reginald Pecock in a passage which returns us to the English context and which throws considerable light on contemporary thought about perceptual priorities.

51   Rosemary Woolf, *The English Mystery Plays* (London, 1972), pp. 88, 366, quoting St. Thomas Aquinas, *Scriptura super Libros Sententiarum*, ed. P. Mandonnet and M. F. Moos (Paris, 1929-47), III, p. 312.

52   Durandus, *Rationale Divinorum Officiorum*, Lib. I, cap. iii, sect. 4, p. 24. 'Pictura namque plus videtur movere animum, quam scriptura. Per picturam quidem res gesta ante oculos ponitur; sed per scripturam res gesta quasi per auditum, qui minus movet animum, ad memoriam revocatur. Hinc etiam est, quod in ecclesia non tantam reverentiam exhibemus libris, quantam imaginibus et picturis'.

In *The Repressor of Over Much Blaming of the Clergy* Pecock defended images against the attacks of the Lollards, and in doing so wrote some interesting observations on the different ways of learning. He explained how much less painful and laborious it was to learn the outline of a story from a visual depiction than from a text. A single glance at a well-made image could convey the information of several pages of a book. Listening to a reader was slow, and even someone who had a text might find himself lacking the services of a reader when he wanted to hear his book. Having got that far, he still had the trouble of fixing what he heard in his mind by conjuring up his own mental pictures, after starting as it were one step back on the route of intellectual processes that passed from image to understanding and memory via mind's eye and mental image. Painted and sculpted images were always on hand in churches; books and readers a much scarcer commodity. It seemed clear (contrary to what Lollards maintained) that there were great advantages, for the learned and lewed man alike, in coming to 'the remembrance of a long story by sight, [rather] than by the hearing of other men's reading, or by hearing of his own reading'.[53] Learning by imagery was easier, faster, and more effective.

Pecock, it is to be noticed (like Durandus), assumes the *speaking* of books, just as the Horatian phrase *ut pictura poesis* assumes the speaking of poetry. As long as it was taken for granted that reading necessitated hearing (muttering or mouthing, if not vocalizing the word on the page) the speed of comprehension was naturally slow: slower than it is for those whose familiarity with letters is such that the written (or printed) words themselves become electric signals, direct referents of reality, more nearly comparable to the painted depiction. We, that is, unlike Pecock's readers, can travel directly, or more directly, from the page in front of us to what the words relate to, without having to articulate, or even form consciously in our minds, every syllable and sentence.[54]

Also important here are the assumptions about the role of mental images. The contemporary theory of memory (clarified for us by Frances Yates), was predicated on a stock of mental pictures, or memory places, in which the mind's collections were housed.[55] The

---

53 Reginald Pecock, *The Repressor of Over Much Blaming of the Clergy*, ed. C. Babington (RS, London, 1860), i, p. 213; cf. my 'Lollardy and Literacy', p. 195 and 'Lollards and Images', p.184. On the aural character of reading in antiquity see the excellent article by G. L. Hendrickson, 'Ancient Reading', *The Classical Journal*, XXV (1929-30), pp. 182-96 (I owe this reference to an American journal to the Philadelphia conference).

54 Havelock, *Origins of Western Literacy*, p. 46; Josef Vachek, *Written Language: General Problems and Problems of English* (Janua linguarum, Series Critica XIV, The Hague, 1973), pp. 37-38, 53; H. J. Chaytor, *From Script to Print* (Cambridge, 1945), pp. 5-21.

55 Frances A. Yates, *The Art of Memory* (Harmondsworth, 1969), esp. Chapters 3-5.

memory process was a great equalizer. It put learned and unlearned in the same boat, since the former as much as the latter had to rely on the *seen* world to form their mental repertory. It also meant that since the mind had to move along visual rails in its recollective process it was, in a sense, irrelevant whether the initial process had started from word or picture – from lettered page or painted wall. Readers and non-readers were on a par.

The spiritual objectives of the devout also levelled to insignificance differences between the tools of learning. There came a moment for every contemplative to drop his book; to turn away from his text to higher things. When St. Francis was ill and a friar thought to console him by reading the Bible, the patient replied that good though such reading was, he had learnt enough for his meditations.[56] 'When thou shalt have read and known many things, thou must needs ever return to one beginning and principle'.[57] The *Imitation of Christ* in which these words appear was written and used by those who shared such a devotional use of letters. 'What need have I, dear daughter', Jordan of Saxony wrote to a nun, Diana of Andalò, 'to write my little letters for your comfort, when you have far better, sweeter consolation, in taking and reading the book which is ever in your mind's eye, the book of life, the volume of law undefiled, converting the soul?'[58] Studying the crucifix as the book of life reduced the need for books of letters. Nor was it only those in religious orders who treated book and image in this way, as alternative aids to rumination. And a text used for meditation was in some ways more like an image than a book which one picks up (preferably indexed) for consultation and reference.

For St. Bernardino and Bishop Pecock and their contemporaries there was an equivalence of books and images which is alien to us. While there was a sense in which letters and books could be images, there was also an unquestionable manner in which images were books. A painting, sculpture or stained glass window was a document or holy text, making its conveyance simultaneously to God and man: it glorified the Creator and it instructed the created. It was intended to speak to those who saw it.

In the last generation we have become more accustomed to thinking of visual imagery as itself a language. But it is still hard, specially for those of us who learn and communicate through the page,

---

56   Smalley, *Study of the Bible*, p. 283, cf. pp. 29, 86 on monastic *lectio divina*; Clanchy, *op. cit.*, pp. 130-31, 144, 216; *Cambridge History of the Bible*, Vol. 2, p. 384.
57   *The Imitation of Christ*, Bk. III, cap. xliii.
58   Smalley, *op. cit.*, p. 283.

to apprehend this medieval parity of painting and letters: *pictura* and *scriptura*. We have become conditioned to a disjunction between the world of art and the world of books. We do not expect a modern painting to teach us something essential for the conduct of our lives; we do not approach a carving with open ears. We tend to think of letters as being more directly linked with abstract messages of the mind, and of imagery as related to the concrete and emotional. Late medieval literacy belongs to another world, in which the arts were an integral part of religious teaching and discourse.[59]

How did this interrelationship of word and image affect the way in which lay people used devotional texts and books? This is not an easy subject to explore, but something can be discovered from teachers as well as learners. For the former we may take two continental examples. John Geiler of Kaisersberg (1445-1510), the famous Strasbourg preacher, gives a recommendation which shows how the unlettered were expected to use pictures and picture-books in their devotions. 'If you cannot read', said Geiler, 'then take a picture of paper where Mary and Elizabeth are depicted as they meet each other; you buy it for a penny. Look at it and think how happy they had been, and of good things.... Thereafter show yourself to them in an outer veneration, kiss the image on the paper, bow in front of the image, kneel before it'. The pictured paper was doubtless a single sheet woodcut of the kind which, as Geiler indicates, became cheap and commonly available in the fifteenth century.[60] This kind of text was a sort of halfway house between church image and illustrated text: a paper icon. It was expected simultaneously to teach the unlettered believer (in this case about the Visitation), and to be venerated by him or her. Book, paper image and carving might all be used with the same devotion.

---

59   Robert Hughes, commenting in his television series 'The Shock of the New' (November 1980) on the didactic purpose of medieval art, its central role of explaining and informing, referred to it as public discourse, painting being 'one of the dominant forms of public speech'. 'Pictures educate; signs command'. Whereas now, art has lost this function. 'Nobody extracts essential information for the conduct of their lives from painting any more'. (I have not found this passage in the published text).

60   S. Ringbom, *Icon to Narrative: The Rise of the Dramatic Close-up in Fifteenth-Century Devotional Painting* (Abo, 1965), p. 29, n. 40, citing Otto Clemen, *Die Volksfrömmigkeit des ausgehenden Mittelalters* (Dresden & Leipzig, 1937), p. 14 (where no citation is given). On the thriving trade along the Rhine of such devotional woodcuts see L. Febvre and H.-J. Martin, *The Coming of the Book*, trans. D. Gerard (London, 1976), p. 46.

A different sort of text, which shows the merging of image and letter in devotional meditation, was an Italian handbook, written as instruction for young girls in 1454 and printed forty years later. This *Zardino de Oration*, the *Garden of Prayer*, includes the following advice, that shows how visualizing memory techniques were to be used by readers in gospel learning and recollection.

> The better to impress the story of the Passion on your mind, and to memorise each action of it more easily, it is helpful and necessary to fix the places and people in your mind: a city, for example, which will be the city of Jersualem — taking for this purpose a city that is well known to you. In this city find the principal places in which all the episodes of the Passion would have taken place .... And then too you must shape in your mind some people, people well known to you, to represent for you the people involved in the Passion....[61]

Christ, the Virgin, St. Peter and others. The rules of the art of memory are here applied to contemplative ends. The text instructs the learner on the making of his mental locations, and the book becomes the passage to the visual memory. The reading led to the imaging.

The experiences of Margery Kempe, as related in her book, offer rare insight into the interactions of heard words and seen images in semi-mystical devotion. Margery was not given to secreting those 'holy inspirations and high contemplations' — 'the best life on earth', as she put it — into which she was so often and so tearfully ravished. The hearing of books and the hearing of sermons both contributed to Margery's meditation – and of course to her ability to hold her own with priests. She describes the kindly ministrations of a priest in Lynn who

> read to her many a good book of high contemplation, and other books, such as the Bible, with doctors thereon, Saint Bride's book, Hilton's book, Bonaventure, Stimulus Amoris, Incendium Amoris, and such others.

This instruction gave her a good grasp of the gospel story, as well as a fund of moralistic tales, which sometimes came in useful. 'Thus', she said, 'through hearing of holy books and holy sermons, she ever increased in contemplation and holy meditation'. But, at the same time, as her narrative makes very clear, when Margery was swept off her feet

61   Michael Baxandall, *Painting and Experience in Fifteenth Century Italy* (Oxford 1972), p. 46.

for 'fullness of devotion', her 'many glorious visions' were suffused with and informed by recollections of the painting and sculpture she had seen in churches. Sometimes it was the sight of a crucifix. On other occasions a Pietà or an Easter Sepulchre overwhelmed her with the reality of the Passion. When Margery (in her words) 'went forth in contemplation', she took with her a mental vocabulary that we cannot uncover, though we know that its components came from books that were graphic as well as verbal. That vanished English library of 'laymen's books' included items from the same shelf that later housed Grünewald's Isenheim Altarpiece. Margery Kempe's vision of Christ's body, 'fuller of wounds than ever was a dove-house of holes.... the rivers of blood flowing out plenteously from every member', surely owed something to images she had seen, as well as to what she had heard of the *Revelations* of St. Bridget of Sweden.[62]

The interlocking patterns of mental image, personal devotion, religious text, and external image, cannot usually be unravelled, though religious currents made a full circuit between them. But there are some rare occasions when we can see into the relationships between these modes of divine communication. The *Revelations* of St. Bridget have been shown to have influenced Grünewald's masterpiece.[63] Nearer home (for a lesser example) there is a representation of the Last Judgment in a window of All Saints Church, in North Street, York, that corresponds with a description in *The Prick of Conscience*.[64] Those who could read would visualize in terms of seen images, and the makers of images were influenced by spoken words as well as by other images — and sometimes directly by texts.

When one turns from readers to texts, the exploration of exactly what literacy amounted to in lay devotions becomes altogether more difficult. For one thing, thanks to the multiplication of vernacular works produced in the fourteenth and fifteenth centuries, we have so many writings that can be dubbed devotional.[65] Perhaps the

62   *The Book of Margery Kempe*, EETS edn., pp. 79, 89, 143-5, 117, 191, 70, cf. 69, 139-40, 148: modern version pp. 101, 115, 188-9, 152-3, 252, 89-90, cf. 88, 183, 193; Pantin, *English Church*, p. 256 ff. On the *Revelations* of St. Bridget, Walter Hilton's *Scale of Perfection*, the *Stimulus Amoris* attributed to Bonaventura, and Richard Rolle's *Incendium Amoris* see notes to the EETS edition pp. 276-77, 320, 323.

63   Otto Benesch, *The Art of the Renaissance in Northern Europe* (London, 1965), pp. 27-34.

64   Pantin, *op. cit.*, pp. 230, cf. 241, 259. On the Prick of Conscience window, c. 1410 (?), in All Saints, North Street, York, which shows the fifteen signs of the end of the world in fifteen days, see Nikolaus Pevsner, *Yorkshire: York and the East Riding* (Harmondsworth, 1972), pp. 115-16; cf. *The Pricke of Conscience* ed. R. Morris (Berlin, 1863), Bk. V, pp. 108-173.

65   See Pantin, *op. cit.*, p. 220 ff. for a survey of religious and moral treatises in the vernacular.

distinctions of letters in the sermon quoted above may act as a guide through this maze. Using this preacher's hierarchy we may divide these texts into three categories: (1) those that were designed for teaching and learning the elements of the faith; (2) those that were related to the rhetorical art of the pulpit; (3) those that had primarily meditative use. Though the boundaries overlap and are far from clear cut, such a division is useful because it helps us to consider the diversity of ways in which people used their texts. We may start with what amounts to a best-selling example, which one might place mainly in category three.

The Book of Hours or Primer (Primmer to contemporaries), to which the name of lay folks' prayer book has been given, was one of the most common books of devotion to be found in the hands of lay people.[66] In a way it is misleading to think of it (whether in Latin or the vernacular) as the layman's prayer-book, since the text was only partially related to the services of the church. Its core, certainly, consisted of parts of the Breviary (the calendar, the hours or office of the Virgin, the penitential psalms, the litany, the office of the dead and suffrages of the saints), but these texts did not enable their possessors to follow or understand ecclesiastical services word by word – nor were they expected to do so. The book of hours was independent of the liturgical cycle and the primer was a text for prayer and meditation, rather than a service-book. It helped the private devotions of its owner (including meditation on death). Such personal prayer and meditation might of course take place at divine office – indeed this was envisaged. The *Lay Folks Mass Book* told people to:

> Behold the elevation reverently.
> Such prayer there then thou make,
> As liketh thee best for to take.[67]

---

66   This is a topic with a considerable literature. On the form of the Book of Hours see the introduction to V. Leroquais, *Les Livres d'Heures Manuscripts de la Bibliothèque Nationale*, 3 vols. (Paris, 1927); John Harthan, *Books of Hours and their Owners* (London, 1977), pp. 12-19; Helen C. White, *The Tudor Books of Private Devotion* (Westport, Conn., 1951, 1979), pp. 53-86; *The Prymer or Lay Folks Prayer Book*, ed. H. Littlehales (EETS, OS 105, 109, 1895-7); Edgar Hoskins, *Horae Beatae Mariae Virginis or Sarum and York Primers* (London, 1901); also the works referred to in n. 73 below.

67   *The Lay Folks Mass Book*, ed. T. F. Simmons (EETS, OS 71, 1879), p. 39. (The title is of course modern). On this text and the layman's part in mass see the valuable chapter on 'The Mass' in B. L. Manning, *The People's Faith in the Time of Wyclif* (1919, rep. Hassocks, 1975), pp. 4-16. Cf. Pantin, *op. cit.*, pp. 256, 276 for the description (in a funeral sermon of 1344) of how Lady Cobham 'at Mass, when the priest was silent, ... said some private prayers in French and some Paternosters and Hail Marys'.

But synchronized worship did not imply connection with the words of the office. The priest celebrated on behalf of the congregation, 'so that his communication is to God, and not to the people' – as an ardent defender of old ways put it in 1554. The understanding that was in question was God's, not man's.[68]

A text which provided the mass-goer with his own vernacular libretto for the Latin service was B. Langforde's *Meditations for spiritual exercise in the time of the mass*, intended to 'move souls to the devotion of the mass'. A dramatic analogy is not unfitting, since the reader, having been introduced to the significance of all the gestures, furnishings, instruments and vestments of the ceremony, is enabled to follow the action by what amount to stage directions. 'When the priest casteth on his overmost vestment....when the priest goeth to the right corner of the altar....when the gospel is read....after *ite missa est* .....': these are all cues for an appropriate meditation and recollection to accompany 'all the secret prayers and gestures of the priest'. The layman, inwardly recalling 'by holy meditation, the whole process of the passion', occupied himself in his vernacular exercise in the nave in parallel with, yet separated from the priest's enactment of the Latin rite in the choir.[69] Seeing the mass (more than hearing it) was the prompter to devout meditation. It could be less an act of communion than the contemplation of a divine tableau vivant – a refiguring of Christ.

Though books without words remained the commonest form of reading, going to church with a book was becoming less of a rarity during the fifteenth century. It has even been suggested that the growing lay fashion for using books in church might have had some influence on ecclesiastical architecture. Was the adoption of lighter-toned stained glass related to the number of the devout who were struggling to see their books in the nave?[70] An Italian visitor to England in 1500 noticed the English habit of hearing mass daily, and how the women went to church with rosaries, 'any who can read taking the office of Our Lady with them, and with some companion reciting it in the church verse by verse, in a low voice, after the manner of

---

68   John Standish, *A discourse wherin is debated whether it be expedient that the Scripture should be in English for al men to reade that wyll* (London, 1554), sig. K. viii[r].

69   *Tracts on the Mass*, ed. J. Wickham Legg (Henry Bradshaw Society, XXVII, 1904), pp. 17-29. Nothing seems to be known about Langforde, and the date of this work is uncertain, the manuscript from which it was printed being late fifteenth or early sixteenth century. On priests' vesting themselves in view of the congregation, see Williams, *Welsh Church,* p. 448.

70   Delaruelle, *L'Eglise au temps du Grand Schisme*, ii, pp. 714-15, 734.

churchmen'.[71] Among those whose habits fitted this description were the mothers of the first Tudor and the two Yorkist kings. Cicely, duchess of York (whose reading matter resembled that of Margery Kempe), got up at seven to say 'her matins of the day and matins of Our Lady' before hearing mass in her chamber; and Lady Margaret Beaufort, according to John Fisher, rose at five each morning for certain devotions, including 'with one of her gentlewomen, the matins of Our Lady'.[72] Besides the thousands of richly illuminated Books of Hours belonging to such nobles, there were countless more humble everyday copies in all sorts of hands. A fifteenth-century London grocer bequeathed at his death 'my primer with gilt clasps whereupon I am wont to say my service'. Hawise Aske of York left five *primaria* in her will of about 1450-51, and in 1461 John Kirkby, a plumber of London, made gifts of three primers to his nephew, son and daughter, respectively. The primer was a book that was owned by the lowly as well as the rich — witness the 'primer for to serve God with' left to a godchild in 1434 by Roger Elmesley, sometime servant of John Bokeler, wax chandler.[73]

Of course primers were not only used for prayer and meditation. The story of William Maldon of Chelmsford who, about 1538, thought to himself 'I will learn to read English', tells otherwise. For Maldon proceeded to learn on an English primer, which he 'plied' on Sundays, in order to gain this skill.[74] The fact that the primer came frequently

---

71   *A Relation .... of England*, ed. C. A. Sneyd (Camden Soc., xxxvii, 1847), p. 23. This use in church is reflected in the directions prefixed to the litany in the official Primer printed in 1545; 'And such among the people as have books, and can read, may read them quietly and softly to themselves: and such as cannot read, let them quietly and attentively give audience in time of the said prayers ....'; White, *op cit.*, p. 119. Cf. Owst, *Preaching* p.171, for a lady found reading her primer in church. Of course lay people also owned missals and breviaries, and according to Orme, *English Schools*, p. 46, these were more common in the wills of townsmen than primers or other more elementary prayer-books.

72   Pantin, *op. cit.*, pp. 254, 260-61; Edmund Waterton, *Pietas Mariana Britannica* (London, 1879), p. 125; Harthan, *op. cit.*, p. 32; *English Works of John Fisher*, ed. J. E. B. Mayor (EETS, ES XXVII, 1876), p. 294, cf. p. 292 on Lady Margaret's understanding of Latin, which amounted to 'a little perceiving specially of the rubric of the ordinal for the saying of her service which she did well understand'; C.A.J. Armstrong, 'The Piety of Cicely, Duchess of York: A Study in Late Mediaeval Culture', in *For Hilaire Belloc*, ed. D. Woodruff (London, 1942), pp. 73-94.

73   C. Wordsworth and H. Littlehales, *The Old Service-Books of the English Church* (London, 1910), p. 249; *Horae Eboracenses*, ed. C. Wordsworth (Surtees Soc., cxxxii, 1920), pp. xxxviii-xxxix (a list of bequests of primers from the fourteenth to the early sixteenth centuries, including one donated in 1513-14 by Lady Elizabeth Scrope, that had been given to her by Lady Margaret Beaufort); *The Fifty Earliest English Wills*, ed. F.J. Furnivall (EETS, OS 78, 1882), p. 102; *The Prymer, or Prayer-Book of the Lay People in the Middle Ages*, ed. H. Littlehales (London, 1891-2), ii, pp. xvii-xviii; Deanesly, *art. cit.*, (n. 18 above), pp. 356-7.

74   *Narratives of the Reformation*, ed. J. G. Nichols (Camden Soc., lxxvii, 1859), p. 349; 'Lollardy and Literacy', p. 214.

to include the elementary items of religious instruction (paternoster, creed, and commandments), lent it the qualities of an ABC: children learnt their faith and letters together, and sometimes the alphabet as such formed part of the text (for instance in a primer for children that was printed in Paris in 1514, and in another of 1543 for the 'tender babes of England' — imitators of Prince Edward).[75] The very name of the book — which may come from *liber primarius* — suggests this educational context, as does Chaucer's description of the seven-year-old conning his lesson from the primer in the Prioress's Tale.[76] The widespread dissemination of primers in the later middle ages makes it likely that this use of the text to learn letters as well as devotion, was spreading long before sixteenth-century reformers gave it such a tremendous boost.

There were a great many other texts that belong more obviously to our first class, and concentrated directly on the instruction of the faithful. Numerous vernacular works were written that taught the elements of the faith, such as Archbishop Thoresby's *Catechism*, or John Mirk's *Instructions for Parish Priests*.[77] The creed, commandments and paternoster were all expounded at length in vernacular tracts. The bulk of this didactic literature was addressed to the parish clergy whose literacy so often failed to reach contemporary standards of latinate *literatus*, and for whom the duty of hearing confession made some knowledge of moral theology more necessary. Works of this kind were to help priests fulfil their duty, examining penitents and explaining the essentials of the faith to their parishioners in the vernacular four times a year (that, at any rate, was the letter of

---

75   C. C. Butterworth, 'Early Primers for the Use of Children', *Papers of the Bibliographical Society of America*, 43 (1949), pp. 374-382; *idem, The English Primers (1529-1545)* (Philadelphia, 1953), pp. 6-7, 251-253, cf. 177-8, 191, 226-7; *Horae Eboracenses*, p. xliii. This association was ancient: cf. Smalley, *op. cit.*, p. xiv for small clerks learning their letters from the psalter in the early middle ages; Bäuml, *art. cit.*, pp. 238-9, n. 4. The loan of a parish psalter to a servant *(famulus)* to read got the rector of Ullingswick (Hereford) into trouble in 1397, when the book was damaged. A.T. Bannister, 'Visitation Returns of the Diocese of Hereford in 1397', *EHR*, XLV (1930), p. 96; cf. p. 97 Bishops Frome.

76   'This litel child, his litel book lernynge, / As he sat in the scole at his prymer'; The Prioress's Tale, 1706-7 ff., cited by Butterworth, *op. cit.*, pp. 3-4. Roger Elmesley's bequest of his primer (above p. 124) was made to a child who was also given child-sized furnishings, including 'a little coffer' for 'his small things.'

77   On the literature of this kind see Wells, *Manual of the Writings in Middle English*, p. 816 ff.; J. Burke Severs and A. E. Hartung, *Manual of the Writings in Middle English 1050-1500* (Hamden, Conn., 1967-), vol. 2, p. 458 ff., 'Instructions for Religious', vol. 3, p. 669 ff., 'Dialogues, Debates, and Catechisms'; Pantin, *op. cit.*, p. 189 ff.; M. T. Brady, '*The Pore Caitiff*: An Introductory Study', *Traditio*, X (1954), pp. 529-48.

the law).[78] Once in circulation, however, there was a good chance of such texts reaching a wider audience. Mirk's *Instructions*, though addressed to and primarily intended for parish clergy (as Thoresby's had been), ended with a specific plea from author to owner not only to read the book himself, but to let others learn from it.

> It is made them to shown
> That have no books of their own,
> And other that are of mene lore,
> That will fain con more.[79]

Early in the fourteenth century Robert Manning made his English verse translation or version of William of Waddington's *Manuel des péchés* for lay people whose love for rhyming tales could help other forms of memorizing, including the requirements of penitential self-examination. Such versified instruction mediated between the worlds of rote and written learning.

> For lewde men I undertook
> On english tongue to make this book.[80]

So much for instructive and meditative texts. Finally we come to our second category: writings related to preaching. The sermon

---

78   On the obligations of Archbishop Pecham's *Ignorantia sacerdotum* 'De informatione simplicium sacerdotum' (1281) and the question of how far these were fulfilled see *Councils and Synods .... relating to the English Church*, ed. F. M. Powicke and C. R. Cheney (Oxford, 1964), ii, pp. 900-905; Pantin, *loc. cit.*; Owst, *Preaching in Medieval England*, pp. 281-2; D. W. Robertson, 'Frequency of Preaching in Thirteenth-Century England', *Speculum*, XXIV (1949), pp. 376-88. It is important (as this article indicates) to distinguish between the parish clergy's obligation to give regular vernacular credal instruction, and the delivering of sermons in general: i.e. one should not base deductions (as has too often been done) about the infrequency of preaching on the 1281 constitution. Thus Mirk's *Instructions* enjoins the parish priest to preach and teach the paternoster and creed twice or thrice a year, in the course of his regular round of instructive preaching; 'thus thou must ofte preach, / And thy parish yerne [carefully] teach'. *John Mirk's Instructions for Parish Priests*, ed. G. Kristensson (Lund Studies in English, 49, 1974), p. 71 ff., cf. 89.

79   *John Mirk's Instructions*, p. 224.

80   *Robert of Brunne's 'Handlyng Synne'*. ed. F. J. Furnivall (EETS, OS 119, 1901), pp. 2-3; Pantin, *op. cit.*, pp. 221, 224-5; *Camb. Hist. Bible*, Vol. 2, p. 379. On verse as 'the most effective method of conveying information' and the use of verse sermons (such as *Handlyng Synne*) see H. G. Pfander, *The Popular Sermon of the Medieval Friar in England* (New York, 1937), pp. 22, 30 and *passim*. For the confessional context of the *Manuel*, and the important point that the instruction required for confession was distinct from catechistical teaching see D. W. Robertson, 'The *Manuel des Péchés* and an English Episcopal Decree', *Modern Language Notes*, LX (1945), pp. 439-447; *idem*, 'The Cultural Tradition of *Handlyng Synne*', *Speculum*, XXII (1947), p. 165.

collections that belong most specifically to the class of 'vocal letters' were more often addressed to speakers than to hearers.[81] They were, that is, intended to help preachers more than to edify members of their congregations. John Mirk's *Festial* and the *Speculum Sacerdotale* (probably both dating from the early fifteenth century) seem to have been designed as manuals for preachers, though the former adopts the direct form of address ('Good men and women'), while the latter reminded priests ('Sires mine') of their duty 'to bring due and needful teaching and doctrine unto the people'.[82] Such texts, close as they are to the spoken word, are a form of prose that reflects the oral character of parish learning. We may well call them — borrowing the preacher's expression — vocal texts.[83]

In this case too (as in the works of instruction) composition for the clergy does not rule out lay readership. The large number of editions of Mirk's *Festial* put out by the early printers argues for a wider than clerical interest.[84] It is quite certain that long before the arrival of printing there was coming into existence an appetite for reading, owning and re-hearing the texts of sermons, something that begins almost to resemble the fervent dissection and consumption of the preached word that characterized the Reformation. We know from her own account how avid Margery Kempe was for sermons.[85]

There are a good many texts of different kinds that reflect this appetite. The fifteenth-century *Jacob's Well* is a long sermon collection of 95 addresses which purports to have been delivered day by day in

---

81   On 'vocal letters' (*litterae vocales*) see above p. 114. Crosby, 'Oral Delivery' (above n. 16), pp. 101-102, points out that lives of the saints and miracles of the Virgin belong to the same category as sermons in that they were intended for recitation — often in church. The Reformation with its priority of 'faith through hearing' naturally affected the ordering of perceptual modes, witness Richard Baxter in his *Christian Directory* (1673), p. 60; 'The writings of divines are nothing else but a preaching the gospel to the eye as the voice preacheth it to the ear. Vocal preaching hath the pre-eminence in moving the affections, and being diversified according to the state of the congregations which attend it': quoted Cressy, *Literacy and the Social Order*, p. 5; cf. Durandus and Pecock above pp. 116-17.

82   *Mirk's Festial*, ed. T. Erbe (EETS, ES 96, 1905), pp. 1, 4, 6, 11 etc.; *Speculum Sacerdotale*, ed. E. H. Weatherley (EETS, OS 200, 1936), pp. 3, 26, 166-7. On both these works see Peter Heath, *The English Parish Clergy on the Eve of the Reformation* (London and Toronto, 1969), pp. 94-103.

83   Cf. Havelock, *Preface to Plato*, p. 53, n. 8 for remarks about texts that were essentially designed to mediate the spoken word. Obviously the versified works of instruction mentioned above were also 'vocal' in this way.

84   There were nineteen editions of the *Festial* 1483-1532 (*STC 2*, Nos. 17957-17975) and there are 26 extant manuscripts. *John Mirk's Instructions*, ed. Kristensson, p. 11; Heath, *op. cit.*, p. 94, cf. p. 88 on the clergy's interest in sermons, witnessed by books named in wills.

85   'If I had gold enough, I would give every day a noble to have every day a sermon'. *Book of Margery Kempe*, EETS edn., p. 142; modern version p. 186, cf. pp. 98 (127), 148 (194).

some kind of homiletic marathon. If the context is obscure, the contents are not, and the audience of 'friends and sires' who were preached to in this vernacular sequence would appear to have been mainly ordinary country people who were reminded of their duty to render tithe, and to whom religion was presented in terms of shovel and spade. Perhaps one should not read too much into the fact that these sermons were recorded, somewhere near the form in which they were heard, complete with the speaker's references back to 'the other day I told you', or explanations that 'this day, for less tarrying', he would not stop to explain a point.[86] But the text would have offered vivid recall to anyone who had been present, and for those who had not, clerk or secular, it provided a full guide to faith and penance.

Already in the fifteenth century the preacher's rhetoric could be a topic for domestic instruction. An Austrian work explained how the head of a household should reinforce at home, post-prandially, the lessons of the sermon. 'Then he sits at home with his good wife and with his children and his servant folk, and asks them what they remember of the sermon, and tells them what he himself remembers....'[87] The transformation of the house into the little church was a process that long antedated Calvin, and it was helped by textual studies before the days of printing. Lollards certainly promoted this sort of learning. They were active in producing and copying vernacular sermons, including transcripts of delivered addresses for perusal by the faithful. William Taylor, whose contentious preaching at Paul's Cross in 1406 attracted a public riposte, saw to it, according to William Thorpe (who heckled this opponent) that his text appeared in both Latin and English, 'and many men have it, and they set great price thereby'.[88]

86   *Jacob's Well*, ed. A Brandeis (EETS, OS 115, 1900), pp. viii-ix, 13, 24, 30, 32 etc; (on this work see Owst, *Preaching in Medieval England,* and *Literature and Pulpit.*)

87   Pierre Janelle, *The Catholic Reformation* (Milwaukee, 1963), p. 19; Owst, *Preaching*, p. 280. A number of suggestive examples show that we should not underestimate the role that exceptional (though not necessarily well off) parents could play in religious education – and the learning of letters. Joan of Arc learnt her paternoster, *ave* and *credo* in French from her mother; John Gerson's parents taught their numerous children; the Bohemian layman Thomas of Štitný (c. 1331 - c. 1401), who wrote religious treatises in the vernacular, says he learnt in youth from his parents, thereby gaining some knowledge of the scriptures; and Vespasiono da Bisticci tells of the learning Alessandra de' Bardi got in infancy from her mother, who first taught her psalms and prayers and then how to read. Delaruelle, *L'Eglise au temps du Grand Schisme,* ii, p. 710; *idem, La Piété Populaire au Moyen Age* (Turin, 1975), pp. 356-7; Pantin, *op. cit.*, pp. 254-5; R. R. Betts, 'Correnti religiose nazionale ed ereticale', in *Relazioni del X Congresso Internazionale di Scienze Storiche* (Rome, 1955), p. 494.

88   *St. Albans Chronicle, 1406-1420,* ed. V. H. Galbraith (Oxford, 1937), pp. 1-2; *Fifteenth Century Prose and Verse,* ed. A. W. Pollard (London, 1903), pp. 159-60; Kightly, 'Early Lollards', pp. 251-2, 456-9. Probably the most outstanding example of a popularised sermon was the pair of addresses delivered by Thomas Wimbledon at Paul's Cross in 1388, which survives in many manuscript and printed versions. Owst, *Preaching*, pp. 360-62; *STC2,* Nos. 25823.3-25839 for the 21 editions or issues between 1540 (?) and 1635.

The lessons of the pulpit could be savoured and digested with the aid of written versions. 'I intend to leave it written among you', announced one Lollard preacher, 'and whoever likes may look over it'.[89] William Swinderby is known to have done just this. After he had preached before Sir Robert Whitney 'and many gentles' and others in the church of Whitney-on-Wye in August 1389, Swinderby gave the knight a copy of his sermon (a fact which came out at the heretic's trial in 1391, when he hoped for testimony of his words on that occasion).[90]

Reginald Pecock was surely indicating a fact of fifteenth-century life (as well as riding his own hobby-horse), when he pointed to the need to allow the lay people written texts of heard sermons. To him the demand was self-evident. Pecock drew attention to the 'great need of our neighbours' souls, asking our help to study and record sermons to be said to them, or for to write fruitful treatises and books for them, which should preach and teach them continually and perpetually unto the world's end'.[91] Preaching and study were necessary to reach the hard knowledge of religious truths, to answer questions, and to ease the doubts of troubled minds. The heretics were not the first to do this, though they helped to give it new publicity. And they offer us, in the person of John Claydon, a rare glimpse of an individual who owned and prized his text of a heard sermon. This London citizen, a book-owner who could not read himself (he was read to by his servant), said he was particularly fond of one of his books because it contained the text of a sermon that had been preached at Horsleydown.[92]

The problem of whether reading prompts questioning more than questioning prompts reading is one of those hen-and-egg imponderables that are doubtless best left alone. But we cannot leave this topic without coming back to the implicit challenge to the church in this lay appetite for books of the kind that were not old-style 'laymen's books'. It was perfectly possible to combine learning (or meditating) in old and

89   *Selections from English Wycliffite Writings*, ed. Anne Hudson (Cambridge, 1978), p. 96; 'Lollardy and Literacy', p. 204.

90   *Registrum Johannis Trefnant*, ed. W. W. Capes (Cant. and York Soc., XX, 1916), p. 245; K. B. McFarlane, *John Wycliffe and the Beginnings of English Nonconformity* (London, 1952), p. 130; Kightly, *op. cit.*, pp. 164, 184. Swinderby called as witness of his preaching 'the lord of the town that has the same sermon written'.

91   Reginald Pecock, *The Reule of Crysten Religioun*, ed. W. C. Greet (EETS, OS 171, 1927), p. 392, cf. 99; cf. 'Lollardy and Literacy', p. 204, n. 54.

92   *Reg. Chichele*, iii, p. 133; 'et ut dixit multum affectavit illum librum propter unum sermonem alias predicatum apud Horsaldowne qui erat scriptus in libro illo'. Jacob identified the place as probably Horsleydown, now united with St. Olave's, Southwark. For what may be a fragment of this sermon in Bodl. MS Douce, ff. 30^r - 32^v see *Selections from English Wycliffite Writings*, ed. Hudson, p. 195.

new ways, and the vernacular religious texts that appeared show this end being encouraged. At the same time attachment to the word and learning from the page (specially the scriptural page) also undermined traditional assumptions.

There were contexts in which the sheer presentation of lay questions seemed to cast a slur on clerical learning. Interest in scholastic theology radiated beyond the schools. In the 1330s William of Ockham remarked that the topic of free will attracted lay disputants, so that 'laymen and old women' were ready to take on 'even learned men and those skilled in theology'.[93] John Mirk's *Festial* included a tract on the ceremonies of Maundy Thursday and Holy Saturday that was designed specifically to help parish priests with vexatious questioners. 'It is seen', started this instruction, 'that lewed men which be of many words and proud in their wit, will ask priests diverse questions of things that touch the service of Holy Church', enjoying the prospect of putting the answerer to shame.[94] Reginald Pecock noticed the same phenomenon among Lollard women, who delighted to 'argue and dispute against clerks' in their domestic confabulations.[95] And according to Walter Hilton (or another writer of his time) for whom the Lollards' pious exterior was a hypocritical disguise to attract the eyes of the world, the heretics' busy cultivation of holy learning and holy writ derived from the desire to 'presume of their own cunning and despise others that are sinful; and they covet state or prelacy, that they might teach all men'. These self-doctored deceivers prided themselves on what they had 'heard and seen in books', and looked down on clerks as having failed in their prime duty of teaching the faithful.[96]

If a desire to put down the clergy seemed like an occupational disease among heretics, the malaise was not confined to the unorthodox. The Lollards presented the most extreme form of a widespread infection. The heretics' attack on images (varied though it was) stemmed in part from a changed orientation towards words and texts, and included a frontal assault on the concept of 'laymen's books' — learning through imagery. William Thorpe (who presented this case to Archbishop Arundel) described his shock and annoyance, as he was preaching in St. Chad's, Shrewsbury, on Sunday 17 April 1407, when

93   Beryl Smalley, *English Friars and Antiquity in the early Fourteenth Century* (Oxford, 1960), p. 29; cf. p. 187 on Holcot.

94   Mirk, *Festial*, ed. Erbe, p. 124; Karl Young, 'Instructions for Parish Priests', *Speculum*, XI (1936), pp. 224-31; Pantin, *op. cit.*, p. 217.

95   Pecock, *Repressor*, I, p. 123, quoted in 'Lollard Women Priests?', p. 51.

96   *Yorkshire Writers: Richard Rolle of Hampole and his Followers*, ed. C. Horstman (London, 1895-6), i, p. 123.

his audience suddenly deserted him at the sound of the sacring bell. They rushed away noisily to watch the elevation of the host. Thorpe · chided them. Seeing the sacrament was of far less value than hearing the word of God. William Thorpe, like some other Lollards, was no believer · in images. 'It suffices .... to all men', he reports himself as telling the archbishop, 'through hearing and knowing of God's word, ... to believe in God, though they see never images made with man's hands'.[97] It came to seem that imagery, far from aiding, impeded true learning · about God.

The devotional interests of lay people reaching towards books, disputing and sometimes rejecting the lessons of church images, undermined and eroded ancient clerical assumptions. The axiomatic superiority of the clerical to the lay estate that for centuries had been firmly bonded to the divide between *literatus* and lewed, was — indirectly if not directly — being tested. The separation of the estates was a separation of mental equipment as well as of secular function. 'For there are two peoples, one of the clerks and the other of laymen ... and they are two types of diverse nature, one superior and the other inferior', wrote Alberic of Rosate in the early fourteenth century.[98] 'You are a chosen people, a royal priesthood, a holy race, you are a peculiar people chosen into the lot of God, you are priests and ministers of God, nay, you are called the very Church of God, as though the laity were not to be called churchmen'.[99] Telling words: put by Richard de Bury in his early fourteenth century *Philobiblon* into the mouth of books, complaining against the clergy; 'as though the lay people were not churchmen'. Their learning and their place in the church militant were of a different order from the priesthood, dedicated and educated to serve God at the altar. Clerks hear in one way, but the lewed should learn in another, as the so-called *Lay Folks Mass Book* put it.[100]

Could God speak directly to an unlettered layman? Could He be

---

97   *Fifteenth Century Prose and Verse*, pp. 130, 136; 'Lollards and Images', p. 166.

98   John H. Mundy, *Europe in the High Middle Ages, 1150-1309* (London, 1973), p. 31.

99   Richard de Bury, *Philobiblon*, trans. E. C. Thomas, ed. M. Maclagan (Oxford, 1960), pp. 36-37. 'Vos estis genus electum, regale sacerdotium, gens sancta, vos populus peculiaris in sortem Domini computati, vos sacerdotes et ministri Dei, immo vos antonomatice [antonomastice] ipsa Ecclesia Dei dicimini, quasi laici non sunt ecclesiastici nuncupandi'. The first phrases are a quotation from 1 Peter II; 9; cf. *Speculum Christiani*, ed. G. Holmstedt (EETS, OS 182, 1933), pp. 174-5.

100   *The Lay Folks Mass Book*, p. 16.

heard in the vernacular? Were not the highest truths expressly couched in arcane tongues to preserve their untouchable holiness? How could the central mysteries of the faith be removed from Latin without placing hidden things in danger of profanation by secular day-to-day affairs? Latin was the reserved language of divinity, the proper medium for expressing certain truths. The idea that divine mysteries were intentionally opaque, veiled to the understanding of the 'irreverent and lewd handling of the multitude' long outlasted the Reformation. 'God's secrets and privy mysteries' could not be entrusted to the language and inhabitants of tavern and market-place. John Standish was reciting an old argument when at Mary's accession he put the case for English scriptures to be removed from 'our new fangled readers', who lacked the 'great fear and reverence' with which 'the mysteries ought to be touched, yea and that only of the learned men'.[101] In exactly the same way, when John Gerson wrote *La Montagne de contemplation* for his sisters, he drew a clear line between the contemplation that belonged to theologians, well-instructed in scripture, and that of 'simple people'. Strong study was also for lay readers, but Gerson's programme did not include Bible reading, and though he allowed saying the Psalter, he did not recommend its translation.[102] Even so ardent a defender of vernacular lay reading as Reginald Pecock admitted this barrier. He was, admittedly, rather a special case, but it was not only prickly defensiveness that made him switch to Latin when discussing the doctrine of the Trinity. 'To move matters immeasurable, to tell of the Trinity' (as Langland put it) was something no self-respecting preacher should undertake unadvisedly in the presence of laymen.[103]

For lay people to prove themselves capable of theology, direct auditors of God, was to change the world. So fundamental a transformation of literacy and clergy seemed mountainously unlikely. How could Christ himself have dictated to St. Bridget the rule of the Order of St. Saviour to be followed at Vadstena? Since it was in *Swedish* was this not inherently improbable? Was it not suspicious that when St. Catherine and St. Margaret spoke to Joan of Arc the words they used were *French*?[104] The lordly clerks who jeered at Margery

---

101   Standish, *A Discourse*, sigs. B 4^r, C 4^r, C 5^{r-v}. Cf. Laqueur,. 'Cultural Origins' (above n. 10), p. 262 for the Declaration of 1538 warning against the unlearned engaging in biblical exegesis in taverns and alehouses.

102   Delaruelle, *Piété Populaire*, pp. 252-3; *idem*, *L'Eglise au temps du Grand Schisme*, ii, pp. 712, 840.

103   *Piers Plowman*, ed. Skeat, i, p. 440, cited Pfander, *op. cit.*, p. 10; Pecock, *Reule*, pp. 87, 90; cf. 'Lollardy and Literacy', pp. 196-7 .

104   Eric Colledge, *'Epistola solitarii ad reges*: Alphonse of Pecha as Organizer of Birgittine and Urbanist Propaganda', *Mediaeval Studies*, XVIII (1956), p. 43.

Kempe's 'good words' on the grounds of her incapacity for letters, had so many centuries of vaunted clerical monopoly behind them that they were insulated against feeling the draughts of change. Old prejudice dies hard. But it became increasingly unrealistic to think of the clergy being (as Richard de Bury put it) 'marvellous in the eyes of the laity' because of their privileged relationship with books, or to define laymen as those who would not notice when a book was upside down.[105] Many different sorts of people had become as text-conscious in their devotions as they were in other parts of their lives, and while they continued to use writings in many different ways, it was clear that instruction and illumination were being sought and found increasingly from the page.

The letters that impregnated late medieval society were holy as well as practical, venerable as well as mundane, eternal as well as ephemeral. Those who left their letter-writing to come down to dinner also retreated to their chambers with a book, knowing — as the *Ancren Riwle* had put it — that 'reading is good prayer'.[106]

---

105   De Bury, *Philobiblon*, p. 161.

106   *The Ancren Riwle*, ed. James Morton (Camden Soc., LVII, 1853), p. 287. On the private retreats of late medieval devotional readers, both domestic closets and chapels, and side chapels in church (where a layman might improve the reading conditions with a glazed window) see W. A. Pantin, 'Instructions for a Devout and Literate Layman', in *Medieval Learning and Literature*, ed. J. J. G. Alexander and M. T. Gibson (Oxford, 1976), pp. 404, n. 2, 406-7, 409; and for a devotional text that directed its users to find 'a prive place from alle manere noyse' for their meditation see J. C. Hirsh, 'Prayer and Meditation in Late Mediaeval England: MS Bodley 789', *Medium Aevum*, xlviii (1979), p. 57.

5

LOLLARDS AND IMAGES

'And in England they are called Lollards, who, denying images, thought therewithal the crafts of painting and graving to be generally superfluous and naught, and against God's laws'.[1]

Stephen Gardiner (letter of 3 May 1547).

'Yet some holden opinion, and say,
that none images should i-maked be:
they erren foul, and go out of the way;
Of truth have they scant sensibility'.[2]

Thomas Hoccleve, *The Regement of Princes.*

The Reformation was a historically orientated movement. The reformers' goal of returning Christianity to its early purity made them acutely precedent conscious and they eagerly added every available card to their pack of justificatory sources. The trumps were not restricted to any single reforming centre. Wycliffe and Huss, despite their differing origins, seemed to belong to reformers at large, and pre-Reformation Latin texts could serve reformist aims in different parts of Europe. Lollardy, however, as an indigenous vernacular movement presented a potential specifically appropriate to English reform, as was realized by those early Protestant investigators who took the trouble to dig out some of the submerged heretical literature and direct it to a wider audience through the medium of print. Lollard heresy was also of value in that despite its heterogeneity (and occasional eccentricity) of belief it had notably anticipated certain parts of the sixteenth-century

---

1   *Letters of Stephen Gardiner*, ed J. A. Muller (Cambridge, 1933), p. 273.
2   *Hoccleve's Works*, III, ed. I. Gollancz (EETS, Extra Series 73, 1925), p. 181.

programme. The Lollards always lacked that central insight of Luther's which became the driving-force of the Reformation; despair about salvation through works never led them into the strong light of justifying faith. But given that lack they had found, or fumbled their way towards several other biblical certainties sufficiently forceful to outlast the fifteenth century and delight the minds of new-style reformers.

Lollard views of images belong to this category of anticipatory discovery. That at any rate was how it seemed to later Protestant propagandists. On this topic, indeed, the English movement offered a more clearly formulated precedent than any other medieval heresy.[3] It is true that Lollard thought on ecclesiastical imagery (as on other matters) was far from uniform or clear-cut. It was unco-ordinated and confused, but one can nevertheless discern a central consistency and (which is important) the main strands seem to have continued throughout the history of the movement.

Opposition to images can be regarded as one of the most consistent features of the Lollard heresy, and was a criterion for distinguishing its adherents at the beginning of the movement and its end.[4] It was one of the points which the chronicler Henry Knighton commented on as characterizing followers of the sect at the end of the fourteenth century. In the middle of the fifteenth century Reginald Pecock, one of the Lollards' chief antagonists, devoted considerable attention to this matter in his various refutations of their views. And John Foxe regarded the rejection of pilgrimage and worship of saints'

---

3   On the Lollard controversy and the general context see W. R. Jones, 'Lollards and Images: The Defense of Religious Art in later medieval England', *JHI*, xxxiv (1973), pp. 27-50; *idem*, 'Art and Christian Piety: Iconoclasm in medieval Europe', in *The Image and the Word*, ed. Joseph Gutmann (Missoula, 1977), pp. 75-105. John Phillips, *The Reformation of Images: Destruction of Art in England, 1535-1660* (Berkeley, 1973), p. 30 ff. has a cursory survey of the Lollards; for earlier medieval heretics' opposition to imagery see M. D. Lambert, *Medieval Heresy* (London, 1977). James Crompton, 'Lollard Doctrine, with special reference to the controversy over Image-Worship and Pilgrimages' (B. Litt. Thesis, Oxford, 1950) is valuable for the academic discussions and the manuscript sources for these.

4   Charles Kightly, 'The Early Lollards. A Survey of Popular Lollard Activity in England, 1382-1428' (D. Phil. Thesis, York, 1975), p. 577. I am most grateful to Dr. Kightly for permission to quote his unpublished work. James Crompton, 'Leicestershire Lollards', *Trans. Leics. Arch. & Hist. Soc.*, xliv (1968-9), p. 38; J. A. F. Thomson, *The Later Lollards* (Oxford, 1965), pp. 245-6, 248 and *passim*. Though he contrasted the 'mainstream' of Lollardy with other (milder or more extreme) forms of dissent Dr. Thomson did not make entirely clear where images fitted into these differing traditions (cf. pp. 28 and 89), nor did he indicate how opposition to images could itself be a means of distinguishing between different schools of heretical opinion.

images as leading tenets of early sixteenth-century heretics.[5]
Investigation of this opposition, however, soon makes it clear that
Lollard iconomachy embraced a wide range of different opinions, from
moderate critics to extreme purifiers and passionate radicals.

We should distinguish these several lines of thought. The
puritanical moralizing common among Lollards shared features of the
continental *devotio moderna*, with its withdrawal from pomp and
formal ceremony to personal acts of private devotion.[6] Purists of this
school could find support in a long line of ascetics, orthodox and
heterodox, who believed the church needed diverting from the
splendours of externals. Other Lollards carried such censure to more
dangerous extremes. Though probably always a minority (but none the
less threatening for that) Lollard radicals denied the lawfulness as well
as the usefulness of the church's imagery, and some of them actually
called for its destruction. The fact that this segment of the movement
left a small mark on events should not blind us to the reality of their
proposals, which were taken seriously enough at the time. Iconomachs
and iconoclasts co-existed throughout the history of Lollardy and
orthodox contemporaries who (unlike their sixteenth-century
counterparts) had no parallel experience on which to draw, were
perhaps more alive to the dangers they presented than prompt to
distinguish between them.

Behind the critics of every stripe there lay — at whatever remove —
the book. Lollard iconomachy (like all other iconomachy) was based in
scripture. And fidelity to biblical injunction covered a wide range of
responses.

W y c l i f f e

'It is evident that images may be made both
well and ill'.[7]
Wycliffe, *De mandatis divinis*.

What guidance did Wycliffe give on this question? He did not
address himself to it specifically, or at length, but several of his works
expounded his objections to images, the veneration of saints and relics,

5   John Foxe, *Acts and Monuments* (hereafter Foxe, *AM*) ed. J. Pratt (London,
1853-68), iv, p. 218; 'Four principal points they [offenders in the diocese of Lincoln] stood in
against the church of Rome: in pilgrimage, in adoration of saints, in reading Scripture-books in
English, and in the carnal presence of Christ's body in the sacrament'.

6   As suggested by K. B. McFarlane, *Lancastrian Kings and Lollard Knights* (Oxford,
1972) p. 225.

7   *Tractatus de Mandatis Divinis*, ed. J. Loserth and F. D. Matthew (Wyclif Soc., London,
1922), p. 156.

and sumptuous church decoration. As might be expected, his 'Treatise on the Decalogue' (the *Tractatus de mandatis divinis* of 1375-76) went fully into the use of imagery in commenting on the prohibition of graven images. It is interesting, in view of later developments, to find that Wycliffe (though he did not make much of this) was conscious of the fact that while the church followed St. Augustine in treating this prohibition as part of the first commandment, there was also patristic authority for separating it off to make a second commandment.[8] Wycliffe's treatment is noteworthy both for its lack of extremism and also for its historical awareness. He made clear (like Luther after him) the difference between the status of images in the Old Testament and in the New. Images were forbidden under the old law because the people, not being 'as learned in faith as Christians', were prone to idolatry. God had not yet taken a corporeal form of which a likeness could be depicted, and it was not until after the marriage of Christ to the church on the cross that, in his long absence, the church had instituted images to commemorate the bridegroom and his family. In the early church imagery did not increase greatly, though St. Sylvester was said to have had pictures of Peter and Paul painted for the emperor Constantine and many miracles were reported to have flourished by means of images. It was after the establishment of the faith that images were introduced to be both books for the laity and commemorative signs for Christians in their proper worship of God's saints.[9]

Wycliffe, who quoted Gregory the Great on the use of images, including the famous letter to Bishop Serenus of Marseilles, which justified pictures as the writings of the unlettered, was ready to accept their educative value. Pictorial teachers of the right kind could stir the minds of the faithful to a more ardent devotion to God. 'It is evident that images may be made both well and ill: well in order to rouse, assist and kindle the minds of the faithful to love God more devoutly; and ill when by reason of images there is deviation from the true faith, as when the image is worshipped with *latria* or *dulia*, or unduly delighted in for its beauty, costliness, or attachment to irrelevant circumstances'.[10] Images, venerated with the wrong kind of worship or

---

8   *Ibid.*, p. 152.
9   *Ibid.*, p. 155. '... introducte sunt ymagines in ecclesiam post firmitatem fidei primitive, ut sint libri laicis et signa recordativa singulis christianis, ut adorent debite sanctos Dei...'; Jones, *art. cit.*, pp. 29-30, and for the term *signa recordativa* see below p. 183, n. 168.
10   *De Mandatis Divinis*, p. 156. 'Et patet quod ymagines tam bene quam male possunt fieri: bene ad excitandum, facilitandum et accendendum mentes fidelium, ut colant devocius Deum suum; et male ut occasione ymaginum a veritate fidei aberretur, ut ymago illa vel latria vel dulia adoretur....'

gloried in for their own sake, could lead people astray. They could also cause misbelief, as when believers thought of the Father, or Holy Spirit, or angels as having bodily forms.

> And thus laymen depict the Trinity unfaithfully, as if God the Father was an aged *paterfamilias*, having God the Son crucified on his knees and God the Holy Spirit descending on both as a dove. And similarly concerning many other likenesses, by which not only laymen but ecclesiastical superiors err in faith, thinking the Father or Holy Spirit or angels to be corporeal.[11]

Many, said Wycliffe, were led into error by thinking that some divine quality was inherent in the image itself, supposing that particular images had particular merit, 'which undoubtedly is idolatry'.[12] This was an argument which, as we shall see, crops up repeatedly in attacks on pilgrimage.

The efficacy of images, according to Wycliffe, resided in their ability to rouse the mind to spiritual intentions, and the sooner the accidents or externals of the representation were left behind the better, since 'dallying in imagery conceals the poison of idolatry'.[13] And this poison — the adoration of the man-made object, instead of what this stood for — was to be avoided at all costs. Therefore before images were admitted it was important to point out to the laity the dangers of their use, all mortals being so prone to idolatry, and

> specially since so-called Christians, like animals or beasts, having forsaken the faith of spiritual believers today exceedingly indulge the senses: the sight, in costly spectacles of church ornaments; the hearing, with bells, organs, and new ways of telling the hours of the day by marvellous striking of bells; and sensuous objects are provided by which all the senses are moved in irreligious ways.[14]

Was Wycliffe, for all his appreciation of Oxford's watery setting, as

11   *Ibid.*, p. 156. Cf. p. 100 for Wycliffe's discussion of whether God is visible except by faith, and the problem of ordinary mortals conceiving of God in a non-creaturely manner.
12   *Ibid.*, pp. 156-7. 'In secundo errant plurimi putantes aliquid numinis esse subiective in ymagine, et sic uni ymagini plus affecti quam alteri adorant ymagines, quod indubie est ydolatria'.
13   *Ibid.*, p. 157.
14   *Ibid.*, p. 158; cf. *Opus Evangelicum*, ed. J. Loserth (Wyclif Soc., London, 1895), pp. 261-2. Wycliffe quoted Bishop Epiphanius of Salamis (c. 315-403), whose tearing of a painted curtain depicting Christ or a saint found in a church door was an early source for iconoclasts. *Iconoclasm*, ed. A. Bryer and J. Herrin (Birmingham, 1977), pp. 9, 180.

visually insensitive as Luther?[15] Or did his own sense of aesthetic temptation heighten his adverse reaction? At all events he had many followers in being so alive to these dangers.

From the purist's point of view (and there was nothing the least unorthodox in this) all works of art were beside the point — as was nature itself. In his examination of idolatry Wycliffe quoted Origen and Grosseteste to the effect that 'all things which the creation of God formed or the imagination invented, or the work of an artificer fashioned, are begotten outside the realm of the divine nature. And although, according to the feigning of the unfaithful, they were introduced to participate in the deity, they have nothing in common with the three divine persons, which alone belong to this realm: therefore they are significantly called "*false gods*", falsely or nominally fashioned'.[16] The true life of the spirit was apart from the delusions of physical structures or material aids. Only fools, wrote Wycliffe in his book 'On the Church' (*De ecclesia* of 1378) would say that the temple built of wood and stone was holy church. The true church, the house of God to which the reverence of God's image was owed, consisted of those spirits who were called by God. And so 'holiness of life and the keeping of justice honour the place of the church more than all the gold and material jewels of this world'.[17] 'It seems that Christ cared little for the sumptuous edifice of the temple'.[18] Imagery and external decoration were tools of the devil's craft. The devil had always seduced people by the illusions of sensible signs.[19] And the man who could not 'raise his mental power to know that the deity is not a creature, but above all individuals, species and genera' was to be written off as *infidelis.*[20]

Yet for all this criticism of the arts and their products Wycliffe did not deny the value and legitimacy of images. 'It is not, however, to be denied that ecclesiastical images can be well made'. As witness he cited Bede on the temple of Solomon, which showed that the figure of Christ on the crucifix and images of apostles and saints could legitimately be in churches, notwithstanding the commandment.[21] The problem

15   *Opera Minora*, ed. J. Loserth (Wyclif Soc., London, 1913), i, p. 18; K. B. McFarlane *John Wycliffe and the Beginnings of English Nonconformity* (London, 1952), p. 31: E. H Erikson, *Young Man Luther* (London, 1972), pp. 170, 188.

16   *De Mandatis Divinis*, p. 159.

17   *Tractatus de Ecclesia*, ed. J. Loserth (Wyclif Soc., London, 1886), p. 265.

18   *Opus Evangelicum*, p. 263. (The context here is how externals hinder rather than help inner prayer).

19   *De Ecclesia*, p. 466.

20   *De Mandatis Divinis*, p. 100.

21   *Ibid.*, p. 159. On Bede as a justificatory source for church imagery see Jones, 'Art and Christian Piety', pp. 79-80. The temple of Solomon was always a prime example for iconodules.

11   The pharisee and the publican at prayer in the temple. The latter
prostrates himself beside a small shrine or tabernacle, with barred doors. (The
Holkham Bible Picture Book, early 14th century. BL Add. MS 47682, f. 26ᵛ)
(p. 143ff.)

Non habebis deos alienos exodi · xx ·

Du salt an beten eynen got
Alz her dir geboten hot

was holdu sdruzen za schaffen
loz beten woruhe vns pfaffen

12 & 13   The first two commandments and the dangers of infringing
them by worshipping the other gods (Exodus 20) and swearing falsely
(Leviticus 19). (Woodcuts in Heidelberg MS 438 from Johannes Geffcken,
Der Bildercatechismus des fünfzehnten Jahrhunderts) (pp. 109, 111, 144)

14   Alabaster (*c*. 1400) of the Trinity (the symbol of the Holy Ghost is
lacking). (Victoria and Albert Museum, A 53 - 1946) (pp. 139, 165)

centred on the idolatry which might arise even from such legitimate images, and to understand this it was necessary to understand the different kinds of worship. *Latria* was the worship owed to God alone; *dulia* meant the reverence due to the creature; *hyperdulia* was the veneration owed to Christ as both creature and creator. Idolatry could be committed either actively or passively; actively by giving to the creature the honour due to God alone; passively by receiving or aspiring to the honour due to God. The first commandment, in fact, summed up all the theological virtues, since the sin of idolatry embraced all other major sins. 'Whoever sins in deed, as when he inordinately loves the creature, offends against the first commandment by committing idolatry'.[22] The poison in the honeycomb, to be avoided at all costs, was worshipping the sign instead of the signified.[23] The cause of many human errors was to be ascribed to the fact that men loved temporal visible goods more than the invisible and delighted in buildings, clothes, ornaments and objects of human invention, more than in the uncreated. 'Therefore', concluded Wycliffe, again citing Grosseteste, 'the variety of apparel, buildings, utensils and other objects invented by pride constitutes the book or graven image of the devil, by which mammon or another is worshipped in the image. Therefore the whole church, or a great part of it, is tainted by this idolatry, because the works of their hands are effectively more highly valued than God'.[24]

Behind such puritanical strictures lay a sound tradition. Yet the corpus of Wycliffe's writings also included words whose import might have seemed more radical. There were several passages in his sermons which touched on idolatry. One of these occurs in the first of a sequence of sermons, (dated by their editor to about 1383), which were (interestingly) delivered at the request of 'a certain devout layman' on the ten commandments.[25] The first sin Wycliffe considered against the first commandment was the twin transgression of worshipping images and the consecrated host.[26] In both cases the law was broken by treating as God what belonged to the world. Those who claimed that

22   *De Mandatis Divinis*, pp. 161-4 (quote at p. 164).

23   *Ibid.*, p. 157.

24   *Ibid.*, p. 166; 'est liber vel sculptile diaboli ...' In this passage Wycliffe expounds the importance of the first commandment and the various forms of idolatrous behaviour..

25   *Johannis Wyclif Sermones*, ed. J. Loserth (Wyclif Soc., London, 1887-1890), i, pp. xxix, 89. For Wycliffe's statement of the need to teach the decalogue in English see 'De nova prevaricancia mandatorum' in *Polemical Works*, ed. R. Buddensieg (Wyclif Soc., London, 1883), i, pp. 111, 116-17, 126.

26   *Sermones*, i, p. 90; 'Contra hoc mandatum faciunt multi stolide adorantes ymagines ac ostiam consecratam'. To put this sin first was itself unusual; cf. below p. 154. For Wycliffe's view of the worship (*latria*) owed respectively to the eucharist and cross as images (sign or sacrament) of Christ see *De Eucharistia*, ed. J. Loserth (Wyclif Soc., London, 1892), pp. 316-18.

their worship of images was vicarious were behaving as idolatrously as the gentiles. The facts were at variance with these claims. Worshipping God in images was idolatry and, 'since this often occurs among laymen, it is evident that this danger would be removed were all such images, as in the old law, to be destroyed'. Lay people were all too prone to worship particular images, to which they were blindly attached. Given the weakness of human nature 'it seems that safety would lie in removing such images, on account of the danger of breaking the first commandment'.[27]

Wycliffe made a similar point in another sermon, again covered by the qualifying proviso '*videtur securum* ...' Here, attacking the worship of relics of saints he remarked that 'it would be to the honour of saints and the advantage of the church were the jewels with which the sepulchres of saints have been foolishly and uselessly adorned, to be distributed to the poor'.[28] Though I know, he added with a final dig at the offenders, that anyone who makes such a suggestion is certain to be deemed heretical by the profiteers of such places.

These carefully worded asides were scarcely offered as prescriptions for direct action. But, as we know, there was no lack of contemporaries ready to hang a great deal on every magisterial hint and parenthesis. Wycliffe's followers took up and developed his criticisms of images, discreetly citing his words and acting on some of his censures. In fact already during his lifetime, as his own words indicate, the consequences of this teaching were being viewed with alarm.

As a whole, Wycliffe's position on images was far from extreme or unorthodox, though he would hardly have been true to himself had he failed to leave an appearance of ambiguity. His interpretation of Old Testament law was not that of an iconoclast. While deprecating the weakness of human nature, he accepted the propensity of all mortals to use sensuous means for spiritual ends. He did not deny the use of images as books of the laity, aware though he was that their legitimate

27   *Sermones*, i, p. 91. Wycliffe agreed that full instruction of the people by suitable clergy – who were notably lacking – could make such sculptures useful books of the laity ('posset facere quod tales sculpture sint libri utiles laicorum'). But Christ and the apostles and scripture did not reverence such images, and it was evident that their multiplication and the enriching of shrines and sumptuous churches were the result of clerical avarice, and defrauded the poor (pp. 91-92).

28   *Ibid*., ii, p. 165. Remarks condemning the delusions of saints' shrines and sumptuous churches (including a passage reminiscent of this) were among the 267 propositions from Wycliffe's works censured in 1411. D. Wilkins, *Concilia* (London, 1737), iii, pp. 342, 349 (nos. 50, 51, 257). No such points were among the errors listed during Wycliffe's lifetime. For other passages expressing views on relics and the avarice of pilgrim centres see *De Ecclesia*, p. 465; *De Officio Regis*, ed. A. W. Pollard and C. Sayle (Wyclif Soc., London, 1887), p. 16; P. Gradon, 'Langland and the Ideology of Dissent', *PBA*, lxvi (1980), pp. 193-4, and below n. 96.

purpose was so easily abused. He issued no theoretical ultimatum for the banning or destruction of imagery. This well-hedged hypothesizing was in character with Wycliffe's treatment of church endowments (another dangerous issue), and it stands in marked contrast to the expressions of some of his followers who aired their views in the vernacular. Academic heresiarch and proselytizing hedge-priests, whatever their community of aim, parted company in practice.

Image-Worship

'To images should no manner worship be done neither genuflexions nor incensing nor other thing of worship'.[29]

William Emayn (trial of 10-14 March 1429).

The most usual Lollard error on images was to deny that these should be worshipped. The dissemination of this teaching had begun before Wycliffe's death in 1384. The bishop of Rochester, Thomas Brinton, reported at Easter 1383 that the heretics 'newly preach and assert that the cross of Christ and images should not be worshipped.[30] The denial of image-worship was repeated thereafter in many texts and by many individual suspects. It seems fairly safe to regard this as the commonest facet of one of the commonest (if not the commonest) of Lollard beliefs, and the view that it was idolatry to serve saints' images with pilgrimage or other acts of devotion secured wide support.

'From this day forward I shall worship images, with praying and offering unto them in the worship of the saints that they be made after, and also I shall never more despise pilgrimage.....'[31] The oath imposed by Archbishop Arundel on four Nottingham suspects in September 1395 was typical of many subsequent submissions. Its wording also

29   *Reg. John Stafford*, ed. T. S. Holmes (Som. Rec. Soc., xxxi-xxxii, 1915-16), i, p. 78. Cf. p. 79 for Emayn's views that 'it is damnable to go on pilgrimage to any sepulchre relics of saints: for a pilgrimage should be done to poor men' and 'it is damnable to offer to any image'. He abjured on 24 March.

30   'Immo de novo predicant and affirmant quod crux Christi vel ymagines non sunt adorande quod est manifeste falsum'; *Sermons of Thomas Brinton*, ed. M. A. Devlin (Camden Third Series, lxxxv-vi, 1954), ii, p. 495; cf. p. 466, also against the teaching of the 'pseudoprophets'; J. M. Russell-Smith, 'Walter Hilton and a Tract in defence of the Veneration of Images', *Dominican Studies*, vii (1954), p. 200, n. 78, and see n. 103 below. In the following decade Roger Dymoke's answer to the attack on images in the 1395 Conclusions concentrated on the denial of image-worship. *Rogeri Dymmok Liber*, ed. H. S. Cronin (Wyclif Soc., London, 1922), p. 186 ff.

31   Wilkins, *Concilia*, iii, p. 225; *Cal. Pat. Rolls, 1385-89*, p. 471; M. Aston, *Thomas Arundel* (Oxford, 1967), pp. 330-31; Kightly, 'Early Lollards', pp. 11-12.

points towards the theology of the question which was certainly very
present to the mind of the archbishop, and to the most informed of the
heretics. To the churchmen there was no doubt that worshipping
images 'in the worship of the saints that they are made after' included,
in the case of cross and crucifix, the highest worship of *latria*. To
heretics bent over their scriptural texts there was equally no doubt that
the first commandment's prohibition of making 'a graven thing' meant
that 'images of saints are not to be worshipped'.[32] The rejection of
conventional devotions to imagery derived from a strict adherence to
the decalogue.

Lollards were earnest about observance of the commandments.
God's law was the foundation on which their vision of the church was
built, and scriptural fidelity embraced the old law with the new. Bishop
Buckingham accused Northampton Lollards of maintaining in 1393
that 'it is lawful for every Christian to inform his brother in the ten
commandments and the holy gospels that he may know and preach
them, and that every householder (*paterfamilias*) shall answer for
himself and those belonging to his household (*familia*)'.[33] Among those
who apparently took this duty seriously were some Leicestershire
suspects who were imprisoned in the Marshalsea in the early summer of
1414, before being handed over to Bishop Repingdon for correction.
John Warwick and William Vany of Saddington were said to be Lollards
'holding and declaring in unlawful places various unlawful opinions
about the ten commandments'.[34] It goes without saying that the
decalogue could spawn many erroneous views, but the opposition to

32   *An Apology for Lollard Doctrines*, ed. J. H. Todd (Camden Soc., xx, 1842), p. 85.
(This is number 24, pp. 85-90, of the 30 questions and answers dealt with in this text).

33   A. K. McHardy, 'Bishop Buckingham and the Lollards of Lincoln Diocese', *SCH*, 9
(1972), pp. 138, 144. Teaching the commandments, like teaching the Gospel, was a Lollard
priority (cf. *English Works of Wyclif hitherto unprinted*, ed. F. D. Matthew [EETS, 74,
1880], pp. 192-3) and this duty towards the decalogue was itself scriptural, as the Lollard Bible
made clear (see below n.143). John of Bath was accused in 1418 of having an English text which
included the words; 'keeping of the behests of God passeth all other virtues and devotions and
vows and religions of man seem they never so holy' (Reg. Chandler [Salisbury], ii, f. 17ᵛ). For
a manuscript tract which stresses the obligation of lay lords to give such instruction see below
p. 153, n. 64. An illuminating example of a knight who took such teaching to heart is Sir John
Clanvowe. His treatise on 'The Two Ways' pointed to 'the keeping of god's hests' as 'the narrow
way that leadeth to life' and included a summary of the decalogue — the rest of his many
Biblical references being New Testament. V. J. Scattergood, *'The Two Ways*: an unpublished
religious treatise by Sir John Clanvowe', *Eng. Phil. Studies*, X (1967), pp. 39, 51-52.

34   The jurors presented them as 'Lollardi tenentes diversa oppiniones et alloquentes de
decem mandatis illicito et locis illicitis contra doctrinam ecclesie sancte Angl' '; PRO KB
27/613, *Rex* m. 6; Crompton, 'Leicestershire Lollards', p. 30.

images was undoubtedly prominent.[35]

John Burell, servant of Thomas Moon of Loddon in Norfolk, who admitted his heresy in April 1429, confessed that three years earlier his brother Thomas had taught him the paternoster, Ave and creed in English. He had also learnt from the same source the commandments in English, 'and that in the first commandment is contained that no honour should be shown to any images sculpted in churches by the hand of man "nor likened after them in heaven above nor after them that be in water beneath earth, to bow to them nor worship them".'[36] The images most immediately discernible as transgressing the commandment were images of God. 'For first', as an early fifteenth-century text put it, 'men err in making of images when they make images of the Godhead....For in the Old Testament God commanded that no man should make any image or likeness of him, neither in likeness of things in heaven, nor in earth nor in water; and this bidding of God stands evermore in place without changing or dispensing'.[37] Particularly objectionable were images of the Trinity, to which Wycliffe drew attention (and on which more below). In a different, most critical category, were crucifixes and images of Christ. John Burell, who belonged to an iconoclastic set, had himself attacked a cross and it is no accident that so many Lollards were examined about their views of the veneration owed to the cross.[38] This lay at the heart of iconomachy since the cross was not only the central Christian image but had also become the subject of the highest reverence. The claim of Aquinas and others that *latria* belonged to the cross was the nub of debate, and Lollard questioning of image-worship fastened on this central issue. Remarks about the qualifications of worship became specially hazardous as soon as crucifix and cross were mentioned and, for all its dilution in popular religion, informed questioning of the

35 Lollard rejection of oaths was another obvious tenet derived from the commandments. The Biblical sources which could be cited against image-worship were legion (for some of the other stock texts see Richard Wyche's list in *Fasciculi Zizaniorum*, ed. W. W. Shirley [RS, London, 1858], pp. 371-2). Foxe pointed to Rev. 9;20 as important; *AM*, iv, p. 240 and cf. p. 237 for Roger Dods, whose Apocalypse reading was linked with opposition to image-worship. For a Lollard commentary on the Apocalypse which reviewed objections to pilgrimages and images see Anne Hudson, 'A Neglected Wycliffite Text', *JEH*, 29 (1978), p. 277.

36 *Heresy Trials in the Diocese of Norwich* ed. N. P. Tanner (Camden Fourth Series, 20, 1977), (cited hereafter as *Norwich Heresy Trials*), p. 73, cf. p. 71 for a similar charge about images, and p. 69 for the English paternoster, Ave and Credo. Burell's abjuration in December 1430 included the denial of honour to 'any images, sculpted or painted, inside or outside churches' (p. 78). On Burell see Thomson, *Later Lollards*, pp. 126, 131.

37 *Selections from English Wycliffite Writings*, ed. Anne Hudson (Cambridge, 1978), p. 83, cited hereafter as *Eng. Wycl. Writings*.)

38 See below p. 172.

church's theology lay behind this Lollard tenet.

John Burell's mention of 'images sculpted in churches' draws attention to another important point. The imagery seen as proscribed by the law was primarily three dimensional: the works of carvers in wood and stone. Lollards were accused of attacking painted as well as sculpted works of art in churches. Hoccleve, for instance, said they were guilty of 'great error' for rejecting images 'be they made in carving or in painting',[39] and Richard Stormsworth's (heavily biased) petition of 1393 about the heretics' activities in Northampton, described a Lollard preacher inveighing against devotions 'of pilgrimage to images, painted tables, the framing of high and costly works of holy church', seemingly damning a great range of church art.[40] Lollards were certainly critical of the work of contemporary painters, but in directing the main burden of their criticism at image-*worship* they had in mind sculpture − 'the craft of graving'[41] − more than painting. It was what Gower called 'the misbelief' of 'many an image of entaile [carving]'[42] that mainly concerned them. The heretic who (probably about 1400) answered the bishops' charge against Lollards for saying 'that neither cross nor images painted or carved' should be worshipped, chose his words carefully when he wrote in reply; 'the making of images *truly painted* is lawful'.[43] The imagery that we know the heretics physically attacked or destroyed was almost without exception three-dimensional, probably free-standing sculpture. The art of painting was of course involved since contemporary statuary − stone and wood alike

39   'And to holde ageyn ymages makynge, / (Be they maad in entaille or ın peynture,) / Is greet errour', wrote Hoccleve in his address to Sir John Oldcastle, 1415. On the context of this charge see below p. 173. *Hoccleve's Works, The Minor Poems*, I, ed. F. J. Furnivall (EETS, Extra Series 61, 1892), p. 21.

40   Gold and silver chalices were also on this list. *The Peasants' Rising and the Lollards*, ed. E. Powell and G. M. Trevelyan (London, 1899), p. 47 gives this text in a seventeenth-century version. For the (damaged) original see Kightly, 'Early Lollards', pp. 99-106.

41   *Select English Works of John Wyclif*, ed. T. Arnold (Oxford, 1869-71), iii, p. 84.

42   *Complete Works of John Gower*, ed. G. C. Macaulay (Oxford, 1899-1902), ii, p. 443, *Confessio Amantis*, v, ll. 1498-1499, at the beginning of a passage on the origins of idolatry. Cf. iv, pp. 98-100, *Vox Clamantis*, chap. x, on the question 'quod in re sculptili .... non est confidendum, nec eciam talia adorari debent', which (referring to familiar Biblical passages such as Isaiah 44 and Psalm 115) rehearsed arguments against a Christian treating as gods 'Ligna sibi, lapides, que cernit ymagine sculpta'. This passage is throughout attached to the *sculptile* of the commandment. Gower was openly critical of the lure of gold and exploitation of offerings attached to saints' statues, but defended their devotional use and championed the worship of the cross − 'venerable wood'. 'Undique signa crucis in honore Ihesu crucifixi / Mentibus impressa sunt adoranda satis'.

43   *English Wycliffite Writings*, ed. Hudson, pp. 19, 23 (my italics), and below pp. 164-5.

— was highly coloured. As one of the objectors put it: 'ignorant wrights hew and form such crosses and images of stocks, and after that ignorant painters glory them with colours'.[44] Such painting or repainting of statuary was itself repugnant. When asked to contribute to the painting of the images in his parish church of South Creake, Norfolk, William Colyn (a local skinner) said he would rather give 12d towards burning any image, than a halfpenny towards painting it.[45] Paintings in their own right, however, did not bear the brunt of Lollard opposition. The *sculptile*, graven image of the commandment text, remained in the forefront.

Denunciations of image-worship might be founded on rudimentary knowledge of the scriptural sources. When Katherine Dertford, a spinster 'strongly suspected' of heresy, appeared before convocation in 1428 and was questioned (among other points) about image-worship and pilgrimage, she claimed she could not reply because she had only been instructed in the creed and the decalogue.[46] Fuller instruction was certainly offered to Lollard proselytes for the heretics (like the sixteenth-century reformers whose decalogue learning became so extensive) had their own versions of the ten commandments, duly glossed and expounded. And there is considerable evidence throughout the history of the movement of the study of these texts. For instance, Thomas Packer of Walford (Herefords.), who was found guilty in 1472 of error on the veneration of images, had been teaching the decalogue in a heretical conventicle and had English books of scripture (perhaps written by himself). Thomas Boughton in Berkshire in 1499 and Thomas Watts of Dogmersfield in Hampshire in 1514, alike accused of impugning images or image-worship, had both been in possession of English copies of the commandments.[47] And John Stilman, who

44 *Norwich Heresy Trials*, p. 44 (Margery Baxter of Martham, 1429).

45 *Ibid.*, pp. 13, 91. William Colyn was clearly eccentric, but his refusal to pray before an image of the Virgin (p. 90) and his disparagement of Walsingham reflected common Lollard attitudes.

46 *Register of Henry Chichele*, ed. E. F. Jacob (Cant. and York Soc., xlii, xlv-xlvii, 1938-47), iii, pp. 187-88.

47 Thomson , *op. cit.*, pp. 40, 42, 81, 83, 88-89, 245, and for other examples of heretics accused of declaring or possessing the Ten Commandments, pp. 75, 162, 168, 242-3; Foxe, *AM*, iv, p. 207. Among the books which Foxe noticed as specially named in the early sixteenth-century proceedings in the diocese of Lincoln was a book 'of the Ten Commandments'. Cf. p. 225 for the case of James Morden accused in these proceedings, who detected his uncle (John Morden) and aunt for reciting the Ten Commandments in their house in English, and cf. Thomson, *op. cit.*, p. 91 for John Morden's possession of a book from which he read out statements against images, image-worship and pilgrimages. For a late-fifteenth century reference to a 'suspect book of commandments' containing material against image-worship see Anne Hudson, 'Some aspects of Lollard book production', *SCH* 9 (1972), p. 156.

attended several readings in Watts' house, was burned as a relapsed
heretic of long standing in 1518 on charges that included teaching that
images should not be worshipped, and owning a book of
commandments which had been given him by Richard Smart, who was
burned fourteen or fifteen years earlier.[48]

In April 1520, when Lutheran doctrine was percolating into
England, the 'seven martyrs of Coventry' whose fate Foxe describes,
were according to him arrested chiefly on account of the domestic
vernacular instruction they had been giving in the Lord's Prayer and
commandments.[49] Given the consistency of their rejection of orthodox
uses of imagery it was to be expected that any Lollard exposition of the
decalogue would give some suspect twist to the prohibition of graven
images, just as the denial of oaths was likely to intrude on the
commandment against taking the Lord's name in vain. Expositions of
this kind rested on oral as well as textual transmission. Thomas Colyns
of Ginge, one of the many accused by Bishop Longland of Lincoln
about 1521, was said to have been instructing his son John for the
previous eight years in the decalogue, 'and namely, that he should have
but one God, and should worship nothing but God alone'. And Richard
Colyns of Ginge (detected for reading the ten commandments and
teaching opposition to image-worship) was the husband of Alice
Colyns, who was known among the heretics for her ability to recite
scripture by heart and was 'commonly .... sent for, to recite unto them
the declaration of the ten commandments' – or other texts.[50]

It is certain then that Lollards (like later iconomachs, who carried
the case much further) based their opposition to church imagery on the
decalogue and that they had writings to support this.[51] But it is not

48   Foxe, *AM*, iv, pp. 207-8; Thomson, *op. cit.*, pp. 83-4, 88, 171.
49   Foxe, *AM*, iv, p. 557; Thomson, *op. cit.*, p. 116. The most popular work read by
Coventry heretics accused in 1511-12 was a version of the Ten Commandments. John Fines,
'Heresy Trials in the Diocese of Coventry and Lichfield, 1511-12', *JEH*, xiv (1963), p. 164; cf.
p. 173 for Foxe's dating of the 'Godly Martyrs'.
50   Foxe, *AM*, iv, pp. 235-6, 238-9, cf. pp. 228, 234 for other cases of heretics accused
of learning or owning the commandments in English. Foxe includes a good deal of evidence
about the various branches of the Colyns family, which is an example of how heresy was
transmitted through the family circle (cf. Gordon Rupp, *Studies in the Making of the English
Protestant Tradition* [Cambridge, 1949], p. 3). Joan Colyns, daughter of Richard and Alice,
was also noted for her learning, including of the Decalogue in which she was instructed by her
parents (and which she herself went on to teach), and Agnes Edmunds was said to have been
taken into the household as a servant so that she could be instructed in God's law, and while
there she 'had learned likewise the Ten Commandments'. Cf. below, Chapter 6, p. 201.
51   Lollard commentaries on the decalogue sometimes pass over the question of images
quite briefly. Cf. the treatise on the commandments in *Select English Works*, iii, pp. 82-92, and
the version printed alongside Thoresby's catechism in *The Lay Folks Catechism*, ed. T. F.
Simmons and H. E. Nolleth (EETS, OS 118, 1901), pp. 33-58, which latter may well have been
an independent tract on the decalogue. (For this suggestion and information on the manuscripts
of this text I am grateful to Anne Hudson). A commentary on the decalogue which goes further

usually possible to identify the actual text or commentary used by individual suspects.[52] One exception is *The Lantern of Light*, which. played an important part in the trial and condemnation of the London skinner, John Claydon, in 1415. This work (composed within the previous five or six years) included an exposition of the ten commandments with strong words against images under the first. This chapter, the longest in the book, constitutes about a third of the text, and it made an impression on one of its auditors. David Berde, Claydon's twenty-three year old domestic servant (illiterate like Claydon himself), who had listened to readings of the book and could vouch for his master's approval of it, knew it contained the decalogue in English. Though hazy as to details Berde said 'he well remembered about the first commandment of our lord Jesus Christ read out by John Fuller' (another of Claydon's servants, who acted as his reader). Among the fifteen errors and heresies that took Claydon to the stake as a relapsed heretic on 10 September 1415, two derived from *The Lantern of Light* are of relevance here: that material churches should not be sumptuously decorated with gold, silver, or precious stones, but the followers of Christ should worship God humbly in a simple house; and that images should not be pilgrimaged to, nor should Christians kneel before them, kiss or otherwise venerate them.[53]

Turning to Claydon's text we find that these views were based on

in this respect is in *English Works of Wyclif*, pp. 7-8. For Lollard commentaries (or interpolated versions of orthodox commentaries) on the Ten Commandments see A. L. Kellogg and E. W. Talbert, 'The Wycliffite *Pater Noster* and *Ten Commandments*', *BJRL*, xlii (1959-60), pp. 363-76; C. F. Bühler, 'The Middle English Texts of Morgan MS. 861', *PMLA*, lxix (1954), pp. 686-92; J. E. Wells, *Manual of the Writings in Middle English* (New Haven, 1916), p. 471; J. Burke Severs, *Manual of the Writings in Middle English* (Hamden, Conn., 1970), 2, pp. 362, 524.

52   For example in the case of William Redhead, maltman of Barnet, who abjured his error and burnt his book in 1427, we have a report that the heretical English book in question contained a tract condemning the worship of images as idolatry, which was evidently important in securing his condemnation, but there is no means of identifying the text. Amundesham, *Annales* ed. H. T. Riley (RS, London, 1870-71) i, pp. xxxvii, 13, 226-229; Thomson, *Later Lollards* p. 56; G. R. Owst, 'A 15th Century Manuscript in St. Albans Abbey', *St. Albans & Herts. Architectural & Archaeological Soc. Transactions* (1924), pp. 45-46.

53   *Reg. Chichele*, iv, pp. 132-138 (arts. 7 and 15, pp. 136-7); cf. *The Lanterne of Light* ed. L. M. Swinburn (EETS, OS 151, 1917), pp. ix-x, 41-43, 84-5 (cf. also art. 10 on church singing and *Lanterne*, pp. 58-9) For Claydon see Thomson, *op.cit.*, pp. 140-42; Kightly, 'Early Lollards', pp. 447-9, 513-19. Claydon had already been in trouble and imprisoned in 1395 and had had to abjure before he regained his freedom. The fifteen points of which he was accused in 1415 were said to have been found in the *Lanterne* and other books: all but one (no. 11 on the eucharist) can be linked with passages in the *Lanterne*.

√ words of St. Bernard and St. Augustine.[54] *The Lantern of Light* shows
how readily orthodox criticism of church splendour could overlap with
unorthodox opposition to imagery. It places such Lollards in a long
descent of purgers and pruners. Chapter 7, 'What is the material church
with her ornaments', which had much to say against rich ecclesiastical
buildings and decoration, supported these arguments with reference to
scripture, St. Jerome, St. Bernard and William of Saint-Amour.[55] The
author made a particular point of contrasting bequests which enriched
the material church with the needs of the deprived poor, harping on the
outstanding failings of the friars and religious orders whose forgotten
duty was to set an example of humble living.

> All holy saints agree in this, that our material church that is
> ordained for parishioners, where they come together, shall be
> made with virtuous means and in an honest measure. But in every
> respect it must be avoided that in this church any pride or luxury
> should show surpassingly, beyond the bounds of poverty, either
> in stone, timber or lead, either in glass, lime or plaster, either in
> bell, lamp or light, either in chalice, book or vestment, either in
> steeple, seats or painting, or other ornaments that belong to the
> church, and diligently this must be marked, that they bow to
> poverty, to eschew vain glory of this world, and glorify the cross
> of God.[56]

But how lamentably contemporary practice differed from this purist
ideal! The very length of the catalogue showed not only the dangers,
but the numbers of those who had succumbed to them. 'Many people
think it a meritorious work to deceive men's eyes with curious building,
and many vain staring sights in their churches'. The religious orders
were the worst offenders in this visual luxury. They constructed

---

54   *Lanterne*, pp. 37-8, 41, 85. It is worth noticing that in both cases the charge is a
condensation, or deduction, rather than an actual quotation from these passages. The author of
the *Lanterne* derived citations, including some of these, from the *Floretum/Rosarium* whose
source for the remark attributed to Augustine on the error of seeking 'God and his saints, not in
books, but in painted walls' remains unidentified; it is also cited elsewhere. *Fasciculi
Zizaniorum*, p. 372; *Apology for Lollard Doctrine*, p. 88; cf. C. von Nolcken, *The Middle English
Translation of the Rosarium Theologie* (Middle English Texts, 10, Heidelberg, 1979), pp. 35,
67, 101.

55   *Lanterne*, pp. 35-43; for some extracts and comments on this text see *Eng. Wycl.
Writings*, pp. 115-19, 195-6; cf. 65, 172, on objections to ornamented church buildings.
Wycliffe's appeals to history on clerical dominion included citation of St. Bernard; e.g. *De
Ecclesia*, pp. 66-67, 109, 316-17, 328, 516; and cf. Thomas Netter, *Doctrinale Antiquitatum
Fidei Catholicae Ecclesiae*, ed. B. Blanciotti (Venice, 1757-59), iii, cols. 898-9.

56   *Lanterne*, p. 41.

enormous buildings, unnecessarily withdrawing people from their parish churches. 'Lord! What meaneth these vast places of these hidden hypocrites, but to tell men by their synagogues where Satan's seat is?'[57]

Such abuse was damaging, dangerous. But nearer to the borderline of heresy was the *Lantern of Light's* open speech against images and pilgrimages which appeared in its exposition of the first commandment. 'The second trap of the fiend is called pilgrimage'.

> The painter maketh an image forged with diverse colours till it seems in the eyes of fools like a living creature. This is set in the church in a solemn place, bound fast with bonds, for it should not fall. Priests of the temple beguile the people with the foul sin of Balaam in their open preaching. They say that God's power in working of his miracles descends into one image more than another, and therefore 'Come and offer to this, for here is showed much virtue'. Lord, how dare these fiends for dread thus blaspheme their God and use the sin of Balaam that God's law hath damned, since Christ and his saints forsook this world's wealth and lived a poor life, as our belief teaches. Why gather riches, you priests, by your painted images, to make yourselves worldly riches in spoiling of the people?[58]

God forbade worshipping images with any godly worship, 'but that they be truly painted' to represent as faithfully as possible Christ and the saints to lay people. And Augustine had said that images should not be sought, sworn by, knelt to, kissed or trusted in.[59]

The idea that any one image was more worthy than another, more holy, more capable of working cures and miracles and therefore to be pilgrimaged to, had (as we have seen) been condemned as idolatrous by Wycliffe. Others repeated his words. Men make idols of images by putting overmuch trust in them, for 'many believe that image to be God, and many believe God's virtue subjectively to be therein, and thus they are more affected to one image than to another; that doubtless is idolatry, as true men say', wrote one Lollard, Englishing a sentence from *De mandatis divinis*.[60] The discriminating respect shown in

---

57   *Ibid.*, pp. 37-38. For another such attack see *English Works of Wyclif*, pp. 321-3.
58   *Lanterne*, pp. 84-85. (Balaam stood for avarice: 2 Peter II; 15).
59   *Ibid.*, p. 85. The remark here attributed to Augustine seems likely to be another from some epitome.
60   *Apology for Lollard Doctrines*, p. 88; cf. p. 139, n. 12 above. This quotation could have derived from the *Floretum/Rosarium*; cf. von Nolcken, *Rosarium Theologie*, p. 100. 'As true men say' is an example of Lollard self-naming; Anne Hudson, 'A Lollard sect vocabulary?' in *So meny people, longages and tonges: philological essays .. .. presented to Angus McIntosh*, ed. M. Benskin and M. L. Samuels (Edinburgh, 1981), p. 21.

pilgrims' treatment of cult statues, even the way in which they referred to them as localized personages ('Our Lady of Walsingham') seemed evidence of idolatrous reverence for the physical object itself. Constant harping on this argument rendered hopelessly suspect an approach which had once been innocuously reformist.[61] Heretical logic (before and after the Reformation) attached this criticism to a radical appraisal of the role of sanctified objects and places in general. To attack images on this score was too, as the *Lantern of Light's* indignant words declare, an aspect of anti-clericalism. Iconomachs who impugned images as a means of priestly profiteering were concerned with the failings of the church's administration as much as with the dangers to individual souls.

As time went on the contrast between the 'dead stones and rotten stocks' and the 'quick images' of God became one of the hallmarks of the Lollards.[62] References to 'dead images' could be seen as a signpost to heresy — even where the argument extended no further than reservations about image-worship. This phrase may be regarded as a component of the sectarian vocabulary in use among the heretics. The following passage, with its repeated harping on 'dead images', comes from a treatise on the ten commandments that expatiated on the dangers of false worship.

> Also he that worshippeth or prayeth to any image i-made of man with that worship and prayers that is only due to God and to his saints, maketh that image his false God. For such dead images be lewed men's books to learn them how they should worship saints in heaven after whom these dead images are shaped. And also that when men behold these dead images [they] should have the sooner mind and the more mind of the saints that be living in heaven, and to make these holy saints their mean between God and them, and not the dead images, for they may not help themselves nor other men. And certis if men had any kindness in themselves or any belief in God, they should not regard or ascribe it to these dead images the miracles that God doth alone by his own power, and believe that the image doth it himself.[63]

61   In 1313 Archbishop Greenfield's reform of a local cult was based on exactly this argument. On the similar criticism of Fitzralph and others see G. A. Benrath, *Wyclifs Bibelkommentar* (Berlin, 1966), pp. 34-5, n. 78; G. R. Owst, *Literature and Pulpit in Medieval England* (Oxford, 1961), p. 141; Jones, 'Art and Christian Piety', in *Image and Word*, ed. Gutmann, p. 90. For Lollard attacks on the localization of saints see below pp.168, 172, and *English Wycliffite Writings*, p. 87.

62   *Eng. Wycl. Writings*, p. 85; Hudson, 'A Lollard sect vocabulary?'. William White, who denied that any honour was due to images, ('any dead idol in church') said that 'trees growing in a wood are of greater virtue and vigour, and bear a clearer likeness and image of God, than stone or dead wood carved to the likeness of man'; *Fasciculi Zizaniorum*, p. 430; Netter, *Doctrinale* iii, cols. 940-1. For Oldcastle on worship to 'dead images' see Wilkins, *Concilia*, iii, p. 355. Lollards were not the first to speak of 'dead images' (Holcot, for instance, uses the term) but they gave it special currency.

63   BL MS Harl. 211, f. 48ʳ. Netter, replying to William White's point (see previous note)

The fullest exposition I have come across of the image prohibition in the decalogue is in a work, interesting for several reasons, that calls itself 'bonus tractatus de decem mandatis.[64] It is indicative of the wide no-man's-land lying between orthodox and unorthodox critics that this text has passed muster as representing the official attitude to images.[65] It does indeed accept and propound legitimate uses of church imagery, but it does a good deal more besides, and close inspection reveals its suspect character. Some of the marginalia draw attention to the arguments on images, suggesting a special interest in this issue.[66]

suggested inconsistency in the heretics for contrasting the dead wood of images with living trees, while at the same time showing such veneration for the gospel – kissing and saluting it and reverencing the very manuscript. By their own logic, surely a live sheep was better than dead skin and letters? *Doctrinale*, iii, col. 942. Cf. above Chapter 4, p. 110.

64   BL MS Harl. 2398, ff. 73^r-106^r, 'Explicit bonus tractatus de decem mandatis'. Two other manuscripts which contain shorter versions of this text, lacking the extended treatment of images, are BL MS Harl. 218, ff. 159^r-167^r and MS Royal 17 A XXVI, ff. 4^r-22^r, and this shorter commentary is printed from BL MS Add. 22283, ff. 92^r-93^v in *The Book of Vices and Virtues*, ed. W. Nelson Francis (EETS, OS 217, 1942), pp. 316-333. I owe this reference and generous help in answering questions about these texts to Miss Rachel Pyper, whose thesis, 'Middle English Prose Commentaries on the Ten Commandments', will include an edition of the MS Harl. 2398 tract and the more outspoken text in York Minster MS XVI L 12 (see n. 73 below). Harl. 2398 is a collection of English religious tracts which also includes a Lollard exposition of the paternoster printed in *Select English Works*, iii, pp. 98-110. Long quotations from the treatment of images in this text are cited by Owst, *Literature and Pulpit*, pp. 141-43, where by a slip this is said to come under the second, instead of the first commandment, and the whole argument is said to show 'very clearly the official attitude to images as set forth by the orthodox pulpit'. If the tract's view of images may be regarded as ambiguous, other passages reflect the author's Lollard sympathies. He harps on the duty of learning the commandments, not only asserting the obligations of priests to teach and publish them with all their might to the common people, but also wishing lords, ladies and gentles 'helping all true Christian people that is holy church' to teach them to their children and servants and to 'commune of them with lewed people that know no letters'. This author was in no doubt of the improvements that would follow if 'each man would busy himself to learn and commune [of] God's hests each with other as Christian men should do' (ff. 74^r-75^r: cf. above p. 144 for this as a heretical activity). Another passage suggestive of Lollard authorship is that on ff. 88^v-89^r on the duties of clerks, knights and labourers: the first should be 'most busy in God's law' and most removed from worldly living and if they failed they took God's name in vain, and 'some saith that antichrist hath changed all these offices for he challengeth to be king of the church of wicked men'; knights should 'show the power of the godhead and by worldly strength maintain god's law', and 'truly know God's law and officers in his church and what they should do and by strength strain them to travail in their office'; labourers should learn to keep God's law.

65   Owst, who describes a variety of criticisms of imagery, pointed out the narrow line dividing orthodox reformers from Lollard iconomachs (*Literature and Pulpit*, p. 49; cf. p. 135 ff. and *idem, Preaching in Medieval England* [Cambridge, 1926], pp. 119 ff., 283, 285, 291 ff.) It is possible that some of the other manuscript discussions of the decalogue referred to by Owst belong to this somewhat ambiguous category of marginal (one might say Wycliffite) Lollardy. This may be the case (though there are difficulties here) with the St. Albans manuscript described by Owst (see n. 52 above) which contains a full exposition of the commandments, critical of image-worship.

66   There are sidenotes throughout MS Harl. 2398. The section on images includes 'nota de ymaginibus' f. 80^v; 'nota bene' f. 82^r (opposite the Holcot quotation described below); 'de veneracione imaginum' f. 82^v.

Even a cursory inspection of the text would surely have given rise to some contemporary doubts. In the first place it was highly unusual for a conventional exposition of the decalogue to devote so much comment to imagery. The examination of the first commandment is longer than any of the others and while it treats (as was to be expected) of gluttony, lechery, covetousness, witchcraft, enchantments and divinations, most space by far is given over to the examination of images. This prohibition is quoted in full: 'Thou shalt have none alien gods before me, thou shalt not make thee an image graven by man's hand....'.[67] How was it to be interpreted? 'Here by this commandment some men peradventure think that it be forbid to make any images'. The anonymous commentator condemned this view. He cited against it the authorities that Bede had cited: the examples of Solomon's temple and Moses making the brazen serpent. 'By much more it is lawful for us to have the image of Christ in the cross. . . it is lawful to paint in holy church images of the twelve apostles and of other saints as we do worship fully and praisably in holy church'. The *making* of images was not forbidden. What was in question was their worship. In effect God had said 'thou shalt not make such images for to praise them or worship them as God'.[68] At this point the discussion moved into debatable territory. It did so with a flavour that is unmistakable.

'But here we shall understand that images may be occasion of good and also of evil. For a great clerk saith that images may be made well and also ill'.[69] The unnamed 'great clerk' was none other than Wycliffe. The words that followed were those from *De mandatis divinis* cited above. Gregory I's letters to Bishop Serenus of Marseilles were then quoted (as they had been by Wycliffe) to show that images should not be worshipped.

Having thus discreetly displayed his colours our author went on to make plain the extent of his reservations about image-worship. He effectively rejected the Thomist argument (upheld by Archbishop Arundel and propounded by Roger Dymoke against the heretics) that *latria* was owed to the crucifix as to Christ. Once more a nameless 'great

---

67   MS Harl. 2398, f. 74r (where the image prohibition is given in full); cf. ff. 78r, 80v-81r for repetitions.

68   *Ibid.*, f. 81r; Owst, *Literature and Pulpit*, pp. 141-2.

69   MS Harl. 2398, f. 81v; Owst, *op. cit.*, p. 142 (which does not identify the source). See above p. 138, n. 10 and *De Mandatis Divinis*, pp. 155-6, 159-60. Bede as well as Gregory had been cited by Wycliffe (above pp. 138, 140 and n. 21). The possibility of an intermediate source arises again, though the Wycliffite material is fuller (and the translation independent) than the *Rosarium*; von Nolcken, *op. cit.*, pp. 98-101.

clerk' was called as witness. 'I worship not the image of Christ for that it is wood, neither for it is the image of Christ, but I worship Christ before the image of Christ for it is the image of Christ and moveth me to worship Christ'.[70] The author cited this time was the Dominican Robert Holcot (d. 1349), who had sailed very close to the wind in discussing this question, and on whom more shortly. The 'good treatise' endorsed the religious use of images. They could increase people's devotion and should be treated with reverence. But they must − all of them − be excluded from *latria*. 'If we do offering and worship that is only appropriate to God to their [saints'] images, we not only then offend God, breaking his commandment, but also we offend all the holy saints of heaven'. This was unexceptionable providing (a big proviso) the crucifix was excluded from the argument. More dangerous words followed about the things, hateful to God, that were done to images 'that be but ... shadows made of wood or stone'.[71]

Worshipping God in his true image meant sustaining 'the meek true poor man that is the true image of God', instead of clothing, visiting and feeding

> dead images that neither thirsteth nor hungereth nor feeleth any coldness neither suffereth disease, for they may not feel nor see nor hear nor speak nor look nor help any man of any disease as the holy prophets witnesseth. And so who that trusteth on them worshipping them with worship that only pertaineth to God he maketh to him false and alien gods and breaketh the commandment of God.

What sort of worship was it (St. Clement had asked) to run about to stone and wooden images, worshipping 'vain images' which were without souls, setting men − the true divine images − at nought? Above all there was scripture. Nowhere in holy writ could Christ be found witnessing that the honours given to images made by men's hands amounted to honours done to him. 'But this is not said for that any man should despise images of holy saints and set them at nought, but for they should truly worship God in the true meek poor man that is a quick image of God'.[72]

70   MS Harl. 2398, f. 82ʳ; Owst, *loc. cit.* (also unidentified). There is a 'nota bene' against this quotation.

71   MS Harl. 2398, ff. 82ʳ⁻ᵛ; Owst, *op. cit.*, p. 143.

72   MS Harl. 2398, ff. 82ᵛ, 83ᵛ-84ʳ. 'Bot we redeth in no place of al holy writ that crist wytnesseth that he holdeth it y do to him that ys y do to any ymage y made of mannes hondes' (f. 83ᵛ), which put a scriptural question mark over the church's theory that the honour done to the image returned to the prototype. Cf. MS Harl. 31, f. 182ʳ, for a reply to the heretical argument 'quod debeamus ymagines facere non legitur in scriptura'. The reference to Clement was a stock source; cf. *Apology for Lollard Doctrines*, pp. 88-89; von Nolcken, *Rosarium Theologie*, pp. 99, 125.

The 'good treatise on the ten commandments' shows the heretics at odds with themselves. In explaining that the decalogue did not prohibit images, but only their false worship, in telling believers not to scorn imagery, but to give their alms rather to the poor, this work refuted would-be iconoclasts from a mildly iconomach position. In a pre-Lollard context the author need have used no evasion. As it was his subterfuge was an attempt to conceal his tendentious purpose. Wycliffite in attitude and academic in approach, he adopted Wycliffe's viewpoint and cited Wycliffe's words to answer the more radical views of 'some men'[73] among the Lollards. We are here privy, in fact, to some of the infighting of the sect in that large hinterland of deviancy on images and image-worship.

At this point it is worth digressing to consider Robert Holcot, because this may tell us something about the antecedents of Oxford heresy, as well as about the changed climate it introduced. Holcot's commentary on the *Book of Wisdom*, for which he was specially famous, was well known and often quoted in the following centuries.[74] The book was printed several times before 1500 and Cranmer's copy of the 1494 edition is in the British Library.[75] *Wisdom* contained a *locus classicus* on the origins of idolatry,[76] so it was natural that anyone interested in this question should turn to Holcot, as a major source. He does indeed include a full discussion of images and the lawfulness of image-worship.[77] This passage would have been of considerable interest to late fourteenth-century Oxford theologians and authors like the

73   On the use of this term (and perhaps also the 'true meek poor man' in the preceding paragraph) see Hudson, 'A Lollard sect vocabulary?' (n. 60 above), pp. 16-17, 20-21. The commentary on the first commandment in York Minster MS XVI L 12, f. 5^{r-v}, presents such a more extreme interpretation. God's opposition to image-making among the Jews was evident in many places in the Old Testament 'and the same God is now, with the same commandment. But here me thinketh that images done both good and harm ...', good as admonitory books, evil when loved for their own sakes, 'so that me would think, save better judgment, that it were more profit unto holy church, that all these images were left, as God bade the Jews ...' The emphasis is different, but we may still detect hidden echoes of Wycliffe's words in *De Mandatis Divinis* and *Sermones* (see above pp. 138, 142, nn. 10, 27). Miss Rachel Pyper kindly sent me a transcript of this passage.

74   B. Smalley, 'Robert Holcot O. P.', *Archivum Fratrum Praedicatorum*, xxvi (1956), pp. 5-97, esp. 10-14; J. C. Wey, 'The *Sermo Finalis* of Robert Holcot', *Mediaeval Studies*, xi (1949), p. 219. The Wisdom commentary, delivered in lectures, is dated by Smalley now to *c.* 1334-6: cf. her remark p. 85, 'How many readers were introduced to the scepticism of the schools through Holcot's plain speaking on Wisdom?'. For examples of authors who drew on Holcot's Wisdom (including Hoccleve and Lydgate) see Owst, *Literature and Pulpit*, pp. 180, n. 4, 221, n. 2.

75   The BL has copies of five incunable editions, including one of 1494 (IB 13732) which bears Thomas Cranmer's 'Thomas Cantuarien' and Lord Lumley's name. In what follows I quote from the 1489 Basel edition (IB 37324).

76   Wisdom, 14, esp. verses 12-15.

77   *Robertus Holkot super librum Sapientie*, Cap. XIII, lectio clvii B, 'Utrum imagines aliquas liceat christianis adorare'. All the following quotations come from this section, listed thus in the table of *questiones*.

writer of the 'good treatise', who were raking over the justifications for image-worship.

Holcot's passage on 'whether Christians may worship any images' looked at some of the main issues with startling clarity. The authorities against image-worship seemed blankly to contradict the usage of the church. There was Exodus (*'non facies tibi imaginem...'*). There was the canon of scripture in which nothing of the kind was to be found. ('It is to be noted that the apostles introduced the use of images into the church although nowhere is this expressed in the canon of the Bible'). At the outset there was ostensible contradiction. 'Therefore it seems superstitious to introduce such images. The rite of the church is to the contrary'.[78]

In explaining how it was that 'largely speaking' it was possible to talk about worshipping the image of Christ (leading up to the sentence quoted anonymously above), Holcot explored objections to the theories of St. John of Damascus and Aquinas about the honour returning to the prototype, and showed the difficulties about granting *latria* to the image of Christ. '*Latria* is the honour due only to God, but no image is God; therefore such honour is due to no image'. It was contradictory to this definition of *latria* to claim that it was owed to the image of Christ. How could the same honour be given to Christ and Christ's image without granting the creature that which belonged to God alone? It might rather be said that no worship should be given to this or any image. Yet, concedes Holcot, switching rather abruptly to expound the orthodox view, because the image of Christ moves us to worship Christ and to make our adoration of him before the representation, it can be said, loosely, that we worship the image. The church's understanding was that by virtue of the representation it was permissible, in front of an image of a saint, to worship whoever was represented by the image. Holcot ends, however, with a proviso. 'I do not think it good to say that the image and God who is imaged are honoured with the same honour'.[79]

78 'Item in canone scripture legitur nihil tale esse processum; ergo supersticiosum videtur tales imagines introducere. Ad oppositum est ritus ecclesie'. And later: 'Est autem notandum quod usum imaginum in ecclesia introduxerunt apostoli licet hoc in canone biblie nullibi exprimatur'.

79 '....latria est honor soli deo debitus, sed nulla imago est deus, ergo nulli imagini debetur talis honor.......Ideo aliter potest dici quod nulla adoratio debetur imagini nec licet aliquam imaginem adorare. Vera enim adoratio est in spiritu et devocione et amore summo et istam nullo modo debemus in aliquam creaturam dirigere. Quia autem propter imaginem christi excitamur ad adorandum christum, et coram imagine adorationem nostram facimus christo, ergo dicitur large loquendo quod imaginem adoramus. Unde videtur mihi dicendum quod nec adoro imaginem christi quia lignum nec quia imago christi: sed adoro christum coram imagine christi: quia est imago christi et excitat me ad adorandum christum .... Nec video pro nunc bene esse dictum quod eodem honore honoratur imago et deus cuius est imago'.

If one could read plenty into this passage, there was also food for thought in what followed. For Holcot next went on to consider the idea of man as the true image of God — in which he was followed by our anonymous commentator. A true living man was a closer image of God than a carving of wood or stone, so why should not God and Christ be worshipped in man rather than in a dead image? The innate qualities of man, as compared with the lack of, or modest worth of an image, accounted for the church's decision since the latter was less likely to be worshipped for itself.

This whole lecture, from which much could have been quarried, particularly on the topic of *latria*, was conducted with a freedom that was endangered by the popular challenge of the Lollards.[80] To suggest that there were difficulties about giving *latria* to the cross assumed a new dimension once ordinary people started refusing worship or kicking crosses. 'He said and asserted', a Lincoln diocese heretic was accused in 1400, 'that all who venerate and worship the sign of the holy cross commit idolatry and are reputed idolaters'.[81] The existence of such talk affected what could be said at all levels. The distinguished academic William Taylor went to the stake in 1423 for his persistent view of the idolatry involved in praying to any creature — whether it were to the saints or the humanity or cross of Christ.[82] The academic debate certainly continued, and was indeed revived and enlarged by the heretics' denials of image-worship. But the atmosphere was charged with contest, suspicion and concealment.

It would be valuable to be able to relate the post-Wycliffe discussions of images in more detail to earlier arguments. Clearly the Lollard challenge to image-worship did not arise in a vacuum. That the topic was a live one at Oxford is suggested by William Woodford's *questio* on 'whether God alone is to be worshipped, and should he be served alone', which formed part of his *Postilla super Matthaeum* of about 1372-3. This passage, which drew on earlier arguments including Holcot's and a commentary on the decalogue by the thirteenth-century Franciscan, Thomas Docking, defended image-worship (both the external act of worship and the internal mental adoration), and the

80   Is it possible that Holcot came to suffer some posthumous guilt by assocation? For an erasure of a remark entered at some time after 1389 in a manuscript containing Holcot's *Sentences*, which stated that some of his *questiones* were hard to obtain, see L. Minio-Paluello, 'Two Erasures in MS. Oriel College 15', *BLR*, iv (1953), pp. 205-7; J. A. Robson, *Wyclif and the Oxford Schools* (Cambridge, 1961), p. 241, cf.p. 134.

81   Wilkins, *Concilia*, iii, p. 249; Kightly, 'Early Lollards', pp. 113, 455.

82   *Reg. Chichele*, iii, pp. 67, 160, 162-9; *Fasciculi Zizaniorum*, pp. 412-13; Thomson, *Later Lollards*, pp. 24-26. In Taylor's case the emphasis was on prayer, not images, but the denial of image-worship is implicit in his premise that *latria* was due to God alone, and he was charged with saying that offering to the cross or any saint was idolatry.

church's use of imagery, in a manner that (it has been suggested) might seem to indicate some rumblings of opposition to image-worship.[83] Such a possibility raises interesting questions about the origins of Lollard iconoclasm, which had such evident difficulty in accommodating itself with Wycliffe.

Profit to Poor Men?

'Also I have read and taught . . . . against the shrining of saints' bones in gold and silver, and hanging about them the same'.[84]

Abjuration of John Croft of Eardisley
(February 1505).

The social injustice of images was a consistent strain of Lollard polemic. It was biblical in origin, harping on the texts that 'God created man in his own image' and 'dwelleth not in temples made with hands'.[85] Man, specially the man whose condition was that of Christ's own poverty, was the only true image of God. Man's creations, unlike God's, could never have life, and to treat them as if they had was worse than an insult; it was a death-sentence to the living. Lollards emphasized, as have many other reformers, the shocking contrast between the living and dead images of Christ. Given their conception of themselves as 'poor priests' and their repeated attacks on church endowments, it was natural for the Lollards to stress the argument that offerings given to images woefully deprived the poor. They enhanced the emotional appeal of this theme by suggesting that such increasing of the rich amounted to murder of the dispossessed. Oblations to 'dead stocks, or stones, or to rich clerks and feigned religious' led to the withdrawal of alms and 'shedding of blood and slaying of poor men'.

These words appear in the General Prologue to the second version of the Lollard Bible, written probably about 1396, a work which in giving a résumé of the Old Testament books necessarily touched on idolatry at a good many points. It also preached its own lesson.

Now men kneel, and pray, and offer fast to dead images, that have neither hunger nor cold; and despise, beat, and slay Christian men, made to the image and likeness of the Holy Trinity. What

83   J. I. Catto, 'William Woodford, O. F. M. (*c* 1330 – *c* 1397)', (D. Phil. Thesis, Oxford, 1969), pp. 150-55: I am grateful to the author for permission to use this work. For a work in defence of images that has been ascribed to Woodford see below p. 175.

84   *Register of Richard Mayew*, ed. A. T. Bannister (Cantilupe Soc. Pubs., 1919), pp. 66-67; Thomson, *Later Lollards*, p. 48.

85   Genesis 1, 27; Acts 7, 48; 17, 24. For a passage of pseudo-Chrysostom which was among the commonplaces cited see *English Wycliffite Writings*, pp. 181, 195.

honour of God is this to kneel and offer to an image, made of sinful man's hands, and to despise and rob the image made of God's hands, that is, a Christian man, or a Christian woman? When men give not alms to poor needy men, but to dead images, or rich clerks, they rob poor men of their due portion, and needful sustenance assigned to them of God himself; and when such offerings to dead images rob poor men, they rob Jesus Christ'.[86]

The case was restated in many of the texts put out by the heretics.

One can see an inevitable vein of anticlericalism running through these arguments. The beneficiaries of offerings to images were 'rich clerks' and 'feigned religious', as well as the gilded statues themselves. Views (like those of William Emayn) condemning both pilgrimage and almsgiving to images were often associated with feelings of outrage at the scale of ecclesiastical profits and possessions. The visible contrast in day-to-day experience between the ragged poor and the plush churchman was seen in terms of the contrast between the scriptural, actual, Christ and the ornate image on the crucifix. The modern church was untrue as well as unjust.

The proper beneficiaries of almsgiving were not parish or conventual or cathedral churches, but the poor. In a later age this reordering of charitable priorities became the official policy of the reformed church. But long before that we can find individuals who were acting on the scriptural belief that Christians should support living, not dead walls; give their alms to the poor, not to the fabrics and adornment of churches. It is a striking feature of the wills of suspect Lollard knights to curtail gifts to the structures and ministrations of the church. The bequests, so common elsewhere, towards making and maintaining images of the saints, are here conspicuously absent. At the lowly burials desired by these testators, and in their bequests, it was the poor and needy, poor men in russet, those who were 'poor and feeble, poor and blind, poor and crooked' who were remembered.[87] We seem here to be near the heart of what much Lollardy was about.[88]

The idea that offerings to images were a diversion of true

86   *Holy Bible*, ed. J. Forshall and F. Madden, (Oxford, 1850), i, p. 34. On the problem of dating the General Prologue see *Eng. Wycl. Writings*, pp. 173-4.

87   The wills of Sir Thomas Latimer and Anne Latimer, in *The Ancestor*, x (1904), pp. 20-21; McFarlane, *Lancastrian Kings and Lollard Knights*, p. 210 ff.; Kightly, 'Early Lollards', pp. 116-17, 347-8.

88   A humbler example of such transferred charity is the case of Thomas Ploman, accused in 1430 of having failed to pay any tithes or offerings to clergy or churches for the previous ten years; he claimed to believe it was lawful to give instead to the poor. It was mainly tithes that were in question here. *Norwich Heresy Trials*, pp. 16, 103: cf. 61, 141, 177, 179, 183, 185; cf. *Fasciculi Zizaniorum*, p. 428, for William White's teaching on this point.

almsgiving was still being voiced in the sixteenth century. James Brewster of Colchester, who was burned at Smithfield on 18 October 1511 together with William Sweeting — both of whom had objected to image-worship — had reportedly 'had much conference with Henry Hert, against oblations and images, and that it was better bestowed money which was given to the poor, than that which was offered in pilgrimage'.[89]

It was not a very long step from such beliefs to the idea (again paralleled in thinking on church endowments in general) that the costly coverings of images might justifiably be taken from them for the benefit of the living. 'Certis, these images of themselves may do neither good nor evil to men's souls, but they might warm a man's body in cold, if they were set upon a fire, and the silver and jewels upon them would profit to poor men, and the wax for to light poor men and creatures at their work'. Hezekiah had destroyed the idolized brazen serpent — even though it had been made by Moses on God's orders — so how much more should this be the treatment of 'false images made by sinful men'.[90] These were highly topical words, penned about the very time that a Leicester heretic was doing penance for having put this injunction very exactly to the test.[91] Breaking up and burning church statuary could be viewed as an act of charity, or at least of social justice. The poor were to benefit from the destruction, since the poor had suffered from the images' erection. Though its effect might look the same, this kind of iconoclasm must be distinguished from that — more true to the name — which smashed images in order to eliminate idolatry.

Censuring images for their wealth — where the gilded and bejewelled statues of pilgrimage shrines were specially in question — was a means of distinguishing between those that were acceptable and those that were not. This school of thought (perhaps broadly representative of moderate Lollard opinion) attacked images on the same lines as the heretics attacked priests: for misrepresenting Christ and their own calling by luxury and the pursuit of riches. Such critics were (like Wycliffe) quite prepared to accept that the right sort of images had a permissible role as teachers. They accepted the convention of images as laymen's books. But they called for action against untrue images, the gilded hypocrites that led to misbelief.

89   Foxe, *AM*, iv, p. 216.
90   From the 'Twenty-five articles', in *Select English Works*, iii, p. 463, which also condemned chanting, saints' days and the 'fat horses' of the clergy (p. 495). This text (on which see H. B. Workman, *John Wyclif* [Oxford, 1926], ii, p. 388-90) dates from before the death of Urban VI on 25 Oct. 1389, and its points were listed by Knighton; *Chronicon Henrici Knighton*, ed. J. R. Lumby (RS, London, 1889-95), ii, pp. 260-63.
91   See below pp. 167-9.

This case was presented in a late fourteenth- or early fifteenth-century 'treatise of images'.[92] 'Almighty God save thy people from erring in images', prayed the author of this work, citing Old Testament prohibitions and declaring that under the law of grace Christ 'commands not to make such images'. The main burden of his argument was directed against the vainglory of images as they were commonly made, rather than towards questioning the overall validity of the church's use of imagery.

> Since Christ was made man, unlearned men are allowed to have a poor crucifix, in order to have in mind the hard passion and bitter death that Christ suffered voluntarily for man's sin. And yet men err foully in this crucifix making, for they paint it with great cost, and hang much silver and gold and precious clothes and stones thereon and about it.[93]

As well as being a wicked waste, when the poor were dying of hunger and cold, simple people were thereby led into error through seeing Christ, the apostles and saints, painted as though they had lived in 'wealth of this world and lusts of their flesh'[94] like the greatest bon-viveur. There were ignorant people who misguidedly believed that images themselves wrought miracles, supposing 'that this image of the crucifix be Christ himself, or the saint that the image is set there for likeness [of]'.[95] And the falsities of shining statues promoted further wrongs, since almsgivers (like modern investors) tended to put their money where they saw evidence of wealth; gold attracted donors. 'For to the gayest and most richly arrayed image will the people soonest offer, and not to any poor image standing in a simple church or chapel'[96] — let alone to the truest of images, their poor neighbours.

92 *English Wycliffite Writings*, p. 83. (This is the first edition of the tract, of which extracts were given by Owst, *Literature and Pulpit*, pp. 143-5).

93 *Eng. Wycl. Writings*, p. 83. A remarkable example of an image decked with jewelled clothes, beads, girdle etc. is the Virgin in the chapel on the bridge at Derby, described in an inventory of 1488; J. C. Cox, *Churchwardens' Accounts* (London, 1913), p. 148. The case against gilding (see below p. 175) would have been reinforced by Baruch 6 (cited by Wycliffe, *De Mandatis Divinis*, p. 157; cf. von Nolcken, *Rosarium Theologie*, p. 100) which repeatedly condemns the falsity of gilded wooden statues.

94 *Eng. Wycl. Writings*, p. 84.

95 *Ibid.*, p. 87.

96 *Ibid.*, pp. 84-5, 88. In a passage similar to this attacking the falsity of gilded sculptures of Christ and the saints, Wycliffe averred that women were attracted to sumptuous statues of the Virgin, of gold, silver, and rich colours, for all the world like Diana of the Ephesians (Acts 19). Benrath, *Wyclifs Bibelkommentar*, pp. 35-6, 337-8. On pilgrims' expectations of dazzling reliquaries and jewelled displays at the shrines they visited see J. Sumption, *Pilgrimage* (London, 1975), pp. 153-55.

The 'treatise of images' included a call, perhaps more theoretical than practical, for the fire. Since images were books for the unlearned, to bring them to meditate on the Passion of Christ, those misleading images that taught vainglory rather than Gospel truths ought to be dealt with like lying books. 'They are worthy to be burnt or exiled, as books should be if they made mention and taught that Christ was nailed on the cross with this much gold and silver and precious clothes'.[97] The assumption is that truthful images (poor crucifixes, simple unadorned statues of saints) could remain, on a par with books. And yet, this Lollard could not help adding, with the idealist's sigh, how much better it would be if men could dispense with these visual aids and believe more spiritually. 'And now men should be more spiritual and take less heed to such sensible signs, as did the apostles of Christ', who did without paintings. 'For our Lord God dwells by grace in good men's souls and, without comparison, better than all images made of man in earth'.[98]

What such Lollards were saying to churchmen was; if you treat images as books, then there is as good a case for burning erroneous images as there is for burning erroneous books. The 'books of the laity' were to be judged on their merits.

> Though images made truly that represent verily the poverty and the passion of Jesus Christ and other saints are lawful, and the books of laymen, according to Gregory and other doctors, nevertheless false images that represent wordly glory and pride of the world as if Christ and other saints had lived thus and deserved bliss by glory and pomp of the world, are false books and worthy to be amended or to be burnt, as books of open error or of open heresy against Christian faith.[99]

No precise date can be put on this conclusion, but it may well have represented the views of a good many early Lollards, including those who were trying to remain faithful to Wycliffe's teaching.

The critics who would accept church sculpture provided it was

---

97   *Eng. Wycl. Writings*, pp. 83-4. (Owst, *op. cit.*, p. 144 misreads 'exilid' as 'exisid').

98   *Eng. Wycl. Writings*, p. 84.

99   H. F. B. Compston, 'The Thirty-Seven Conclusions of the Lollards', *EHR*, xxvi (1911), p. 743; cf. *Remonstrance against Romish Corruptions*, ed. J. Forshall (London, 1851), p. 23. This is Article 10 of the 37 Conclusions, which exist in both a short Latin form and a longer (and more extreme) English version. It is to be noted, for example, that the end of this article in the Latin reads 'sunt libri falsi et corrigendi vel *eciam* comburendi' (my ital.). The text has similarities to the General Prologue of the Lollard Bible, and has been postulated as being the larger book referred to in the 1395 'manifesto' (*Fasciculi Zizaniorum*, pp. 368-9) though there are reasons for doubting this. *Eng. Wycl. Writings*, pp. 198-99 (plausibly suggesting a date before 1401); cf. M. Deanesly, *Lollard Bible* (Cambridge, 1920), pp. 257, 282-3, 374-6, 379-81; Workman, *John Wyclif*, ii, p. 166.

truthful were focussing their attention on the painters and gilders rather than the carvers. It was those who 'paint...with great cost' who were at fault, rather than those who sculpted in the first instance. Sculptures must, it was repeated, be *'truly* painted', and that meant avoiding the contemporary fashion of decorating Christ and his saints with silver shoes and mantles of gold and the dazzle of worldly finery. Painting, to be valid, must be completely truthful, 'and not too splendid'.[100] (Would not such believers have approved Tilman Riemenschneider's innovation of using monochrome, instead of polychrome and gilding, on the finish of his altarpieces?).[101] The Elizabethan homilist who castigated the statues of 'men-saints' and 'women-saints' as all too similar to 'princes of Persia' or 'nice and well trimmed harlots' was elaborating on the same theme.[102] It was an approach not radical in itself — even if it was sometimes associated with remarks about giving images to the fire. Poor followers of Christ should have art that was suitable — humble and self-effacing.

One early Lollard who attempted, at least in self-justification, to retain this distinction between permissible true images and unlawful false ones was William Swinderby. Among the fifteen points of which Swinderby was accused by the bishop of Hereford in 1391 was that of having preached to his followers that they should in no way worship the image 'of him that was done on the cross', or the images of the Virgin or other saints, reproving such worship as idolatry. But, replied Swinderby, in a long defence which was in part prevarication, I did not speak in these terms. God surely forbade the worship of graven images (witness much biblical chapter and verse) and equally surely many men fell into the sin of idolatry by worshipping 'such dead images'. Yet he did not deny that 'images are good to those men to whom they are but calendars, and through the sight of them they know better and often worship God and his saints'. As laymen's books they could be beneficial; but when men trusted in them and worshipped them they were harmful, as Pope Gregory had written to Bishop Serenus.[103]

100   *Eng. Wycl. Writings*, pp. 83, 23 (my ital.), 84, 103, Cf. above p. 151 for the *Lanterne of Light* on this point.

101   M. Baxendall, *The Limewood Sculptors of Renaissance Germany* (New Haven & London, 1980), pp. 18, 186-89.

102   *Certain Sermons or Homilies* (Oxford, 1844), p. 235.

103   *Registrum Johannis Trefnant*, ed. W.W. Capes (Cant. and York Soc., xx, 1916), pp. 249-50; McFarlane, *John Wycliffe*, pp. 130-31. Compare Swinderby's list of Old Testament prohibitions of image-worship with Walter Brut's, 'concerning idols and their worship I feel the same as Moses, Solomon, Isaiah, Jeremiah and other prophets...' (*Reg. Trefnant*, p. 357, cf. pp. 364, 392). Swinderby's remarks about images as laymen's books, in which he quoted from Gregory's letter, are grammatically involved, but seem to be unambiguous in upholding images providing they remain only teachers; '...to tho men ben ymages goode to wham thai ben bot kalenders ...'). Russell-Smith, 'Walter Hilton', *Dominican Studies*, vii (1954), p. 201, n. 81, points out that the charge about images was raised against Swinderby after his first trial in 1382 — perhaps an indication of the emergence of the issue (see above p. 143).

Swinderby's defence was thus in line with a common Lollard view that images as lay books were acceptable, while image-worship was to be deprecated. It was the nature of this worship (that had troubled others long before Wycliffe) that was the problem. The Lollard case, specially when presented for ecclesiastical hearing, was not intransigent. It might be granted, for instance, that images could be reverenced as silent teachers in the way that clerks reverenced their books, without committing the sin of idolatry. Sculptures and paintings of saints must not be 'worshipped as God' (i.e. with *latria*), nor must the rood or even the very cross that Christ had died on, but that did not exclude the making and usefulness of imagery.

> But nevertheless the making of images truly painted is lawful, and men may lawfully worship them in some manner as signs or tokens; and that worship men do to them, if they love them and use them to that end that they are ordained for, as clerks do their books, despising the vows, prayers and sacrifices and misbeliefs unlawfully done to them.[104]

The Lollard case against images as potential books of error was therefore well argued, much of it narrowly unorthodox. This applied to the damning of one image in particular. Lollards, like Wycliffe, proscribed as a special source of error images of the Trinity, so often represented in the form of the crucified Christ sustained by the Father, with the Holy Ghost descending as a dove. Images of this kind were given prominence by receiving special mention in the Twelve Conclusions drawn up for parliament's attention in 1395. The eighth paragraph of this document objected that 'pilgrimage, prayers, and offerings made to blind roods and to deaf images of wood and of stone, are near kin to idolatry and far from almsgiving. And though this forbidden imagery is a book of error to the lay people, yet the usual image of Trinity is most abominable.'[105]

A Lollard who presented a full account of his view of images was William Thorpe. He was accused of having preached at Shrewsbury on 17 April 1407 (among other matters) 'that images should in no wise be worshipped'. Thorpe's determination on this point, and the related matter of pilgrimages, was given full treatment in his own description of his trial, in which the accused is never denied the opportunity of

104 *Eng. Wycl. Writings*, p. 23, cf. pp. 19 and 145 for the suggestion that these model answers were possibly intended for use in Lollard schools. Another of the points in this text was the danger of idolatry in setting lights before crucifix or other images.

105 *Fasciculi Zizaniorum*, pp. 364-5; H. S. Cronin, 'The Twelve Conclusions of the Lollards', *EHR*, xxii (1907), pp. 300-301; *Rogeri Dymmok Liber*, p. 180; *Eng. Wycl. Writings*, p. 27, and notes pp. 153-4. See above p. 139 for Wycliffe on this question.

speaking his mind in full. His opposition to images was based on both the Old Testament prohibitions and patristic authorities, the former clearly including the Decalogue (though there is no report of any discussion of the commandment text) and Hezekiah's destruction of the brazen serpent. Among the latter Gregory's letter to Serenus appears again as an authority against image-worship. Thorpe, however, was denying much more than the idolatry and erroneous doctrine that stemmed from mistaken attitudes towards images. He had reached a position that took him well beyond the 1395 manifesto — indeed well beyond the thinking of a good many early Protestants — to the point of denying that images should be accepted at all in their traditional role as books of the illiterate.

Men of the highest authority had, Thorpe recognized, looked on carving, casting and painting as 'a calendar to ignorant men that neither can nor will be learned to know God in his word, neither by his creatures, nor by his wonderful and divers workings'.[106] To Thorpe (as to many subsequent reformers) this was an admission of failure. If the faith were truly preached and God's works truly studied and known, no 'sinful and vain craft of painting, carving, or casting' would be needed by the church. It had had to call upon imagery because it had failed in other ways.

> For certes, sir, if the wonderful working of God, and the holy loving and teaching of Christ and of his apostles and prophets were made known to the people by holy living and true and busy teaching of priests; these things, sir, were sufficient books and calendars to know God by, and his saints, without any images made with man's hand.

Imagery was superfluous where the word of God was truly preached. 'When the faith of God is published in Christendom, the word of God suffiseth to man's salvation, without .... miracles; and thus also the word of God suffiseth to all faithful men and women, without any such images'.[107]

Thorpe, therefore, represents himself as arguing the ultimate case of

---

106   *Fifteenth Century Prose and Verse* ed. A. W. Pollard (London, 1903), pp. 121, 133-4. The accusations against Thorpe centered on the contents of this sermon. On Thorpe's narrative see *Eng. Wycl. Writings*, pp. 155-6.

107   *Fifteenth Century Prose and Verse*, pp. 135, 137. The word calendar, which appears elsewhere in this context, has the meaning of the most elementary, horn-book type of instruction in letters. For an example of its application to the cross see R. M. Haines, ' "Wilde wittes and wilfulness": John Swetstock's attack on those "poyswunmongeres", the Lollards', *SCH*, 8 (1972), pp. 150-51.

word against image, exalting the one to the exclusion of the other. Though he did not frame it thus, this was the cause of iconoclasm; the total repudiation of ecclesiastical imagery. Not surprisingly it met with a sharp rejoinder. Archbishop Arundel denounced Thorpe and his fellows as a rabble of would-be image-breakers. 'Then the archbishop said to me, "I hold thee a vicious priest, and a cursed! and all them that are of thy sect! for all priests of holy church and all images that move men to devotion, thou and such others go about to destroy! Losel! Were it a fair thing to come into a church and see therein none image?"'[108]

If such an exaggeration was really voiced by Arundel perhaps it was under the stress of extreme irritation. It was certainly not the case that all or even most of the Lollards who opposed the church's use of images were of Thorpe's thinking. But the call to destroy had been sounded in more than one context, and it is not surprising that the authorities paid attention. Iconoclasm for them was something that had been in the air from the very moment that the pernicious 'sect' first began trespassing on hallowed ground.

Destruction

'Whereof serve these images? I would they were brent every one'.[109]

Dives in *Dives and Pauper*

To what extent did the Lollards advance from advocacy to action, from speeches against imagery to actual image-breaking? Acts of iconoclasm were rare, but there were enough sporadic examples to keep the authorities on the alert through the fifteenth century and to penetrate their fears of Lollard intentions in general.

The first reported Lollard iconoclast was a layman, William Smith, a smith of Leicester. Henry Knighton, who described in detail this convert's ascetic existence (ostentatiously renouncing fish and flesh, women and wine) represented his eccentricities as the result of worldly disappointment. But there seems to have been a certain consistency in the smith's adopted way of life, including one incident which evidently caused particular local scandal.

William Smith, together with a chaplain called Richard Waytestathe, had established himself in the chapel dedicated to St. John the Baptist that stood near a leper house outside the east gate of Leicester. Here

---

108   *Fifteenth Century Prose and Verse*, p. 135.
109   *Dives and Pauper*, ed. P. H. Barnum (EETS, OS, 275, 280, 1976-80) i, p. 82; *Dives & pauper* (1496), sig. a vii^r.

they held meetings and taught their heretical views. According to the story the two Lollards one day found themselves short of fuel to cook their vegetarian meal, and looking about their chapel discovered in one corner an old painted statue of St. Catherine. It seemed an admirable opportunity to kill two birds with one stone; the saint could simultaneously cook their cabbage and be put to the final test of axe and fire. Let us try her sainthood, they said. If she is truly worthy of adoration she will bleed: if not, into the fire with her. So while one of them held the figure, the other took an axe and cut off its head.

The St. Catherine was burnt because it was a sham. It evinced no sign of life; it could not prove itself. Henry Knighton, commenting on the story of the image-burning (an event he deemed worthy of commemoration in verse), regarded it as a manifestation of a general heretical deviation. 'It was', he wrote, 'a feature of this Lollard sect to hate and attack images, and they preached that they were idols, and scorned them as likenesses (*simulacra*). And in referring to the blessed Mary of Lincoln or the blessed Mary of Walsingham, they called them witches, "the witch of Lincoln and witch of Walsingham" and so forth'.[110]

Knighton was not always dependable, even in his reporting of events at Leicester, and we cannot be sure of the exact date of this incident. But the chronicler's account of William Smith's treatment of the St. Catherine statue is corroborated by the record of the submission of Smith and Waytestathe before Archbishop Courtenay in November 1389.[111] Smith's penance was designed to make amends for his humiliation of the saint. He was to walk barefoot, bare-headed, in his shirt, before the procession in the collegiate church of St. Mary's, Leicester, carrying in his right hand an image of St. Catherine, and to kneel devoutly three times — at the beginning, middle and end of the procession. This object-lesson was to be repeated in the market-place of

---

110   *Chronicon Henrici Knighton*, ii, pp. 182-3, cf. 183-4 for the Latin verse on the incident. Knighton says that immediately after this affair Smith and Waytestathe were ejected from the Leicester hospice. For Smith's activities see Crompton, 'Leicestershire Lollards', pp. 19-20, 24-25; and on Knighton's limitations as a reporter, *ibid.*, pp. 15-16; McFarlane, *Lancastrian Kings and Lollard Knights*, p. 141; Kightly, 'Early Lollards', pp. 52-55 (suggesting that Waytestathe may have been an officially appointed guild chaplain, not just a squatter in a deserted building, as Knighton insinuates). For Lollard sarcastic punning on the names of great pilgrim centres see Thomson, *Later Lollards*, p. 126 and below p. 172.

111   Knighton's chronology may not be right and (as the 1389 penance perhaps suggests) the image-burning may have taken place after, rather than (as Knighton indicates) before the spring of 1382. The chronicler wrote this passage some eight years after that date, and certainly made some mistakes. Kightly, *op. cit.*, pp. 54, 85; V. H. Galbraith, 'The Chronicle of Henry Knighton', in *Fritz Saxl ... Essays*, ed. D. J. Gordon (London, 1957), p. 139.

Leicester during the Saturday market, and again in his parish church the following Sunday. Two other offenders, Roger Dexter and his wife Alice, were ordered to do penance with Smith. They each had to carry a crucifix, evidently in token of their refusal to worship 'any cross'. While the smith was sufficiently literate to be ordered to recite an antiphon and collect for St. Catherine, the unlettered Dexters were to say the Ave Maria and paternoster.[112]

Another early report of action against images is specially interesting in being attributed to one of the suspect Lollard knights. The sole narrator in this case was Thomas Walsingham, but he might well have had inside information since the manor where the event took place was only six or seven miles from St. Albans. According to the chronicler, at some time either during or before the year 1387 (the date is not clear), Sir John Montagu (later earl of Salisbury) had all the images removed from the chapel of his manor at Shenley in Hertfordshire. He had them all 'taken down and hidden in secret places, allowing only one, an image of St. Catherine, the privilege of being taken to the bakehouse, because many people were fond of it'.[113] The estate at Shenley, which had come to Montagu between 1381 and 1383 through his marriage with the widow of two prominent Londoners, was the knight's place of residence, and this action cannot be dismissed as a domestic quirk.[114] It was an example of behaviour which other Lollards, who did not enjoy the advantage of possessing a private chapel, would have liked to imitate. The humble William Smith in effect did enjoy such a privilege. There was, however, a great difference between the knight's and the blacksmith's treatment of their images. Montagu did not break up his statues or put them to trial by fire. He simply put them away, where they would not be worshipped and could do no harm. Though their horror of idolatry may have been equal, iconomach and iconoclast, the image-hater and the image-breaker, used wholly contrasting methods.

As I show more fully elsewhere, there could be good reasons for choosing *burning* for the destruction of idols, rather than any other method.[115] Apart from the fact that a wooden carving would make

112 *The Metropolitan Visitations of William Courtenay*, ed. J. H. Dahmus (Illinois Studies in the Social Sciences, xxxi, No. 2, Urbana, 1950), pp. 170-72; *Chronicon Henrici Knighton*, ii, p. 313; Crompton, 'Leics. Lollards', pp. 24-25; McFarlane, *John Wycliffe*, p. 140. Waytestathe was reconciled with the church with no mention of penance.

113 *Chronicon Angliae*, ed. E. M. Thompson (RS, London, 1874) p. 377; *Thomae Walsingham Historia Anglicana*, ed. H. T. Riley (RS, London, 1863-64), ii, p. 159, cf. p. 244. (Kightly, 'Early Lollards', pp. 356-7, relates Walsingham's statement that Nicholas Hereford visited Shenley to the heretic's movements).

114 Workman, *John Wyclif*, ii, p. 383 was sceptical; cf. McFarlane, *John Wycliffe*, pp. 146-7; *idem, Lancastrian Kings and Lollard Knights*, pp. 168, 175, cf. 199; W. T. Waugh, 'The Lollard Knights', *Scottish Hist. Rev.*, xi (1914), pp. 73, 88.

115 This is discussed in my forthcoming 'England's Iconoclasts'.

good fuel (and so reduce the miseries of the poor) the burning of idols, like the condemnation of their worship, was based on Old Testament injunctions. The old law might indeed be regarded as having specifically enjoined the destruction of false images by fire. 'These images of themselves may do neither good nor evil to men's souls, but they might warm a man's body in cold, if they were set upon a fire'.[116] There was Old Testament fidelity in such a view, whether or not the writer had in mind any particular passage, such as Deuteronomy 7 ('burn the graven images') or Isaiah 44, deriding the vanity of the idol that was made from the selfsame trunk which the carpenter used to warm himself and to bake his bread.[117] Whatever the degree of their biblical knowledge, William Smith of Leicester and some of the heretics who followed him were as true to Old Testament prescription as were subsequent reformers who followed the same path.

It is clear too, that for Lollards, like many other iconoclasts, chopping up or burning an image was not just a way of eliminating wooden carvings of saints that had been wrongly venerated. It was a method of disproving supposed miraculous powers, the best argument there could be of the lack of relationship between lifeless represent-ation and actual saint. Denying images meant repudiating their mira-culous properties.[118] No power could make a dead image bleed. The Leicester iconoclasts were making the same point as Richard Wyche, who twenty years later renounced his view that 'God cannot by his ordained power make an image bleed or alter [i.e. ? liquify] blood'.[119] A barely recorded incident of image-burning at Loddon in Norfolk in the 1420's was associated with talk about crosses not being able to bleed.[120] And the idea of fire as the ultimate disproof of an image's alleged supernatural powers seems to lie behind the words of Elizabeth

---

116   Above, p. 161, n. 90.

117   Deut. 7, 5 ff.; 12, 3 ff., in *Holy Bible*, ed. Forshall and Madden, i, pp. 484, 496; 'But rather thes thingis ye shulen doo to hem; the auters of hem underturneth, and brekith togidres the ymagis, and the mawmet wodis hewith down, and the graven thingis brenneth': 'Scatre ye the auters of hem, and brekith togidre the ymagis; the mawmet wodes brenneth with fier, and the mawmettis destruy ye'. Isaiah 44 was cited in Wycliffe's *De Mandatis Divinis*, p. 157; cf. von Nolcken, *Rosarium Theologie*, p. 100.

118   This was a point made in the 'Twenty-five articles', *Select English Works*, iii, p. 462; '...and that God does not any miracle by them'; cf. *Chronicon Henrici Knighton*, ii, p. 261.

119   'Deus non potest facere de sua potentia ordinata imaginem sanguinare vel sanguinem minuere'; *Fasciculi Zizaniorum*, p. 501; BL MS Royal 8 F XII, f. 16r. It seems possible that *'minuere'* (to alter, modify) is a mistranscription of *'minere'* (to colour red). On Wyche see below p. 171 and M. G. Snape, 'Some evidence of Lollard activity in the diocese of Durham in the early fifteenth century, *Arch. Aeliana*, 4th Series, xxxix (1961), p. 359; Kightly, 'Early Lollards', p. 18.

120   Below p. 172.

Sampson, cited for heresy by Bishop FitzJames of London in 1509. Our Lady of Willesden, she was reported to have said, 'was a burnt arse elf and a burnt arse stock, and if she might have helped men and women which go to her on pilgrimage, she would not have suffered her tail to have been burnt'.[121]

Monastic chroniclers and diocesan bishops alike did not discount the possibility that those who aired views about burning or breaking might act on their words. Heretics continued to crop up who were accused not only of denying that images should be worshipped, but also of advocating their destruction, in particular their destruction by fire. 'I am charged with having preached that images should not be worshipped, but rather put to the fire', wrote Richard Wyche, defending his opposition to image-worship with a tapestry of quotations, biblical and patristic.[122] In the year that Wyche was eventually burned, 1440, a weaver of Farnham in Surrey, Adam Millward or Sims, was charged with having planned to burn an image of the Virgin.[123] Among the subjects of Bishop Alnwick's proceedings in Norfolk in 1429-30 we have already met William Colyn preferring to have his parish images burnt rather than repainted, and another man, Richard Fletcher of Beccles, abjured the view 'that no worship should be done to any images, but that all images ought to be destroyed and done away'.[124] Alice Hignell of Newbury, who abjured early in 1491, was suspect for denying images on various scores, including the desire to chop them up for firewood, and Foxe recorded the opinion of Richard Hegham, one of eight Coventry suspects of 1486, that if the image of Our Lady of the Tower were put into the fire, it would make a good fire.[125]

Iconoclasm was practised as well as preached by some of the heretics in the diocese of Norwich who were investigated at the end of the 1420s. At a gaol delivery held at Norwich Castle in February 1429, the justices (acting in accordance with the statute of the Leicester

---

121   Reg. FitzJames (London), f. 4ʳ; Foxe, *AM* (1641), i, p. 1012; *AM*, ed. Pratt, iv, p. 126. These words suggest that the statue had been damaged in some fire. Elizabeth Sampson was also said to have called the image of St. Saviour at Bermondsey 'Sim Saviour with kit lips'. Thomson, *Later Lollards*, pp. 160-61, on the dating of this case.

122   *Fasciculi Zizaniorum*, p. 370. On Wyche see Thomson, *op. cit.*, pp. 148-50; McFarlane, *John Wycliffe*, p. 162. Obviously it has to be borne in mind that the questions put to suspects may reflect the suspicions of the authorities quite as much as (or more than) the actual tenets of individual heretics. Thomson, *op. cit.*, p. 224 ff.; Anne Hudson, 'The Examination of Lollards', *BIHR*, xlvi (1973), pp. 145-59.

123   Thomson, *op. cit.*, p. 64. The charge against Millward included plotting the death of the king and spoliation of the church, suggesting association with the ideas of Oldcastle's circle.

124   *Norwich Heresy Trials*, pp. 86, 91 and above p. 147; Thomson, *op. cit.*, pp. 124, 126.

125   Thomson, *op. cit.*, pp. 77, 104; Foxe, *AM*, iv, p. 133.

Parliament of 1414) assigned to the bishop of Norwich six men arrested as suspect Lollards, several of whom were examined by Bishop Alnwick during the coming months. Among the charges against them was one of which the surviving trials make no mention. It was stated that two husbandmen, John Skilly of 'Bergh' (probably Bergh Apton) and William Wardon of Loddon (a village a few miles away) on the night of 5 February 1427, had made an armed entry into the cemetery of the church of St. Andrew at Trowse Newton. They had there taken possession of an image of the church's patron saint, valued at two shillings, which they carried away to Bergh Apton, 'and there they falsely and treacherously burnt the said image'.[126]

Though we cannot follow this incident any further it does not stand quite on its own. John Skilly may perhaps be identified as John Skylan of Bergh Apton, who abjured his heresies before the bishop of Norwich in the chapel of the episcopal palace on 4 August 1430. This abjuration included acknowledgement of his assocation with various well-known heretics, including Hugh Pye, and recantation of his rejection of images as idols and his attack on pilgrimages done to 'the Lefdy of Falsyngham, the Lefdy of Foulpette and to Thomme of Cankerbury'.[127] William Wardon may have been present at another near-iconoclastic incident at Loddon in July 1428, when a heretic hit out against a cross. We also learn from a terse report in the trial of this offender that the clerk of Loddon 'burnt images in Loddon'.[128] This suspect John, clerk of Loddon, cannot be identified but it seems reasonable to link these goings-on with the case of Hugh Pye, chaplain of Loddon, who was burned in 1428. No official record of his trial survives, but Foxe reports three charges brought against him in July 1424 by Alnwick's predecessor, Bishop Wakering, of which the third was; 'that the image of the cross and other images are not to be worshipped; and that the said Hugh had cast the cross of Bromehold into the fire to be burned, which he took from one John Welgate of Loddon'.[129] The evidence is fragmentary but it seems likely that Hugh

---

126   *Norwich Heresy Trials*, p. 218. Trowse Newton is just outside Norwich, about five miles from Bergh Apton, eight from Loddon.

127   *Ibid.*, pp. 144-151 (quote at 148), punning on Walsingham, Woolpit, and Canterbury. ('Lefdy' = lady).

128   *Ibid.*, p. 76 and n. 45, p. 46.

129   Foxe, *AM*, iii, p. 586. (Foxe's 'Ludney' may be identified as Loddon, and 'Bromehold' as Bromholm.) On Hugh Pye, whose influence on the heretics of Norwich diocese is evident in twelve of Bishop Alnwick's trials, see Thomson, *Later Lollards*, pp. 120, 125; Amundesham, *Annales*, i, p. 29 (where he is seen as the chief of those burned at Norwich in 1428); F. Wormald, 'The Rood of Bromholm', *JWCI*, I (1937), pp. 41-2.

Pye — whom one contemporary considered a Lollard of some standing — was responsible for this nest of iconoclasts in Loddon.

Some of the extremist Lollards who desired or dared the destruction of images supported Sir John Oldcastle's radical plans. Roger Swan, one of the men of Daventry charged with complicity in the 1414 rising, was also accused of having violated an image of the Holy Trinity. And Walter Coggeshall, an Essex weaver who had moved to London by the time of the revolt, was indicted by jurors in Braintree for his Lollard views, which included a recommendation that the image of St. Saviour in Bermondsey — disparagingly dubbed 'Sim Saviour' — should be thrown down.[130] Whiffs of these associations drifted about for years. The parish clerk of Byfield in Northamptonshire who went so far as to cut off and burn the head of an image of the Virgin in his parish church on the night of 26 December 1416, was accused of knowing Oldcastle. Nearly a decade later John Walcote, a west country shepherd of Hazleton, near Northleach in Gloucestershire, who had had links with Sir John and another rebel of 1414, expressed views against images, including a readiness to burn them.[131]

The Oldcastle rising also brought to light the only known example of Lollards destroying a painted image. In 1417 — when Oldcastle himself was believed to be concealed in the neighbourhood of St. Albans — the abbot's men undertook a nocturnal search. Among the discoveries were some service-books in which the names and illuminated haloes of saints had been blasphemously defaced. One such text was sent to the king who passed it on to the archbishop of Canterbury to serve as an object-lesson for Londoners.[132] Possibly this revelation and the publicity it received reinforced the impression conveyed by some defenders of orthodoxy, including Hoccleve in the reprimand he addressed to Oldcastle in 1415, and Thomas Netter some years later in his *Doctrinale*, that the heretics condemned paintings as well as sculpture.[133]

Our knowledge of the image-breakers is fortuitous, incomplete. Contemporary reporting may alert us to the disappearance of what was common knowledge, once notorious, now impenetrable. An example of this appears in the sole Middle English poem exclusively devoted to the

130   Kightly, 'Early Lollards', pp. 142, 384, 387. Cf. above n. 121 on the nickname of the Bermondsey image.

131   Thomson, *op. cit.*, pp. 27-8, 100; Kightly, 'Early Lollards', pp. 147-8, 260-61, 463.

132   *The St Albans Chronicle 1406-1420*, ed. V. H. Galbraith (Oxford, 1937), p. 115; *Historia Anglicana*, ii, p. 326, cf. p. 317; Thomson, *op. cit.*, p. 13; Kightly, *op. cit.*, pp. 403-4.

133   Netter, *Doctrinale*, iii, col. 920; 'Cum imaginum sculpturas, *aut picturas* aspiciunt, idola vocant, et earum artifices et cultores jungunt idololatris' (my ital.). See also above p. 146.

Lollards. 'Defend us from all lollardry', written not long after Oldcastle's rising, blames the heretics for their hatred of pilgrimage statues and alludes to what was evidently a well-known example of Lollard iconoclasm.

> And namely James among them all
> for he twice had tournament,
> Much mischance may him befall
> that last beheaded him in Kent;
> and all that were of that assent.[134]

There appears to be no other reference to this repeated beheading of a statue of St. James, located somewhere in Kent.

Not all image-breakers were necessarily Lollards. A curious affair at Exeter was brought to the attention of Archbishop Chichele by the Franciscans of the city in 1421. Ill-disposed locals (it was complained) had profaned the friars' close, the Friernhay, by illicit entry and sacrilegious treatment of the noble tombs and imagery inside. The offenders broke the barred door of the friars' chapel and then 'tore to pieces and pulled down the image of the Virgin' and the arms of Henry V depicted in the windows. The report was taken seriously by the archbishop. He directed letters to the parochial clergy throughout his province ordering them to publish the excommunication of the offenders, and to try to discover their identity. If the culprits were found they were to be examined by Chichele himself or before his court of audience.[135]

No mention was made here of Lollardy or heresy. Yet there are suspicious reverberations in this incident. The heretics' notorious hostility towards the mendicants was accompanied, as we have seen, by attacks on the wicked costliness and ornamentation of their churches. In this case the recent restoration of the Franciscan chapel may have added provocation. The fact that it housed the tombs of 'many nobles' would also have condemned it in the eyes of those who disapproved of

---

134   *Historical Poems of the XIVth and XVth Centuries*, ed. R. H. Robbins (New York, 1959), pp. 156, 331-32. Kightly, 'Early Lollards', p. 405 points out that this incident, though obscure to us, was apparently well known at the time.

135   R. Foréville, 'Manifestations de Lollardisme à Exeter en 1421?', *Le Moyen Age*, lxix (1963), pp. 691-706 (quoting from p. 705, which seems to be somewhat misread p. 691). Kightly, 'Early Lollards', p. 352, n. 1 is sceptical of Lollard influence on this incident. It is worth noting in this context a later case from Exeter diocese in which a statue of the Virgin was dishonoured. In 1441 Hugh Knight, husbandman, was excommunicated for having used candle smoke to give a beard to the image of the Virgin at Newport chapel, in the parish of Bishop's Tawton, Devon, saying derisively, 'Mable, ware thy berde'. F. D. Logan, *Excommunication and the Secular Arm in Medieval England* (Toronto, 1968), pp. 52, n. 48, 190.

lavish displays for the dead. Riot behaviour has its own patterns and fashions. Though no charge of heresy followed this occasion it remains possible that there were some elements of imitative action at work — just as in the sixteenth century image-breaking entered the vocabulary of rioters once protestant iconoclasts had given the lead.

Lollard logic pointed in contrary directions. Trenchant criticism of the arts produced a variety of conclusions, some more radical than others. One opponent of the heretics (possibly William Woodford) suggested that

> if it were true that the making of images or carvings is in general against the first commandment, then it would follow that all artists, painters, illuminators of books, moneyers, carpenters, goldsmiths, sculptors, and in short all craftsmen who make likenesses or images of things by carving, weaving or painting would be sinning mortally and their arts illegal and to be destroyed.[136]

Such reductive reasoning was to be used against iconomachs after the Reformation. And Lollard proscription of the arts does seem in some cases to have moved beyond the church. The Twelve Conclusions of 1395 included among its controversial paragraphs a condemnation of the 'waste, curiosity and disguising' fostered by the church's unnecessary multitude of crafts. These were to be destroyed for the increase of virtue.[137] Goldsmiths were singled out with armourers for special mention, objections to the former doubtless being linked with thoughts about those gilded statues that stole from the backs and bellies of the poor.[138] It sounds as if William Bate, an East Anglian heretic of 1430 who attacked the 'crafts of painters and gravers' as unnecessary, shared this line of thinking.[139] The makers of images as well as the images themselves came under Lollard criticism. And in the

136   'Si ymagines facere vel aliquod sculptile sit generaliter contra preceptum prime tabule, sequitur tunc quod omnes tinctores, pictores, illuminatores librorum, monetarii, carpentarii, aurifabri et sculptores et breviter omnes artifices qui solent facere et earum similitudines vel ymagines sculpendo, texendo vel pingendo peccarent mortaliter cum eorum artes sint illicite et per consequens destruende'. BL MS. Harl. 31, f. 182[r-v]; cited *Eng. Wycl. Writings*, p. 155.

137   Cronin, 'Twelve Conclusions' (n. 105 above), p. 304; *Fasciculi Zizaniorum*, p. 368; *Rogeri Dymmok Liber*, p. 292; *Eng. Wycl. Writings*, pp. 28, 154. It is to be noted that while the text in the *Fasciculi* refers to the arts 'in nostro regno', the Cronin version has 'in nostra ecclesia'.

138   Roger Dymoke, replying to this article, justified the art of goldsmiths' work in the service of the church with reference to the example of the tabernacle in Exodus 31. For a contrary Biblical case in the heretics' repertory see n. 93 above.

139   *Norwich Heresy Trials*, pp. 158, 160; cf. 148; Thomson, *Later Lollards*, p. 129; cf. p. 160 for a woman of Southwark, 1508, who condemned image-makers as well as image-worshippers.

sixteenth century there were painters who seem to have been swayed by the heretics' arguments. William Smith of Ombersley (Worcs.) was examined in 1511 for his refusal to paint St. Paul as an apostle on the grounds that the Bible made no mention of this calling, and the same year the bishop of Coventry and Lichfield wrote to the bishop of Lincoln about two painters who were living together at Leicester, and both reported to be against image-worship and to deny the true faith of the eucharist.[140]

Doctrinaire consistency took some Lollards to a position as extreme as that of many later separatists. The charge that intending rebels aimed to despoil cathedrals and other churches and religious houses of their relics and possessions and raze them to the ground may sound unrealistic to the point of fantasy,[141] but it consorts with other opinions. If it was the duty of the king to withdraw temporalities from offending clergy, the secular authorities also had obligations to purify church buildings. The Christian ruler should follow the example of Hezekiah and 'with assent of his lords and true clergy should break or burn dumb idols'.[142] Ultimately God's word called them to 'destroy the places wherein heathen men did idolatry'.[143] John Lydgate, rising to the defence of the church, pointed the prince in the opposite direction, against those

> that of presumption
> Dispraven her [holy church] , and her ornaments,
> And therewithal, of indignation
> Withdraw would her rich paraments.[144]

The other face of the reforming coin was quietist withdrawal. Some people prefer to turn their backs in retreat rather than throw stones. Lollards disparaged church buildings as unnecessary, as well as offensively gaudy. There were others like Anne Palmer of Northampton who thought that 'it suffices every Christian to serve God's commandments in his chamber, or to worship God secretly in the field, without call for public prayers in a material building'.[145] Those who denied the

---

140   Thomson, *op. cit.*, p. 49; Fines, 'Heresy Trials', *JEH*, xiv (1963), p. 171.

141   Cf. the note of caution about the 'exaggeration on all sides' sounded by R. H. Hilton, in *Peasants, Knights and Heretics* (Cambridge, 1976), p. 8. For one such exaggeration see above p. 167, n. 108.

142   *Remonstrance against Romish Corruptions*, ed. Forshall, p. 25.

143   *Holy Bible*, ed. Forshall and Madden, i, p. 6, in a summary of Deuteronomy (see n. 117 above). Cf. the preceding sentences on the duty of learning the commandments (Deut. 11; 19-20).

144   John Lydgate, *Poems*, ed. J. Norton-Smith (Oxford, 1966), p. 33: (paraments are decorations, hangings).

145   McHardy, 'Bishop Buckingham', *SCH*, 9 (1972), p. 143.

spiritual value of images were consistent when they also believed that churches were an irrelevance in the face of God's universal presence. 'Material churches be but of little avail and ought to be but of little reputation, for every man's prayer said in the field is as good as the prayer said in the church'. [146] The repudiation of images could mean the repudiation of a great deal else besides.

The Defence of Images

'Were it a fair thing to come into a church and see therein none image?'[147]

Archbishop Arundel to William Thorpe (1407)

The church's response to the Lollard challenge to images was impressive. A series of replies appeared in Latin and in the vernacular, some devoted specifically to this question, and since the university texts remain in manuscript the scale of this reaction has not been properly appreciated.[148] When it has been fully explored we may have to revise some of our ideas about first generation Lollardy. Central to the debate was the honour owed to the crucifix which, as indicated above, was already proving bothersome before the mid-fourteenth century. One of the more interesting aspects of this whole controversy is the fact that it was not a topic that had excited Wycliffe. On this matter his followers, willy nilly, had to break their own ground. This applied to Bohemian disciples of the Oxford master, as well as English ones.

Both sides had to admit that Wycliffe had not written much about images. 'Search as you will', wrote Netter, 'and you will not find him against the makers [*conditores*] of images, or to have said much about their ecclesiastical use'. And this, Netter went on (exploring the issue at some length in his *Doctrinale*), was upsetting to Wycliffe's followers who 'accused him of senselessness for not having dared expressly to condemn them. Therefore they themselves did not cease to preach and make tracts and public attacks on holy images.'[149]

In Bohemia Peter Payne, or some other English Wycliffite, took it

146   *Norwich Heresy Trials*, p. 58, cf. p. 53.
147   *Fifteenth Century Prose and Verse*, p. 135.
148   For references to the manuscript sources see the works of Jones ('Lollards and Images') and Crompton, cited n. 3 above, and *Eng. Wycl. Writings*, p. 180. Cf. also E. Ruth Harvey's summary of the defence of images in *Complete Works of St. Thomas More*, Vol. 6, Pt. II, ed. T. M. C. Lawler et al. (New Haven & London, 1981), pp. 748-59.
149   Netter, *Doctrinale* iii, col. 902.

on himself to fill this gap. In 1417, when images became an issue in Prague and Jakoubek of Stříbro began preaching against their misuse, the evangelical doctor was defended in a treatise 'De ymaginibus'. While pointing out (like Wycliffe) that the early church had no images, this author expounded Wycliffe's view that images could serve as books of the laity, but ran the danger of both misleading and being treated as idols. He used the example Wycliffe had used of Trinity imagery, but he seems to have extended (as English heretics did) Wycliffe's comments on the kinds of worship into a denial of the acceptability of giving *latria* to the cross. 'All lawful worship [*adoracio*] of the image of the saviour is *dulia*; no *dulia* is *latria*. Therefore no lawful worship of the image of the saviour is *latria*'.[150] This was to cross the critical line that turned so many critics of image-worship into heretics.

The defenders of images were in no doubt that the case they had to answer was at least in part iconoclastic. It was taken for granted that the heretics who rejected church images talked in terms of destruction. 'Whereof serve these images? I would they were all burnt'. Dives, the devil's advocate, put the case to Pauper in the discussion of the first commandment in *Dives and Pauper*, a popular work of the early fifteenth century which reflects the impact of Lollard teaching on images and presents the arguments of both sides. Pauper, in answering Dives' probing question, proceeded to present a conventional defence of images which explained and (most unconventionally) Englished the scholastic terms for worship. In doing so he refuted the would-be image-breakers. As the author realized, the case that Gregory I expounded to Bishop Serenus of Marseilles had itself been an answer to image-breaking. 'We find that a bishop [i.e. Serenus] destroyed images as thou wouldest do, and forbade that any man should worship images. He was accused to the pope, St. Gregory, which blamed him greatly for that he had so destroyed the images. But utterly he praised him for that he forbade men to worship images'. It was all too contentious an issue, and the very openness of the book's discussion as to how images could be worshipped without idolatry could have laid it open to suspicion. *Dives and Pauper* made plain that images were 'venerable and worshipful', and therefore nobody should 'despise them nor defile them, burn

150   Prague Univ. MS. X.E.9, f. 211[r]. The argument here (f.210[v]) that 'the image of the saviour should not be worshipped with latria', seems to show familiarity with Holcot (above p. 157). I am most grateful to Anne Hudson for sending me her transcript of this text. W. R. Cook, 'John Wyclif and Hussite Theology, 1415-1436', *Church History*, 42 (1973), pp. 336-7, n. 13. No evidence is cited here for attributing this tract to Payne. Cf. Anne Hudson, 'Contributions to a Bibliography of Wycliffite Writings', *Notes and Queries*, 218 (Dec. 1973), p. 447, n. 28.

them nor break them'.[151] At the same time Pauper placed limits on the worship of images which in the early fifteenth century (specially after the publication of Archibishop Arundel's Oxford constitutions) could be read as challenging.

One of the early academic defences of images was a determination 'On the worship of images' by the Cambridge Augustinian, Walter Hilton. This treatise, which probably dates from the decade 1385-95 (though it could have been earlier), was professedly framed against those 'who wish to destroy the images gathered in churches'.[152] There were preachers, stated Hilton, who were openly asserting in their sermons that images of the saints placed in churches led the faithful into idolatry, instead of instructing them. And therefore, they proclaimed, such images should be taken down and publicly destroyed. Such insidious objects 'should be destroyed and burnt', said the heretics. 'It is a work of merit to destroy such images lest the simple people err in idolatry'.[153] Hilton, expounding the accepted idea of images as lay people's books ('as it were writing gross and palpable'),[154] set out case for representing the Trinity and worshipping the crucifix but clearly saw the Lollard threat as more than the rejection of image-worship. It was the iconoclasts whom he feared, with their incitement to destruction. Like Archbishop Arundel and others, Walter Hilton did not underestimate the implications of the attack on ecclesiastical images. That 'their removal would be the ruin of the church'[155] — as another defender put it — it was a common feeling at the time.

Another tract 'on the veneration of images' (doubtfully attributed to William Woodford) tried to answer the Lollard objection to images as 'books of error' by rolling the fundamentalist log back against them. If one had to burn images because they occasioned abuse, then by the same token, argued this author, one ought to burn bibles and holy

151   *Dives and Pauper*, ed. Barnum, i, pp. 82-83, 108-109; *Dives & Pauper* (1496), sigs. a vii[r], b v[r]. It is to be noted that *Dives and Pauper* stresses (pp. 83, 85) that worship must not be given *to* the image though prayer and offerings may be offered *before* it. The most dangerous point in this discussion concerned the honour owed to cross and crucifix. At this juncture the author's deductions from his explanation of *latria, hyperdulia,* and *dulia* (for which he struggled to find English equivalents in adoration, honoration, and veneration), were debatable.

152   BL MS. Royal 11 B X, f. 183[v]; Owst, *Lit. and Pulpit*, p. 137, n. 4. For the dating of this work see Russell-Smith, 'Walter Hilton', *Dom. Studies,* vii (1954), pp. 199-204 (Hilton died in March 1396).

153   BL MS. Royal 11 B X, f. 178[r-v]; Russell-Smith, *art. cit.*, p. 202.

154   BL MS. Royal 11 B X, f. 179[r]; 'velut quadam grossam scripturam quasi palpabilem de christo et sanctis eius oculis omnium laicorum et clericorum offert....'

155   Russell-Smith, *art. cit.*, p. 204. 'Opinion has it that images ought *neither to be in churches,* nor to be worshipped', wrote a doctor replying to Walter Brut in 1393 (my ital). *Reg. Trefnant,* p. 392. Cf. R. Pecock, *The Repressor of Over Much Blaming of the Clergy,* ed. C. Babington (RS, London, 1860), i, p. 138.

scripture for having produced heretics.[156] This was an argument that, like many others, did the rounds in iconoclastic controversies.

Thanks to the activity of the Lollards, images came to the fore as a topic of academic controversy in the last decade of the fourteenth century. Clearly the issue was familiar in the schools (the nature and varieties of worship were considered by Peter Lombard as well as by St. Thomas), and the scholastic justification of image-worship gave rise to questioning before Wycliffe. In the 1390s, however, the question assumed new urgency and there were masters in both universities who turned their attention to the justification of images and image-worship.[157] The considerable number of surviving manuscripts reflects the liveliness of this debate. These texts need fuller study but it seems that those who defended images against the heretics about this time included the Oxford masters Robert Alington and Nicholas Radcliffe, and Cambridge's John Devereux or Deveros, and Walter Hilton.[158]

Images were of absorbing interest both inside and outside university circles, and lay opinion (and laymen's errors) reflected back on learned discussions. The tone became acrimonious. John Devereux referred to the opponents of images as 'execrable hypocrites and Lollards'.[159] His writings on behalf of images and pilgrimage (of which there were several) were occasioned in the first instance by a conversation in which he found himself involved with a (nameless) squire in the country. It was after this talk that Devereux wrote up his conclusions and sent them in summary form (in Latin) to this same gentleman. At this point the debate widened. Devereux's text came into the hands of an Oxford scholar (was he also canvassing the squire?) who produced a reply — which shows that the schools could still find spokesmen for the Lollard cause. This riposte caused Devereux to put together a more scholarly version of his text.[160] The development of these arguments is of the

---

156   BL MS. Harl. 31, f. 187ʳ. On this work (cf. n. 136 above) see Jones, 'Lollards and Images', pp. 40-41, 45; Catto, 'William Woodford', p. 314 (questioning the attribution to Woodford).

157   Crompton, 'Lollard Doctrine' (n. 3 above), pp. 131, 208 and cf. 118 for the suggestion that Roger Dymoke's Determinations against the Twelve Conclusions of 1395 might have been delivered in the first instance as lectures.

158   Crompton's work, so far the fullest examination of these manuscripts, was particularly concerned with the contribution of John Devereux, and in defining this shows (pp. 139-40, 165-6, 179) the error of attributing some of these texts to John Sharpe. Cf. Jones, *art. cit.*, p. 39, n. 63; *Eng. Wycl. Writings*, p. 180. A. B. Emden, *Biog. Reg. Cambridge* (Cambridge, 1963), p. 186, 'Deveros', corrects A. B. Emden, *Biog. Reg. Oxford* (Oxford, 1957-59), iii, p. 1680, 'Sharpe'.

159   Russell-Smith, *art. cit.*, p. 202 (from Merton MS. 175 on which see Crompton, *op. cit.*, p. 138 ff.).

160   Crompton, 'Lollard Doctrine', pp. 169-177, including references n. 1, p. 171 and n. 2, p. 172 to 'uni armigero' and the summary sent 'ad quendam venerabilem generosum', which

greatest interest in showing (as, rather differently, did the case of Walter Brut) how theological controversy could weave to and fro between country houses and the universities.[161] Devereux envisaged his defence of images and pilgrimage reaching an audience beyond the schools, even though it was in Latin. 'I wrote in Latin', he said, 'as if I had been preaching in English'.[162] He seems deliberately to have tried to break down the barrier of scholastic terminology.

The writer who made the most radical effort to convert popular theologisers was, of course, Reginald Pecock. His remedy — that of satisfying the appetite for lay theology in its own staple diet of English — proved too revolutionary. Pecock's style seemed dangerously like the converse of Devereux's: writing in English as if he had been preaching in Latin. As a result much of what Pecock wrote was destroyed. Among his lost works is the one which probably contained his fullest answer to the Lollards' views on images: *The Book of Worshipping*.[163] The completion of this book did not, however, deter Pecock from subsequently devoting a long and prominent section of his *Repressor of Over Much Blaming of the Clergy* to a refutation of errors about images. Images came first of the eleven points of clerical governance which the treatise set out to justify. The 'having and using of images in churches' was something which the 'lay party' was out to prevent, believing that 'no images of God or of saints [should] be in churches'.[164]

Crompton, needlessly, took to indicate a 'nobleman'. For Devereux's objection to his opponents trying to use the example of Bishop Serenus (above p. 138) as a justification for iconoclasm see von Nolcken, *Rosarium Theologie*, p. 126. For references to Devereux's Lollard opponent see Crompton, pp. 142, 170-71, 173, 184, and for the dating of Devereux's text, pp. 198-99.

161   For an example of a different kind of extramural influence in the 1390s, cf. the allegation that John Fox, mayor of Northampton, obtained Lollard preachers from Oxford — passing them off as 'great clerks' in borrowed hoods and gowns. *Peasants Rising and Lollards*, pp. 48-49.

162   Crompton, 'Lollard Doctrine', p. 172, n. 2 quotes Devereux's apology for writing 'grosso stilo, non attendens situationem ad suppositionem terminorum logicalium, sed scripsi in latino ac si predicassem in anglico'.

163   This lost work was concerned with image-worship and the more general meaning of worship and Pecock constantly adverted to it in the *Repressor*. See *Repressor*, ed. Babington, i, pp. 119, 166, 188, 230, 254-5, 273, and cf. Introduction, p. lxxvii, and Pecock's *Donet*, ed. E. V. Hitchcock (EETS. OS 156, 1921), p. 126; V. H. H. Green, *Bishop Reginald Pecock* (Cambridge, 1945), p. 242. According to Crompton, 'Lollard Doctrine', p. 219, at least part of the 'Book of Worshipping' was known to John Foxe.

164   *Repressor*, i, pp. 4, 138, cf. 48-9, 111, 117. For Pecock's treatment of images see Green, *op. cit.*, p. 143 ff. and Jones, 'Lollards and Images', p. 41 ff. Green, pp. 89-90, raises the question of whether the *Repressor* 'formed a reply to Wyclif's own works or to works written by his followers'. Certainly, on the leading question of images, it seems abundantly plain that Pecock was (as Green indicated) concerned with the contemporary mid-fifteenth century state of affairs, which (in both writings and actions) had developed a great deal since Wycliffe's death.

Pecock started by listing Lollard objections to imagery and pilgrimage. The bishop's understanding of the heretics as people of the book, Bible men whose chief error was to believe themselves capable of all truth through 'poring in the Bible alone', gave him a firm grasp of the 'known men's' sense of priorities. He apprehended the opposition of word against image. Where the word truly lived no images were needed. Images and pilgrimages served purely commemorative purposes which could and should be attained by knowledge of the scripture. If bishops and priests had been less negligent in preaching and teaching, lay people would never have been driven to the cost and trouble of finding these alternative methods; 'the having and using of images and the doing of pilgrimages are idle and wasteful.....writings may serve better than them'. So (ran the heretical argument) the labour and costs expended on images could much more profitably be devoted to such services as 'visiting of poor men, and teaching of unwise men, and busy study in devout books and in other books of spiritual learning'.[165]

Since the Lollard case was so determinedly scriptural, Pecock was careful to refute it by the same means. As his opponents stood 'so busily and so fervently and sturdily' upon the Decalogue text, Pecock assembled additional Old Testament passages to demonstrate that the words 'Thou shalt not make to thee any graved thing' was a prohibition not of *all* graven images not only of 'a graved false pretended God'.[166] The commandment must not be applied against images in general. Similarly in the New Testament, St. Paul's words in Acts when he stood on Mars Hill and told the men of Athens that 'God dwelleth not in temples made with hands' was a reproof of heathen idols, not of images legitimately used in temples. And Christ's words to the woman of Samaria — 'God is a spirit; and they that worship him must worship him in spirit and in truth' — were spoken of the idolatry of the Samaritans and not relevant to Christians' use of images. Scriptural proscriptions of graven images should not be prised out of context: the idolatry of serving and believing and worshipping images as gods. Pecock was confident that this could not be said of contemporary veneration of images; 'no person doth in these days [worship as gods] the images had and used in the church'. Scripture, the 'doom of reason' and long accustomed church belief and practice all sanctioned the use of images. The most that could be made of Hezekiah's destruction of the brazen serpent was that 'images may lawfully be broken, when they be used to idolatry irremediably'. Since this was clearly not the case with the

---

165   *Repressor*, i, pp. 53, 85, 192, 195.
166   *Ibid.*, pp. 137-8, 142, 175. Pecock regarded the prohibition of images as an integral part of the first commandment. On this critical point see above p. 138.

English church, those who were so uncompromising in their condemnation of imagery were 'foolish and simple persons' whose mistaken views should be utterly rejected. The iconomachs must be
rebutted and rebuked 'as fastidious, befooled, wilful, wanton, schism-
sowers and disturbers of the people, in a matter on which they can
never bring about their intention'.[167]

Pecock was ready to admit that one might have too many as well as
too few images. There should be enough to stimulate the 'solemn and
fervent and devout remembrance' of the faithful, but not so many that
'at each church, at each chapel, at each street's end, or at each hedge's
end in the country be set such an image', which would cheapen their
respect. In saying this the bishop was thinking of the human responses
which iconomachs pushed aside. Images served a psychological need
which Lollards blindly refused to admit. Human frailty was such that
believers needed what Pecock (doing his best with a Latin term) called
'seeable rememorative signs' as well as 'hearable rememorative signs',
such as Holy Scripture and other devout writings. Even if — as the
heretics desired — all men and women learnt to read the vernacular in
their youth, reading alone would not bring them to Christ. Visible signs
were necessary to 'pluck him [man] upward and for to hold him
upward in good thoughts', and these had been devised and intended by
Christ. The sacraments were one form of 'seeable signs': sculptures and
pictures another. 'If hearable rememorative signs had been sufficient for
all the needful spiritual remembering of Christian men, why should
Christ have given Christian men under commandment seeable rememorative signs, such as are his sacraments of the New Testament?'
Visible sacraments, in short, were an argument for visible images,
whether engraved, carved or cast, of Christ's person, passion and death,
'to make us remember him, and his Passion and death'.[168] Images,
contrary to the extreme Lollard view, were perfectly permissible as
laymen's books. 'It is not against the first commandment of God....
[for] images to be had as books or calendars to remember and bring
into [the] mind [of] the beholder' his duty to follow, worship and
pray to Christ and his saints.[169]

This justification of images in apposition to books and texts rested
in part on the differing values of the different senses. Pecock, like
others before and after, stressed the faculty of seeing over that of

---

167   *Ibid.*, pp. 139, 145-7, 156-7, 196-7, 233-5 (Acts 17;24: John 4; 24).
168   *Ibid.*, pp. 183-4, 192-3, 208-9, cf. 164-5. Pecock's 'rememoratijf signes' is a
translation of the scholastic 'signa recordativa', used regularly in discussions of imagery. Cf.
above n. 9, and cf. Wilkins, *Concilia*, iii, p. 255 for Sawtry's use of the term.
169   Pecock, *Donet*, p. 121.

hearing. More could be learnt, and learnt more quickly and painlessly, by the eye than by the ear. The learning of six or seven pages of a book could be conveyed by a glance at one well-wrought image.

> The eyesight showeth and bringeth into the imagination and into the mind within the head of a man much matter and long matter sooner, and with less labour and travail and pain, than the hearing of the ear doth. And if this now said is true of a man who can read stories in books — that he shall much sooner and in shorter time and with less labour and pain in his brain come to the remembrance of a long story by sight, than either by hearing other men's reading, or by hearing his own reading — much more is this true of all those persons who cannot read in books; namely, since they shall not find men so ready to read a dozen leaves of a book to them as they shall find ready the painted walls of a church, or a stained cloth, or images spread abroad in diverse places of the church.[170]

Pecock was here stating, in his own unique way, a fact of human perception that was known in antiquity and is with us still: that visual images are more readily assimilated and more lasting than acoustic messages: the picture's advantage over the page. Centuries later the painter Delacroix said almost the same thing. 'Your picture you can see at a single glance but in a manuscript you do not see the whole page, that is to say your mind cannot take it in as a whole'.[171]

Reading in Pecock's day, as these remarks indicate, was for many readers a much more laborious process than it is now. This passage also reminds us that those who were weighing the respective values of book and image really were, for the most part, considering hearing and seeing as alternative modes of learning. For even though books had to be seen they were also mediated to nearly everybody by the ear ('hearable signs of writings', as Pecock puts it), whether a reader was mouthing words for himself, or reading aloud for the benefit of others.[172] There is an obvious sense, therefore, in which reading imagery — as claimed here —

---

170   *Repressor*, i, pp. 212-13 (I have repunctuated this passage). Cf. also the following passage, pp. 213-14, where Pecock writes of how images reduced the 'pain and labour' of recollection, both by their visible presence, and as mental images. Cf. above Chapter 4, p. 117.

171   *Journal of Eugène Delacroix*, ed. H. Wellington, trans. L. Norton (London, 1951), p. 128. Delacroix was here talking about the free flow of ideas in *composing* on the page and canvas respectively, not about the *comprehending* of page as opposed to picture, but the point still holds. For Neoplatonic interpretations of the instantaneity of visual apprehension see E. H. Gombrich, *Symbolic Images* (London, 1972), p. 158, and for a perceptive account of the differences between acoustic and visual learning see H. J. Chaytor, *From Script to Print* (Cambridge, 1945), pp. 5-21.

172   *Repressor*, i, p. 209, cf. p. 213, and cf. below, Chapter 6, p. 195 ff.

had the advantage of speed over book-reading, for few readers were in a position to scan pages (manuscript ones at that) with the rapidity which we now take for granted. On the other hand both sides, the defenders of images and the defenders of books, could make play with the availability of their medium. Wall-paintings and pictures in churches, argued Pecock, were available to all comers — men, women and children — at all times of day, whereas they might not always be able to get access to a book or to call on the services of a reader.[173]. But the heretics could just as easily make out a case for the continuous availability of the page. Indeed Pecock might here have been replying to the words of one Lollard who argued the merits of learning the faith from books and nature instead of through painting and sculpture.

It is a common saw, and sooth it is, word and wind and man's mind is full short, but letter written dwelleth. And as St. Austin saith, *ad Volusianum*, that [which] man or woman hath in writing or in book, he may read it alway; when he hath time and tome to read, he may read when he will, and stop when he will, without trouble, but he may not alway have preaching or teaching when he would, and oft when he may have a teacher, he hath no tome.[174]

Of course images were much more than teachers. If they were loved and cultivated, that was no detriment to the faith. Pecock's appreciation of the devotional value of imagery shows him sensitive to human need, aware of how physical consolations can bolster spiritual belief. Human feelings are nourished by physical proximity and visual contacts, and religion (argued Pecock) would be the poorer without these. God and the saints, like ordinary men and women whose portraits enabled their friends to recall them vividly when absent, were the better loved and better served the better they were represented. The affections are most moved by that which most nearly resembles the physical presence of the departed. So the Christian was specially stirred by beholding the image of Christ on the crucifix, and his mental picture was clearest at such moments as the Palm Sunday procession (representing Christ riding into Jerusalem) or on Good Friday (when the worshipper could imagine himself creeping towards Christ in person).

173 *Repressor*, i, pp. 213-14. A similar point was made by John Martiall in the sixteenth century, who said that people could always see the sign of the cross, but might not always be able to hear a good preacher.

174 *Holy Bible*, ed. Forshall and Madden, i, p. xiv, n. k, from CUL MS. Ii 6 26, p. 41. Cf. the similar argument for printed sermons put by Richard Baxter in his *Christian directory* (1973), cited by David Cressy, *Literacy and the Social Order* (Cambridge, 1980), p. 5.

Just as the love of two individuals, or of a man for a child, naturally finds expression in physical touch and embrace, so the physical treatment of images (kissing them, creeping to the cross) 'ought not to be scorned or rebuked'. 'Why, in like manner, may not the more love and good affection be engendered towards God or a saint by such touch.....?'[175]

Pecock in fact refuted the Lollards in an altogether individual way. His exploration of the traditional role of ecclesiastical images (as instruction and aids to devotion and recollection) led him into psychology. He showed how 'laymen's books' far exceeded their instructional role, and were deeply enriching to religious experience. To deny such aids was to deprive every kind of believer, literate and illiterate alike, of an approach to God which few could afford to dispense with. It was a means which God himself sanctioned. God had chosen to promote men's devotions by preferring certain places and certain images above others, in which to manifest himself by working miracles and bestowing special grace. To show respect to such places and images by pilgrimaging to them was therefore a legitimate form of devotion.[176] 'And therefore, since images and pilgrimages are lawful and may profitably be used, . . . and people are so set that they will not lack and leave that use, it is a great folly to fight against it'.[177]

---

175 *Repressor*, i, pp. 164-5, 268-72. Pecock here expounded the devotional values of imagining, inner visualizing (or as he put it, p. 270, 'the inward imaginative deed') which lay behind the theory and practice of medieval religious art. Imagination, he explained elsewhere, was 'as a treasury to the...common wit', retaining the impression of sensible things; *Folower to the Donet*, ed. E. V. Hitchcock (EETS, 0S 164, 1924), p. 26. Cf. M. W. Bundy, *The Theory of Imagination in Classical and Medieval Thought* (Univ. of Illinois Studies in Language and Literature, xii, 1927, rep. 1970), p. 158ff. esp. 165 on Augustine.

176 The fourth of the fifteen Lollard objections to images which Pecock listed was the argument that since God is present and ready to grant his grace everywhere alike, 'therefore no place in earth is holier than another place is, and no image is holier than another similar image is. Wherefore it is vain waste and idle to trot to Walsingham rather than to every other place in which there is an image of Mary, and to the rood at the north door at London [St. Pauls], rather than to any other rood, wherever it may be'. (*Repressor*. i, pp. 193-4). Pecock's answer to this attempted an explanation of the ways in which things could be holy, and made clear that this was an important issue, for it had been 'a full great let' against the use of images and doing of pilgrimages.

177 *Ibid.*, p. 254. In these concluding passages Pecock argued from history. In general his refutation was unacademic: he did not try to expound *latria* and *dulia*, nor did he have much recourse to patristic authority. But here he points a historical moral, and referred his readers to the example of eastern iconoclasts. Leo III and his son Constantine V had broken images and punished those who used them, but they had been opposed by western Christendom and papal authority, and by the Council of Nicaea in which 'the right use of images was again confirmed'. It was a warning lesson. 'And certainly in like manner it will happen, whoever strives against the said use of images'.

I have given a good deal of attention to Pecock not simply on account of the fullness of his treatment, but because he penetrated to so many important aspects of the questions raised by church imagery. Pecock's approach was original and he managed to lift the topic (as of course did some Lollards) out of the well-worn rut of scholastic argument and citation. He had a grasp of essentials, combined with a sense of the range of human experience attached to the ecclesiastical arts. As a result the bishop succeeded in sawing his way into the core of several issues that became central in sixteenth-century iconoclastic controversy. Admittedly these issues remained the same in every period of iconoclastic dispute: problems of the validation of Christian use of visible signs and symbols, and the respective capacities of hearing and seeing as modes of learning and remembering. But Pecock, because he seems to have been provoked by Lollard questioning into working out so much for himself, makes one vividly aware of the contemporary threat to imagery. A great deal seemed to be at stake — far more than might at first sight appear. 'Thou shalt not make unto thee any graven image.....' interpreted in a fundamentalist spirit opened the door to challenges that were social as well as doctrinal and spiritual, to discussions about the role of the sacraments and the external apparatus of Christian worship, as well as to enquiries about the complex ways in words and pictures respectively may teach people and move their feelings. Religious, political, educational and aesthetic questions were all at issue. That had been made clear and was in some part understood as the result of Lollard iconomachy.

'Knees not bent before Baal'[178]

Lollard views on images formed an important part of the heresy and throw light on the movement as a whole. We can see both continuity and divergence in the conflicting threads of opinion spun out across the fifteenth century for, as Thomas Netter pointed out, the heretics differed deeply among themselves. Where one Wycliffite was for priestly marriage another was for continence; there were those who said and those who denied that the eucharist was bread. Some accepted images while others condemned them, and Lollardy developed a split

---

178   The extravagant Lollard letter (?1411) addressed to 'the synagogue of Satan', described the Lollards as those 'quorum genua non sunt curvata ante Baal'. *Snappe's Formulary*, ed. H. E. Salter (Oxford Hist. Soc., lxxx, 1924), p. 132.

(not unlike that which went so much further among the Hussites) between image-reformers and image-breakers.[179] The iconomachs also alert us to the large reservoir of marginal dissent that lay behind the heresy. Lollardy emerged in a society that was worried (and increasingly articulate in its worries) about the external apparatus of the church, and there was uncertainty about where orthodox criticism ended and unorthodox dissent began. There was a wide range of critical opinion about images and doubts about the church's position long before the appearance of doctrinal heresy, and what Wycliffe wrote on this matter could not be faulted as unorthodox. This area of the critical and ambiguous remained after Lollardy had arrived and been recognized as a heretical movement. The difficulties experienced by twentieth-century scholars in identifying Lollard texts reflect the difficulties of fifteenth-century bishops.[180]

Heresy was not like a door that is either shut or open. The ajar segment of the heterodox was determined by the currents of contemporary opinion. As Lollard writings and actions developed, the climate of tolerable criticism changed and ambiguity acquired a different face. Long-voiced doubts about the theory of image-worship came to seem more dangerous. Remarks of Wycliffe (like those in *De mandatis divinis*) lifted out of context and translated into the vernacular, appeared with new meaning and looked more challenging in a popular setting. There was a sense in which it was the Lollards who hereticated Wycliffe.

Opposition to images shows us heresy both derived from and developing away from Wycliffe. The magisterial impetus from which the popular movement stemmed was weak at this point. Wycliffe had said enough for his view of images to be deducible, but he had not gone into this matter at length. It was only after his death that the topic came to the fore in debate, both academic and popular. Lollards were at one in opposing the existing use of images. They disagreed quite profoundly in the lines of their dissent. Some tried to remain faithful to Wycliffe in believing that images had uses as books of the illiterate but must be safeguarded from abuse. Others moved to a more extreme iconoclastic position.

By the end of the fourteenth century imagery had become a leading point of controversy. Though much of the matter in dispute was familiar, the heretics pointed it in a new direction. They gave it fresh

179   Netter, *Doctrinale*, iii, col. 942.
180   On this difficulty of determining the degree of unorthodoxy, and the effect of simplified expression on the definition of heresy, see von Nolcken, *Rosarium Theologie*, pp. 34, 38-39.

focus by their emphasis on the commandment text, accenting a clause in the decalogue that was usually disregarded, or given little attention. The very harping on this part of God's law itself became a pointer to unorthodoxy. It seems that there were many Lollards who took the view that it was in the worship (not the use) of images that the contemporary church was chiefly at variance with scripture. The idea that the sheer making or placing of imagery in churches was unlawful may have been held by only a small minority, but that did not prevent it affecting contemporary judgment of Lollard critics at large. Thanks to the talk of burning and some well publicized examples of image-breaking, all opponents of images tended to become tarred with the iconoclastic brush. To regard every moderate dissenter as an extremist in the making is part of all codes of repression.

Wycliffites took theology — including the scholastic theory of image-worship — into the tavern and market-place, but the mere fact of doing so necessarily altered its content. Thoughts were metamorphosed as they were lifted out of the scholastic Latin of the lecture-room and turned into the English texts and vernacular terminology suitable for heretical schooling. The nuggets of Wycliffe's prose that entered this heretical writing were transposed into a setting altogether different from that in which they orginated. And it is an undoubted indication of the altered nature of the heresy that what had, as Netter pointed out, been of marginal importance to Wycliffe became so central for his later followers.

Popular religion had its own order of priorities, not necessarily at all the same as Wycliffe's. The aspects of imagery that bothered many accused Lollards were often more social than doctrinal. The denial of image-worship to many of them, though based on scripture, amounted to questioning the false values of pilgrimage centres and the church's maladjusted economy, more than worries about the validity of *latria*, *hyperdulia* and *dulia*. The issue of images stood midway between the theology of the eucharist on one side and church polity on the other. It was logical for those who denied transubstantiation to doubt the legitimacy of worshipping the cross or praying to saints through their representations. Many fifteenth-century Lollards, however, were not constrained by logic, nor primarily concerned with sacramental theology. It is significant that so many of the heretics who were guilty of denying image-worship were *not* accused of eucharistic error. [181] Their

---

181   This is not to deny that leading heretics, including those who were burned, such as William Sawtry, William White, and Thomas Bagley, were guilty on both scores. Kightly, 'Early Lollards', pp. 577-78 found that of 37 heretics in the period 1382-1428, 26 doubted images and pilgrimages, and 21 questioned transubstantiation. Cf. the figures for error on the eucharist and images in *Norwich Heresy Trials*, p. 11.

concern with church images was practical rather than theological, linked with the question of ecclesiastical temporalities and criticisms both anticlerical and social.

Lollard controversy over images covered a good deal of the ground that was explored so fully in the sixteenth century. The heretics developed a number of the arguments that were employed by later reformers of images. They reformulated the priorities of decalogue teaching, indicating the lapses of conventional expositions. They put the biblical case for destruction alongside the prohibition of graven images. They contested the traditional theory of images as books of the laity, and directed alms towards the living instead of the lifeless images of Christ. But it is also important to consider what the Lollards did *not* do. They did not reach the point — despite some suggestive hints in this direction — of making the decalogue text into a separate second commandment. Though they had sounded they do not seem to have stressed the call to destroy. Nor did they, so far as we know, ever produce an iconoclastic riot, though perhaps they were not far off that on one or two occasions. In general what the Lollards did amounts to a great deal less than what they wrote or said, which makes the study of their views just as important as a head count of their adherents.

The irony was, of course, that in the short term the heretics' efforts had the reverse effect of what they intended. Though a general reform of images was never at all likely in the late medieval church, heretical concentration on this matter made far more difficult even such efforts as there had been to curb particular local abuses. Here, as in the promotion of vernacular Bible reading, Lollardy rendered suspect aspirations that were in themselves laudably reformist. The genuine case of moderates was submerged in the suppression precipitated by extremists. Yet the fact was the iconomachy, once launched, was there to stay. And it was not without effect on the iconoclasm of a later period, though Reformation opponents of images provided a fresh initiative.

Subsequent controversialists on both sides were well aware of this precedent. 'In England they are called Lollards, who, denying images, thought therewithal the crafts of painting and graving to be generally superfluous and naught, and against God's laws', Bishop Gardiner wrote warningly to the captain of Portsmouth in 1547, after there had been rioting in the town against images.[182] The English heretics could be used, like Karlstadt, as a warning of what to avoid. They could also be regarded as gloriously justificatory. Foxe, looking back with hindsight on the last generation of pre-Reformation Lollards, saw their op-

182   Above, n. 1.

position to images as effectively undermining the defence put up for ecclesiastical imagery in his own day. The Lollard precedent seemed to declare the essential falsity of the traditional case for image-worship, with its argument that the worship passed from representation to prototype. The examples of those earlier heretics who abhorred 'the idolatrous worshipping of the dead images' seemed to the martyrologist to give

> just occasion to condemn the wilful subtlety of those, who, in this bright shining light of God's truth, would yet, under colour of godly remembrance, still maintain the having of images in the church.

Mercifully the hearts of the elect had become wiser, understanding — like some heretics of old — that 'the word of God doth so manifestly forbid as well the worshipping of them [images], as also the making or having them for order of religion'.[183]

Lollard opposition to images was a valuable precedent. New-style reformers were delighted to discover that previous heretics had anticipated their own views, so helping to answer the question of where the true church had been before Luther. Some of the early printed editions of Lollard texts helped to publicize the continuity of thought on this issue. *The Lantern of Light* and William Thorpe's account of his trial (both of which, as we have seen, contained expositions of the case against imagery) were in print by about 1530, and the preface to the latter drew the reader's attention to its treatment of image-worship and pilgrimage, among other matters.[184] Another book, which appeared not long after, was *The praier and complaynte of the ploweman unto Christe*, which printed an old English text in order to show how prelates were defaming the doctrine of Christ as new learning. This tract likewise showed the antiquity of the case against image-worship. 'But Lord God', ran one passage, 'men maketh now great stone houses full of glazen windows, and call them thy houses and churches. And they set in these houses idols of stocks and stones, and before them they kneel privily and openly, and make their prayers. And all this they say is thy worship and a great praising to thee. Ah lord, thou forbiddest some time to make such idols, and who that had worshipped such had be worthy to be dead'.[185]

---

183   Foxe, *AM*, iv, p. 176.
184   *Fifteenth Century Prose and Verse*, p. 100; quoted below, Chapter 7, p. 226.
185   *The praier and complaynte of the ploweman unto Christe*, [Antwerp, 1531] sig. C

Lollard iconomachy neither caused nor enabled Reformation iconomachy . The attacks on images that moved forward in the 1530s to become part of royal reform started from a new power base and were reinforced by continental precept and example. That is not to say, of course, that the long-standing Lollard cause made no contribution to the arguments and actions of a new generation of iconomachs, or that it lost all ongoing momentum of its own. No adequate method has yet been found to test the plausible hypothesis that there was some continuity between pre- and post-Reformation dissent. At the critical period of transition, however, we can see some fusing of views. From the years 1530-32 images became an important issue in England's developing Protestantism. There was little enough in common between Henry VIII and the obscure individuals who had spoken out for so long against the abuses of images, but the dismantling of the gilded shrines of Canterbury, Walsingham and elsewhere, and the destruction of pilgrimage statues, created at least a semblance of common interest. Image-breaking became official and entered a new era. A cause for which people had been prepared to risk or lose their lives was publicly launched — on an unforeseeably long course. Lollard image-haters and image-breakers sank from view in the rising tide of Protestant iconomachy.

---

iiii[v], cf. preface 'To the Christen reader' (see below, pp. 224, 233). W. A. Clebsch, *England's Earliest Protestants 1520-1535* (New Haven, 1964), pp. 163, 336, thought this text was probably edited by Tyndale. It has also been attributed to George Joye; *Complete Works of St. Thomas More*, Vol. 6, Pt. II, ed. T. M. C. Lawler et al. (New Haven & London, 1981), p. 744, n. 2.

6

LOLLARDY AND LITERACY

'The voice of books', wrote Thomas à Kempis, 'informs not all alike'[1]. In the later middle ages the truth of that statement was learnt by many people in England. Thanks to the literary endeavours of the Lollards and the acoustic properties of books it came to be accepted that different readers read in different ways and with differing effects; accordingly they were to be treated differently. Literacy was not a neutral topic. It had then, as in some places it still has, serious social implications.

The fifteenth century was a time of generally increasing literacy and of growing opportunities for lay people to learn to read and write. Doubtless many took their chance to acquire these skills as a way of opening vocational doors, and what has been called 'pragmatic literacy'—literacy as a tool of trade—brought reading and writing within the range of increasing numbers of craftsmen and men of business.[2] As always, however, people wanted to read for a variety of reasons. And one aspect of the acquisition of letters which must not be left out of account is the revelatory.

Since most of us nowadays (in this society) become readers and writers in childhood, it may need an act of imagination to comprehend the element of spiritual discovery which can accompany adults' first direct communication with the page. This has been seen in our days in Latin America and Portugal. Paulo Freire showed the 'inevitable link between literacy and political awakening' in Brazil, where the obstacles to learning were overcome once the peasants gained insight into the nature of their oppression. 'Whole villages learn to read in weeks. They gain an emotional relationship with written language which means something to them for the first time'.[3] A Portuguese exile described how, as one of the few literate people in a small hamlet, he gained early insight into the rural problems of his country. 'I made pocket money by reading newspapers and writing letters for most people in the area'.[4] Such evidence throws light upon the workings of literacy in non-reading peasant communities of earlier periods. Literates in predominantly illiterate societies have power to influence other people's lives, particularly if their own reading is of the variety we may call revelat-

* A version of this paper was delivered to the Historical Society of Queen's University, Belfast, in October 1976, and I am grateful for the comments offered there. I also wish to thank Professor R. H. Hilton and Miss Anne Hudson for their help.

[1] Thomas à Kempis, *Of the Imitation of Christ*, Bk. III, chap. xliii (World's Classics edn., London, 1961, p. 188).

[2] For this term see M. B. Parkes, 'The Literacy of the Laity', in *The Mediaeval World*, ed. D. Daiches and A. Thorlby (London, 1973), pp. 555–577. (I owe this reference to Miss Pamela Robinson). In addition to the works on literacy listed here p. 577, see also Carlo M. Cipolla, *Literacy and Development in the West* (Penguin Books, Harmondsworth, 1969), and H. S. Bennett, *English Books and Readers 1475–1557* (Cambridge, 1952), Chapter II.

[3] Christopher Price, 'The Right to Read', *New Statesman*, 24 May 1974, p. 719; on Paulo Freire's work for the education of adult illiterates see his *Pedagogy of the Oppressed* (Penguin Books, Harmondsworth, 1972), pp. 9, 12.

[4] Antonio de Figueiredo, 'Power to the people?', *The Guardian*, 16 April 1975, p. 14.

ory. Some self-taught readers, in late medieval as in modern times, were caught up in a process that was revolutionary both for themselves and for the communities which shared their aspirations.

The Portuguese boy who read the newspaper to his villagers serves also to remind us that there are different sorts of reading, just as there are many different degrees of literacy. In the first place we must remember that in the period we are considering, as in that village in Portugal, reading was more often than not a *social* or at least a shared activity—as amongst ourselves it now only is exceptionally. 'Reading a book', it can now be said, 'is essentially a private activity'.[5] Reading, as we most commonly practise and think of it today, is a silent enclosed occupation of the kind which makes it possible for fifty studious people to sit, inaudible and detached in one room reading fifty different books. There was a time when the reverse was true. Reading was not private and closed but acoustic and open. When you read you were audible, so that reading might be social, or anti-social, but if you wanted to read privately you had to be alone.

A well-known passage in the *Confessions* of St. Augustine describes the reading habits of St. Ambrose. 'As he read, his eyes glanced over the pages and his heart searched out the sense, but his voice and tongue were silent'. It is indicative of his surprised reaction to this manner of reading that St. Augustine found it necessary to account for it. Was it that Ambrose was thus enabled to refresh his mind without the interruptions which would otherwise have ensued? Perhaps he feared (mused Augustine) that if he had been reading some obscure passage aloud, some interested or puzzled listener would have called upon him to explain it. Or was he anxious to preserve his voice? There is a hint that in a man less holy, Ambrose's silent reading *to himself* might have been blamed as selfish for the very reason that being silent it could not be shared.[6]

Vocalized reading was still taken for granted in the seventeenth century. The chapter in Grimmelshausen's *Simplicissimus* which describes how the hero learnt to read and write tells how he was set upon this road by observing a hermit reading the Bible. 'When for the first time I saw the hermit reading the Bible, I could not imagine with whom he could be having such a secret and, as I thought, earnest conversation. For I saw the movement of his lips, and heard the murmuring, but yet I saw and heard nobody talking with him'.[7]

[5] Fenella Crichton, 'Book for book's sake', *The Listener*, 2 September 1976, p. 282.

[6] Saint Augustine, *Confessions*, Bk. vi, chap. 3, trans. Albert C. Outler (Library of Christian Classics, Vol. VII, London, 1955), p. 116. Cf. G. G. Coulton, *Five Centuries of Religion*, I (Cambridge, 1923), p. 38 for the case of a thirteenth-century Cistercian who found his 'inward understanding' disturbed by his own vocalization.

[7] *Simplicissimus*, Bk. i, chap. 10. I have slightly amended the version of this passage in *Simplicissimus the Vagabond*, trans. A. T. S. Goodrick (London, 1912), p. 20. This is cited among other relevant quotations by H. J. Chaytor, *From Script to Print* (Cambridge, 1945) in the illuminating chapter on 'Reading and Writing', pp. 5–21, to which I owe much. But when did silent reading become general, and was it really due to 'the dissemination of printed matter' rather than the (concomitant but separable) increase of reading facility among many more readers? The fact that much printed matter was less taxing to the eye than manuscripts; that after printing more people were able to own books for private perusal, to read and re-read them at leisure, did not of themselves eliminate age-old habits. Reading and hearing, hearing and reading, were still accepted as twinned activities well into the English Reformation.

In the later middle ages, though there must have been a growing number of expert 'professional' readers who could scan a page to themselves inaudibly like St. Ambrose, silent reading was still exceptional. This meant that reading was generally much more co-operative than it has since become. Reading went with hearing. It was, as Reginald Pecock put it, 'by the hearing of other men's reading or by hearing of his own reading' that an individual learnt about the contents of books.[8] Both practised readers and pupils learning to read were able to promote the learning of others who were present and listened to them. Adults might be educated by children. What Archbishop Whitgift describes as happening in the sixteenth century was a process that had undoubtedly started long before. 'God', he said, 'by his word read of a child, may, and doth oftentimes, teach us. And hereof we have (God be thanked) many examples in England, of those which, being not able to read themselves, by the means of their children reading to them at home, receive instruction and edifying'.[9]

The common practice of reading aloud also meant that a knowledge of letters and book-learning were compatible with very little direct contact with the page itself. (Rote learning, on which more shortly, could be very extensive among illiterates.) One could even be an author without knowing how to read or write. An interesting example of this is Margery Kempe whose title to fame rests on the fact that she left an account, in English, of her life and religious experiences. But Margery did not pen her book herself, and seems never to have learnt to read or write. She was, nevertheless, closely in touch with, and influenced by, the world of books and her decision to compose her treatise, long pondered before being acted upon, accorded fully with the tendencies of the time. Among those who seriously advised her to do it was a man who had behind him a youth of mis-spent heretical fervour: Philip Repton or Repingdon, the bishop of Lincoln.[10]

The example of Margery Kempe indicates that when we speak of literacy in the later fourteenth and fifteenth centuries, we are using a word which covers a wide range of abilities. Book learning did not necessarily imply a capacity for letters. And leaving aside the distinction between *literati* and *illiterati*, there were many degrees of skill belonging to the lettered page. For one thing reading and writing are separate arts. Between the fourteenth century and the seventeenth there were many readers, highly educated and otherwise, who considered penmanship a matter for the experts. Meanwhile books themselves might be penetrated vicariously and remained objects to be heard as well as seen—after, as before, the invention of printing. In many cases they were used primarily for acoustic communication. And to hear a book might, or might not, be the first step along the road to learning to read it.

*   *   *   *

[8] Reginald Pecock, *The Repressor of Over Much Blaming of the Clergy*, ed. C. Babington (Rolls Series, London, 1860), i, p. 213; cf. p. 209 where 'hearable signs of writings' are contrasted with 'seeable signs of images'.

[9] *The Works of John Whitgift*, ed. John Ayre, iii (Parker Soc., Cambridge, 1853), p. 39.

[10] *The Book of Margery Kempe*, ed. S. B. Meech and H. E. Allen (E.E.T.S., O.S. 212, 1940); modern version by W. Butler-Bowden (World's Classics, London, 1954). Margery, who describes herself as unlettered, speaks in various places of the books she had 'heard read', including the Bible.

It is necessary to bear in mind these features of contemporary reading habits in order to understand both the Lollards' activities and their reception. The fact that reading as generally practised was itself a social activity, was of profound importance in the spread and condemnation of the heresy. It also helps to explain the limits that were set upon even orthodox religious reading and learning.

The advance of lay literacy went with the advance of the vernacular, in affairs of state, in business, in bill-posting[11]—and in religion. In the later fourteenth century it was becoming possible to believe more, as well as to do more, by means of English. Besides the appearance of mystical works of devotion like those of Richard Rolle, the church and churchmen were showing themselves more aware of the needs of congregations whose understanding was limited by vernacular horizons, even if partially literate. Various vernacular works appeared, such as the *Catechism* of Archbishop Thoresby of York (issued in both English and Latin in 1357), or John Mirk's *Instructions for Parish Priests* (of about 1400), or *The Lay Folks Mass Book*, which were intended to reduce the gap between the Latin rites of the church and the understanding of most of its members. People attending mass, even if they could not follow word by word, should at least know what the priest was doing and attend to their own devotions in an appropriate manner:

> Though ye understand it nought
> ye may well wite that God it wrought,[12]

as a work explaining the 'manner and mede of the mass' put it, about the year 1370. Not to understand did not mean not to participate. Yet despite this recognition of the needs of laymen who, though 'lewed' by contemporary definition, might yet be intellectually demanding, the church's attitude remained definitely reserved. It was not only a question of what people *could* not understand, but also of what they *should* not. Some things were inappropriate for the layman's language, for lay tongues and ears. 'The highest and subtlest and hardest truths . . . ought not to be delivered

---

[11] For a charge of 1424 against a man who had posted English bills in Norwich see J. W. Adamson, 'Literacy in England in the Fifteenth and Sixteenth Centuries', in '*The Illiterate Anglo-Saxon' and Other Essays on Education* (Cambridge, 1946), p. 41. Charges against Lollards of posting 'diversas bullas et scripturas' in 1431 appear in P.R.O. K.B.27/686, *Rex* m. 1v. (charges against John Pleysee of Thatcham, Berks., labourer) and elsewhere; cf. *Peasants, Knights and Heretics*, ed. R. H. Hilton (Cambridge, 1976), p. 317. On the posting of Lollard 'schedules' see Anne Hudson, 'A Lollard Quaternion', *Review of English Studies*, N.S.xxii (1971), pp. 441–2; *idem* 'Some Aspects of Lollard Book Production', in *Schism, Heresy and Religious Protest*, ed. Derek Baker (*Studies in Church History*, Vol. 9, Oxford, 1972), pp. 149–50. See above 45.

[12] From 'A Treatise of the Manner and Mede of the Mass', in *The Lay Folks Mass Book*, ed. T. F. Simmons (E.E.T.S., 71, 1879), p. 140. This text was intended for laymen, in particular for reading aloud to those who could not read. For this and other works of vernacular instruction see B. L. Manning, *The People's Faith in the Time of Wyclif* (Cambridge, 1919, rep. 1975), p. 4 ff., and W. A. Pantin, *The English Church in the Fourteenth Century* (Cambridge, 1955), p. 189 ff.

to laymen'.[13] For all the advance of vernacular religious instruction there was still a boundary of belief between Latin and English which there were obvious dangers in crossing.

From their first beginnings the Lollards devoted much attention to attacking this boundary. At the outset, and deriving from Wycliffe's inspiration, it was primarily a question of the Bible: the conviction that 'holy scripture containeth all profitable truth' and (after Jerome) that 'holy writ is the scripture of peoples, for it is made that all peoples should know it'.[14] Busy study and teaching and preaching of God's law should be the primary occupation of the whole clerical profession, and all Christian men 'should stand to the death for maintaining of Christ's Gospel, and true understanding thereof, gotten by holy life and great study', setting no faith in sinful prelates and their 'cursed clerks' who were blind to the truth of Holy Writ.[15] Language held no barriers—if it did so these were barriers that called for crossing. As the translator of the second version of the Lollard Bible made clear, lack of latinity must be no bar to direct scriptural understanding. Nor, as experience was to show, was even lack of literacy a bar to extensive Biblical learning. 'God grant to us all grace to kunne well, and keep well holy writ, and suffer joyfully some pain for it at the last!'[16] was the prayer of the translator. Succeeding generations of dissent seem amply to have answered this entreaty. Lollard enthusiasm for their English Bible translations lasted through the fifteenth century to assist the beginnings of the Reformation.

As well as, and as part of this stress upon Biblical understanding, Lollard writers laid emphasis upon the necessity for reading which, fervently adopted by some of the heretics, in certain cases led away from or beyond the Bible. One defender of their labours said that all Christians could be divided into three kinds: the lettered for whom were ordained books in Hebrew, Greek and Latin; the completely unlettered; and lastly those who—both clerks and others—'can read but little, or not understand', and for whom there were books in the vernacular.[17] These last were the 'studiers in Christ's church' (as another work referred to them)[18] to whom Lollard endeavours were directed and who were to be increased in number. It was *study*, by knights and clerks and others, which was to be the means of redemption. Read this book once a week and it will do you more good than saying your beads, one writer admonished his readers.

[13]Reginald Pecock, *The Reule of Crysten Religioun*, ed. W. C. Greet (E.E.T.S., 171, 1927), p. 87. Pecock was here on the defensive, forestalling the objections of a critic, but he did not dissent from the premise. Cf. the ensuing passage on the Trinity in Latin, and the remarks on pp. 90 and 21. Pecock also refers (p. 401) to the reading of 'unlettered man . . . when they read their Psalter or their pater noster in Latin' as being valuable, even though not properly comprehended.

[14] *The Holy Bible, in the earliest English versions made from Latin Vulgate by John Wycliffe and his followers*, ed. J. Forshall and F. Madden (Oxford, 1850), i, pp. 49, 56, from the Prologue. On this topic there is the valuable study by Margaret Deanesly, *The Lollard Bible* (Cambridge, 1920) to which my debts are large.

[15] *The English Works of Wyclif Hitherto Unprinted*, ed. F. D. Matthew (E.E.T.S., O.S.74, 1880) (henceforth *English Works*), pp. 258–9; cf. p. 159 on the duty of every layman to teach the commandments to his children and household.

[16] Sven L. Fristedt, *The Wycliffe Bible*, Part I (Stockholm, 1953), p. 9.

[17] *The Holy Bible*, ed. Forshall and Madden, i, p. xiv, n. k; Deanesly, *op. cit.*, p. 272.

[18] *The Lanterne of Lizt*, ed. L. M. Swinburn (E.E.T.S., O.S. 151, 1917), p. 62.

> For the science of God cometh of diligence of reading: truly ignorance of God is daughter of negligence. Truly if not all men reading know God, how shall he know that readeth not?

cited another early adherent of the movement.[19] Moreover, for all the decrying of useless university learning which appeared in some Lollard circles, there seems for some time to have been a branch of heretics who believed in the possibility of regenerating university studies. So at least one might judge from the proposal put forward for the benefit of parliament in 1410, that the revenues of the ecclesiastical possessioners might be used (among other purposes) for the endowment of fifteen new universities. As time went on perhaps a Lollard 'university' became more and more of a contradiction in terms—and even as thought of here it may have been more 'lewed' then 'learned'. As the author of the 'General Prologue' to the Lollard Bible remarked warningly. 'god both can and may, if it liketh him, speed simple men out of the university, as much to know holy writ, as masters in the university'.[20] The learned had no prerogative over mastery of the scriptures.

Oxford firmly closed its doors to the heretics. But drummed out of the university though they were, the Lollards did succeed in establishing a firm tradition of Bible study and vernacular learning which maintained its continuum despite all efforts to uproot it. They may also have managed to retain at least some meaningful contact with Wycliffe's works and other sources of Latinate learning until well into the fifteenth century.[21] At present that remains somewhat speculative. What is certain is the continuity of their vernacular writings and learning.

At the beginning of the fifteenth century the statute *De Heretico Comburendo* drew attention to the Lollards' literacy as an aspect of their sedition. 'They make', it stated, 'unlawful conventicles and confederacies, they hold and exercise schools, they make and write books, they do wickedly instruct and inform people'.[22] References to such Lollard schools crop up from time to time from the first appearance of Lollardy until the sixteenth century. One such case is that of Richard Belward of Earsham in Norfolk, accused in 1424 (according to Foxe) on a number of scores including that he 'keepeth schools of Lollardy in the English tongue, in the town of Ditchingham, and a certain parchment-maker bringeth him all the books containing that doctrine from London'.[23] Though our knowledge of them is derived almost entirely from the records of the prosecution, it is clear that Lollard schools existed throughout the fifteenth century, and that they were considered important both by the authorities and by the heretics, one

---

[19] E. Colledge, '*The Recluse*. A Lollard Interpolated Version of the *Ancren Riwle*', *Review of English Studies*, xv (1939), p. 9; cf. pp. 135–6 for the admonitions to readers both to read and instruct; Deanesly, *op. cit.*, p. 450, (expounding Chrysostom).

[20] *The Holy Bible*, ed. Forshall and Madden, i, p. 52 (cf. p. xiv, n. k). For the hostility to Oxford and Cambridge (the apostles had no degrees) see *English Works*, pp. 420, 427–8.

[21] For instance Ralph Mungyn, accused in Convocation in 1428, had two of Wycliffe's Latin works. It seems likely that more work on Lollard texts could elucidate this question further.

[22] *Statutes of the Realm*, ii, p. 126, cf. p. 127; *Documents of the Christian Church*, ed. H. Bettenson (London, 1963), p. 252.

[23] John Foxe, *Acts and Monuments* (henceforth *A. and M.*) ed. S. R. Cattley and G. Townsend (London, 1837–41), iii, p. 585; cf. below p. 202 and n. 38 for the heretical school reported to have been held by William Smith.

of whom maintained in 1485 that a man must be 'occupied in school for one year before he knows the true faith'.[24] We cannot know precisely what went on in these centres of instruction, but whether or not they taught reading as well as vernacular doctrine it was undoubtedly the case that the heretics (like later Protestants) regarded the acquisition of literacy as part of a religious vocation. And there is ample evidence of their informal study groups.

The picture which John Foxe gives of Lollard activities on the eve of the Reformation seems to have been true—at least of one wing of the heretics—all through the fifteenth century. He praised them for their 'fervent zeal',

> sitting up all night in reading and hearing; also by their expenses and charges in buying of books in English, of whom some gave five marks, some more, some less, for a book: some gave a load of hay for a few chapters of St. James, or of St. Paul in English.[25]

Groups of fervent readers, listeners and learners attending scriptural meetings, are characteristic of the Lollards from the days when their translated text first became available. William Wakeham of Devizes, who was caught by the bishop of Salisbury as a relapsed heretic in 1437, making rash pronouncements among the weavers of Marlborough, had three years earlier admitted 'that I with other heretics and Lollards was accustomed and used to hear in secret places, in nooks and corners, the reading of the Bible in English, and to this reading gave attendance by many years'.[26] Early in the 1490s a man called Richard Sawyer, late of Newbury, confessed similarly to secret night readings with men of Newbury. And in the early years of the sixteenth century such underground reading parties were still being discovered by the authorities; in the diocese of Hereford, for instance, or in Hampshire where Thomas Watts of Dogmersfield had been reading the English New Testament to his wife and family and to five others who were later accused.[27] Fields and hedges were as good as secret hideouts for such gatherings. James Brewster, an illiterate carpenter of Colchester, was said to have 'been five times with William Sweeting in the fields keeping beasts, hearing him read many good things out of a certain book: at which reading were also present at one time Woodroof or Woodbinde, a netmaker, with his wife; and also a brother-in-law of William Sweeting; and another time

---

[24] Anne Hudson, 'A Lollard Compilation and the Dissemination of Wycliffite Thought', *Journal of Theological Studies*, N.S. Vol. xxiii, Pt. i (1972), p. 80; for further evidence of Lollard schools see *idem*, 'A Lollard Sermon-Cycle and its Implications', *Medium Aevum*, xl (1971), p. 152; *idem*, 'Some Aspects of Lollard Book Production', p. 150. The heretics certainly caused the authorities to pay unwonted attention to school-teaching, and one of Archbishop Arundel's Constitutions of 1409 concerned schoolmasters. D. Wilkins, *Concilia* (London, 1737), iii, p. 317; Nicholas Orme, *English Schools in the Middle Ages* (London, 1973), pp. 143, 253–4.
[25] Foxe, *A. and M.*, iv, p. 218; cf. *The Lanterne of Liȝt*, p. 62. Of the four 'principal points' Foxe says the Lollards 'stood in against the church of Rome', one was 'reading Scripture-books in English'.
[26] Bishop Neville's Register (Salisbury), ff. 52 r.-v., 57 v.
[27] J. A. F. Thomson, *The Later Lollards, 1414–1520* (Oxford, 1965), pp. 78, 48, 88–89; cf. 113–14 for the books used and owned by the Midlands heretics investigated in 1511–12. For other evidence of Lollard readings see Hudson, 'Some Aspects of Lollard Book Production', pp. 148, 156–7; Deanesly, *op. cit.*, Chapter xiv, esp. p. 363 ff.

Thomas Goodred, who likewise heard the said 'William Sweeting read'.[28]

These readings were not confined to translated Biblical books, though when texts are actually named these occur more often than any others. Most frequently, as one might have supposed, it was the New Testament, or individual books from it, for not everyone was as fortunate as Thomas Watts in being able to come by a complete New Testament. Copies of the Epistles of St. Paul and St. James, of separate Gospels, of the Acts, or the Apocalypse were within the reach of many humble heretics, and a Coventry Lollard who had on loan a copy of St. Paul's Epistles also owned the complete Old Testament.[29] As Foxe's account justly comments, the heretics set a high value upon their books. A glossed Epistle of St. James cost a Lollard of the Chilterns, who bought it from a man who was eventually burned in 1522, the sum of two nobles.[30] Another enterprising sixteenth-century heretic managed to barter the tick of a feather-bed for a book.[31] And early in the previous century an East Anglian Lollard paid 4 marks 40 pence for a New Testament which he bought in London.[32] The text of the complete Lollard Bible would therefore have been a very valuable possession, but although it is not known to have been revealed in any trials of the later artisan Lollards, it does not follow that none of them owned it. They seem to have acquired considerable expertise in the concealment of their books, and while very little is known about the early owners of still extant copies of the Lollard Bible, at least two of them seem to have been in the hands of fifteenth-century heretics, and a rare bequest of two English Bibles was made in 1507 by a Coventry mercer who had Lollard connections.[33]

Their appreciation of the value of books made the heretics avowedly jealous of the inaccessible supplies in monastic libraries. The religious— they tried to make out—were playing dog-in-the-manger by not making these resources available through gift, loan or sale, to secular clerks who would have made proper use of them in study and teaching. As it was they were sitting on 'hidden buried treasure' and many valuable texts ('books of holy writ and holy doctors and other needful sciences') were 'rotting' in their libraries. The result of this lack of monastic charity was that 'seculars and curates may almost get no book of value', and parishes were starved of essential texts. When curates and parish clergy did have books they were

---

[28] Foxe, *A. and M.*, iv, pp. 215–6, 'Ex. Regist. Lond.' Thomson, *op. cit.*, pp. 137, 162. Brewster and Sweeting (whom Foxe reports to have been holy water clerk at Boxted and later at Colchester in Essex) were burned together at Smithfield in 1511.

[29] Thomson, *op. cit.*, p. 113; cf. pp. 42, 65, 81, 89, 105, 115, 162, and Foxe, *A. and M.*, iv, p. 176. For books of the Coventry heretics of 1511–12 (who included more readers than writers) see John Fines, 'Heresy Trials in the Diocese of Coventry and Lichfield, 1511–12', *Journ. Eccl. Hist.*, xiv (1963), pp. 164–5.

[30] Thomson, *op. cit*, p. 91. See below p. 206 for Pecock's description of how the heretics prized their books.

[31] Fines, *art. cit.*, p. 164.

[32] Thomson, *op. cit.*, p. 131; Foxe, *A. and M.*, iii, p. 597; Deanesly, *op. cit.*, p. 358. Nicholas Belward, who paid this high price, may probably have been related to Richard Belward, the Lollard schoolmaster, above p. 198.

[33] I. Luxton, 'The Lichfield Court Book: a Postscript', *B.I.H.R.*, xliv (1971), pp. 120–22, 125; Deanesly, *op. cit.*, pp. 365–6, cf. pp. 334–6 and 343. For the 'pulcherrimos libros de herese' of 'magistri Wiggiston et Pysford', see Fines, *art. cit.*, p. 162, and Luxton, *art. cit.*, pp. 122–3.

the wrong sort: books not of God's law, but of man's. 'But few curates have the Bible and expositions of the Gospels' and little did they study them or act upon them. 'Would God that every parish church in this land had a good Bible and good expositors of the Gospels' was a Lollard pipedream.[34]

There may have been many heretics for whom familiarity with texts—Biblical or otherwise—remained purely aural, and for whom learning by rote was a substitute for books. Reginald Pecock commented on the Lollard practice of learning scriptural texts by heart to 'pour them out thick at feasts, and at ale drinking, and upon their high benches sitting'.[35] Learning of this kind could be remarkably extensive, as orthodox cases also show. Henry Tuck, a wiredrawer of Bristol, knew the whole Apocalypse by heart and John Gest, a Birmingham cobbler, had memorized parts of the Epistles of St. Paul.[36] Alice Colyns, wife of Richard Colyns of Ginge in Berkshire, had apparently become a 'famous woman' among the heretics for her ability to memorize and recite much of the Scriptures, and would be sent for when they held their conventicles.[37] In this respect the behaviour of the Lollards resembled that of the Waldensians, against whose scriptural recitations the inquisitors had constantly proceeded. Concentrated enthusiasm and rote-learning could supply many deficiencies of books and readers. They could also act as a stimulus to the acquisition of literacy, and this certainly occurred.

Individuals like Henry Tuck and Alice Colyns who learnt books as well as hearing them studied and expounded, might go on to become book-owners, and the conviction that the knowledge which really mattered was that derived direct from the text, provided a powerful motive for learning to read. Indeed Alice Colyns, who was a member of a literate family may herself (like her husband) have been able to read, as well as to recite. An early example of the promptings of self-education is that of the Leicester blacksmith, William Smith, reported to have been a man of 'despicable and deformed appearance', who was one of the very first Lollards. He apparently became a convert out of a variety of frustrated enthusiasms which

---

[34] *English Works*, pp. 49, 128, 145, 221, 223. Cf. the remark on p. 194 comparing the study and work 'wasted' on service-books with the needed making and study of Bibles, with the thanks rendered in another tract (p. 290) for the mass-books witnessing to the Gospel in every church. The translator of the Wycliffite Bible who referred to his labours in assembling manuscripts to make 'one Latin Bible sumdel true', would doubtless have sympathized with these complaints about the inaccessibility of texts; Fristedt, *op. cit.*, p. 138. See also n. 54 below.

[35] Pecock, *Repressor*, i, p. 129; cf. p. 89 for an attack on the mindless rote-learning of ill-educated preachers. See A. G. Dickens, *The English Reformation* (London, 1964), pp. 13, 30, for remarks on Lollard rote-learning, and for that of the Waldensians, Deanesly, *op. cit.*, pp. 28, 38–9, 62–4.

[36] Thomson, *op. cit.*, pp. 47, 114. Cf. p. 68 for the case of James Willis.

[37] Foxe, *A. and M.*, iv, p. 238; cf. pp. 235, 239, for reports of her biblical learning. Heresy seems (on Foxe's account) to have been well entrenched in the Colyns family. Richard Colyns, Alice's husband, owned quite a heretical library of English books: 'Wickliff's Wicket', the Gospel of St. John, the Epistles of Paul, James and Peter, an Exposition of the Apocalypse, 'a book of our Lady's Matins in English', 'a book of Solomon in English', and the *Prick of Conscience*. He also read a book called 'The King of Beeme' [Bohemia] to a group in Burford (where other members of the Colyns family lived). Meanwhile Joan, daughter of Alice and Richard, was reported to have learnt from her parents the ten commandments, seven deadly sins and, with other teaching, the Epistle of St. James. Foxe, *loc. cit.*, pp. 235–6; Thomson, *op. cit.*, pp. 90, n. 5, 93.

included disappointed love, vegetarianism and teetotalism. As part of the profession of his new calling he learnt to read and write. Smith seems to have put these skills to true Lollard uses, for when he was caught and examined some years later in 1389, he confessed to having spent eight years copying English books of the Gospels and Epistles and Fathers, which he had to hand over to the archbishop of Canterbury. He is also recorded to have held a heretical school.[38] At the other end of the movement, from the early sixteenth century, comes the story of Roger Dods of Burford, servant of John Drury the vicar of Windrush. The vicar, so it was related, 'taught him the ABC to the intent he should have understanding in the Apocalypse, wherein he said, that he should perceive all the falsehood of the world, and all the truth.'[39] Literacy was the apple on the tree of prophetic knowledge.

Between the days of William Smith and Roger Dods many heretical book-owners and readers were revealed. Those who owned books were not by any means always able to read them. John Claydon, a London skinner who died for his faith in 1415 after many years adherence to the sect, had been in possession of a recently composed book called *The Lantern of Light*, which he had had copied and bound, and read aloud by his servant John Fuller, though he was never able to read it for himself.[40] Errors or heresies, however, as numerous cases suggest, could just as easily—indeed (as the authorities doubtless realized) probably more easily—be derived from the vicarious knowledge of texts.[41] Some of the literate or semi-literate Lollards who are disclosed in the trials were clerks (such as Richard Preston, a chaplain of Cookham in Berkshire, who owned the English Gospels and abjured in 1443), but more of them were artisans of one kind or another—weavers, woolwinders, fullers, wiredrawers, or simply labourers.[42] Individual Lollards from all these trades were discovered who in varying degrees and ways had become book-conscious or literate. But the processes by which they had been introduced to this world of heretical

[38] *Chronicon Henrici Knighton*, ed. J. R. Lumby (R.S. 1895), ii, pp. 180–81, 313 (Knighton mistakenly placed Courtenay's 1389 proceedings at Leicester under the year 1392); cf. p. 182 for the report that while Smith was staying with the chaplain Richard Waytestathe in the chapel of St. John the Baptist outside the walls of Leicester, members of the sect met there and 'conventicula fecerunt', and also 'ibi habuerunt gignasium malignorum dogmatum et opinionum, et errorum haereticorumque communicationem'. K. B. McFarlane, *John Wycliffe and the Beginnings of English Non-conformity* (London, 1952), pp. 103–4, 139–41, 173; James Crompton, 'Leicestershire Lollards', *Trans. Leics. Arch. and Hist. Soc.*, xliv (1968–9), pp. 19–20, 24–5.

[39] Foxe, *A. and M.*, iv, p. 237.

[40] *The Register of Henry Chichele*, ed. E. F. Jacob, iv (Canterbury and York Society, Vol. xlvii, 1947), pp. 132–8; *The Lanterne of Lizt*, pp. viii-xiii; James Gairdner, *Lollardy and the Reformation in England*, i (London, 1908), pp. 89–90. *The Lantern of Light* can be dated on internal evidence to 1409 × 1415. Claydon valued it so highly he was reported to have said he would rather have paid thrice the price he had, than be without it. Another parallel case is that of James Brewster (above, p. 199) who though unable to read owned 'a certain little book of Scripture in English, of an old writing almost worn for age'. Foxe, *A. and M.*, iv, p. 216.

[41] This was a point made by Pecock who argued that hearers of difficult points were more likely to report and understand amiss than were readers of the same. *Reule*, p. 99 and see below p. 208. For the contrary view (reading is more productive of error than hearing) see William Butler's Determination in Deanesly, *op. cit.*, p. 403.

[42] Thomson, *op. cit.*, p. 65. On the social status of the Lollards see Fines, *art. cit.*, pp. 162–3; Dickens, *op. cit.*, p. 30.

learning are rarely revealed, for all the anxiety displayed by the authorities
to make detection an obligation upon those who abjured. Members of the
sect learnt their own methods of concealment and deception, and they had
the strongest motives to conceal their books. They might go so far as to
destroy them in the hope of avoiding detection.[43]

On occasion even heretics who were caught and recanted, or burned,
managed to secrete their books for the benefit of other followers. Two
treatises by imprisoned heretics of the first Lollard generation were preserved and copied for posterity.[44] The wife of a wright of Martham in
Norfolk, whose husband used to read to her at night, came into possession
of a book that had belonged to William White, a Kentish refugee who was
burned in Norwich in 1428.[45] And a Lollard by name of John Stilman who
died in 1518, had been able at his abjuration before the bishop of Salisbury
about eleven years earlier, to hide away for two years, 'in an old oak', the
books which he had inherited from a condemned heretic, and then took
them with him to London where these doings were laid against him by the
bishop in 1518.[46]

The family circle, the household—including servants as well as
relatives—might well have been the commonest group in which some sort
of literacy could be acquired, and perhaps also the likeliest way of coming
into possession of heretical reading matter. A good many of the Coventry
Lollards examined in 1511–12 were found to have learnt their heresy
through domestic, familial introductions.[47] Sometimes we can see into the
ways in which books as well as doctrines passed down in heretical family
groups. For instance there is the sixteenth-century case of John Morden of
Chesham, whose son-in-law inherited his book of heresy, and then came to
attend Bible-readings with Morden's nephew James.[48] It was fears of such a
literary bequest which led Bishop Blythe of Coventry and Lichfield to write
on 3 November 1511 to warn the bishop of Lincoln about the 'many books
of heresy' of one Master William Kent, who had probably died the previous
year having been the 'master of divers heretics'. These books, capable of
corrupting many others, were thought to have probably descended to William's nephew and executor, Ralph Kent, priest.[49]

For some heretics the anxiety to get hold of these underground treatises
might have entailed careful cultivation of personal contacts and considerable expenses or travel. Owing to the need for concealment we do not,

[43] Luxton, *art. cit.*, pp. 124–5; Thomson, *op. cit.*, p. 89.
[44] Namely William Thorpe's account of his trial and the commentary on the Apocalypse
known as the *Opus Arduum*.
[45] Thomson, *op. cit.*, pp. 122–3, 130. Margery Baxter, wife of William Baxter a wright of
Martham, was tried in October 1428 and put to penance. The vicar of Halvergate, who was
accused of receiving William White, had also received unnamed books from both White and
Baxter. For White's confession of the 'many books' he had made and dictated see *Fasciculi
Zizaniorum*, ed. W. W. Shirley (R.S. 1858), p. 432.
[46] Foxe, *A. and M.*, iv, pp. 207–8; Thomson, *op. cit.*, p. 83. The books in question were
'Wickliff's Wicket' and a book of the ten commandments which Richard Smart (who was
burned at Salisbury about 1503–4) had given him. John Stilman had read English books at the
house of Thomas Watts of Dogmersfield (above p. 199) who in turn was taught by John
Hacker (below n. 57). Thomson, *op. cit.*, pp. 88–89.
[47] Fines, *art. cit.*, pp. 165–6, gives examples of conversions through domestic readings.
[48] Thomson, *op. cit.*, p. 91.
[49] Fines, *art. cit.*, pp. 170–2.

of course, know much about the centres where the heretical literature was produced or copied—and no doubt these changed with the leadership and opportunities of the sect. But some of the manuscripts of a surviving sermon-cycle have been shown to contain evidence which suggests that there existed (at any rate at some stage) a fairly tight organization for supervising the production and correction of texts.[50] Early in the fifteenth century it was possible for visiting Bohemian scholars to get access to works of Wycliffe at the country parishes of Kemerton in Gloucestershire and Braybrooke in Northamptonshire, as well as—still—in Oxford.[51] Braybrooke was still such a centre at the time of Sir John Oldcastle's rising some years after this, when a man named Thomas Ile was busy there writing out the broadsheets with which it was hoped to muster supporters for the rebellion.[52] Later on we catch glimpses of individuals who may have helped to keep up the supplies of secreted texts—for instance a man from a Gloucestershire group who in 1472 had to promise the bishop of Hereford not to keep quires or rolls written by himself or others containing heresies or errors.[53]

Visiting missionaries apparently sometimes left behind copies of their sermons for the benefit of the congregations they had been addressing. We can deduce this from the following words which appear in a tract against the clergy holding property—two copies of which survive in the same handwriting.

> Now sirs, the day is over and I may keep you no longer, and I have no time to make now a recapitulation of my sermon. Nevertheless, I intend to leave it written among you, and whoever likes may look over it . . . [54]

[50] Hudson, 'A Lollard Sermon-Cycle' (above n. 24), pp. 145–6, 149–50, 152; *idem*, 'Some Aspects of Lollard Book Production', pp. 152–5; *idem*, 'Contributions to a Bibliography of Wycliffite Writings', *Notes and Queries*, December 1973, p. 448.

[51] The three works were the *De ecclesia, De dominio divino*, and *De veritate sacre scripture*, which Nicholas Faulfiš and George Knĕhnic were able during their visit of 1407–8 to copy in the country and correct at Oxford—where Gascoigne reports a burning of Wycliffe's books at Carfax in 1410. Braybrooke and Kemerton can both be linked with Lollard suspects. The former rectory was occupied by Robert Hook, who was in trouble for heresy three times between 1405 and 1425; the rector of Kemerton in 1401–2 was Robert Lechlade, who was banished from Oxford from 1395–99 for teaching suspect doctrine. Both men were associated with the suspect Lollard knight Sir Thomas Latimer: Anne Hudson, 'The Debate on Bible Translation, Oxford 1401', *E.H.R.*, xc (1975), pp. 11–13; Thomas Gascoigne, *Loci e Libro Veritatum*, ed. J. E. Thorold Rogers (Oxford, 1881), p. 116.

[52] McFarlane, *John Wycliffe*, p. 146; *idem, Lancastrian Kings and Lollard Knights* (Oxford, 1972), pp. 195–6; Hudson, 'Some Aspects of Lollard Book Production', pp. 155–6 on Braybrooke as a possible midlands centre for the production of Lollard works of instruction.

[53] Thomson, *op. cit.*, pp. 40–42. For such an abjuration formula see n. 66 below.

[54] Hudson, 'Contributions to a Bibliography of Wycliffite Writings', p. 449. Cf. *idem*, 'A Lollard Compilation and the Dissemination of Wycliffite Thought', p. 68 for the *Floretum*, intended as a preaching aid for those who lacked books; 'veraces libri multiplicati, sed religiosis privatis incarcerati, in collegiis concatenati, ita quod pauperes sacerdotes . . . propter penuriam pecunie libros emendi impediti . . .' (my thanks to Miss Hudson for this quotation). For a reference to poor priests who 'think with God's help to travel about where they should most profit by evidence that God gives them', see *English Works*, p. 253. John Claydon confessed that one reason why he so valued his red leather-bound volume containing *The Lantern of Light* was because it contained a sermon that had once been preached at Horsleydown; *Register of Henry Chichele*, iv, p. 133. Pecock fervently recommended that preached truths should be conveyed to lay people in writing, having in mind 'the great need of our neighbours' souls asking our help to study and record sermons to be said to them'; *Reule*, pp. 99, 392, and below p. 208.

It seems reasonable, too, to suppose that the parchminers and scriveners who appear among the accused, had something to do with the heretics' book-production: men such as the Michael Scrivener and William Parchmener who were among those charged by Archbishop Courtenay at Leicester in 1389. And we have already encountered the report of a parchment-maker bringing books from London in the 1420s to a Lollard schoolmaster in Norfolk.[55]

As time went on and particularly after the advent of printing (marginally though that affected them), perhaps the Lollards' book world, like that of others, came to focus especially on London. The capital, apart from its other resources, had the advantage of providing better cover for illicit copyists than could most country outposts. It was there, in the aftermath of Perkins's revolt of 1431, that a ceremonial burning of Lollard books is reported. In 1508 the rector of Letcombe Basset in Berkshire, himself a possessor of heretical English books, admitted to having been told by one of his Lollard associates that if he ever went to London he would find rich supplies of reading matter there.[56] It also appears—at any rate by this period—that there were individuals acting as agents or purveyors of Lollard books, and some of them (who seem to have had widespread contacts in the world of underground manuscripts) went on to help in the dissemination of printed Lutheran texts.[57]

We may observe that the readings to which the Lollard texts were put and of which the authorities became so suspicious, were of several different kinds.[58] At one end of the scale was the solitary study of individuals like William Smith and Roger Dods, wrestling initially with their own inadequacies as readers, as well as with the problems of textual comprehension. At the other extreme were the readings (chiefly Biblical) of a more or less ritual nature, which called for expert readers (or prophetic reciters like Alice Colyns) who pronounced the word to gatherings of heretics met specifically for this purpose. In between these two a variety of domestic groupings joined together in study as opportunity offered, within the ramifying circles of household and kin: servants read to masters (John Claydon); husbands to wives (William and Margery Baxter); fathers to families (Thomas Watts); in-laws to in-laws (William Sweeting or John Morden). Probably among all such Lollard readers silent reading was

---

[55] Crompton, 'Leicestershire Lollards, p. 23, cf. p. 30 for the arrest in 1414, after Oldcastle's rising, of William Mably parchminer, perhaps the same as the William Parchmener of 1389. See above p. 198 for the parchminer who supplied Richard Belward, and below n. 66 for a scrivener's form of abjuration. For general observations about Lollards in the book-trade see McFarlane, *John Wycliffe*, p. 180.

[56] *Peasants, Knights and Heretics*, p. 318. Above, 46; Thomson, *op. cit.*, pp. 85–6. For book-links between Coventry and London see *ibid.*, p. 114 and Fines, *art. cit.*, p. 164.

[57] John Hacker or Hakker ('old father Hacker') of Coleman Street in London, where he was a water-bearer, may very well have been such a colporteur of Lollard (and later Lutheran) texts. When questioned in 1521 it emerged that he had links with heretics in various areas, and he admitted taking two books to Burford Lollards. Despite his abjuration in 1521 Hacker's activities continued, and he was called upon to abjure again in 1527. Thomson, *op. cit.*, pp. 89, 93, 138; Dickens, *English Reformation*, pp. 28–9, 32–3; *idem*, 'Heresy and the Origins of English Protestantism', *Britain and the Netherlands*, ed. J. S. Bromley and E. H. Kossmann, ii (1964), pp. 55, 58, 60–61; Foxe, *A. and M.*, iv, pp. 234, 236, 239–40; John Strype, *Ecclesiastical Memorials*, Vol. I, pt.i (Oxford, 1822), pp. 114–117.

[58] As pointed out by John Fines, *art. cit.*, p. 166.

scarcely to be expected, and we may surmise that the expertise of this kind of reading was rarer among heretically inclined craftsmen than it was among upper class or professional readers.

Biblical books were far from being the only texts which were the object of Lollard studies. The large number of manuscripts of their literature which still survive (some of them bulky and handsome in appearance) is itself a tribute to the vitality of the heretics' literary activity.[59] But since the Bible had a unique role Bishop Pecock was perhaps right to distinguish two sorts of readers among the heretics. One kind, he said, held 'so stiffly and so singularly' to the vernacular Bible—above all the New Testament—that they dismissed all other books, Latin or English, as unnecessary and redundant. The other school of heretics admitted other books alongside the reading and study of the Bible, and these (to Pecock 'sorry and unsavoury and insufficiently teaching' books) they cherished as rich jewels, to be 'embraced, loved and multiplied' abroad among all Christian people.[60]

* * * *

Undoubtedly then, though obviously many Lollards were neither readers nor textual learners, a significant number were. This was true at the beginnings of Lollardy in the 1380s, and it was still true in the 1520s when the literate members of the sect no longer included any university men, but were clerks and tradespeople. Although we cannot begin to calculate the total numbers of such persons it is clear that at the later date, as at the earlier, it was the literate who were likely to be the most influential members of the movement. It is certain that they were recognized as such. Seldom, in fact, has such humble learning been received with so much and such elevated alarmism. Those who wrote against the Lollards, those who acted against them, and those who devised new procedures to deal with them, all similarly concentrated upon the heretics' use and dissemination of vernacular texts—particularly the Bible.

This Master John Wycliffe, the chronicler Henry Knighton wrote accusingly some years after his death, translated the Gospel from Latin into English so that it was more open to laymen and ignorant people, including 'women who know how to read', whereas previously it had been the preserve of well-read clerks of good understanding.[61] It was Wycliffite reliance upon the text of scripture which Thomas Netter of Walden specially set out to refute in his long Latin *Doctrinale*. It was in their capacity of 'Bible-men' that Bishop Reginald Pecock embarked upon his series of English writings to undermine the heretics, pointing out that even if (as the Lollards idealistically recommended) 'it might be ordained that all men and women in their youth should learn to read writings in the language in which they live and dwell', reading alone would not suffice to bring them to Christ.[62]

As time went on and the church improved its anti-heretical procedures, its attention became increasingly directed towards the reprobation and

[59] Hudson, 'Some Aspects of Lollard Book Production', pp. 147, 149; *idem*, 'A Lollard Sermon-Cycle', pp. 150–151.

[60] Pecock, *Reule*, pp. 17–18.

[61] *Knighton*, ii, pp. 151–2 ('laicis et infirmioribus personis'); Adamson, *art. cit.*, (above n. 11), p. 40.

[62] V. H. H. Green, *Bishop Reginald Pecock* (Cambridge, 1945), pp. 106–7; Pecock, *Repressor*, i, pp. 192, 208–9.

discovery of vernacular Lollard tracts and readers. Whereas in 1382, when the university of Oxford was ordered to seize all books or tracts of Wycliffe or Nicholas Hereford, no mention had been made of English works, by 1388 the enquiries were extended further afield and specifically refer to English as well as Latin texts.[63] Archbishop Arundel formulated fuller controls over the extension of the vernacular—controls which earned him abusive comment at the hands of heretical writers—by making it obligatory to obtain ecclesiastical permission for any Biblical translation.[64] And when, after Oldcastle's rising of 1414, a settled procedure for anti-heretical actions was decided on in the convocation of 1416, the two main points which were to be regularly enquired into were the holding of Lollard conventicles and the possession of suspect writings in English.[65] The questions asked of heretics in individual cases show that the possession or reading of vernacular texts became a leading criterion.[66] Was the suspect familiar with the heretics, or did he or she have books in English containing error? Simply to be a reader of English or to own a religious text written in English became in certain circumstances and among certain sorts of people potentially incriminating. Literacy pointed an accusing finger towards heresy. As one Lollard author put it, 'truth moveth many men to speak sentences in English that they have gathered in Latin, and therefore are men held heretics'.[67] It was as a vernacular literate movement that Lollardy had gathered momentum and it was as a vernacular literate movement that it was suspected and persecuted.

Suspicions, however, easily breed misunderstandings. They certainly did so in this case. Both individuals and writings were brought up for examination or censure, the questioning of whose orthodoxy might now seem surprising. In their different ways both Margery Kempe and Reginald Pecock were the victims—at least in part—of such misunderstandings. Margery Kempe, though she has now earned a title for discussion in the annals of English mysticism, was challenged by her contemporaries as a Lollard and twice examined by churchmen for her suspected unorthodoxy. She was exonerated. Pecock, on the other hand, was not. Having spent many years and much labour producing a corpus of English writings to counter the Lollards' position, he was himself convicted of error in 1457, saw his books publicly burnt, and spent the remainder of his days in ignominious exile in Thorney Abbey in Cambridgeshire. Pecock had

[63] It is significant of the changing direction of the movement that in 1382, when the Oxford followers of Wycliffe were being tried and condemned at the Blackfriars Council, John Aston took the step of circulating through London copies of his 'confession' written in both Latin and English. *Fasciculi Zizaniorum*, pp. 329–30; cf. pp. 312–14 for the 1382 orders; *Chronicon Henrici Knighton*, ii, pp. 264–5 for a copy of the 1388 letters patent; McFarlane, *John Wycliffe*, p. 111.

[64] Wilkins, *Concilia*, iii, p. 317; Deanesly, *op. cit.*, pp. 295–6.

[65] *Register of Henry Chichele*, iii, p. 18.

[66] On the formulas devised to standardize proceedings against suspect Lollards see Thomson, *op. cit.*, p. 200 ff. and Anne Hudson, 'The Examination of Lollards', *B.I.H.R.*, xlvi (1973), pp. 145–59. These procedural instructions make clear the importance attributed to the heretics' English writings, and the abjuration formula appears to have been framed for a Lollard scribe. Cf. below p. 208 for the St. Albans enquiries about English books in 1426–7, and Fines, *art. cit.*, pp. 164–5 for the Coventry proceedings of 1511–12 displaying more interest in books than in doctrine.

[67] Hudson, 'A Lollard Quaternion', p. 441.

undoubtedly fallen into doctrinal error, for which he was deservedly condemned. But in his case, as in Margery Kempe's earlier in the century,
alarm was partly caused by long-bred suspicions.[68] Both of them had displayed too great a fondness for trying to improve others by 'good words' in
the vernacular, either spoken or written. Indeed Pecock upheld quite as
earnestly as the Lollards his deep conviction that books, vernacular books
of doctrine for the lay people, 'which they may often read or hear often
read', were essential to supplement preaching.[69] Such enthusiasm seemed
dangerously akin to that of the heretics. Pseudo-mystic and pseudo-
theologian were equally reminiscent of Lollardy, equally liable to err.

It was the same story with texts.[70] Among the orthodox writings which
were brought to the attention of the authorities in heretical proceedings
were the *Prick of Conscience* (a long English poem covering nearly the
whole of contemporary theology, which was popular enough by 1350 for
there to be versions in both northern and southern dialects);[71] Chaucer's
Canterbury Tales (named in proceedings of the 1460s);[72] *Dives et Pauper*
(owned by a chaplain of Bury St. Edmunds who abjured in 1430-31);[73] and
a book called the *Shepherd's Kalendar* which had been printed in four
editions before it was found, about 1521, in the hands of a heretic of
Lincoln diocese who said 'that he was persuaded by this book . . . that the
sacrament [of the altar] was made in remembrance of Christ'.[74]

The suspicion attached to these works might be attributed to the
development of a general ecclesiastical obsession about the dangers of all
works written in English when read by the wrong sort of people: an obsession which produced for instance ordinances at St. Albans in 1426–7
against 'all false preachers and possessors of books in the vulgar tongue',
on the grounds that heresy was largely caused by 'the possession and read-

---

[68] For Pecock's recantation see Green, *op. cit.*, pp. 59–60; cf. pp. 34–5, 45, 89, 202–3 for
the suspicions Pecock aroused through writing in the vernacular. His own works witness to his
defensiveness, as well as his defence, on this score; e.g. his *Reule*, pp. 87 ff., 99 (see above
n. 13); or *The Folower to the Donet*, ed. E. V. Hitchcock (E.E.T.S., O.S. 164, 1924), p. 7, cf.
pp. 176–8.

[69] Pecock, *Reule*, pp. 19–20, cf. 97, 99, 392 and n. 54 above.

[70] In the following paragraphs I do not attempt a complete account of texts interpolated by
the Lollards, but offer some salient examples. For further references to such works see *A
Manual of the Writings in Middle English*, ed. J. Burke Severs, ii (Hamden, Conn., 1970),
p. 357; and for the *Ancren Riwle* above n. 19.

[71] For Richard Colyns of Ginge, detected in 1521 for possession of the *Prick of Conscience*,
see above n. 37. Two occasions on which this work was handed over for examination were in
1473, by Richard Rider to the bishop of Winchester, and 1514, when it was one of the books
which Richard Hunne surrendered to the bishop of London. Thomson, *op. cit.*, pp. 73–4,
168–9. On this work see also Deanesly, *op. cit.*, pp. 214–15; H. E. Allen, *Writings Ascribed to
Richard Rolle of Hampole* (London and New York, 1927), pp. 386–7.

[72] 'The second book of the tales of Canterbury' was named (with other books) in Lincoln
diocese proceedings of 1464 against John Baron of Amersham. Deanesly, *op. cit.*, p. 363;
Thomson, *op. cit.*, p. 70.

[73] Robert Bert was accused on 2 March 1430 of possessing a book called 'Dives et Pauper',
which contained many errors and heresies. He denied all knowledge of its heretical nature.
Edwin Welch, 'Some Suffolk Lollards', *Proc. Suff. Inst. Arch.*, vol. xxix (1964), p. 160;
Hudson, 'The Examination of Lollards', p. 145. Above, pp. 96, 178–9.

[74] The *Shepherd's Kalendar* was named in Longland's proceedings, suspect because of these
words spoken by John Edmunds *alias* John Ogins, of Burford, denying the real presence.
Foxe, *A. and M.*, iv, p. 238, cf. pp. 240–41. There were English editions in 1503, 1506, 1508
and 1520 [?] (*STC* 22407–22410).

ing of books which are written in our vernacular tongue'.[75] Much mis-
apprehension derived from this conviction that for certain people to read,
above all to read English, was to err. There were however better grounds
than this for the church's alarmism. The need for wariness, even of
orthodox texts, was suggested by the heretics' own preaching and practising.

In their anxious search for precedents the Lollards (specially the early
Biblical translators) eagerly hunted out the church's weak points: its own
admissions about the uses and needs of the vernacular. They had of course
no lack of examples—from Jerome onwards. Some of the more valuable
and telling ones lay nearer to hand in contemporary England.[76] In the
English version of Richard Ullerston's early fifteenth-century defence of
Bible translation, we find the following passage.

> Also a noble holy man, Richard Hermit [Rolle], drew the psalter into English,
> with a gloss of long process . . . by which many Englishmen have been greatly
> edified . . . Also sir William Thoresby, archbishop of York, had a treatise drawn
> into English by a worshipful clerk whose name was Gaytrik, in the which were
> contained the articles of the faith, seven deadly sins, the works of mercy and the
> ten commandments, and sent them in small pamphlets [*pagynes*] to the common
> people to learn this and to know this.[77]

It was certainly a useful argument. But the Lollards did more than argue.
They also acted. And their actions included, in addition to the provision
of their own texts—Biblical, homiletical, poetical—the adaptation of
orthodox writings to suit less orthodox views. Both the texts named in this
passage were accorded such treatment.

Richard Rolle's translation of the *Psalter,* together with the glosses of
Peter Lombard, was written before 1349 and having appeared so long
before the days of Wycliffe was safely exempted from the 1409 ban upon
unsponsored Bible translations.[78] It was copied and circulated freely in the
fifteenth century, and indeed acquired the status of a standard version. But
while one group of texts adheres to the original, another was produced with
many additions and alterations, which was a doctored version. One
fifteenth-century copy of Rolle's *Psalter* has prefixed to it a metrical prologue which was concerned to assure the reader of the book's orthodoxy
since, the writer said:

> Copied has this Psalter been, of evil men of lollardry:
> And afterward it has been seen, ympyd in with heresy.
> They saiden then to lewed fools, that it should be all entire,
> A blessed book of their schools, of Richard Hampole the Psalter.

---

[75] Deanesly, *op. cit.,* p. 327, quoting Amundesham, *Annales*, ed. H. T. Riley (Rolls Series,
1870–71), i, p. 225.

[76] For the use made of the *pater noster* in this case see Appendix.

[77] Curt F. Bühler, 'A Lollard tract: On translating the Bible into English', *Medium Aevum*,
vii (1938), p. 175. On the authorship of this text see Hudson, 'The Debate on Bible Translation, Oxford 1401', *E.H.R.,* xc (1975), pp. 1–18.

[78] For Rolle's Psalter (which had a wide circulation and 'appealed to gentry of no special
asceticism') and the Lollards' treatment of it see Allen, *Writings Ascribed to Richard Rolle*,
pp. 170 ff. esp. 173–6, 188–92; Deanesly, *op. cit.,* pp. 145–6, 231, 304; *Manual*, ed. J. Burke
Severs, ii, pp. 386, 538–9.

Thus they said, to make them believe, on their school through subtlety,
To bring them in, so them to grieve, against the faith in great folly,
And slandered foul this holy man, with their wicked cursed wiles.[79]

The Lollards had indeed edited the *Psalter,* keeping Rolle's text but introducing some of their own teaching as commentary.

The other work referred to by Ullerston is also a clear illustration of Lollard editorial methods. The manual of instructions which (as we have seen) Archbishop Thoresby issued in 1357 and for which he had the same year obtained the approval of the convocation of York, likewise survives in two versions: orthodox and heretical. Here too the editor did not alter the text so much as introduce interpolations, which include lengthy commentaries upon both the *pater noster* and the apostles' creed, neither of which has any parallel in the original.[80] The interpolator's Lollardy is clearly displayed by his attitude towards the church, and by such statements as 'secular lords should in default of prelates learn and preach the law of God in their mother tongue'.[81]

It is evident that in both these instances the work of Lollard editing might be explained by the fact that here, as Ullerston indicated, were to be found ready-made versions of Biblical texts which carried full official approval. The opportunities for propaganda were obvious and were utilized. But some other examples of heretical association with orthodox writings are less easily accounted for.

In the case of the *Canterbury Tales* we know that at any rate by the sixteenth century a heretical connection had been acquired by the insertion of the tendentious *Plowman's Tale*—an insertion which was enough to help persuade one good Protestant that he had in Chaucer an upright Wycliffian forbear.[82] The *Prick of Conscience* (which was suspect more than once) was for long, but wrongly, attributed to Richard Rolle, and its very popularity might have held some attraction for editors of doubtful standing. At all events there were such. In this text the interpolated passages may seem more anti-clerical than heretical, though they have been thought to show Lollard influence, and the emphasis upon 'God's law' might itself have been enough to arouse contemporary suspicion.[83]

[79] Allen, *op. cit.,* p. 174, quoting from Bodl. Laud Misc. 286 of the early fifteenth century (ympyd=grafted). Cf. p. 190 for the reference to a psalter being taken from William Thorpe by Archbishop Arundel. (Whether or not one accepts the suggestion that Thorpe was responsible for the glosses, it is possible that he owned one of the interpolated Psalters).

[80] For the interpolated version see *The Lay Folks' Catechism, or the English and Latin Versions of Archbishop Thoresby's Instruction for the People*, ed. T. F. Simmons and H. E. Nolleth (E.E.T.S., O.S. 118, 1901); A. L. Kellogg and E. W. Talbert, 'The Wyclifite *Pater Noster* and *Ten Commandments*, with Special Reference to English MSS. 85 and 90 in the John Rylands Library', *Bull. John Rylands Lib.,* Vol. 42 (1959–60), pp. 356–8; Pantin, *op. cit.,* pp. 211–12.

[81] *The Lay Folks' Catechism*, p. 15.

[82] See my 'Lollardy and the Reformation: Survival or Revival?' *History.* See below, pp. 229-30. As regards this view of Chaucer it is worth pointing out that Foxe (and John Gough before him) attributed *Jack Upland* to Chaucer; *Jack Upland*, ed. P. L. Heyworth (Oxford, 1968), pp. 5–6. See below pp. 219ff.

[83] There are more than a hundred surviving manuscripts of the *Prick of Conscience*. For a description of them, including the interpolated text, see Allen, *op. cit.,* pp. 372–97, and J. E. Wells, *A Manual of the Writings in Middle English* (New Haven, 1916), pp. 447–9. Allen suggested (*op. cit.,* p. 3) that the attribution to Rolle might have been due to a desire to give the poem a safe-conduct from Lollard associations.

Lastly there are the English books called *Dives et Pauper* and the *Kalendar of Shepherds*. These were both popular manuals of general instruction which seem to have been written and to have circulated in unimpeachable circles, and both appeared in early editions before 1510. The author of *Dives et Pauper* who was writing about 1405–10, appears to have been a mendicant—quite possibly a university man.[84] The work is shaped as an exposition of the Decalogue in dialogue form and starts with a discussion 'of holy poverty', perfectly orthodox in tone. How was it possible for this book to be labelled heretical? Did the sheer openness of the discussion over such vexed questions as images come to seem insidious? The *Shepherd's Kalendar* is still more of a puzzle. It was a sort of layman's guide to general knowledge, and it is hard to see how the heretic under trial by the bishop of Lincoln could have derived from it his allegedly erroneous views on the eucharist. While the work expounds the articles of the faith, the *pater noster* and the commandments, the editions which survive hardly appear to touch on this sacrament, and Richard Pynson (whose version appeared in 1506) was careful to edit the text so as to stress its orthodoxy—though he did not refrain from putting in a good word for the French who were 'so fortunate' as to have the Bible and Apocalypse in their mother tongue, which 'in English may not be'.[85]

How are we to account for these interpolated texts, and the broader suspicions to which they gave rise? After all, Wycliffites and Lollards alike were clearly not short of material of their own to write, copy and disseminate. Why did they find it necessary to make use of existing orthodox works? In the first place, obviously, there was the value of disguise. Under cover of an ostensibly unimpeachable author or title it might be possible to pass off the views of the sect or infiltrate them into the hands of unsuspecting readers.[86] It could be a process of unobtrusive undermining of the other side's defences. It is noticeable that the works chosen for this sort of treatment were popular ones which enjoyed a wide circulation. Insinuating Lollard views into Rolle's *Psalter* or the *Prick of Conscience* was a means of climbing onto the laps of people—including the gentry—who had come to fight shy of heresy. We might therefore see the interpolated texts as part of a bid to win a wider circle of readers and to escape from the literary underworld. Secondly (and not unconnected with this) is the fact that the views expressed in these editorial additions tend to fall into the category of what may be described as marginal unorthodoxy. The difficulty modern editors have experienced of deciding whether or not interpolated passages are to be defined as specifically Lollard,[87] reflects the difficulties of con-

[84] H. G. Pfander, '*Dives et Pauper*', *The Library*, 4th series, xiv (1934), pp. 299–312; H. G. Richardson, '*Dives and Pauper*', *Notes and Queries*, 11th series, iv (1911), pp. 321–3; H. G. Richardson, '*Dives and Pauper*', *The Library*, 4th series, xv (1935), pp. 31–37. H. G. Richardson showed that Bale's ascription of the work to Henry Parker was erroneous. There were editions of *Dives et Pauper* in 1493, 1496 and 1536 (*STC* 19212–19214). The first modern edition is that now being edited by P. H. Barnum (E.E.T.S., 275, 1976).

[85] From the concluding verses added by Pynson at the end of the 1506 edition, which he had had freshly translated from the French, on the grounds that the English of the earlier edition was incomprehensible. For the earlier continental editions see *The Kalender of Shepherdes*, ed. H. O. Sommer (London, 1892).

[86] As indicated by Kellogg and Talbert, *art. cit.*, pp. 349, 376–7.

[87] For instance *ibid.*, p. 350 ff. or Allen, *op. cit.*, pp. 170–71, 367–8, 374–5, 391–2.

temporary prelates in discerning and weeding out contaminated texts. Heresy (and not only that of the Lollards) always presented a problem of definition, for behind each hardline adherent who was prepared to die for his faith there may always have stood half a dozen fellow-travellers of varying degrees of dissent. This border country of sympathizers which (as the story of the Lollard knights shows) was all-important to the heretics, might have been reached by interpolated orthodox texts, when most other methods were failing.

*   *   *   *

By the end of the fifteenth century, thanks to a century of action and counter-action, the attitude of the church authorities towards certain uses of the vernacular had become excessively wary. About 1400 it had been possible for Mirk to press the advantages of the use of English upon the parochial clergy. 'It is much more useful and meritorious for you to say your *pater noster* in English than in such Latin as you do. For when you speak in English, then you know, and understand well what you say; and so by your understanding you have liking and devotion to say it'.[88] By 1500 there had been too many people urging the use of English for the wrong sort of understanding: too many people like William Wakeham of Devizes who twisted the case into statements like 'it is no better for laymen to say the *pater noster* in Latin than to say "bibble babble" '.[89] Sayings like this played their part in helping to discredit even some perfectly orthodox uses of the vernacular, which might otherwise have gained ground in England. As it was, such developments were arrested—unhealthily arrested. England was unlike other parts of Europe in that no printed editions of the Bible in the vernacular appeared in the fifteenth century.

Lollardy has been described as 'a series of attitudes from which beliefs evolved, rather than . . . a set of doctrines'.[90] The heretics as we can now see them were indeed a divergent crew. Their views were erratic as well as erroneous, and they seem to have included loose-livers as well as tavern-talkers. Yet for all their aberrations and despite the fact that they came to consist mainly of tradespeople and humble persons against whom the combined resources of order and orthodoxy were arrayed, they survived and, in the course of a century, produced a number of adherents who were ready to die for their beliefs. The contemporary prosecutors, upon whose proceedings we must largely rely, continued throughout to regard the Lollards as a movement. Were they altogether wrong?

If we take the Lollards on this contemporary hostile estimate, they seem to have looked dangerous above all as vernacular readers, of the Bible primarily, but also of various other texts. They were articulate, and to some extent consistent, because they had a backbone of literacy. There is indeed a considerable body of writings which survives to buttress this contemporary viewpoint, and if we want to study the Lollards on their own terms it is essential to study them together with the literature they pro-

---

[88] *Mirk's Festial*, ed. Theodor Erbe (E.E.T.S., Extra Series, xcvi, 1905), p. 282, cf. p. 299; Manning, *The People's Faith*, p. 44. See also Appendix.

[89] *Peasants, Knights and Heretics*, 287. Above, 15 ; Thomson, *op. cit.*, pp. 32–33.

[90] Thomson, *op. cit.*, p. 244, cf. pp. 239, 250. See also the similar view of E. W. Talbert in *A Manual of Writings in Middle English*, ed. J. Burke Severs, ii, p. 380.

duced.[91] To study them without it might seem (as they themselves would have been pleased to think) rather like studying St. Jerome without mention of the Vulgate. Seeing the heretics as readers, and seeing their literature as an inherent part of their work, we can understand better the problem of the authorities. Or, to put it another way, it becomes clear that the heretics continued to survive and to make recruits because they reflected developments which were widespread and which were taking place in the whole of society, not merely in unorthodox circles.

So, looking on to events of the sixteenth century, did the alarmist attitudes which the Lollards had aroused towards the religious literacy of lesser laymen have any discernible bearing upon the Reformation? The answer must surely be that they did, though it is only possible here to give a few indications.

Consider first the case of John Colet, dean of St. Paul's. Probably early on in the year 1513—at a time when there was considerable activity against the Lollards—Colet was suspected of heresy and, reportedly, threatened with excommunication. In July the bishop of London suspended him from preaching for several months. Among the reported reasons for this, one (given by Tyndale) was that Colet had translated the *pater noster* into English.[92] The Lord's Prayer in English! What a harmless action, one might think—and so indeed it seemed, not so many years later. In 1513, however, translating the *pater noster* was a suspect enterprise, linked with heretical views. The Lollards had brought the English Lord's Prayer into discredit by making it part of their case for vernacular scripture, and a few years afterwards some of them were burned for this very teaching. It is not inconceivable that Colet was temporarily tarred with the Lollard brush. Were not Lollards reported as attentive auditors at Colet's sermons? Was not the dean jestingly dubbed as 'some Wycliffite, I suppose' in one of Erasmus's *Colloquies* 'I don't think so', ran the answer, though Colet had read Wycliffe's books. 'Where he got hold of them isn't clear', though this would be less of a mystery if we were to suppose (without any firm evidence for doing so) that Colet, like Tyndale, Coverdale, Robert Barnes and other later

---

[91] For a recent plea by one who is doing much to this end see Anne Hudson 'Contributions to a Bibliography of Wycliffite Writings', p. 443 ff. Obviously we should not neglect the Latin sources, but as time went on Lollardy became more and more exclusively vernacular and further removed from Wycliffe's Latin writings, which owed their preservation more to the Hussites than to the Lollards.

[92] For the proceedings against Colet see P. S. Allen, 'Dean Colet and Archbishop Warham', *E.H.R.,* xvii (1902), pp. 305–6; Thomson, *op. cit.,* p. 252; H. C. Porter, 'The Gloomy Dean and the Law: John Colet, 1466–1519', in *Essays in Modern English Church History in Memory of Norman Sykes*, ed. G. V. Bennett and J. D. Walsh (London, 1966), p. 23; F. Seebohm, *The Oxford Reformers* (London, 1887), pp. 254–5; Tyndale, *Answer to More's Dialogue*, ed. H. Walter (Parker Soc., Cambridge, 1850), p. 168; *Sermons of Hugh Latimer*, ed. G. E. Corrie (Parker Soc., Cambridge, 1844), p. 440. Colet's English paraphrase of the Lord's Prayer appeared in print in the 1530s, but it is worth noting that in the *Accidence* he prepared for St. Paul's School, the *pater noster* was left in Latin. C. C. Butterworth, *The English Primers (1529–1545),* (Philadelphia, 1953), pp. 7–8, 89, 122.

reformers, thought it worth while to ferret out texts which had been preserved in the Lollard literary underground.[93]

The fears about Colet occurred in the pre-Lutheran world. My next
example comes from the period when England, post Luther, post divorce,
had herself turned to heresy. In 1538 Henry VIII took the decisive,
revolutionary step of ordering the English Bible to be placed in all churches
(thereby answering an ancient Lollard prayer). The year that this happened
an apprentice aged about 20, called William Maldon, was living with his
parents in Chelmsford in Essex. He recalled years later how immediately
after the royal orders for the Bible were given, various poor men of
Chelmsford bought the New Testament for themselves, and sat reading at
the lower end of the church on Sundays, 'and many would flock about them
to hear their reading'. Maldon himself was happy to join in these occasions
and (as he put it), 'to hear their reading of that glad and sweet tidings of the
Gospel'. Unfortunately though, his father had no sympathy for this new
world. Incensed, he came repeatedly to fetch William home to say the
Latin matins. William's response is illuminating. 'Then thought I, I will
learn to read English, and then will I have the New Testament and read
thereon myself'. He did so. He succeeded in both aims, learning to read
from an English primer, and clubbing together with another apprentice to
buy an English New Testament, which they hid in their bed straw.[94]

Maldon's story tells us a good deal about the motives and methods which
(among Protestants as among Lollards) led individuals to acquire vernacular literacy: and also about the fears entertained by those whose world
was that of the Latin mass and ancient ceremonial, towards the opening of
divine matters to English reading and English discussion. And here also we
can see once more how reading, vernacular scriptural reading, was a social
activity. It was the group of townsmen sitting in the nave of Chelmsford
church, listening to the New Testament, which set William Maldon on the
path to English literacy and reform. He *heard* first; thereafter he came to
read.

Finally, it was this social aspect of the new reading of new readers which
caused more than a hiccup in the process of Henrician reform. In 1543 the
king decided that it was too dangerous to allow unlimited Bible reading.
The act passed that spring 'for the advancement of true religion and for the
abolishment of the contrary', restricted the use of the Bible on a social
basis. The nobility and gentry might read to their households at home,
providing this was done quietly and without disturbance; more substantial
merchants, noblewomen and gentlewomen were allowed to read the Bible
and New Testament to themselves, so long as this was done 'privately',
'alone and not to others'—i.e. in nobody else's hearing. Humbler people,

---

[93] *The Colloquies of Erasmus*, trans. Craig R. Thompson (Chicago, 1965), p. 305; cf. *Opus
Epistolarum Des. Erasmi Roterdami*, ed. P. S. Allen and H. M. Allen, iv (Oxford, 1922),
p. 523, for Erasmus's statement about Colet's reading of heretical books. For Lollards going
to hear Colet preaching see Foxe, *Acts and Monuments*, iv, p. 230, and for the suspicions
attaching to the Englished *pater noster* Appendix below.

[94] *Narratives of the Reformation*, ed. J. G. Nichols (Camden Society, lxxvii, 1859),
pp. 348–51; Dickens, *English Reformation*, p. 190. As Adamson, *art. cit.*, p. 44 points out,
Maldon may already have been able to construe Latin before he taught himself to read
English.

those of the 'lower sort', listed as 'women, artificers, apprentices, jour-
neymen, serving-men of the degree of yeomen or under, husbandmen
[and] labourers', were not allowed to read the Scriptures at all, whether to
themselves or anyone else, privately or openly. The old fear has surfaced
again—and in the old form. This is not to say that specific memories of
Lollard experience brought about this enactment. Rather, that given the
old limitations of the English horizon (the restrictions on vernacular scripture, the fears of artisans' religious reading) there was perhaps a tendency
for reactions to repeat themselves.[95]

Education has often seemed to threaten the equilibrium of society, and
self-education may carry potential dynamite. In the middle ages, when
religious dissent bore inevitable implications of political disorder, the
advance of literacy was a force to be reckoned with in social and political
terms—as it still is in some parts of the world. The Lollards, by fostering
the religious reading of humble artisans, hinged the revelations of reading
to the phenomenon of dissent and revealed a fact which was not thereafter
forgotten. Literacy was a key which could unlock heresy and sedition, as
well as spiritual insights.

This is not to deny that the Lollards were both more and less than
studiers of God's law, or to say that the words on the page meant more to
them than the word living on the lips of the enlightened. Preaching was
always accounted the most worthy work of the servants of God, and the
essential task of salvation. We cannot afford to forget those Lollards whose
claim to fame was that of *excellens locutor*, the Speakwells of the fifteenth
century whose eloquence could gather and hold illicit heretical congregations.[96] Access to scriptural sources (at this time as later) was
achieved in various ways, but it was the sense of directness that counted.
Their own 'good books' strengthened the heretics' assurance in their own
'good steadfast belief'.[97] Their certainty of having their eyes and ears and
spiritual fulcrum centred upon the word of God gave the Lollards the
confidence of their convictions—whether these concerned the eucharist,
pilgrimages, images, saints, or other matters. There was some sort of consensus in the issues upon which they erred, right up to the Reformation.
And behind that consensus lay such means as they had of holding together:
their texts, their writers, their readers.

There was an appetite for reading, vernacular reading on religious subjects, sharing the experience of the Bible in English, before the Reformation as well as after it. If the history of the Lollard movement proves
anything, it surely proves the claim of one of its founders that 'the lewed
people crieth after Holy Writ, to kunne it and keep it'.[98] Given the ways in
which literacy spread and acted, that appetite tended to satisfy itself in
communal group activities, as well as in individual private perusal. We

[95] *Statutes of the Realm*, ii, pp. 894–6; Dickens, *op. cit.*, pp. 189–90. The act itself, as others
have pointed out, presupposes a fairly widespread ability to read English. It is also suggestive
(cf. note 7 above) of the vocalizing habits of most readers. For a conjecture that the enactment
of 1543 could still have carried implications of 'the association of Lollardy with artisans', see
Jack Upland, ed. Heyworth, p. 12, n. 2.

[96] Hudson, 'A Lollard Sermon-Cycle', p. 152; Crompton, 'Leicestershire Lollards', p. 28.

[97] Fines, *art. cit.*, p. 162.

[98] Deanesly, *op. cit.*, p. 258, cf. p. 454; *The Holy Bible*, ed. Forshall and Madden, i, p. 57.

must always remember that books themselves became voices. Wherever they existed they were heard as well as seen, and the reverberations of vocalized texts resounded outwards, with diminishing accuracy and immediacy, away from the readers and hearers who worked directly upon the page. This was something contemporaries never forgot. And since the conviction had established itself by the end of the fifteenth century that scripture in the hands of the humble inevitably produced undesirable sectarian behaviour, so the conservatives after the Reformation remained afraid of the social dangers of Bible-reading. Of course they were right in a way. England was not alone in sensing the threat of Biblical revolution. But luckily (we may think) the alarmism of the sixteenth century was not strong enough to damp down permanently the process of change. Literacy and Bible-reading went forward. Lollardy and the fears of Lollardy faded out under the impact of greater events.

APPENDIX

LOLLARDS AND THE PATER NOSTER

Apart from innocuously emphasizing the Lord's Prayer as the most worthy form of prayer (e.g. *English Works,* pp. 82, 320), the heretics also used the *pater noster* as a precedent justifying the translation of the whole Bible. They pointed to the example of the York plays in which the *pater noster* was said in English; why therefore, 'since the paternoster is part of Matthew's gospel, as clerks know, may not all be turned to English truly, as is this part?' (*ibid.,* pp. 429–30; cf. *Select English Works of John Wyclif,* ed. T. Arnold (Oxford, 1869–71), iii, pp. 98–99). This association with the heretics' whole case for vernacular scripture doubtless helped to bring discredit upon some English versions of the Lord's Prayer.

The fact that neither Thoresby's *Catechism* (in its original form) nor the *Lay Folks Mass Book* included translations of the *pater noster* was no doubt because of the expectation that this prayer should be familar in Latin. The Lollards, however, added a long section to Thoresby's text on the *pater noster*. For examples of heretics possessing suspect books containing the Lord's Prayer, *Ave Maria* and Creed in English, see Thomson, *op. cit.,* pp. 89, 105. The 7th treatise of Pecock's *Reule* included an exposition of the *pater noster,* and it has been suggested that possibly the 'heresy' of this treatment explains the loss of this part of the work. (*The Reule of Crysten Religioun,* ed. W. C. Greet, p. 8; cf. *Repressor,* ed. C. Babington, i, pp. lxxvii–lxxviii).

Foxe records cases of heretics charged with learning the *pater noster* in English. According to him the chief cause of the accusations against the 'Seven Godly Martyrs' at Coventry in April 1520 was 'for teaching their children and family the Lord's Prayer and Ten Commandments in English'. (Foxe, *Acts and Monuments,* iv, p. 557, Thomson, *op. cit.,* p. 116; Deanesly, *op. cit.,* p. 367). A Buckinghamshire woman, Alice Dolly, claimed in 1520 that John Hacker of London (on whom see n. 57 above) was as expert in the gospels and other things belonging to divine service, and the *pater noster* in English, as any priest, and it did one good to hear him. Foxe also records the case of John Ryburn, testified to have said that the service of the church was nought, because it was not in English. ' "For", said he, "if we had our Paternoster in English, we would say it nine times against once now".' (iv, pp. 582–3).

It seems therefore, as if by the early sixteenth century the English *pater noster* had become inseparably linked with the general hereticated case for vernacular scriptures. And accordingly when the tables were turned and the teaching of the Lord's Prayer in English became part of England's new orthodoxy, we find individuals objecting to this new learning as part of the new heresy. The injunctions of 1536 enjoined parish clergy, fathers, mothers and others to see that children learnt the *pater noster*, creed and commandments in English, and to make sure that those who could read knew where to find this in print. In November the same year one John Page's wife declared that neither king nor council would make her learn the *pater noster*, creed and decalogue in English–and she hoped the northern rebels would prevail. *Visitation Articles and Injunctions of the Period of the Reformation*, ii, ed. W. H. Frere and W. M. Kennedy (Alcuin Club Collections, xv, 1910), pp. 6–7 (injunction 5, 1536) cf. pp. 36–7 (injunctions 4 and 5, 1538); *Letters and Papers of the Reign of Henry VIII*, Vol. xi, p. 446, no. 1111. See Butterworth, *The English Primers*, pp. 8, 32 ff. 82 ff. for early printed versions of the English Lord's Prayer.

Additional Notes to Chapter 6

7   For a full examination of the evidence for silent reading, and its extension from the sphere of Latin books and learning into aristocratic vernacular culture, see Paul Saenger, 'Silent Reading: Its Impact on Late Medieval Script and Society', *Viator*, 13 (1982), pp. 367-414.

10   See the penetrating paper on Margery Kempe by Anthony Goodman, 'The piety of John Brunham's daughter of Lynn', in *Medieval Women*, ed. Derek Baker, *SCH*, Subsidia 1 (Oxford 1978), pp. 347-58.

34   FitzRalph had similarly charged friars with cornering books, so perhaps this complaint was an inherited exaggeration. But see William Woodford's defence – in the 1380s or 1390s – of the friars' keeping their books on Holy Scripture and other works locked up, so secular clerks were excluded from using them; J. I. Catto, 'New Light on Thomas Docking', *Med. and Ren. Studies*, vi (1968), p. 147.

54   Parts of this text are now printed in *English Wycliffite Writings*, ed. Anne Hudson (Cambridge, 1978), pp. 93-96 (quote at p. 96). On the *Floretum* see *The Middle English Translation of the Rosarium Theologie*, ed. C. von Nolcken (Heidelberg, 1979).

65   The question of the stages by which the dangers of vernacular theology were perceived by the authorities has now been examined by Anne Hudson in 'Lollardy, the English Heresy?', *SCH*, 18 (1982), pp. 261-83. Cf. also, on the wider context of these developments, Janet Coleman, *English Literature in History 1350-1400* (London, 1981).

67   *Four English Political Tracts of the Later Middle Ages*, ed. J.-P. Genet (Camden Fourth Series, 18, 1977), p. 5.

81   The relationship of these texts is far more complex than I indicated here. Anne Hudson's – as yet unpublished – study of the manuscripts suggests that the EETS version (Lambeth Ms. 408) represents an assemblage of independent treatises, rather than a single revision of Thoresby. I am grateful to her for information on this point.

7

LOLLARDY AND THE REFORMATION:
SURVIVAL OR REVIVAL?

LOLLARDY AND THE REFORMATION: it is a phrase which, ever since Dr. James Gairdner produced his four volumes under the title fifty years ago, has raised more doubts than it has resolved. Just how significant were the Lollards on the eve of the Reformation? Had their opinions as transmitted through the minds of artisans and country bumpkins maintained continuous semblance to a creed? To what extent were there significant traceable connections between the old heretics and the new?[1]

Though research is adding to our knowledge there are still many uncertainties about Lollard continuity up to the 1530s, and the numbers and opinions of those who were brought to light, or suffered for their faith, in the later years of the fifteenth century and the early years of the sixteenth. But an obvious and, it may be, an important way of approaching the matter is as a literary question. We have only to open the pages of Foxe to see the most conspicuous way in which there was a connection between Lollardy and the Reformation. Wycliffe, Hereford, Repton, Aston, Swinderby, Sawtry, Badby, Oldcastle and the others are all there, their careers and achievements commemorated and immortalized in that great valhalla of the English Reformation. They were considered worthy and vital links in a great and consummated tradition. But how and when did the Lollards acquire this new *post-mortem* fame? The first (Latin) version of Foxe's work did not appear until 1554, after the main foundations of the English Reformation had been laid. It was not until after the making of the Elizabethan church settlement that in 1563 the *Acts and Monuments* first appeared in English on the scale by which we know it. Was it then only as a justificatory act

---

* I am grateful to Professor A. G. Dickens, Mr. K. B. McFarlane and Mr. James Crompton, for having read and commented on this article.

[1] This article cannot attempt to deal with the evidence for sixteenth-century Lollardy. The most recent examinations of this are: A. G. Dickens, 'Heresy and the Origins of English Protestantism', in *Britain and the Netherlands*, ed. J. S. Bromley and E. H. Kossmann, ii (1964), pp. 47–66; J. Fines, 'Heresy Trials in the Diocese of Coventry and Lichfield, 1511–12', *Journal of Ecclesiastical History*, xiv (1963), pp. 160–74. Various Lollard cases are described in the *Victoria County Histories*, in particular, *London*, vol. i. Aspects of the problem of relations between Lollards and Protestants are considered by A. G. Dickens, *Lollards and Protestants in the Diocese of York, 1509–1558* (1959), and E. G. Rupp, *Studies in the Making of the English Protestant Tradition* (1947). Though it is clear that there was continuity of belief and that certain identifiable Lollard characteristics remained, it is also clear that there was debasement (as well perhaps as change of emphasis) in Lollard 'theology'.

of faith that the Lollard martyrs found their elevated niche in the new order of the sixteenth century? Or did their views make some contribution towards the establishment of this order?

Quite apart from the possibility of active proselytizing by the sixteenth-century inheritors of the old Lollard school, it was likely that the new reformers would be interested in the views of their protesting predecessors, both for the chance of adding vernacular arguments to their own armoury, and to show that they themselves were not the founders of a new tradition. If they could demonstrate their possession of brave English ancestry, the way of truth and justice could be pushed backwards as well as forwards, and they might be regarded as the continuators of those who through a long persecuted past had been defending the cause of the true, primitive church in England. It is clear too that there were a number of ways in which Wycliffite and Lollard arguments had anticipated and could help sixteenth-century reformers. If the image of Wycliffe as the Reformation morning star was able, for so long, to carry conviction, one of the reasons must be that protestantism, in its origins, is less like a hydra than a cyclops. When views on the central matters of scriptural authority and ecclesiastical possessions tend to recur in similar shapes in all reforming protests, the mere coincidence of opinion on these and other issues can tell us little on the all-important matter of influences. One method, though, of investigating sixteenth-century reformers' interest in Lollardy is to trace the appearance of certain pieces of Lollard literature in print. And it is not necessary to look far to see the value which, in the early stages of the Reformation, was attached to them.

In November 1531 Richard Bayfield, sometime monk and chamberlain of Bury St. Edmunds, was examined by the bishops of London and Winchester, and sentenced as a relapsed heretic for having (among other charges) imported forbidden heretical works from abroad.[2] On 3 December, the day before Bayfield was degraded, and burnt at Smithfield, Bishop Stokesley of London had a sermon preached at St. Paul's Cross, strictly forbidding under penalty of suspension the sale, purchase or reading of thirty named books.[3] Most of these were the works of exiled English reformers, Tyndale, Frith and Roye. But two which are worth considering further were Lollard tracts. They were the *A.B.C. ayenst the Clergye*, and *A boke of thorpe or of John Oldecastelle*. If the

---

[2] *The Acts and Monuments of John Foxe*, 4th edn., revised J. Pratt (1877), (referred to hereafter, in this edition unless otherwise indicated, as *Acts and Mons.*), iv, pp. 680–8; *Dict. Nat. Biog.*, iii, p. 440; *V.C.H. London*, i, pp. 254–5, 258–9. Bayfield had abjured in 1528. No record of the proceedings against him appears in the register of Bishop Stokesley, and the documents Foxe used seem to be lost.

[3] *Political, Religious and Love Poems*, ed. F. J. Furnivall (E.E.T.S., O.S. 15, 1866), pp. 34–5; *Three Fifteenth-Century Chronicles*, ed. J. Gairdner (Camden Society, N.S. xxviii, 1880), pp. 89–90; *Wriothesley's Chronicle*, ed. W. D. Hamilton (Camden Soc., N.S. xi, xx, 1875–7), i, p. 17. The close correspondence between the works condemned in the episcopal prohibition, and those Bayfield was accused of importing, makes it clear that his case was the direct occasion for Stokesley's action.

former of these can, as seems most probable, be identified with *A proper dyaloge betwene a Gentillman and a husbandman*, subheaded *An A.B.C. to the spiritualte*,[4] we have here two books, each consisting of two parts, which provided together four separate Lollard texts. In addition to these tracts two others may be considered which, though not noticed in Bishop Stokesley's list, appeared about this time. They were *The Lanterne of lyght*, a work sometimes attributed to Wycliffe, printed about 1530, and *The praier and complaynte of the ploweman unto Christe*, which was issued with a preface dated February 1531/2.

All these works, and others which appeared later, were edited and adapted to a greater or lesser extent for modern purposes and modern readers. And in doing so the sixteenth-century editors made various mistakes about both the date and authorship of the texts they were handling—matters which, after all, have continued to plague and obscure present-day Wycliffite studies. It is conceivable that the tract called *Wickliffe's Wicket* (on which more later) dates from the reign of Richard II, but if its composition was to be placed in the year 1395, as its editor supposed, it clearly could not have been Wycliffe's own work.[5] *The praier and complaynte of the ploweman* was said to have been written 'not long after' the year 1300, which put it about a century too early, and well outside the range of Wycliffe and the Lollards.[6] On the other hand John Purvey's defence of the translation of the Bible (which formed part of the *A.B.C. to the spiritualte*) was rightly dated to about 1400, though the version printed in fact contained references to events after that date.[7]

---

[4] This identification was rejected by Edward Arber in his edition of the tract in *English Reprints*, 28 (1871), p. 128, where he alludes to Foxe's reference (*Acts and Mons.*, iv, p. 685) to the 'A.B.C. of Thorpe's', and 'A Dialogue betwixt the Gentleman and the Ploughman'. But it appears from comparison with the bishop of London's list that Foxe has here elided the *A.B.C. ayenst the Clergye*, with the *Boke of Thorpe or Oldecastelle*, and that three separate works were condemned. The identification of the *A.B.C.* with the *Proper dyaloge* is confirmed by the fact that Foxe gives the acrostic alphabet with which the latter begins, with the title of 'The A.B.C. against the pride of the clergy', saying that he had found it 'in the margin of a certain old register' attributed to William Thorpe (*Acts and Mons.*, iv, p. 259). (This is perhaps a reference to the register of Bishop Tunstall, Guildhall Library, London, MS. 9531/10, f. 143 v.) Since this would appear to be the name by which it was known to contemporaries I have generally referred below to the *Proper dyaloge* as the *A.B.C. to the spiritualte*. Both it and (probably) the *Boke of Thorpe* were condemned again in 1542. *Acts and Mons.*, v, Appendix x (unpaged). *Cf.* p. 225 n. 19 below.

[5] *Wycklyffes Wycket: whyche he made in Kyng Rycards days the second in the yere of our lorde God MCCCXCV; S[hort]-T[itle] C[atalogue]*, compiled by A. W. Pollard and G. R. Redgrave (1926), no. 25590, *cf.* p. 234, n. 61 below. There appears to be no extant manuscript version of this work. J. E. Wells, *A Manual of the Writings in Middle English* (1916), pp. 470, 842; G. Lechler, *Johann von Wiclif und die Vorgeschichte der Reformation* (1873), i, pp. 627–8, n. 1; H. B. Workman, *John Wyclif* (1926), ii, p. 39, n. 1. The ascription to Wycliffe is (as with other English Wycliffite works) doubtful.

[6] *S.T.C.*, 20036; W. Nijhoff and M. E. Kronenberg, *Nederlandsche Bibliographie van 1500 tot 1540* (1923–40), 2, ii, p. 734, no. 3763. This work was reprinted in the *Harleian Miscellany*, vol. vi (1745), pp. 84–106. Similarly John Gough in 1541 thought that the General Prologue (*cf.* below, p. 230) was written 'more than two hundred years past'. Such antedating might of course have been done deliberately, to conceal the Wycliffite origin of works. *Cf.* M. Deanesly, *The Lollard Bible* (1920), p. 334.

[7] E. Arber, *English Reprints*, 28, pp. 128, 178, noting the reference to the death of Bishop Richard Fleming of Lincoln, who died in 1431, was thereby misled to date the whole treatise as 'clearly not much earlier than 1450'.

Further, as well as these (perhaps largely unavoidable) errors, the editors showed signs of the current Tudor propensity to make history a moral hunting ground. In this case the moral purpose was to demonstrate the virtue of the Lollards' aims, as the true forerunners of the present-day reformers, and the iniquity of their opponents. And here, as elsewhere, the demonstration meant doing violence to the actual course of history. Tyndale put the case in his *Prophet Jonas*: 'Wicleffe preached repentaunce un to oure fathers not longe sens: they repented not for their hertes were indurat and theyr eyes blinded with their awne Pope holy rightwesnesse . . .' [8] And what was the result? Regicide; three unlawful kings; slaughter of lords and commons, and decay of cities and towns. The civil wars were a useful and obvious sign of God's displeasure for the neglect of this earlier admonitory voice, and the unlawful suppression of His word. But—as a palatable concession to the popular view, soon to appear in the works of Polydore Vergil and Hall—Henry V might be excepted from this version of retribution for Lollard failure. As the husbandman put it to the gentleman in their dialogue, when the gospel was being 'prosecuted fiercely' by the clergy in the reign of Henry V, the king began to give the matter 'serious consideration' and,

> to note the clergyes tyranny
> And what temporaltees they dyd occupye
> Their spirituall state ferre a mysse.
> Wherfore he determyned certenyly
> To depryve theym temporally
> Of all theyr worldly gouvernaunce.[9]

The clergy, however, saw what was coming, and sagely packed the king off to France, where he remained too busy to carry out his plans. This version of the aims of the victor of Agincourt reads as a laughable parody of the facts. History serves polemics with a large discount of truth.

But no distortion of the Lollard texts themselves was needed to make them serve the reformers' purposes. Lollard insistence on the degeneration of the church since its acquisition of secular property, and the rights of lords and knights to deprive delinquent clergy, could provide useful arguments for those in the sixteenth century who were concerned with similar problems. In the *A.B.C. to the spiritualte*, which was published about a year after the meeting of the Reformation Parliament, the two complainants were discussing in their versified exchanges leading questions of the day. A general summary of clerical failings showed that more radical steps were necessary, for though the clergy had been offered scripture 'mekely without any provocacion', they had refused it

---

[8] *The prophete Jonas*, sig. B iii v.; *Doctrinal Treatises . . . by William Tyndale*, ed. H. Walter (Parker Society, Cambridge, 1848), p. 458. This passage was later echoed by Foxe, *Acts and Mons.*, i, p. 93; cf. W. Haller, *Foxe's Book of Martyrs and the Elect Nation* (1963), pp. 138, 167.
[9] Arber, *op. cit.*, p. 166.

indignantly.[10] The only remedy for all the abuses and troubles which had arisen since the church's usurpation of secular lordship was by deprivation, namely, to apply to parliament. But there too difficulties would arise, for the clergy in all their 'great multitude' would be bound to have 'a mischefe in the ende'.[11] It was only necessary to see what happened to King John, or Sir John Oldcastle, to realize what they could do. They had found arguments (said the gentleman) against the *Supplication for the Beggars*, and the views of the Lutherans, whom they dubbed 'a secte newe fangled', and they raised precedent on their side saying,

> none presumed till nowe a late
> Against the clergye to beare any hate
> Or grudged at their possession.[12]

To which the husbandman indignantly exclaims:

> By seynt mary syr, that is a starcke lye
> I can shewe you a worcke by and by
> Against that poynte makinge obiection.
> Which of warantyse I dare be bolde
> That it is above an hundred yere olde
> As the englishe selfe dothe testifye.
> Wherin the auctour with argumentes
> Speaketh against the lordshippes and rentes
> Of the clergye possessed wrongfully.[13]

And so the reader is introduced, with apologies for its incompleteness, to the last four chapters of a Lollard treatise on the illegality of the clergy holding property. We, unlike this protagonist who so boldly led the Lollards into the lists of current controversy, are fortunately in possession of the whole work, and are able to see that apart from some minor modernizations of language, the Reformation editor was content to leave this record as he found it. The text, which gathered together a variety of sources to prove the wrongfulness of ecclesiastical lordship, and considered the nature of perpetual alms and tithes, was reproduced with considerable accuracy.[14] Precedent, the husbandman was able triumphantly to point out, lay with reform.

The activity of Wycliffe's followers also provided precedents on another crucial issue; the translation of the Bible. The emphasis on return to the scriptural text as the basis of authority, and the Bible translations

---

[10] *Ibid.*, p. 132. [11] *Ibid.*, p. 145. [12] *Ibid.*, p. 149.
[13] *Ibid.* E. G. Rupp, *Studies in the Making of the English Protestant Tradition* (1947), p. 59. *Cf.* also C. H. Herford, *Studies in the Literary Relations of England and Germany in the Sixteenth Century* (1886), pp. 45–6.
[14] The complete text (which Arber did not have the opportunity of identifying) is printed in *The English Works of Wyclif Hitherto Unprinted*, ed. F. D. Matthew (E.E.T.S., O.S. 74, 1880), pp. 359–96, under the (modern) title of 'The Clergy may not hold Property'. The sixteenth-century editor (though he included the postscript on the wrongfulness of priests holding secular office) lacked, as he lamented, the first half of the work, and began at the middle of chapter 7 (p. 382 in Matthew's edition), not, as he stated, at the beginning of chapter 6. Internal evidence neither confirms nor contradicts the suggestion that it was 'made aboute the tyme of kynge Rycharde the seconde'. Arber, *op. cit.*, p. 150.

which resulted from Wycliffe's inspiration, were probably the most important part of the Lollard heritage. It was both pleasing and convenient for new reformers to find not only such antecedents for their own arguments, but also the collection of Biblical (and other) sources to prove them. Their spiritual ancestors had already done a lot of homework. As the gentleman replied happily to the husbandman:

> Nowe I promyse the after my iudgement
> I have not hard of soche an olde fragment
> > Better groundyd on reason with scripture.
> Yf soche auncyent thynges myght come to lyght
> That noble men hadde ones of theym a syght
> > The world yet wolde chaunge peraventure.[15]

So the second part of the *A.B.C.* was devoted to the publication of 'A compendious olde treatyse shewynge howe that we ought to have the scripture in Englysshe'. Once again the work was excused, this time for being 'olde, clothed in barbarous wede, Nothynge garnysshed with gaye eloquency'.[16] But this surely was nothing, set beside such a venerable authority, and its ability to show the 'furious frenesy' of those who called it heresy to have English scriptures. The tract, which is again easily identifiable, is a version of John Purvey's defence of the translation of the Bible.[17] It too was allowed to speak for itself, for the sources it mustered on its side could only add to the force of sixteenth-century argument, as well as showing—so it seemed now, as it had seemed to the Lollards themselves—that modern prelates feared and suppressed the publication of vernacular scripture as the illuminator of their own defects.

Other tracts recovered from Lollardy and given to Reformation readers by 1532 were presented in the same spirit; the desire above all to muster precedent and example. So anxious indeed was the editor of *The praier and complaynte of the ploweman unto Christe* to show 'it ys no new thinge, but an olde practyse of oure prelates . . . to defame the doctrine of Christe with the name of new lerninge and the teachers thereof with the name of new masters', that he deliberately left archaic words in the text, conceding to his readers' difficulties only the assistance of an introductory glossary of the most outlandish examples. He was ostensibly very pleased with his edition, and promised to repeat the labour, if he should happen to acquire 'any more soch holy reliques'.[18]

Relics of another kind—one destined in the end for more celebrated

[15] Arber, *op. cit.*, p. 165.

[16] *Ibid.*, p. 170. The *Compendious olde treatyse* was also printed separately, by the same (Antwerp) press, likewise with date 1530. *Nederlandsche Bibliographie*, 2, ii, p. 836, no. 3980, 2, i, p. 277, no. 2775; R. Steele, 'Notes on English Books Printed Abroad, 1525–1548', *Transactions of the Bibliographical Society*, xi (1909–11), pp. 206, 211.

[17] M. Deanesly, *op. cit.*, pp. 437–45. The text printed in the sixteenth century was a longer and later English version of the tract *De Versione Bibliorum* than that printed by Miss Deanesly. There are some omissions, as well as extended passages.

[18] *S.T.C.*, 20036, Preface 'To the Christen reader', sig. A iii r.; *Harleian Miscellany*, vol. vi, p. 86.

15a   Woodcut of St. Matthew from the only surviving fragment of the first [Cologne, 1525] printing of Tyndale's translation of the New Testament. (p. 231)

15b   Title-page of Bale's *Brefe Chronycle* (1544) showing Sir John Oldcastle as a 'valyaunt warryoure' in pseudo-classical armour (note shield with crucifixion) (p. 236)

16   Title-page of Foxe's 1563 *Actes and Monuments*, depicting the persecuted church (left) and the persecuting church (right). (p. 238)

reverence—were accounts of the trials and sufferings of notable Lollards. The *Boke of thorpe or of John Oldecastelle* belonged to this class, and included two such narrations, which passed through the hands of various reformers, before they were finally enshrined in the *Acts and Monuments*.[19] It is easy to see why such relations were so highly valued, for they provided persecuted Protestants with the comforting spectacle of their own cause (or so it seemed) being defended by their allies in spirit, in similar circumstances, against similar opponents. Past suffering became present precept. As Thorpe's editor (perhaps Tyndale) expressed it to his readers, unholy churchmen made 'all their examinacions in darkenes', and to be able to read about these matters from the other point of view was a means by which 'the lorde of all lyght shall lighten the with the candle of his grace, for to se the trewth'.[20]

Testimony to the truth in the shape of so valuable a record as a personal account of his trial before Archbishop Arundel, had elevated William Thorpe by 1530 to a place of celebrity in the annals of Protestant scholarship alongside a far more notable leader of the Lollard movement: Sir John Oldcastle, Lord Cobham. From what is known of their respective fates and achievements this seems surprising, for though it might, conceivably, have been fair to both, neither we nor those who originally crowned them with the laurels of Protestant martyrdom could justifiably say so. As both Bale and Foxe freely admitted, there is no record of how William Thorpe ended his days. There were indeed some who told Foxe that he had been burnt in August 1407, but there was no authority for this, and the supposition that he died in prison of sickness, torture or privation, was founded on equal uncertainty.[21] In the end though, this did not matter. 'The cause, not the punishment, makes the martyr.'[22] Thorpe fitted easily into Foxe's canon. He certainly seems to have been a long and faithful follower of the Lollard cause. When he came for trial in 1407 he was said (apparently) to have 'this twentie winter and more, traveiled about besilie in the north countrey

---

[19] W. T. Waugh thought that Bale's *Brefe Chronycle* was the earliest surviving printed edition of Oldcastle's trial, and that the edition of 1530, already rare in Bale's day, was lost. It certainly appears from the way in which Bale considers Bonner's charge of 1541 against William Tolwyn for possessing (among other works) 'A boke called Thorpe and oldecastell', that Bale did not know the 1530 edition. 'Thorpe and oldecastell', he said, 'are the names of ii dyverse menne, and not of one severall boke . . . For a monstruouse thynge yt were ii menne to be one boke', and he goes on to summarize the points of their respective examinations. Bale, *Yet a course at the Romyshe foxe* (1543), ff. 46 v.–48 v. The *Boke of thorpe or Oldecastelle* may, however, be identified with Brit. Mus. G. 12012 (*S.T.C.*, 24045), of which there is a modern printed version in *Fifteenth Century Prose and Verse*, ed. A. W. Pollard (1903), pp. 97–189. *Cf.* W. T. Waugh, 'Sir John Oldcastle', *Eng. Hist. Rev.*, xx (1905), p. 434, n. 1. The compilation of this work can be dated to 1530 from the reference to 'that good preaste and holye martyr Syr Thomas hitton', who 'was brente now thys yere at maydstone yn Kent'. *Cf. Acts and Mons.*, iv, p. 619; viii, pp. 712–15.

[20] From the preface 'Unto the Christen Reader'; *Fifteenth Century Prose and Verse*, p. 100.

[21] J. Foxe, *Commentarii rerum in ecclesia gestarum* (Strasbourg, 1554), ff. 156 v.–157 r. *Cf. Acts and Mons.*, iii, p. 285.

[22] 'Si non poena, sed causa martyrem faciat, cur non unum Cranmerum sexcentis Becketis Cantuariensibus non conferam, sed praetulerim?' From the 1563 preface 'Ad doctum Lectorem', *Acts and Mons.*, i, p. xi; quoted and translated by J. F. Mozley, *John Foxe and his Book* (1940), p. 134.

and in other diverse countries of England',[23] and one of the matters about which he was examined was a sermon which he had delivered at Shrewsbury, attacking pilgrimages, images and shrines. The record which Thorpe left to posterity was a long, confident, incautious testimony to his views on these and other matters, given in his own words. It is not surprising that so remarkable a document should have been thought worthy of translation into Latin for the benefit of Czech reformers,[24] as well as of publication, in both Latin and English, in the sixteenth century.

> I exhorte the good brother [wrote the editor of 1530], who so ever thou be that redest thys treatyse, marke hit well and consyder it seryouslye, and there thou shalt fynde . . . what the chyrche ys, theyre doctryne of the Sacramente, the worshyppynge off ymages, pylgremage, confessyon, Swerynge and payinge of tythes . . .[25]

So the survival of records brought Thorpe and Oldcastle to posthumous fame together. The prominence and activities of the latter—in particular, of course, the notoriety of the Lollards' most highly placed supporter, the circumstances of his trial, his attempted rebellion, and discovery and death after several years in hiding—all meant that there was much to be discovered and said about one who was indeed a martyr to the most conspicuous failure of the Lollard movement: the failure to capture widespread support among the knightly classes. The short English account of Oldcastle's trial and opinions which was published in 1530 seems to have been the first effort to probe and exploit these sources for a wider fame. It marks the launching of Oldcastle into a new renown which had far-reaching repercussions.

The earliest dated Lollard writing to be printed for Reformation purposes appears to have been one which, after some interesting travels in the service of reform, returned to England in the sixteenth century with a commendation from Luther himself. The *Commentarius in Apocalypsin ante Centum Annos æditus* appeared at Wittenberg in 1528, having been sent to Luther by Dr. Johann Brismann early the previous year.[26] It was a highly polemical tract, written in 1390 by an imprisoned English heretic, and the extant manuscript versions show that it had found considerable popularity in Czech circles.[27] The author, to judge

[23] *Acts and Mons.*, iii, p. 252; *Fifteenth Century Prose and Verse*, p. 107.
[24] Latin versions of this work are to be found in Vienna Nationalbibliothek, MS. 3936; Prague Chapter Library MS. O 29, and there was once also a version of it in MS. IV H 17 of Prague University.
[25] From the preface, *The examinacion of Master William Thorpe*, sig. A ii r.; *Fifteenth Century Prose and Verse*, p. 100.
[26] *Martin Luthers Werke*, Weimar edition, 26 (1909), pp. 121, 131.
[27] The commentary, with an introductory passage which does not appear in the 1528 edition, exists in a number of Czech manuscripts. I am grateful to Professor F. M. Bartoš for drawing my attention to it, and hope to deal more adequately with it on a future occasion. The influence of this work upon the Hussites has been demonstrated (from one angle) by A. Molnár, in an article entitled 'Apocalypse 12 dans l'interpretation hussite', which is due to appear shortly in the *Revue d'Histoire et de Philosophie Religieuses* of Strasbourg, and which I am grateful to have had the opportunity to read in typescript.

from his learning, must have belonged to the circle of Wycliffe's Oxford followers, and the Lollard characteristics of the work remain (despite some curtailments) in the printed version.[28] Luther was in no doubt of the value of the treatise, despite the limitations of its author who, 'among the first' of his time though he might have been, was at a disadvantage compared with those who 'in this age are so much more learned and freer'.[29] In his preface Luther besought the pious reader to give credence to the commentary, as having been sent to him 'by the best men from the furthest parts of Germany, namely from the regions of Sarmatia and Livonia, disfigured by the letters and syllables which accurately testify to its age'.[30] Age was a strong comforter. Quite rightly, Luther stressed the relevance of the commentary to the papal schism.[31] The author had been greatly concerned by that event, in particular the papal warfare so notoriously and wickedly demonstrated by the Flemish crusade on behalf of Urban VI, conducted by Bishop Despenser in 1383. It was an episode to which he frequently returned as a primary illustration of the contemporary crimes of Antichrist. And Luther (like Bale after him)[32] found encouragement in the insistence on the Babylonish fall of the Roman church.

> Understand therefore, good reader [he continued], that we have made this preface to make known to the world that we are not the first to interpret the papacy for the reign of Antichrist . . . For this author [was] . . . a witness preordained by God, so many years before us, for the confirmation of our doctrine.[33]

In the editions we have so far considered, the work of recovery was openly acknowledged. Antiquity, since it was valuable, was avowed. But other Reformation editors proceeded on different principles. It was one thing to publish a text, more or less as it stood, archaisms and all, to prove that new reformers were but old reformers writ large, with the right of precedent on their side. It was another to take over an old text, and rewrite it (without acknowledgement) to serve a new purpose, or alter it sufficiently to obscure its origin. And this also happened.

It may have been about 1530 that Robert Redman printed a work

---

[28] *Commentarius in Apocalypsin* (Wittenberg, 1528), ff. 67 v., 120 v., have references to the Lollards. The question of authorship was considered by F. M. Bartoš, 'Lollardský a Husitský Výklad Apokalypsy', *Reformační Sborník*, vi (1937), pp. 112–14, where the claims of Richard Wyche are argued against those of John Purvey.

[29] *Commentarius*, sig. A 2 v.   [30] *Ibid.*, sig. A 2 r.

[31] Though Luther himself rightly understood the general context of the composition of the work, a note at the end of the 1528 edition, following a faulty passage in the text, placed it in the year 1338 (*Commentarius*, ff. 195 v., 170 r.). This is impossible, and is contradicted elsewhere in the printed text (e.g. ff. 170 v., 122 v.), which makes it quite clear that the year of composition was 1390, as Bale realized.

[32] It appears to have been in the 1528 edition that the commentary was referred to by Bale, in his own work on the Apocalypse, and later he quoted from this version of the text in his catalogue of British writers, where he attributed it to John Purvey. Bale, *The Image of bothe churches* (? 1548), part i, sig. A vii v., part ii, sig. K vii r.; *Scriptorum illustrium maioris Brytannie Catalogus* (1557–9), cent. septima, pp. 516, 528–9, 542–3; cf. *Commentarius*, ff. 61 v., 62 v., 95 r., 103 v.–104 r., 115 r., 122 v., 128 r., 170 r.

[33] *Commentarius*, sigs. A 2 v.–A 3 r.

called *The Lanterne of lyght*.[34] It contained no indication whatever of its editorship or origin, though it is in fact one of the rare Lollard works which can be fairly closely dated, and having been composed between the years 1409 and 1415, when the heretics were faced by increasing controls, opposition and the penalty of burning, it was specially appropriate for publication.[35] Some passages gained new significance in new circumstances: 'The well, the begynnynge, and the cause of all ruine and myschyefe is the courte of Rome'; or 'The iii assaulte of Antechrist is inquisicion as y⁰ prophete sayth, that Antechrist enquyreth secheth and harkeneth, where he maye fynde any man or woman that wryteth lerneth redith or studyeth goddes lawe in theyr mother tonge . . .'[36] In fact to the undiscerning eye the Lollard origin of this work of comfort and exhortation might not at once have been apparent, although the editor's only emendations consisted of some changes of vocabulary, and the omission of the Latin passages which the author (probably an Oxford man) had been careful always to quote before his translations.

But change in the interests of change might go much farther than this. Two Lollard works ended up, almost unrecognizable in shape, in early editions of the works of Chaucer. A long poem called *The Complaint of the Plowman*, or *The Plowman's Tale*, lampooning the abuses of the clergy in eight-line stanzas, is both a literary and a religious muddle. Though unfortunately no manuscript version survives, it seems clear that while the work as a whole dates from the sixteenth century, its basis was an original fourteenth-century Lollard poem. This seems to have been taken over and remodelled—chiefly by the addition of two long interpolations—to bring it up to date in the current religious controversies.[37] In a lengthy dialogue which takes place between the pelican (representing the assailant of ecclesiastical corporations in the cause of true religion), and the griffon (the defender of the corrupt established order),[38] a rather clumsy insertion produced a topical sixteenth-century discussion on the nature of ecclesiastical authority. 'Shuld holy churche have no heed? Who shuld be her governayl?' asks the griffon, challengingly.[39] To which the pelican, with a 'houge cry', replies:

> Christ is our heed that sitteth on hy,
> Heddes ne ought we have no mo.
>
> . . . .
> All other maysters ben wicked and fals,

[34] *S.T.C.*, 15225, 'Here begynnethe the Lanterne of lyght'; colophon, 'Imprynted at London in Fletestrete / by me Robert Redman / dwellynge at the sygne of the George / nexte to Saynt Dunstones church'.

[35] *The Lanterne of Liȝt*, ed. from MS. Harl. 2324 by L. M. Swinburn (E.E.T.S., O.S. 151, 1917), pp. vii–xiii. The editor makes no reference to, or use of, the Redman edition.

[36] Redman, ff. ix r., x r.–v.; Swinburn, pp. 16, 18.

[37] J. E. Wells, *op. cit.*, pp. 267–8; H. Bradley, 'The Plowman's Tale', *The Athenaeum*, 2 July 1902, p. 62; *cf. Chaucerian and Other Pieces*, ed. W. W. Skeat (1897), pp. xxxi–xxxv.

[38] *Cf.* the reference to the clerical party as 'greedy Griffons and vile todes terrestial', in Wilfrid Holme's *The Fall and Evill Success of Rebellion*, quoted by A. G. Dickens, *Lollards and Protestants in the Diocese of York, 1509–1558*, p. 122.

[39] *Chaucerian and Other Pieces*, p. 181.

That taketh maystry in his name,
Gostly, and for erthly good;
Kinges and lordes shuld lordship han,
And rule the people with mylde mode.[40]

It may perhaps be of some significance that this work appeared in print under the name of *The Plowman's Tale*, as an ultimate Canterbury Tale, in William Thynne's second edition of the works of Chaucer in 1542.[41] This edition, dedicated to Henry VIII at a time when religious persecution was going on under the Act of Six Articles, made no attempt to veil the religious purport of its preface. While the king, defender of the faith, was besought in his likeness to Constantine to

Do forthe do forthe, contynue your socour
Holde up Christes baner lette it nat falle,[42]

the 'shynyng' lords were urged to 'shove on' in the same cause, and it was lamented that

This yle or this had ben but hethnesse
Nad be of your fayth the force and vigour
And yet this day the fendes crabbydnesse
Weneth fully to catche a tyme and hour
To have on us your lieges a sharpe shoure.[43]

The distinctly polemical *Plowman's Tale* did not discord with the tone of this admonitory preface. It may have been due to objections that the poem was not included in Thynne's earlier edition, and according to his son Francis it was only 'with muche ado' that it was finally able to appear.[44]

Another Lollard piece which appeared in print about this time was likewise attributed to Chaucer. *Jack up Lande*, a scurrilous and vituperative attack on the friars, dating from the early fifteenth century, was published about 1536 to 1540 by John Gough.[45] He was a bookseller of undoubtedly reforming sympathies, who had been in trouble

[40] *Ibid.*, p. 182.
[41] Skeat warns us against too readily charging early collectors of Chaucer with false ascriptions. Thynne's collection was from the beginning one of the works of Chaucer *and other writers*, but later changes ascribed to Chaucer more than Thynne had intended. Thus the Plowman's Tale was in Stow's 1561 edition of Chaucer placed before the Parson's Tale. Already before this there had apparently been an edition expressly stating it was by Chaucer. *Chaucerian and Other Pieces*, pp. ix–x, xxxi–xxxii.
[42] *The workes of Geffrey Chaucer newlye printed* (London, 1542), prefatory ballad.
[43] *Ibid.*
[44] *Francis Thynne's Animadversions upon Speght's first (1598 A.D.) Edition of Chaucer's Workes*, ed. F. J. Furnivall (Rolls Series, Chaucer Society, Second Series 13, 1876), pp. xli–iii, 9–10. There are various difficulties about Francis Thynne's story, but his father's (reported) protection of Skelton would certainly not have endeared him to Wolsey.
[45] *Chaucerian and Other Pieces*, pp. xxxv–xxxviii, 191–203; cf. *Political Poems and Songs*, ed. T. Wright (Rolls Series, 1859–61), ii, pp. 16–39. A copy of Gough's version (not listed under *S.T.C.*, 5098, but used by Skeat) exists in the library of Gonville and Caius College (Aa. 3. 9/6). The work, which consists of sixty-four prose paragraphs, is headed 'Jack up Lande Compyled by the famous Geoffrey Chaucer'. Skeat thought that this edition could be 'safely' dated 1536, and that there must have been an earlier text of *Jack up Lande*. For Foxe's edition see *Acts and Mons.*, ii, pp. 357–63.

in 1525 and 1528 for dealing with heretical books, and found himself
again imprisoned in the Fleet in 1541 for similar reasons, which may
well have been connected with his production this year, under the title
of *The dore of holy scripture*, of the General Prologue to the Wycliffite
Bible.[46] According to John Bale, who saw a copy of *Jack up Lande* in the
office of John Day, this tract was ascribed by some to Chaucer—a
suggestion upon which he did not vastly improve by substituting John
Wycliffe.[47]

A good deal has been fathered on Chaucer through six centuries of
literary opinion. But it is understandable that by 1570 the poet seemed
to John Foxe 'to be a right Wiclevian, or else there was never any'.[48]
The martyrologist was neither undiscerning nor altogether mistaken in
the character he attributed to *The Testament of Love*, and *The Plowman's
Tale*, of which latter he asked,

> Under whiche *Hypotyposis*, or Poesie, who is so blind that seeth not by the
> Pellicane, the doctrine of Christ, and of the Lollardes to bee defended
> agaynst the Churche of Rome?[49]

If Chaucer had been wronged, it was not for lack of good intentions.
And there may have been other factors, apart from the limitations of
sixteenth-century textual criticism, which earned him this misplaced
eulogy.

By the middle of the century more Lollard works, and more editions,
had been made available to English readers. In 1546 and 1548 appeared
editions of *Wickliffe's Wicket*, a Lollard work expounding the eucharist
in a figurative interpretation, of which its second editor, Coverdale,
remarked that 'no one man hath more briefly and playnely declared
the true understanding of the wordes of the lordes supper, than dyd this
authoure in thys treatyse . . .'[50] In the 1540s John Bale produced several
editions of an improved version of Oldcastle's trial, and by the end of
1546 this work together with *The praier and complaynte of the ploweman*,
The Lanterne of lyght and *The dore of holy scripture*, had joined the lists of
proscribed books.[51] In 1550, in different circumstances, a second (and
very accurate) version of the General Prologue to the Lollard Bible
was printed by Robert Crowley. The authority of Bale was cited for
printing this work as Wycliffe's, and the editor was able to claim
with pride that he had followed an original 'written in an olde English

---

[46] John Gough also translated the *Image of Love*, which was said to contain heretical matter,
and his *Dore of holy scripture* (dated 12 March 1540/1) was prohibited in 1546. *Letters and
Papers of the Reign of Henry VIII*, ed. J. S. Brewer and J. Gairdner (1862–1910), iv, pt. ii,
pp. 1803–4, no. 4073; C. Sturge, *Cuthbert Tunstal* (1938), pp. 140–1; *Acts and Mons.*, v, pp.
448, 568, 831, and Appendix; Deanesly, *op. cit.*, p. 255, n. 3; A. W. Reed, *Early Tudor Drama*
(1926), pp. 166–8, 184–5.

[47] *Index Britanniae Scriptorum*, ed. R. L. Poole and M. Bateson (1902), p. 274.

[48] *Acts and Mons.*, iv, p. 249; *cf.* i, p. xxiii, where Chaucer and Gower find their place in a
list of 'faithful witnesses', headed by Wycliffe, Thorpe and others.

[49] *Acts and Mons.* (1570), ii, p. 965.

[50] *S.T.C.*, 25591ᵃ, from the preface 'To the studiouse readers . . .' sig. A ii r.

[51] H. McCusker, *John Bale* (1942), pp. 16–17; *Acts and Mons.*, v, pp. 566–8, 838–9, Appendix
xviii (unpaged).

Bible bitwixt the olde Testament and the Newe, Whych Bible remayn-
eth now in yᵉ Kyng hys maiesties Chamber'.[52] This 'preciouse Jewell',
composed in a time 'ryght dayngerouse', had, the reader was told,
been wonderfully preserved through all the storms and fires of persecution by men who had paid a high price to secure it, and now, at a
moment when 'true religion biginneth to floryshe', it was made
accessible to all, at little cost.[53]

The days of extreme peril and literary smuggling were indeed, temporarily, over. But a number of Lollard works had been brought out in
the 1530s and '40s, in those dangerous years of the printing underground which brought Tyndale and others to their end. Protestant
readers were then presented with at least ten Lollard texts, providing
the opportunity to read and become acquainted with the views of earlier
English reformers on the eucharist, the translation of the Bible, church
endowments, and other leading questions. Literary activity may have
been haphazard, but it had produced a fairly comprehensive result.
Lollardy, in one shape or another, had certainly found a market through
twenty years of Reformation history. What does this tell us about
Lollard survival, and the thorny problem of influence? Who was responsible for these texts, and what effect may they have had?

Some interesting conclusions emerge from these examples. First, it is
clear that already by 1532 Protestant reformers had done some research
into Lollard literature—research which we may suppose was assisted by
the clubbing together of old and new reformers. Strype gives an illuminating picture of the kind of thing which must have happened. John
Tyball, a Lollard of Steeple Bumpstead, who was arraigned for heresy
in 1528, confessed that he had gone to London in the autumn of 1526
to buy one of the new New Testaments. He, and a companion in his
faith (one Thomas Hilles), showed to their acquaintance of the new
learning, Robert Barnes (the Cambridge Lutheran who was proceeded against in 1526), 'certayne old bookes that they had'. In this
case the manuscripts were Lollard translations of some of the epistles
and the four gospels, and not of much interest to their contacts in the
wider world of learning, who considered that these works compared but
poorly with the new printed version 'of more cleyner Englishe'.[54] In

[52] *The true copye of a Prolog wrytten about two C yeres paste*, title.
[53] *Ibid.*, from the preface 'to the Reader'.
[54] J. Strype, *Ecclesiastical Memorials* (Oxford, 1822), I, pt. i, p. 131, pt. ii, pp. 54–5, quoted
by T. M. Parker, *The English Reformation to 1558* (London, 1950), pp. 28–9. The case of Barnes,
and some other examples, are considered by Professor Dickens, 'Heresy and the Origins of
English Protestantism', *loc. cit.*, pp. 60–1, from the point of view of the converse and important
question of Lollard reception and distribution of Lutheran literature. B.M. MS. Harl. 421,
ff. 7 r.–35 r., contains valuable material relating to proceedings against heretics in the
diocese of London 1527–8, and provides further information about the Steeple Bumpstead
Lollards. In addition to the very selective use to which Foxe put these documents, Strype
made an abstract (*op. cit.*, I, pt. i, pp. 113–34), and printed some further selections (*ibid.*,
I, pt. ii, pp. 50–65). The 'original papers' of these enquiries which remain in MS. Harl. 421,
appear to be leaves from a London register of Bishop Tunstall—or his vicar-general (they
have the original pagination running, with many omissions, from xxxi to cccclxi). Among

other cases though, with different individuals and different texts, such meetings might have had another outcome, and it is permissible to suppose that such exchanges between old reformers and new helped some of these Lollard manuscripts to find their way into print, actively to assist the Reformation in its early stages.

Secondly, it is clear that whether or not Lollards of the old and various school were significantly active in person, turning old arguments to new purposes as latter-day reformers, there certainly were Lollard texts being transformed in this way to help the evolution of reforming arguments, even, it might be, to proselytize. The kind of influence which a Lollard writing could have in moulding or preparing the minds of new reformers is illustrated by the conversion of Thomas Topley, an Austin friar of Clare in Suffolk, as recounted at his recantation in 1528.

> It fortuned thus, about half a year ago, that the said sir Richard [Foxe, curate of Steeple Bumpstead, himself a heretical suspect who had already introduced Topley to a work of Erasmus] went forth, and desired me to serve his cure for him; and as I was in his chamber, I found a certain book called Wickliff's Wicket, whereby I felt in my conscience a great wavering for the time that I did read upon it, and afterwards, also, when I remembered it, it wounded my conscience very sore. Nevertheless, I consented not to it, until I had heard him preach, and that was upon St. Anthony's day. Yet my mind was still much troubled with the said book (which did make the sacrament of Christ's body, in form of bread, but a remembrance of Christ's passion), till I heard sir Miles Coverdale preach, and then my mind was sore withdrawn from that blessed sacrament, insomuch that I took it then but for the remembrance of Christ's body.[55]

Lollards might not actually make Protestants, but they could sow fertile seeds of doubt.

It seems reasonable to suppose also, from the availability and acquisition of these texts, that there was still a variety of Lollard works, apart from Bible translations, in active use and circulation on the eve of the Reformation. Some of them are referred to in heretical proceedings. In particular *Wickliffe's Wicket* was discovered in the course of enquiries by Bishops FitzJames of London and Longland of Lincoln to be in use among various heretics between 1510 and 1521, and Thorpe's examination was owned by a heretic of Oxfordshire.[56] On the other hand one cannot ignore the fact that none of the texts we have been considering

---

[55] *Acts and Mons.*, v, p. 40. It may be significant that these proceedings are to be associated with those referred to above, for Richard Foxe and Thomas Topley were both connected with John Tyball. Strype, *op. cit.*, I, pt. ii, pp. 60–2.

[56] *Acts and Mons.*, iv, pp. 176, 207–8, 226, 234–6, 238, 240.

the confessions is that of Edmund Tyball (ff. 28 r.–29 v.), referred to by Foxe, *Acts and Mons.*, iv, p. 585; *cf. Letters and Papers of Henry VIII*, iv, pt. ii, pp. 1984–5, no. 4545, p. 2095, no. 4850. This was made on 21 July 1528, and reveals Richard Foxe as being defamed of heresy, holding erroneous views about images, pilgrimages and fasting, and denying transubstantiation. Another interesting confession (ff. 34 r.–35 r.) which bears no name, but is evidently that of Thomas Hilles, tells more of the doings of Foxe, Topley and John Tyball, including the visit to Robert Barnes in London (see Appendix), which may be compared with Tyball's account, as printed by Strype.

appears to have been composed after about 1420. One aspect of the Lollards' dwindling academic support was their reliance on old theology, and though old theology may be the best theology, it needs direction to prevent it degenerating. The Lollard underworld lacked that direction, and pure texts, however carefully preserved, could not make up for it.[57] Moreover there seems to be no evidence that printed editions of any of these works existed before the Reformation was well under way with the production of its own literature. This might be an accident of survival, but it seems altogether more likely that it was the new blood, new interest, and the methods and abilities of the new reformers, which brought these hoarded texts to light in the days of printing.

The responsibility for this transfusion is largely obscured by the necessity for editorial anonymity. But we know the names of a number of reformers who handled Lollard texts, and there is no doubt that Tyndale is to be associated with several of the early editions. There is also the possibility that an important part may have been taken by the Christian Brethren, a mysterious organization which appears to have linked together reformers of various kinds at home with the exiles abroad, and to have played a significant rôle in the sponsoring and distribution of heretical literature. Bayfield seems to have been an important agent, and the rhymed *Dyaloge betwene a Gentillman and a husbandman,* or *A.B.C. to the spiritualte,* which he imported, was by Jerome Barlow, working for William Roye (the sometime amanuensis of Tyndale), both of whom may have had some connection with the Christian Brethren.[58]

It seems that Tyndale had something to do with both Thorpe's and Oldcastle's examinations. Foxe had a version of Thorpe in Tyndale's own handwriting, and Bale refers to the latter's edition of both this and the Oldcastle text.[59] Both reformers also attribute to Tyndale *The praier and complaynte of the ploweman.* Another work which might perhaps be thought to have enjoyed Tyndale's acquaintance was *Wickliffe's Wicket,* for its first known edition, printed with the date 1546, was given alongside the *Testament of William Tracy,* with the statement that after Tyndale had been 'judaslie betrayed', certain things of his were found which he had intended to have 'put forth to the furtheraunce of godes worde'.[60]

[57] *Cf.* Rupp, *op. cit.,* p. 5.

[58] *Ibid.,* pp. 6–14 on the Christian Brethren, and pp. 9, 53, 59 for Roye's contacts with them, and his making of rhymes, including the *Dyaloge.*

[59] *Acts and Mons.,* iii, p. 249; J. Bale, *Scriptorum illustrium maioris Brytannie Catalogus* (Basel, 1557–9), cent. octava, p. 659; *A brefe Chronycle,* f. 3 v.; *Select Works of John Bale,* ed. H. Christmas (Parker Society, Cambridge, 1849), p. 6. *The examinacion of Master William Thorpe,* the *Proper Dyaloge,* and the *Compendious olde Treatyse,* were all products of the so-called 'Marburg' press, which produced various of Tyndale's works, and which has been identified with the press of Johannes Hoochstraten at Antwerp. M. E. Kronenberg, 'De geheimzinnige drukkers Adam Anonymus te Bazel en Hans Luft te Marburg ontmaskerd', *Het Boek,* viii (1919), p. 272; *Nederlandsche Bibliographie,* 2, i, pp. 277, 390, nos. 2775, 3007; 2, ii, p. 836, no. 3980.

[60] *Wycklyffes Wycket* (1546); preface to the testament of William Tracy. Tracy's will, with the expositions of Tyndale and Frith, had already been published in 1535. *Nederlandsche Bibliographie,* 2, ii, pp. 845–6, no. 3997; J. F. Mozley, *William Tyndale* (1937), pp. 240–1.

The *Wicket* however, though it remained attached to Tracy in the new edition of 1548, was then 'faythfully overseene and corrected after the originall and first copie', because of the 'innumerable and shamfull erroures in the other edicion', over the initials of M. C.[61] Miles Coverdale, who presumably this was, added a preface to the tract, and this connection is specially interesting in view of Thomas Topley's statements. Other names associated with these texts were George Constantine (with Thorpe's account),[62] and Robert Barnes, whom we have seen being shown Lollard manuscripts, and who was one of those whom John Gough claimed to have perused his *Dore of holy scripture* before its publication.[63] In general, though, the sixteenth-century editors and their associates must remain—and for the same reasons—as doubtful as the earlier authors.

It can be seen from the publication of these tracts that Protestant scholarship had made no small headway in finding Lollard texts and examples well before John Foxe ventured into print. And in the end the antecedents and genesis of the new martyrology must be looked for in the cataclysmic event which began a new phase of historical research in England: the dissolution of the monasteries. Among the group of antiquaries who concerned themselves with collecting and preserving the books and documents from monastic libraries a leading rôle should be ascribed to John Bale. He also played an important, though less recognized, part in the literary revival we are considering.

Personal disposition, and the unfortunate accidents of his interrupted career, conspired to make Bale's fame that of a cataloguer and compiler, rather than that of a writer. But at a time when the need for action was pressing and imperative, Bale performed various services, and though he was never able to recover the bulk of his own huge library, he seems to have been a central figure, helping others and suggesting the course which future work was to take. He is found in 1560 replying to a request of Matthew Parker with a long list of sources on different subjects.[64] He was a close literary companion of John Leland, whose *Laboryouse Journey* he edited, and his feeling about the loss of manuscripts and books at the suppression—so bitter that he could 'scarsely utter it wythout teares'—should not be forgotten when considering the impetus for the royal antiquary's commission.[65] But it was Bale's friendship with John Foxe which may have been the most fruitful of his associations.

Bale was perhaps moved primarily by a passionate desire for actual

---

[61] *Wicklieffes Wicket* [1548], title. J. F. Mozley, *Coverdale and his Bibles* (1953), p. 331. The 1548 title shows that there had been two earlier editions, and there were in fact (*cf. S.T.C.* 25590) two versions printed with the 'Norenburch 1546' colophon. There are copies of both in the Bodleian Library, one of which belonged to George Joye.

[62] *The workes of Sir Thomas More* (London, 1557), i, p. 342.

[63] *The dore of holy scripture* (end), 'Perused by doctor Taylor and doctor Barons, Master Ceton, and Master Torner'.

[64] H. McCusker, *John Bale*, pp. 58–68.

[65] J. Bale, *The laboryouse Journey* (London, 1549), John Bale to the reader, sig. A vii v.

literary preservation. It was this which led him to praise the example of that 'valyaunt captayne syr Johan Oldecastell', who, seeing the 'outrage' of the papacy against John Wycliffe, 'caused all hys workes to be coppyed oute by moste fayre wryters, at his owne great cust and charge, and so convayed them into the lande of Beme, that they myghte be there preserved from destruccyon'.[66] But the vitriolic ex-Carmelite, who spent his last years as canon of Canterbury trying to recover books from the library he had left behind in Ireland, was concerned with the use, as well as the saving of documents. To him, more perhaps than to anyone, must be attributed the credit of seeing that the exile of the papacy from England meant the ending of a whole historical tradition, and that the advent of a Protestant settlement meant the need to reshape and rewrite English chronicles with a new, reformist outlook.

> I wolde wyshe [he wrote in 1544], some lerned Englyshe manne (as there are now most excellent fresh wyttes) to set forth the Englyshe chronycles in theyr ryght shappe . . . all affeccyons set a part. I can not thynke a more necessarye thynge to be laboured to the honour of God, bewtye of the realme, erudicyon of the people, and commodite of other landes, next the sacred scripturs of the Byble, than that worke wolde be.[67]

And he launched, with all the unrestrained violence of his pen, into a broadside on the 'Romish' errors of Polydore Vergil. Bale may even have hoped to accomplish this remedial task himself, for he said in 1560 that he needed his books for the 'perfourmance of an Englysh chronycle, whych I have begonne and not fynyshed'.[68] This was not to be. But already his aims had in some measure been achieved, as was shown by the long list of books forbidden by royal proclamation in June 1555, which started with those of Calvin and Luther, and ended with the chronicles of Edward Hall.

An integral part of this new history was the production of a new martyrology; the dethronement and deposition of the annals of Catholic martyrs, and the elevation and crowning of a new Protestant series. Bale's connection with this aspect of the work of revision is more directly traceable. Already by 1536 he had—in propagandist circumstances—made some contribution to it, with his play 'on the impostures of Thomas Becket', which may have helped to prepare the ground for the final assault, led by his patron Thomas Cromwell, on the shrine of Becket in 1538.[69] The editions of some Lollard texts had, with other literature, been leading in the same direction. But the literary reversal of making old heretics into new heroes involved more, as Bale saw, than

---

[66] *Ibid.*, sig. F iii v.; *cf. A brefe Chronycle* (1544), f. 8 r.

[67] *A brefe Chronycle*, f. 5 v. This emphasis of Bale's work was noticed by J. W. Harris, in *John Bale, A Study in the Minor Literature of the Reformation* (1940), p. 13, *cf.* p. 127, and is now given fuller recognition by W. Haller, *Foxe's Book of Martyrs and the Elect Nation*, pp. 58–70.

[68] McCusker, *op. cit.*, p. 30.

[69] Bale's play of this name is referred to in his *Anglorum Heliades* of 1536. J. W. Harris, *op. cit.*, p. 98, *cf.* p. 134; *cf.* Bale, *Scriptorum illustrium maioris Brytannie Catalogus*, cent. octava, p. 704, *Illustrium Maioris Britanniae scriptorum summarium* ([Wesel], 1548), f. 244 r.

the piecemeal editing of heretical literature. It meant taking over enemy territory, and using enemy ammunition. Official records, works compiled by the authorities to condemn and eradicate heresy, were to be used as they had never been used before; for an anti-Catholic purpose. This was a task in which, of course, John Foxe pre-eminently excelled. But it is here that Bale's career is particularly interesting and important, suggesting the process which Foxe was to consummate.

Some six years after the campaign for the destruction of the English shrines, Bale produced a new edition of the examination of John Oldcastle, in which he contrasted the 'false myracles, erronyouse writtynges, shrynes, relyques', of the papists, with those 'godlye and valeaunt warryours' who had given their lives fighting for the cause of Christ against Antichrist.[70] Among these warriors an elevated place was to be assigned to Sir John Oldcastle, that 'verye specyall membre' and 'vessell of Gods elecyon'[71]—so special in fact that Bale raised him to take the place of Thomas Becket in the new canons of English martyrs. Becket (he said) died as the result of 'his owne sekynge onlye'; Oldcastle 'at the importune sute of the clergye, for callynge upon a Christen reformacyon in that Romyshe churche of theyrs'.[72] Could there be any doubt, for those who were able to 'plucke from [their] eyes the corrupted spectacles of carnall or popyshe iudgementes', as to who was the real martyr of Christ?[73]

> Whan the Gospell laye dead, gloryouse Thomas Becket was a saynct, and Johan Oldecastell a forgotten heretyque. But now that the lyght thereof shyneth, we are lyke to se yt farre otherwyse. For proude Becket hath alredye hydden his face, and poore Oldecastell begynneth now to apere verye notable . . .[74]

The main source for Bale's edition (which to judge from its several reprintings enjoyed some success) was, as he tells us, an official record, taken from the 'bokes and writtynges of those Popyshe Prelates which were present both at his condempnacyon and iudgement'.[75] It is almost certain that the 'great process' of Archbishop Arundel to which Bale here alludes was known to him from a manuscript called the *Fasciculi Zizaniorum*. This Carmelite collection of Wycliffe's 'tares' (which has still not been printed in its entirety) was—and is—an important source book for the views and history of Wycliffe and the Lollard movement, and it holds a most interesting place both in Bale's own career, and in the history of Lollard revivalism. He made numerous additions to it, including (characteristically) an index, a collection of short biographies of leading Lollards, and a translation into Latin of part of William

---

[70] *A brefe Chronycle* (1544), Preface, ff. 2 v.–3 r.   [71] *Ibid.*, f. 3 r.
[72] *Ibid.*, ff. 52 v.–3 r. The Reformation transformation of Oldcastle has been considered in various places; e.g. W. Baeske, *Oldcastle-Falstaff in der englischen Literatur bis zu Shakespeare* (1905); R. Fiehler, 'How Oldcastle Became Falstaff', *Modern Language Quarterly*, 16 (1955), pp. 16–28; L. M. Oliver, 'Sir John Oldcastle; Legend or Literature?', *The Library*, Fifth Series, i (1946–7), pp. 179–183.
[73] *A brefe Chronycle*, f. 53 v.
[74] *Ibid.*, f. 55 r.–v.   [75] *Ibid.*, f. 2 r.

Thorpe's examination, which he made in 1543. And when Bale went into exile at the fall of Cromwell in 1540, he took the *Fasciculi* with him, and had it rebound in Germany.[76] And this returns us to our starting point. For Bale and the *Fasciculi Zizaniorum* undoubtedly had no small influence on John Foxe and his *Acts and Monuments.*

Bale and Foxe, despite their considerable difference in age, became and remained good friends. In 1548, when Bale returned from exile, they lived together in the London house of the duchess of Richmond. Foxe was then thirty-one, with years of hardship and disappointment behind him; Bale in his early fifties, an acknowledged author and re-former. They spent part of Mary's reign under the same roof in Basel, where Bale penned a tribute to his faithful 'Achates' of the previous ten years. And to judge by the greetings sent from Oporinus to Bale via Foxe in 1560 the friendship continued after their return.[77]

Foxe's *Commentarii rerum in ecclesia gestarum*, a Latin work which appeared at Strasbourg in 1554, was in effect the first version of what was to become the *Acts and Monuments.*[78] Most of the work for it appears to have been done before the author left England, but it seems nowhere to have been noticed what a large debt it owed to Bale and his manu-script, the *Fasciculi Zizaniorum.*[79] The book—which did not enjoy a great success, and was reprinted ten years later under a different title—touches on some foreign martyrs (Huss, Jerome of Prague, and Savo-narola), but was mainly devoted to Wycliffe and the Lollard movement, and in doing so follows both the text of the *Fasciculi* itself, and also Bale's additions to it. Of the two hundred odd pages of the *Commentarii* the first hundred or so drew largely on these sources, including the examina-tion of John Oldcastle (of which Bale had already printed an English version). There followed a Latin version of Thorpe's trial (Foxe's own translation), and a miscellaneous collection of English and continental martyrs, which appears to have been Foxe's own compilation, an error of which, repeated in his 1563 English work, he later admitted, with the excuse that this edition had been 'so hastely rashed up'.[80]

[76] The history of the Fasciculi has been described by J. Crompton in '*Fasciculi Zizaniorum*', *Journal of Ecclesiastical History*, xii (1961), pp. 35–45, 155–66. It is here (p. 41) established that Bale owned the manuscript by 1540.

[77] W. Haller, *Foxe's Book of Martyrs*, pp. 56, 70–1; J. F. Mozley, *John Foxe and his Book*, pp. 29–30, 51, 64; J. W. Harris, *op. cit.*, p. 119; J. Bale, *Scriptorum illustrium maioris Brytannie Catalogus* (Basel, 1557–9), cent. nona; p. 733—misnumbered p. 763; *Acts and Mons.* (1570), p. 830.

[78] A consideration of the *Commentarii* appears in J. F. Mozley, *op. cit.*, pp. 118–19; W. Haller, *op. cit.*, pp. 13, 70–1.

[79] W. Haller, *op. cit.*, pp. 164, 166, in a general survey of the *Acts and Monuments* account of Wycliffe and the Lollards, refers to Foxe's use of the *Fasciculi*.

[80] Bale, *Scriptorum illustrium maioris Brytannie Catalogus*, cent. nona, p. 733; *Acts and Mons.* (1570), i, pp. 830–1; cf. *Commentarii*, f. 177 r.; *Acts and Mons.* (1563), p. 371. Foxe's sources for the work as a whole were, clearly, various, but for his English material the *Fasciculi* played an important part, and some facts could have been derived only from it. Since the text as edited by W. W. Shirley (Rolls Series, 1858) excludes Bale's annotations, the full extent of Foxe's borrowing can only be realized by a comparison with the original (Bodley MS. e Museo 86). Thus, for example, Foxe's note on Purvey, *Commentarii*, f. 43 v., comes from f. 84 v. of the manuscript, and his list of Wycliffites on f. 44 v. is derived from Bale's bio-graphies on ff. 54 v.–56 v.

The main part of the *Commentarii* must, in fact, have been carried out with Bale's co-operation and the loan of his manuscript, probably when the two reformers were living together in London.[81] And Foxe was far from concealing his indebtedness. On a later occasion he was to refer to 'a certain old written book in parchment, borrowed once of J. B.', and both now and afterwards he cites as sources both Thomas Walden (to whom Bale attributed the *Fasciculi*), and Bale himself.[82] The compiler of the *Commentarii* left on record his praise and esteem for the latter:

> through whose exquisite labour and diligence it is brought to pass, that not only certain titles and arguments of his [Wycliffe's] books, but also certain monuments, as I do hear, are recovered out of darkness; a man who, not in this respect alone, hath well deserved of good students.[83]

The older man—and Bale was now getting on in years—seems to have given the younger every encouragement and help to achieve an objective which, we have seen, he had himself so much at heart. Together with the loan of his manuscript Bale must have passed on much advice and support, and it is sad to think that he did not live to see its full fruition. He died in 1563, the very year in which the *Acts and Monuments* first appeared in the English shape which was to earn its lasting popularity.

No deep inspection of the work is necessary to see how fully it realized Bale's desires, and how it incorporated the material which others had already prepared. In a number of cases—the trials of Thorpe and Oldcastle, the *Compendious olde treatyse*, *The praier and complaynte of the ploweman*, *Jack up Lande*[84]—Foxe was merely reproducing the editions of earlier reformers. But he was of course doing a great deal more. To realize his debts is not to belittle him. Genius, after all, lies in execution more than in inspiration. And placing Foxe's work in the perspective of his predecessors and contemporaries, we can see how far he rises above them.

The *Acts and Monuments*, for all its faults, was undoubtedly a work of grandeur, which can be seen as the culmination of a process, the completion of a generation's efforts.[85] It raised Protestant scholarship from the level of tractarian and bibliographical collections, and turned it into monumental history. And it carried to a logical conclusion the work of editing and collecting official (as well as unofficial) records, so establishing not only a valuable source-book, but a firm basis of historical

---

[81] At any rate before Bale left for Ireland in 1552, taking the *Fasciculi* with him. Crompton, *art. cit.*, pp. 42–3.

[82] *Acts and Mons.*, iii, p. 292; *Commentarii*, ff. i v., 32 r.–v., 43 v., 59 v., 107 v., 117 v. (including references to other works of Walden).

[83] *Acts and Mons.*, iii, p. 54; *Commentarii*, f. 32 v. Bale was able to return the compliment a few years later in his catalogue, where he quotes Foxe's *Commentarii*; *Scriptorum illustrium maioris Brytannie Catalogus*, cent. sexta, p. 469, cent. septima, p. 557; *cf.* cent. nona, p. 733.

[84] The last two tracts were first included in the 1570 edition.

[85] In addition to W. Haller, *Foxe's Book of Martyrs*, recent estimates of Foxe's work are to be found in A. G. Dickens, *art. cit.*, pp. 49–51, and J. Fines, *art. cit.*, pp. 173–4.

method. It was in fact a landmark in the launching of English Protestant history, and Foxe had done something for which the Church of England had lasting reason to be grateful. He provided it with a tradition, with the historical evidence of spiritual ancestry reaching back through the annals of English martyrs towards the pure standards of the primitive apostolic church. It was not for nothing that in 1571 orders were given for the latest edition of the work to be provided for common reading in all cathedral churches. The Anglican settlement had acquired its own historical textbook, and the foundations of a long tradition had been well and truly laid.

'We have,' remarked the martyrologist in 1572, 'great cause to geeve thankes to the high providence of almighty God, for the excellent arte of Printing, most happely of late found out, and now commonly practised everywhere, to the singular benefite of Christes Church.' It was an invention which he saw as intended above all for spiritual purposes, for the aid of religion, to restore true doctrine, repair the church, repress abuses, and 'to revive agayne the lost lyght of knowledge to these blynde tymes, by renuing of holsome and auncient writers: whose doinges and teachinges otherwise had lyen in oblivion, had not the benefite of Printing brought them agayne to light, or us rather to light by them'. There was reason to be thankful for what it had been possible to collect of the 'ringleaders' of the latter reforming days. But he still had regrets:

> And woulde God the like diligence had beene used of our aunccient forelders, in the tyme of *Wickliffe, Purvey, Clerke, Brute, Thorpe, Husse, Hierome,* and such other, in searching and collecting their workes and writings. No doubt but many thinges had remayned in lyght, which now be lefte in oblivion. But by reason the Arte of Printing was not yet invented, their worthy bookes were the sooner abolyshed.[86]

It is difficult to escape the impression that in so far as the work of sixteenth-century reformers touched upon the textual bases of the Lollard movement, it was a work of recovery and revival. For Lollardy had lived long in a dark uncertain underground. Its adherents may have been numerous, but they lacked the power of spiritual regeneration; they were living on old texts, old arguments, and a seemingly moribund tradition. They had failed in a number of old aspirations. But for those who survived to these new days of travail, may it not have seemed like a long-awaited dawn? Scriptural strength and assistance from new quarters moved—with the help of the printing press—towards old objectives with greater, though still persecuted, assurance. Heretics of the old school were able to acquire new English Bibles; some of their texts reached print and new readers through the new reformers; and the Lollards themselves could have found little to quarrel with in some of the reformers' views on image worship, pilgrimage and clerical endowments.

[86] *The whole workes of W. Tyndall, John Frith, and Doct. Barnes* (London, 1572-3), Foxe's Epistle or Preface to the Christian Reader, sigs. A ii r.–A iii r.

The processes of the Reformation included some mutual recognitions. And the Lollards did not have to wait long to see their heroes and martyrs receiving acclamation in new quarters—an acclamation which, within not much more than a generation, had gained the stamp of official recognition. It did not do, as Shakespeare discovered, to impugn the sanctity of that hardly established 'Golden Legend' of the Anglican settlement. It had no room for laughable buffoons, now that Sir John Oldcastle had been so surely rescued from the annals of traitors and royal rebellion. He died a martyr—and he led the fame of those other Lollard martyrs who blossomed to such high renown in a new, more lasting, and more fruitful spring.

APPENDIX

B.M. MS. Harl. 421, f. 35 r. Part of the examination of Thomas Hilles (? 15 October 1528)[87]

Also he saith that abowt whytsontyde was twelf moneth he came to london with John Tyball, and spoke with frear barons at frears augustyns in his chambre, and the said John Tyball told the said frear barons that they came from Cantebrige to by some of the new testaments. And in his chambre they fownde a young gentelman whom he did not know, havyng a chayne about his neck, to whom the said frear did rede in the new testament. And this respondent saith that the said John Tyball and this respondent taryed still in his chambre, and herd hym rede a chapitre of powle as he remembrith. And that done Tyball moved the said frear barons of sir Richard Fox, and shewed that sir Richard was well lerned, and rekened that he wold do well, wherfore he desyred frear barons that he wold wryte a lovyng lettre to the said sir Richard. Which frere barons so wrote a lettre to the said sir Richard, which lettre after he had wryten it he did rede it to this respondent and John Tyball, how be it he doth not now remembre what was conteyned in it, and delivered to Tyball. And afterward eche of them bowght a new testament in English of hem, and paid iii s for a pere, which he kept after that it was forboyden untyll the sunday before myd lent last past. In which new testament he red in Roger a Tanners house of bowres Gyfford, bowerhall, mother bocher's and mother charite's, and at last sold the said new testament to sir Richard Fox.

[87] I have extended all obvious abbreviations, and modernized the punctuation. The date 15 October appears on f. 34 r.

Additional Notes to Chapter 7

1 A lot of work has been done since this article appeared, including the following: J. A. F. Thomson, *The Later Lollards 1414-1520* (Oxford, 1965); M. D. Lambert, *Medieval Heresy: Popular Movements from Bogomil to Hus* (London, 1977); Claire Cross, *Church and People 1450-1660* (Glasgow, 1976); idem, 'Popular Piety and the Records of the unestablished Churches 1460-1660', *SCH*, 11 (1975) pp. 269-92; J. F. Davis, 'Lollardy and the Reformation in England', *Archiv für Reformationsgeschichte*, 73 (1982), 217-36; idem, 'Joan of Kent, Lollardy and the English Reformation', *JEH*, 33 (1982), pp. 225-33.

4 For the probability that the first edition of *A proper dyaloge* was the unique *STC2* 1462.3 (1530), which does not include 'A compendious olde treatyse' (unlike *STC* 6813), see A. Hume, 'English Protestant Books Printed Abroad, 1525-1535. An Annotated Bibliography', in *The Complete Works of St. Thomas More*, 8, ii, ed. L. A. Schuster *et al.* (New Haven and London, 1973), pp. 1076-77, and below n. 16.

5 Cf. *A Manual of the Writings in Middle English 1050-1500*, 2, ed. J. Burke Severs (Hamden, Conn., 1970), pp. 361-2, 523.

7 For misattribution of this text to Purvey see below n. 17.

14 On this text see *Manual of Writings in Middle English*, 2, ed. Severs, pp. 375, 531.

16 On the separate edition, *STC* 3021, probably preceding the joint one, *STC* 6813, see Hume, *loc. cit.*

17 · On this text, wrongly attributed to John Purvey by Miss Deanesly, datable to 1401 x c. 1407, and written by Richard Ullerston, see Anne Hudson, 'The Debate on Bible Translation, Oxford, 1401', *EHR*, xc (1975), pp. 1-18; idem, 'John Purvey: A reconsideration of the Evidence for his Life and Writings', *Viator*, 12 (1981), p. 377. Cf. also C.F. Bühler, 'A Lollard tract: On translating the Bible into English', *Medium Aevum*, vii (1938), pp. 167-83.

18 Cf. *STC2* 20036.5 for another edition [T. Godfray, *c.* 1532] with initials 'w.T.' to the Preface. See also Hume, *op. cit.*, pp. 1078-79.

19 Bale's words about 'two men' and 'one book' form part of his invective against Bonner and do not (as I suggested) indicate his ignorance of the double text. Bale summarized the main points covered in the two treatises, to indict the bishop for condemning 'manye godly thynges that owr gracyouse prince hath done by the auctoryte of gods worde....Lett menne dylygentlye serche those ii treatyses, and they schall easelye perseyve what a faythfull part ye have played here, in condemnynge in a maner all thynges that he hath made lawfull by the scripturs'. *Yet a course at the Romyshe foxe*, *loc. cit.*

24 See *Selections from English Wycliffite Writings*, ed. Anne Hudson (Cambridge, 1978), pp. 29-33, 155-6, for the manuscript versions of this work, and for part of the fifteenth-century English text.

27 Molnar's article appeared in the journal mentioned in vol. xlv (1965), pp. 212-31. For a full examination of this text see Anne Hudson, 'A Neglected Wycliffite Text', *JEH*, 29 (1978), pp. 257-79. Nicholas Hereford is here considered a possible author.

32 Bale, who attributed this work to John Purvey, referred to it in his *Illustrium maioris Britanniae scriptorum....summarium* (1548), f. 181ʳ, but the only firm evidence for his knowledge of the text is in the 1557-9 *Scriptorum illustrium maioris Brytannie Catalogus*, cent. septima, pp. 516, 528-9, 542-3, where he quotes it, using the 1528 edition. It seems therefore (contrary to my suggestion) that Bale gained access to this work too late to draw on it for his own work on the Apocalypse, *The Image of bothe churches*. Richard Bauckham *Tudor Apocalypse* (Appleford, 1978), p. 27; cf. Hudson, 'John Purvey', p. 369.

33 See Bauckham, *op. cit.*, p. 43, on this text influencing Luther's view of the Apocalypse, and cf. p. 46 for Bullinger's use of it.

34 *STC2* 15225 suggests [1535 ?] for the date of this book.

36 For the influence of this work in making accessible Lollard apocalyptic ideas, and a possible echo of it in a sermon of 1579, see Bauckham, *op. cit.*, pp. 32, 252 ff., 347, 351, n. 29.

37   *Manual of the Writings in Middle English*, 4, ed. A. E. Hartung (1973), pp. 1068-9. For a new assessment of *The Plowman's Tale*, which rejects Bradley's conclusion and establishes it as an early fifteenth-century Lollard poem that was resurrected and printed in 1536 to aid Henrician propaganda, see Andrew N. Wawn, 'The Genesis of *The Plowman's Tale*', *Yearbook of English Studies*, 2 (1972), pp. 21-40; *idem*, 'Chaucer, *The Plowman's Tale* and Reformation Propaganda: The Testimonies of Thomas Godfray and *I Playne Piers*', *BJRL*, lvi (1973-74), pp. 174-92.

41   For the 'discretionary arguments' for putting Chaucer's name to outspoken religious texts, in view of the exemption of Chaucer's works from the 1542-3 act prohibiting forbidden books, see P. L. Heyworth, 'The Earliest Black-letter Editions of *Jack Upland*', *Huntington Library Quarterly*, xxx (1967), p. 314, n. 32, cf. p. 312.

45   See now the edition by P. L. Heyworth, *Jack Upland, Friar Daw's Reply and Upland's Rejoinder* (Oxford, 1968), and on the early editions see Heyworth, *art. cit.*, where it is suggested that *Jack Upland* was part of Thomas Cromwell's printing propaganda – John Gough's edition appearing probably in 1536.

46   On *The Ymage of Love*, (STC2 21471.5, 21472), see *The Complete Works of St. More*, 6, ii, ed. T. M. C. Lawler *et al.* (New Haven and London, 1981), p. 729 ff.

48   For the sixteenth-century view of Chaucer see *Chaucer and Chaucerians*, ed. D. S. Brewer (London, 1966), pp. 249-50; John N. King, *English Reformation Literature: The Tudor Origins of the Protestant Tradition*, (Princeton, 1982), pp. 50-52, 227, 229, 323.

57   See *English Wycliffite Writings*, ed. Hudson, pp. 10-11.

59   See Hume, *op. cit.*, pp. 1077-79, where the attribution of these two editions to Tyndale is rejected on the grounds that he is not known to have published anonymous works after 1526. George Joye is preferred for *The praier and complaynte*; George Constantine for *Thorpe and Oldcastle*. Tyndale's handling of the Thorpe text might, however, be another matter, and Foxe carefully distinguished between Tyndale's copy and the original manuscript held by Constantine. Cf. also n. 18 above.

61   *STC2* 25590; 25590.5.

67   See also L. P. Fairfield, 'John Bale and the Development of Protestant Hagiography in England', *JEH*, xxiv (1973), pp. 146-60; *idem*, *John Bale: Mythmaker for the English Reformation* (West Lafayette, Ind., 1976); King, *op. cit.*, pp. 56-75; and below Chapter 9, n. 29.

69   See T. B. Blatt, *The Plays of John Bale* (Copenhagen, 1968), pp. 34, 48-52, 125.

72   See also Alice-Lyle Scoufos, *Shakespeare's Typological Satire. A Study of the Falstaff-Oldcastle Problem*, (Athens, Ohio, 1979).

78   For the influence of Grindal's publication projects on Foxe's work after the appearance of the *Commentarii*, see D. M. Loades, *The Oxford Martyrs* (London, 1970), pp. 263-6.

84   For citation of 'that godlie man *William Thorp*', and 'that auncient and godlie writing intituled *The prayer and complaint of the Ploughman*', to show that judicial oaths 'were not first misliked by Jesuits and seminarie priests', but by earlier 'true Christians', see [James Morice], *A briefe treatise of Oathes exacted by Ordinaries and Ecclesiasticall Iudges* [Middelburg, 1590?], pp. 15, 18.

85   See now also V. N. Olsen, *John Foxe and the Elizabethan Church* (Berkeley, 1973); K. R. Firth, *The Apocalyptic Tradition in Reformation Britain 1530-1645* (Oxford, 1979); F. J. Levy, *Tudor Historical Thought* (San Marino, 1967); and the works of Bauckham and King referred to above nn. 32, 48.

8

JOHN WYCLIFFE'S REFORMATION REPUTATION

JOHN WYCLIFFE, LIKE SOME OTHER GREAT PROBLEMATICAL FIGURES, has acquired a historical ghost.   As one of the most studied and most celebrated figures of the English middle ages he remains one of the most controversial.   Too many and too deep disputes have raged over his name for historians to enter lightly into any new assessment of his character and aims.   The bulk both of earlier discussions and of Wycliffe's own works preclude any brief estimation of his fame.   But in Wycliffe's as in other cases where the task of understanding is a matter of historical recovery, it is necessary to begin with the removal of various layers of posthumous commentary and interpretation.   And one important stage of this process concerns the level of sixteenth-century Protestant acclamation and accretion.   It may help towards a clearer view of Wycliffe to try to trace the genesis and assess the truth of the celebrity which he gained in the pages of Protestant polemics.   For it is not always sufficiently realized how large a debt modern estimates of Wycliffe continue to owe to the features of his portrait as delineated and retouched by early generations of Protestant reformers.

There is indeed a sense in which the modern study of ecclesiastical history can be dated from the work of those writers and reformers of the sixteenth century who so anxiously searched out historical precedents to justify and buttress their cause.   Their achievements were of the utmost significance, and brought to new celebrity and publicity the work of earlier English heresy, and of John Wycliffe, its originator.   The Lollards were given new fame as the spiritual ancestors of sixteenth-century reformers.   Wycliffe gained a notoriety he has never since lost.   These Protestant investigators and historians were, however, writing under the pressure of great convictions and great events, and not surprisingly their own views left strong impressions upon their estimates of Wycliffe.   Since the imprint of these convictions has left an indelible mark through a line of later histories, it is of special importance to consider how and where the authors may have distorted or erred in selecting and interpreting their materials.   Certain features of their long-lived portrait of Master John Wycliffe have held uncritical acceptance for too long.

* A shortened version of this paper was read to the Cambridge Historical Society on 28 November 1963.   I am grateful to Mr. K. B. McFarlane for reading and commenting on it.

There can be no doubt that in the sixteenth and seventeenth centuries a number of people came to be concerned with Wycliffe's faith and achievements, and that certain of them were also acquainted with some of his authentic works. The book which contained what is probably the first formal Reformation eulogy of Wycliffe was produced abroad. In the prologue to the earliest printed edition of Wycliffe's *Trialogus*, which appeared at Worms in 1525, Wycliffe was described as the "true and pious witness of Christ", who was "undoubtedly inscribed in the book of life before the foundations of the world", and who announced Christ and His word despite the atrocious threats of Antichrist. The Christian reader was admonished to behold him "now that the sun is shining again, driving back the darkness and thickest mists inimical to light", appearing (thanks to a skilful printer) restored to light and life.[1] It may have been the first of a long series of luminary metaphors. Not many years later Tyndale called attention to the disastrous consequences which had overtaken England as the result of failure to heed a clear pre-Reformation call to repentance:

> Wickliffe [he said in his Prologue to Jonah (1531)] preached repentance unto our fathers not long since. They repented not; for their hearts were indurate, and their eyes blinded with their own pope-holy righteousnesss, wherewith they had made their souls gay against the receiving again of the wicked spirit . . . .

As the result of which neglect Richard II was murdered, and the civil wars of the fifteenth century brought the land "half into a wilderness".[2]

Wycliffe was already launched into a position of new prophetic influence. But it was John Bale who in this matter (as in others in these formative years) took a decisive step in the unfolding of Wycliffe's historical fame. He seems to have been the first to apply the words from Ecclesiasticus which subsequent repetition has worn into a threadbare cliché. The morning star, *stella matutina*, was one of the descriptions accorded, in a passage of fulsome praise, to the Oxford master by the ex-Carmelite in his catalogue of British writers, which first appeared abroad in 1548. The phrase as Bale there applied it is an indication of the forcefulness of his perception, as well as of his convictions and his vocabulary. It is worth translating his words:

---

[1] *Joannis Wiclefi viri undiquaque piissimi dialogorum libri quattuor* ([Worms], 1525), sig. A ii b; *Joannis Wiclif Trialogus*, ed. G. Lechler (Oxford, 1869), pp. 13-14; *Short-Title Catalogue of Books Printed in The German-Speaking Countries* (London, 1962), p. 913.

[2] *Doctrinal Treatises and Introductions to Different Portions of the Holy Scriptures by William Tyndale*, ed. H. Walter (Parker Society, 1848), p. 458.

John Wycliffe, Englishman, the greatest theologian of his time, held alone for many years the magisterial chair (as it is called) in teaching and disputing at Oxford. Apart from the truly apostolic life which he led, he far excelled all his fellows in England by his ability, eloquence, and erudition . . . . He was roused by the spirit of the eternal father to stand for His truth in the midst of the darkness of impious locusts, as the magnanimous warrior of Jesus Christ, and he became the most invincible organ of his day against Antichrists. He was indeed the most strong Elias of his times to reform all distortions. He was one and the first after the loosing of Satan to bring the light of truth in that age of darkness, and who dared before the whole synagogue of the devil to confess Christ, and to reveal the abominable turpitude of the great Antichrist. For he shone like the morning star in the midst of a cloud, and remained for many days as the faithful witness in the church. As the radiant sun he shone in the temple of God, and like incense burning in the fire. He was always of the most irreproachable faith, and most absolute attachment to the truth . . . .[3]

And so the analogies multiplied. Bale had already testified elsewhere to his confidence in the divine desire for Wycliffe's spiritual exhumation. "I think not the contrary", he wrote two years before this, "but, ere the world be at a full end, God will so glorify that twenty times condemned heretic, execrated, cursed, spitted, and spatted at, that all your popish writers, before his time and after, will be reckoned but vile swineherds to him, for the good favour he bare to Christ's holy gospel".[4] Among the remaining points of Bale's accounts of Wycliffe, two are worthy of notice. First that having lived securely in the reign of Edward III he suffered several years' exile under Richard II, but returned to die at Lutterworth in 1387, leaving behind him "no small number of godly disciples . . . to defend the lowliness of the gospel against the exceeding pride, ambition, simony, avarice, hypocrisy, whoredom, sacrilege, tyranny, idolatrous worshippings, and other filthy fruits of those stiff-necked Pharisees".[5] Second, that he published "for the advantage of the Christian state"

---

[3] J. Bale, *Illustrium maioris Britanniae scriptorum . . . summarium*, ([Wesel], 548), (cited hereafter as Bale, *Summarium*), f. 154 v; cf. J. Bale, *Scriptorum illustrium maioris Brytannie . . . Catalogus* (Basel, 1557-9), (cited hereafter as Bale, *Catalogus*), cent. sext. p. 450, where Bale quotes from Leland. See . Leland, *Commentarii de Scriptoribus Britannicis*, ed. A. Hall (Oxford, 1709), i, pp. 378-9.

[4] *Select Works of John Bale*, ed. H. Christmas (Parker Society, 1849), pp. 140-1, from the preface to *The First Examination of Anne Askewe* (1546). Other eulogies of Wycliffe are to be found elsewhere in Bale's writings, for example *Select Works*, pp. 15, 171; *Summarium*, ff. 165 r., 246 r.; *Index Britanniae Scriptorum*, ed. R. L. Poole and M. Bateson (Oxford, 1902), p. 270.

[5] *Select Works of John Bale*, p. 15. Bale repeats the date 1387 elsewhere: *Summarium*, f. 157 v.; *Catalogus*, cent. sext. p. 456; *Index Britanniae Scriptorum*, p. 268. The idea of the exile could have been derived from Polydore Vergil's *Anglica Historia* (Basel, 1534), p. 395. This fiction was repeated as late as 1608 by Thomas James, in the short life of Wycliffe appended to his *Apologie for John Wickliffe* (Oxford, 1608), and in the frontispiece to the 1753 continental edition of the *Trialogus*.

numerous works, "partly in Latin, partly in the vulgar tongue", and "translated the whole Bible into English".[6]

John Foxe the martyrologist followed where Bale had led. In his *Commentarii rerum in ecclesia gestarum*, a work which owed much to Bale and which appeared at Strasbourg in 1554 as the first (not very successful) Latin version of the later *Acts and Monuments*, Foxe devoted the opening section to the history of Wycliffe and the Lollards. For, as he explained, "although it be manifest and evident enough, that there were divers and sundry before Wickliff's time, who have wrestled and laboured in the same cause and quarrel that our countryman Wicliff hath done", yet it was in his time that "this furious fire of persecution seemed to take his first original and beginning".[7] And so he plunged into the opening of a historical narrative which was to be his life's work. Wycliffe's place in it remained a leading one, though in later editions it was prefaced by Foxe's descriptions of the primitive church, European heretical precedents, and earlier English ecclesiastical history and resistance to the tyranny of Rome. The martyrologist praised the English arch-heretic in a passage which, passing from the Latin edition into the English *Acts and Monuments* of 1563 and later, borrowed eulogistic images and phrases from John Bale:

> he, being the public reader of divinity in the university of Oxford, was, for the rude time wherein he lived, famously reputed for a great clerk, a deep schoolman, and no less expert in all kinds of philosophy; . . . this is out of all doubt, that at what time all the world was in most desperate and vile estate, and that the lamentable ignorance and darkness of God's truth had overshadowed the whole earth, this man stepped forth like a valiant champion, unto whom that may justly be applied which is spoken in the book called Ecclesiasticus, of one Simon, the son of Onias: "Even as the morning star being in the midst of a cloud, and as the moon being full in her course, and as the bright beams of the sun; so doth he shine and glister in the temple and church of God".[8]

But Foxe was not a blind borrower, and he adopted a somewhat more

---

[6] Bale, *Catalogus*, cent. sext., pp. 451, 456; cf. *Summarium*, ff. 155 r., 157 v., and J. Leland, *Commentarii de Scriptoribus Britannicis*, ii, p. 380. See also p. 250 and notes 25 and 30 below.

[7] J. Foxe, *Commentarii rerum in ecclesia gestarum* (Strasbourg, 1554), f. 1 r. - v., as later given in the English version, *The Acts and Monuments of John Foxe*, 4th edn. revised J. Pratt (London, 1877), (cited hereafter in this edition unless otherwise indicated, as *Acts and Mons.*), ii, pp. 790-1. In the first English edition of 1563, this passage comes at the opening of the second part, p. 85.

[8] *Acts and Mons.*, ii, pp. 791-2, conflating the 1563 and 1570 editions; cf. Ecclesiasticus, l. 6-7. Foxe's first version of this passage is *Commentarii rerum in ecclesia gestarum*, ff. 1 v. - 2 v. For Foxe's account of Wycliffe, and the enlargement of his English edition, see W. Haller, *Foxe's Book of Martyrs and the Elect Nation* (London, 1963), pp. 158-9, 162-3.

cautious attitude than Bale on certain points in his account.   On the matter of Wycliffe's reputed exile, though he at first accepted the (wrong) date of 1387 for the heresiarch's death, he was careful to remark that between 1382 and then Wycliffe's history was obscure, and that it was on the authority of Thomas Netter that the deduction of the exile was made.[9]   Later Foxe was able to correct 1387 to 1384, though he still did not entirely abandon the possibility of exile, and referred to Wycliffe's death after his return "within short space, either from his banishment, or from some other place where he was secretly kept".[10]   Foxe seems also (wisely in the circumstances) to have been somewhat more hesitant than Bale in the literary output which he was prepared to ascribe to this champion's pen.   Having referred in his earliest edition to the large number of works produced by Wycliffe, he later fell back on the authority of John Cochlaeus who, said Foxe in 1570.

> testifieth that he wrote very many books, sermons, and tractations . . . [and] recordeth also, that there was a certain bishop in England, who wrote to him, declaring, that he had yet remaining in his custody two huge and mighty volumes of John Wickliff's works, which, for the quantity thereof, might seem to be equal to the works of St. Augustine.[11]

But for his own testimony Foxe, compared with Bale, showed restraint. "Among other of his treatises, I myself also have found out certain . . .", he said, "which I intend hereafter, the Lord so granting, to publish abroad".[12]   The titles were three, and they were all Latin works: "On the Sense and Truth of Holy Scripture", "On the Church", and "Wycliffe's Confession on the Eucharist".   It might seem that Foxe was not prepared to swallow the whole of Bale's Wycliffite canon.[13]

---

[9] Foxe, *Commentarii*, f. 32 r.; cf. *Acts and Mons.*, iii, p. 49.

[10] *Acts and Mons.*, iii, p. 53; cf. p. 49.

[11] *Ibid.*, iii, p. 54; 1570 edition, i, p. 547; cf. 1563 edition p. 98; J. Cochlaeus, *Historiae Hussitarum Libri Duodecim* (Mainz, 1549), pp. 7-8.   Cf. Bale's remark in his preface to *The First Examination of Anne Askew:* "I have at this hour the titles of a hundred and forty-four of them [Wycliffe's books] which are many more in number: for some of them under one title comprehendeth two books, some three, some four; yea, one of them containeth twelve" (*Select Works of John Bale*, p. 140).   A decade later, when Bale published the full version of his catalogue, there were 238 items listed under Wycliffe's name.   See n. 69 below for some of the errors in these attributions.

[12] *Acts and Mons.*, iii, p. 54; 1570 edition, i, p. 547.   It appears that Foxe's intention was never realized.

[13] In the case of an English Lollard work called *Jack up Lande*, which was printed in the late 1530s, and included by Foxe in the 1570 edition of the *Acts and Monuments*, he repeated the erroneous ascription to Chaucer which Bale emended (also erroneously) in favour of Wycliffe: *Acts and Mons*, ii, p. 357; Bale, *Catalogus*, cent. sext., p. 454; *Index Britanniae Scriptorum*, p. 274.   See also n. 37 below.

Having passed from Bale's acclaim to such an elevated niche in the *Acts and Monuments*, Wycliffe's morning-star reputation was fairly assured, and after this launching was to sail (sometimes stormily) through many generations of Protestant histories. Early in the seventeenth century Wycliffe's most distinguished apologist was Bodley's first librarian, Thomas James, whose *Apologie for John Wickliffe* (1608), like his scheme for the frieze on the walls of the Bodleian Library, shows how deeply he was imbued with the Protestant view of history as expounded by Bale and Foxe. And Wycliffe was a key figure. He headed the list of those "Authors of the middle age, that wrote in the defence of that Religion, which is now (thanks be to God) publikely established in the Church of England", whose works James was anxious to see faithfully transcribed, collected and collated.[14] And he found an honourable place between Pierre d'Ailly and John Hus in the series of painted portraits which still remains to illustrate the librarian's concept of ecclesiastical history. Among all the writers who had defended Christ against Antichrist, and opposed themselves as "Arch-pillers, against the Arch-hereticks and Caterpillers" of their times, none said James had

behaved himselfe more religiously, valiantlie, learnedlie, and constantlie, then this stout Champion, reverend Doctor, & worthie preacher of Gods word *John Wickliffe* . . . .[15]

The prime concern of the *Apologie* was to demonstrate Wycliffe's "conformitie with the now Church of England", refuting the recent "slaunderous obiections" raised by the Jesuit Robert Parsons, and showing Wycliffe as a "sound", "absolute", "resolved true, Catholike, English Protestant".[16] It was an argument which had already been employed in 1593 by an accused Brownist, who thought it worth while trying to defend his writings as being in the cause of true religion with a plea that they contained points held by John Wycliffe, once accounted heresy and Lollardy.[17] Likewise in 1626 Sir Edward Coke, when trying to escape exclusion from parliament, based his

[14] T. James, *The Humble and Earnest Request . . . to the Church of England* [? Oxford, ? 1625], p. 4. James's theological interests are considered by G.W.W[heeler], "Thomas James, Theologian and Bodley's Librarian", *The Bodleian Quarterly Rec.*, iv (1923), pp. 91-5.

[15] T. James, *An Apologie for John Wickliffe, shewing his conformitie with the now Church of England* (Oxford, 1608), p. 1. Though its tendentious nature is evident from its title, this first published monograph on Wycliffe makes praiseworthy use of source material to prove Wycliffe's "Anglicanism". For Wycliffe's place in the Bodleian Library frieze see J. N. L. Myres, "Thomas James and the Painted Frieze", *The Bodleian Lib. Rec.*, iv (1952-3), pp. 30-51.

[16] T. James, *Apologie*, title and pp. 2, 10, 14, 25.

[17] J. Strype, *Annals of the Reformation* (Oxford, 1824), iv, p. 192. (To improve the case reference was made to Foxe.)

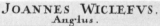

17a   Woodcut from John Bale's *Illustrium maioris Britanniae Scriptorum Summarium* (1548). This cut was also used in *The true copye of a Prolog* (1550) (pp. 251-2)

17b   Anon. engraving from *Les Vrais Pourtraits des Hommes Illustres* (1581), a French translation of Theodore Beza's *Icones*.

17c   Engraving by H. Hondius in J. Verheiden, *Praestantium aliquot Theologorum* (1602).

17d   Engraving from Samuel Clarke, *The Marrow of Ecclesiastical History* (London, 1654).

18 & 19   Illuminated leaves of 1550 added to the 15th-century copy of the Lollard Bible from which Crowley printed the General Prologue that year. (Cambridge University Library, MS Mm 2. 15, f. 274r-v) (pp. 253-4)

The true copie of a Prologe whiche Iohn wickliffe wrote to this Bible which he translatid into Englishe about two hundrid yers past, that was in the tyme of kynge Edwarde the thrid, as may iustly be gatherid of the mention that is had of him in diuers auncient Cronicles.

Anno domini . 1550 .

20b Title-page of James Verheiden's *Praestantium aliquot Theologorum* (1602). Note the inset busts, probably of Wycliffe (left) and Hus (right). See Plate 17c.

20a Title-page of the first edition of Wycliffe's *Trialogus* ([Worms], 1525) – the first of his Latin works to be printed. (p. 264)

refusal to take the sheriff's oath on its (then arguably archaic) clause for the suppression of "all manner of Heresies and Errors, commonly called Lollaries", maintaining that Lollard was now only another name for Protestant.[18]   Not much later Milton answered his own rhetorical question of why "was this Nation chos'n before any other, that out of her as out of Sion should be proclam'd and sounded forth the first tidings and trumpet of Reformation to all Europ", with the proud assertion that

> had it not bin the obstinat perversnes of our Prelats against the divine and admirable spirit of Wicklef, to suppresse him as a schismatic and innovator . . . the glory of reforming all our neighbours had bin compleatly ours.[19]

By the second half of the seventeenth century Fuller found no difficulty in calling Wycliffe "that glorious saint", qualifying it only with the reasonable admission that "he was a man, and so subject to error, living in a dark age, more obnoxious to stumble, vexed with opposition, which makes men reel into violence".[20]   The old phrases were borrowed, twisted and refurbished by new writers returning to the old theme.   "The famous *John Wickliffe*, the Morning-Star of the Reformation", was how he appeared in the eighteenth century to the historian Daniel Neal,[21] and a generation later William Gilpin began his lives of reformers with a description of how the "intuitive genius" of Wycliffe had "explored the regions of darkness, and let in not a feeble and glimmering ray; but such an effulgence of light, as was never afterwards obscured".[22]   And finally, a new biography of the following century produced a still more romantic elaboration:

> The age of Chaucer and Wycliffe was as the morning light in our history; the streaks of day which then crossed the horizon, and threw their beautiful influences over the world beneath, were for a season over-clouded: but they were as heralds, nevertheless, proclaiming the sure rising of the sun.[23]

[18] C. D. Bowen, *The Lion and the Throne* (London, 1957), p. 408; J. Rushworth, *Historical Collections* (London, 1659), pp. 201-2.   Coke's plea was allowed, the clause was omitted, and he was excluded from parliament.   The clause in the oath relating to the suppression of Lollardy dated from the Leicester Parliament of 1414, and Coke's action resulted in an order for its permanent abolition.

[19] *Complete Prose Works of John Milton*, gen. ed. D. M. Wolfe (New Haven, 1953—), ii, pp. 552-3; cf. i, pp. 525-6, ii, pp. 231-2, 707.   Foxe was one of Milton's sources.

[20] T. Fuller, *The Church History of Britain*, ed. J. S. Brewer (Oxford, 1845), ii, p. 316.

[21] D. Neal, *The History of the Puritans or Protestant Non-Conformists* (London, 1732-38), i, p. 3.   Though others had thus clearly shown the way, Daniel Neal appears to have been the first to use the phrase "morning star of the Reformation".

[22] W. Gilpin, *The Lives of John Wicliff; And of the most Eminent of his Disciples* (London, 1766), p. 58.   The edition of this work which appeared in 1809, five years after the author's death, was called *The Lives of Reformers*.

[23] R. Vaughan, *John de Wycliffe D.D.* (London, 1853), p. 317.

And so on — through this long succession of Protestant star-gazers.[24]

But if Protestants and Anglicans of so many kinds and generations were thus proud of their Wycliffite dawn, in what particularly was this seen to have resided? We must turn back again to look more closely at the beginnings from which the metaphor was elaborated.

*   *   *   *

In claiming Wycliffe as their spiritual ancestor, Protestant writers looked to him as one who had singularly proclaimed and defended the causes for which they themselves were, or had been, struggling. Wycliffe's light shone brightly for them in his work as an opponent of the Popish corruptions and Romish enormities of his time — against the dissolute lives of clergy, monks and friars, and against miracles, pilgrimages, images and (to their thinking) other errors and abuses. And these endeavours were seen to have been based, in the fourteenth century as in the sixteenth, upon a return to the authority of scripture, and the restoration of evangelical standards. Wycliffe, like his successors in a later age, was regarded as having restored the word of the gospel and scriptural understanding to the forefront of Christian life and profession.

High, therefore, among the heresiarch's extolled achievements, came to be placed his part in the production of an English Bible, and in the composition of vernacular works to make God's truth available to all. The idea that Wycliffe himself translated the whole Bible into English was one which could be drawn from some of his posthumous medieval critics, as well perhaps as from oral Lollard tradition.[25] Here as elsewhere we find old condemnation becoming new commendation. John Bale found support in Aeneas Silvius for his statement (repeated in several places) that Wycliffe "translated the whole Bible into English, adding prefaces and arguments to each

---

[24] It is impossible to explore here the ramifications of Wycliffite historiography as it passed through the hands and controversies of Roman Catholics, non-jurors, anabaptists and non-conformists, in the seventeenth and eighteenth centuries. For a brief treatment of this part of the story see M. Burrows, *Wiclif's Place in History* (London, 1882).

[25] In 1411 Hus wrote that "it is said by the English that he [Wycliffe] himself translated the whole Bible from Latin into English": M. Deanesly, *The Lollard Bible* (Cambridge, 1920), p. 240; *Historia et monumenta Joannis Hus* ([Frankfurt], 1715), i, p. 136. The statements of Archbishop Arundel and of the chronicler Henry Knighton on this matter are considered by Miss Deanesly, pp. 238-40. It is to be noted that neither of them went so far as to say that Wycliffe had translated the whole Bible.

book", and also a general prologue of fifteen chapters.[26] Bale's authority meant much to later generations, and it is therefore of some importance that his statement was clearly applied to the later version of the Lollard Bible, the General Prologue of which can be dated to about 1396. This prologue was printed more than once in the sixteenth century. The first known occasion was in 1541, when John Gough published it under the title of *The dore of holy scripture.* While the preface stressed the antiquity of "this lytell codicell", as having been written "more then two hondred yeares past", to readers of this edition the "fyrste translatoure of the byble out of latyn in to Englyshe" remained nameless as "a simple pore clark".[27] Whatever the editor's private convictions, such anonymity was not inadvisable when some Lollard tracts had already, twelve years earlier, been publicly condemned. And as it was John Gough was imprisoned in the Fleet and within six years *The dore of holy scripture*, with Wycliffe's English works in general, had been stigmatized by public prohibition.[28]

By 1550, however, circumstances were very different. That year saw a new edition of the General Prologue, printed this time by Robert Crowley, and called the "pathwaye to perfect knowledge".[29] Now that "true religion beginneth to floryshe", the tract was entitled *The true copye of a Prolog wrytten about two C yeres paste by John Wycklife,* and Bale's recently published Summary of Writers was quoted in

---

[26] Bale, *Catalogus*, cent. sext., pp. 456, 451; *Summarium*, f. 157 v.; *Index Britanniae Scriptorum*, pp. 266, 268-9, 273. See note 30 below. For Sir Thomas More's similar belief (expressed in 1528), see Deanesly, *The Lollard Bible*, pp. 5-6.

[27] *The dore of holy scripture*, (S[hort] T[itle] C[atalogue]), compiled A. W. Pollard and G. R. Redgrave, [London, 1926], no. 3033), from the preface "To the Reader".

[28] For the Lollard tracts condemned by Bishop Stokesley of London in December 1531, and further references to *The dore of holy scripture*, see my article "Lollardy and the Reformation: Survival or Revival?", *History*, xliv (1964). Above 219ff. John Gough was imprisoned in the Fleet in January 1541 for printing and selling seditious books. The colophon of *The dore of holy scripture* is dated 12 March 1540/1. *Three Fifteenth-Century Chronicles*, ed. J. Gairdner (Camden Soc., N.S., xxviii, 1880), pp. 89-90; *Letters and Papers, Foreign and Domestic, of the Reign of Henry VIII*, ed. J. S. Brewer and J. Gairdner, v, App. 18, pp. 768-9; xxi, pt. i, p. 611; Foxe, *Acts and Mons.*, v, pp. 448, 568, 831; *Tudor Royal Proclamations*, ed. P. L. Hughes and J. F. Larkin, i (New Haven and London, 1964), pp. 181-6 [early 1530, not 1529], 373-6 [8 July 1546]. By the middle of the sixteenth century Wycliffe's writings had been publicly condemned not only in England but also in the Netherlands (1529) and France (1544), and at Louvain (1546) and Lucca (1549).

[29] It is perhaps worth noticing that Tyndale's edition of Luther's preface to the New Testament was called "A pathway to the holy scripture". *S.T.C.*, nos. 24462-4.

support of the ascription.[30]　　There followed a short versified account
of the current Protestant view of England's arch-heretic:

> Kyng Edward the iii did Wicklife defend
> Wherebi he did florish in Oxford longe while
> But Richard ye ii King did somthing bend
> To papistis bi whom Wicklife was in exile
> Yet dyd thys good man never alter his stile
> But wrot mani volumis whils he was alive
> To extinguish errour, and truth to revive
> At the last he returnid to his contrei againe
> And lyvid at Lutterworth . . . .[31]

The large number of extant manuscripts of the Lollard Bible, many
of which have sixteenth-century annotations, shows that orthodox and
unorthodox readers alike were able to derive from it spiritual comfort
and exhortation.　　The notes of these readers show also that some of
them approached the translation in the same spirit as the editors of
the General Prologue.　　"This ancient monyment of the holy scripure
dothe show", wrote one, "how the Lord God in all ages and tymes
wold have his blessed woorde preserved for the comforte of his elect
children and church in all tymes and ages, in despyte off Sathane,
Antichrist, and all his enemyes".[32]　　Already too, before the printed
word enlarged its currency, the view that Wycliffe was the author of
the General Prologue and responsible for the work of translation, may
have been not uncommon.　　"Note the baseness of Wycleff against
the university of Oxford . . ." wrote Bishop Blyth of Coventry and
Lichfield in Latin in the margin of his copy, "here he argues that a
free entry to holy scripture should be made open to all the unlearned,

---

[30] The full title of this edition reads "The true copye of a Prolog wrytten
about two C yeres paste by John Wycklife (as maye iustly be gatherid bi that,
that John Bale hath written of him in his boke entitled the Summarie of famouse
writers of the Ile of great Britan) the Originall whereof is founde written in an
olde English Bible bitwixt the olde Testament and the Newe.　Whych Bible
remaynith now in ye Kyng hys maiesties Chamber".　Bale's 1548 *Summarium*,
f. 157 v. states of Wycliffe: "Transtulit quoque in Anglicum sermonem Biblia
tota, cum quibusdam veterum doctorum tractatibus", and the list of Wycliffe's
works (f. 157 r.) includes (without an *incipit*) "Introductorium scripturae".
Clearer statements of the ascription of the General Prologue to Wycliffe are
those of the *Catalogus*, cent. sext., p. 451, and of Bale's autograph notebook,
Index Britanniae Scriptorum, pp. 266, 268.

[31] All the facts for these lines could have been derived from Bale's *Summarium*,
ff. 154 v. - 158 r.　Both Bale and Crowley made play for Edward VI's benefit
with the protection which Edward III had allegedly given to Wycliffe: *ibid.*,
f. 165 r. - v.

[32] *The Holy Bible . . . in the Earliest English Versions*, ed. J. Forshall and
F. Madden (Oxford, 1850), i, p. lx, no. 149, written in a fifteenth-century copy
of the later version of the Lollard Bible, now MS. A.I.5 of Trinity College
Dublin.　Forshall and Madden's edition was the first printed text of the whole
Lollard Bible, though there had already been editions of the New Testament,
including that of the later version produced by John Lewis in 1731.

so that he might at least corrupt the simple with the poison of his error . . .".[33]

The richly illuminated manuscript of the Lollard Bible which Robert Crowley used in preparing his edition of the General Prologue, appears to have been rebound, very probably for the king's own benefit, in that same year, 1550. It was enriched by the addition of some decorated title pages, one of which bears the name "EDOVERDVS SEXTVS", and the title "The true copie of a Prologe whiche John Wicklife wrote to this Bible which he translatid into Englishe about two hundrid yers past, that was in the tyme of kynge Edwarde the thryd, as may iustly be gatherid of the mention that is had of him in divers auncient Cronicles".[34] It may well have

---

[33] *Ibid.*, p. lv, no. 116, from Corpus Christi College, Cambridge, MS. 147. It was upon the notes in this manuscript that A. Ogle, *The Tragedy of the Lollards' Tower* (Oxford, 1949), pp. 118-31, constructed a somewhat dubious argument by identifying this copy as "the actual volume produced in evidence against Hunne" in 1514.

[34] Cambridge University Library, MS. Mm. II. 15, f. 274 r. - v.; cf. note 30 above. Another inserted leaf, likewise illuminated to match the manuscript, is f. 4. For a description of this manuscript see *The Holy Bible*, ed. Forshall and Madden, i, pp. liv-lv. Since the binding is sixteenth century, and appears, to judge by a note on f. 307 r. which was cut when the leaves were trimmed, to have been after 1519, there is a strong probability that it was executed at the time of these additional leaves, in 1550. Various sixteenth-century names are noted in the manuscript, of which the most interesting is that of Lady Elizabeth Tyrwhitt. A note written on paper, stitched to the beginning of the book, includes these words:

> sethen I knowe my lyf is short
> and that my book and I must part
> to you my dere and faythful frende
> my chefest iuel I doo comend.
>   your pooer and faythful frend in the lord
>   Elyzabeth Tyrwhyt.

Lady Elizabeth Tyrwhitt (d. 1578), wife of Sir Robert Tyrwhitt (d. 1572), was a notable Protestant and highly placed at court. Her husband was master of the horse to Queen Catherine Parr, whose first husband, Sir Edward Borough, was his cousin. Lady Elizabeth herself was long attached to Catherine Parr's entourage, and in 1548 was appointed governess to Princess Elizabeth. Lady Elizabeth Tyrwhitt's Morning and Evening Prayers formed part of the contents of the elaborately bound Girdle Prayer Book which she is reported (though there are difficulties in the story) to have presented to Elizabeth. In 1548 Sir Robert Tyrwhitt described his wife as "not sayne in Dyvinnity, but is half a Scripture woman", and two years earlier, according to Foxe, when Catherine Parr was under a cloud on account of her religious views, there were plans for arresting and accusing under the Act of Six Articles, Lady Elizabeth together with two other ladies of the queen's chamber. The interests, education and standing of Lady Elizabeth Tyrwhitt make it possible to surmise that she might have had something to do with the treatment, and perhaps also the printing, of this manuscript, and conceivably with its deducible presentation to Edward VI. R. P. T[yrwhitt], *Notices and Remains of the Family of Tyrwhitt* [1872], pp. 18, 24-6; Foxe, *Acts and Mons.*, v, 557, 560; G. H. Tait, "Historiated Tudor Jewellery", *Antiquaries Jl.*, xlii (1962), pp. 232-4; J. Nichols, *The Progresses and Public Processions of Queen Elizabeth* (London, 1788), i, pp. xxvi-xxvii, n.

been this copy to which Thomas James referred when in 1608 he came to praise the scriptural side of Wycliffe's attainments.[35]   And to James it seemed one of the reformer's prime achievements that, as the "worthie instrument & chosen vessel of Gods glorie", he had been moved "to carrie his name before the Gentiles, to translate the whole Bible, to comment upon some parts therof, & chiefly those parts of Holy Scripture which are most in use".[36]   Here once more, Wycliffe stood forth as the "absolute Protestant".   His title of first translator of the Bible into English had acquired firm foundations, upon which a long-lasting edifice was built.   Wycliffe the translator and English author had come to stay.[37]

Part and parcel of this supposed Biblical achievement was the publication of other works in English for (it was pleasant to think) the common benefit.   Bale referred to Wycliffe's vernacular productions, and Leland stressed the fact that it was this part of his writings which was specially popular, being read also "by certain people in our time".[38]   John Lewis, writing in 1720, adapted Polydore Vergil's remarks about Wycliffe's dangerous concern to infect "even the peasants" with his opinions, which had born such fruit that "even now", in the days of Henry VII, people were going to the stake for his English writings.   According to his eighteenth-century biographer, Wycliffe "wrote and Published a great many Tracts . . . . Many of these Tracts he first published in *Latin*, and afterwards in *English*", so that it was complained of him that he " 'composed Books written in his Country's Language, and forthwith published them,

---

[35] T. James, *An Apologie for John Wickliffe*, p. 14, notes Wycliffe's translation of the whole Bible as being "extant in his Maiesties librarie at White-Hall".
[36] *Ibid.*, p. 14.
[37] The growth of the legend was such that Montagu Burrows, in his *Wiclif's Place in History* (London, 1882), describing Foxe's picture of Wycliffe and noticing his reticence on this point, remarked: "Above all, he [Foxe] unaccountably omitted all mention of the Reformer's chief claim to notice, the translation of the Bible" (*op. cit.*, p. 24).   The first person to sound a salutary, though half-hearted, note of caution in this matter appears to have been John Lewis, who in 1731 discussed the contemporary evidence for Wycliffe's part, and wrote of the Wycliffite Bible with some qualifying phrases: "Dr. Wiclif's Translation of the Bible, or however of the New Testament . . ."; "the New Testament of this Version, of which Dr. Wiclif is commonly reputed the Author . . ." Lewis also pointed out Bale's mistaken attribution of the New Testament prologues to Wycliffe.   J. Lewis, *The New Testament . . . Translated out of the Latin Vulgat by John Wiclif* (London, 1731), pp. 6 ff.   Cf. the statements in J. Lewis, *The History of the Life and Sufferings of the Reverend and Learned John Wicliffe* (London, 1720), pp. 66, 69 ff.
[38] J. Leland, *Commentarii de Scriptoribus Britannicis*, ed. A. Hall (Oxford, 1709), ii, p. 380.

that he might make even the Country People skilful in his mischievous Superstition' ".[39]

Next in this catalogue of Protestant praise we may notice the stress which was laid by Wycliffe's eulogizers on the apostolic nature of his ministry. Bale, Foxe and others emphasized (as we have seen) the pure and blameless life which Wycliffe led in rude, dark, corrupt times. And in practising the piety which he preached he was (they thought) concerned that others should participate in his good works and perpetuate his standards. He collected disciples and he sent them forth. The concept of Wycliffe as the founder of a ministry of poor preaching priests has had a long history. We find Foxe referring to Wycliffe "with his fellows going barefoot and in long frieze gowns, preaching diligently unto the people".[40] And already before this Leland had found a source describing how Wycliffe gathered to himself in Oxford followers of one sect, who dressed in long gowns of russet, and went round the country barefoot, preaching to the people.[41] It was an idea which satisfied the Protestant desire for an earlier ministry of the faithful which had foreshadowed their own, in taking Christ's word to those depressed and deprived by Antichrist. And here too there seemed to be some authority in (hostile) medieval report. So Wycliffe, the pre-Protestant apostolic Wycliffe, was regarded as the deliberate founder of a persecuted sect. As put by John Stow:

> John Wicliffe, who with his Disciples, were of the common people called Lollards, they went bare-footed and basely clothed, to wit in course russet garments downe to the heeles, they preached, especially against Monks . . . .[42]

[39] J. Lewis, *The History of . . . John Wicliffe* (London, 1720), pp. 143-4; P. Vergil, *Anglica Historia* (Basel, 1534), p. 395; D. Hay, *Polydore Vergil* (Oxford, 1952), p. 90. A modern reiteration of Lewis's views appears in *Wyclif: Select English Writings*, ed. H. E. Winn (Oxford, 1929), p. xxx.

[40] *Acts and Mons.*, iii, p. 4; cf. ii, p. 799, which suggests that Foxe derived both statements from Walsingham. An eighteenth-century repetition of them is to be found in W. Gilpin, *The Lives of Wicliff; And . . . his Disciples* (London, 1766), p. 34.

[41] J. Leland, *Collectanea*, ed. T. Hearne (Oxford, 1715), iii, p. 379. Various antiquaries had access to Leland's manuscripts and might have known of this passage before it came eventually to be printed. Leland's source was apparently a continuation of the Polychronicon; cf. *Chronicon Angliae*, ed. E. M. Thompson (Rolls Series, 1874), App., p. 395, and *Thomae Walsingham Historia Anglicana*, ed. H. T. Riley (Rolls Series, 1863-4), i, p. 324.

[42] J. Stow, *Annales* (London, 1631-2), p. 272. Stow may well have been relying on the same medieval source as Leland for this passage, and it is worth noticing that the continuation of the Polychronicon printed in the Appendix to the *Chronicon Angliae* (see previous note), survived among Stow's miscellaneous papers in the Harleian manuscripts: *Chronicon Angliae*, *loc. cit.*, and p. lxiv.

Another important issue for this Reformation estimate of Wycliffe was the doctrine of the eucharist. Here again, it seemed to some of the Reformers that they had a ready-made precedent to hand. In his controversy with Cranmer on the sacrament of the altar, Gardiner placed among the disadvantages of the archbishop's view that "there is nothing present but in a sign", the fact that Wycliffe had "enterprised the same" not much more than a century earlier and God had not prospered his teaching. Cranmer countered with the defence that any word spoken against Rome's teaching on this matter would be taken as heresy, and "as for John Wickliff, he was a singular instrument of God in his time to set forth the truth of Christ's gospel".[43] By Mary's reign confidence in Wycliffe's doctrine was able to comfort Protestant sufferers such as Thomas Wats, who died in 1555 believing in a purely commemorative eucharist and holding that

> Luther, Wickliff, Dr. Barnes, and all others that have holden against the sacrament of the altar, and suffered death by fire, or otherwise, for the maintenance of the said opinion, were good men and faithful servants and martyrs of Christ in so believing and dying.[44]

Under Elizabeth, John Jewel argued that one of the reasons why Wycliffe and Hus had been unjustly condemned was for having maintained that "the pope and his clergy, by these new articles of transubstantiation and other like fantasies, had deceived the people", for (in their view) "Christ is not in the sacrament really".[45] To Foxe Wycliffe's views on this sacrament seemed part of a well-conceived objective, since "it was his chief and principal purpose and intent, to revoke and call back the church from her idolatry, to some better amendment; especially in the matter of the sacrament of the body and blood of Christ".[46] And to Thomas James it appeared that Wycliffe had held a doctrine of a sacramental and figurative presence which precisely anticipated the position of the Anglican church.[47]

---

[43] *Writings and Disputations of Thomas Cranmer*, ed. J. E. Cox (Parker Soc., 1844), pp. 13-14, 196.

[44] Foxe, *Acts and Mons.*, vii, p. 120.

[45] *The Works of John Jewel*, ed. J. Ayre (Parker Soc., 1845-50), iii, p. 162. In defending Wycliffe against the charges of Thomas Harding, Jewel provides an interesting example of the false positions into which, in the state of contemporary knowledge, it was possible to be led. In answer to Harding's statement that Wycliffe had held that a bishop in a state of mortal sin is no bishop, and that God ought to obey the devil, Jewel said: "These and other like errors were alleged against him forty years after he was dead, and could not be present to make his answer" (*ibid.*, p. 162). In fact these points were both among the heresies in Wycliffe's writings which were condemned in 1382.

[46] Foxe, *Acts and Mons.*, ii, p. 796.

[47] T. James, *Apologie for John Wickliffe*, p. 29.

Here also however, as in the question of the Bible translation, some of those helping to hoist Wycliffe on to his Anglican pedestal were using some doubtful material. It included a work named *Wickliffe's Wicket*, a short English tract on the eucharist, which seems to have enjoyed some popularity in Lollard circles on the eve of the Reformation. The refutation of it, which was apparently written by William Grocyn (who died in 1519), might have been inspired by the revelations of its use in the dioceses of London and Lincoln during the last decade of his life.[48] From the Lollards the *Wicket* passed into the hands of Protestant reformers. It was printed twice in 1546, twice again in 1548, (re-edited by no less a person than Miles Coverdale), and once more in 1612 by Henry Jackson of Corpus Christi College, Oxford. The first (anonymous) editor made no doubt of the authorship of the treatise; *Wycklyffes wycket: whyche he made in Kyng Rycards days the second*, it was entitled. Bale in the 1550s included it in his list of Wycliffe's works, and Henry Jackson, prefacing the tract two generations later, was able to quote the recent authority of Thomas James for the demonstration that "in this discourse hee [Wycliffe] teacheth the true doctrine of the sacraments with the now Church of England".[49] Whether Coverdale had subscribed to the attribution is perhaps more doubtful, but he did not refute it any more than did his contemporaries.[50] The *Wicket* seems to have passed unchallenged into the accepted canon of Wycliffe's works.

The justice of the ascription is, to say the least, extremely doubtful. The *Wicket* expounds the eucharist in a figurative interpretation, and explains the words of consecration as "set for a mynde of good thynges passed of Christes body".[51] Although it would be possible

---

[48] Bale, *Catalogus*, cent. decimatertia, p. 164. Grocyn's work is no longer extant, and it has also been suggested that it might have been written in the 1470s. *Collectanea*, 2nd ser., ed. M. Burrows (Oxford Hist. Soc., xvi, 1890), pp. 365-6. The *Wicket* ("a slender enough tract") is referred to, together with some other pieces of the Lollards' sixteenth-century reading, by E. G. Rupp, *Studies in the Making of the English Protestant Tradition* (Cambridge, 1949), pp. 4-5, 10; cf. also above pp. 230, 232-4.

[49] *Wickliffes Wicket or A Learned and Godly Treatise of the Sacrament, made by John Wickliffe* (Oxford, 1612), from the preface "To the Christian Reader". Bale, *Catalogus*, cent. sext., p. 453, "Hostiolum Vuiclevi, Lib. I. Obsecro vos fratres per Dominum".

[50] Coverdale, referring to "this authore in thys treatyse" and "this godly wryter", did not commit himself, though it is doubtful whether one should read anything into this. *Wicklieffes Wicket. Faythfully overseene and corrected* [? 1548], sig. a ii r. - v. Two editions of Coverdale's version are extant, *S.T.C.*, nos. 25591, 25591 a.

[51] *Wicklieffes Wicket* [? 1548], sig. b iii r. J. Stacey, *John Wyclif and Reform* (London, 1964), pp. 141-2, regards such statements as disqualifying Wycliffe from the authorship.

to provide parallels from Wycliffe's Latin works for certain of its arguments, the presentation of the tract as a whole is cruder and more blatant in both its methods and conclusions, than what we are accustomed to read from the pen of the master. Whatever his shortcomings, Wycliffe cannot be accused of failing to deal with subtle and complex problems in an appropriate manner. Had his viewpoints been more categorical, and less subject to qualification, his reputation might be less controversial. Apart from the question of its language, the very clarity, simplicity, and affirmativeness of the *Wicket* seem to separate it from Wycliffe.

One further part of this sixteenth-century rescue operation of Wycliffe's name became important because of the celebrity and influence of the *Acts and Monuments*. For Foxe himself, concerned as he was with tracing the continuous succession of sufferers in the Protestant cause, it was desirable that Wycliffe should have shared some of the hardships which others endured in the struggle for truth. This was one significance of the supposed exile which, we have seen, Foxe did not entirely abandon. Wycliffe, rather than desert his faith, had taken himself abroad, where his kindly reception in Bohemia bore lasting fruit. It was not a happy suggestion — though it partially met the need to find medieval England's arch-Protestant subjected to some form of persecution. And although in general the place which Wycliffe had found in the Foxian canon satisfied many successors of Protestant sympathies, this account contained certain inherent difficulties. It was not long before they were pointed out.

The most devastating and thorough early onslaught on the *Acts and Monuments* was that of the Jesuit Robert Parsons, who in his *Treatise of Three Conversions* fastened on the crucial difficulty that Wycliffe not only did not die for his faith, but was not even as much as imprisoned for it. Quite rightly Parsons pointed out that Wycliffe had died on 31 December 1384, not in 1387, and that the only form of exile which could properly be attributed to him was the literary exile of his exported works, which had such momentous consequences for the Bohemian reformers, Hus and Jerome of Prague.

> And how then [Parsons pertinently demanded] may *John Wickliffe* be put downe for so solemne a Martyr, who never was so much as imprisoned for his Religion? Truly I see not: except Fox hath a licence to canonise whome he will. And yf he will say, that he did yt for that his bones were taken up 40 yeares after his buriall, and burned by the commandement of the Councell of *Constance*, that discovered his heresies, which in his life he had dissembled: then must he say also, that a man may be made a Martyr without sense or feeling, or without the consent or concurrence of his owne will, which is most absurd and ridiculous.[52]

[52] R. Parsons, *The Third Part of A Treatise of Three Conversions . . . the First Six Monethes* ([St Omer], 1604), p. 185. (Parsons did not explicitly deny that Wycliffe went to Bohemia.)

Parsons was launched upon a radical attack on the basic premises of the *Acts and Monuments*. It was a matter of volumes rather than words. And it took him back to John Bale and his catalogue of epithets, including the morning star. Parsons called in to his aid critical statements of both Luther and Melanchthon about Wycliffe and his errors. The chain of Foxian continuity was, Parsons suggested, very weak when some of its later martyr-links had so little respect for earlier ones. Wycliffe, that so-called "holy *Elyas*, and brother-like Saint *Wickliffe*", was in fact "one of the most pernicious, wicked, dissembling, hipocriticall impugners of Christ and his doctrine, that ever was in the Church of God".[53] He was a time-server, a disappointed place-seeker, who had developed his opinions to suit temporal advantages, and to win approval in high places. "And this", said the Jesuit with triumphant contempt, "is the protestants great grandfather, so much bragged of by Fox and Bale".[54]

That the Protestant picture survived this attack was by no means due to ignorance or disregard. Thomas James, as we saw, wrote with the specific intention of refuting Parsons, and another author of his century deliberately adopted one of the latter's contemptuous suggestions. Thomas Fuller, in remarking it to be "Admirable, that a hare so often hunted with so many packs of dogs should die at last quietly sitting in his form", went on to answer Parsons's snarls at Wycliffe as a Foxian martyr on the very grounds that

the phrase may be justified in the large acception of the word — for a witness of the truth; besides, the body of Wicliffe was martyred as to shame, though not to pain, as far as his adversaries' cruelty could extend . . . .[55]

Wycliffe in fact, thanks to the labours of these Reformation revivers, and their belief in his evangelism, his doctrine, and his vernacular productions, had acquired and retained fame as a *reformer*, with practical systematic plans for the redemption of the church. "This Wickliff", wrote Foxe, "after long debating and deliberating with himself . . . at the last determined with himself to help and to remedy such things as he saw to be wide, and out of the way", and seeing the difficulties to be such that it was necessary to proceed from lesser to greater "taking his original at small occasions, thereby opened himself a way or mean to greater matters".[56] His efforts, in more ways than one, seemed a foreshadowing of the Reformation.

[53] *Ibid.*, pp. 187-9.
[54] *Ibid.*, p. 194. Thomas Harding in *A Confutation of a Booke Intituled An Apologie of the Church of England* (Antwerp, 1565), f. 263 v., had referred to "the heresies of your great grandfather Ihon Wicklef".
[55] T. Fuller, *Church History*, ed. J. S. Brewer (Oxford, 1845), ii, pp. 362-3.
[56] Foxe, *Acts and Mons.*, ii, p. 796.

"He lived", according to Thomas James, "in a very corrupt time, when the tares had so far over-growne the good corne, that he stood doubtfull where to begin his reformation: whether with the head, or with the taile, with the inferiour sort of Clergie men, or with the Superiours . . .". "Reformation is that which he sought, which God . . . did afterwardes . . . establish in this kingdome".[57]

Although however, there are features of this Reformation portrait which have survived criticism, controversy and rebuke through four centuries, some of them do not well withstand close inspection. For Wycliffe did not personally translate the whole Bible into English; nor can we imagine him writing a series of vernacular treatises for the benefit of his followers, or setting out, in the way that Reformation authors thought of it, to found a sect and to reform the doctrine of his day. It remains to be proved that Wycliffe wrote anything in English and while his share in the production of the Lollard Bible is still disputable, it seems likely that at most it did not extend to more than inspiration, supervision, or partial supervision.[58] Of the large number of English tracts, treatises and sermons which have been fathered upon Wycliffe some are demonstrably false, others extremely probably so, and none provably his. The fact that they are in a number of cases simplified, popularized, sometimes distorted versions of Wycliffe's views and writings may tell us more about his followers than it does about Wycliffe himself. The idea that he sat down to compose some of his works in triplicate for different sorts of followers seems ludicrously unlike the rest that is known of his character and interests.[59]

Nor does the idea of a sect of poor priests constituted under

[57] T. James, *Apologie for John Wickliffe*, pp. 48-50.

[58] The most important discussions of Wycliffe's share in the translation of the Bible are those of Deanesly, *The Lollard Bible*, and S. L. Fristedt, *The Wycliffe Bible* (Stockholm Studies in English, iv, 1953). Cf. also K. B. McFarlane, *John Wycliffe and the Beginnings of English Nonconformity* (London, 1952), pp. 118-9, 148-9. Even if it is allowed that Wycliffe might have played some significant part in the production of the early version, it should be noticed that Reformation writers' views on this matter appear to have been based largely on what they knew of the later version, and its Lollard prologue which is datable to about 1396.

[59] Cf. n. 39 above. As Winn pointed out (*Wyclif: Select English Writings*, p. xxx) the degree of correspondence between the Latin works and their English equivalents varies considerably. This is not surprising, but the rarity of close translations might perhaps be thought to argue (along with other considerations) against Wycliffe's own hand. Some salutary cautions upon the ascriptions of various of the English works to Wycliffe are to be found in H. B. Workman, *John Wyclif* (Oxford, 1926), i, pp. 329-332; Fristedt, *The Wycliffe Bible*, p. 106; Deanesly, *The Lollard Bible*, pp. 241, n.i., 248-9, 317; W. W. Shirley, *A Catalogue of the Original Works of John Wyclif* (Oxford, 1865), pp. viii-ix.

Wycliffe's direction, to follow his orders and evangelical example as a preaching ministry, fit any better. That there were Lollard missionaries who thought of themselves in some such terms, and that some of them fitted contemporary strictures in their appearance and behaviour, is clear.[60] But we know next to nothing, and are unlikely to discover more, about the precise nature of their links with Wycliffe. He himself, for all his emphasis on the duties of evangelical office, could not be described in the missionary sense as an evangelist. And though the heretical missionaries who began to vulgarize his views were already active during the last two years or so of his life, and Wycliffe himself did not refrain from drawing some morals from their activities, nobody ever officially accused him of being responsible for them, and there are other ways of explaining their origin than his conscious reforming directive.[61]

And how justifiable were Reformation interpretations of Wycliffe's views on the matter of the eucharist? It should at once be admitted that this is an issue upon which it is hard, even now, to be categorical.[62] It was by a gradual unplanned process that Wycliffe's eucharistical thinking became explicit, and the negative aspects of his thought on this question remained, to the end, clearer than the positive. For him the substantial presence of the bread in the host was indissolubly linked with the presence of Christ; to suppress the one would be to suppress the other. Wycliffe therefore, applying his realist philosophy to this issue, did deny the disappearance of the substance of the bread in the consecrated host. But in what did the sacrament consist? In reading some of the passages where Wycliffe explored these delicate questions one might conclude that those reformers were

[60] Henry Knighton provides the fullest description of the early Lollards, and a careful reading of his account may seem to suggest that he endorses Thorpe's statement (see p.270 below) about the nature of their connection with Wycliffe: "sicut magister eorum Wyclyf potens erat et validus in disputationibus . . . sicut isti . . . ad sectam illam attracti . . .". For a categorical assertion we are left with Walsingham, and it is to be noticed that the passage on which the reformers' account was constructed was an embellishment to Walsingham's first version. *Chronicon Henrici Knighton*, ed. J. R. Lumby (Rolls Series, 1889-95), ii, pp. 176-87; *Thomae Walsingham Historia Anglicana*, i, p. 324, ii, p. 188; cf. *Chronicon Angliae*, pp. 115-6, 338.

[61] The case is put by J. A. Robson, *Wyclif and the Oxford Schools* (Cambridge, 1961), p. 243: "That Wyclif himself had any direct connection with Lollardy is open to doubt; but that a number of Oxford masters lent their support is certain". Cf. also Deanesly, *op. cit.*, p. 225.

[62] Recent discussions of Wycliffe's views on this matter to which this paragraph owes much are those of P. de Vooght, *Hussiana* (Louvain, 1960), pp. 292-9; M. Hurley, " 'Scriptura Sola': Wyclif and his Critics", *Traditio*, xvi (1960), pp. 299-304; C. W. Dugmore, *The Mass and the English Reformers* (London, 1958), pp. 52-55. See also D. Stone, *A History of the Doctrine of the Holy Eucharist* (London, 1909), i, pp. 364-8.

Lollards and Reformers

justified, who thought that he had anticipated some of their conceptions of the sacrament as a spiritual sign and figurative representation. His writings contain such expressions of the eucharist as that it was "an efficacious sign" of the Lord's body which should be taken "to figure sacramentally". Yet it is important to remember that although Wycliffe asserted time and again that the sacrament could not consist in an accident without a substance, he never admitted to the denial of the real presence, and he died in full communion with the church. And although he never made altogether explicit what he thought constituted the essential nature of the consecrated host, in one of his last full treatments of the matter Wycliffe stated clearly that "the sacrament *is* the body of Christ, and not merely that it *shall* be, or that it *figures* sacramentally the body of Christ".[63] The real presence of Christ in the eucharist was, in fact, retained in Wycliffe's belief. Though Protestant reformers justly drew attention to his treatment, they seem in some cases to have arrived at a much less unqualified view of Wycliffe's interpretation of the eucharist than we must now allow for.

*   *   *   *

The Protestants and Anglicans who so extolled Wycliffe's fame produced, therefore, a picture which was in some ways erroneous and misleading in its emphasis. But we need not suppose that they resorted to deliberate or conscious falsification. To understand how they arrived at the judgements they did it is necessary to consider the imperfect knowledge from which they were working, and the texts upon which their views were based.

One possible contributory source, which cannot be explored, but which should not be left out of account, is that which continuous oral tradition may have made to Wycliffe's posthumous fame. For it seems clear that Lollards on the eve of the Reformation looked upon Wycliffe as their founder, and (despite the distortions which popularization had in fact effected) saw themselves as the faithful perpetuators of his teaching. Possibly also, Wycliffe's name, which was already reverenced in the days of Oldcastle and Jerome of Prague, obtained a new kind of sanctification through the exhumation

---

[63] *Joannis Wiclif Trialogus*, ed. G. Lechler (Oxford, 1869), p. 255. A discussion of the eucharist which Wycliffe wrote during the last year of his life is in *Iohannis Wyclif Opus Evangelicum*, ed. J. Loserth (Wyclif Soc., 1895-6), ii, pp. 142-70.

and burning of his bones by Bishop Fleming of Lincoln in 1428.[64] Certainly by the autumn of that year Wycliffe was referred to as "blessed", and soon after there are signs of more explicit heretical canonization.[65] William Emayn of Bristol (whose home country was Byfield, Northamptonshire, not so very far distant from Lutterworth), in March 1429 abjured before the bishop of Bath and Wells heresies which included the opinion that "Maister John Wyclif was holier and now is more in blisse and hier in heven glorified than Seint Thomas of Canterbury the glorious Martir", and two years later the Convocation of Canterbury encountered similar views in Thomas Bagley, vicar of Manuden in Essex.[66] Such opinions were not eradicated during a century of Lollard history. Among the heretics proceeded against and burnt by Bishop FitzJames of London in 1518 was one John Stilman, condemned for having relapsed, among other matters, over the view maintained eleven years earlier before the bishop of Salisbury, that "Wickliff is a saint in heaven, and that the book called his Wicket is good, for therein he showeth the truth".[67] Though it was hardly consistent with some other articles of Lollard belief, John Stilman was certainly not the last — as he was also not the first — to hold such a view of Wycliffe. In 1531 similar reverence was displayed by another heretic in the diocese of London, George Bull, a draper of Much Hadham. As well as holding erroneous views on the nature of confession, and maintaining that Luther was a good man, he was said to have "reported, through the credence and report of Master Patmore, parson of Hadham, that where Wickliff's bones were burnt, sprang up a well or well-spring".[68]

Religious movements need a father figure, and there could be no doubt who should fill that rôle for the Lollards. There was justice, as well as inconsistency, in their reverence. But it also assisted the growth of misconceptions, and they were misconceptions which enlarged in the hands of those making a new historical tradition.

[64] The Hussite contribution to Wycliffe's posthumous fame cannot be described here, but for the charge of the Council of Constance that Jerome of Prague had a picture of Wycliffe, venerated as a saint, in his room at Prague, see H. von der Hardt, *Magnum oecumenicum Constantiense Concilium* (Frankfurt and Leipzig, 1697-1700), vol. iv, cols. 654, 751.

[65] William White in his trial at Norwich in September 1428 was accused of quoting words of "beatus Wyccliff" in support of unlicensed preaching. *Fasciculi Zizaniorum*, ed. W. W. Shirley (Rolls Series, 1858), p. 429.

[66] *Register of John Stafford*, ed. T. S. Holmes (Somerset Rec. Soc., xxxi-xxxii, 1915-16), i, p. 79; *The Register of Henry Chichele*, ed. E. F. Jacob (Cant. and York Soc., xlii, xlv-vii, 1937-47), iii, p. 222; J. F. Davis, "Lollards, Reformers and St. Thomas of Canterbury", *Univ. of Birmingham Hist. Jl.*, ix (1963), p. 5.

[67] Foxe, *Acts and Mons.*, iv, pp. 207-8.

[68] *Ibid.*, v, p. 34.

Works, as well as views, came to be ascribed to Wycliffe which could not possibly have been his. And, apart from these fragmentary suggestions of the possible influence of oral Lollard tradition, it is through the works which they studied and printed that understanding of the reformers' attitude may best be approached.

It is of the greatest importance for the understanding of Wycliffe's historical reputation to realize that until the foundation of the Wyclif Society in 1881, knowledge of him was often or largely based upon very imperfect materials: upon the works of writers who were concerned to refute him; chroniclers who were writing from a hostile point of view; and works which were falsely ascribed to his pen. The large majority of surviving manuscripts of Wycliffe's Latin works are in European libraries (chiefly Prague and Vienna), and though there were undoubtedly more originals available to English researchers of the sixteenth century than there are now, it remains the case that until the nineteenth century only one indisputable work of Wycliffe had found its way into print, and this was published abroad.[69] It was the *Trialogus*, printed at Worms in 1525, a late work which reflected the more extreme development of Wycliffe's views.[70]

The estimates of the reformers whose views we have been considering were clearly not based only on printed sources. Leland refers to several Latin works of Wycliffe which he had seen; Foxe, as we saw above, mentioned three which he intended to publish, and both he and Bale made use of the manuscript known as the *Fasciculi Zizaniorum*.[71] One of the Marian exiles, John Aylmer, when attacking ecclesiastical temporalities in his *Harborowe for Faithfull and Trewe Subjectes* (a work designed for Elizabeth's attention in 1559), regretted that Wycliffe's views on this question were not in print.

[69] This fact, as well as ignorance, provides some excuse for Fuller's lament. "But now, alas!" he wrote of Wycliffe's works, "of the two hundred books, which he wrote, being burnt, not a tittle is left, and we are fain to borrow the bare titles of them from his adversaries": *Church History*, ed. Brewer, ii, p. 339. Bale's fullest list, which credited Wycliffe with 238 titles, derived from references as well as from direct knowledge, includes numerous mistaken ascriptions. And of the titles in his shorter list in the *Index Britanniae Scriptorum*, ed. R. L. Poole and M. Bateson, pp. 264-74 (in which Bale gives his various sources), about one third are English works of doubtful authenticity. The false ascriptions here include as well as the prologue to the later Lollard Bible, *Jack up Lande*, Richard Rolle's Commentary on the Psalms, and the *Poor Caitiff*.

[70] *Joannis Wiclefi viri undiquaque piissimi dialogorum libri quattuor* ([Worms], 1525). There was another edition published at Frankfurt and Leipzig in 1753. See n. 1 above.

[71] J. Leland, *Commentarii de Scriptoribus Britannicis*, ed. A. Hall (Oxford, 1709), ii, p. 380; Haller, *Foxe's book of Martyrs and the Elect Nation*, pp. 62, 164, 166; and p.247, n. 12 above.

I would [he wrote] our country man Wicliefes boke whych he wrote *de ecclesia*, were in print, and there shoulde you see that your wrinches and cavillations, be nothing worthe. It was my chaunce to happen of it in ones hand that brought it out of Bohemia.[72]

The earliest independent accounts to be given of Wycliffe's life and opinions, those of Thomas James and John Lewis (in 1608 and 1720 respectively) both make numerous citations from his works, and the former refers to at least four major Latin works.[73] But this documentation had its own, and serious, pitfalls. For along with the genuine a great deal of the suppositious was unhesitatingly ascribed to Wycliffe, and used to delineate his opinions. This is clearly evident in Bale's long list of Wycliffe's works, which includes a good many identifiable Lollard titles. John Lewis, who was the first to give some sort of critical examination to this list, pointed out that it contained items which Bale had never seen, but merely collected as names from other works. But though Lewis was quite right in remarking that "Dr. Wiclif being the most noted and eminent, several books, though written by others, seem to be reckoned *his*",[74] he (and it is hardly surprising) fell into precisely the same errors. The quotations in Lewis's work on the "suffering" doctor were in very large part derived from English tracts which can with no certainty be called Wycliffe's, and he even tried to add to the list.[75]

The appetite for research had been growing, but so had dependence on the printed word. And for printed matter Wycliffe's early eulogizers could turn to various accounts; to the works of Polydore Vergil, whose *Anglica Historia* appeared at Basel in 1534; to John Cochlaeus's *Historia Hussitarum*, published in 1549, and to the works of Pope Pius II.[76] All these were, it is to be noticed, in one sense at least foreign compositions, and all of course wholly hostile to Wycliffite aspirations. Later on the equally (or more) hostile accounts of the English chroniclers Walsingham and Knighton were added to these

[72] J. Aylmer, *An Harborowe For Faithfull and Trewe Subiectes* ([London], 1559), sig. O 4 v.
[73] Namely the *De veritate sacre scripture, De civili dominio, De blasphemia, De ideis*.
[74] J. Lewis, *The History of the Life and Sufferings of John Wiclif* (Oxford, 1820), p. 217. Cf. 1720 edition, p. 142.
[75] Quite unwarrantably Lewis suggested attributing to Wycliffe the famous sermon (it was printed several times in the sixteenth century) which was preached at Paul's Cross in 1388 by Thomas Wimbledon: *ibid.* (1720), pp. 156-7.
[76] P. Vergil, *Anglica Historia* (Basel, 1534); J. Cochlaeus, *Historiae Hussitarum Libri Duodecim* (Mainz, 1549). There were several early editions of Pius II's *Historia Bohemica*, and his *Commentariorum de Concilio Basileae* was printed 1525 (?).

publications.[77]   As well as these narratives, fuller and closer treatment of Wycliffe's doctrine was to be found in the refutations of Thomas Netter of Walden (whose *Doctrinale* was first printed in the years 1521-32) and of William Wodeford (whose late fourteenth-century treatise against condemned points from the *Trialogus* reached print in both 1525 and 1535).[78]   Both these had as their primary objective the condemnation and refutation of Wycliffite doctrine, and in doing so made numerous citations from Wycliffe's works.

Apart from these narrative and source collections other, more misleading material came into print.   It is certainly significant of the Reformation concept of Wycliffe that four of the first five works to be printed as his were either certainly, or very probably, Lollard productions.   For after the *Trialogus*, the next works to be printed as Wycliffe's were *Wickliffe's Wicket*, the General Prologue to the Lollard Bible, and two texts which were edited by Thomas James in 1608.   The *Wicket* and the General Prologue we have already considered, and seen how the editions of them may have been fruitful in disseminating misconceptions.   Doubts must also surround the authenticity of Thomas James's two tracts.   One of these has a better case than the other, being a shortened English version of Wycliffe's memorial of seven points (or "imprecations") produced for the May parliament of 1382.   There is, however, no evidence that Wycliffe was himself responsible for this redaction.   But the text is obviously closer to the master than James's other tract, on fifty heresies and errors of friars, which was almost certainly of a later date than Wycliffe, and might conceivably have been the work of John Purvey.[79]

---

[77] *Historia Brevis Thomae Walsingham ab Edwardo Primo ad Henricum Quintum* (London, 1574); *Historiae Anglicanae Scriptores*, ed. R. Twysden (London, 1652), vol. ii.

[78] Works originally written to refute Wycliffite doctrine might be printed in the sixteenth century to serve both Catholic and reforming interests.   Thus while Thomas Netter's *Doctrinale* was printed after a resolution of the theological faculty of Paris that this would help to combat Lutheran doctrine, the work of Ortwin Gratius which included William Wodeford's treatise against points from Wycliffe's *Trialogus* was put on the Venetian Index in 1554. *Doctrinalis antiquitatum ecclesiae Iesu Christi* ([Paris], 1521); *Sacramentalia F. Thome Walden* (Paris, 1523); *Tomus Primus Doctrinalis Fidei Ecclesiae Catholicae* (Paris, 1532); *Commentariorum Aenae Sylvii Piccolominei Senensis de Concilio Basileae* [Basel, 1525 ?]; *Fasciculus rerum expetendarum ac fugiendarum*, ed. O. Gratius ([Cologne], 1535).   Wodeford's treatise was printed in both these last two works.

[79] *Two Short Treatises, against the Orders of the Begging Friars*, ed. T. James (Oxford, 1608).   Modern editions of these two texts are to be found in *Select English Works of John Wyclif*, ed. T. Arnold (Oxford, 1869-71), iii, pp. 507-23, 366-401.   In both cases James had Bale's ascription to go on: Bale, *Catalogus*, cent. sext., pp. 452, 454.   (The title of the latter text, *Fifty Heresies and Errors of Friars*, is modern.)

These false ascriptions, the failure to arrive at any kind of accurate Wycliffite canon, the fairly extensive reliance upon doubtful English works, and the absence for so long of any printed edition of Wycliffe's undoubtedly authentic works,[80] are significant both of the relationship between the Lollard movement and its ostensible founder, and of the relationship between Wycliffe, Lollardy, and the Reformation. Lollardy survived, as the Reformation was to live, on the basis of a vernacular literature. And though there certainly were English reformers in the sixteenth and seventeenth centuries who had explored beyond the reaches of earlier English heretical literature into its Latin originals, these last were not destined to find a Reformation market. Such works of earlier English heresy as were printed and marketed by Reformation Protestants were with two (both of them continental) exceptions, vernacular tracts.[81] And as such they were Wycliffite only in the second degree; the works, we may suppose, not of Wycliffe himself, but of his successors, publishers, and popularizers.

Wycliffe himself, at best, could only make an imperfect "morning star". And the lights which his Anglican defenders failed to find, or failed to emphasize, may be as significant as those which they did. Most striking, perhaps, is that to which John Aylmer drew attention in 1559. For if Wycliffe was consistent in anything, it was in his insistence upon the evils of ecclesiastical endowment, and the ability and duty of secular powers to remove temporalities from a habitually offending church. Such views were clearly available to reformers, in the *Trialogus* and elsewhere. Clearly, too, there were moments when such arguments could have been turned to advantage, as in the 1530s, when a Lollard text which considered this very matter was printed and utilized as a precedent.[82] Just at this very moment in fact, Henry VIII himself (though for his own reasons) was giving some official sponsorship to Wycliffite researches.[83] And in 1540, ten

---

[80] This tendency to publish doubtful English tracts persisted until the foundation of the Wyclif Society. William Gilpin joined to his account of Wycliffe the treatise "Why many priests have no benefices" (printed in *The English Works of Wyclif*, ed. F. D. Matthew [Early Eng. Text Soc., Orig. Ser., lxxiv], 1880, pp. 244-253); there was a new edition of the *Wicket* in 1828, edited by T. P. Pantin from the 1546 version; *The Last Age of the Church* was edited as "very probably" Wycliffe's in 1840 by J. H. Todd (Dublin, 1840); and the *Tracts and Treatises of John de Wycliffe*, ed. R. Vaughan (London, 1845) — a first abortive Wycliffe Society endeavour — included the two texts printed by James in 1608, *Wycliffe's Wicket*, and *Why Poor Priests have no Benefices*.

[81] The exceptions were the *Trialogus*, and the Lollard *Commentarius in Apocalypsin ante Centum Annos aeditus*, which appeared at Wittenberg in 1528.

[82] Above, pp. 221-3.

[83] A. Wood, *The History and Antiquities of the University of Oxford*, ed. J. Gutch (Oxford, 1792-6), ii (1), p. 50; *Letters and Papers of the Reign of Henry VIII*, ed. J. S. Brewer and J. Gairdner (1862-1910), iv, pt. iii, p. 2946, no. 6546; p. 2990, no. 6637, pp. 3000-1, no. 6656.

years after the king had sent to Oxford for the tenets on which Wycliffe had been condemned in the university and at Constance, we find some of these same points being cited against an enthusiastic supporter of the English Reformation, who had been hoping to extend the good works — including a clerical deprivation — to Scotland.[84]

On the other hand Wycliffe's deducible (if ambiguous) extremism on this issue was such as to invite criticism, and as time went on and Anglicanism became settled into a new establishment, the "morning star" and the English church here demonstrably parted company. Already in 1530 Melanchthon had pointed out that Wycliffe "contends that it is not lawful for priests to possess any property", and Robert Parsons, quick to light upon such serviceable discrepancies, indicated that one of the articles "wherin he [Wycliffe] differeth from our Protestants as well as from us, and therby maketh a distinct Sect", was in maintaining the unlawfulness of ecclesiastical persons holding temporal possessions, and the ability of lay lords to deprive them in case of need.[85]   His ground was here well chosen.   Did not Hooker himself admit as much?

> If Wickliff therefore were of that opinion which his adversaries ascribe unto him (whether truly or of purpose to make him odious I cannot tell, for in his writings I do not find it) namely, "That Constantine and others following his steps did evil, as having no sufficient ground whereby they might gather that such donations are acceptable to Jesus Christ"; it was in Wickliff a palpable error.[86]

Wycliffe's authentic words could prove an embarrassment.   There was some truth in one of Peter Heylin's "Animadversions" upon Fuller's *Church History* which described the "wheat" of Wycliffe as "intermingled with so many and such dangerous *Tares*, that to expose it to the view, were to mar the market".[87]

The Church of England never became as evangelical as some of the statements of the "evangelical doctor" might appear to have advocated. Wycliffism and Anglicanism went different ways.   If the history of the Lollard movement had been seriously jeopardized by the public attention given to the matter of ecclesiastical endowments, Protestant historians were wise to avoid emphasizing this matter.   They served Wycliffe better than some of the Lollards — though perhaps with no more   justice.   Given   the   inherent   ambiguity   of   the   master's

---

[84] *Letters and Papers*, xv, pp. 334-5, no. 714; Foxe, *Acts and Mons.*, v, p. 614.

[85] *Philippi Melanthonis Opera*, ed. C. G. Bretschneider in *Corpus Reformatorum*, ii (1835), col. 32 (letter to Myconius); Parsons, *Three Conversions . . . First Six Monethes*, p. 112.

[86] R. Hooker, *Works*, ed. J. Keble, 7th edn. revised R. W. Church and F. Paget (Oxford, 1888), iii, pp. 287-8.

[87] P. Heylin, *Examen Historicum* (London, 1659), p. 68.

utterances, it was hard for anyone to represent him without some distortion, and Lollards and Protestants alike were guilty of misrepresentation. At some points perhaps, and in some ways, Wycliffe's Catholic opponents of the Reformation saw him more clearly than his new-style defenders, and through criticism and polemic they contributed to his newly found fame. Yet from both sides much remained obscured. Though the Catholic Nicholas Harpsfield made the pregnant suggestion that Wycliffe's "disciples went far beyond him", and though Fuller saw that "the tenets of his followers in after-ages might be falsely fathered upon him",[88] friends and foes alike left the pursuit of these considerations to later generations. Such distinctions were dependent upon textual criticism of a kind which Reformation writers had neither the time nor the equipment — nor always the inclination — to tackle. Wycliffe and Lollardy entered Protestant history together, inextricably associated.

     *   *   *   *

These Protestant misconceptions tell us, in fact, something in turn about Wycliffe, the Lollard movement, and sixteenth-century attitudes towards them. Bale, Foxe and the others were doing pioneering work in a large and important field, and like most pioneers they necessarily had to sacrifice some details to the broader issues. And they were working under many disadvantages. The nature of their sources, the limitations of their evidence, and their own predispositions, all meant that in a number of ways and cases they were inclined to attribute to Wycliffe more than was his in both works and intentions. Others since them have continued to do the same. And perhaps we shall find it easier to understand the limitations of England's major heretical movement, if we understand the limitations of its founder.

For all his originality and importance, Wycliffe began and ended his career essentially a schoolman. Despite his incursions into publicity and politics, despite all his emphasis upon ecclesiastical debasement, upon Scripture and the scriptural text, at heart he was not a popularizer, and the writings he produced were of a learned, burdened, scholastic Latin which could never make general reading. There are no positive grounds for believing that Wycliffe himself "was responsible for a single sentence" of the Bible translations, or of the

---

[88] N. Harpsfield, *Historia Anglicana Ecclesiastica* (Douai, 1622), p. 678. (Harpsfield died in 1575. This remark was applied to church rites and ceremonies.) Fuller, *Church History*, ed. Brewer, ii, p. 320.

numerous English heretical treatises which have been ascribed to his name. Equally doubtful is the justice of attributing to Wycliffe any direct concern or positive initiative in the origination of the Lollard movement. Upon both scores recent research has warned us into an attitude of wariness, and such wariness is not lessened when it is realized upon what premises and in what circumstances such affirmations originated.

Yet in the last resort we must allow some remnants — and they may be thought significant remnants — of truth to Wycliffe's impassioned Reformation defenders. Though their case rested on some false assumptions it also had sufficient plausibility to gain long-lasting acceptance. For all his failure as a practical reformer, for all his impractical ruthlessness, there was an infecting fire in Wycliffe's logic. If he did not personally translate the Bible, he consistently emphasized conformity to the law of God in Scripture as the one sure sign and criterion of all that is truly Christian, and as time went on he grew more impatient of other forms of authority.[89] He himself had written of Holy Scripture as "the pre-eminent authority for every Christian, and rule of faith and of all human perfection"; and had stated that "all Christians, especially secular lords, ought to know and defend the holy scriptures".[90] And even if he did not primarily set out to practise what he preached, he had said that "evangelization exceeds prayer and administration of the sacraments to an infinite degree", and that "in order that the truth may be more widely spread abroad it behoves the faithful to set forth their opinions both in Latin and in the vernacular".[91] If it was easy to misunderstand Wycliffe, it seems that it was also easy to be inspired by his words and his very existence. Among the rare personal testimonies from his followers, this passage from the pen of a Lollard describing his own trial in 1407 before Archbishop Arundel is worth considering:

> Sir, [William Thorpe reports himself as saying] Maister John Wickliffe was holden of full mainie men, the greatest clearke that they knewe then living; and therewith hee was named a passing rulie man and an innocent in his living: and, herefore, great men communed oft with him, and they loved so his learning, that they writ it, and busilie inforced them to rule themselves therafter.[92]

[89] On this question see in particular Hurley, *art. cit.* (above, n. 62); McFarlane, *John Wycliffe*, p. 91; Deanesly, *The Lollard Bible*, p. 242.

[90] *De veritate sacrae scripturae*, ed. R. Buddensieg (Wyclif Society, 1905-7), i, pp. xxv, 39, 136, 377.

[91] *De officio pastorali*, ed. G. V. Lechler (Leipzig, 1863), p. 33; *Opera Minora*, ed. J. Loserth (Wyclif Society, 1913), p. 74.

[92] Foxe, *Acts and Mons.*, iii, p. 257. A fifteenth-century Latin version of this passage reads: "Domine, magister Johannes Wyclyff reputabatur a valde multis hominibus maximus clericus quem viventem noverunt suo tempore super

It sounds like a voluntary association of disciples who came to listen to the master, and who needed no bidding in their concern to make his teaching available to a wider circle. And we know that William Thorpe was not the only man who felt called to Oxford by the fame of Wycliffe's repute.

Wycliffe was in a sense the founder of a movement in default of, despite himself. As the greatest and most influential schoolman of his day, others were drawn to him, and felt the compulsion to publicize his ideas, to implement his convictions, and to take them into a wider world than the university of Oxford. And we know that they had some success — a success which produced offspring its parent would hardly have recognized. But though the magnetism of his personality and the force of his speech and writings were so powerful that others could not be prevented from utilizing his name and his ideas, Wycliffe himself was too doctrinaire and introverted a thinker to have formulated such precise reformation thoughts as Reformation writers foisted upon him. He was a man whose concerns took him deeper into thought and study, rather than further into action and example. And the fact that the reformers of the sixteenth century had to start again on a new footing was due at least in part to the academic limitations of their fourteenth-century predecessor; limitations which they were the last to be able to recognize. What they wanted they had found. And we are still haunted by its ghost.

terram, et cum hoc nominatus fuit digne ut estimo excellens regularis homo et innocens in tota vita sua. Et propter hoc vir magne literature et alii similiter multum adherebant sibi et communicaverunt frequenter cum ipso et sic sapiebant doctrinam eius quod scripserunt eam solicite et regere se ipsos secundum eam nitebantur". Vienna Nationalbibliothek, MS. 3936, f. 5 r.

Additional Notes to Chapter 8

Note*   The historiography of Wycliffe now includes James Crompton, 'John Wyclif: A Study in Mythology', *Transactions of the Leicestershire Archaeological and Historical Society*, xlii (1966-7), pp. 6-34; Vaclav Mudroch, *The Wyclyf Tradition*, ed. A. C. Reeves (Athens, Ohio, 1979). John F. Davis, 'John Wyclif's Reformation Reputation', *The Churchman*, 83 (1969), pp. 97-102, criticizes this and the preceding chapter.

3   It is worth noting that Ecclesiasticus 50;6 ('He was as the morning star in the midst of a cloud') was a text used in medieval canonizations; J. Moorman, *A History of the Franciscan Order* (Oxford, 1968), pp. 86, 281. It also – probably more relevant to Bale's experience – formed part of Carmelite devotion to the Virgin; L. P. Fairfield, *John Bale: Mythmaker for the English Reformation* (West Lafayette, Ind., 1976), p. 191, n. 8. Cf. also p. 94 for Bale's unrealised plan to write a large work on Wycliffe, to be called 'The battayle of John Wycleff'.

8   For the importance of Wycliffe in Foxe's periodizing of church history see V. N. Olsen, *John Foxe and the Elizabethan Church* (Berkeley, 1973), pp. 23, 35-6, 38, 66, 70-74, 114, 126, and the works referred to in Chapter 7, n. 85, and Chapter 9, n. 23, at pp. 242, 311.

24   See also the works of Crompton and Mudroch noted above.

27   STC2 25587.5: on the dating of the General Prologue see *English Wycliffite Writings*, ed. Hudson, pp. 173-4, 176, and for Gough's edition see P. L. Heyworth, 'The Earliest Black-letter Editions of *Jack Upland*', *Huntington Library Quarterly*, xxx (1967), p. 309.

29   On this and other editions of Robert Crowley see J. N. King, *English Reformation Literature* (Princeton, 1982), p. 96 ff., esp. 98-100.

58   In addition to the work of Fristedt (Stockholm Studies in English, iv, xxi, xxvii, 1953-73) see C. Lindberg, *MS Bodley 959. Genesis – Baruch 3.20 in the earlier version of the Wycliffite Bible...(Baruch 3.20 – end of OT edited from MS Christ Church 145)*, (Stockholm Studies in English, vi, viii, x, xiii, xx, xxix, 1959-73). For a recent appraisal of the authorship question, which makes the all-important distinction between the New Testament translation and that of the whole Bible, see M. Wilks, 'Misleading manuscripts: Wyclif and the non-Wycliffite Bible'. *SCH*, 11 (1975), pp. 147-61. Cf. also H. Hargreaves, 'The Wycliffite Versions', in *The Cambridge History of the Bible*, ii, ed. G. W. H. Lampe (Cambridge, 1969), pp. 387-415.

61   For another view of this question see M. Wilks, '*Reformatio regni*: Wyclif and Hus as leaders of religious protest movements', *SCH*, 9 (1972), pp. 119-21; *English Wycliffite Writings*, ed. Hudson, p. 9.

62   See also Gordon Leff, *Heresy in the Later Middle Ages* (Manchester, 1967), ii, pp. 549-57; *idem*, 'John Wyclif: the Path to Dissent', *PBA*, lii (1966), pp. 143-80, esp. 176 ff.; *English Wycliffite Writings*, ed. Hudson, pp. 142-3.

79   A doubtful attribution: see Anne Hudson, 'John Purvey', *Viator*, 12 (1981) p. 378.

92   For the fifteenth-century English version of this passage see *English Wycliffite Writings*, ed. Hudson, p. 32.

9

RICHARD II AND
THE WARS OF THE ROSES

'our eyes do hate the dire aspect
Of civil wounds plough'd up with neighbours' sword'
King Richard II, I. iii. 127–8.

'I am Richard II. know ye not that?' Queen Elizabeth's words
amounted to a rhetorical question for their recipient, William
Lambarde.[1] Now, they may act as a reminder of how the Tudors
stand between us and Richard II. History being what it is every
historian has some duties towards historiography, but for historians of the later middle ages in England, where the Tudor imprint is still powerful, the need is specially great. Such is the hold
of poetry and accepted myth, the impact of oral and typographical
repetition, that Shakespeare and the Reformation remain media-
tors of the past. Historical textbooks continue to repeat clichés
about fifteenth-century bloodshed and the decimation of the
nobility which stem from sixteenth-century interpretations.[2] The

I wish to thank Professor William Haller and Mrs Elizabeth Eisenstein for their
helpful criticisms of this paper. To avoid misunderstanding I ought perhaps to
stress the limitations of my argument. It does not attempt to discuss the 'Tudor
myth' in its entirety—the important question of Tudor views of British history
has been left altogether aside, not to mention other aspects. Nor have I explored
the Yorkist case for Richard, which produced such favourable statements as a
poem of the 1460s that looked back to his reign as a time of wealth and plenty.

[1] *The Progresses and Public Processions of Queen Elizabeth*, ed. John Nichols, iii
(London, 1823), p. 552. This reported conversation of 1601 has received considerable
attention in Shakespearean scholarship because of the queen's allusion to the playing of the tragedy of Richard II; cf. *King Richard II*, ed. Peter Ure (Arden Shakespeare, London, 1961), pp. lvii ff.
[2] For instance A. L. Rowse, *Bosworth Field and the Wars of the Roses* (London,
1966), p. 144 remarks 'we see the way in which families were being decimated'; or
E. Harris Harbison, *The Age of Reformation* (Ithaca, N.Y., 1955), p. 15 speaks of how
'In Spain, France, and England the civil wars of the fifteenth century had decimated

Tudor myth has long been recognized, but it has not yet been banished. Nor has the full extent of this historical reconstruction ever been properly displayed. The idea of the Wars of the Roses, which was a framework for understanding the whole of the late medieval past, had a profound and pervasive influence, ecclesiastical as well as secular. Among the reigns and personalities whose interpretation it affected, Richard II was prominent. He held a critical position in the Tudor historical scheme, and it should help to clear the path to our own understanding to see more of the range and outcome of earlier misreadings.

★   ★   ★

It is a mistake to dismiss the term 'Wars of the Roses' as the invention of Sir Walter Scott. He may have been the first to use the phrase as such and to popularize its use, but very little credit, or discredit, need go to him for this.[3] The name, to all intents and pur-

---

the feudal nobility'. There have, of course, been warnings enough, both tentative and firm, against such statements and exaggerations of the casualties, destruction and dislocation caused by fighting in fifteenth-century England. Cf. K. B. Mc-Farlane, 'The Wars of the Roses', *Proceedings of the British Academy*, l (1964), pp. 87–119, including the caveat (p. 115) 'if any generalization about the Wars of the Roses is sure of wide agreement it is that they resulted in the extermination of most of the "old nobility"; and none is more demonstrably false'; J. R. Lander, *The Wars of the Roses* (London, 1965), pp. 20–3; J. R. Lander, *Conflict and Stability in Fifteenth-Century England* (London, 1969), pp. 161–4; R. L. Storey, *The End of the House of Lancaster* (London, 1966), p. 7; V. H. H. Green, *The Later Plantagenets* (London, 1955), pp. 330, 351, 356, 381, 395–6; C. H. Williams, 'England: The Yorkist Kings, 1461–1485', *Cambridge Medieval History*, viii (Cambridge, 1936), pp. 421, 423–4; C. L. Kingsford, *Prejudice & Promise in XVth Century England* (Oxford, 1925), pp. 33, 48. Among earlier works credit for challenging the accepted view should be given to T. L. Kington Oliphant, 'Was the Old English Aristocracy destroyed by the Wars of the Roses?' *T.R.H.S.*, i (1872), pp. 351–6, which aimed to prove 'that the common notion of the old English aristocracy having been destroyed by the Wars of the Roses is a mistake'.

[3] S. B. Chrimes, *Lancastrians, Yorkists and Henry VII* (London, 1964), pp. xi–xiv; S. B. Chrimes, 'The Fifteenth Century', *History*, xlviii (1963), p. 24, where E. F. Jacob is praised for not using the term 'Wars of the Roses' in *The Fifteenth Century* (Oxford, 1961); Lander, *The Wars of the Roses*, p. 15. For the reference to Scott's *Anne of Geierstein* see n. 9 below. The most astringent objections to the use of the term are those of Professor Chrimes, who seems to weaken his case by saying 'The civil wars of that [the fifteenth] century were not about roses, badges, or other symbols'; moreover it is only literarily correct to state that Tudor writers 'stopped short of calling the series of battles "the wars of the roses"'; Chrimes, op. cit., pp.

poses, had been invented together with the idea, centuries earlier. 'The horrible murthers and bloody battels, that were of long time between the factions of the red rose and the white, the houses of York and Lancaster, for the crown of this realm, by the happy marriage of king Henry VII. and Q. Elizabeth, were ended': so ran a motion to parliament, on lines that were already conventional, about the succession in 1571.[4] If Elizabeth I's subjects were kept mindful of the inestimable benefits which had accrued to England through the joyful union of her grandparents, they in turn made sure that the queen remained conscious of the infinite perils which threatened the land if she should fail it. Sir Thomas Smith, putting the case in 1561 for Elizabeth to marry an English nobleman, chose a dialogue form which enabled him with somewhat less than his usual bluntness to appeal to her—in words spoken by the realm itself—to perpetuate 'the race of the mixed rose, which brought again the amiable peace long exiled from among my children by the striving of the two roses'. His elaboration of the horrors of such strife described it in terms which had already become standard.

I am afraid to speak, and I tremble to think, what murders and slaughters, what robbing and rifling, what spoiling and burning, what hanging and heading, what wasting and destroying, civil war should bring in, if ever it should come. From the time that King Richard II. was deposed, in whom all the issue of the Black Prince was extinct, unto the death of King Richard III. the unkind and cruel brother of Edward IV. whose daughter was married, as ye know, to King Henry VII. by reason of titles this poor realm had never long rest. Noble men were beheaded, poor men spoiled, both one and th'other slain in battle, or murdered at home. Now this King prevailed, now th'other. No man sure of his Prince, no man of his goods, no man of his life: a King to-day, to-morrow a prisoner; now hold the sceptre, and shortly after fly privily the realm. And when this fell upon the head, how sped the body, think you? Those two blades of Lyonel and John of Gaunt never rested

---

xii, 177; cf. Storey, op. cit., Introduction, pp. 1–28 on 'The Wars of the Roses' where the name is criticized for directing over-much attention to the dynastic issue.

[4] John Strype, *Annals of the Reformation* (Oxford, 1824), II, ii, p. 425, from 'A motion in parliament, 13 Elizab. about the succession to the crown; according to K. Henry VIII. his will'. Cf. J. E. Neale, *Elizabeth I and her Parliaments*, i (London, 1953), pp. 226–34.

pursuing th'one th'other, till the red rose was almost razed out, and the white made all bloody; and as it were Eteocles and Polynices, they ceased not till they had filled their country full of bloody streams. They set the father against the son, the brother against the brother, the uncle slew the nephew, and was slain himself. So blood pursued and ensued blood, till all the realm was brought to great confusion. It is no marvel though they lost France, when they could not keep England. And England in the latter end of King Henry VI. was almost a very chaos: parishes decayed, churches fell down, towns were desolate, ploughed fields waxed groves, pastures were made woods; almost half England by civil war slain, and they which remained not sure, but in moats and castles, or lying in routs and heaps together.[5]

It was a concept of civil discord—duly turned into a lesson for royal ears—which minimized no terrors in accounting for all England's calamities of the fifteenth century. The striving roses were the cause of all, from Richard II to Richard III.

To think of the red rose as a device of warring Lancastrians was certainly misleading and historically incorrect. Whereas the white rose was a recognized badge of York in the fifteenth century, evidence for the use of the red rose as a Lancastrian symbol is rare before 1485. The development of the red rose, like the whole idea of the factious roses, was the work of the Tudors, who had themselves been using the red rose in Wales long before Bosworth and who were as anxious to draw attention to their Lancastrian lineage as they were to harp upon the glorious theme of dynastic and civil union.[6] The warring roses, as much as the union rose which grafted them together, were successful Tudor plantings upon the Plantagenet past. There is no need to look far for results; it was an idea with luxuriant growth.

And for that the discendents of . . . the dukes of Lancaster and Yorke, came afterward to strive who had the best title to reigne, therof it came, that the controversie had his name of these two famiies, which for more

---

[5] John Strype, *The Life of the Learned Sir Thomas Smith* (Oxford, 1820), pp. 216, 221–2; Mary Dewar, *Sir Thomas Smith: A Tudor Intellectual in Office* (London, 1964), pp. 84–6. It is to be noted that Strype, like Tyndale (see below p. 285), connected the civil wars with the effects of late medieval depopulation.

[6] Sydney Anglo, *Spectacle, Pageantry and Early Tudor Policy* (Oxford, 1969), pp. 36–7; C. L. Kingsford, *English History in Contemporary Poetry*, ii, *Lancaster and York, 1399 to 1485* (London, 1913), pp. 41, 45; Howell T. Evans, *Wales and the Wars of the Roses* (Cambridge, 1915), pp. 7–8; *Bishop Percy's Folio Manuscript. Ballads and Romances*, ed. John W. Hales and Frederick J. Furnivall, iii (London, 1868), p. 194.

distinction sake, & the better to be knowne, tooke uppon them for their ensignes a rose of two different colures, to wit, the white rose, and the redd, as al the world knoweth, wherof the white served for Yorke, and the redd for Lancaster.[7]

The world seems mistakenly to have been making this assumption long before Robert Parsons wrote these words in the 1590s. According to Polydore Vergil in the first Tudor reigns, seventy to eighty years earlier, 'the common people even at this day call the one [faction] the red rose, the other the white, for the white rose was the emblem of one family and the red rose of the other'.[8]

To refer, therefore, as Scott did in 1828–9, to 'the civil discords so dreadfully prosecuted in the wars of the White and Red Roses' was to do little more than capitalize and extend the currency of a long-established denomination.[9] The formula may itself have been mistaken, but if one wishes to contest its premises there is very little point in taking issue with the name which summarizes it. The 'Wars of the Roses', like the 'Renaissance', might as well be accepted as a term which has come to stay, given the proviso that it belongs more to historiography than to history. And though, like the 'Renaissance', it was not generally adopted by historians until the nineteenth century, it has its own long ancestry, and acts as a shorthand for the idea of civil discord which permeated Tudor views of the fifteenth century.[10]

[7] Robert Parsons [R. Doleman *pseud.*], *A Conference About the Next Succession to the Crowne of Ingland* ([Antwerp?], 1594), pt. ii, p. 38.

[8] Polydore Vergil, *Anglica Historia* (Basel, 1534), p. 315; Denys Hay, *Polydore Vergil, Renaissance Historian and Man of Letters* (Oxford, 1952), p. 143 quotes this passage from the later editions; for the composition of Vergil's work see pp. 79ff.

[9] Sir Walter Scott, *Anne of Geierstein or The Maiden of the Mist* (Boston, 1894), i, p. 111, a passage in Ch. vii in which the main emphasis is on Edward IV's intention of regaining 'those rich and valuable foreign possessions which had been lost during the administration of the feeble Henry VI'. The novel is set in the mid-fifteenth century and in Ch. iii (p. 66) appears a conventionally exaggerated sketch of the impact of the wars. '"Alas!" he said, "I deserve to feel the pain which your words inflict. What nation can know the woes of England that has not felt them—what eye can estimate them which has not seen a land torn and bleeding with the strife of two desperate factions, battles fought in every province, plains heaped with slain, and scaffolds drenched in blood! Even in your quiet valleys, methinks, you may have heard of the Civil Wars of England?"'

[10] Thus although the red and white roses were in the sixteenth century commonly associated with the Lancastrian and Yorkist factions, nineteenth-century writers must be held responsible for adopting and popularizing the name 'wars of the roses' as a title. The earliest book to be published with this name which I have

Now that we have so long become accustomed to the use and abuse of the idea of the warring roses, it is important to realize not only how it arose, but also how in its modern application it differs from its origin. The nineteenth-century writers who popularized the term narrowed its context—perhaps unconsciously, certainly unavowedly. In this we have followed them. Historians today who continue, somewhat defensively, to write about the wars of the roses, generally concern themselves with thirty years in the second half of the fifteenth century (1455 to 1485 or 1487) when Henry VI's incapacity and Yorkist claims brought the country to armed conflict and bloodshed. Writers of the sixteenth and seventeenth centuries, on the other hand, had in mind much more than this. They thought in terms of a whole century of dissension, brought to a happy conclusion when Henry VII married Elizabeth of York and, still more completely, when the last Yorkist pretenders had been snuffed out and Henry VIII, heir to both houses, succeeded. Not unnaturally the main focus of attention was upon the reign of Henry VI, but the beginning of the wars was placed long before this. They ran, as indicated by Sir Thomas Smith's rhetorical plea of 1561, from the reign of Richard II to the death of Richard III.[11]

discovered (but not seen) is J. G. Edgar, *The wars of the roses: or, stories of the struggle of York and Lancaster* (London, 1859).

[11] Modern historians who accept the limit of thirty years in the second half of the century include Lander, Storey, Green, Williams, Oliphant and Evans, in the works cited in notes 2 and 6 above. Plenty of other examples could be cited, including the classic over-statement of *The Encyclopaedia Britannica*, 11th edn. (Cambridge, 1911), s.v. Roses, Wars of the; 'a name given to a series of civil wars in England during the reigns of Henry VI., Edward. and Richard III . . . They were marked by a ferocity and brutality which are practically unknown in the history of English wars before and since'. R. B. Mowat's *The Wars of the Roses, 1377–1471* (London, 1914), despite its title, restricts the name to the years after 1455, while recognizing it as 'an invention of the sixteenth century'; p. 232, cf. pp. 10, 17, 34, 50–1, 95. A. L. Rowse, in *Bosworth Field and the Wars of the Roses*, though surveying the period 1377 until the Tudors, reserves the term 'Wars of the Roses' until ch. vii and events of the 1450s; pp. 127 ff., 281. Historians of the sixteenth and seventeenth centuries might differ over the exact period of the wars, but it is clear that where there is now a consensus on about thirty years there was once a consensus of a duration of about a hundred. In addition to the works cited in the following paragraph see n.18 below and pp. 275 and 292 for quotations from Thomas Smith and Robert Parsons; according to John Taylor, *A Briefe Remembrance of all the English Monarchs, From the Normans Conquest, until this present* (London, 1618), sig. C 2r, by the time of Edward IV 'These bloody broyles had lasted threescore yeares, . . . [and] wasted fourescore of the Royall Peeres'. Perhaps one might see evidence of this disjunction

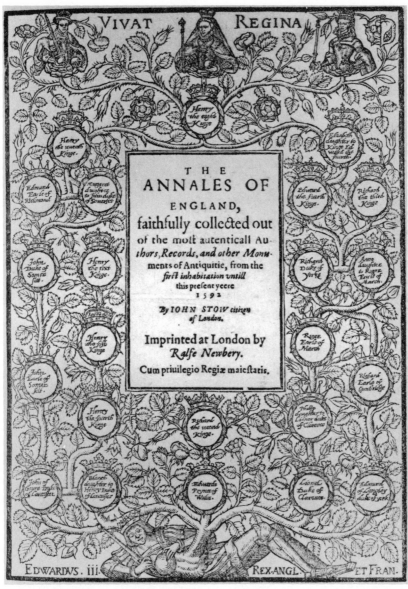

21   The title-page of Stow's *Annales of England* (1592), which was also used in his *Chronicles* (1580). (p. 281)

22 Biondi's *History of the Civill Warres* (1641) used as its
title-page an adapted version of Reynold Elstrack's engraving for Henry
Holland's *Baziliωlogia* (pp. 281-2)

23   Wenceslaus Hollar's 1639 etching of the Wilton Diptych, dedicated to Charles I (to whose collection the painting belonged) with verses by Henry Peacham. (pp. 304-5, 311)

24a   Richard II as delineated in Thomas Tymme's *Booke, containing the true portraiture ... of the kings of England* (1597), which repeats the tradition that 'this king was comely of personage'. (p. 305)

24b   Reynold Elstrack's engraving of Richard II from Henry Holland's

Shakespeare might well have been surprised that a wars of the roses version of his historical cycle should limit itself to his plays about Henry VI and Richard III; for him the wars embraced the whole historical sequence. 'The blood of English shall manure the ground, . . . tumultuous wars Shall kin with kin, and kind with kind, confound.' The bishop of Carlisle's prophecy of 1399 was fulfilled by a continuous train of disorder until—in echoing words —it was closed up at the end of *King Richard III.* 'We will unite the white rose and the red: . . . England hath long been mad and scarr'd herself; The brother blindly shed the brother's blood.'[12] For Shakespeare and his contemporaries it was a commonplace that the roses had striven for a full century.

One important result of this viewing of the past was seriously to prejudice the history of Richard II. Placed in the context of the divided succession and civil disturbance, Richard's reign tended to be looked at for explanations of coming strife, focused upon the circumstances leading to the deposition, unnaturally detached from events of the fourteenth century to act as the explanatory prelude to those of the fifteenth. Changes in the succession, or fears of such changes, renewed civil war, or fears of civil war, caused the struggles of York and Lancaster and the fate of Richard II to be re-examined and re-written. During the last decade of Elizabeth's reign several disputants, joining issue with Robert Parsons on the succession question, combed through the rights and wrongs of Richard II's deposition and the rival claims to the throne thereafter.[13] In the mid-seventeenth century the Italian Giovanni

of opinion between modern and Tudor writers in the remark of Professor Hay, op. cit., p. 143 on Vergil's *Anglica Historia*; 'The actual outbreak of the "Wars of the Roses" is, of course, quite properly explained . . . when the rivalry of the Lancastrians and Richard duke of York finally provokes an open conflict; but there is no doubt that the main catastrophe for Vergil was Henry IV's seizure of the throne'. It should be noted that while accounting for the divisions of the factions of Lancaster and York in 1453, both then and in 1451 Vergil (op. cit., 1546, pp. 497, 502) speaks of the revival and renewal of domestic discord. Cf. Bernard André's slightly earlier description of the outbreak of civil war in the 1450s; *Historia Regis Henrici Septimi a Bernardo Andrea Tholosate Conscripta*, ed. James Gairdner (London, 1858), pp. 18–20. I owe this reference to the kindness of Professor Haller.

[12] *King Richard II*, p. 133, IV. i. 136–47; *Richard III*, ed. John Dover Wilson (Cambridge, 1954), p. 139, V. v. 19–31; Hay, op. cit., pp. 144–5; E. M. W. Tillyard, *Shakespeare's History Plays* (Harmondsworth, 1962), pp. 7, 59 ff, 304.
[13] Much of this controversy focused upon Robert Parson's *Conference About the*

Francesco Biondi produced *An History of the Civill Warres of England betweene the two houses of Lancaster and Yorke*, which carried lengthily into prose the topic of Samuel Daniel and Shakespeare and detailed the history of eight reigns, starting with Richard II and ending with Henry VII.[14] Later in the same century a new wars of the roses history appeared in a new succession context. *England's Happiness in a Lineal Succession; And the Deplorable Miseries Which ever attended Doubtful Titles to the Crown, Historically Demonstrated, By the Bloody Wars Between the Two Houses of York & Lancaster* aimed in 1685 to show England's fortune in the succession of James II by contrast with 'that Bloody, Unnatural and Fatal War, which had lasted about 106 Years' between York and Lancaster—traced here from Richard II's reign to the execution of the earl of Warwick by Henry VII.[15]

Next Succession, a work which was remarkable for its extremist arguments and which has been described as 'the chief storehouse of facts and arguments drawn upon by nearly all opponents of the royal claims for a century'; it was reissued in whole or in part in 1648, 1655 and 1681. In examining the titles of the various claimants to the English throne Parsons went fully into 'the great and generall controversie and contention' between Lancaster and York, and the justice of Richard II's deposition, showing reasons for supposing that the latter was 'iust and lawful'. He was assailed for this demonstration, combined with the assertion that 'the best of al their titles [to the crown] . . . depended of this authority of the common wealth', being 'ether allowed confirmed altered or disanulled by parlaments'. In this controversial literature on the succession Richard II remains attached to the Lancastrian–Yorkist dispute. Parsons, op. cit., pt. i, p. 195, pt. ii, pp. 56 ff., 72; *The Political Works of James I*, ed. C. H. McIlwain (Cambridge, Mass., 1918), pp. l–li, xcii–xciii; John E. Parish, *Robert Parsons and the English Counter-Reformation* (Rice University Studies, vol. 52, 1966), pp. 43–7.

[14] The rest of the title makes plain that Richard II's reign belonged to the wars; 'The originall whereof is set downe in the life of *Richard* the second; their proceedings, in the lives of *Henry* the fourth, the fifth, and sixth, *Edward* the fourth and fifth, *Richard* the third, and *Henry* the seventh, in whose dayes they had a happy period.' Giovanni Francesco Biondi (1572–1644) spent the years 1609–40 in England, where he enjoyed the patronage of James I, who knighted him in 1622, and Charles I, to whom the *Civill Warres* was dedicated. The first edition, in Italian, was published in Venice in three volumes in 1637–44, entitled *L'Istoria delle guerre civili d'Inghilterra, tra le due case di Lancastro, e di Iorc*. Henry Carey's translation, not completed until after the author's death, was begun 'out of [his] written Papers, whilst he was here in England': the preface to the second part, issued in 1646 after Biondi's death, expressed the hope that, appearing in a time of civil war, the book might offer persuasions of peace. Biondi, *History of the Civill Warres*, pt. ii, sig. A 2r–v; *D.N.B.*, s.v. Biondi, Sir Giovanni Francesco.

[15] Warwick's execution is dated 'about' 1504 (it was in fact 1499) so the 106 years run from 1398 to 1504. The wars were luridly described to add force to the

Title-pages—even of books which were not specifically concerned with the civil wars as a topic—represent graphically this attachment of Richard II to the Tudor scheme. John Stow's *Annales of England* dealt with English affairs from the first inhabitants and the legendary Brutus up to the author's own times, but the segment of history which was singled out for illustration on the title-page was that from Edward III to the reigning queen. It was a depiction of the divided roses which illustrates the central position of Richard II (Plate 21). The descent—or ascent—of the crown is shown as a rosework genealogical tree that springs from the side of a recumbent warrior king Edward III.[16] The branches of York and Lancaster rise to right and left, and the bust of Elizabeth placed centrally at the top appropriately occupies a position exactly comparable to that of Richard II beneath: her stem was terminating in the 1590s quite as clearly as had his in the 1390s. At the front of Biondi's history is another version of the same theme. Here the kings whose reigns bounded the wars are shown as full-length figures. Between Richard II, erect and regal, clasping orb and sceptre, and Henry VII, martially triumphant, his sword resting negligently on his shoulder, lie strewn the corpses—royal and otherwise—of the century that divided them. Below, linked with this century of domestic strife, is a vignette of the battling troops of that other, associated century of foreign warfare. Reynold Elstrack's engraving was no more new to Biondi than the

argument: 'it is almost incredible to believe, how many Bloody Battels were fought, what Multitudes of Men were slaughtered, how many Treasons and horrid Conspiracies were carried on and perpetrated, how much Noble Blood was spilt, how many Families were ruined, how many Barbarous Executions, how many unreasonable Fines, and perpetual Banishments hapned, during this unfortunate War . . . the many miseries, which attended that Unfortunate Quarrel, may serve, at once, to shew us their misery and our own happiness, under the Influence of the most Auspicious and Promising Reign of our present Sovereign, James the Second, who derives his Title from the happy Union of the two Houses, whereby that War was ended'. *England's Happiness* (London, 1685), sigs. A 3r-v, A 6r, p. 228. This book, like Biondi's, carries an illustration which shows how the Tudors' union theme was adapted to the Stuarts; it also covers the same period as Biondi, and of its 228 pages 63 are devoted to the reign of Richard II.

16 Stow's *The Annales of England* (London, 1592) was an enlarged version of his *The Chronicles of England* (London, [1580]), which carried the same illustration as its title-page. For the use of such genealogical trees in London pageants, including a discussion of Richard Grafton's role in their planning and their possible relationship to the frontispiece of Hall's *Chronicle* (1550), see Anglo, op. cit., pp. 194–5, 334–5, 354.

idea which it depicted, but he followed it with a text more directly applied to its subject-matter than had Henry Holland's *Bazili⍵logia*, whence it was borrowed.[17] (Plate 22.)

Richard II, sculpted thus as a figure annexed to the civil wars, was a monarch whose realities were no less (though less notoriously) blurred than those of Richard III. The two kings stood as the two poles of the Tudor historical sequence, and others besides Biondi found their roles to be special and specially unfortunate. 'All the (Kings) *Richards*, and all the Dukes of *Gloucester* came to violent ends'.[18] Richard II as well as Richard III had been guilty of grave regnal injustices. Both were discrowned; both met untimely deaths; both gave way to new departures in history. The second Richard, unlike the third, was not regarded as a monster but he too, seen through the distorting glass of sixteenth-century interpreters, emerged—more convincingly but nevertheless markedly—as a constructed type. The facets of his reign and character which were selected and emphasized and known were those which best fitted the Tudor formula.

★   ★   ★

[17] H. Holland, *Bazili⍵logia, A Booke of Kings* (London, 1618), title-page. In Biondi's work the portraits of Charles I and Henrietta Maria were substituted for those of James I and Anne, and the figures of Richard II and Henry VII are identified, but otherwise the engravings are the same. The upper part of Richard's figure, like the separate portrait of him in this volume, seems to be related to the Westminster painting; cf. below p. 306. The portraits of Holland's book, like its title-page, were used again elsewhere; H. C. Levis, *Bazili⍵logia, A Booke of Kings. Notes on a Rare Series of Engraved English Royal Portraits from William the Conqueror to James I* (New York, 1913), pp. 1, 18–20, 28–9, 60–1; Freeman O'Donoghue, *Catalogue of Engraved British Portraits Preserved in the Department of Prints and Drawings in the British Museum*, iii (London, 1912), pp. 567–9.

[18] Biondi, op. cit., pt. ii, bk. viii, p. 115. Biondi was apologetic about devoting the final book of his history to Henry VII; 'The Civill wars whereof I write, ought to end with the death of *Richard* the 3. without any further progress', but could not because of the pretenders Simnel and Warbeck; ibid., pt. ii, bk. ix, p. 219. In 1651 Lambert van den Bos (or Bosch) published at Amsterdam his *Roode en Witte Roos. of Lankaster en Jork*, a play on Richard III which was possibly translated into Dutch from a lost English original. The action is focused on Richard III, but 'the feud begun of old by our ancestors' is discussed with explicit reference to the defects of Richard II, and his 'sly tricks'. In 1658 Bos published a prose account of the struggles of Lancaster and York which also took Richard II as its starting-point and allocated a hundred years to the subject. O. J. Campbell, 'The Position of the *Roode en Witte Roos* in the Saga of King Richard III', *University of Wisconsin Studies in Language and Literature*, No. 5 (Madison, 1919), pp. 1, 18, 103–7. The historical reputation of Richard III has been helpfully described by A. R. Myers, 'Richard III and Historical Tradition', *History*, liii (1968), pp. 181–202.

It is neither possible nor necessary here to trace the emergence of the wars of the roses myth in the political context in which it has received most salient recognition.[19] The pivotal place of Richard II was already recognized by sixteenth-century disputants, who pointed out that divergences of opinion about him belonged to the wars themselves.[20] Whereas for the Yorkists all wrongs stemmed from the criminal deeds of 1399–1400, Lancastrian supporters had every reason to go back behind the deposition to demonstrate the misdeeds which justified Richard's removal. Two major features of the Tudor thesis were already enunciated in the declaration of the Yorkist title in the first parliament of Edward IV; namely the idea that the deposition and death of Richard II had involved the land in untold tribulation, and secondly an elaborately exaggerated view of the scale of fifteenth-century troubles. The usurping Henry of Lancaster, it was asserted,

the same Kyng Richard, Kyng enoynted, coroned and consecrate, and his Liege and moost high Lord in the erth, ayenst Godds Lawe, Mannes Liegeaunce, and oth of fidelite, with uttermost punicion attormentyng, murdred and destroied, with moost vyle, heynous and lamentable deth; wherof . . . this Reame of Englond, . . . therfore hath suffred the charge of intollerable persecution, punicion and tribulation, wherof the lyke hath not been seen or herde in any other Cristen Reame, by any memorie or recorde . . . unrest, inward werre and trouble, unrightwisnes, shedyng and effusion of innocent blode, abusion of the Lawes, partialte, riotte, extorcion, murdre, rape and viciouse lyvyng, have been the gyders and leders of the noble Reame of Englond.[21]

The next Yorkist reign, according to More's *History of King Richard III*, saw another link attached to the chain of supposition— the idea of the decimation of the nobility.

In which inward warre among our self, hath ben so gret effucion of the

[19] In addition to the works of Tillyard, Hay, and Lander already referred to, see Lily B. Campbell, *Shakespeare's "Histories": Mirrors of Elizabethan Policy* (San Marino, 1947), pp. 119–25, 168, ff.

[20] Both Robert Parsons and his opponent Sir Thomas Craig stressed this prejudice in Lancastrian and Yorkist disputants. Parsons, op. cit., pt. ii, pp. 62–3; Thomas Craig, *Concerning the Right of Succession to the Kingdom of England, Two Books; Against the Sophisms of one Parsons a Jesuite, Who assum'd the Counterfeit Name of Doleman* (London, 1703), p. 322. The 1703 translation was apparently the first edition of this work which the title-page states was originally written in Latin 'above 100 Years since'.

[21] *R.P.*, v, p. 464.

auncient noble blood of this realme, y^t scarcely the half remaineth, to the gret infebling of this noble land, beside many a good town ransakid & spoiled, by them that have ben going to ye field or cumming from thence. . . . So that no time was ther in which rich men for their mony, & gret men for their landes or some other for some fere or some displesure were not out of peryl.[22]

So, from the arguments of the disputants themselves Tudor writers were able to develop that conception of divine punishment and deliverance which Shakespeare inherited from Polydore Vergil through the chronicle of Edward Hall.

The idea of the wars of the roses arose therefore in the thick of political contest as a political moral which looked back to 1399 as a critical turning-point. Powerful moralizations are not, however, usually restricted in their application, and this one was no exception in that it grew in different contexts and was applied in different fields. The Tudor myth of history was not only a political myth relating to the secular order of the universe. Quite as evidently it was also a reshaping of the religious past, and here too the reign of Richard II was regarded as a point of departure which had profoundly affected the course of England's development. This tendentious patterning likewise magnified the disasters of the fifteenth century as the indicator of divine displeasure. But in this case it was the affairs of the church at the turn of the fourteenth century which Richard's reign and fate were seen to have so greatly affected. This part of the Tudor legend failed (for reasons which quickly become apparent) to establish itself so successfully,

[22] *The Complete Works of St Thomas More*, ed. Richard S. Sylvester, ii (New Haven, 1963), p. 71. Tales of mortality—royal and common as well as noble—grew in the telling and were used as warnings to both crown and subjects. Cf. Tyndale, 'and of their noble blood remaineth not the third, nor I believe the sixth, yea, and if I durst be so bold, I wene I might safely swear that there remaineth not the sixteenth part. Their own sword hath eaten them up'; a letter to Elizabeth on the subject of her marriage spoke of 'great ruines of great families, and great effusion of the bloud royal' in the time of Henry VI, and alleged that between the death of Richard II and the accession of Edward IV 'there was in the mean season slain fourscore of the bloud royal'; Thomas Craig said that as the result of Henry IV's usurpation 'Of all his most numerous Family *There was not one left to piss against the Wall*, to make use of a Scripture phrase; This gave beginning and rise to those Lamentable and deadly Factions between the Families of *York* and *Lancaster*; which was not expiated but with the slaughter and blood of a hundred thousand *Englishmen*'. William Tyndale, *Expositions and Notes on Sundry Portions of the Holy Scriptures*, ed. Henry Walter (Parker Society, Cambridge, 1849), p. 53; Strype, *Annals of the Reformation*, II, ii, p. 655; Craig, op. cit., p. 331, cf. p. 322.

and has therefore been less noticed by modern historians. Yet it was equally a part of contemporary theory, and is equally revealing of the ways in which interpretations of Richard's life and character were bent to shape Tudor preoccupations.[23]

In the Tudor Protestant myth Richard II is presented as the would-be defender of the Gospel, and the turmoils of the fifteenth century were attributed to the suppression of Wycliffe's admonitory voice. This view of things was propounded by William Tyndale when the Reformation in England was still very much in the making, and it was carried further by others who built on his suggestions.

Wickliffe preached repentance unto our fathers not long since. They repented not; for their hearts were indurate, and their eyes blinded with their own pope-holy righteousness, wherewith they had made their souls gay against the receiving again of the wicked spirit . . . But what followed? They slew their true and right king, and set up three wrong kings a row, under which all the noble blood was slain up, and half the commons thereto, what in France, and what with their own sword, in fighting among themselves for the crown; and the cities and towns decayed, and the land brought half into a wilderness, in respect of what it was before.[24]

The land was devastated by dissension because it had failed to hear the contemporary call to repentance. Tyndale's exposition of the divine judgement manifested in fifteenth-century events was a variation of the theory which Polydore Vergil first published a few years later. But it was a theory with a difference, in that the fatal breach between Plantagenet and Lancaster was envisaged in strictly religious terms, and the deposition and death of Richard II were laid at the door of hypocritical prelates who were out to silence the prophetical voice of Wycliffe. It was they who 'to quench the truth of his preaching, slew the right king, and set up three false kings a row: by which mischievous sedition they caused half England to be slain up, and brought the realm into such ruin and desolation that M. More could say, in his Utopia,

[23] So far as I know the only person who has directed attention to this significant variant of the Tudor myth is William Haller, *Foxe's Book of Martyrs and the Elect Nation* (London, 1963), pp. 167–9.

[24] William Tyndale, *Doctrinal Treatises and Introductions to Different Portions of the Holy Scriptures*, ed. Henry Walter (Parker Society, Cambridge, 1848), p. 458, from the Prologue to the Prophet Jonas (1531).

that as Englishmen were wont to eat sheep, even so their sheep now eat up them by whole parishes at once'.[25] According to Tyndale's interpretation, the murderous leaders of the church were unable during Richard II's reign to carry out their wish to eradicate the true preachers of God's word, but they found their way out of the impasse in what proved to be both a political and religious crisis. While the king was in Ireland 'our prelates had another secret mystery a brewing. They could not at their own lust slay the poor wretches which at that time were converted unto repentance and to the true faith, to put their trust in Christ's death and blood-shedding for the remission of their sins, by the preaching of John Wicliffe'. So no sooner was Richard out of the realm on his way to subdue the Irish (who had been deliberately incited to rebellion by the scheming popish prelates) than Archbishop Arundel was up against him, and on his return took him prisoner and did him to death most cruelly. 'O merciful Christ!' Tyndale apostrophized, 'What blood hath that coronation cost England!'[26] This was the event that had turned England into a veritable sheep-walk, dimi-nished towns, villages and people by a third, and eaten up the nobility so that only a fraction remained in the land. For Tyndale it was the bloodshed of religious martyrs more than of warring political factions. 'And then, when the earl of Derby, which was king Harry the fourth, was crowned, the prelates took his sword, and his son's Harry the fifth after him (as all the king's swords since), and abused them, to shed Christian blood at their pleasure.'[27] It was the spirituality, the pope and his abettors, who were crimi-nally responsible, who had slain in England 'many a thousand, and slew the true king and set up a false, unto the effusion of all the noble blood and murdering up of the commonalty'.[28]

Improbable though this interpretation of events was, it did not end with Tyndale. Protestant propagandists saw to it that Angli-can monarchs as well as Anglican martyrs should have good fore-

[25] Tyndale, *Expositions and Notes*, pp. 224-5, from the Exposition of the first Epistle of St John (1531). These views of Tyndale's were published before the first edition of the *Anglica Historia*, though Polydore Vergil was writing this work more than a decade earlier (see n. 8 above).

[26] Ibid., p. 296, from The Practyse of Prelates ([Antwerp], 1530).

[27] Ibid., p. 297.

[28] William Tyndale, *An Answer to Sir Thomas More's Dialogue*, ed. Henry Walter (Parker Society, Cambridge, 1850), p. 166.

bears, and though Richard II did not stay the course in this role there was a time when he was apparently being tailored for it. John Bale did nothing so striking for Richard II as he did for King John, who was well set by Thomas Cromwell's playwright upon a Protestant stage which he continued to occupy until seventeenth-century constitutionalists found better boards for him. Bale did, though, place both Edward II and Richard II alongside the supposedly poisoned hero of 1215, together with burned Lollard leaders and 'an infynite nombre of poore symple soules' who were victims of the persecution of Antichrist.[29] And John Foxe, taking up Tyndale's story, even his very words, made full use of the fact that no heretics were burnt in England during the first twenty years of the Lollard movement. If Henry IV seemed set as the staunch defender of cruel Catholic orthodoxy and inaugurator of persecution, could not a reverse case be made out for his predecessor?

In the *Acts and Monuments* Foxe considerably expanded and embellished the interpretation of the civil wars and Richard II's place in them which Tyndale had propounded. Near the beginning of his book, in his section on the primitive church, Foxe reproduced—without acknowledgement—almost verbatim a passage from Tyndale's *Prophete Jonas* (1531) with its examples of 'the terrible plagues of God against the churlish and unthankful refusing or abusing the benefit of his truth'.

Not many years past, God, seeing idolatry, superstition, hypocrisy, and

---

[29] John Bale, *The Image Of bothe Churches* (London, [1548?]), pt. i, sigs. P viiv–viiir; John Bale, *Select Works*, ed. H. Christmas (Parker Society, Cambridge, 1849), p. 351. Bale evidently wanted Richard to be included with the emperors and kings, some of whom 'were accursed, some deposed, some slaine, some poysoned', who suffered at the hands of the 'slayne sort'. Cf. F. J. Levy, *Tudor Historical Thought* (San Marino, 1967), pp. 89–92 for Bale as 'The first of the English church historians' and his suggestion that Arundel had arranged the deposition of Richard II in order to proceed against the Lollards with *De heretico comburendo*. The way in which Bale developed historical ideas in Tyndale's works (especially the presentation of King John) has been pointed out by Rainer Pineas, 'William Tyndale's Influence on John Bale's Polemical Use of History', *Archiv für Reformationsgeschichte*, 53 (1962), pp. 79–96. It should be noted that Bale, who apparently never completed the third and fourth parts of his *Actes of English votaryes*, planned that the final book should cover the years I Henry IV to the present (1550 or 1551). This would have fitted with both Tyndale's and Foxe's view of Richard II's deposition as a dividing-line in ecclesiastical history. *The first two partes of the Actes or unchaste examples of the Englyshe Votaryes*, (London, 1560), pt. ii, sigs. T viiv–viiir.

wicked living, used in this realm, raised up that godly-learned man John Wickliff, to preach unto our fathers repentance; and to exhort them to amend their lives, to forsake their papistry and idolatry, their hypocrisy and superstition, and to walk in the fear of God. His exhortations were not regarded, he, with his sermons, was despised, his books, and he himself after his death, were burnt. What followed? They slew their right king, and set up three wrong kings on a row, under whom all the noble blood was slain up, and half the commons thereto. What in France, with their own sword in fighting among themselves for the crown; while the cities and towns were decayed, and the land brought half to wilderness, in respect of what it was before. O extreme plagues of God's vengeance![30]

Although he did not elaborate on the civil wars as such, Foxe's interpretation of their significance was essentially an expansion of that already outlined by Tyndale. They were to be seen, that is, in the context of religious developments, in which the reign of Richard II held a key position. The martyrologist can here be watched struggling with certainly intractable material to make of Richard II a youthful hero who had attempted to maintain the true cause of the gospel in the face of bloodthirsty popish prelates. The king was exonerated from any direct responsibility in the proceedings against Wycliffe and his Oxford followers. Foxe stressed that he being 'but young and under years of ripe judgement' was not to be held personally answerable for the action of 1382, and his association with the statute of that year was explained by his having been 'partly induced, or rather seduced, by importunate suit' of the archbishop of Canterbury.[31] Foxe was trying to claim Richard as the would-be protagonist of Wycliffe and the Lollards. He opened his account of the reign with the statement that the youthful king, following in the steps of his grandfather Edward III, was 'no great disfavourer of the way and doctrine of Wickliff', though unfortunately, owing to circumstances, he could not accomplish all

---

[30] John Foxe, *The Acts and Monuments*, ed. Josiah Pratt (London, 1877), i, p. 93; cf. Tyndale, *Doctrinal Treatises*, p. 458, quoted above p. 285. Professor Haller, op. cit., p. 167, comments on this passage in Foxe, but does not note its debt to Tyndale.

[31] Foxe, op. cit., iii, p. 37; cf. p. 42 'The young king also, moved by the unquiet importunity of the archbishop' wrote to Oxford ordering the suppression of Wycliffite teaching there. Foxe agreed with his contemporaries in this emphasis on Richard's youth, but he used it as an argument to forgive, rather than blame the king.

that he would have liked. 'Notwithstanding, something he did in that behalf; more perhaps than in the end he had thank for of the papists . . .'[32] To bolster up his case the martyrologist inserted a fictitious admonitory letter from Richard to William Courtenay, in which the king, marvelling at the archbishop's desire for blood and recalling various telling historical precedents (in order to contrast royal lenity with ecclesiastical cruelty), cited Courtenay and the heretic Nicholas Hereford to be tried as equals before the king at the bar of scripture.[33] Richard was to be envisaged as the aspiring advocate of the gospel.

Foxe was, however, unable to sustain his attempted defence of Richard to the end. His praises could not extend beyond the fact that the followers of the gospel in this reign, though they were proceeded against, did not have to suffer the extreme penalty. Thus no great harm came to William Swinderby until after Richard's deposition. 'I find none who yet were put to death on that account during the reign of this king Richard; whereby,' Foxe concluded, 'it is to be thought of this king, that although he cannot utterly be excused for molesting the godly and innocent preachers of that time . . . yet neither was he so cruel against them, as others that came after him.'[34] Richard himself was not of a fierce disposition towards the heretics, and the actions which he took against them were to be explained by his fear of popes and prelates who egged him on to these 'strait and hard' dealings against the Wycliffites. 'Thus king Richard, by the setting on of William Courtenay, archbishop of Canterbury and his fellows, taking part with the pope and Romish prelates, waxed somewhat strait and hard to the poor Christians of the contrary side of Wickliff . . . albeit, during all the life of the said king I find none expressly by name that suffered burning'.[35] And of course there was Richard's end to be accounted for. Foxe did not go into details of the deposition but this event had its place in the course of his ecclesiastical history. Richard, to the martyrologist, was a man of virtues as well as vices,

[32] ibid., p. 1.
[33] Ibid., pp. 48–9. The letter, an imagined answer to the archbishop's formal signification of excommunication of Nicholas Hereford, is headed by Foxe; 'To this letter of the archbishop, might not the king, gentle reader, thus answer again, and answer well'. Its fictitious content is also stressed in the marginal 'Prosopopoeia. What the king might have answered again'.
[34] Ibid., p. 202; cf. p. 130.   [35] Ibid., p. 197.

who had shown signs of promise but ultimately failed. He was at fault above all in that 'he, starting out of the steps of his progenitors, ceased to take part with them who took part with the gospel'. The church historian drew a moral which bore very little relation to the articles of deposition. The judgement against Richard was a judgement of God and it was caused by the way in which the king had first supported and then abandoned the defence of the gospel. Richard II was forsaken by God because he had forsaken the Word, and 'considering the whole life and trade of this prince', nothing 'seemeth to be of more weight to us, or more hurtful to him, than this forsaking of the Lord and his word'.[36]

John Foxe, therefore, looked back upon the accession of the Lancastrians as a lamentable turning-point which marked the inception of bloodshed and disorder. For him, as for Tyndale before him, the blood was the blood of martyrs and the disorder the disorder of spiritual malaise. The death of Richard II brought the end of an era, the beginning of a melancholy new chapter of ecclesiastical history. He was the last king in whose time faithful followers of the gospel were not called upon to suffer death for witnessing to the Word. 'This is to be noted', wrote Foxe (again echoing Tyndale), 'that since the time of king Richard II, there is no reign of any king to be assigned hitherto, wherein some good man or other hath not suffered the pains of fire, for the religion, and true testimony of Christ Jesus.'[37] It was the Lancastrians who were responsible for this changed state of affairs. Henry IV, who was 'altogether bent to hold with the pope's prelacy' was 'the first of all English kings that began the unmerciful burning of Christ's saints for standing against the pope'. While the reign of the first Lancastrian was 'full of trouble, of blood and misery', the ruin of the last was also to be associated with the burning of good gospellers.[38] The troubles of the house of Lancaster, like the fate of

---

[36] Ibid., p. 216; cf. Haller, op. cit., pp. 168–9 where it is pointed out that for Foxe 'the deciding reason for the judgment which overtook Richard II was his yielding to the dictation of the Pope in the suppression of Wyclif and the gospel'. Foxe excuses himself for not going further into the deposition on the grounds that it was to be found in other works and 'for that it is not greatly pertinent to my argument'.

[37] Foxe, op. cit., iii, p. 755, referred to by Haller, op. cit., p. 169; cf. above p. 286 for Tyndale's similar statement.

[38] Foxe, op. cit., iii, pp. 229, 753; Haller, loc. cit.

Richard II, were to be explained on the same lines—persecution of the faithful.

Accepting and adapting to his own story the now hardy myth of fifteenth-century strife, with all its attendant slaughter and sacrifice, Foxe looked back, as the originators of the myth had looked back, to the reign of Richard II as a fatal cross-roads in English history. The advent of the house of Lancaster meant the arrival of a deplorable new distemper in the English church, from which there was no alleviation right up to his own day. Richard II had not persecuted to the death; Henry IV had started to burn the witnesses of Christ and thereafter the fires of persecution were never extinguished.

This feature of the *Acts and Monuments* did not escape the eye of Foxe's searching opponent, Robert Parsons. He took pains to point out the weakness of this visible seam lying between the fourteenth and fifteenth centuries, peculiarly differentiating the periods before and after. For, argued the Jesuit, it being Foxe's aim 'to exhibit unto us a reall visible Church on his part, that is to say, a succession or rather representation of divers professors of his religion', with continuous descent from early times onwards, it was to be remarked that it was not until he reached the time of Wycliffe and his followers that he succeeded in making this ecclesiastical lineage visible, despite the variety of 'sectaryes in former ages' whom he acclaimed. 'It is to be noted, that scarse ever throughout this whole volume of acts, and monuments from Christ downward (for the space of 1400. yeares) doth Fox talke of any visible Church on his side, but only now, when he commeth to these *Wickliffians* and other like sectaryes.'[39] But once Wycliffe arrived on the scene Foxe markedly began to change his tune, making martyrs of heretics, 'canonizinge them for Saints that were any way punished or called in question' from Richard II's time onwards.[40]

The argument might be attacked, but the moral and the myth remained. They were irresistibly accommodating and Parsons picked up the well-worn threads and wove them into his own

[39] Robert Parsons [N.D. *pseud.*], *A Treatise of Three Conversions of England from Paganisme to Christian Religion* ([S. Omer], 1603–4), i, pp. 484–5, 502.

[40] Ibid., p. 508. Of course Foxe's case did change with changes in the law; it was the cruelties of the persecutors, as well as the stand of the persecuted, which constituted the break between the reigns of Richard II and Henry IV.

polemic. The historical rift which had been made out of Richard II's reign served many causes, and what had reinforced Foxe's Protestant case was now made to support the Catholic position of his opponent. For Parsons too the sufferings of the fifteenth century had religious explanations, though in his case, of course, they were to be looked for not in the persecution of the Wycliffites but the precise opposite—the failure to take heresy firmly and speedily to task. It is amusing to see how, in turning the Protestant argument upside down, the Jesuit himself echoed its resounding emphases.

But what followed of this? I meane of this negligence in resistinge this sect of *Wickliffe* at the beginning? Truly there followed or rather flowed such seas of calamities, as were never seene in our countrey before, nor scarse heard of in others.

  For wheras *K. Edward* the 3. had byn a most glorious king, his end was pittiful: his heyre *K. Richard* after infinite sedition, contention, and bloudshed of the nobility, and others was deposed, and made away. The bloudy division of the house of *Lancaster* and *Yorke* came in, & endured for almost an hundred years, with the ruine not only of the royall line of *Lancaster,* by whom specially *Wickliffe* was favoured at the beginning ... but with the overthrow also of many other noble princes, and familyes, and most pernicious warres & garboyles continued, both at home and abroad with the losses of all our goodly *States, Provinces & Countreyes* in France. Unto àll which, the division of harts, mynds and iudgments brought in by *Wickliffes* doctrine did help not a little, and the calamityes so continued untill the tyme of the most wise, Christian, and Cath. *K. Henry* the 7. Who as he extinguished the reliques of this wicked *Wickliffian* seed ... so did he happily also extinguish all temporall division, about the succession of our Imperiall crowne.[41]

Richard II's role in the wars of the roses myth was therefore as various as it was inescapable. His reign being, by general consent, the seed-bed for the ensuing century of troubles, was accorded the moral which most suited the moralist. Whereas for Robert Parsons the misfortunes of the house of Lancaster might be traced back to the protection which John of Gaunt had afforded Wycliffe, for Tyndale and Foxe they were to be accounted for in exactly the opposite way: by Lancastrian failure to follow Richard II's tolerant example. It can scarcely be surprising that the *Acts and Monuments'*

---

[41] Ibid., pp. 544–5.

essayed portrayal of Richard as a proto-Protestant monarch never gained much currency. It was much too conspicuously at variance with known facts. If Richard flinched, as his successor did not, from making it legal to burn heretics, he certainly brought the law to bear against them in other ways, and there is not the slightest evidence of his wishing to encourage them. Everything rather pointed the other way, as proceedings against the Lollards were stepped up from 1382 onwards, and indeed the king seems to have prided himself for his efforts in this direction—witness his epitaph in Westminster Abbey. 'He protected the church . . . He overwhelmed heretics, and laid low their friends.' Though John Weever, who transcribed it, found the epitaph as a whole 'strange, if not ridiculous' in the qualities it attributed to Richard, given his ending, it was not easy to attack the substance of these phrases.[42] Even so, Foxe's story was not without some later echoes—even additions. John Lewis, in his *History of the Life and Sufferings of the Reverend and Learned John Wicliffe*, having written of how his subject was 'very happy' in the royal favour of Edward III and patronized by his 'very zealous Protector' the duke of Lancaster, added that 'K. *Richard* II was, at first, no Enemy to Dr. *Wicliffe*. He made him his Chaplain, and grac'd him with his Royal Favour. However afterwards he suffered himself to be made use of by the Ruling Clergy to be the Instrument of wreaking their Spight on him and his Followers'.[43]

★   ★   ★

In a variety of ways the Tudors' periodization influenced their assessment of Richard II. One particularly obvious result was the tendency to telescope events of the reign and to concentrate un-

---

[42] Royal Commission on Historical Monuments, *London*, i (London, 1924), p. 31; H. G. Richardson, 'Heresy and the Lay Power under Richard II', *E.H.R.*, li (1936), p. 23; John H. Harvey, 'The Wilton Diptych—A Re-examination', *Archaeologia*, xcviii (1961), p. 8, n. 6, p. 18; John Weever, *Ancient Funerall Monuments* (London, 1631), pp. 471–2. Weever, who found the epitaph too flattering to Richard (he quoted lines Fabian wrote 'to extenuate the force of such palpable grosse flattery') seems to have thought that the tomb and epitaph were the work of Henry V, when he moved Richard's body to Westminster. In fact the epitaph, together with the tomb, was presumably of Richard's own choosing in 1395–7 (a specially topical moment for the heresy question).

[43] (London, 1720), p. 198.

duly·upon the critical happenings at its end, that were specially provocative of subsequent strife. This disposition began before and lasted long after Shakespeare, who was far from alone in focusing attention on the closing eighteen months of the reign, starting with the Hereford-Norfolk quarrel and ending with the display of Richard's corpse in March 1400.[44] The same, or similar perspectives were adopted by historians. John Hayward's history of the first year of Henry IV's reign devoted two-thirds of its space to the reign of Richard II but had little to say of the years before 1387.[45] To take the affairs of 1387-8 as a significant starting-point was natural for those, such as Hayward, who were concerned to trace the rising star of the future Henry IV, or who looked back, as did others, to the encounter at Radcot Bridge as the first battle of the wars of the roses. 'By reason of the contention of York and Lancaster were foughten sixtiene or seventiene pitched fieldes, in lesse then an hundreth yeares. That is, from the eleventh or twelfth yeare of K. Richard the second his reigne (when this controversie first began to bud up) unto the thirtienth yeare of K. Henrie the seventh.'[46] *Leicester's Commonwealth* (as this very outspoken book of 1584 later came to be called) regarded the activities of the Lords Appellant as the true beginning of England's prolonged troubles. Samuel Daniel likewise, spelling out the 'fatall causes of this civile Warre', returned to Richard II and the events of 1387-8.

> In this mans Raigne, began this fatal strife
> (The bloudie argument whereof we treate)

[44] The action of the play runs from 29 April 1398 (when the king appointed the day for the Norfolk–Hereford combat) to March 1400 (when Richard's body was displayed in London). Shakespeare's starting-point was the same as Edward Hall's, though opinions differ as to the extent of this debt. *King Richard II*, ed. Ure, pp. xxxi, xlix–l; Tillyard, op. cit., pp. 40–9, 237 ff.

[45] J. Hayward, *The First Part of the life and raigne of King Henrie the IIII. Extending to the end of the first yeare of his raigne* (London, 1599). On p. 12 Hayward reaches the year 1387, and of the total of 149 pages, 99 concern Richard II. Cf. *King Richard II*, ed. Ure, pp. lviii–lxii for the extensive literature on Hayward's book and the troubles he got into over its publication.

[46] *The Copie of a leter, wryten by a master of arte of Cambrige, to his friend in London* ([Antwerp?], 1584), pp. 121–2. Cf. Hayward, op. cit., pp. 23–4 on the significance of the battle joined at Radcot Bridge at which though 'scarse ten ounces of bloud was lost on both sides', yet 'this was the firste acte whereby reputation did rise to the side, and the greatnes began, whereunto the Earle [of Derby] afterwards attained'—thanks to his magnanimity on this occasion.

That dearely cost so many a Prince his life;
And spoyld the weake, and even consum'd the great.[47]

The same posthumous prejudice continued in seventeenth-century histories. John Trussell published in 1636 a history of England which was designed to fill the gap between Daniel's prose history, which ended with Edward III, and Bacon's *Henry VII*. Of his opening forty-nine pages devoted to Richard II only the first twenty, however, are spent on the years 1377–96. The main concentration was upon 1397–9, when the catastrophic weakness of a king 'so blinded and bewitched with continuall custome of flatteries' became fully apparent.[48] As long as Richard's life and reign were overshadowed by Lancastrian-Yorkist struggles it was a distortion of balance which was with difficulty avoided. The imminent clash of the contending factions meant that the end was already present in the beginning. 'It is not my purpose to write all the acts of this king, a great part whereof I passe over; I will onely treat of such things as caused his ruine', Biondi explained candidly at the outset of his history, to make clear that he had no intention of writing the entire story of Richard II. 'I take my rise from the unfortunate reigne of *Richard* the second, who comming to the Crowne at eleven yeares of age, doth prove the miserable condition of such States as are governed by an infant King.'[49] Richard, like Oedipus, enters the stage to set in motion the unfolding of foreknown disaster.[50]

But whatsoever mov'd him; this is sure,
Hereby he wrought his ruine in the end;
And was a fatall cause, that did procure
The swift approaching mischiefes that attend[51]

[47] Samuel Daniel, *The Civil Wars*, ed. Laurence Michel (New Haven, 1958), pp. I, 77.

[48] John Trussel, *A Continuation of the Collection of the History of England* (London, 1636), p. 22.

[49] Biondi, op. cit., Introduction, sig. C 2v; p. 3.

[50] This parallel was pointed to in the sixteenth century by Sir Thomas Smith, with his allusion (above p. 276) to Eteocles and Polynices, warring sons of Oedipus and Jocasta.

[51] Daniel, op. cit., p. 82; M. M. Reese, *The Cease of Majesty; A Study of Shakespeare's History Plays* (London, 1961), pp. 227–9. In a similar vein of heralded disaster John Taylor opened his sonnet to Richard II, 'A Sunshine Morne, precedes a showry day, A Calme at Sea ofttimes foreruns a storme': Taylor, op. cit., sig. 3 6r.

—and the foreknowledge was a historical commonplace before Daniel and Shakespeare.

It suited 'wars of the roses' portrayers of Richard to single out some incidents of the reign at the expense of others. The appointment of the parliamentary committee of 1398 had been highlighted among the doings of Richard's later years long before it received the attention of constitutional historians. It was pointed to as a signal of the unbridled abuse of power at the reign's most critical period; of all the thirty-three articles of deposition it seemed the most egregious example of royal perversion. It revealed the extremes to which the king was prepared to go in putting personal desires and sycophantic friends before public interests. 'And finaly', wrote Robert Parsons,

in the last parlament that ever he held, which was in the 21 yeare of his reigne, commonly called *the evel parlament*, he would needs have al authority absolute graunted to certaine favorits of his, which Thomas Walsingham saith, were not above 6. or 7. to determine of all matters with al ful authority, as if they only had bin the whole realme, which was nothing in deede but to take al authority to him selfe only.[52]

What cut across parliamentary rights on one hand seemed on the other to be a supreme illustration of Richard's lifelong propensity to rule through the favours of his friends. By the 1640s the example of the Shrewsbury commission had gained heightened interest in the context of the proceedings of the Long Parliament. William Prynne, who examined the precedent of Richard II's deposition in more than one context, in January 1649 utilized the 1398 committee as an instructive reprimand for that 'Unparliamentary Junto', the Rump. For, he argued, ingeniously—perhaps rather too ingeniously—turning Richard's precedent upside down, the reduced parliament of 1649 was just as unlawful in its form and quite as derogatory to the privileges and power of parliament as the committee of 1398, which had been prominent among the reasons for the king's deposition. The Rump, in fact, with its

---

[52] Parsons, *Conference*, pt. ii, pp. 65–6. Richard Grafton, in words which were still being echoed in the seventeenth century, said the commission was 'in derogation of the state of the house, and to the great disadvantage of the king, and perillous example in time to come'; *A chronicle at large* (London, 1569), p. 394. For modern historians' attention to the question see R. H. Jones, *The Royal Policy of Richard II: Absolutism in the Later Middle Ages* (Oxford, 1968), pp. 118–20.

designs of deposing Charles I, was guilty of one of the very usurpations of power for which Richard II had been deposed.[53]

Modern historians find the first important moment of Richard II's reign in the Peasants' Revolt, when the young king asserted himself to face the rebels at Smithfield.[54] This famous incident was recounted in full by Froissart and was therefore readily available to sixteenth-century readers in the various editions of his chronicles. Later on there was also the full account of the rising which was printed by Stow, drawn from various sources.[55] This glimpse of Richard as the royal saviour of the hour, worthy successor to his martial father and grandfather, had its Elizabethan stage version in *The Life and Death of Jack Straw*. The Richard of this play is the pattern of a youthful king whose justice, clemency and regality are the true counterpoise to the rebellious upsetters of the civil order. He shows himself in the height of crisis just as a monarch should show himself. And the earl of Salisbury observes to the queen mother,

> For though your sonne my Lord the King be young,
> Yet he will see so well unto him selfe,
> That he will make the prowdest Rebell know,
> What tis to moove or to displease a King,

[53] William Prynne, *A Breife [sic] Memento To the Present Unparliamentary Iunto Touching their present Intentions and Proceedings to Depose and Execute, Charles Steward, their lawfull King* (London, 1648), p. 9; (the pamphlet is dated 'From the Kings Head in the Strand Jan. 1. 1648'); cf. pp. 12–14 where Prynne denies that the depositions of Edward II or Richard II were precedents since they were not Protestant monarchs, 'And those Proceedings were only by Popish parliaments in time, of ignorance'. Unfortunately Prynne's position was not consistent (though he himself could claim the great alteration of circumstances), and he had earlier turned this argument from religion and the example of Richard II in the opposite direction, citing the Shrewsbury committee and Richard's 'judicial' dethronement in answer to 'the clamourous tongues of all ill Counsellours, Courtiers, Royalists, Malignants, Papists, and Cavaliers', to show that 'Popish Parliaments, Peeres, and Prelates', Lords and Commons, had previously exercised much greater powers and jurisdiction over kings than the contemporary parliament or any parliament in modern times. William Prynne, *The Soveraigne Power of Parliaments and Kingdomes* (London, 1643), pt. i, pp. 7–8, 28–30, 33, 78ff.; W. M. Lamont, *Marginal Prynne 1600–1669* (London and Toronto, 1963), p. 89.

[54] See, for instance the comments of Anthony Steel, *Richard II* (Cambridge, 1962), pp. 76–82, 123–4; Jones, op. cit., pp. 18–20, 22, 125–6; G. Mathew, *The Court of Richard II* (London, 1968), pp. 15–16, 18; M. McKisack, *The Fourteenth Century* (Oxford, 1959), pp. 411–14, 423, 425–6; V. H. Galbraith, 'A New Life of Richard II', *History*, xxvi (1942), p. 230; Harvey, art. cit., p. 17.

[55] The first English edition of Froissart's chronicles was published in 1523. Stow's long and detailed account of the rising in *The Annales* (1592) gave full recognition to the king's courage and initiative.

And though his looks bewray such lenitie,
Yet at advantage hee can use extremitie.[56]

But the view of Richard's maturity which was common in the sixteenth century was not related to this image of his early promise. Writers who were more concerned with fitting the reign into their general historical scheme than with welding together discrepant facets of the king's character, were inclined to omit or diminish the dramatic action of 1381. Smithfield was an occasion which displayed Richard's qualities probably at their best, and perpetuators of the wars of the roses mythology accordingly played it down. Daniel omitted the rising altogether. Polydore Vergil had already set the stage by describing the dangerous encounter at Smithfield with no reference to Richard's bravery, while William Warner attributed the laurels of that day not to the king who 'begun that civell warre', but to the mayor of London, William Walworth, 'because his courage chiefly gave an ende to that uprore'.[57] Later on neither Biondi, who launched his account of the reign straight into royal favouritism and Richard's impatience with the limitations of the law, nor the author of *England's Happiness in a Lineal Succession*, for all the fullness of his version of events, had any time for the daring deeds of 1381.[58] Obviously there were writers who made good such omissions, but it is surely noteworthy that the wars of the roses focus had this effect of blurring so outstanding an illustration of Richard's personality.

The most remarkable myth to be perpetuated about Richard II existed already during his own lifetime, thanks to his critics and political opponents, and was incorporated into the Tudor picture

[56] *The Life and Death of Jack Straw 1594*, ed. K. Muir and F. P. Wilson (Malone Society Reprints, 1957), sig. B 3v. This play was entered in the Stationers' Register on 23 October 1593 and printed at the turn of this year. Apparently nothing is known about its date of composition or authorship. For the picture it presents of Richard see David Bevington, *Tudor Drama and Politics* (Boston, 1968), pp. 236–8.

[57] Vergil, op. cit., (1546), p. 404; William Warner, *The First and Second parts of Albions England* (London, 1589), ii, p. 125.

[58] Others who—for their own prejudiced reasons—made little of the king's independent role at Mile End and Smithfield were John Trussell, op. cit., pp. 4–7, and Sir Robert Howard who, in his *Historical Observations Upon the Reigns of Edward I. II. III. And Richard II* (London, 1689), though he included a summary of the revolt, gave no stress to Richard's brave role and (p. 95) showed the city of London coming to his rescue. Cf. the same author's *The Life and Reign of King Richard the Second* (London, 1681), p. 22, where the king's exceptional courage is emphasized.

since it perfectly fitted that distorted landscape. This was the myth of the king's youth. Succeeding to the throne at the age of ten and dying in his thirty-fourth year, Richard seemed cut out to be the pattern of a feckless royal minor who demonstrated to the full the extreme insecurity of kingdoms ruled by infant kings. He was seen to exemplify these dangers not only during those early years when he was still technically a minor, but right up to the very end of the reign.

The effects of the minority were a feature of political argument during Richard's lifetime, as well as being insistently stressed thereafter. Richard II's minority was by no means the longest of medieval English sovereigns, but it was exceptional in that its political usage was unduly protracted. The king was over twenty-two when in that well-known scene of 3 May 1389 he declared that having passed the age at which ordinary subjects reached their majority, he intended to be full master of his own house. The circumstances were certainly peculiar. No doubt part of the peculiarity must be attributed to the king's own taste for theatrical scene-setting. Yet there are signs enough that contemporary politicians were making moral capital out of the situation, just as later writers were to do so. In January 1380 when Richard was thirteen, a year younger than Edward III had been at his accession, the commons (petitioning against government expenditure and for a reduction of the continual council) took the opportunity to suggest that the king 'being now of a good discretion and fine stature' and almost of the age at which his grandfather was crowned, might make do, as Edward had done, with only the five great officers.[59] It was clearly an argument of convenience, but those who chose to regard the king as politically immature continued to find his youth a useful platform for years to come. For as long as Richard could be treated as a minor he could be considered neither the only nor the best judge of his own and his country's interests; individuals whom he favoured unduly could be attacked for having abused the king's tender years and the innocence of the royal person. This approach, exploited to the full by the Appellants in 1388, has a conspicuous air of special pleading, given Richard's age.[60] Yet

[59] *R.P.*, iii, p. 73. The petition was made 'aiant regard, que notre Seigneur le Roi si est ore de bone discretion & de bele stature; aiant regard de son age . . .'
[60] Ibid., pp. 230, 241; McKisack, op. cit., p. 456.

eleven years after, at the end of the reign, it was still possible to make play with the same political fiction. The text chosen by Archbishop Arundel for his oration in support of Henry IV's claim to the throne on 30 September 1399 was from I Samuel ix: 'vir . . . dominabitur populo'—'Behold the man . . . this same shall reign over my people'. It was a theme which he artfully embroidered with reference to other texts, including I Corinthians xiii ('When I was a child, I spake as a child') to lay every possible emphasis on the advantages of having a *man*, not a child, as ruler. And England could now rejoice, for the perils of childish speech and behaviour were past, since a man not a boy was to govern.[61] The message cannot have been lost upon those of Richard's subjects who had so long been harping upon the errors of his youth. But it is an astonishing performance when one remembers that Henry, far from being Richard's senior was actually three months younger.

'Woe to thee, O land, when thy king is a child.' Richard had appeared in literature as a model for this proverbial lesson long before Polydore Vergil. The poet John Gower (who, unlike Henry of Lancaster, was old enough to have been Richard's father) criticized his monarch for damaging childish behaviour, and did not scruple to exaggerate the youthfulness of the king's favourites, or to rebuke the 26-year-old king as an 'undisciplined boy'.[62] Sixteenth-century writers, reading the reign backwards, as it were, from 1399, constantly harped upon this topic. Richard became the prototype of the wayward boy king, whose years of juvenility were prolonged by his circle of miscreant young friends. His image became frozen with the features of disastrously misspent youth.

Richard was firmly set into this scheme of things in the *Mirror for Magistrates* (1559), whose exemplary tragedies were largely chosen from periods of royal minority. It was intended to be 'a memorial of suche Princes, as since the tyme of King Richard the

[61] *R.P.*, iii, p. 423. Elaborating on the dangers of childish weakness and love of flattery, Arundel stressed the evils from which the realm was freed.

[62] In his revisions of Book vi of the *Vox Clamantis*, made about 1393, Gower changed 'puer immunis culpe' to 'rex, puer indoctus', *The Complete Works of John Gower*, ed. G. C. Macaulay, iv (Oxford, 1902), pp. 246, 399; *The Major Latin Works of John Gower*, trans. Eric. W. Stockton (Seattle, 1962), pp. 13, 21, 232–3, 445.

secunde, have been unfortunate in the Realme of England'. Richard's own 'vicious story' was no exception.

> I am a Kyng that ruled all by lust,
> That forced not of vertue, ryght, or lawe,
> But alway put false Flatterers most in trust,
> Ensuing such as could my vices clawe:
> By faythful counsayle passing not a strawe.
> What pleasure pryckt, that thought I to be iust.[63]

And the fate of Robert Tresilian was an example of how the king had turned everything topsy-turvy 'by synister advyse', ignoring the limits of the law and 'not raygning but raging by youthfull insolence'.[64] The implicit assumption was that Richard's misdeeds, even those of his adult years, were in intention and effect the actions of an errant minor. This interpretation, which gained ground with the development of his allotted role in Tudor history, was clearly formulated by Polydore Vergil.

Is there anything more shameful than that one who ought to rule should through his own idleness and ignorance be compelled to obey others like a child under age—not of eight or ten years, but of twenty, thirty or more—and be ruled instead of ruling? Such a king was Richard II . . . a youth not of the worst disposition to begin with, inasmuch as he was not everywhere of such deficiency of understanding, or weakness of character, or poverty of judgement, that he could not take, receive, and retain good advice, but profligate counsellors finally took control of him.[65]

This concept of perennial political immaturity was the burden of numerous other accounts, and it is remarkable how in literature, as in his own lifetime, the fiction of Richard's youth was preserved to the end of his days.

In Samuel Daniel's *Civil Wars* Richard, the 'unbridled King'

[63] *The Mirror for Magistrates*, ed. Lily B. Campbell (Cambridge, 1938), pp. 5–10, 70–1, 112–13.

[64] Ibid., pp. 78–9.

[65] Vergil, op. cit., (1546), p. 439; Hay, op. cit., p. 141 (where this passage is quoted); Tillyard, op. cit., p. 33. Vergil stresses Richard's youthful failings throughout his account of the reign; for instance pp. 400, 407 (quoting Ecclesiastes, x. 16 'Vae tibi, terra, cujus rex puer est'), 418 (Richard's failure to revenge the Scots in 1388), 425 (Edmund of York on the king's adolescent errors, 1399), 427–8 (Richard's confession of the offences of youth at his abdication).

who had been spoiled by youthful counsel, private gain and partial hate, was still the 'wanton young effeminate' at the time of Hereford's banishment near the end of the reign, as he was 'th' indiscreete young King' at its beginning. When finally challenged by Bolingbroke he excuses himself on the grounds of his youth and the argument that he is now moving towards a 'calmer state'.[66] John Hayward, like Edward Hall, put into Richard's mouth a speech of resignation in which, while admitting his faults, he offered the plea of youthful misjudgement. The unfortunate Richard who was deposed in Hall's account was a young king 'in whom if there were any offence it ought more to be imputed to the frailtee of his wanton youth then to the malice of his heart or cankerdnesse of his stomacke'. Richard is presented pleading to his deposers in the Tower that he was 'partely led by the frailtie of young waveryng and wanton youth', and had intended to correct his offences 'especially in my old age', the accustomed time for such improvements, in which he like other young men might, given riper years, have mended his ways and turned the proverbial ragged colt into a good horse.[67] The convention that Richard's defects were attributes of his youth became so well established that there was nothing unusual about attributing his undoing to his childishness.

> But, if this *King* had not so *childish* bin
> When *Mowbray* peacht th' *Usurper* of Treason,
> He might have bin secure from al his *Kin*:
> But blinded *Iudgment* is the *hire* of *Sinne*.[68]

John Davies of Hereford's summary assessment of 'Disastrous Richard' was based upon premises which left some marks on Shakespeare's play. Clearly the dramatist was not alone in glossing over the exact contemporaneity of Richard and his supplanter. 'Cousin, I am too young to be your father, Though you are old enough to be my heir'. Richard's words to Bolingbroke may be deftly ambiguous, but earlier remarks of the royal uncles leave no

[66] Daniel, op. cit., pp. 79, 85, 88.

[67] Edward Hall, *The Union of the two noble and illustrate famelies of Lancastre & Yorke* (London, 1548), ff, vir–v, viiiv–ixr; Hayward, op. cit., pp. 86–8. Cf. n. 69 below. Vergil (op. cit., 1546, pp. 427–8) had given Richard such a speech.

[68] *The Complete Works of John Davies of Hereford*, ed. Alexander B. Grosart (Privately Printed, 1878), i, p. 55 (from *Microcosmos*, 1603).

doubt that in their eyes, at least, the king was an 'unstaid youth'.

> The king is come, deal mildly with his youth,
> For young hot colts being rein'd do rage the more.[69]

This civil war type-casting of Richard II was reinforced, as was that of Richard III, by reference to the king's appearance. Just as the later Richard's unnatural cruelties were mirrored in his bodily deformity, so the earlier Richard's effeminate weakness was associated with his exceptional beauty. Richard II was generally acknowledged to have been of outstanding personal appearance, but this was itself regarded as a sign and cause of his deficiencies. He was the lover of minions instead of those feats of martial prowess appropriate to his estate; the very attractiveness of his features accentuated the unmanliness which determined his destiny. 'He was the goodliest personage of all the Kings that had been since the conquest; tall of stature, of streight and strong limbes, faire and amiable of countenance; and such a one as might well be the Son of a most beautifull mother', reported Richard Baker in 1643, embroidering some inherited facts.[70] But the other side of this desirable exterior had long been indicated, to the king's notorious disadvantage.

> In beauty, bounty and liberality, he farre passed all his Progenitors; but was overmuch given to rest and quietnesse, little regarding matters of Armes: and being young, was most ruled by young Counsell, regarding little the Counsell of the sage and wise men of the Realm. Which thing, turned this Land to great trouble, & himselfe to extreme misery.

Ralph Brooke's brief biography of Richard II in his *Catalogue and Succession of the Kings, Princes, Dukes, Marquesses, Earles, and Viscounts of this Realme of England, since the Norman Conquest, to this present yeare 1619*, echoed the words of Grafton and Stow, fifty and

---

[69] *King Richard II*, ed. Ure, pp. 47, 54–5, 116; II. i. 2, 69–70; III. iii. 204–5; see p. 55 for a comment on Hall's use of the proverb 'Of a ragged [shaggy, untamed] colt comes a good horse'. Shakespeare's 'rein'd do rage' sounds like an echo of the *Mirror for Magistrates* 'not raygning but raging', quoted above.

[70] Richard Baker, *A Chronicle of the Kings of England From the Time of the Romans Goverment* [sic] *unto the Raigne of our Soveraigne Lord King Charles* (London, 1643), pt. ii, p. 27; cf. *England's Happiness*, p. 2; 'He was of such a comly and graceful Personage, that he is said to be the most Beautiful Prince, that ever wore the *English* Diadem.' The comment was so often repeated it became virtually a set piece.

thirty years earlier.[71] Richard's outstanding beauty had come, like so much else, to be appropriated to his defects: his youthful weakness, his preferment of young advisers, his dislike of military affairs. 'O flatt'ring glass, Like to my followers in prosperity, Thou dost beguile me.' Richard's face was part of his fate, and its failure to reflect his ultimate abasement might be taken as the final measure of the lifelong damages of his looks. Shakespeare's scene in which Richard calls for the looking-glass to read the book 'where all my sins are writ',[72] was not history, but was closely linked with Tudor versions of it.

As time went on pictorial evidence could be called upon to lend weight to statements about Richard's appearance. Thomas Hearne, who in 1729 published his edition of the chronicle attributed to a monk of Evesham, with its full description of the king, pointed out in his introduction that it was scarcely surprising—given his loveliness—that men as well as women loved Richard so much, and that his manners were affected by excessive praises. In support of the king's beauty Hearne referred to the Wilton Diptych and the engraving of it by Wenceslas Hollar, inscribed to Charles I, in 1639.[73] The diptych could certainly have reinforced stereotyped Tudor views of Richard's youth and beauty. Whether or not Richard had purposely had himself depicted in the guise of his past adolescence, as seems quite possible, the king of the painting is a youth, not a man.[74] But, since the whereabouts of the diptych is

[71] Ralph Brooke, *A Catalogue and Succession of the Kings, Princes, Dukes, Marquesses, Earles, and Viscounts* (London, 1619), sig. **. 6v. Cf. Grafton, op. cit., p. 324, and Stow, *Annales*, p. 434, for almost identical passages. Cf. also the modern view of Rowse, op. cit., p. 9; 'Richard's appearance was attractive, though of a distinctly feminine cast'.

[72] *King Richard II*, ed. Ure, pp. lxxxi–lxxxiii, 140–1; IV. i. 275, 279–81.

[73] *Historia Vitae et Regni Ricardi II. Angliae Regis*, ed. Thomas Hearne (Oxford, 1729), pp. vii–viii, xxvii–xxviii, 169, 402. On the Hollar engraving see Gustav Parthey, *Wenzel Hollar, Beschreibendes Verzeichniss seiner Kupferstiche* (Berlin, 1853), pp. 42–3, no. 229; George Vertue, *A Description of the Works of the Ingenious Delineator and Engraver Wenceslaus Hollar* (London, 1759), pp. 4, 139–40. According to Vertue the painting was in the Arundel collection when Hollar engraved it. The 1639 catalogue of Charles I's pictures, which contains the first certain mention of the diptych, records it as having come to the king from one Lady Jenings. Harvey, art. cit., pp. 2–4; Mrs Reginald Lane Poole, 'Notes on the History in the Seventeenth Century of the Portraits of Richard II', *The Antiquaries Journal*, xi (1931), pp. 145, 147–8.

[74] Richard's youthful appearance in the diptych has, of course, often been commented on. Harvey, art. cit., p. 13 n. 1 argues that there has been a tendency to

unknown during the sixteenth century—an obscurity which might well be connected with its iconography—nothing can be said of the influence of this image on the Tudors. The case is different with another well-known portrayal of Richard, the large panel in Westminster Abbey. If Tudor Protestant monarchs might have found unwelcome, or distasteful, a view of a royal ancestor 'kneeling in his golden robes to our Lady',[75] they could have no objection to this thoroughly regal portrait of Richard, crowned and enthroned with orb and sceptre. The Westminster painting, unlike the Wilton Diptych, was already known before the end of the sixteenth century and various copies of it existed by the time that Queen Elizabeth asked Lambarde whether he knew of 'any true picture, or lively representation' of Richard's countenance and person.[76] By this time interest in royal portraiture was becoming widespread, and though for many individuals imagined features might serve as truth, there were authentic sources for delineating Richard II and they were reproduced. The face of the king which appeared in Thomas Tymme's *Booke, Containing the true portraiture of the countenances and attires of the kings of England* in 1597, though

exaggerate this, and cites evidence which suggests that Richard did not start to grow a beard until 1394–5. Even if, however, he did preserve exceptionally youthful looks until he was 27–28, it is hard to accept this as his represented age in the painting, though the late 1390s seem on other grounds most probable for its composition. For suggestions that the king's appearance was deliberately idealized in a youthful form see Francis Wormald, 'The Wilton Diptych', *Journal of the Warburg and Courtauld Institutes*, xvii (1954), p. 202; Galbraith, art. cit., p. 238. Cf. also Mathew, op. cit., p. 41, for a miniature portrait of Richard 'still shown as a beardless adolescent although he was already twenty-four', and pp. 11, 114, 200 for several suggestive remarks about the adolescent qualities which were 'so prized in the international court culture'.

[75] As he was described in Charles I's catalogue; Mrs R. L. Poole, art. cit., p. 147. The objections of Protestants and the actions of iconoclasts against pictures, statues and idolatrous worship of the Virgin might well have provided reasons for concealing the diptych, especially at certain moments, in the sixteenth century.

[76] *Progresses and Public Processions of Queen Elizabeth*, p. 553; David Piper, 'The 1590 Lumley Inventory: Hilliard, Segar, and the Earl of Essex—I', *The Burlington Magazine*, xcix (1957), 227; Lionel Cust, 'The Lumley Inventories', *The Walpole Society*, vi (1917–18), pp. 21–2. Roy Strong, *Tudor and Jacobean Portraits* (London, 1969), i, p. 261, states that the painting which Elizabeth describes Lord Lumley as having discovered 'fastened on the backside of a door of a base room', and presented to her to 'put it in order with the Ancestors and Successors', was the Westminster painting—which Lumley certainly had copied. For an alternative suggestion that the gift was of the smaller of the two paintings of Richard II listed in the 1590 Lumley inventory, see Mrs R. L. Poole, art. cit., pp. 156–9.

not very lifelike was clearly based upon some known representation—witness the king's bushy hair and characteristic forked beard.[77] And in 1618 appeared Henry Holland's *Baziliωlogia: A Booke of Kings Beeing The true and lively Effigies of all our English Kings from the Conquest untill this present*, with an engraving by Reynold Elstrack which was reproduced in various seventeenth-century works. This 'true pourtraicture of Richard the 2' was certainly derived, though perhaps not directly, from the Westminster panel, a painting which in the original at least, helped to sustain belief in Richard's beauty: 'that beautifull picture . . . which witnesseth how goodly a creature he was in outward lineaments', wrote Weever.[78] (Plates 23, 24a, b.)

Finally, appropriate in a consideration of this wars of the roses image, something may be said of Richard's own views of war. Military success being an established part of the conventional image of the successful monarch, Richard II was naturally blamed for his attitude to war, for being 'overmuch geven to rest and quietnesse' and for having 'loved litle dedes of armes and Martiall Prowes'.[79] Not surprisingly, a king who had not only failed to campaign in France but had also made peace and a marital alliance was contrasted unfavourably with those 'two thunderbolts of warre', Edward III and the Black Prince.[80] This aspect of Richard's shortcomings was linked with his domestic failure, for the hundred years' war with France and the hundred years' discord in England were seen to have an intrinsic see-saw relationship. Losses abroad meant faction at home; native turmoils were successfully buried

[77] T[homas] T[ymme], *A Booke, containing the true portraiture of the countenances and attires of the kings of England, from William Conqueror, unto our Soveraigne Lady Queene Elizabeth now raigning* (London, 1597), sig. D 1r. This reproduction may be compared, for instance, with the king's features in the Dymoke manuscript (see the frontispiece of Steel, op. cit.). An imaginary portrayal of Richard appears in the series of royal heads in the Pictorial Commonplace Book of Thomas Trevelyan (1608), Folger Shakespeare Library Ms. V.b.232, fo.111v (I owe this reference to the kindness of Professor John Hale). For Elizabethan portrait collections, and the fashion for sets of kings, both painted and, later, engraved, see Ellis Waterhouse, *Painting in Britain 1530 to 1790* (Harmondsworth, 1953), pp. 2–3, 25–6; Roy Strong, *The English Icon: Elizabethan and Jacobean Portraiture* (London, 1969), pp. 44–8.

[78] Weever, op. cit., p. 473; cf. Baker, op. cit., p. 28; Mrs R. L. Poole, art. cit., pp. 153, 156. I have not seen Henry Holland's *Baziliωlogia*; Levis, op. cit. reproduces the Richard II engraving on p. 60 and states (p. 2) that the portraits were originally issued as separate sheets. Cf. also Strong, *Tudor and Jacobean Portraits*, p. 261.

[79] Grafton, op. cit., p. 324.   [80] Daniel, op. cit., p. 76.

in foreign conquest. The idea of a century of duplicated inter-
acting warfare existed long before Biondi made it a central feature
of his narrative. His work, with its extensive interweaving of the
troubles and fighting in France and England makes abundantly
clear how foreign affairs reflected back upon English events, to
make of the fifteenth century a double tale of war, resounding
with the alternating clash of alien and domestic battles.[81]

Time, however, effected a change even upon such traditional
judgements. Ultimately it became possible to see that England's
continental ambitions were misguided, and Richard II, instead of
being blamed for his pacifist endeavours, could be exonerated—or
even praised for an innovatory policy.[82] Some steps in this direction are discernible even in the sixteenth century, taken by those
who judged the right and wrong of these affairs in the light of
their own domestic history. Once England, thanks to Mary Tudor,
had lost her last foothold in France, and Elizabeth's subjects had
had time to come to terms with this, the long-acclaimed achievements of Crécy and Agincourt could be regarded in a fresh light.
'*Edward* the third was most victorious, . . . Yet were his *Conquests* hurtfull to his *State*, For they the same did but debilitate.'[83]
The idea that continental possessions were an unwarrantable drain
upon domestic resources, and had themselves contributed to the
disasters of Richard II's reign, had been propounded well before
John Davies published these lines in the year of James I's accession.
It seemed to Sir Thomas Smith, two years after Elizabeth came to

[81] Shakespeare was following Holinshed in using the argument at the beginning
of *Henry V*, that the king's foreign exploits were intended to divert attacks on the
church at home. Biondi saw Henry V as appeasing his kingdom and burying all its
civil contentions through his foreign campaigning, while the renewal of the civil
wars under Henry VI was chiefly to be ascribed to losses in France. That this inter-
action of foreign and domestic faction was indicated does not mean, of course, that
there was any clear idea of the 'Hundred Years' War' with France, which is another
term with its own history. For its development see Kenneth Fowler, *The age of
Plantagenet and Valois: The struggle for supremacy 1328–1498* (New York, 1967), pp.
13–14.

[82] For praise of Richard's negotiations as 'the most statesmanlike effort to mend
the breach between England and France since the days of St Louis', see J. J. N.
Palmer, 'The Anglo-French Peace Negotiations, 1390–1396', *T.R.H.S.*, 5th
Series, xvi (1966), p. 94.

[83] *Complete Works of John Davies*, i, p. 55. Such views are in noteworthy contrast with the more common untempered glorification of Edward III and Henry V,
and show that the Elizabethan attitude was not as monolithic as has sometimes been
supposed; cf. Jones, op. cit., p. 118.

the throne, that just as Henry VIII had undone his father's good work and beggared England by gaining Boulogne, so the misfortunes of Richard II and Henry VI were associated with the French acquisitions of their predecessors. 'But because we shall better and more near at hand see the advantage of heaping realms together, King Edward III and the Black Prince got almost all France. His next successor therefore must needs have his power marvellously increased. So it may appear. For though he were confessed the right heir, yet a nobleman of this realm of England bereaved him of both France and England.'[84] It was quite misleading to suppose that the territorial conquests of either Edward III or Henry V had been assets for their successors; in both cases the inheritors of such supposedly marvellous gains had been dispossessed of the crown. Although the argument (which was admittedly tendentious) was not pursued, Richard II was implicitly acquitted for his reluctance to prosecute the French war; his continental inheritance was seen to excuse, rather than magnify his failure. English lands in France were more expensive than glorious, more enervating than elevating. So, it seemed to Thomas Craig, Edward III's triumphs were misguided. Granted, this king had grievously plagued France, but he had 'exhausted *England* of its Men and Money for carrying on the War', and eventually Normandy, Maine, Aquitaine and Anjou were all lost. 'And all those toils and attempts with the vast Expences of Blood and Treasure which were made to the irreparable loss of *England*, vanish'd into Smoak. It had been much to the advantage of that Nation if it had never attempted any such thing.'[85] It was a chink, albeit a small one, in the armour of Richard II's traditional critics.

* * *

Historical interpretation had to change considerably before Richard II could be judged in modern times in a dispassionate light. Above all it was necessary for interpreters of the later middle ages to shift

[84] Strype, *Life of the Learned Sir Thomas Smith*, p. 256, cf. p. 249. This comes from the dialogue quoted above, and Smith was admittedly pleading a special case, though the speaker Axenius, or Homefriend, who argued so cogently against continental possessions (as among the disadvantages of a royal marriage with a foreigner) was clearly voicing the opinions of the author.

[85] Craig, op. cit., p. 180.

their attention away from the idea of the wars of the roses and the genesis of long and damaging conflict. The profound success of the Tudor thesis endowed the century preceding 1485 with the outstanding features of warfare, bloodshed and aristocratic mortality—all of which gained exaggerated scale in the retrospective view. The whole period, 1377–1485, was cast into a single distorting mould, a mould of disharmony and disturbance. Its lessons were equally instructive whether they were applied to church or state, directed at sovereigns or subjects. And the king whose reign lay at the beginning, whose times were regarded as the breeding-ground and starting-point for this century of disaster, was as damagingly affected as the royal tyrant whose death brought it to a close.

The portrait of Richard II which emerged was largely a literary construction. His was the stock image of the weak, over-influenced minor, who failed in counsel, in religion, and in war, whose inability to rise above the deficiencies of his youth was the overriding reason for his downfall. Those occasions when he was to be seen at his best, facing the rebels of 1381 or (as it is now possible to think) refusing to be pressed into conventional hostilities against France, tended to be discounted or isolated from the general view. Some parts of his character were emphasized at the expense of others. Reading even a part of the great amount of historical narration which, one way or another, was printed about Richard II during the first century or so of English renaissance historiography, one can see how little was lacking from the matter that we use today, but how much of it failed to be integrated. Divergent aspects of the king's character remained separated like individual icons, or different pictures by different artists of one sitter in varying moods.

Four hundred years should be enough time to gain some historical perspective, and the Tudors' history now seems very unlike our own. Yet for all our doubts about the wisdom of preferring 1485 before various other dates as terminal or seminal for England's well-being, or of ascribing unparalleled benefits to Henry VII, or to Henry VIII and his children, we have failed to free ourselves from some of the most outstanding platitudes of sixteenth-century historians. We quarrel with their terms—but we go on using them. We remark their exaggerations—but we continue to repeat them in attenuated forms. Dissatisfied with the whole concept of the wars of the roses we have half-consciously whittled it down to suit our own knowledge of events. As a result Richard II, fortunate in being prised away sooner than Richard III from this stultifying scheme, can now be recognized as a monarch who, more than an effete and misled minor, held bold and imaginative ideas of kingship, was courageous in his approach to the French war, and showed himself a discriminating patron of the arts.

Richard II held an exceptional and peculiarly unfortunate place in Tudor historical thought. It was important that he had been deposed—but he was not unique in that. More important was the fact that he had been deposed and replaced in a way which initiated England's most damaging century, the century of the wars of the roses. And by the time that Tudor rule and successful myth-making had themselves filled out a century, it was hard to take a fresh look back at that reconstructed past. Queen Elizabeth, in any case, was in no position to do so when, ageing, childless, and struggling to prevent the tarnishing of her own long-polished image, she conversed with Lambarde at Greenwich on 4 August 1601. The one thing which cannot have been absent from her mind that day, as she 'fell upon' the reign of Richard II with those accusing, self-accusatory words—'I am Richard II. know ye not that?'—was the notion of civil disturbance. Was not Richard II indelibly associated with a great, never to be forgotten lesson—the inauguration of the wars of the roses? For that offence he well deserved to find a last quietus.

Additional Notes to Chapter 9

2   More recent works on the topic include: Charles Ross, *The Wars of the Roses* (London, 1976); Anthony Goodman, *The Wars of the Roses: Military Activity and English Society, 1452-97* (London 1981); John Gillingham, *The wars of the Roses: peace and conflict in fifteenth-century England* (London, 1981); Colin Richmond, 'The Nobility and the Wars of the Roses, 1459-61', *Nottingham Mediaeval Studies* xxi (1977), pp. 71-85.

23   Cf. also Glanmor Williams, *Reformation Views of Church History* (London, 1970), chapter II on Tyndale, esp. p. 29.

29   For Bale see also the works referred to in the additions to note 67, Chapter 7 above.

56   Cf. also, for delineation of the events of 1381 in the Lord Mayor's pageants in London in 1590 and 1616, David Bergeron, *English Civic Pageantry 1558-1642* (London, 1971), pp. 133-4, 156.

57   Cf. also May McKisack, *Medieval History in the Tudor Age* (Oxford, 1971), pp. 175-6.

73   See also Richard Pennington. *A descriptive catalogue of the etched work of Wenceslaus Hollar 1607-1677* (Cambridge, 1982), pp. 27-28, No. 229; Antony Griffiths and Gabriela Kesnerová, *Wenceslaus Hollar Prints and Drawings* (Brit. Mus. Exhibition Catalogue, London, 1983), pp. 31, 79-80, No. 48.

75   Cf. Henry Peacham's text appended to Hollar's engraving; 'Quem [i.e. Christ with the Virgin] Rex suppliciter pronus adorat'.

82   See also J. J. N. Palmer, *England, France and Christendom, 1377-99* (London, 1972).

10

ENGLISH RUINS AND ENGLISH HISTORY:
THE DISSOLUTION AND THE SENSE OF THE PAST

> Neare to the ruinous walls of the Castle, stood a Priory
> pleasantly seated, which in the shipwracke of such
> religious structures, was dasht all a peeces.
> John Weever on Tunbridge Priory.[1]

> Where the Choir was, now grass grows, where
> anciently were buried Kings and great men.
> John Aubrey on Malmesbury Abbey.[2]

Ruins may make historians. Few can be inspired to the heights of Gibbon, but the prospect of decaying grandeur is necessarily moving to those for whom the past itself consists of fragments awaiting reconstruction. And the greater the ruin the greater the wonder of the onlooker. Roman remains were already a source of inspiration to the Anglo-Saxons.

> Splendid is this masonry—the fates destroyed it;
> the strong buildings crashed, the work of giants moulders away.[3]

However uncomprehended the nature of the builders, the human mind is daunted by the endurance of walls and stones, in contrast with architects, inhabitants and bones.

> The clutch of the grave,
> the strong grip of the earth, holds the master-builders,
> ...Often has this wall,
> grey with lichen and mottled with red, endured one sovereignty after another,
> and stood firm under storms.[4]

In the sixteenth century England acquired a whole suite of ruins. They proved to be peculiarly fertile in stimulating consciousness of the past and in promoting historical activity. The many shells of monastic buildings which were left behind as permanent, telling witnesses to the efficiency of Henry VIII's treatment of the religious houses were not, to be sure, the only notable architectural remains to be found in the English landscape. Nor was this the first time that English monasteries had been sacked and despoiled. It was, however, the first time that religious foundations had been thoroughly attacked and stripped with the deliberate intention of effecting a physical and institutional break with the past. It was the first time that it had seemed possible to wipe out for ever a whole department of religious life. The very

---

[1] John Weever, *Ancient Funerall Monuments within the united Monarchie of Great Britaine, Ireland, and the Ilands adiacent, with the dissolved Monasteries therein contained; their Founders, and what eminent Persons have beene in the same interred*, London 1631, p. 322.

[2] *Wiltshire. The Topographical Collections of John Aubrey F.R.S., AD 1659–70*, ed. J. E. Jackson, Devizes 1862, p. 255.

[3] *The Exeter Book*, part ii, ed. W. S. Mackie (Early English Text Society, Original Series, no. 194), 1934, p. 199, from The Ruin. It is clear from the nature of the ruins described in the poem that they must have been Roman, and the reference to hot baths makes it most probable that the place was Bath.

[4] *Ibid.*

ruthlessness of the idea and its vigorous enactment shocked contemporaries into a sense of loss. And the architectural fossils which remained as testimonies to the royal guillotining of the monastic past fostered a growing nostalgia for what had been swept off in this break.[5]

Historical studies were profoundly affected by the Reformation.[6] The appeal to the past, which had for long formed part of efforts to regenerate the Church, and which was so greatly strengthened by humanist techniques of textual criticism, now gained a new stature. History had to be rewritten to suit the profound reshaping of the Church, and the events of the present helped to heighten contemporary consciousness of historical change. The visible rupture with the past prompted a passionate urge to preserve, as well as to straighten out, the sequence of history. The agonizing sight of wholesale destruction spurred people into activity—even those whose Protestant convictions made them wholly endorse the process at large. The spectacle of physical loss, which already in the 1530's motivated antiquarian researches, was thereafter a continuous element in the English countryside. The landscape held a series of signposts to the destroyed monastic era, and they led to nostalgia and poetry, as well as to antiquarianism and history. From this time on, the ruins of the monasteries entered into English consciousness of the past.

*   *   *

Already in the sixteenth and early seventeenth centuries English literature bears witness to an awareness of the departed monastic period. It is present in Donne's 'winds in our ruin'd Abbeyes rore',[7] and in Shakespeare's 'bare ruin'd choirs where late the sweet birds sang'.[8] Accustomed as they had

---

[5] The losses entailed by the Dissolution are considered in many works; see, for example, D. Knowles, *The Religious Orders in England*, iii, Cambridge 1955–59, pp. 383 *et seq.*, 456 *et seq*; J. C. Dickinson, *Monastic Life in Medieval England*, London 1961, pp. 131 *et seq.*; Geoffrey Baskerville, *English Monks and the Suppression of the Monasteries*, London 1937, pp. 275 *et seq.* These discussions do not, however, attempt to pursue the point under consideration in this article. Suggestive remarks about this are to be found elsewhere: Rose Macaulay, *Pleasure of Ruins*, London 1953, p. 17, 'The Dissolution did much to add the dimension of ruin to British life', and cf. the discussions and citations (several of which I have quoted here) pp. 14–18, 335–67; Kenneth Clark, *The Gothic Revival*, London 1962, p. 23, 'Antiquarians appeared long before Gothic architecture had fallen into general disfavour. Perhaps they owe their origin to the Reformation, for they saw monasteries destroyed and libraries dispersed, and were moved to perpetuate their vanishing glories'; Joan Evans, *A History of the Society of Antiquaries*, Oxford 1956, pp. 2–3, 'Continuity was broken and familiarity des-

troyed by the English Reformation. The dissolution of the monasteries between 1535 and 1539 arrested the stream of English life by an unparalleled catastrophe. The "bare ruined fanes" became at a blow historical monuments, because they no longer fulfilled their functions'; Philip Styles, 'Politics and historical research in the early seventeenth century', *English Historical Scholarship in the Sixteenth and Seventeenth Centuries*, ed. Levi Fox, London 1956, p. 65, 'It [the Dissolution] was the visible sign, such as had never been seen before, of the breach with the past'.

[6] Discussions of the significance of the Reformation for historical thought appear in F. J. Levy, *Tudor Historical Thought*, San Marino 1967, chapter iii, and F. S. Fussner, *The Historical Revolution*, London 1962, pp. 17–25.

[7] John Donne, *The Satires, Epigrams and Verse Letters*, ed. W. Milgate, Oxford 1967, p. 9, from Satire ii.

[8] *Shakespeare's Sonnets*, ed. W. G. Ingram and Theodore Redpath, London 1964, pp. 168–9. Given 16th-century circumstances it seems almost obscurantist to rule out the

become to the dismembered remains of their religious revolution, Elizabethans could have taken as their own the setting of *Titus Andronicus*, when a Goth comes on stage and says:

> ... from our troops I stray'd
> To gaze upon a ruinous monastery;
> And as I earnestly did fix mine eye
> Upon the wasted building, suddenly
> I heard a child cry underneath a wall.[9]

By the 1590's two generations of decay—helped by natural and human agencies—had mellowed and continued the work of Henry VIII's commissioners. Monastic ruins were plundered, quarried, adapted, abandoned. And they went on being remembered for what they were.

> This fortification
> Grew from the ruines of an auncient Abbey:
> And to yond side o' th' river, lies a wall
> (Peece of a Cloyster) which in my opinion
> Gives the best Eccho, that you ever heard;[10]

says Delio in John Webster's *The Duchess of Malfi*. The same sometime abbey moved Antonio to ruminate in response that 'all things have their end: / Churches, and Citties (which have diseases like to men) / Must have like death that we have'. It was an age of special sensibility to the ruins of time and Antonio enjoyed his contemplation of mutability.

> I doe love these auncient ruynes:
> We never tread upon them but we set
> Our foote upon some reverend History.[11]

The echoes of 'reverend history' sounded by monastic ruins were certainly far-reaching; they sounded down to Walter Scott and the Gothic revival (Pl. 25a).[12]

Pre-Reformation relics could be powerful even by virtue of their absence. When Euphues and Philautus arrived in Canterbury 'like two pilgrims' at the turn of 1579 in Lyly's *Euphues and his England*, they seem to have been astounded by the invisible past as well as the impressively visible present. In the cathedral city 'somewhat decayed yet beautiful to behold' they were greatly affected by the cathedral itself, 'the very majesty whereof struck them into a maze'; there they saw many monuments, and also 'heard tell of greater than either they ever saw or easily would believe'.[13] The golden

---

possibility that Shakespeare's line may allude to ruined architectural as well as arboreal tracery. Cf. below p. 323 and note 41.

[9] *Titus Andronicus*, ed. J. C. Maxwell, London 1953, p. 103, V, i.

[10] John Webster, *The Duchess of Malfi*, ed. F. L. Lucas, London 1958, p. 124, V, iii. The play was produced before 1614 (p. 13), and printed in 1623.

[11] *Ibid.* For a similar contemplation of mortality inspired by the ruins of Verulamium in 1627 see J. Evans, *op. cit.*, p. 19.

[12] The plate of which this is part was contributed by John Twistleton of Rawcliffe 'Least that time, which has now near demolished, should utterly eradicate and destroy all traces of this once magnificent Monastery.'

[13] The two travellers 'took shipping' on 1 December 1579; Lyly's work was published in 1580. John Lyly, *Euphues: The Anatomy of Wit; Euphues & his England*, ed. Morris William Croll and Harry Clemons, London 1916, pp. 205, 232; G. K. Hunter, *John Lyly: The Humanist as Courtier*, p. 37. Memory of the

shrine of Thomas Becket (Pl. 26),[14] English Mecca for centuries of pilgrims, whose destruction in 1538 had so greatly shocked Catholic Europe, evidently continued to be a wonder-worker even in the telling, forty years after its jewels and ornaments had been carted off for Henry VIII's enrichment.[15]

The losses of the 1530's passed into common parlance. 'It is a common speech amongst the people, and much used,' said Latimer in a sermon of 1552, 'that they say, "All religious houses are pulled down."' [16] The wanton destructiveness of Henry VIII's actions exposed him to Protestant as well as Catholic reproaches. Indeed the monasteries, for some, came to belong to a blurred and gilded vision of the vanished past. 'Many do lament the pulling downe of abbayes,' wrote Francis Trigge, a Lincolnshire cleric, in 1589. 'They say it was never merie world since.'[17] Another Anglican clergyman, who belonged to this school of thought, in the later years of Elizabeth's reign set down in no uncertain terms his views of the fall of the religious houses. This Yorkshireman, Michael Sherbrook, romantically idealized the condition of the monasteries, but it is not hard to find others, unimpeachably Protestant, who regretted as profoundly as he did the damaging effects of the Dissolution. In 1640 the royalist John Denham was inspired into an angry poetical parenthesis by the sight of a hill which until the Dissolution had

---

celebrated shrines and pilgrimage centres continued long after the Reformation, both in the recollections of people who had had direct knowledge of them and also in Protestant teaching against them. Lyly himself had reason to know about Canterbury as he was brought up there. The *Catechism* of 1548, admonishing children against the superstition and idolatry of the images at Walsingham, Ipswich, Canterbury and Buxton, told them that 'your owne fathers, yf you aske theym' could declare these abuses from their own experience. Twenty years later William Lambarde was still drawing on the memories of 'many of the aged' to record the frauds and impostures at the roods of Chatham and Boxley, and this oral tradition carried over into the 17th century, by means of print, and further direct inquiry. *A Short Instruction into Christian Religion*, ed. E. Burton, Oxford 1829, p. 23; William Lambarde, *A perambulation of Kent*, London 1576, pp. 181–2, 286–7; Weever, *op. cit.*, pp. 343–4 (repeating Lambarde). Cf. below p. 332 on John Aubrey's questions about roods, and p. 329 for Lambarde's remarks, contemporaneous with Lyly's, on the decay of Canterbury.

[14] John Stow's description of the shrine in his *Annales*, 1592, p. 972, corresponds with this depiction; 'This shrine was builded about a mans height, all of stone, then upwarde of tymber plain, within the which was a chest of

yron, conteining the bones.'

[15] Henry's destruction of Becket's shrine played an important part in expediting the papal bull of excommunication which had been threatening him since 1533. In 1535 Paul III had renewed the sentence of 1533, but the first bull to be (at least partially) published was that of 17 December 1538 which specifically mentioned the desecration of Becket's remains and the spoliation of St. Augustine's, Canterbury. D. Wilkins, *Concilia Magnae Britanniae et Hiberniae*, iii, London 1737, pp. 792–7, 840–1; *Letters and Papers of the Reign of Henry VIII*, ed. J. S. Brewer and J. Gairdner, 1862–1910 (hereafter referred to as *Letters and Papers*), XIII, ii, no. 1087, p. 459; J. J. Scarisbrick, *Henry VIII*, London 1968, pp. 318, 320, 334; cf. H. Maynard Smith, *Henry VIII and the Reformation*, London 1948, pp. 151–2; Edward Lord Herbert of Cherbury, *The Life and Raigne of King Henry the Eighth*, London 1649, pp. 437–8.

[16] *The Works of Hugh Latimer*, ed. G. E. Corrie (Parker Society), i, Cambridge 1844–1845, p. 391.

[17] Quoted in *Tudor Treatises*, ed. A. G. Dickens (Yorkshire Archaeological Society, Record Series), cxxv, 1959, p. 38. Sherbrook's authorship of the work on 'The Fall of Religious Houses', written *c.* 1567–91, is established here 'with something like certainty', pp. 28 *et seq.*

been crowned by a chapel. He interrupted his windy topographical outpourings with a diatribe against Henrician ruthlessness.

> Tell me (my Muse) what monstrous dire Offence,
> What crime could any Christian incense
> To such a rage? was't Luxury? or lust?
> Was he so temperate, so chast, so just?[18]

Denham outspokenly deplored the king's actions, wishing (as others wished)
that monastic lethargy could have been cured by some other less drastic
method. The sight of the ruin filled him with a mixture of anger, shame,
and fear—anger for the despoiling, shame over the motivation, fear of future
sacrilege.

> Who sees these dismall heaps, but would demand,
> What barbarous Invader sackt the land?
> But when he heares, no Goth, no Turk did bring
> This desolation, but a Christian King;
> When nothing, but the Name of Zeale, appeares
> 'Twixt our best actions and the worst of theirs,
> What does he think our Sacriledge would spare,
> When such th'effects of our devotions are?[19]

The prejudice against monkery, as part of banished popery, was indeed deep-
seated, but not universal. The way in which it had been eradicated meant
that already in the seventeenth century a number of individuals were coming
to think, as did Browne Willis in the early eighteenth, that 'the pulling down
and desecrating' of religious buildings was 'the chief Blemish of the Reformation'.[20] Even in Elizabeth's reign Sampson Erdeswicke wrote almost ap-
provingly, in his survey of Staffordshire, of the monks' solicitude for their
founders and benefactors.[21] Antiquarian enthusiasm produced, in fact, some
strong defences of monastic institutions, whether it was merely to point out,
as John Weever did, the piety of monastic founders, or to argue like Browne
Willis and others before him, that monastic buildings could well have been
saved and turned to parochial or other non-cenobitic purposes. 'There are
not extant,' wrote Weever, 'any other more conspicuous and certaine Monuments of [our Ancestours'] zealous devotion towards God, than these Monasteries with their endowments, for the maintenance of religious persons', and
although they were done away with because of 'their owne abominable
crying sinnes', Henry VIII's action had been motivated by a 'greedie desire
to enrich his coffers' and had brought in its train a lamentable wave of
destruction.[22] 'And indeed,' wrote Francis Godwin, 'even they who confesse

---

[18] John Denham, *Coopers Hill. Written in
the yeare 1640. Now printed from a perfect Copy;
And a Corrected Impression*, London 1655, p. 7.
The address to the reader says that there had
been five previous impressions of the poem,
but that this one was the only true copy.
According to the *D.N.B. s.v.* Denham,
John, the 1655 edition was the final form of
the poem. It is quoted by Browne Willis,
An History of the Mitred Parliamentary Abbies and

Conventual Cathedral Churches, i, London 1718–
1719, p. 2, and also by Thomas Southouse,
Monasticon Favershamiense in Agro Cantiano,
London 1671, p. 130.

[19] John Denham, *op. cit.*, p. 8.

[20] Browne Willis, *loc. cit.*

[21] May McKisack, *Medieval History in the
Tudor Age*, Oxford 1971, pp. 137–8.

[22] Weever, *op. cit.*, sig. A 1ʳ, pp. 104, 115.

the rowsing of so many unprofitable Epicures out of their dennes, and the abolishing of Superstition, wherewith the Divine Worship had by them beene polluted, to have beene an act of singular Justice and Piety; do notwith-standing complaine of the losse of so many stately Churches dedicated to Gods service.' God was said to have been offended alike by Henry VIII and Thomas Cromwell for subverting so many religious houses.[23]

New zeal, new desolation, new nostalgia: where Henry VIII led others followed. The wrecking of the monasteries was but a beginning, and by the middle of the seventeenth century pietistic sackings of various kinds had piled up the causes for regret. The dangers of iconoclastic enthusiasm had been made all too evident and it became possible to grieve not only for the ravaging of monastic buildings, but for the departure of the very institution itself. 'I wished monastrys had not been putt downe,' wrote John Aubrey, 'that the reformers would have been more moderate as to that point. Nay, the Turkes have monasteries. Why should our reformers be so severe?' They would, he thought, have been such convenient resting-places on journeys about the countryside. 'It was fitt that there should be receptacles and provision for contemplative men, and what a pleasure 'twould have been to have travelled from monastery to monastery.'[24] Monasteries, indeed, for some dedicated seventeenth-century antiquaries took on something of the air of vanished convivial inns, conveniently disposed for the refreshment of cultivated travellers.

As time went on it became possible to envisage a new kind of monasticism, which meant retirement without Rome. And changes of religion, together with a change of dynasty, loosened the tongues of critics of the Tudors. Henry Spelman spent twenty years collecting material for his *History and Fate of Sacrilege*, though it was not published until 1698, more than fifty years after his death. His views on the 'ocean of iniquity and sacrilege' which flowed from Henry VIII's 'insatiable avarice' and 'tempest of indignation against the clergy' were more than denunciatory—they expounded English history in terms of prophetic doom. The loss of the monasteries on this reading was enough to damn not only the Tudor line, but half the gentry of England. The land was cursed in the ruin of sacrilegious families, who were punished by disaster or misfortune as the result of their taking over consecrated pro-perty. The king had sacked and razed the monasteries like an enemy action; desolation followed dissolution; 'the axe and the mattock ruined almost all the chief and most magnificent ornaments of the kingdom', and virtually nothing was done—despite laudable suggestions—to retain some of the abbeys for pious charitable purposes. James I, on the other hand, would have acted differently. Had he found monastic buildings standing, reported Spelman, he would have kept them, 'not meaning to continue them in their superstitious

[23] Francis Godwin, *Annales of England*, London 1630, p. 175.

[24] '*Brief Lives*' *chiefly of Contemporaries, set down by John Aubrey, between the years 1669 & 1696*, ed. A. Clark, i, Oxford 1898, p. 41; H. B. Walters, *The English Antiquaries of the sixteenth, seventeenth and eighteenth centuries*, London 1934, p. 20; cf. Aubrey, *Wiltshire*, p. 9. Aubrey's monastic longings had some basis of reality for in 1671, at a critical moment of his life, he considered withdrawing to a monastic house on the Continent. Anthony Powell, *John Aubrey and his Friends*, London 1963, pp. 137–8, 140–2, cf. 156.

25a   West view of the ruins of St. Mary's Abbey, York, from Francis
Drake's *Eboracum* (London, 1736). (p. 315)

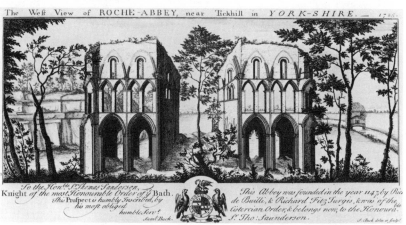

25b   Transepts of Roche Abbey, Yorkshire, 1725. (p. 322)

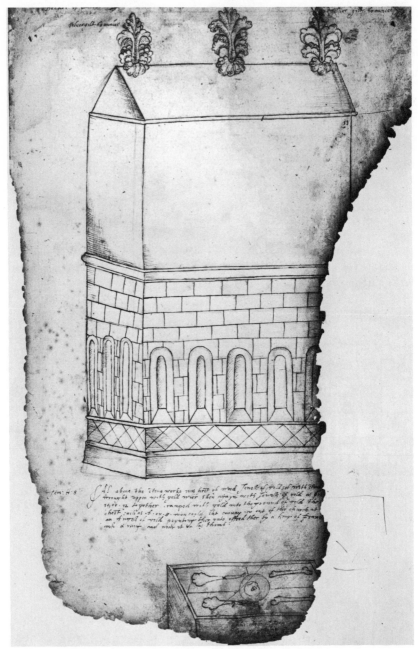

26   Antiquary's drawing of the shrine of Thomas Becket at Canterbury, showing (below) the chest containing his bones. (London, British Museum, MS Cotton Tiberius E viii, fol. 278ᵛ) (p. 316)

27a   Aerial view of Buckland Abbey, Devon. (p. 324)

27b   Aerial view of Fountains Abbey, Yorkshire. (p. 324)

28a   East view of Walsingham Priory, Norfolk, 1738. (pp. 322, n. 37, 325)

28b   Malmesbury Abbey, showing the part of the nave licensed for parochial use in 1541, and remains of the central tower of which the spire fell about that date. (p. 326)

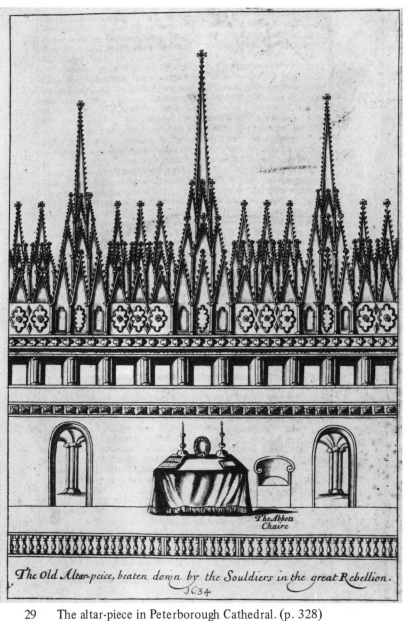

The Old Altar-peice, beaten down by the Souldiers in the great Rebellion.
1634

The Abbots
Chaire

29   The altar-piece in Peterborough Cathedral. (p. 328)

Loe here's mine Effigie, and Turkish suite;
My Staffe, my Shasse, as I did Asia foote:
Plac'd in old Ilium; Priams Scepter thralles:
The Grecian Campe design'd; lost Dardan falles
Gird'd with small Simois: Idaes tops, a Gate;
Two fatall Tombes, an Eagle, sackt Troyes State.

30   William Lithgow (1582-1645?), depicted in Turkish garb, standing
in the ruins of Troy. (p. 332)

Prospectus Ruinarum Abbatiæ de OSNEY, juxta Oxon:

31   Ruins of Osney Abbey, Oxford. (p. 332)

32a   Anthony Wood's drawing of Eynsham Abbey ruins near Oxford.
(p. 334)

32b   Detail of title-page, engraved by Hollar, to Roger Dodsworth and
William Dugdale, *Monasticon Anglicanum* (1655-73), vol. i. (p. 334)

uses, but to employ them, as Korah's censers, to some godly purposes'.[25]

In the later years of the seventeenth century two Scottish Protestant churchmen were lamenting the disappearance of monastic institutions from the Reformed Church, and advocating the usefulness of monasteries as places of spiritual retreat and culture. Robert Leighton, Archbishop of Glasgow (1611—84), 'a monastic man' who was sympathetically disposed towards Jansenism, thought (according to his friend Gilbert Burnet) that

> the great and fatal error of the Reformation was, that more of those houses, and of that course of life, free from the entanglements of vows and other mixtures, was not preserved: so that the Protestant churches had neither places of education, nor retreat for men of mortified tempers.[26]

Similar views were expressed in *The Reformed Bishop*, a work of the Scottish parson, James Gordon, which appeared in 1679 as the work of 'a Well-wisher' to the present government of the Church of Scotland. The then Bishop of Edinburgh, however, found highly disturbing its nineteen proposals for transforming the church militant into the church triumphant by restoring the episcopal office more nearly to early church patterns. Among these articles was the recommendation that monasteries should be built as places where Christians could be free to pursue a 'Speculative Life' of virtue; they could be 'Cities of Refuge' for contemplative souls and ladies of noble descent; there was no doubt that they could serve many useful purposes.

> Necessary Reformations [it was concluded] might have repurged Monasteries, as well as the Church, without abolishing of them: and they might have been still Houses of Religion, without having any dependence upon Rome.[27]

By this time, with the examples of Port Royal and Little Gidding, monasteries and religious retreats did not have to be thought of so automatically as shrines of papal abuses. But already, long before, anger at monastic outrages had been offset by anger at the ravages of those who eradicated them. To church historians, as to poets, looking back upon the events of the English Reformation, the material losses of that time had the air of a barbarous massacre. Much that was destroyed had been rubbish, perversion, corruption, but the effects were devastating and lamentable—for Europe as well as for England. 'These cruel cormorants, with their barbarous beaks and

[25] Henry Spelman, *The History and Fate of Sacrilege*, ed. C. F. S. Warren, London 1895, pp. 99–101, 104–5; *D.N.B., s.v.* Spelman, Henry. Spelman, whose peculiarly obsessive interests in monastic property (connected with his own lawsuits in Norfolk) have unfortunately been followed by later editors, started this work about 1613. He evidently travelled with his eyes open for monastic ruins; *op. cit.*, p. 158. The argument of this work shows why it remained so long unpublished; Philip Styles, *art. cit.*, pp. 66–68;

Keith Thomas, *Religion and the Decline of Magic*, London 1971, pp. 98–99, 101–3.

[26] D. Butler, *The Life and Letters of Robert Leighton*, London 1903, p. 544; Ruth Clark, *Strangers & Sojourners at Port Royal*, Cambridge 1932, p. 137; *Burnet's History of my own Time*, ed. O. Airy, i, Oxford 1897–1900, pp. 246–7.

[27] [James Gordon], *The Reformed Bishop: or XIX Articles* (Printed for the Author), London 1679, pp. 23, 25–27; Butler, *op. cit.*, p. 109, n. 2.

greedy claws, rent, tore, and tattered these inestimable pieces of antiquity.'[28] What Thomas Fuller felt about the irreparable losses of books others felt about monastic buildings. The Dissolution came to seem a major blot upon England's Protestant conscience. It was already beginning to do so at the very time when the monasteries were being plundered and defaced.

*   *   *

In order to appreciate the intensity of these antiquarian passions, it is necessary to recall the drastic workings of Henry VIII's commissioners. 'I defacyd the churche wyndoes and the sellys of the dorter as I dydd in every place saving in Bedford and Aylisbury wher were few byars,' John London conscientiously reported back to Thomas Cromwell in 1538 about the friaries he had been dissolving. 'I pullyd down no Howse thorowly at noon of the Fryers: butt so defacyd them as they shuld nott lyghtly be made Fryerys agen.'[29] The royal agents received specific instructions for demolition. And the work of destruction, intentionally designed to make it impossible for monastic 'nests' ever to be settled in again, concentrated upon those parts of the buildings which were specially devoted to the communal conventual life. 'Hit may please your good Lordship to understond,' John Freman, another of Cromwell's deputies, wrote to his master in August 1539, 'that the King's Commyssion commaundeth me to pull downe to the grownde all the walls of the Churches, stepulls, cloysters, fraterys, dorters, chapter housys, with all other howsys, savyng them that be necessary for a farmer.'[30] It was not the labour of a day, given the solidity of thick-walled medieval buildings, and the fulfilment of Freman's commission was made more difficult by the fact that it was harvest time and—as he said—a hundred men 'be skant sene in a wekke in sum Howsys'. But the commissioners, as usual tailoring royal commands to fit local circumstances, duly went about their work, and during those years of the later 1530's many monastic buildings were wrecked or dismantled. Many of those who witnessed it must have found it a mournfully memorable sight. For the ending of monastic life in England was accomplished in quite as spectacular a way as that of revolutionary France, and the physical impact of the scenes of directed destruction which accompanied it were certainly equally dramatic. Some of the surviving English records convey almost as graphically as later French descriptions of the ending of great abbeys like Royaumont or Cluny, the scale of what was involved.

In the spring and early summer of 1538 work was in progress at Chertsey Abbey for nearly three months. Besides masons, carpenters, bricklayers and plumbers, sometimes as many as ninety labourers were needed. One wonders how far their wages were covered by the sales of the materials recovered, which

[28] Thomas Fuller, *The Church History of Britain*, ed. J. S. Brewer, iii, Oxford 1845, p. 434. Fuller, whose *Church History* was published in 1655, was referring to the purchasers of monastic buildings.

[29] *Original Letters, Illustrative of English History*, ed. Henry Ellis, III, iii, London 1824–1846, pp. 131–2; *Letters and Papers*, XIII, ii,

no. 719, p. 275; Knowles, *op. cit.*, iii, p. 363.

[30] *Original Letters*, III, iii, pp. 268–9; *Letters and Papers*, xi, no. 242, p. 105. This letter was calendared under the year 1536, but Professor Knowles, *op, cit.*, iii, p. 384, n. 3, pointed out that the year is clearly 1539. Cf. G. H. Cook, *Letters to Cromwell and others on the Suppression of the Monasteries*, London 1965, pp. 181–2.

included the stones and pinnacles of the steeple, carefully dismantled and preserved with the aid of baskets and straw.[31] A full account of these drastic and melancholy proceedings survives for Lewes Priory. This house was granted to the son of the king's vicar-general, Gregory Cromwell, who moved into the prior's house and reported to paternal headquarters that his wife found it 'so comodious that she thinketh hir self to be here right well settylled.'[32] The church of Lewes Priory was of massive proportions, requiring careful planning of the demolition by Giovanni Portinàri, who sent Cromwell bulletins on its progress, giving the exact measurements of the building with its thirty-two pillars, eight of which ('verry bygge') were fourteen feet thick and forty-five in circumference, and the others ten feet thick and twenty-five in circumference. The works began to the right of the high altar, with the destruction of its vaults and surrounding chapels. For this purpose the foundations were undermined, props put in and then fired, with results which were successful in the third week of March 1538.[33] In the case of Stanley Abbey in Wiltshire (which was so thoroughly despoiled by its new owner that there was hardly anything left to see by the time that John Aubrey wrote about it around 1665) excavations carried out early this century revealed that here, too, part of the church had been pulled down in similar fashion by mining operations and props, apparently killing one of the workmen in the process.[34] It was not labour for the unskilled, and Portinari took down to Lewes from London seventeen men (including carpenters, smiths, plumbers and a furnace man) who were deemed more experienced than local labour—and possibly also less likely to be inhibited by any local sympathies for an old familiar building. Even those (and they included all sorts) who hoped to profit from the distribution of monastic goods might well have had qualms about assisting in the thunderous ruin of a church in or near which they and perhaps their forebears had been accustomed to worship.

Yet the scrabble for spoils accounted for a great deal. It was not only the well-placed—whose interest in monastic lands has received so much attention —who profited. This ecclesiastical dismemberment put a whole mass of different materials on the market (timber, glass, furniture, lead, household goods of all descriptions) and local buyers and filchers of every kind clearly had their ears and eyes open. Richard Layton may well have been exaggerating a little (to emphasize his own forethought) when he described how a fire broke out on his visitation of Christ Church, Canterbury, and he had set a watch and 'bandoggs' to keep care of the rich shrine of St. Thomas, on the grounds that 'If I hade not taken that order for spoile within the Churche, ther wolde have bene harme done'.[35] And as it was, he wrote, poor people took advantage of the circumstances to make off with the bedding which had

[31] *Letters and Papers*, XIII, i, no. 1238, p. 457. According to Fuller (*op. cit.*, iii, pp. 361–2) at the pulling down of Holy Trinity Priory in London, Sir Thomas Audley 'was fain to be at more charges than he could make of the materials'.

[32] *Original Letters*, III, iii, p. 193; *Letters and Papers*, XIII, i, no. 734, p. 277;

[33] *Three Chapters of Letters relating to the Sup-* pression of the Monasteries, ed. Thomas Wright (Camden Society), xxvi, 1843, pp. 180–2; Cook, *op. cit.*, pp. 138–40; Knowles, *op. cit.*, iii, p. 384.

[34] Harold Brakspear, 'The Cistercian Abbey of Stanley, Wiltshire', *Archaeologia*, Second Series, X, ii, 1907, pp. 495, 500–2.

[35] *Original Letters*, III, iii, p. 165; *Letters and Papers*, ix, no. 669, p. 226.

been thrown into the cloister. There must have been a large amount of unrecorded pilfering and fiddling, and it may be assumed that a goodly proportion of monastic property found its way into the households of those who, without necessarily being motivated in any particular direction towards the religious, were watchful for such opportunities.

> The power [poor] people thorowly in every place be so gredy upon thees Howsys [of friars] when they be suppressyd that by night and daye, nott oonly of the townys, butt also of the contrye, they do contynually resortt as long as any dore, wyndoo, yren, or glasse, or lowse [loose] ledde remaynythe in any of them.[36]

What John London experienced in Warwick was not peculiar to that place. It was a 'universal greediness'—most human and comprehensible. And so, thirty years after he had bought up part of the timbers of the dissolved Cistercian abbey of Roche in Yorkshire (Pl. 25b),[37] a father found himself being examined by his clerical son. How was it, questioned this filial conscience, that you, thinking well of the religious, could have participated in their spoliation? 'What should I do, said He: might I not as well as others have some Profit of the Spoil of the Abbey? For I did see all would away; and therefore I did as others did'[38]—he got what he could.

The fate of Roche was typical of many houses. The church (as we learn from the story of this saddened son) was the first part of the buildings to suffer. Then followed the abbot's lodging, the dorter and frater and cloister and neighbouring buildings inside the abbey walls. The writer's uncle, being then a young unmarried man, and not having any immediate use for household utensils, refused the offer to buy a monk's cell door for 2d. Others, however, were less restrained. 'Such Persons as afterward bought their Corn or Hay or such like, found all the doors either open or the Locks and Shackles plucked away, or the Door itself taken away, went in and took what they found, filched it away.' Local cormorants lent helping hands to the work of the central agents. 'Nothing was spared but the Ox-houses and swinecoates and such other Houses of Office, that stood without the Walls; which had more Favour shewed them than the very Church itself.'[39] Events at Roche followed the usual pattern.

What we know of the labours at Lewes and elsewhere makes it most unlikely that in general, as Fuller put it, church building was 'a cripple in going up, but rides post in coming down'.[40] There might, indeed, be cases—specially, perhaps, after rain and frost and pillagers had followed up the first decisive steps—where a day's determined effort could do a great deal. The remains of Repton Priory in Derbyshire, which was Fuller's example, were apparently pulled down one Sunday in Mary's reign by Gilbert Thacker

[36] *Original Letters*, III, iii, p. 139; *Letters and Papers*, XIII, ii, no. 757, p. 294; Knowles, *op. cit.*, iii, p. 363.

[37] From S. and N. Buck, *A Collection of Engravings of Castles, Abbeys, and Towns in England and Wales*, [London] 1726–52, vol. i. (Pl. 28a is from vol. ii.) Michael Sherbrook records that at the Suppression his father bought all the timber in the steeple including the bell frame.

[38] *Tudor Treatises*, p. 125, from the work by Sherbrook referred to in n. 17 above; Dickinson, *op. cit.*, pp. 133–4.

[39] *Tudor Treatises*, pp. 123–4.

[40] Fuller, *op. cit.*, iii, p. 486.

(son of Thomas Cromwell's zealous steward, Thomas Thacker), who was fearful of the Queen's plans of monastic restoration and said 'he would destroy the nest, for fear the birds should build therein again'.[41] In general, though, the very expense of the demolition procedures imposed some limits upon hopes of razing all conventual buildings to the ground—and there were reportedly still enthusiasts who had ideas about carrying on the work in the days of James I.[42] Henry VIII's servants realized the limits to envisageable destruction. As John Freman told Cromwell about the substantial houses of Lincolnshire, 'I sertefy your Lordship that yt will be chargabull to the Kynge, the doune pullyng of them, if I sholde folow the Commyssion, by the Leste M^{li} [£1,000] within the shere.' What he recommended, therefore, was the removal of the bells and lead, the sale of which would realize a large sum, 'and this donne, to poull downe the rovys, batilments, and stayres, and lete the wallis stonde, and charge som with them as a quarre of ston to make salys of, as they that hathe nede will fetche'.[43] The number of extant monastic ruins owes something to the obvious soundness of this argument, as well as to the staunchness of medieval buildings.

There certainly were sites of religious houses which were left with little to show. This may have been decided in some cases by the poor state of the buildings before the appearance of the royal vandals. 'I have sold in some ffrire (friary) houses all the buyldynges,' one agent reported, having acted thereby contrary to his instructions, which directed the sale of 'housyng' only from churches, cloisters and dorters. 'The cause was for that they werre so spoyled and torne by suche as solde the goodes, that in manner they werre downe,' and had they not been sold the king would have gained nothing at all.[44] In many cases, however, roofless walls were left standing after the more valuable materials had been dismantled and removed. As the reports of the commissioners make clear, after the jewels and plate (gold and silver chalices, the rich ornaments of the various pilgrimage shrines) it was the lead of bells

---

[41] *Ibid.*; *V.C.H. Derbyshire*, ii, p. 62. Scornful references to religious houses as monastic 'nests' appear elsewhere in the 16th century. Lambarde (*op. cit.*, p. 166) describing the first appearance of the Carmelites in England says that they 'made their nest at Newendene', and the Scottish iconoclasts are reported to have shouted 'Pull down the nests and the rooks will depart' at their destruction of monasteries; Frederick Ross, *The Ruined Abbeys of Britain*, i, London [1882], p. 64.

[42] In the historical preface to his elegy on Netley Abbey, George Keate related that a Puritan in the reign of James I 'is said to have defaced many of its [the abbey's] ornaments, and to have intended the demolition of the whole' but was killed by a fall of masonry while giving orders to his workmen. *The Poetical Works of George Keate*, London 1781, p. 175, cf. 187–8. Another case of post-Henrician destruction is quoted by Dugdale, who records that Adrian Stokes, holding the lordship of Astley, Warwicks., as part of the dowry of his wife, Frances, Dowager Duchess of Suffolk, pulled down the walls of the collegiate church of Astley, and also the spire, which was such a landmark that it was known as the 'Lanthorn of Arden'; as the result of which the tower and much of the church collapsed in 1600; William Dugdale, *The Antiquities of Warwickshire*, London 1656, p. 75; *V.C.H. Warwicks.*, vi, p. 18.

[43] *Original Letters*, III, iii, pp. 268–9. This is the same letter quoted above p. 320.

[44] *Three Chapters of Letters*, pp. 281–2. Government policy, as the Rev. J. C. Dickinson points out (*op. cit.*, pp. 138–9) was clearly divided between the dual aims of making the monasteries uninhabitable for conventual purposes, yet sufficiently desirable to attract new lay owners. The retention of an 'honest continual house' was specifically ordered in the act dissolving the smaller houses in 1536.

and roofs which was considered the most desirable perquisite of the monastic buildings, and which was everywhere carefully reserved to the king's use. In some places we can see the attention which was given to preserving the lead of the roofs when the buildings were to be pulled down. 'I have taken down all the leade of Jarvaxe and maid it in pecys of half foders,' Richard Bellasis wrote to Cromwell on 14 November 1537, explaining at the same time that it could not be carted away until the following summer 'for the ways in that cowntre are so foule and deape that no caryage can passe in wyntre'—a delay which in this case cost the king his profits, for the lead of Jervaulx was still lying by the west wall, in the pigs into which it had been cast, in 1923, when it was discovered and used for re-leading the windows in York Minster. On account of the shortness of autumn days Richard Bellasis was also disposed to postpone till the spring the pulling down of the house—which work would itself be promoted by the winter weather, once the roof was gone.[45] The stripped carcases of the conventual establishments must sometimes have been a bare investment to the new owners, for whom the subsidiary domestic buildings may often have been the best part of the buy, though they might be able to carve new houses for themselves out of monastic stones.

> And all that Neighbour-Ruine shows
> The Quarries whence this dwelling rose.

Andrew Marvell's lines on the Fairfax house of Nun Appleton Hall in Yorkshire could well have been applied elsewhere[46] (Pl. 27 a,[47] b[48]).

The fate of the monastic buildings was indeed far from uniform, but it was surely decisive. Zealous or self-interested individuals continued to hack and quarry religious walls for many years to come, but Thomas Cromwell and Henry VIII had seen to it that these were only supplementary efforts. For those who lived through these years, part of the shock of the Dissolution must have derived from seeing this process of sudden ruination, a spectacle of physical desolation which lasted longer and must have been quite as impressive as the accompanying human upheaval. It may well have been more so. The dispossessed religious, despite the rupture and hardships which dislocated their lives, took their pensions and capacities and went their various ways, to be absorbed into the rest of society. The sites which they had inhabited, on the other hand, remained—mutilated, dismembered, or converted—as constant reminders of the corporate life which had been so abruptly terminated. 'The ruins of many churches, with the monasteries which formerly belonged to friars and nuns, greatly disfigure the city,' wrote the Venetian ambassador in 1554, contrasting these blemishes with London's otherwise beautiful riverside view.[49] Though ruined or unkempt buildings

---

[45] *Three Chapters of Letters*, pp. 164–5; Cook, *op. cit.*, pp. 136–7.

[46] *The Poems & Letters of Andrew Marvell*, ed. H. M. Margoliouth, i, Oxford 1963, pp. 61, 230–1.

[47] The church at Buckland, the only part of the monastic complex to remain, was turned into a house in Elizabeth's reign by Sir Richard Grenville, who ingeniously converted

to secular use nave, chancel and central tower.

[48] Fountains Hall, an early 17th-century mansion (which lies to the west, outside the plate) was built largely of monastic materials taken from the south-east of the site.

[49] *Relazioni degli Ambasciatori Veneti al Senato*, ed. E. Albèri, ser. i, vol. iii, Florence 1853, pl 51; cf. *Calendar of State Papers, Venetian*, ed. Rawdon Brown, vol. v, London 1873, p. 543.

were no doubt more familiar to sixteenth-century eyes than they are to ours, these were ruins of a new kind: great ruins of great buildings—deliberately created. Like the gashes in an urban landscape continuing long after the Second World War, they remained to cauterize on another generation's consciousness the scars of earlier destruction.

*   *   *

> Bitter, bitter oh to behould the grasse to growe,
> Where the walls of Walsingam so stately did shew.
> Such were the works of Walsingam while shee did stand,
> Such are the wrackes as now do shewe of that holy land.
> Levell levell with the ground the towres doe lye,
> Which with their golden, glitteringe tops pearsed once to the skye.[50] (Pl. 28a)

Passionate feelings of regret such as this could still be extremely intense two generations after the Dissolution. The pilgrimage centres and reliquaries of pre-Reformation England remained enshrined in literary consciousness— Protestant as well as Catholic—many years after their contents had been swept into the chests and wagons of Henry VIII's officials. Mourning for the passing of the old religion, different in kind from the mourning of historians—yet in some ways overlapping with that sentiment—also focused poignantly on the 'wracks' which the Reformation had left behind.

> It would have made an Heart of Flint to have melted and weeped to have seen the breaking up of the House, and their sorrowfull departing; and the sudden spoil that fell the same day of their departing from the House.[51]

The Elizabethan clergyman who wrote so feelingly in the late sixteenth century about the dissolution of Roche Abbey, was only a child of four at the time of that event. He was deeply conscious of living in the aftermath of iconoclastic revolution, in daily contact with its resultant decay. In Rotherham, where he went to school, there still stood the building of Rotherham College which, he wrote, 'is a fair House yet standing; but God knoweth how long it shall stand; for certain Brick Chimneys and other Brick Walls (for it is all made of Brick) is decayed and fallen down for lack of Use.' And Rotherham, a small chantry college, founded in 1483 by the Archbishop of York and dissolved in 1547, had fared better than the abbey of Roche and a great many other foundations. He relived those moments of dissolution with anguish. 'It would have pitied any Heart to see what tearing up of the Lead there was, and plucking up of Boards, and throwing down of the Sparres; and when the Lead was torn off and cast down into the Church, and the Tombs in the Church all broken . . . and all things of Price, either spoiled, carted away or defaced to the uttermost.'[52]

[50] J. C. Dickinson, *The Shrine of Our Lady of Walsingham*, Cambridge 1956, p. 67; *Bishop Percy's Folio Manuscript. Ballads and Romances*, ed. John W. Hales and Frederick J. Furnivall, iii, London 1867–68, pp. 471–2. The 'she' in these lines refers to the Virgin 'Queen of Walsingham'. A suggested author for this Catholic poem is Philip, Earl of Arundel (1557–95) who became a Catholic in 1584 and spent the last ten years of his life in the Tower.

[51] *Tudor Treatises*, p. 123; Knowles, *op. cit.*, iii, p. 402, n. 1.

[52] *Tudor Treatises*, pp. 124, 126. Sherbrook says that he himself saw the bells of Roche

By some of those who saw them go, or who strenuously resisted their going, the religious houses were appreciated for their looks, as well as their functions. The monasteries, pleaded Robert Aske, putting up the case for them on behalf of the rebels of the Pilgrimage of Grace in 1536, were 'one of the beauties of this realm to all men and strangers passing through the same'.[53] Nor was such appreciation limited to those of Catholic sympathy. The glories of sometime monastic buildings were being extolled long before the fashions of romantic travellers—and by men of sound Protestant conviction. John Leland, whose itinerary through England and Wales in the 1530's and 1540's was undertaken for reasons quite other than aesthetic, was clearly alive, as he shows from hints in various places, to the beauty of monastic churches. At Malmesbury (Pl. 28b) the spire had collapsed before Leland's visit[54] and the remains of the abbey church had been made parochial, thanks to the mediations of 'one Stumpe', a rich clothier who had filled up all the domestic offices with his weaving gear. 'Thabbey chirch,' noted Leland, 'a right magnificent thing.' And of Neath in Glamorgan he wrote that 'It semid to me the fairest abbay of al Wales.'[55]

Individual distress over the processes of destruction turned to activity—to some almost hectic efforts of salvage and reconstruction. In the first instance, for those with literary sensibilities, the greatest loss of the Dissolution seemed to be the loss of books. The destruction of liturgical and other manuscripts was enormous, and itself a goad to antiquarian endeavours. Since the libraries of the religious houses were one of the main depositories of medieval learning a very substantial proportion—now impossible to estimate—of England's bibliographical resources was housed within monastic walls. With the Reformers proudly discarding medieval superstition and banishing the schoolmen from the centres of learning, the efforts which were made to save these works—liturgical, scholastic, patristic—were minimal. One of the vast, irretrievable and long-bewailed losses of the Reformation years was the

hanging in the steeple more than a year after the Suppression; his questions were put to his father thirty years after it. The 1547 Chantries Act made provision for charitable and educational purposes—of which Rotherham was an example—but the chantries, like the monasteries, came in for their share of demolition, which continued through Edward VI's reign. Weever gives examples of this Edwardian razing in the diocese of London, the buildings being replaced in one case by a wine tavern, in another by a garden. G. H. Cook, *Mediaeval Chantries and Chantry Chapels*, London 1947, pp. 44–45, 60, 116, 167; Joan Simon, *Education and Society in Tudor England*, Cambridge 1966, pp. 37, n. 3, 238; Weever, *op. cit.*, pp. 378–9, 390–1.

[53] *Letters and Papers*, XII, i, no. 901, pp. 405–6. A 15th-century traveller who recorded his appreciation of English ecclesiastical architecture (in this case a secular cathedral) was Aeneas Silvius Piccolomini

who went to York 'where there is a cathedral notable in the whole world for its size and architecture and for a very brilliant chapel whose glass walls are held together by very slender columns'. *The Commentaries of Pius II*, ed. F. A. Gragg and L. C. Gabel (Smith College Studies in History), Northampton, Mass. 1936–57, book i, pp. 20–21. Cf. James E. Oxley, *The Reformation in Essex to the Death of Mary*, Manchester 1965, p. 48, for Richard Redman's praise of the beauty of Beeleigh Abbey buildings, in 1500.

[54] Another part of the tower was shaken down by the celebrations for the return of Charles II in 1660, according to John Aubrey, who knew the ruins from his youth. Powell, *John Aubrey*, p. 97.

[55] *The Itinerary of John Leland*, ed. Lucy Toulmin Smith, London 1906–10, part ii, pp. 130–2, part vi, p. 51; Aubrey, *Wiltshire*, pp. 255–60; Walters, *op. cit.*, p. 3. The clothier was William Stump.

wanton dispersal of monastic libraries.[56] The pages of many books were undoubtedly used as fire-lighters, or for other more degrading purposes. 'We have sett Dunce in Bocardo, and have utterly banisshede hym Oxforde for ever,' Richard Layton wrote from Oxford with satisfaction in 1535. The discredited schoolman now seemed to have been truly put in his place, 'nowe made a comon servant to evere man, faste nailede up upon postes in all comon howses of easment.'[57] The second time the king's commissioners came to New College they found the quadrangle full of blown leaves of Duns Scotus, and a certain Mr. Grenefelde of Buckinghamshire 'getheryng up part of the saide bowke leiffes (as he saide) therwith to make hym sewelles or blawnsherres [i.e. scarecrows, scaring-sheets] to kepe the dere within the woode, therby to have the better cry with his howndes'.[58] Such happenings were heartbreaking to historians. Books were reduced to the value of waste paper—or waste parchment—and the uses it could be put to were manifold. The service books of Roche Abbey were taken off by the local inhabitants to mend their wagons.[59] Others found other uses, as described by John Bale, in his 1549 edition of John Leland's 1546 New Year's Gift to Henry VIII, which his antiquarian friend was unable to publish himself, being by then 'besides his wittes'.[60]

Bale could not find words sufficient to decry the losses of English libraries at the Suppression. It was an infamy which would redound for ever to England's dishonour—even though he was the first to admit that the monasteries themselves were rank with error and superstition.

> To destroye all without consyderacyon, is and wyll be unto Englande for ever, a moste horryble infamy amonge the grave senyours of other nacyons. A great nombre of them whych purchased those superstycyouse mansyons, reserved of those lybrarye bokes, some to serve theyr iakes, some to scoure theyr candelstyckes, & some to rubbe their bootes. Some they solde to the grossers and sope sellers, & some they sent over see to yᵉ bokebynders, not in small nombre, but at tymes whole shyppes full, to the wonderynge of the foren nacyons.[61]

The universities themselves were not free from blame, and Bale knew one merchant who had purchased the contents of two noble libraries for forty shillings and had been using them as wrapping paper for ten years without having exhausted his supply.[62] It was certainly a grievous spectacle—and one which went on being remembered. More than a hundred years later Fuller echoed Bale's cry, expatiating on the 'irreparable loss of learning' at the Dissolution, bewailing the beautiful Bibles, rare fathers, subtle schoolmen, valuable historical and mathematical works, which had all been 'massacred' together. 'But alas! those abbeys were now sold to such chapmen, in whom

---

[56] On this question see C. E. Wright, 'The Dispersal of the Libraries in the Sixteenth Century', *The English Library before 1700*, ed. Francis Wormald and C. E. Wright (University of London, The Athlone Press), 1958, pp. 148–75.

[57] *Letters and Papers*, ix, no. 350, p. 117; *Three Chapters of Letters*, p. 71; *Original Letters*, II, ii,

p. 60.

[58] *Ibid.*

[59] *Tudor Treatises*, p. 124 and n. 1.

[60] John Bale, *The laboryouse Journey & serche of Johan Leylande for Englandes Antiquitees*, London 1549, sig. D viʳ.

[61] *Ibid.*, sig. B iʳ.

[62] *Ibid.*, sig. B iᵛ.

it was questionable whether their ignorance or avarice were greater, and they made havoc and destruction of all.'[63]

This lamentation did not remain confined to words. Bale and Leland turned their horror to action, and their efforts to rescue what they could of monastic libraries gave a new impetus to historical and antiquarian researches. Already in 1533 Leland had been given authority by Henry VIII to search monastic and college libraries for the works of ancient authors.[64] It was thanks largely to Leland that some of the finer books were saved from the general dispersion for the royal library—whence they eventually passed into the British Museum. Bale himself was at work among the manuscripts of the Carmelites before he left that Order to join the ranks of Thomas Cromwell's propagandists. Besides putting Leland's New Year's Gift into print he published—mainly in catalogue form—the results of his own notable researches into medieval English writers—monastic and other.[65] It seemed to Bale, as to others afterwards, that the iniquities of monastic life could in no way excuse the iniquities which accompanied the Suppression.

> Thys is hyghly to be lamented, of all them that hath a naturall love to their contrey, eyther yet to lerned Antiquyty, whyche is a moste synguler bewty to the same. That in turnynge over of ye superstycyouse monasteryes, so lytle respecte was had to theyr lybraryes for the savegarde of those noble & precyouse monumentes . . . this would I have wyshed (and I scarsely utter it wythout teares) that the profytable corne had not so unadvysedly and ungodly peryshed wyth the unprofytable chaffe, nor the wholsome herbes with the unwholsome wedes, I meane the worthy workes of men godly mynded, and lyvelye memoryalles of our nacyon, wyth those laysy lubbers and poppyshe bellygoddes. But dvyerse were the workers of thys desolacyon, lyke as the thynges dyssypated were dyverse.[66]

It was truly a 'wycked age . . . muche geven to the destruccyon of thynges memorable'.[67]

The onslaught which started with monastic walls and idolatrously abused shrines, relics and images of saints, moved on to ecclesiastical sculpture, stained-glass windows, and even the inscriptions and tombs of secular persons erected for purely commemorative purposes. The awareness of ruin came to extend from lost manuscripts and battered walls to mutilated statues, razed altars (Pl. 29),[68] defaced funeral monuments, vanished vestments and chalices. The accumulated evidence of loss left its mark in topographical research, as well

---

[63] Fuller, *op. cit.*, iii, p. 433. Fuller quoted Bale's lament over these losses (pp. 434–5).

[64] The nature of Leland's commission is discussed by Arnaldo Momigliano, 'Ancient History and the Antiquarian', in \ *JWCI*, XIII, 1950, pp. 313–14. For the work of Leland and Bale and the 'unique stimulus to historical research' of the dispersal of monastic libraries see McKisack, *op. cit.*, pp. 1 *et seq.*

[65] Namely his *Illustrium Maioris Britanniae Scriptorum . . . Summarium*, [Wesel] 1548, and *Scriptorum illustrium maioris Brytannie . . . Catalogus*, Basle 1557–59.

[66] Bale, *The laboryouse Journey*, sigs. A vii^v–viii^r.

[67] *Ibid.*, sig. D iii^v.

[68] The eye-witness account appended to Simon Gunton, *The History of the Church of Peterburgh*, London 1686, pp. 333–34, describes how this altar was 'destroy'd by Sacrilegious hands' in 1643. This 'stately Skreen', painted and gilded, 'because it bore the name of the High Altar, was pulled all down with Ropes, lay'd low and level with the ground'.

as repeated lamentation. People began to trace out the sites, as well as search
out the manuscripts, of the ravaged Catholic past. Antiquarian activity held
hazards for the amateur archaeologist, however orthodox his religious position,
when, it was said, 'a broken Statue would almost make him an Idolater'.[69]
Idolatry was dangerous ground after 1547. The amount of print and passion
(as well as action) which many Reformers expended upon it was sufficient to
cut across a number of antiquarian interests. Yet the recollection of vanished
objects of Roman Catholic veneration was not only a way of satisfying curiosity
or nostalgia; it could also be presented as a means of combating superstition, by
recording for posterity exemplary abuses of the religious past.

To the Kent historian William Lambarde (1536–1601), sadly surveying
the state of the city of Canterbury in 1570, it seemed that the Dissolution was
the main cause of the extensive decay he saw around him. He could not but
applaud the cause, yet he sorely deplored the results. Fire and flame had
played their part, but it was the 'finall overthrowe of the Religious houses'
which had done most of all, for these had attracted patronage and riches and
helped the advancement of cities.

> And therfore, no marvaile, if after wealth withdrawn, and opinion of
> holynesse removed, the places tumbled headlong to ruine & decay: In
> whiche part, as I can not on the one side, but in respect of ye places them-
> selves, pitie & lament this general desolation, not only in this Shyre, but
> in all other places of the Realme: So on the other side, considering the
> maine Seas of sinne and iniquitie, wherein the worlde (at those dayes)
> was almost whole drenched, I must needs take cause, highly to prayse
> God, that hath thus mercifully in our age delivered us, disclosed Satan,
> unmasked these Idoles, dissolved there Synagoges, and raced to the
> grounde all Monumentes of building, erected to superstition and un-
> godlynesse: And therefore let every godly man ceasse with me from
> hencefoorth to marvail, why Canterbury, Walsingham, and sundry suche
> like, are nowe in these our dayes become in manner waste, since God in
> times paste was in them blasphemed most.[70]

The sight of such places was wretched, but divine retribution had taken its
course. 'By the iust iudgement of God, therfore, Canterbury came soudenly
from great wealth, multitude of inhabitaunts, and beautiful buildings, to
extreme povertie, nakednes, and decay.'[71] To embark, as Lambarde did,
upon recalling and recording the monuments and antiquities of that happily
departed time of 'Popish illusion' (including the supposed miracles and
mechanical devices of some of the notable Kent images) seemed justifiable as
a means of the 'keping under of fained & superstitious religion', as well as
being itself a pleasurable pursuit. And realization of the sheer number of
religious houses with which popery had been provided in those outmoded

[69] John Earle, *Micro-Cosmographie*, ed.
Edward Arber, London 1869, p. 28.

[70] Lambarde, *op. cit.*, pp. 235–6. The title
of this work says that it was 'Collected and
written (for the most part) in the yeare 1570'.

Francis Godwin in his *Annales of England*,
London 1630, p. 40, likewise linked the decay
of Canterbury with the Dissolution.

[71] Lambarde, *op. cit.*, p. 236.

times was an admonition to the cold charity of contemporary Elizabethans.[72] Living memories of the monasteries could still be called upon. Yet their practices and their buildings were allocated to a past sufficiently far removed to become an exemplar in the resuscitation.

Tudor iconoclastic operations were on a grandiose scale, and the very bulk of what had gone was a deterrent as well as an urgent summons to recorders of antiquities. To have done justice to the many religious houses cast down by the axes of Henrician hewers would, John Speed announced in his *History of Great Britaine* (1611), greatly have interrupted the flow of his narrative of that reign. Yet the destruction of 'so many beautifull Monasteries' which had been borne down in the 'sudden deluge of those tempestuous times, whilst the world stood amazed', was a duty owed both to 'the example of their Founders holy zeale' as to 'venerable Antiquity' itself.[73] He therefore inserted a separate catalogue of the religious houses (provided by Cotton), giving details of their founders, orders and revenues. The work of resurrection was well under way.

The tides of destruction also ebbed as well as flowed. In 1631, when John Weever published his *Ancient Funerall Monuments*, work had begun—thanks to the impetus provided by Laud—on repairing decayed chapels and churches. Weever explained in his preface how he had been inspired to make extended travels with 'painefull expences' over most of England and part of Scotland, collecting inscriptions and recording monuments, because he was so tormented by the scale of contemporary losses.

> Knowing withall how barbarously within these his Maiesties Dominions, they are (to the shame of our time) broken downe, and utterly almost ruinated, their brasen Inscriptions erazed, torne away, and pilfered . . . grieving at this unsufferable iniurie offered as well to the living, as the dead, out of the respect I bore to venerable Antiquity

he had set himself to work. He feared, in fact, such was the extent of contemporary erasing, defacing and abusing of inscriptions and memorials which seemed to smack of popery and idolatry, that 'nothing will be shortly left to continue the memory of the deceased to posteritie'.[74]

Seventeenth-century antiquaries, living as they were in a denuded time, and themselves witnessing still further deprivation, doubtless did not minimize the amount that was lost.[75] Yet their very lack of moderation emphasizes

---

[72] Lambarde, *op. cit.*, pp. 230, 286; Evans, *op. cit.*, pp. 5–6. Lambarde's Protestantism is in no doubt. Yet various historians and antiquarians found it desirable to stress that laments for monastic losses did not imply a condoning of monastic abuses. Cf. below p. 335 note 95 for such disclaimers.

[73] John Speed, *The History of Great Britaine*, London 1611, pp. 778, 786; *The English Library before 1700*, p. 203.

[74] Weever, *op. cit.*, from the Epistle to the Reader, and p. 18.

[75] Consider, for example, the lamentations

over church plate and vestments. There are no church robbers today, said Weever, because there is so little left to rob. 'For what man will venture a turne at the Gallows, for a little small silver chalice, a beaten-out pulpit cushion, an ore-worne Communion-cloth, and a course Surplisse? ther are all the riches and ornaments of the most of our Churches' (*op. cit.*, p. 49). And Fuller: 'foor private men's halls were hung with altar-cloths, their tables and beds covered with copes instead of carpets and coverlets. Many drank at their daily meals in chalices; and no wonder if, in the keenness of their concern for the vanished or vanishing past. Weever, like others, was stirred by the visible evidence of ruin. 'We have,' he wrote, 'many examples here in England of the small continuance (as I may so call it) of magnificent strong buildings, by the sudden fall of our religious houses,' and he went on to quote a poem by 'a late nameless versifier' on this subject.

> What sacred structures did our Elders build,
> Wherein Religion gorgeously sat deckt?
> Now all throwne downe, Religion exild,
> Made Brothell-houses, had in base respect,
>   Or ruind so that to the viewers eye,
>   In their owne ruines they intombed lie:[76]

The writer's verse could hardly do justice to his feelings, but we cannot impugn the latter on that account. And to the antiquarian Weever, striving to recapture the piety as well as to record the monuments of the past, it seemed that ruins and funeral statuary alike had a religious value. Were not the many people who flocked daily to look at the monuments in Westminster Abbey struck with 'religious apprehension' at seeing the stately entombment of such venerable ashes? Could not ancient buildings do the same?

> We desire likewise to behold the mournfull ruines of other religious houses, although their goodly faire structures bee altogether destroyed, their tombs battered downe, and the bodies of their dead cast out of their coffins; for that, that very earth which did sometimes cover the corps of the defunct, puts us in minde of our mortalitie, and consequently brings us to unfained repentance.[77]

Certainly by this time monastic ruins were already attracting visitors— though their motives were no doubt more mixed than this passage would imply. It was probably curiosity, rather than piety, which took crowds from London and elsewhere to inspect the coffins dug up in the remains of Lessness Abbey in Kent, at the time when Weever was writing.[78] Sir John Oglander (1585–1655), on coming into his inheritance in the Isle of Wight, was sufficiently interested in the fate of a great Cistercian abbey to undertake actual excavation.

proportion, it came to the share of their horses to be watered in rich coffins of marble' (*op. cit.*, iv, p. 96).

[76] Weever, *op. cit.*, p. 4.

[77] *Ibid.*, p. 41. Weever here provides an early example of the advocacy of ruins for their contemplative inspiration. As was pointed out by Rose Macaulay, this kind of meditative delight in 'mournful ruins' does not become explicit until the 17th century. Sixteenth-century antiquaries were too obsessed with rage and resentment at loss and decay to be ready to indulge in the pleasures of meditative melancholy, and perhaps the early Elizabethans were too near the actual process of destruction to be able to enjoy ruins like later generations. On the other hand it is clear that this sense of melancholy delight was being expressed well before the middle of the 17th century, and the awareness of ruins, and passionate regrets for the process of ruination, began long before. Macaulay, *op. cit.*, pp. 342, 346–7, 366, 454.

[78] Weever, *op. cit.*, pp. 41, 336–7. Weever had reason to know about this because, as he tells us, he himself for a time held the rectory of Lessness. Linked with such curiosity in monastic remains was the propensity to ascribe a monastic origin to Tudor and Stuart prophecies, several of which were reported to have been unearthed in the ruins of religious houses. Keith Thomas, *Religion and the Decline of Magic*, London 1971, pp. 269, 391.

At my fyrst cominge to inhabit in this Island Anno 1607 I went to Quarr, and inquyred of divors owld men where ye greate church stood. Theyre wase but one, Father Pennie, a verye owld man, coold give me anye satisfaction; he told me he had bene often in ye church whene itt wase standinge, and told me what a goodly church itt wase; and furthor sayd that itt stoode to ye sowthward of all ye ruins, corn then growinge where it stoode. I hired soome to digge to see whethor I myght finde ye fowndation butt cowld not.[79]

Other individuals set off to trace out monastic sites with deliberate historical intent, and it was possible by 1628 to depict the antiquary, a character 'strangely thrifty of Time past', in the guise of one who 'will goe you forty miles to see a Saints Well, or ruin'd Abbey'.[80] A man who had gone thousands of miles further than this in pursuit of antiquity was William Lithgow (Pl. 30),[81] who after extensive travels in the East was this year, 1628, journeying in his native Scotland. He saw the levelled sites of the Scottish religious houses 'which were the greatest beauty of the Kingdome' with the eyes of one who had measured the remains of Troy, and compared what was left of his country's 'admirable Edifices' to 'the Ruines of Troy, Tyrus, and Thebes, lumpes of Wals, and heapes of Stones'.[82] A less ambitious antiquarian tourist was the learned Englishman William Backhouse (1593–1662), of Swallowfield in Berkshire, whose custom was, according to Aubrey, 'once every summer to travel to see Cathedrals, Abbeys, Castles &c'.[83] And John Aubrey (1626–97), who was himself a more celebrated enthusiast of this kind, gives what is perhaps the fullest account of how monastic ruins could stir the antiquarian soul.

'I was inclined by my Genius from my childhood, to the love of antiquities: and my Fate dropt me in a countrey [i.e. county] most suitable for such enquiries'. Aubrey relates in his *Brief Lives* how the direction taken by this 'strong and early impulse to antiquitie' was such that he was 'always enquiring of my grandfather of the old time, the rood-loft, etc., ceremonies, of the priory, etc.'. One of his early achievements was to get a drawing made of Osney Abbey, Oxford, before these remains were demolished during the Civil War, which sketch became incorporated as a plate in Dugdale's *Monasticon* (Pl. 31).[84] Such was Aubrey's lifelong enthusiasm that his eye became sensitively trained in observant appraisal of monastic (and other) sites—even at a distance. 'When a traveller rides along by the ruins of a Monastery: he knows by the manner of building, sc. Chapell, Cloysters, &c., that it was a

---

[79] Stuart Piggott, 'Antiquarian thought in the sixteenth and seventeenth centuries', *English Historical Scholarship*, ed. Levi Fox, p. 105, quoting from the *Oglander Memoirs*.

[80] Earle, *op. cit.*, p. 28.

[81] He visited Troy in 1610 in the course of his nineteen years' travels. Frontispiece to William Lithgow, *The Totall Discourse, Of the Rare Adventures, and painefull Peregrinations of long nineteene Yeares Travayles*, London 1632.

[82] *Ibid.*, p. 500; *The English Library before 1700*, p. 178.

[83] John Aubrey, *Miscellanies upon Various Subjects*, London 1857, p. 127.

[84] Engraved by Hollar for the *Monasticon*, vol. ii, illustration between pp. 136–7, from a drawing contributed by John Aubrey whose arms are shown on the shield. Aubrey was an undergraduate at Trinity College when he had several drawings made of the ruins— his first achievement in practical antiquarianism. The abbey remains were demolished in the Civil War soon afterwards.

Convent, but of what Order, *sc.* Benedictine, Dominican, &c., it was, he cannot tell by the bare view.'[85]

Aubrey only had one book published during his lifetime, and that scarcely of a kind to do justice to his ranging antiquarian inquiries.[86] He was, however, closely associated with a group of men who shared his passionate interests, and between them produced some great works of historical scholarship. And it was he who expressed most clearly the way in which the imaginative contemplation of monastic ruins affected the seventeenth-century antiquary.

> In former daies the Churches and great houses hereabout did so abound with monuments and things remarqueable that it would have deterred an Antiquarie from undertaking it. But as Pythagoras did guesse at the vastnesse of Hercules' stature by the length of his foote, so among these Ruines are Remaynes enough left for a man to give a guesse what noble buildings, &c. were made by the Piety, Charity, and Magnanimity of our Forefathers.
>
> > 'And as in prospects wee are there pleased most,
> > Where something keeps the eie from being lost,
> > And leaves us roome to guesse;'
>
> so here, the eie and mind is no lesse affected with these stately ruines than they would have been when standing and entire. They breed in generous mindes a kind of pittie; and sett the thoughts a-worke to make out their magnificence as they were when in perfection. These Remaynes are 'tanquam tabulata naufragii' (*like fragments of a Shipwreck*) that after the Revolution of so many yeares and governments have escaped the teeth of Time and the hands of mistaken zeale.[87]

'The eye and mind' moved to 'a kind of pity' made more powerful by the very awareness of what was lacking: Aubrey's reaction to those ruins which had escaped the zeal and shipwreck of the Reformation sums up sentiments which had long been breeding and which, in the works of his friends, were given monumental birth. If those who retrieved forgotten things from oblivion

[85] Aubrey, *Wiltshire*, pp. 314, 317; *Brief Lives*, i, pp. 36–39, 51; *Miscellanies*, pp. vii–viii; Powell, *John Aubrey*, pp. 50–51; *D.N.B.*, *s.v.* Aubrey, John; Roger Dodsworth and William Dugdale, *Monasticon Anglicanum*, ii, London 1655–73, illustration between pp. 136–7. Aubrey provides an interesting example of how—despite all the Reformers' destructive and instructive work—human memories as well as physical remains helped to span the gap between pre-Reformation Catholic usages and the first great works of scholarship on the monasteries (cf. note 13 above). A significant result of Aubrey's observations was his *Chronologia Architectonica*, an (unprinted) attempt to establish the chronology of medieval English architecture, based upon detailed studies and drawings of about eighty buildings. H. M. Colvin, 'Aubrey's *Chronologia Architectonica*', in *Concerning Architecture. Essays on Architectural Writers and Writing presented to Nikolaus Pevsner*, ed. John Summerson, London 1968, pp. 1–12.

[86] This was his *Miscellanies*, London 1696, on which see Powell, *John Aubrey*, pp. 291–2. The dedication to this work says that Aubrey's description of Wiltshire was already half finished but on account of his age he had 'devolved' the task of completing it upon Thomas Tanner. The *Topographical Collections of Wiltshire*, though used by Tanner, were not, however, published in full until the nineteenth century.

[87] Aubrey, *Wiltshire*, p. 4. The lines of verse quoted are by Sir John Suckling.

were, as he suggested, like conjurers, raising the dead from their graves to walk, then he moved in a circle of magicians.

John Aubrey's generation produced the first great works of scholarship on monastic history. And he himself, though remaining the heir of Bale and Leland—more of a traveller, collector and compiler than an author—made his contributions to the works of Dodsworth and Dugdale, Thomas Tanner and Anthony Wood. These other more productive antiquaries, the authors of the *Monasticon* and the *Notitia Monastica* and the *History and Antiquities of the University of Oxford*, were also moved by the architectural, as well as the documentary desolation of the past.

> Of the *Religious Houses, Hospitalls* and *Chantries* (those signall Monuments of our Forefathers Pietie) I have shewed their Foundations, endowments, and continuance, with their dissolutions and ruine, which gave the greatest blow to Antiquities that ever *England* had, by the destruction and spoil of so many rare Manuscripts, and no small number of famous Monuments.[88]

It was a 'barbarous generation' which had subverted 'those goodly structures of that kind, wherewith *England* was so much adorned'.[89] The words are Dugdale's in his *Antiquities of Warwickshire*, which appeared in 1656, a year after the first large volume of the *Monasticon Anglicanum* (1655–73), whose title-page,[90] engraved by Wenceslaus Hollar, had already given them pictorial expression (Pl. 32b). There can be seen, depicted in miniature, Henry VIII as destroyer, pointing imperiously with the words 'sic volo' at the shell of a ruined monastery, which did duty for that 'common ruin' that had resulted from the king's 'fatal survey'. On the other side, in the period when kings were still faithful to God and the Church, we see a thoroughly intact church, representing those 'magnificent and costly Structures' by which, as a 1693 epitome of the *Monasticon* explained, 'the greatest Kings, Princes, and Noblemen of this Island were once thought to have eternized their names', though (it was erroneously stated) 'not one remains at this day; nay the very Ruines of many are become invisible'.[91]

Yet the piles that remained themselves surely constituted an argument. Did not Anthony Wood, 'wonderfully stricken' by the venerable remains of the abbey of Eynsham (Pl. 32a) in 1657, find that place able 'to instruct the pensive beholder with an exemplary frailty'?[92] Crumbling monastic walls

[88] Dugdale, *Antiquities of Warwickshire*, Preface, sig. b 3ᵛ. Perhaps obsession with past losses contributed to Dugdale's hasty travels and work on the eve of the Civil War, which he rightly feared would entail more destruction. Simon Gunton, *The History of the Church of Peterburgh*, London 1686, Preface; David C. Douglas, *English Scholars, 1660–1730*, London 1951, p. 34.

[89] Dugdale, *Warwickshire*, p. 492.

[90] Eastlake wrote in his *History of the Gothic Revival*, 1872, referring to the vignettes at the foot of this page, 'It is impossible to mistake the spirit which found vent in these

symbols.' Charles L. Eastlake, *A History of the Gothic Revival*, ed. J. Mordaunt Crook, Leicester 1970, p. 8.

[91] K. Clark, *op. cit.*, pp. 25–26 (referring to the title-page of the 1682 edition of the *Monasticon*); Dugdale, *Antiquities of Warwickshire*, pp. 134, 492, 500; William Dugdale, *Monasticon Anglicanum, or the History of the Ancient Abbies, and other Monasteries*, Epitomized, London 1693, sig. A 2ᵛ.

[92] *The Life and Times of Anthony Wood, antiquary, of Oxford, 1632–1695, described by Himself*, ed. A. Clark (Oxford Historical Society), i, 1891–1900, pp. 228–9, and pl. iii

could act as a stimulus to research—especially after the appearance of the *Monasticon*.

> Having lived so many years within the verge and precincts of so remarkable an Abbey as this once was, & observing with how ruinous and maimed an aspect it now beholds us, expecting it every day to sink under the heavy pressure of its own weight, and lie entombed in the rubbage of its ruines amongst the rest of its no less comely parts, and the history thereof be quite forgotten, I thought my self in duty bound . . . to rescue from the teeth of all devouring time and oblivion some memorials concerning the primitive state & condition thereof.[93]

Thus did Thomas Southouse explain to his readers the motivation of his *Monasticon Favershamiense*, a historical survey of the abbey of Faversham, which was published in 1671. And Thomas Tanner, whose *Notitia Monastica* of 1695 was intended to supplement as well as epitomize Dodsworth and Dugdale's monumental work, invoked monastic ruins to his aid to combat the virulence of Protestant prejudice. 'From the Popular Clamours, that have been raised and carried on against the Old Monks ever since the Reformation, it is easie to foresee what cold reception a Book of this nature must meet with,' he wrote in his dedicatory epistle to the Warden of All Souls'.[94] Delvers into the monastic past were indeed, in the hostile climate of Anglican opinion, all too liable to be construed as papal sympathizers—as John Stow and Anthony Wood both discovered.[95] But the grandeur of surviving monastic architecture, itself so provocative of questioning interest, seemed to offer a way of circumventing this prejudice.

> So that [wrote Tanner] to satisfie the curiosity of those who are willing to know, when, by whom, and for whom these Religious Houses were Founded, (the Majesty of whose very ruines strike Travellers with Admiration:) To preserve some remembrance of these Structures, once the Glory

(here Pl. 32a), cf. pp. 241, 344-6; B.M. MS Harl. 5409, fols. 48ᵛ-49ʳ. Wood, who describes the 'two high towers at the west end of the church' and the walls still standing on the north, lived to see these 'much lamented ruins' which he had sketched with 'melancholy delight' also pulled down.

[93] Southouse, *op. cit.*, sigs. a4ʳ-a5ʳ, from the Epistle to the Reader.

[94] Thomas Tanner, *Notitia Monastica or A Short History of the Religious Houses in England and Wales*, Oxford 1695, from the Epistle.

[95] Stow cleared himself in 1569 of charges that he was a papist, and Anthony Wood, who reported of himself in 1673 that 'I am generally taken for a Papist', was examined by the university authorities at Oxford at the time of the Popish Plot. In the reign of Elizabeth the very possession of medieval texts could cause suspicions of papal sympathies, and Camden

referred to those who 'take it ill that I have mention'd Monasteries and their Founders' in the *Britannia*. Fears that the study of monastic antiquity would lead people into (or were a sign of) popery were long lasting, and taken into full account by historians. Cf. Weever's defence of the piety of monastic founders, quoted above p. 317, and the disclaimers of Fuller ('I protest myself not to have the least inclination to the favour of monkery') and Browne Willis ('I shall forbear speaking farther of this Matter, lest I render my self traduced and suspected of retaining too superstitious an Affection for these Buildings')— all in conjunction with regrets for monastic losses. Fussner, *op. cit.*, p. 215; Powell, *op. cit.*, pp. 147, 172-4, 205-6; McKisack, *op. cit.*, pp. 43, 153; Fuller, *op. cit.*, iii, p. 437; Browne Willis, *op. cit.*, i, p. 3; Douglas, *op. cit.*, p. 246; Evans, *op. cit.*, p. 5.

of our *English* Nation, and of their Founders, that so highly deserved of the several Ages they lived in, is the design of this Book.[96]

By the end of the seventeenth century long-felt regrets for the losses of the monastic past had matured into some of the best early fruits of English historical scholarship. Individuals for whom monastic sites were the admonitory receptacles of a vanished yet recoverable past, brought antiquarian researching to bear closely upon religious institutions. And eventually it became possible to pursue that part of the papal past without fears of Anglican suspicions. So, when the Gentlemen's Society of Spalding, which was established in 1710 and closely linked with the revived Society of Antiquaries, opened correspondence with the London body, it could be said of its members that 'in the true style of monastic antiquity, [they] assumed to themselves the modest denomination of a *Cell* to that of London'.[97] Thus closely had the feeling for the monastic past become entwined with antiquarian sensibility.

* * *

That sense of the past which is so integral a part of English literary consciousness has many roots. One of them, which struck deep, was that put down by the Dissolution. The sight of destruction gives a powerful impulse to preserve and record, is itself conducive to a nostalgia which can merge with concerns for history.[98] The very thoroughness of the Reformation shocked people into action. So much was seen to be going at once—manuscripts, church plate, sculpture and buildings. For some of those who witnessed it, this royal whirlwind could not be justified even in terms of the monstrous perversions of monastic life. For others, later, Henry VIII's reign seemed like a barbarous holocaust, cutting a brutal swathe through the English landscape and the ecclesiastical past. Anger and frustration at this unjustifiable desolation took creative directions, with a momentum which continued.

The writing of English history was permanently affected by the stimuli which it received at the Reformation, and the feeling for those—largely irrevocable—losses of the past reached out beyond the work of antiquarians and historical researchers into more indefinable areas of literary consciousness. Where historians delved and annotated and recorded others wandered and hinted and alluded. There is a real sense in which English awareness of ruins was turned in a direction both gothic and monastic in the sixteenth century. Clearly a great deal more than ruin-gazing goes to the writing of history. And many forces, apart from those of physical loss, contributed to the growth of English historical studies from the sixteenth century onwards. But what historians seek is affected by what they see, and had England had

---

[96] Tanner, *op. cit.*, sig. A 5[v], from the Preface.

[97] John Nichols, *Literary Anecdotes of the Eighteenth Century*, vi, London 1812–15, pp. 5–6; Walters, *op. cit.*, p. 37; Evans, *op. cit.*, pp. 53–54, and cf. pp. 22 and 42 for the concern with the foundation of religious houses, together with castles and public works, in the 1638 regulations of the Society of Antiquaries,

and for the extensive scheme for monastic researches in Wanley's proposals of 1708.

[98] For remarks about the way in which 'a newfound nostalgia' for the medieval past combined with a living Gothic tradition in Elizabethan secular architecture, see J. Mordaunt Crook's remarks in his edition of Eastlake, *A History of the Gothic Revival*, p. ⟨28⟩.

more Roman walls, more Roman baths and theatres and triumphal arches set beside its castles and monastic masonry, the early interest in its history might have taken a more decisively Roman direction. The first antiquaries were certainly intent upon Roman sites and medieval castles as well as ecclesiastical remains, and these parts of British history also received their early due. But Britain's secular ruins, though they contributed to the growth of anti-quarian interests, did not carry with them the same profound sense of shock as that left by the cataclysm of the Dissolution. Henry VIII's monastic ruins proved formative as well as evocative, because they stood for a thousand years • of English history, shut off and largely destroyed. A decisive historical orientation was initiated by the first iconoclastic monarch to grace, or dis-grace, the English throne. The very process of casting off the past generated nostalgia for its loss. And with nostalgia came invigorated historical activity.

INDEX